**FRANÇOIS-RÉGIS GAUDRY
AND FRIENDS
PRESENT**

LET'S EAT
PARIS!

ARTISAN | NEW YORK

To Alexandra, Gabrielle, and Suzanne,
my three favorite Parisians.

WHY LET'S EAT PARIS?

I was not born in Paris, but Paris is where I nurtured my love for food. My parents raised me in Lyon and taught me to love eating well. My grandmother from Bastia raised me on Corsican cooking, but Paris is where my emotions for food ignited, thus whetting my immense appetite for French gastronomy and creating my insatiable curiosity about foods from all cultures.

Although I went to Paris for my formal studies, I became obsessed with another goal: discovering all the foods the city had to offer!

Eating became a passion for me, and now it has become my profession. Paris has never ceased to be my favorite place for culinary exploration. For over twenty years—for the press, radio, television, and publishing—I have been "consuming" the capital from end to end, confirming that the City of Light remains the world's gastronomic beacon.

Paris is where large-scale gourmet food halls and the restaurant were invented.

This city has given birth to a unique culinary heritage and many of the world's iconic recipes, from the baguette to the croque-monsieur and from veal blanquette to the jambon-beurre.

Paris has also conquered pastries like no other city. It has created the world's pastry terminology and is the origin of world-famous cakes and confections, including the macaron, mille-feuille, Saint-Honoré, and Paris-Brest.

Paris benefits from an exceptional expertise in production and agriculture, which has developed in the terroirs of the Île-de-France region.

Parisian gastronomy holds steadfast to its traditions but has never isolated itself. It is a constantly moving, exciting, and creative scene brought to life by great chefs, restaurateurs, and food artisans from all over France and around the globe. From street food to bistronomy, from pizza to kebabs, from small bars to large restaurants, the capital remains a fascinating melting pot of cultures I never tire of exploring.

Paris was well worth a new opus highlighting its living heritage. This book is a tremendous accomplishment, written with the dedication of my close collaborators and an expanded circle of fine connoisseurs. Our goal? Amass everything we love about the capital into a vast cultural encyclopedia, a cookbook, and an abundant visitor's guide of the city's best places. *Let's Eat Paris!* is a well-nourished and witty bible not only for native Parisians but also for those visiting the capital just for a day.

Bon appétit et vive Paris!
François-Régis Gaudry

A GOURMET CHRONOLOGY

FIRST-THIRD CENTURIES → Wines, olive oils, garums, and oysters are unearthed in the archaeological remains of Gallo-Roman Paris.

MIDDLE AGES → Île-de-France is an important wine region, with Paris as its first commercial outlet.

EIGHTH CENTURY → The *Consile d'Apostle* attests to the reputation of several local products from the Île-de-France region: (geese from Beauce, Brie cheese, shallots from Étampes, tripe from Saint-Denis . . .).

1137 → Establishment of the Marché du Roi (King's Market) in Les Champeaux, the future Halles de Paris.

1183 → Construction of two long halls in the Marché du Roi, intended for storing goods.

THIRTEENTH-FIFTEENTH CENTURIES → The "petits pâtés de Paris" become preparations emblematic of the city, are made for easy transport, and are inexpensive.

AROUND 1265 → Publication of *Crieries de Paris*, by G. de La Villeneuve, a collection of poems that recalls the cries of Parisian street vendors.

1266-1269 → É. Boileau, provost of the merchants of Paris, begins drafting general regulations for Parisian trades (bread bakers, wine criers, tavern keepers, beer makers, secondhand merchants . . .).

LATE THIRTEENTH-EARLY FOURTEENTH CENTURIES → Copies, in Paris, of the two oldest French culinary manuscripts: *Les Enseingnemenz qui enseingnent a appareil toute manieres de viandes* and *Le Viandier*.

JANUARY 6, 1378 → Charles V hosts a memorable feast at Palais de la Cité.

AROUND 1393 → Writing of the *Mesnagier de Paris*, which includes many recipes.

AROUND 1486 → First cookbook printed in France, *Le Viandier*.

SIXTEENTH-EIGHTEENTH CENTURIES → Butter from Vanves grows in reputation, loved by Parisians through the eighteenth century.

AROUND 1539 → Publication of *Livre de cuysine tres utille & prouffitables*. This is the only new cookbook printed in France in the sixteenth century.

1543-1572 → Reconstruction of Les Halles with covered galleries (the "pillars of Les Halles").

SEVENTEENTH-NINETEENTH CENTURIES

→ The talmouses (a pastry) of Saint-Denis enjoy a flourishing reputation.

→ Parisian bakers begin offering more products.

1607 → First mention, in *Thrésor de santé* (Lyon), of "gafteaux fueilletez" (a reference to a flaky cake) that "is made in Paris."

1650s → First known recipes of modern puff pastry.

MID-SEVENTEENTH CENTURY → Parisian upper classes discover ice cream.

1651 → Publication of La Varenne's *Cuisinier françois*, a testimony to the emergence of an aristocratic and Parisian French cuisine, breaking with traditions practiced since the Middle Ages.

1653 → Recipes for macarons, gâteau feuilleté (a flaky cake), marzipan, petits choux . . . appear in *Le Pastissier françois*.

1670s → Rise of outdoor cafés.

1686 → Opening of Le Procope, the oldest café in Paris.

1690 → Introduction of *chouquette* under the name of *chou* in the *Dictionnaire universel* by Furetière.

→ Fame of Montmorency cherries attested by Merlet in *Abrégé des bons fruits*.

EIGHTEENTH CENTURY → Paris reigns supreme over culinary publishing in France.

→ Rise of the popularity of cafés, a mecca of intellectual life.

→ Appearance of the "artichoke of Paris."

→ Specialization of the Vexin area in "veal blanc" (veal blanquette).

→ Montreuil specializes in the production of peaches.

→ French Gâtinais chicken develops its reputation for excellence.

1730s → First plantings of Chasselas grapes in Thomery.

1746 → *La Cuisinière bourgeoise*, J. Menon, becomes a bestselling culinary book.

1756 → Move of the Vincennes porcelain factory, built in 1740, to Sèvres.

1762-1767 → Construction of the new wheat market, today the Bourse de Commerce (commercial exchange) in Paris.

1766 → Birth of the modern restaurant attributed to Monsieur Roze de Chantoiseau. The Palais-Royal becomes the center of Parisian gastronomy.

1782 → Mention of two kinds of Brie cheeses (round and flat and flowing) in *Histoire de la vie privée des Français* by P. J. B. Legrand d'Aussy.

AROUND 1800 → Probable invention of frites (fried potatoes) in the form of round slices by female vendors on Pont-Neuf. "Stick" fries appeared around 1840.

EARLY NINETEENTH CENTURY → Opening of Rocher de Cancale, specializing in consumption of oysters.

1801 → First appearance of the term *gastronomy* in the poem "*La gastronomie, ou l'homme des champs à table*" by J. Berchoux.

1802 → Founding in Massy of the factory by N. Appert, inventor of appertization (the canning process).

1803 → First delivery of Grimod de La Reynière's *Almanach des gourmands*.

1803-1804 → A. Carême (1783-1833) is hired by the minister and gastronome Talleyrand.

1804 → Appearance of the word *mayonnaise* in *Souvenirs de Paris* by A. von Kotzebue.

1806 → *Le Cuisiner impérial* by A. Viard mentions the tomato in Parisian (and French) cuisine.

1810 → Abolition of Parisian slaughterhouses by Napoléon I, replaced by five other slaughterhouses (Montmartre, Ménilmontant, Villejuif, Roule [Miromesnil], and Grenelle).

AROUND 1810 → Use of underground quarries in the Île-de-France region for cultivating *Agaricus bisporus*, the white button mushroom (champignon de Paris).

1810s → Appearance of the description *à la parisienne* to describe different dishes garnished with savory jellies and served with mayonnaise.

1814 → Publication of *Guide des dineurs* by H. Blanc, a review and critique of the most popular restaurants in Paris.

1814-1815 → Triumph of Parisian cuisine by chef A. Carême at the Vienna Congress.

1825 → Publication in Paris of Brillat-Savarin's *Physiology of Taste*. This is the first book that makes good food the subject of philosophical reflection.

1830 → Founding of silverware manufacturer Christofle.

1830s → Migration of Parisian haute cuisine from the Palais-Royal to boulevards du Temple and des Italiens.

AROUND 1838 → Opening of the Boulangerie Viennoise (Viennese Bakery) by Austrian A. Zang on rue Richelieu.

AROUND 1840 → Appearance of brasseries in Paris. Brasserie Andler on rue Hautefeuille is the first of its kind.

AROUND 1845 → Creation of the *savarin* by the Julien brothers.

1846 → Publication of *Paris à table*, by E. Briffault, a collection of food and gastronomic traditions of the capital.

AROUND 1850 → Appearance of soupe à l'oignon, later as a gratin, on tavern menus in Les Halles.

- **1850s** → Appearance of the first recipes for the Saint-Honoré cake.

- **1850-1900** → Beginning of an effervescent Parisian culinary scene with the opening of the prestigious Maxim's, Weber, Lucas (later Lucas-Carton), Pavillon Ledoyen, Pavillon de l'Élysée, Fouquet's, Pré Catelan, Tour d'Argent, and Lapérouse, among others.

- **1853** → Probable first recipe for "breads called croissants," without butter, in *Les Substances alimentaires* by A. Pan.

- **1854** → First *bouillon* restaurant opened by the butcher B. A. Duval on rue de la Monnaie.

- **1856** → Publication of *Consommations de Paris*, by J. C. A. Husson, a vast study on the eating habits of Parisians.

- **1857** → Opening of the Baltard pavilions at Les Halles de Paris.

- **1859** → Bercy, the largest wine market in the world, becomes part of Paris.

- **1860s-1870s** → Creation of Argenteuil asparagus, notably by L. Lhérault, considered the "Parmentier of asparagus."

- **1865-1915** → The golden age for hens from Houdan.

- **1866** → First daily culinary chronicles in the newspaper *La Liberté* by Baron Brisse.

- **1867** → Entry of the adjective *bourguignon* in the *Grand dictionnaire universel* by Larousse, marking the first time that a dish of Parisian bourgeois cuisine becomes a regional specialty.

- → Opening of the slaughterhouses and livestock market at La Villette.

- **JUNE 7, 1867** → "Three Emperors Dinner" at Café Anglais.

- **1869** → Jambon de Paris is defined as a boneless, salted, reconstituted, cooked ham, according to J. Gouffé in his *Livre des conserves*.

- **SECOND HALF OF THE NINETEENTH CENTURY** → Collapse of the Île-de-France vineyard due to competition from southern wines, the phylloxera crisis, and urbanization.

- **SEPTEMBER 1870-JANUARY 1871** → The siege of Paris. Horses, dogs, cats, rats, and zoo animals kept at the Jardin d'Acclimatization (elephants, antelopes, etc.) become part of the menu for hungry Parisians.

- **1870-1890** → Following the phylloxera crisis, pears became the dominant crop in Groslay (Val-d'Oise).

- **1873** → *Le Ventre de Paris* by Émile Zola is published, a novel about the new Halles de Paris.

- **1879** → Creation of the bûche de Noël by A. Charabot, chef at M. Sanson, rue de Buci.

- **1880** → Creation of Grand Marnier liqueur in Neauphle-le-Château by the Lapostolle distillery.

- **1880s** → The word *bistrot* enters Parisian slang.

- **1882** → First culinary exposition organized by chef T. Génin.

- → First recipe for tartlettes à la bourdaloue (poached apricots in frangipane) in U. Dubois's *Cuisine artistique*.

- **1886** → Opening of the Fauchon gourmet foods store.

- **1891-1892** → Introduction by C. Lefèvre of watercress cultivation in Méréville.

- **1894** → Opening of the Arpajonnais, a train line supplying Les Halles from Arpajon.

- **1896** → Birth of Le Cordon Bleu culinary school.

- **1898** → Opening of the Ritz Hotel at Place Vendôme. Heading the restaurant is chef A. Escoffier.

- **1900** → Banquet for the mayors of France (more than 22,000 guests) in the Tuileries Gardens.

- → Opening of what is probably the first Parisian Japanese restaurant, Tomoe-Tei, on rue Bonaparte.

- **1903** → *Guide culinaire*, by A. Escoffier, becomes the reference text of French haute cuisine.

- **FEBRUARY 26, 1903** → First of the monthly lunches of the "Ten" of the Académie Goncourt, at the Grand Hôtel. The jury moved to Drouant in 1914.

- **1904** → First known use of the word *baguette* for long breads.

- **1909** → Appearance of flan Parisien (Parisian flan) in the *Traité de pâtisserie moderne* by É. Darenne and É. Duval.

- **INTERWAR PERIOD** → Rise in the 13th, 14th, and 19th arrondissements of simple Breton establishments, which quickly took the form of typical *crêperies*.

- **1920** → Founding by the Petrossian brothers of the *maison* of the same name, specializing in caviar.

- **1920s** → Publication of *La France gastronomique: guide des merveilles culinaires et des bonnes auberges françaises* by Curnonsky, M. Rouff (three volumes on Paris and the Île-de-France).

- **1923** → Launch of Radio Cuisine, the first cooking radio program, by É. de Pomiane.

- → Le Bon Marché opens a food boutique on rue de Sèvres, which becomes La Grande Épicerie in 1978.

- **1927** → Opening on December 20 of La Coupole on boulevard du Montparnasse.

- **1930s** → Probable creation by the Clichy pâtisserie of the *clichy*, later renamed the *opéra*.

- **1932** → Planting of a small vineyard on Butte Montmartre.

- **1933** → Creation of the Michelin Guide star classification. Out of twenty-three three-star establishments, six are Parisian: Le Café de Paris, Foyot, Lapérouse, Larue, Lucas-Carton, and La Tour d'Argent.

- **1936** → *L'Art culinaire moderne* by H.-P. Pellaprat presents the recipe for Paris-Brest, perhaps created in 1910 by pastry chef L. Durand at Maisons-Laffitte.

- **1952** → The Tarte Tatin, a dessert from Sologne, is added to Maxim's menu and becomes a national icon.

- **1957** → G. Lenôtre opens his shop at 44, rue d'Auteuil (Paris 16th).

- **1960s** → Proliferation of Chinese and Vietnamese restaurants in the capital.

- **1963** → *Guide Julliard de Paris*, the first guide by the duo H. Gault and C. Millau.

- **1965** → Planting of a municipal vineyard in Suresnes.

- **1969-1973** → Move of Les Halles Centrales to Rungis.

- **1972** → Opening in Créteil of the first McDonald's in France.

- **1973** → Publication in the magazine *Gault & Millau* of the ten commandments of Nouvelle Cuisine, a Parisian movement begun in the 1960s.

- **1974** → Closure of La Villette slaughterhouses.

- **1980s** → Rise of municipal vineyards, Bagnolet (1980), Bagneux (1982), Joinville-le-Pont (1989), Argenteuil (1997), Sannois (2003), etc.

- **1980s-1990s** → Le Grand Véfour, Vagenende, Au Chien Qui Fume, La Coupole, Pharamond, Prunier, Lipp, and Fouquet's are classified as historic monuments.

- **1989** → Premiere of J. C. Brisville's *Souper* at the Montparnasse theater: a fictitious dinner between Talleyrand and Fouché in Paris on July 6, 1815.

- **1990s** → Invention by several haute cuisine chefs of bistro cuisine. In 2004, this trend was dubbed *bistronomy* by the *Le Fooding* movement.

- **1990s-2000s** → Thanks to pastry chef P. Hermé, the macaron becomes one of the emblems of Parisian pastry.

- **2007** → Release in theaters of *Ratatouille* by Pixar Studios.

- **2011** → Launch of Camion Qui Fume, the first food truck in Paris.

- **2015** → First edition of the gastronomic festival Taste of Paris.

- **2019** → Creation of the Parcours de la Gastronomie en Île-de-France to promote local products from the Île-de-France region across six premier sites.

- **2020** → New PGI (Protected Geographical Indication) appellation for Île-de-France wines.

- **2024** → Opening of the Cité de la Gastronomie Paris-Rungis.

—LOÏC BIENASSIS

TYPES OF DINING ESTABLISHMENTS

Whether for a quick bite or a special occasion, the capital's restaurants offer seemingly endless options for dining. Here is an overview of the types of establishments where you can choose an experience that suits your mood—from the most luxurious to the everyday.

1 THE GRAND RESTAURANT

These establishments offer all the luxuries of French gastronomy, from decor to service to dishes and wines. Appropriate dress is required, and the bill is always high. According to the ratings in the Michelin Guide, the experience will be "worth a detour" (two stars) or "worth a special trip" (three stars).

ORIGIN: *These prestigious establishments developed in the aftermath of the Revolution around the gardens of the Palais-Royal and spread, starting in the nineteenth century, along the Grands Boulevards.*

2 THE RESTAURANT DE PALACE

These are grand restaurants, but within luxury hotels. They are intended to provide an exceptional dining option for guests, but they also welcome nonguests of the hotel. The George V and the Plaza Athénée were the first such Parisian establishments to be awarded three Michelin stars in 1934.

ORIGIN: *Opened in 1898 in Place Vendôme, the Ritz Hotel was the first luxury hotel in Paris to offer a grand restaurant for the first time in Paris, orchestrated by César Ritz and chef Auguste Escoffier.*

3 THE BRASSERIE

These are large establishments with historic decor (art nouveau or art deco) with uniformed servers and upscale service. They offer sauerkraut, seafood platters, and Parisian specialties.

ORIGIN: *Starting in the 1860s, brasseries were devoted to the brewing and consumption of beer. Then, under the impetus of Alsatians, they began offering sauerkraut and beer on tap in an upscale setting.*

4 THE BISTRO

A small neighborhood restaurant with checkered tablecloths, simple specialties, and a warm ambience. Bistros are popular and referred to as *gargote, bistroquet,* or *troquet.* Some upscale bistros offer a more upscale cuisine.

ORIGIN: *The term* bistro *first appeared in French in 1884, then* bistrot *in 1892. Perhaps from the Russian* bystro *meaning "fast" or from Poitevin dialect* bistraud *(meaning "small servant" of* cabaretiers*) or from* bistrouille *(meaning "bad alcohol" in northern France and Belgium). The origin remains uncertain.*

5 THE BOUILLON

A large-scale restaurant for working classes that serves a great number of customers at once. The original broth-based specialties have given way to traditional and inexpensive dishes (oeuf mayonnaise, leeks vinaigrette, roast chicken with fries, etc.).

ORIGIN: *In 1855, the butcher Baptiste-Adolphe Duval opened the first* bouillon *in the Halles district, soon followed by many other locations. The genre has flourished to the present day.*

6 THE CAFÉ

An establishment where coffee and other beverages and snacks are consumed throughout the day in a dining room or at the counter.

ORIGIN: *Called* salles de café *(coffee rooms) or* salons de café *(coffee salons) in the seventeenth century, these became meeting places for political groups of the Revolutionary era and gathering places for intellectuals ("literary cafés") and later* cafés chantants *(singing cafés; 1850), then* cafés-concerts *(concert cafés; 1852), des* caf' conc' *(1878), and* cafés-théâtres *(1867).*

7 THE CABARET

An establishment offering dinner with a show, adapted from artists' cafés and *goguettes* where you could drink, eat, and smoke while watching a play, concert, or a revue.

ORIGIN: *Originally a place for drinking (tavern) where patrons could sit down to eat and sometimes stay overnight (inn), the cabaret developed its artistic style at the end of the nineteenth century.*

8 THE GUINGUETTE

This is an establishment with a green space where patrons drink, eat, and dance, located in suburban areas or along waterways.

ORIGIN: *The word appears as early as 1694, derived from the old French* guinguet *(sour wine) or from* guinguer *(to skip or frolic), and refers first to suburban establishments, then to a cabaret where* guinguet *(a light local sour green wine) was served that made "goats dance."*

9 THE BAR

A drinking establishment where patrons consume drinks standing or sitting near the counter. In Paris, these are also called *zinc* and *bar à vin* (wine bar) when offering a wide choice of vintages. In the twentieth century, the expression replaced *marchand de vins* (wine seller).

ORIGIN: *The word appears in French in 1857 as an abbreviation of the Anglo-American term "bar-room," inherited from the French* barre, *designating the wooden or metal bar attached to the counter.*

10 THE BAR À COCKTAILS

A bar specializing in cocktails, which have become popular within Parisian luxury hotels, although they have been present in Paris since the beginning of the twentieth century.

ORIGIN: *Opened in 1911, Harry's New York Bar (Paris 2nd) is the oldest cocktail bar in Europe. It was not until the 2000s that the cocktail scene in Paris was revived.*

11 THE CAVE À MANGER

A wine shop offering small bites (charcuterie board, cheeses, and simple dishes) for dining in. A corkage fee is charged for tasting the shop's wines.

ORIGIN: *The expression was coined by the* Le Fooding *movement in 2004 when these establishments, offering natural wines, were increasing.*

12 THE COMPTOIR À EMPORTER

À emporter meaning "to go," such as from a *crêperie,* salad bar, healthy coffee shop, street kebabs, etc. There are many on-the-go food establishments offering a variety of choices and which now number 6,500 locations, making up 35 percent of Paris's restaurants.

ORIGIN: *Street foods were already popular among Parisians in the Middle Ages, including butchers, enriched breads and pâté vendors, etc.*

DINING PARIS-STYLE

AT THE RESTAURANT

Parisian dining establishments have standard rules regarding decor, service, and etiquette, depending on the type of restaurant.

DECOR

The decor of Parisian restaurants is codified when it comes to their choice of furniture, materials, and accessories. Let's explore three different ones.

IN A GRAND RESTAURANT

AT A BISTRO

AT A CAFÉ

DINING GUIDES

The quality of a restaurant is often judged by the number of stickers attached to its windows. Here are the most common stickers seen in Paris from gastronomic guides.

GUIDE LEBEY

Founded by Claude Lebey in 1987

GUIDE PUDLO PARIS

Founded by Gilles Pudlowski in 1990

GUIDE FOODING

Founded by Alexandre Cammas and Emmanuel Rubin in 1999

GUIDE DU ROUTARD

Founded by Michel Duval and Philippe Gloaguen in 1973

GUIDE MICHELIN

Founded by André and Édouard Michelin in 1900

GAULT & MILLAU

Founded by Henri Gault and Christian Millau in 1969 / Guide Île-de-France in 2012

A LITTLE GALLANTRY, PLEASE!

Men first! Traditional etiquette dictates that a man is expected to enter an establishment first, leading the lady who accompanies him. Why? Parisian inns of the past were sometimes infamous for lurking dangers, so a man had to check that the woman accompanying him would not be at risk. Today, a gentleman walks in front of a lady to open the door for her.

MAJOR FOOD STREETS

Some Parisian streets are dedicated entirely to the pleasures of eating.

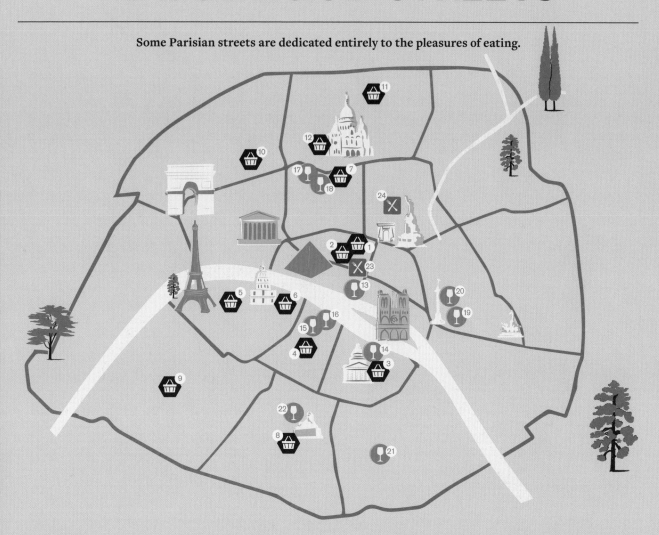

STREETS FOR
FOOD SHOPPING

These streets are a concentrated collection of food shops that allow you to quickly do all your food shopping in one convenient area.

1. *Rue Montorgueil, 2nd*
2. *Rue du Nil, 2nd*
3. *Rue Mouffetard, 5th*
4. *Rue du Cherche-Midi, 6th*
5. *Rue Cler, 7th*
6. *Rue du Bac, 7th*
7. *Rue des Martyrs, 9th (top half, starting from Notre-Dame-de-Lorette to Pigalle)*
8. *Rue Daguerre, 14th*
9. *Rue du Commerce, 15th*
10. *Rue de Lévis, 17th*
11. *Rue du Poteau, 18th*
12. *Rue Lepic-rue des Abbesses, 18th*

STREETS FOR DRINKS

With an exceptional offering of cafés, bars, and pubs, these streets are nighttime gathering places for students, partygoers, and tourists.

13. *Rue des Lombards, 1st and 4th*
14. *Place de la Contrescarpe, 5th*
15. *Rues des Canettes, Princesse, and Guisarde, 6th*
16. *Rue de Buci, 6th*
17. *Rue Pierre-Fontaine, 9th*
18. *Rue Jean-Baptiste-Pigalle, 9th*

19. *Rue de Lappe, 11th*
20. *Rue Oberkampf, 11th*
21. *Rue de la Butte-aux-Cailles, 13th*
22. *Rue de la Gaîté, 14th*

STREETS FOR COOKS

Whether an amateur or a professional, cooks frequent these streets to outfit their kitchens with equipment or tableware.

23. *Rue Montmartre, 1st and 2nd (utensil shops around Saint-Eustache)*
24. *Rue de Paradis, 10th (tableware)*

RESTAURANTS AND FOOD SHOPS IN NUMBERS

RESTAURANTS (INCLUDING FAST FOOD OUTLETS): **19,538**

BAKERIES: **1,405**

BUTCHER SHOPS: **708**

PASTRY SHOPS: **251**

SEAFOOD SHOPS: **132**

CHARCUTERIES: **98**

CHOCOLATE SHOPS: **55**

Source: *INSEE et Observatoire des métiers de l'Alimentation en Détail, 2021.*

FOOD SERVICE PROFESSIONALS

In cafés, hotels, or restaurants, these four primary Parisian professions are a mainstay. But they each have a little mystery surrounding their origins and responsibilities. Let's unpack each one.

Where did bartending in Paris originate?

FROM ONE SIDE OF THE ATLANTIC . . .

Bartending as a profession emerged in the eighteenth century in England and the United States with the appearance of cocktails. The profession arrived in Paris for the first time in 1900 during the Universal Exposition. Cocktails, which at the time were rather sweet, became very popular among wealthy clientele, who were usually accustomed to bitter or aniseed-based spirits (absinthe, gentian, etc.).

. . . TO THE OTHER!

While the 1920s marked the beginning of Prohibition on one side of the Atlantic in the United States, Europe entered the Roaring Twenties on the other side. Losing work due to the ban on alcohol sales, American bartenders set sail for Europe and Paris. Three

big names in the bar industry shook up the Parisian scene: Scotsman Harry MacElhone, the owner of Harry's New York Bar; Frank P. Newman, an English-born bartender at the Grand Hôtel; and Frank Meier, an Austrian and the bar manager at the Ritz.

THE HOTEL BARTENDER

During World War II, cocktails were consumed mainly in hotel bars. The classy and attentive service counted as much as the quality of the drinks, and the sophisticated clientele who frequented these places contributed to the growth in the popularity of cocktails. The hotel bartender was the master of their space, knew their regular customers well, and invented refined cocktails. The profession grew to become more professional, and it gained prestige.

THE MODERN BARTENDER

From the mid-2000s, bartenders started to appear in the many bars throughout the city, and restaurants increasingly included cocktails on their menus. Paris became an important place for the creation and consumption of these beverages. Several Parisian establishments are regularly included in the list of the World's 50 Best Bars, such as The Little Red Door (Paris 3rd), which has appeared on the list since 2014. The bartender profession was modernizing, with suit jackets giving way to shirts with pushed-up sleeves. More women are now bartenders, in a world that remained very masculine for a long time.

Why does a chef wear a hat . . . or not?

FOR HYGIENE

Although the origin of the chef's hat is unknown, one thing about the hat is certain: the chef's hat was first worn for the purposes of hygiene. To contain a cook's hair or sweat while working in enclosed spaces among hot ovens and bubbling pots, the soft black cotton hats, the first types of hats worn, served a primarily practical purpose.

BECAUSE IT'S A TITLE

The invention of the white toque is attributed to Antonin Carême in 1820 while he was working as a chef in Vienna. Inspired by the military uniforms of the Congress of Vienna, he developed a pristinely white and rigid cap trimmed with a cardboard circle. It symbolized the rigor of the chef in their appearance and the quality of

their work represented on the plate. It was also a way to codify uniforms in the kitchen and give the uniforms a certain allure. Another great name, Auguste Escoffier, gave the chef's hat its final shape: straight and pleated, which was synonymous with integrity and cleanliness. It was first worn by Parisian chefs before eventually ending up on all heads in professional kitchens.

TO COMMUNICATE IMPORTANCE

The higher the hat, the more important the position! With an open top, the chef's hat is supposed to be cooling to the wearer. Antonin Carême would have agreed, as he never wore a hat less than 17 inches (45 cm) tall.

TO COMMUNICATE A LEVEL OF EXPERTISE

Originally starched and handmade by pressers, the chef's hat's pleats are shrouded in many myths. Some think the number of pleats represents the number of recipes a chef knows, or a chef's years of experience, or the number of ways to prepare an egg, but there were originally a hundred folds in total. Starting in the 1970s, thicker, disposable hats started to appear.

TO BE STYLISH

Today, most chefs wear a hat only as official representation, or perhaps for other reasons. But bandanas, caps, or bare heads have gradually replaced the traditional white and rigid tubelike hats that were eventually deemed impractical, therefore modernizing the chef's outfit.

Why does the server seem in a bad mood?

In a poll posed in the French newspaper *Le Figaro*, 85.79 percent of respondents answered no to the question: "Are Parisian waiters friendly enough?" So where does this bad reputation come from?

THE CULTURAL EXPLANATION

Critiqued by the foreign press and tourists, servers' bad reputations often originate from a cultural gap between Anglo-Saxon practices—where smiling and tipping are expected—and the presumed position that French people are not fond of insincere actions. The Paris Chamber of Commerce turned it into a campaign in 2013, encouraging establishment managers to "be more welcoming" to tourists.

THE ECONOMIC EXPLANATION

A server's job can often be underappreciated, thankless, precarious, poorly compensated, stressful, physically exhausting, and subject to an intense pace. In 1907, servers went on strike to be granted a day off during the week . . . and the right to sport a mustache, which was once reserved for military personnel and gentlemen of higher classes.

THE SARTRIAN POINT OF VIEW

In *L'Être et le Néant*, Jean-Paul Sartre seems to disagree with this urban legend of the server: "He approaches consumers a little too lively, he bows with a little too much eagerness, his voice, his eyes, express an interest a bit too full of solicitude for the customer's order." (Perhaps these servers were trying to get one of the philosopher's generous tips . . . unlike those from average Parisian customers!)

AN ARISTOCRATIC UNIFORM

The iconic black-and-white outfit appeared in the nineteenth century in the cafés along the Grands Boulevards, to distinguish servers from customers. The uniform consists of:

→ a white shirt and black bow tie.

→ a *gilet* or *rondin*: a multipocketed short black vest with rounded tails.

→ a *tablier*: a long, white apron at waist height, open in the back and tied in a bow.

IN FRENCH CINEMA

Le Petit Café by Raymond Bernard (1919) with Max Linder; *Garçon!* by Claude Sautet (1983) with Yves Montand; *Quatre Aventures de Reinette et Mirabelle* by Éric Rohmer (1987).

THE WAITERS' RACE

Paris is credited with the origin of this unique sporting event. A waiters' race is organized every year, earning winners a little more prestige in their craft. The first photos of the race, dating to 1918, show the one-day athletes being cheered on by thousands of spectators along Paris's boulevards. The goal? Cross the finish line first while holding a tray full of glasses without letting any fall over.

Why is the oyster shucker so resilient against the cold?

THE SAVOYARDS

In the early twentieth century, flourishing brasseries offered platters of open oysters, ready for savoring. This idea was a success, and establishments hired many oyster openers ("shuckers"). One of the first was a Savoyard from the village of Montaimont, and he was soon joined by others from the region. With little access to work in the winter, these men enjoyed a serious income in Paris when oysters were offered during months whose names have an "r." The Savoyards developed a good reputation because, accustomed to the cold, they could work for hours with their hands in ice.

The Savoyard workers' numbers declined from the 1960s to the 1970s, but the famous Opinel knife remains, to which the No. 09 oyster knife pays tribute.

THE KABYLE CONNECTION

Arriving in Paris with the first wave of North African immigrants in the 1960s, the Kabyle people gradually replaced the Savoyards in the marquees of large brasseries. As hardworking as they are resilient, they also had the advantage of being used to the cold since they were raised in the mountain highlands of northern Algeria. The Kabyles co-opted each other for a long time to maintain their posts at the stalls.

A FEW COMMANDMENTS . . .

→ Oyster stands must be installed at least 28 inches (70 cm) above the ground and inclined, protected from the weather, and not exposed to the sun.

→ Have a potable water station and cold storage between 41° and 59°F (5° and 15°C).

→ Shellfish packages cannot be placed on the ground.

→ Keep health safety labels and quality labels visible to the consumer and clean each table and the floor after each working day.

A typical oyster shucker can open nearly two thousand oysters in a day and, on competition days, a hundred in nearly six minutes.

MARKETS

There are more than eighty food markets in Paris; some are covered while others are open-air.

PARIS 1ST

1 Saint-Eustache-les-Halles
📍 *Rue Montmartre*
🕐 Thursday and Sunday, all day

2 Saint-Honoré
📍 *Place du Marché-Saint-Honoré*
🕐 Wednesday and Saturday, all day

PARIS 2ND

3 Bourse
📍 *Place de la Bourse*
🕐 Tuesday and Friday, all day

PARIS 3RD

4 Les Enfants-Rouges (covered)
📍 *39, rue de Bretagne*
🕐 Tuesday to Sunday, all day

PARIS 4TH

5 Baudoyer
📍 *Place Baudoyer*
🕐 Wednesday, and Saturday morning

PARIS 5TH

6 Maubert
📍 *Place Maubert*
🕐 Tuesday, Thursday, and Saturday morning

7 Monge
📍 *Place Monge*
🕐 Wednesday, Friday, and Sunday morning

8 Port-Royal
📍 *Blvd. de Port-Royal*
🕐 Tuesday, Thursday, and Saturday morning

PARIS 6TH

9 Biologique Raspail
📍 *Blvd. Raspail*
🕐 Sunday morning

10 Raspail
📍 *Blvd. Raspail*
🕐 Tuesday, and Friday morning

11 Saint-Germain (covered)
📍 *4–6, rue Lobineau*
🕐 Tuesday to Saturday all day, Sunday morning

PARIS 7TH

12 Saxe-Breteuil
📍 *Av. de Saxony*
🕐 Thursday, and Saturday morning

PARIS 8TH

13 Aguesseau
📍 *Place de la Madeleine*
🕐 Tuesday, and Friday morning

14 Treilhard (covered)
📍 *Rue Corvetto*
🕐 Every day all day

PARIS 9TH

15 Anvers
📍 *Place d'Anvers, on the side of Square d'Anvers*
🕐 Friday all day

PARIS 10TH

16 Alibert
📍 *Rue Alibert, odd-numbered side*
🕐 Sunday morning

17 Saint-Martin (covered)
📍 *31–33, rue du Château-d'Eau*
🕐 Tuesday to Saturday all day and Sunday morning

18 Saint-Quentin (covered)
📍 *85 bis, blvd. Magenta*
🕐 Tuesday to Saturday all day and Sunday morning

PARIS 11TH

19 Bastille
📍 *Blvd. Richard-Lenoir*
🕐 Thursday, and Sunday morning

20 Belleville
📍 *Blvd. de Belleville*
🕐 Tuesday, and Friday morning

21 Biologique
📍 *Place du Père-Chaillet*
🕐 Saturday morning, Wednesday all day

22 Charonne
📍 *Between blvd. de Charonne and rue Alexandre-Dumas*
🕐 Wednesday, and Saturday morning

23 Ménilmontant
📍 *Blvd. de Ménilmontant*
🕐 Tuesday, and Friday morning

24 Popincourt
📍 *Blvd. Richard-Lenoir*
🕐 Tuesday, and Friday morning

PARIS 12TH

25 Beauvau (or d'Aligre) (covered)
📍 *Place d'Aligre*
🕐 Tuesday to Friday 8 a.m. to 1 p.m. and 4 p.m. to 7:30 p.m., Saturday continuously, and Sunday morning

26 Bercy
📍 *Place Lachambeaudie and rue Baron-le-Roy*
🕐 Sunday morning, Wednesday all day

27 Cours de Vincennes
📍 *Cours de Vincennes*
🕐 Wednesday, and Saturday morning

28 Daumesnil
📍 *Between rue de Charenton and Place Félix-Éboué*
🕐 Tuesday, and Friday morning

29 D'Aligre
📍 *Rue d'Aligre and Place d'Aligre*
🕐 Tuesday to Sunday morning

30 Ledru-Rollin
📍 *Av. Ledru-Rollin*
🕐 Thursday, and Saturday morning

31 Porte Dorée
📍 *Av. Daumesnil*
🕐 Thursday, and Sunday morning

32 Saint-Éloi
📍 *Rue de Reuilly*
🕐 Thursday, and Saturday morning

PARIS 13TH

33 Alésia
📍 *Rue de la Glacière, even-numbered side*
🕐 Wednesday, and Saturday morning

34 Auguste-Blanqui
📍 *Blvd. Blanqui, between Place d'Italie and rue Barrault*
🕐 Tuesday, Friday, and Sunday morning

35 Bobillot
📍 *Rue Bobillot, odd-numbered side*
🕐 Tuesday, and Friday morning

36 Jeanne d'Arc
📍 *Place Jeanne d'Arc*
🕐 Thursday, and Sunday morning

37 Maison-Blanche
📍 *Av. d'Italy, even-numbered side*
🕐 Thursday, and Sunday morning

38 Salpêtrière
📍 *Blvd. de l'Hôpital*
🕐 Tuesday, and Friday morning

39 Vincent-Auriol
📍 *Blvd. Vincent-Auriol*
🕐 Wednesday, and Saturday morning

PARIS 14TH

40 Biologique Brancusi
📍 *Place Constantin-Brancusi*
🕐 Saturday until 3 p.m.

41 Brune
📍 *Blvd. Brune*
🕐 Thursday, and Sunday morning

42 Edgar-Quinet
📍 *On the median of blvd. Edgar-Quinet*
🕐 Wednesday, and Saturday morning

43 Jourdan
📍 *Rue Émile Faguet*
🕐 Wednesday, and Saturday morning

44 Mouton-Duvernet
📍 *Place Jacques-Demy*
🕐 Tuesday, and Friday morning

45 Villemain
📍 *Av. Villemain*
🕐 Wednesday, and Sunday morning

PARIS 15TH

46 Cervantes
📍 *60, rue Bargue*
🕐 Wednesday, and Saturday morning

47 Convention
📍 *Rue de la Convention*
🕐 Tuesday, Thursday, and Sunday morning

48 Grenelle
📍 *Blvd. de Grenelle*
🕐 Wednesday, and Sunday morning

49 Lecourbe
📍 *Rue Lecourbe*
🕐 Wednesday, and Saturday morning

50 Lefebvre
📍 *Blvd. Lefebvre*
🕐 Wednesday, and Saturday morning

51 Saint-Charles
📍 *Rue Saint-Charles*
🕐 Tuesday, and Friday morning

PARIS 16TH

52 Auteuil
📍 *Place Jean-Lorrain*
🕐 Wednesday, and Saturday morning

53 Passy (covered)
📍 *Place de Passy*
🕐 Tuesday to Saturday 8 a.m. to 1 p.m. and 4 p.m. to 7 p.m., and Sunday morning

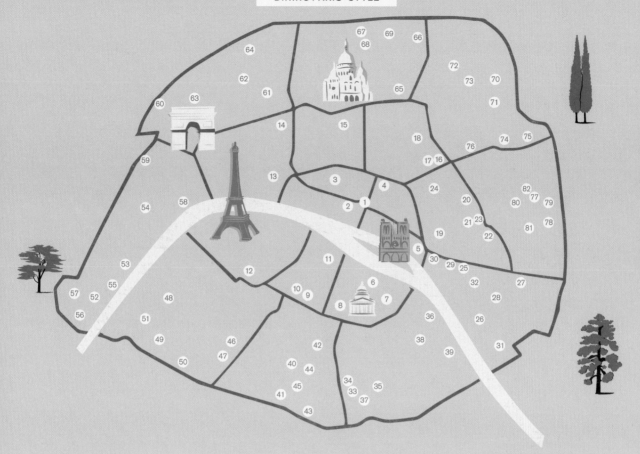

54 **Saint-Didier (covered)**
- *Rues Mesnil and Saint-Didiers*
- Monday to Friday all day and Saturday morning

55 **Gros-la-Fontaine**
- *Between rues Gros and Jean-de-La-Fontaine*
- Tuesday, and Friday morning

56 **Point du Jour**
- *Av. de Versailles*
- Tuesday, Thursday, and Sunday morning

57 **Porte Molitor**
- *Place de la Porte-Molitor*
- Tuesday, and Friday morning

58 **President Wilson**
- *Av. du Président-Wilson*
- Wednesday, and Saturday morning

59 **Admiral Bruix**
- *Blvd. Bruix*
- Wednesday, and Saturday morning

PARIS 17TH

60 **Berthier**
- *Blvd. de Reims, along the Square André-Ulmann*
- Wednesday, and Saturday morning

61 **Biologique des Batignolles**
- *On the median of blvd. des Batignolles*
- Saturday until 3 p.m.

62 **Batignolles (covered)**
- *96 bis, rue Lemercier*
- Tuesday to Friday 9 a.m. to 2 p.m. and 4 p.m. to 8:30 p.m., Saturday continuously, and Sunday morning

63 **Ternes (covered)**
- *8 bis, rue Lebon*
- Tuesday to Friday 8 a.m. to 2:30 p.m. and 4 p.m. to 7:30 p.m., Saturday continuously, and Sunday morning

64 **Navier**
- *Rue Navier*
- Wednesday, and Saturday morning

PARIS 18TH

65 **Barbès**
- *Blvd. de la Chapelle*
- Wednesday, and Saturday morning

66 **La Chapelle (covered)**
- *10, rue de l'Olive*
- Tuesday to Saturday all day, and Sunday morning

67 **Ney**
- *Blvd. Ney*
- Thursday, and Sunday morning

68 **Ordener**
- *Rue Ordener*
- Wednesday, and Saturday morning

69 **Ornano**
- *Blvd. Ornano*
- Tuesday, Friday, and Sunday morning

PARIS 19TH

70 **Crimée-Curial**
- *Rue de Crimée, even-numbered side*
- Tuesday, and Friday morning

71 **Jean-Jaurès**
- *185, avenue Jean-Jaurès*
- Thursday, and Sunday morning

72 **Halles Secrétan**
- *29, avenue Secrétan*
- Every day all day

73 **Joinville**
- *Place de Joinville*
- Thursday, and Sunday morning

74 **Place des Fêtes**
- *Place des Fêtes*
- Tuesday, Friday, and Sunday morning

75 **Porte Brunet**
- *Av. de la Porte-Brunet*
- Wednesday, and Saturday morning

76 **Villette**
- *Blvd. de la Villette*
- Wednesday, and Saturday morning

PARIS 20TH

77 **Belgrand**
- *Rues Belgrand and de la Chine and Place Édith-Piaf*
- Wednesday, and Saturday morning

78 **Marché Davout**
- *Blvd. Davout*
- Tuesday, and Friday morning

79 **Mortier**
- *Blvd. Mortier, even-numbered side*
- Thursday, and Sunday morning

80 **Pyrénées**
- *Rue des Pyrénées*
- Thursday, and Sunday morning

81 **Réunion**
- *Place de la Réunion*
- Thursday, and Sunday morning

82 **Télégraphe**
- *Rue du Télégraphe*
- Wednesday, and Saturday morning

IN THE NAME OF PARIS

These culinary specialties and ingredients have Paris in more than just their history—they have it in their names!

"PARIS"

1 CHAMPIGNON DE PARIS

From the gardens of the Palace of Versailles to the quarries of Île-de-France, *Agaricus bisporus* (the white button mushroom) is one of the best-known emblems of the capital.

2 JAMBON DE PARIS

A boneless ham cooked in an aromatic broth and sold in slices. It's an essential component of the jambon-beurre sandwich, croque-monsieur, and salade Parisienne.

3 BOUDIN DE PARIS

Blood sausage that is one-third blood, one-third fat, and one-third onions, originating from a medieval recipe.

4 BOULE BOISSIER DE PARIS

A hard candy in the shape of a ball, flavored with cherry, created by Maison Boissier. Other flavors have been developed (orange, lemon, violet, mint . . .).

5 PARIS-BREST

Created at Maisons-Laffitte in 1910, this tribute to the eponymous bicycle race is in the shape of a wheel of choux pastry sprinkled with sliced almonds and filled with a praline mousseline cream.

6 PARIS-DEAUVILLE

A delicious cake in the shape of savarin (ring shape), with a texture between a soufflé and a crème caramel. It was created in 2013 by chef Éric Fréchon in his brasserie Lazare, Gare Saint-Lazare (Paris 8th) as a tribute to his native Normandy.

"PARISIEN"/ "PARISIENNE" (PARISIAN)

7 SANDWICH PARISIEN

This is the real name of the jambon-beurre sandwich, which is a half baguette spread with unsalted butter, jambon de Paris, and cornichons.

8 POTAGE PARISIEN

A peasant-style soup from the Paris region, from a base of leeks and potatoes. It has been refined in the capital under the name "potage bonne femme."

9 SALADE PARISIENNE

This is the emblematic salad of neighborhood cafés and is composed of lettuce, hard-boiled egg, jambon de Paris, and Emmental cheese, all with a mustard vinaigrette.

10 SAUCE PARISIENNE

Previously called "German sauce" but renamed "sauce blonde" by Auguste Escoffier following World War I, then finally "sauce Parisienne." It is made from a white stock, egg yolks, cream, lemon, and sometimes champignons de Paris (button mushrooms). It's used to top a vol-au-vent or fish.

11 POMMES PARISIENNES

These are fried potato balls. Their rounded shape comes from using a melon baller to shape them.

12 BAGUETTE PARISIENNE

The name suggests the possibility of other baguettes, but there is only one true baguette, a long loaf made with white wheat flour and invented in the capital! It is also called baguette de Paris or Parisienne in Lorraine.

13 L'ESCALOPE PARISIENNE

This is the French version of its Austrian cousin, which is a thin slice of veal that swaps the breadcrumb coating for a simple mixture of egg and flour. This *Pariser Schnitzel* was introduced at the 1889 Universal Exposition.

14 GALETTE PARISIENNE

This is the other name for the galette des rois (kings' cake), composed of puff pastry filled with almond cream or frangipane.

15 FLAN PARISIEN

Also called flan pâtissier. Describes a flan baked into a crust made from flaky pastry or puff pastry.

16 BRIOCHE PARISIENNE

With a small top and fluted larger bottom, this brioche has long distinguished itself from its provincial cousins by its use of fresh yeast, which makes it particularly light and fluffy.

"À LA PARISIENNE" (IN PARISIAN STYLE)

17 GNOCCHIS À LA PARISIENNE

Far from the Italian gnocchi most of us know, which is made with potatoes, these small bites of salted choux pastry are gratinéed with a béchamel or Mornay sauce (the cheese version).

18 SAUMON À LA PARISIENNE

Codified by Auguste Escoffier in Le Guide culinaire (1903), this center-cut salmon fillet dish is served with mayonnaise, diced and cooked vegetables, artichokes, and herbs.

19 LANGOUSTE À LA PARISIENNE

The spiny lobster was long considered the king of the crustaceans at Parisian markets. It was often enjoyed cold with the same topping as the saumon à la Parisienne (see above), or just simply with mayonnaise.

20 CHARLOTTE À LA PARISIENNE

In 1800, pastry chef Antonin Carême created this French version of the British charlotte. It is distinguished by its use of ladyfingers (as opposed to pain de mie, or a plain white bread), a Bavarian filling, and fresh fruit (as opposed to a compote). It is served chilled.

UTENSILS

21 CUILLÈRE PARISIENNE

This is a spoon (a melon baller) whose scoop is a half sphere ⅓ to 1 inch (1 to 3 cm) in diameter, originally intended for making pommes Parisiennes (see page 147). It is also called the cuillère à pomme Parisienne. Today, it is typically used to make small balls of melon, tomato, or other vegetables.

22 LE PARISIEN

This is the name for the proofing rack used when making bread, constructed of wooden supports or stainless steel racks. A liftable or removable door allows for shutting the rack.

DON'T BE FOOLED

SAUCE CAFÉ DE PARIS

The term de Paris can sometimes be misleading. The sauce café de Paris is composed of butter, eggs, and mustard to which aromatic herbs and spices are added. This is an ideal sauce to accompany red meats and was popularized in the 1930s by a brasserie named Café de Paris located in the heart of . . . Geneva!

PARISIAN PRICES

AVERAGE PRICES

1 SANDWICH: about €6
1 PIZZA: between €8 and €12
1 COMPLETE MEAL (*starter, main course, dessert, no beverage*): between €15 and €20, depending on the district
1 HALF-PINT OF BEER AT THE CAFÉ: €4

Source: *Office du tourisme et des Congrès de Paris, 2022.*

THE RESTAURANT BILL

The price of a meal at a restaurant costs €15 per person on average. The same meal costs around €20 to €40 in a bistro, €40 to €60 in a gourmet bistro, and much more in a Michelin-starred establishment.

Some gourmet restaurant menus have significantly higher prices. Here are the menus of establishments with three Michelin stars, priced as of 2022. The prices quoted do not include a beverage.

1 **Kei, Paris 1st** (Kei Kobayashi): *Menu Horizon, €385.*

2 **Plénitude Cheval Blanc Paris, Paris 1st** (Arnaud Donckele): *Menu Symphonie in 6 acts, €405.*

3 **L'Ambroisie, Paris 4th** (Bernard Pacaud): *No menu, but an à la carte price around €400.*

4 **Guy Savoy, Monnaie de Paris, Paris 6th** (Guy Savoy): *Menu Couleurs, Textures et Saveurs in 13 courses, €585.*

5 **L'Arpège, Paris 7th** (Alain Passard): *Menu Terre & Mer, €490.*

6 **Alléno Paris, Paris 8th** (Yannick Alléno): *Collection en 10 Émotions, €395.*

7 **Le Cinq, Hotel George V, Paris 8th** (Christian Le Squer): *Menu of signature dishes, €530.*

8 **Pierre Gagnaire, Le Balzac, Paris 8th** (Pierre Gagnaire): *Menu Esprit Pierre Gagnaire, €365.*

9 **Épicure, Le Bristol, Paris 8th** (Éric Fréchon): *Menu, €420.*

10 **Le Pré Catelan, Paris 16th** (Frédéric Anton): *Le menu du Pré, €330.*

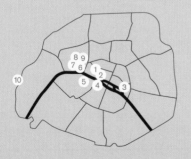

THE PRICE OF A TRADITIONAL BAGUETTE

The average price of a baguette in Paris, considering all arrondissements combined, is about €1.07 compared to €0.89 in other parts of France. *The French government raised the price of a baguette tradition in Paris's traditional boulangeries in April 2022.*

ESTABLISHMENT	ADDRESS	PRICE
TOUT AUTOUR DU PAIN	34, rue de Turenne, 3rd	€1.40
LA PARISIENNE SAINT-GERMAIN	52, blvd. Saint-Germain, 5th	€1.20
MAISON MULOT	6, rue de Seine, 6th	€1.45
AU PAIN RETROUVÉ	18, rue des Martyrs, 9th	€1.10
BOULANGERIE DU PAIN	20, blvd. des Filles-du-Calvaire, 11th	€1.10
BOULANGERIE FLORENT TOUPIN	65, av. des Gobelins, 13th	€1.20
L'ARTISAN DES GOURMANDS	60, rue de la Convention, 15th	€1.20
BOULANGERIE BACILLUS	100, rue des Dames, 17th	€1.20
AU PAIN COMPLET DE PARIS	59 bis, rue du Mont-Cenis, 18th	€1.30
AU LEVAIN DES PYRÉNÉES	44, rue des Pyrénées, 20th	€1.20

THE PRICE OF COFFEE

In Paris, coffee is more expensive than anywhere else in France, costing €2.48 on average in inner Paris, compared to €1.56 in France. There is often a price difference between coffee served at the counter and coffee served in the dining room or on the terrace, but more and more establishments have set a single price. *The French government raised the price of coffee in Paris's traditional cafés in April 2022.*

ESTABLISHMENT	ADDRESS	PRICE AT THE COUNTER	PRICE AT A TABLE
CAFÉ MARLY	93, rue de Rivoli, 1st	NA	€5
LE PETIT VENDÔME	8, rue des Capucines, 2nd	€1.30	€2.50
LE SORBON	60, rue des Écoles, 5th	€1.40	€3
LE SELECT	99, blvd. du Montparnasse, 6th	€1.70	€3.60
AUX FOLIES	31–33, rue Juliette-Dodu, 10th	€1.20	€2.20
FOUQUET'S	99, av. des Champs-Élysées, 8th	NA	€6
PAUSE CAFÉ	41, rue de Charonne, 11th	€1.20	€2.20
LE CAFÉ DAGUERRE	4, av. du Général Leclerc, 14th	€1.40	€2.60
L'AÉRO	3, pl. de Passy, 16th	€1.20	€2.30
LE CAFÉ DES DEUX MOULINS	15, rue Lepic, Paris 18th	€1	€3

TIPPING

In Paris, as in the rest of France, prices include taxes and service (about 15 percent of the total price). But if the service has been particularly kind and attentive, you can leave a tip, especially when you know that, considering the cost of rent in the capital, the cost of living for servers can be difficult. The amount to tip is usually 5 to 10 percent of the total bill.

NAMES TO CHEW ON

In Paris, the passion for gastronomy is evident even in the names of some of its streets and metro stations.

Streets

PASSAGE ANTOINE-CARÊME, 1ST
Marie-Antoine Carême (1784–1833), French chef and pastry chef, nicknamed "the king of cooks and the cook of kings."

RUE DU PONT-AUX-CHOUX, 3RD
Named after a bridge leading to a path that crossed through vegetable crops.

RUE BRISEMICHE, 4TH
The name of this street refers to the loaves of bread distributed to the canons of the cloister Saint-Merri located nearby. It absorbed the old rue Taille-Pain.

RUE DE LA COUTELLERIE, 4TH
Many cutlery manufacturers were established here under Henry II.

RUE DES BOULANGERS, 5TH
The location of many bakeries during the Middle Ages.

RUE DE L'ÉCHAUDÉ, 6TH
Blocks of houses in the shape of an échaudé, a triangular pastry invented in the Middle Ages.

RUE GÎT-LE-COEUR, 6TH
Alteration of the name Guy le Queux, a cook of King Odo of France.

RUE CAMBACÉRÈS, 8TH
After Jean-Jacques-Régis de Cambacérès (1753–1824), a statesman, jurisconsult, and voracious gastronome.

AVENUE PARMENTIER, 10TH AND 11TH
Antoine-Augustin Parmentier (1737–1813), military pharmacist, agronomist, and nutritionist known for his actions to promote the potato.

RUE NICOLAS-APPERT, 11TH
Nicolas Appert (1749–1841) was a French industrialist who invented the canning process to preserve foods.

RUE ESCOFFIER, 12TH
Legendary cook, author of *Le Guide Culinaire*, Auguste Escoffier (1846–1935) most notably launched luxury hotels.

TERRASSE DES NÉGOCIANTS, 12TH
Located in the former warehouses of Bercy, a former site for wine trade.

RUE CURNONSKY, 17TH
Maurice Edmond Sailland (1872–1956), known as Curnonsky, was a novelist, gourmet journalist, and food critic. He was nicknamed the "prince of gastronomes."

RUE EUGÈNE-JUMIN, 19TH
The name of the butcher Eugène Jumin (1855–1913) who most notably served as president of the Federation of Butchers of France.

RUE RAMPONEAU, 20TH
In honor of the creator of grand popular cafés, Jean Ramponeau (1724–1802).

Metro stations

ALEXANDRE-DUMAS ②
11TH and 20TH
French writer, cook, and gastronome (1802–1870).

BERCY ⑥ ⑭
12TH
An old village, which housed the largest wine market in the world in the nineteenth century.

CHEMIN VERT ⑧
3RD and 11TH
An old path that ran through the middle of vegetable crops.

COUR SAINT-ÉMILION ⑭
12TH
To avoid rivalry between the vineyards of Bordeaux and Burgundy, the station was originally to be called "Pommard-Saint-Émilion," but the name "Cour Saint-Émilion" was retained.

GAÎTÉ ⑬
14TH
From the name of the rue de la Gaîté crowded with *guinguettes*, theaters, and restaurants.

GLACIÈRE ⑥
13TH
From the rue de la Glacière connecting the places where ice blocks from the Bièvre River were stored, used for the manufacture of ice cream.

GONCOURT ⑪
10TH and 11TH
Brothers Edmond and Jules de Goncourt, originally French gourmet writers who originated the Prix Goncourt, awarded each autumn at the restaurant Drouant.

JUSSIEU ⑦ ⑩
5TH
Takes its name from Jussieu–Halle-aux-vins, where a small wine exchange created by Napoléon I existed. Jussieu is the surname of several botanists of the seventeenth and eighteenth centuries.

LES HALLES ④
1ST
From Les Halles de Paris food market, which was located here starting in the twelfth century.

MAISONS-ALFORT–LES JUILLIOTTES ⑧
MAISONS-ALFORT
Takes its name from the former "lands of Juliotte," former mushroom farms on vacant land and in quarries.

MARAÎCHERS ⑨
20TH
From the rue des Maraîchers, once lined with vegetable gardens, including the famous peach trees of Montreuil.

MARCADET-POISSONNIERS ④ ⑫
18TH
From Mercade, a hamlet in the Middle Ages where there was a market (*marcadus* in Latin). In 1930, the name of the station was changed to Marcadet and merged with the station Poissonniers, located nearby.

POISSONNIÈRE ⑦
9TH and 10TH
On the *poissonière*'s (fishmonger's) way, the fish merchants of the North Sea to Les Halles.

REAUMUR-SEBASTOPOL ③ ④
2ND and 3RD
René-Antoine Ferchault de Réaumur (1683–1757) was a French physicist and naturalist, the inventor of the alcohol thermometer, an artificial incubator called a "chicken oven," and a way to preserve eggs by coating them in a fatty substance.

THE GALLERY OF DINERS

The capital is a gastronomic ecosystem that can accommodate every type of eater.

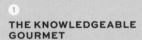

① THE KNOWLEDGEABLE GOURMET

Paris is the perfect place for this type of artistic eater, who is not only omnivorous and curious but also demanding. This eater will travel multiple metro stops just to try a new Vietnamese hole-in-the-wall or a forty-five-day aged prime rib of Aubrac beef.

UNIQUE TRAIT

Reserves a table using the chef's personal cell number.

② THE WINE LOVER

What is in the glass is more important that what is on the plate for this oenophile, who chooses a restaurant according to the wine list and the mood of the sommelier. These diners are attentive to the brand of stemmed glassware used, refuse to drink Champagne from a flute glass (it's too narrow!), and become indignant when a restaurant's wine list doesn't offer the perfect wine choice with the steak.

UNIQUE TRAIT

Always tries to bring a good bottle to a restaurant, subject to a corkage fee.

③ THE HEARTY EATER

No doubt this eater would have been a worthy guest at the copious banquets common in the nineteenth century. The quantity of meats consumed (pâtés, game, dishes in sauce or butter and cream) can be as important as the quality, origins, and preparation of the dishes. This eater typically avoids lighter vegan dishes and low-sugar desserts.

UNIQUE TRAIT

Thinking about the next meal while eating!

④ THE SWEET TOOTH

In Paris, the pastry capital of the world, the sweet tooth hits the jackpot! Between the classics and new creations, this eater burns calories by running from one end of Paris to the other to try "so-and-so's" macaron or "so-and-so's" Paris-Brest.

UNIQUE TRAIT

Dessert always comes first!

⑤ THE STREET-FOOD FAN

During the twentieth century, this eater had to be content with a simple jambon-beurre as the choice for on-the-go street food, but now exotic specialties from around the world, such as smash burgers, banh mi, sando, and pitas are all at their fingertips.

UNIQUE TRAIT

The fork is an unfamiliar utensil.

⑥ THE HEALTHY EATER

Flexible dieting, veggie, vegan, raw foods, gluten-free . . . whatever this modern-day eater's passion, the goal is to stay healthy, scouring the city for calorie-conscious foods such as buddha bowls, lacto-fermented vegetables, barley juice, and pastries with no added sugar.

UNIQUE TRAIT

Asking for a kombucha at the local bistro.

⑦ THE FOOD CRITIC

Eating is this person's job, always consuming everything no matter where, to report for a newspaper or other media outlet, moving from bars to grand restaurants, from new street-food hot spots to local market cafeterias.

UNIQUE TRAIT

Spotted eating alone at the table, to minimize expenses.

⑧ THE INFLUENCER

Gastro-obsessed and gastro-connected, posting on Instagram all the new food spots and taking photos, this newfangled eater wants to make the passion of eating into a business by promoting all the great eating locations on social networks while getting paid to do so.

UNIQUE TRAIT

Constantly holding a smartphone and switching between photo and video mode when even the smallest edible object is nearby.

ÎLE-DE-FRANCE TERROIR

From the limestone plateau of the French Vexin to the clay soils of Brie, the agricultural lands of the Île-de-France region represent nearly half its area. Truck farming, arboriculture, and livestock farming provide an exceptionally rich and diverse selection of products and know-how, despite current threats to some of France's traditional production processes. Here is an inventory. —**ALESSANDRA PIERINI AND ILARIA BRUNETTI**

VAL-D'OISE

Cergy

Pontoise

Groslay

Montmorency

Argenteuil

Mantes-la-Jolie

La Seine

Poissy

Croissy

Gennevilliers

Montreuil

Nanterre

PARIS

Versailles

HAUTS-DE-SEINE

Créteil

VAL-DE-MARNE

Houdan

YVELINES

Rambouillet

ESSONNE

Évry

Arpajon

Étampes

Milly-La-F

Méréville

PARIS

HISTORIC TERROIRS

- ◆ Brie
- ○ Gâtinais
- ⊖ Beauce
- ✕ Hurepoix
- ▽ Mantais
- ▨ Vexin
- ⌒ Valois
- ▥ Champagne

FORMER TRUCK-FARM PLAINS

- Ⓐ Plains of Vertus
- Ⓑ Plains of Bonneuil
- Ⓒ Plains of Freneuse
- Ⓓ Plains of Croissy

FRUITS

1. Cherry from Montmorency
2. Chasselas grapes from Thomery
3. Strawberry of Paris
4. Peach from Montreuil
5. Pear from Groslay
6. Reine-Claude de Chambourcy (*plum*)
7. Faro apple

VEGETABLES

8. Artichoke from Paris or the Gros Vert de Laon
9. Asparagus from Argenteuil
10. Swiss chard from Paris
11. The Paris Market carrot
12. Red Long lisse de Meaux carrot
13. Carrot from Croissy
14. Red poppy from Nemours
15. Button Mushroom of Paris
16. Cabbage from Pontoise
17. Watercress from Méréville
18. Chinese artichoke
19. Giant spinach from Viroflay
20. Flageolet bean from Arjapon
21. Peppermint from Milly-la-Forêt
22. Île-de-France turnip
23. Dandelion from Montmagny
24. Leek from Gennevilliers
25. The belle de Fontenay potato (or Parisienne, Hénaut, or Boulangère)
26. The bright red pumpkin from Étampes
27. Lettuces
28. Onions

PANTRY GOODS

29. Honeys from Paris
30. Honey from Gâtinais
31. Rose petal jam from Provins
32. Barley sugar of the nuns of Moret-sur-Loing
33. Saffron from Gâtinais
34. Moutarde de Meaux Pommery
35. Vinegar from Lagny

CHEESES

36. Brie de Meaux
37. Brie de Melun
38. Boursault
39. Brillat-Savarin
40. Coulommiers
41. Délice de Saint-Cyr
42. Explorateur
43. Fontainebleau
44. Mozzarella
45. Saint-Foin (or Saint-Jacques)

MEATS

46. Île-de-France lamb
47. Boudin noir from Paris (*blood sausage*)
48. Jambon de Paris (ham)
49. Rabbit from Gâtinais
50. Garlic sausage from Paris
51. Gâtinais chicken
52. Houdan chicken

SPIRITS

53. Clacquesin
54. Noyau de Poissy
55. Grand Marnier

Meaux · Saint-Cyr-sur-Morin · Le Grand Morin · Lagny-sur-Marne · Coulommiers · Saint-Siméon · SEINE-ET-MARNE · Melun · Provins · Thomery · La Seine · Fontainebleau · Moret-sur-Loing · Nemours

"God knows that I admire, on the fickle lands of Île-de-France, the orchards. Worked and reworked, loosened, tormented by man, enriched by him; there is not an inch of land within the worked cantons that hasn't borne cherry or pear, gooseberry or raspberry. Gobelet pruning puts us on the level with the fruit, shaping the vine so that the sun's rays and the breeze descend into it. To whom shall we award the prize, choosing among the misty raspberry of purple blooms, the Montmorency [cherry] of a flesh so fine that the core shines through it in the light, and the Mirabelle [plum] plump as a cheek?"
—Colette, *Flore et Pomone*, 1943

FRUITS

Cherry from Montmorency

A cherry with a long or short stem. Round, with thin bright red skin, tender flesh with colorless and tangy juice. Also called gobet, coularde, or gaudriole.

SCIENTIFIC NAME
Prunus cerasus Montmorency

SEASON
🗓 *Mid-June to mid-July*

PLACE OF ORIGIN
📍 *Montmorency (Val d'Oise)*

HISTORY
Louis XV loved cherries and encouraged the cultivation of many varieties, including Montmorency, which remained for a long time the most esteemed variety. The fruit is described as "admirable to eat & use in preserves" in *L'Abrégé des bons fruits* by Jean Merlet (1690). In the eighteenth century, it was sold at auction in the streets of the capital. Rousseau, Voltaire, and Madame de Sévigné mention it in their works. This cherry is also cultivated in the United States and Canada. Today in France, it has become rare and largely replaced by the sweeter Bigarreau variety.

A CURIOUS FACT
In the nineteenth century, Parisians rented cherry trees by the hour so they could enjoy their fruit. Bélissaire Boissier, a famous confectioner, eventually discovered these cherries and decided to produce the first candies in the shape of red balls.

IN COOKING
The name "Montmorency" is used for various savory or sweet recipes that include these cherries, such as with duck, tarts, ice creams, bombes. The cherry is prepared as a preserve, as a jelly, or preserved in brandy. Butcher-caterer Jean-Luc Maurice has been making headlines for decades with his roast leg of Montmorency recipe. The dish consists of a large turkey roll stuffed with duck-liver mousse, veal, pork, and Montmorency cherries in eau-de-vie, baked with cognac and butter.

🗄 PRODUCERS
Les Vergers de Champlain (orchard)
📍 *RN4, La Croix Saint-Nicolas, La Queue-en-Brie (Val-de-Marne)*
Les Légumes de Laura (vegetable vendor)
📍 *Rogenvilliers, Fontains (Seine-et-Marne)* 💧 ORGANIC

Chasselas grapes from Thomery

Also called Chasselas Doré de Fontainebleau, this golden grape has a thin, crunchy skin with few seeds, and is both fragrant and sweet.

SCIENTIFIC NAME
Vitis vinifera Chasselas

SEASON
🗓 *September to October*

PLACE OF ORIGIN
📍 *Thomery (Seine-et-Marne)*

HISTORY
The Charmeux family started growing the fruit in 1730 on the land occupied by the king's vineyards in Fontainebleau, using the first trellis technique in history, which consists of growing the vine horizontally against a south-facing wall. The walls, still visible today, are classified as historical monuments. Found in these traditional vineyards since the Renaissance, these delicious grapes were sought after by the richest consumers in Europe until the end of the nineteenth century. As a result of the World Wars, cultivation practically disappeared and today only survives thanks to a few individuals.

A CURIOUS FACT
The bunches are kept fresh using a unique traditional method, which involves immersing the end of the shoot in a mixture of water and charcoal to nourish them with sugar. This keeps the grapes fresh until the following May.

🗄 PRODUCER
Today grown only by individual growers.

Strawberry of Paris

Round, fleshy, and red, the fruit is also called the "strawberry of Marcoussis" and "Linas" (Vallé de l'Orge), from the Bièvre and Yvette river valleys.

SCIENTIFIC NAME
Fragaria ananassa (common strawberry)

SEASON
🗓 *June to September*

PLACE OF ORIGIN
📍 *Montreuil (Seine-Saint-Denis)*

HISTORY
Until the eighteenth century in Paris, only wild strawberries were consumed. Eventually Île-de-France's truck farmers produced the Montreuil strawberry, which was larger and able to compete with the arrival of new American varieties. Until the mid-nineteenth century, the Parisian variety dominated the market. Today, although having been continuously grown, the crop is in sharp decline and is almost exclusively farm produced.

IN COOKING
Used in cakes, jellies, preserves, syrup.

🗄 PRODUCERS
La Fraiseraie du Plessis
📍 *1, rue des Blancs Manteaux, Le Plessis-Gassot (Val-d'Oise)*
Les Saveurs de Chailly
📍 *7, av. de Villeroy, Chailly-en-Bière (Seine-et-Marne)*

Peach from Montreuil

The peaches from Montreuil, now almost disappeared, are grown using "peach walls," which give the fruit a superior quality. There are a dozen varieties of peaches, some of which are still cultivated today, such as the Téton de Vénus (Nipple of Venus), or Late Admirable: a very large juicy and fragrant peach with yellow skin and white flesh.

SCIENTIFIC NAME
Prunus persica (common peach)

SEASON
📅 *July to September*

PLACE OF ORIGIN
📍 *Montreuil (Seine-Saint-Denis)*

HISTORY
Originally from Asia, most likely from China, the peach tree appeared in France in the twelfth century, and peach production in the Paris region was quickly recognized as among the best. Initially, Corbeil vine peaches were sold at Les Halles, but, starting in the seventeenth century, peaches from Montreuil stole the spotlight. The knight Girardot, a musketeer of Louis XIV, made famous the technique for growing fruit trees on a trellis, which he practiced in his garden in Bagnolet. His neighbors in Montreuil soon began to imitate his technique. Today, only 93 acres (38 ha) remain out of the 1,200 acres (500 ha) that were cultivated in Montreuil during its peak production period.

PEACH WALLS
From the seventeenth century until the end of the nineteenth century, on Montreuil's plateau, horticulturists separated the cultivated plots with plaster walls, thanks to gypsum-rich soil. This technique made it possible to store the heat from the sun and create a warmer environment at night, thus guaranteeing peach trees a temperature higher than the actual outside temperature (up to 54°F/12°C). The branches are kept close to the walls, facing north–south, using strips of fabric (called trellising) to make the most of this microclimate. Some growers install removable wooden roofs on the walls to protect the trees and fruits from the rain.

CURIOUS FACTS
It is said that in 1670, Girardot gave a basket of his peaches to King Louis XIV, who appreciated their quality so much that he asked for a basket every year, elevating the peaches from Montreuil to the most prized of any served on the tables of the kings of Europe.

Émile Zola, in *Le Ventre de Paris* (1873), described the peaches of Montreuil compared to those from the South: ". . . peaches, especially the blushing Montreuils, have fair and thin skins, like girls from the north, while the peaches from the south, yellow and sun-kissed, are tanned, like girls from Provence."

🏭 PRODUCER
The technique is only practiced by individuals. The garden museum of the Regional Horticultural Society of Montreuil, open every second Sunday of the month, offers a tour of the orchard and a tasting.

Pear from Groslay

Groslay is not the name of a variety but of a place, emblematic for its production of pears during the nineteenth and twentieth centuries. The Williams Pear, the Doyenné du Comice (or just Comice), and other varieties, were grown here. Today, only a few orchards remain.

SCIENTIFIC NAME
Pyrus communis (common pear)

SEASON
📅 *Fall to winter*

PLACE OF ORIGIN
📍 *Groslay (Val d'Oise)*

HISTORY
Until 1900 in Groslay, vineyards were the main crop, but when phylloxera attacked the vines, they were replaced by pear trees. Orchard growing has drastically decreased since the 2000s because of urbanization.

A CURIOUS FACT
Under the reign of Louis XIV, pears were a royal offering that only the court could claim. They remained a luxury product for a long time.

IN COOKING
Tarte Bourdaloue, composed of pears and frangipane.

🏭 PRODUCER
Les Vergers des Rougemonts
📍 *Rue Émile-Aimond, Groslay (Val-d'Oise)*

⌒ SKIP TO
The Tarte Bourdaloue, p. 268.

Reine-Claude de Chambourcy

This late-variety plum is round, medium-large, green, and tinged with red. The early variety has smaller, gold-green fruits. The flesh is juicy, fragrant, and sweet.

SCIENTIFIC NAME
Prunus domestica Reine-Claude de Chambourcy

SEASON
📅 *Mid-August (early variety)*
📅 *Late September to October (late variety)*

PLACE OF ORIGIN
📍 *Chambourcy (Yvelines)*

HISTORY
It was the Romans who introduced the plum, originally from Syria, to Gaul, but the fruit was not adopted until the Renaissance. In the sixteenth century, there were only seven varieties compared to four hundred at the beginning of the twentieth century. It wasn't until 1840 that people began talking about the late-ripening Reine-Claude de Chambourcy, where fruit orchards were anchored in the area's history. Thanks to the plum's taste, production grew rapidly, and in 1950 it was the best-selling variety in France! Today, the early variety is more widespread.

IN COOKING
Used in jams and tarts, or just for eating.

🏭 PRODUCER
Maison Gaillard
📍 *110, route Royale, Les Alluets-le-Roi (Yvelines)*

Apples and ciders

Île-de-France boasts of the largest number of indigenous apple varieties in France, especially in the Brie region, where all varieties of apples can be found. They are juicy when eaten raw or even when you drink them . . . sparkling!

FROM THE ORCHARDS OF BRIE TO SEINE-SAINT-DENIS
The Brie region (Seine-et-Marne) has become a renowned site for cider production. There are many local apple varieties suitable for eating, such as Nouvelle France or Marie Madeleine; to produce cider, such as Vérité, Bassard, or Sebin; or for both purposes, such as the Faro. Other varieties of apples can be found in the Val-d'Oise, such as Belle de Pontoise or even the Bondy (Seine-Saint-Denis), near Paris, from the town of the same name.

Faro apple

Bloodred skin, yellowish-greenish flesh, crunchy, juicy and sweet, fragrant.

SCIENTIFIC NAME
Malus communis Faro

SEASON
📅 *End of September to end of March*

PLACE OF ORIGIN
📍 *North of the Seine-et-Marne*

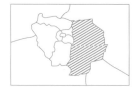

HISTORY
A document from 1350 attests that this apple was already renowned in the Middle Ages. It was also grown in the Chartreux de Paris nursery (currently Luxembourg Garden).

IN COOKING
Enjoyed raw or used for cider.

🍶 PRODUCER
Cidre Fahy
📍 *Carr, de Saint-Blandin, Guérard (Seine-et-Marne)*
💧 *ORGANIC*
A family sibling took over the Fahy family farm, which produces ciders using ancient local organic varieties.

Cider from Brie

This sparkling drink is obtained by grinding apples on canvas and leaving the must behind. Calcium chloride and a natural enzyme are then used to ferment the product for two to three months before bottling.

HISTORY
Cider was being produced on farms in Brie as far back as the sixteenth century, but the cider had not yet gained the same level of fame as the ones from its Norman or Breton neighbors. The consumption of cider increased starting in 1880 due to the onset of the phylloxera that devastated grapevines. Transporting cider was expensive, but thanks to new techniques, production in Brie increased to satisfy demand from Parisians.

THE MIGNARD CIDER HOUSE
Adolphe Mignard began his cider production as a "traveling cider maker," using a press that was affixed to wheels, before creating one of the first cider houses in France in 1909 in Bellot (Seine-et-Marne). Pernod Ricard bought the family-owned business in 1991 and closed the Bellot site in 1995. Michel Biberon, who at the time produced apples for the cider house, revived the Jehan de Brie vintage (the only one produced with indigenous apple varieties) and embarked on his own production, thus continuing the local tradition.

🍶 PRODUCER
Ferme de la Bonnerie
📍 *Verdelot (Seine-et-Marne)*

VEGETABLES

Artichoke from Paris or the Gros Vert de Laon

This cultivar has a rounded flower head with a broad, thick bottom, and fleshy, short, pointed, light green leaves (bracts). The artichoke resembles the Gros Camus de Bretagne, but it is smaller, rough in appearance, and flavorful.

SCIENTIFIC NAME
Cynar acardunculus var. *scolymus* (common artichoke)

SEASON
📅 *July to September*

PLACE OF ORIGIN
📍 *Paris region*

HISTORY
Indigenous to the Mediterranean countries, in particular Spain and Arabic Sicily during the Middle Ages, the artichoke arrived in France in the sixteenth century. Cultivation developed in Avignon and around Paris to satisfy the demands by the aristocracy for this now-fashionable vegetable, which was favored by Catherine de' Médicis and Louis XIV. The Gros Vert de Laon was the most famous variety until the twentieth century, but after World War II, production in the Paris region could no longer compete with the Italian variety that was rapidly gaining popularity.

IN COOKING
Enjoyed raw or boiled.

🏛 PRODUCER
Laurent Berrurier
📍 *1, imp. des Clos, Neuville-sur-Oise (Val-d'Oise)*

↪ **SKIP TO**
Poultry, p. 42.

Asparagus from Argenteuil

White asparagus has thick stalks with purple tips. The stalks can reach about 10 inches (25 cm) long and 1 inch (3 cm) in diameter. There is a more common early variety and a late variety. Planting is in March and April in soil enriched with manure. The shoots will be harvested three years later. One month before harvest, each asparagus plant is covered with a thick mound of dirt to protect the buds from the sun, which explains the pale color. The flavor is delicate and subtle, with a pronounced bitter aftertaste.

SCIENTIFIC NAME
Asparagus officinalis Argenteuil

SEASON
📅 *April*

PLACE OF ORIGIN
📍 *Argenteuil (Val-d'Oise)*

HISTORY
The cultivation of white asparagus developed in Argenteuil (Val-d'Oise) in 1860 by horticulturist Louis Lhérault, creator of the Belle d'Argenteuil. He selected plants imported from the Netherlands and increased yields using a technique of growing rows of asparagus in the middle of rows of grapevines. This method, introduced at the Universal Expositions of 1867 and 1878, allowed winegrowers, whose vineyards were decimated by phylloxera, to recover. The technique eventually disappeared from Argenteuil, although it continued in the Cergy region.

A CURIOUS FACT
In the 1930s, farmers competed to produce huge asparagus, up to nearly 1½ pounds (600 g) per stalk and 6 to 7 inches (16 to 18 cm) in circumference!

IN COOKING
Used in Argenteuil soup, scrambled eggs Argenteuil-style, or simply *à l'anglaise* (boiled), accompanied by a vinaigrette.

🏛 PRODUCER
Laurent Berrurier
📍 *1, imp. des Clos, Neuville-sur-Oise (Val-d'Oise)*

Swiss chard from Paris
🐌 *Slow Food Ark of Taste*

With broad and fleshy green to yellowish leaves. The stems are white and thin. Its ribs have a pronounced flavor.

SCIENTIFIC NAME
Beta vulgaris var. *cycla* (chard or common chard)

SEASON
📅 *June to November*

PLACE OF ORIGIN
📍 *Île-de-France*

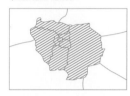

HISTORY
Chard was a despised vegetable during antiquity, then widely used for a soup called porée. In the fourteenth century, recipes based on chard could be found in *Le Viandier* and *Le Mesnagier de Paris*. In the sixteenth century, the cultivation of different varieties began. In the seventeenth century, white chard was sold in markets.

IN COOKING
Chard with béchamel, or chard soup.

🏛 PRODUCER
Vergers de Cossigny
📍 *9, av. des Peupliers, Chevry-Cossigny (Seine-et-Marne)*
◈ *ORGANIC*

A STAR TRUCK FARMER
Joël Thiébault comes from a family of farmers, arborists, and winegrowers who have been rooted for generations in Carrières-sur-Seine (Yvelines) and have been present in Parisian markets since 1873. Managing 49 acres (20 ha), on which he grows 1,500 vegetables, Joël supplied vegetables to many chefs before retiring in 2016.

The Paris Market carrot

Slow Food Ark of Taste

This carrot is round and small, 1 to 1½ inches (3 to 4 cm) in diameter, and orange. Its texture is tender, and its taste is very sweet. This is a very early spring variety.

SCIENTIFIC NAME
Daucus carota subsp. *sativus* Marché de Paris

SEASON
June to November

PLACE OF ORIGIN
Seine-Saint-Denis (Yvelines)

HISTORY
Carrots in Europe had been white since ancient times. The orange color appeared in the sixteenth century thanks to hybridization with other varieties imported from Afghanistan and Asia. A legend says that the Dutch, close to the House of Orange (a French Protestant principality), created this vegetable as a sign of their loyalty. In Île-de-France, carrots were favored by truck farmers on the plains of Vertus, around Aubervilliers, and the plains of Croissy, Montesson, and Chatou starting in the eighteenth century, when the land was wet and the working classes were large consumers of vegetables.

IN COOKING
Beef with carrots

PRODUCER
Fabrice Robert
Ferme des Alluets, 3, rue Traversière, Les Alluets-le-Roi (Yvelines)

Red Long lisse de Meaux carrot

This carrot has a long and cylindrical taproot with an intense red color. The greens are light in color and sparse. The carrot tastes sweet.

SCIENTIFIC NAME
Daucus carota subsp. *sativus* Longue Lisse de Meaux

SEASON
August to November

PLACE OF ORIGIN
Meaux (Seine-et-Marne)

HISTORY
Thanks to its long shelf life, this carrot was sold at Les Halles at the end of winter. Today, it has almost disappeared from commercial outlets. The strategic location of the city of Meaux on the outskirts of the Marne has undoubtedly contributed to cultivating this carrot in the area's truck farms. At the beginning of the twentieth century, Meaux had at least a hundred truck farmers who supplied the capital with fresh fruits and vegetables.

A CURIOUS FACT
In the village of Varreddes (Seine-et-Marne) near Meaux, growing carrots and other root vegetables called "raves" was so important that its inhabitants were nicknamed "Ravetons."

IN COOKING
In salad or soups, such as potage Crécy.

PRODUCER
Gaec Maurice de Poincy
440–44, rue de Dampleger, Poincy (Seine-et-Marne)
ORGANIC

Carrot from Croissy

This carrot is conical, medium long, and very light red with a yellow core.

SCIENTIFIC NAME
Daucus carota (common carrot)

PLACE OF ORIGIN
Croissy-sur-Seine (Yvelines)

HISTORY
Starting at the end of the nineteenth century, Croissy became an important center for truck farming with 850 acres (344 ha) growing mainly carrots, parsnips, onions, and leeks, which earned the city the nickname "queen of Les Halles de Paris." During World War II, carrot cultivation began to disappear due to the introduction of lettuces and greens, whose roots contained a milk favored by a fungus that attacked the carrots.

A CURIOUS FACT
Although the cultivation of this carrot has disappeared from Croissy, the annual Carrot Festival still celebrates it.

PRODUCER
Laurent Berrurier
1, imp. des Clos, Neuville-sur-Oise (Val-d'Oise)

Red poppy from Nemours

These wildflowers grow in untreated fields. They are as beautiful as they are delicate, and their petals are picked by hand in the morning then dried and macerated. An average of 440 pounds (200 kg) are harvested each year.

SCIENTIFIC NAME
Papaver rhoeas (common poppy)

SEASON
Mid-May to end of June

PLACE OF ORIGIN
Nemours (Seine-et-Marne)

HISTORY
The tradition of poppy candies originated in Nemours in the mid-nineteenth century thanks to confectioner François-Étienne Desserey. The tradition was revived in the 1990s by the confectionery house Des Lis. Today, other poppy products are made by local confectioners and chocolatiers.

IN COOKING
In candies, chocolates, jams, and liqueurs.

CONFECTIONERS

Des Lis Chocolat

- 📍 *1, rue de Boissettes, Melun (Seine-et-Marne)*
- 📍 *ZI du Rocher-Vert, 6, rue Louis Blériot, Nemours (Seine-et-Marne)*
- 📍 *Commercial center at Villiers-en-Bière (Seine-et-Marne)*

Distributed at Maison du Sucre d'Orge de Moret

- 📍 *Place Royale, Moret-sur-Loing (Seine-et-Marne)*

Chinese artichoke

A small yellowish-white root vegetable with a caterpillar shape. It has a nutty, sweet taste, similar to common artichoke, salsify, and Jerusalem artichoke.

SCIENTIFIC NAME

Stachys affinis
(common Chinese artichoke)

SEASON

📅 *Winter*

PLACE OF ORIGIN

📍 *Crosne (Essonne)*

HISTORY

This tuber, originally from Asia, takes its French name *crosne* from the town Crosne (Essonne), where it was cultivated in 1882 for the first time in Europe by industrialist Nicolas-Auguste Paillieux and botanist Désiré Bois. Large quantities were sold at Les Halles de Paris until the end of the nineteenth century, then the tuber disappeared at the end of the twentieth century due to periods of famine.

A CURIOUS FACT

The famous Parisian restaurateur Paul Brébant honored this vegetable in his Japanese-style salad after a legendary potato salad described in the play *Francillon* (1887).

IN COOKING

In soups, gratinéed, sautéed, or in salad. Charlotte Paillieux, great-great-granddaughter of Nicolas-Auguste Paillieux, created this recipe: Clean the artichokes by rubbing them in a cloth with coarse salt to remove the thin skins and dirt. Blanch the artichokes in boiling water for 10 to 15 minutes. Next, fry them in butter with chopped shallots and a garlic clove and sprinkle with chopped fresh flat-leaf parsley.

PRODUCER

Produced in France, but no longer in Île-de-France.

Giant spinach from Viroflay

◉ *Slow Food Ark of Taste*

A variety of spinach with leaves that can reach 24 inches (60 cm) in diameter. The leaves are large, smooth, and fleshy, hence its other name: "elephant ear spinach." It can only be harvested by hand.

SCIENTIFIC NAME

Spinacia oleracea
Monstrueux Viroflay

SEASON

📅 *March to May and September to November*

PLACE OF ORIGIN

📍 *Viroflay (Yvelines)*

HISTORY

Accounts of this variety date to the seventeenth century, but it was marketed for the first time in 1880 by Maison Vilmorin in Viroflay, near Versailles. Madame Vilmorin herself most likely gave this vegetable its name. It was grown along the royal road on the Right Bank and sold in the stalls of Les Halles. This variety has become rare because its cultivation requires a great deal of work.

A CURIOUS FACT

France is the leading producer of spinach, mostly frozen or canned, but the giant spinach of Viroflay is only sold fresh.

IN COOKING

Raw in salad; cooked; in a Viroflay omelet.

PRODUCERS

Laurent Berrurier

- 📍 *1, imp. des Clos, Neuville-sur-Oise (Val-d'Oise)*

Fabrice Robert

- 📍 *Ferme des Alluets, 3, rue Traversière, Les Alluets-le-Roi (Yvelines)*

Flageolet bean from Arpajon

A small, green shell bean, cultivated using a harvesting method in which the plants are pulled from the ground to dry out, then covered with rye straw. The beans thus maintain a green color and have a more pronounced taste than that of a common flageolet.

SCIENTIFIC NAME

Phaseolus vulgaris
Chevrier Vert Flagrano

SEASON

📅 *July to October*

PLACE OF ORIGIN

📍 *Arpajon, Dourdan, Limours (Essonne)*

HISTORY

Beans were imported as a crop from America at the beginning of the sixteenth century. Cultivation developed a century later in the Paris region. Parisians quickly grew to love beans, especially flageolets. At the end of the nineteenth century, a farmer from Brétigny-sur-Orge, Gabriel Chevrier, discovered, thanks to a lucky coincidence, the technique for growing flageolets, to which he lent his name (*haricot chevrier* in French). He placed straw on top of plants pulled from the ground and, a few days later, found open pods containing beans that were still very green. The popularity of his growing method for flageolets spread rapidly in the region, particularly in Dourdan, Limours, and Arpajon—which had a rich fruit- and vegetable-farming tradition since the Middle Ages—and eventually throughout France.

A CURIOUS FACT

Since 1922, the Bean Fair has been held in Arpajon on the third Sunday of September, recognized since 1970 as a national fair. The flageolet inspired a nougatine-based sweet treat that is bean-shaped.

IN COOKING

Purée Musard, or as an accompaniment to a mutton stew or leg of lamb.

PRODUCER

Le potager d'Olivier

- 📍 *Le Mesnil Racoin, La Ferté-Alais (Essonne)*

Peppermint from Milly-la-Forêt

Slow Food Ark of Taste

Peppermint with dark green lanceolate leaves, perennial, and vigorous; its taste is strong and fragrant.

SCIENTIFIC NAME

Mentha piperita Mitcham Milly

SEASON

June to August

PLACE OF ORIGIN

Milly-la-Forêt (Essonne)

HISTORY

The commune of Milly-la-Forêt (Essonne) has been linked to the cultivation of aromatic and medicinal plants since the Middle Ages. Such production, attested by official acts that mention marsh mallow and mallow crops, was developed at the end of the nineteenth century by truck farmer Armand Darbonne, who invented a specific drying bed called the "Milly dryer." The story of peppermint begins when Darbonne brought back mitcham (black mint) from England that was used for the famous Bêtise de Cambrai (a boiled sweet), which he hybridized with spearmint.

CURIOUS FACTS

Jean Cocteau, who lived for several years in Milly-la-Forêt, painted medicinal plants in the chapel of Saint-Blaise. A National Conservatory of Edible, Medicinal, Aromatic &

Industrial Plants (CNPMAI) was created in 1987.

IN COOKING

Used in condiments, infusions, confections, and drinks.

PRODUCERS

Ferme du Clos d'Artois

4, rue de l'Église, Oncy-sur-École (Essonne)

Émile et Une Graine

Fremigny, Soisy-sur-École (Essonne)

RECIPE

Pears from Orgeval with Pepper and Mint from Milly (by Guy Savoy)

Serves 4. Peel and halve 4 pears. Bring 3 cups (700 ml) water to a boil with 1½ cups (300 g) sugar, 1¼ cups (300 ml) dry white wine, and 10 crushed peppercorns. Immerse the pears in the boiling liquid for 10 minutes. Let cool, and refrigerate. Blanch 8 fresh mint leaves in boiling water, then transfer them to the pan with the pears. Place the pears on paper towels to drain. Serve the pears in the cold syrup, topped with a mint leaf.

Île-de-France turnip

The Croissy variety is Slow Food Ark of Taste.

This root vegetable can be found in different forms depending on the variety, whose name is determined by the place where it is grown. The Virtus is round with white flesh, supple and soft; The Freneuse has a drier flesh that is sweet and mild. The Croissy is round or semi-long and white. The Montesson, Montmagny, and Meaux varieties (available at the end of winter) have a yellow flesh.

SCIENTIFIC NAME

Brassica rapa (common turnip)

SEASON

Year-round

PLACE OF ORIGIN

Freneuse, Croissy-sur-Seine, Montesson, Gargenville (Yvelines), Plaine des Vertus (Seine-Saint-Denis), Meaux (Seine-et-Marne)

HISTORY

The turnip was commonly consumed in the Middle Ages as it had been present in France before the arrival of potatoes and beans. In the eighteenth century, the varieties Freneuse and Virtus appeared around Aubervilliers. Other varieties soon arrived.

IN COOKING

In ragouts and stews.

PRODUCERS

Gaec Maurice de Poincy

40–44, rue de Dampleger, Poincy (Seine-et-Marne) ORGANIC

Les Jardins de Courances

14, rue du Moulin, Courances (Essonne)

SKIP TO

Lamb Stew, p. 231.

Dandelion from Montmagny

Slow Food Ark of Taste

Dandelion with long, green, toothlike leaves.

SCIENTIFIC NAME

Taraxacum officinale Vert de Montmagny

SEASON

November to April

PLACE OF ORIGIN

Cergy (Val-d'Oise)

HISTORY

This dandelion appeared toward the end of the nineteenth century. Known as "lion's tooth" (*dent de lion*), it is whiter and less bitter than other varieties thanks to a special cultivar created in 1857 by Joseph Châtelain, resulting in a more tender plant. It was for a long time one of the most consumed greens in the capital, but today it is rare.

IN COOKING

Salade Parisienne (with lardons, boiled eggs, and croutons).

PRODUCERS

Le Petit Maraîcher du Bois de Cergy

49, chemin des Patis, Cergy (Val-d'Oise)

Maison Paulmier

2519, route Royale, Orgeval (Yvelines)

Leek from Gennevilliers

Slow Food Ark of Taste

A vegetable with a long, white bulb and dark, stiff greens.

SCIENTIFIC NAME

Allium ampeloprasum var. *porrum* (common leek)

SEASON

🗓 *Winter*

PLACE OF ORIGIN

📍 *Gennevilliers (Hauts-de-Seine)*

HISTORY

Since the early twentieth century, Gennevilliers (Hauts-de-Seine) has given its name to a variety of leek with a delicate and sweet taste, now grown in other agricultural areas in the Île-de-France. The history of truck farming in Gennevilliers is linked to Parisian wastewater, which was discharged into the Seine. In the nineteenth century, Alfred Durand-Claye, an engineer of the city of Paris, proposed to divert the use of wastewater to fertilize the fields of the northwestern suburbs. This solution worked miracles and allowed the richer soils to accommodate vegetables in addition to the more traditional crops, such as grains.

IN COOKING

In the famous recipe of Michelin-starred chef Éric Fréchon in his restaurant Épicure at Le Bristol (Paris 8th), described as "Leeks from Île-de-France grilled whole with seaweed butter, white pearl oyster tartare, scallions, and lemon"; potage Parisien (vegetable soup) or potage bonne femme (leek and potato soup).

⚒ PRODUCER

Les Jardins de Courances

📍 *14, rue du Moulin, Courances (Essonne)*

↷ **SKIP TO**

Paris in the Soup, p. 266.

The belle de Fontenay potato

(or Parisienne, Hénaut, or Boulangère)

Small to medium in size, oblong, smooth, light yellow skin, firm and dark yellow flesh.

SCIENTIFIC NAME

Solanum tuberosum Belle de Fontenay

SEASON

🗓 *May to July*

PLACE OF ORIGIN

📍 *Fontenay-sous-Bois (Val-de-Marne)*

HISTORY

This variety was created at the end of the nineteenth century in Fontenay-sous-Bois, although the origin of its cultivator is not known with certainty. The first written testimony of it dates to 1885. It has been listed since 1935 in the *Catalogue officiel français des espèces et variétés végétales* (*The Official French Catalogue of Vegetable Varieties and Species*).

IN COOKING

It lends itself to any type of cooking, especially when steamed, fried, or gratinéed.

⚒ PRODUCER

Fabrice Robert

📍 *Ferme des Alluets 3, rue Traversière, Les Alluets-le-Roi (Yvelines)*

The bright red pumpkin from Étampes

A voluminous, ribbed, spherical, and squat fruit with fine, shiny orange-red skin and a thick, melting orange flesh.

SCIENTIFIC NAME

Cucurbita maxima Rouge Vif d'Étampes

SEASON

🗓 *Autumn*

PLACE OF ORIGIN

📍 *Étampes (Essonne)*

HISTORY

The Portuguese popularized this American plant in Europe and Asia during the sixteenth century. This variety was among the most consumed in France and was discovered by chance by a truck farmer from Étampes in the mid-nineteenth century.

IN COOKING

In soups, as a purée, gratinéed.

⚒ PRODUCERS

Laurent Berrurier

📍 *1, imp. des Clos, Neuville-sur-Oise (Val-d'Oise)*

Cueillette de Chanteloup en Brie

📍 *Rue de la Cueillette, Chanteloup-en-Brie (Seine-et-Marne)*

Lettuces

Different varieties of lettuce (Batavia, romaine, chicory, oakleaf, escarole, lamb's lettuce, curly endive) and shoots.

SEASON

🗓 *Year-round*

PLACE OF ORIGIN

📍 *Plains of Chailly-en-Bière (Seine-et-Marne), of Milly-la-Forêt (Essonne), and Montesson (Yvelines)*

HISTORY

At the time of Louis XIV, fifteen varieties of lettuce were grown in the king's garden. The consumption of lettuce in the Paris region exploded starting in the 1960s. Today, the cultivation of Montesson lettuce represents 40 percent of production in Île-de-France and 5 percent of all French lettuce.

A CURIOUS FACT

In the 1980s, in memory of the former truck farming terroir of Croissy-sur-Seine (Yvelines), the town named one of its parks after a lettuce grown in the area, the blonde paresseuse (*paresseuse* meaning "lazy") a large, slow-growing sweet lettuce.

⚒ PRODUCERS

Jean-Claude Guehennec

📍 *2, rue du Port, Le Mesnil-le-Roi (Yvelines)*

Marc Beausse

📍 *Rue de Forges, Chailly-en-Bière (Seine-et-Marne)*

Béhuret

📍 *18 bis, rue de la Fromagerie, Chailly-en-Bière (Seine-et-Marne)*

Button Mushroom of Paris

This button mushroom was originally cultivated in Parisian quarries. Though the practice is rare, a handful of farmers are bringing back the seventeenth-century methods for producing this fungus.

The button mushroom is also referred to as the "champignon de couche" (layered mushroom) because it was grown on layers of horse manure. It is not commonly found in the wild, and there are white and brown varieties. It is plump with a smooth skin, and its gills are pink to black-brown. Its flesh is firm, and its taste is mild and delicately woody. The brown variety is more fragrant.

SCIENTIFIC NAME
Agaricus bisporus

SEASON
🗓 *Year-round*

PLACE OF ORIGIN
📍 *Île-de-France*

HISTORY
Images of this mushroom appear on the walls of tombs of Egyptian pharaohs dating to 1450 BCE. The Romans were fond of the mushroom, according to poets Horace and Ovid, but it was not until the seventeenth century that agronomist Olivier de Serres described its cultivation in his *Théâtre d'agriculture* (1600). De Serres recounts that once cultivated in the royal gardens, the mushroom would appear on the table of Louis XIV at Versailles. Scientists began developing a controlled cultivar to increase the production of this popular vegetable. The Parisian subsoil and its cellars became the first French mushroom farms to perfect its cultivation thanks to their darkness, constant temperature, good ventilation, and high humidity—necessary factors for the mushroom's production quality.

A CURIOUS FACT
Around 1810, Parisian horticulturist Chambry had the idea of growing mushrooms in abandoned quarries under the Palais du Trocadéro, in the catacombs of Montrouge, and around the 14th arrondissement. This new method of cultivation spread quickly into other quarries, which allowed large volumes of production, but the construction of the Paris metro at the end of the nineteenth century put an end to this growing method. Today, there are only a few families of producers in the Paris region who continue this traditional growing method, far from the competing industrialized mushroom farms in Asia and other countries of the East.

IN COOKING
The mushroom is eaten raw when young and firm, tossed with a little cream or a vinaigrette. The larger heads can be stuffed, while the stem is often prepared in a duxelles (chopped with onion and shallot). It is sautéed in butter to form the base of some sauces. When sautéed, it accompanies meat, fish, poultry; is used in a fricassee; and is an addition to a vol-au-vent, omelet, sole Normande, or veal blanquette.

🏛 PRODUCERS
Le Clos du Roi

📍 *11, rue Pagnère, Saint-Ouen-l'Aumône (Val-d'Oise)*

Grégory Spinelli is one of the last producers in Île-de-France. He grows only button mushrooms in a limestone quarry founded by his family in 1949.

Champignonnière des Carrières

📍 *Rue des Carrières, Évecquemont (Yvelines)*

Champignonnière de la Marianne

📍 *3, rue Thérèse Lethias, Méry-sur-Oise (Val-d'Oise)*

Champignons de l'Orme Rond

📍 *7, rue du Pressoir, Villeneuve-sur-Bellot (Seine-et-Marne)*

Ferme de la Haye

📍 *Ch. de la Haye, Les Mureaux (Yvelines)*

Cabbage from Pontoise

Although it faded in popularity by the 1980s, this bulbous vegetable does not disappoint.

Also called "chou pommé" (apple cabbage) for its slightly flattened apple shape, this is a late-summer variety, hardy, and resistant to cold. It is purplish green in color with an imposing size and delicate, tender, and smooth veined leaves. Its taste is mild, delicate, almost sweet, and it has the distinction of being very digestible, unlike other cabbages.

SCIENTIFIC NAME

Brassica oleracea (common cabbage)

SEASON

🗓 *Winter*

PLACE OF ORIGIN

📍 *Plain of Cergy-Pontoise (Val-d'Oise)*

HISTORY

Originally from Milan, Italy (thus called *chou Milan* in French), this cabbage has been cultivated around Paris since the sixteenth century. The vegetable's production occupied most of the land in the region until the nineteenth century before being reduced to a few acres due to increased urbanization.

A CURIOUS FACT

In the city of Pontoise, each family had its cabbage seed, which was treated as an inheritance that was respectfully handed down and could be neither sold nor exchanged. The selection of plants for seed production is quite specialized. Truck farmers choose the most resistant and attractive cabbages during winter and according to their own criteria, thus determining a select family type. The town maintains traces of this glorious gastronomic past, the most notable of which is the Chou (cabbage) district, along the Oise to Auvers-sur-Oise.

IN COOKING

Served as an accompaniment to poultry; stuffed with sausage and braised; in pot-au-feu; stews with meat and potatoes; grated into salads. Featured as the flavor of the day by Michelin-starred chef Yannick Alléno in his famous recipe poularde Houdan au chou de Pontoise (Houdan chicken with Pointoise cabbage).

🏭 PRODUCERS

Laurent Berrurier

📍 *1, imp. des Clos, Neuville-sur-Oise (Val-d'Oise)*

Laurent Berrurier, one of the last to possess the original strain for this cabbage, which is a family treasure that has been handed down for four generations, grows it using sustainable agricultural methods.

Ferme de la Brie

📍 *570, ch. des Caves, Couilly-Pont-aux-Dames (Seine-et-Marne)* ⬤ ORGANIC

↷ **SKIP TO**
Chicken Recipes, p. 236.

AUBERVILLIERS CABBAGE
In the same family of cabbages is the Virtus or Aubervilliers type, produced in Seine-Saint-Denis, so called because of the many "miracles of rain" produced in the nearby church of Notre-Dame-des-Vertus. It is an early-autumn cabbage, blue-green in color with yellowish tinges and frizzy and crinkled leaves. It is tender and tasty.

Watercress from Méréville

🌀 *Slow Food Ark of Taste*

Farming of this "green gold," as it's called, from Essonne reached its peak in the nineteenth century, but even today, the know-how is handed down from generation to generation, and the *cressonnières* (watercress growers) carve out impressive landscapes south of Paris for its cultivation.

Watercress (not to be confused with garden cress or land cress) has a wide, oval, dark green leaf that is thin and crunchy, with a slightly pungent taste. It is almost an aquatic plant and grows in humid environments. Essonne supplies 35 percent of French production. The watercress grows in pits 8 to 16 inches (20 to 40 cm) deep and slightly sloping so the water can drain. The seeds are planted in July, and about ten days later they are covered in water. The first cut is done by hand using a knife five to six weeks after planting, then about every twenty-five days until the end of the season in June.

SCIENTIFIC NAME
Nasturtium officinale (common watercress)

SEASON
📅 *Year-round*

PLACE OF ORIGIN
📍 *Valleys of the Essonne, Juine, and École*

HISTORY
Wild watercress has been consumed in Europe since antiquity, and the farming of watercress appeared in Germany in the seventeenth century. Dr. Cardon, manager of the hospitals of the Grande Armée, noticed it in the nineteenth century and decided to introduce it in the Oise. The cressonnière Sainte-Anne, created in 1856 in the Gâtinais, was the first in Essonne; in 1894, crop growing arrived in Méréville.

Production in the valleys of the Essonne, École, and Juine helped satisfy strong demand from the capital. From 1900, production decreased, and today there are only a dozen producers in Méréville, and less than thirty throughout Essonne.

A CURIOUS FACT
The commune of Méréville is listed as a Site Remarquable du Goût (a site known for its local produce excellence) and the cressonnières of Essonne as a *paysage de reconquête* (area of reclamation). In an interview with author Michel Manoll, the poet Blaise Cendrars revealed that in the summer of 1917, although wounded during the Great War, he "rejuvenated" himself in Méréville and experienced a poetic "revolution" that he mysteriously summarized as follows: "There was watercress, I drew salt from the watercress, and I sold my formula." Watercress grower Villa Paul (Méréville) opened a museum named Maison du Cresson.

IN COOKING
Watercress can be eaten raw such as in salads, or cooked in soups, sauces, or purées.

Watercress soup is popular, and the plant plays a dominant role in the dish entrecôte vert-pré (a classic steak frites dish served with watercress).

🏛 PRODUCERS
Cressonnière Sainte-Anne
📍 *Rue de l'Église, Vayres-sur-Essonne (Essonne)*
💧 *ORGANIC*

The Sainte-Anne cressonnière was taken over by the Morizot family in 1984. Since 2019, Mikaël has been growing organic watercress.

Cressonnières de la Vallée de la Juine
📍 *23, rue du Tour-de-Ville, Le Mérévillois (Essonne)*
💧 *ORGANIC*

The Barberon family owns five watercress farms, most of which grow organic watercress.

Cressonnières de la Villa Paul
📍 *17, rte. de Courcelles, Le Mérévillois (Essonne)*
💧 *ORGANIC*

Olivier Barberot (president of the Association Syndicale Libre de la Cressiculture Essonnienne, and vice president of the National Federation) manages 9 acres (3.5 ha) of an organic watercress farm created in 1897 by his great-grandfather.

↻ SKIP TO
Paris in the Soup, p. 266.

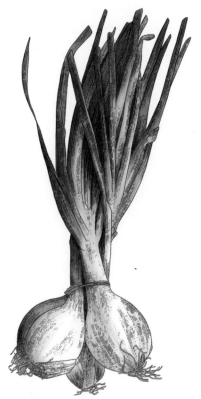

Onions

Until the first half of the twentieth century, onions were one of the most widespread crops in the areas around Paris. They were an essential food in the capital and in parts of Europe during winter months. Onions were stored in bundles using dried and braided greens to tie them.

Historically, the onion was widely cultivated throughout the Paris region. It is an indispensable vegetable and condiment, and it's a common vegetable in the truck farming areas surrounding the country's large cities. The names of the three oldest varieties that survive today testify to where they were originally farmed, but there are few farms that cultivate them today.

SCIENTIFIC NAME

Allium cepa (common onion)

SEASON

📅 *Spring*

PLACE OF ORIGIN

📍 *Île-de-France*

White onion from Vaugirard

◉ *Slow Food Ark of Taste*
Its name comes from a former commune in the Seine department, which, until the early nineteenth century, was a rural farming region before being integrated into Paris's 15th arrondissement. This white onion is a hardy and semi-early variety with a medium-size round and slightly squat bulb. It has a mild and fresh flavor and crunchy texture. When the leaves are still green, they are bundled and sold in markets in early spring as "spring onions." Those harvested in midsummer are called *de garde* (storage onions).

White onion from Paris

A hardy and semi-early variety with large round and squat white bulbs. When harvested while still young, small, and green, it is referred to as the "Parisian spring onion." It can be eaten raw. It has a mild and slightly sweet flavor.

White onion from Malakoff

This is the earliest variety of the white onion and has small round bulbs. It has a mild taste when young but becomes more pungent when mature.

Yellow onion of Vertus

A hardy, quite early variety and very productive, with thick skin and very large straw yellow round bulbs that are slightly squat with white flesh. Formerly farmed by truck farmers on the Plains of Vertus in Aubervilliers, it is highly appreciated for its taste and long storage. It has a strong taste and tolerates long cooking times.

IN COOKING

Au gratin, in sauce soubise, mixed with peas, Parmentier (shepherd's pie), soups, pickled in vinegar.

🍴 **PRODUCERS**

Ferme du Logis
📍 *Lieu-dit Le Logis, Jumeauville (Yvelines)*

Ferme des Prés Neufs
📍 *90, rue de Villiers, Longpont-sur-Orge (Essonne)*

⌒ **SKIP TO**
The Onion Soup of Les Halles, p. 204; Peas à la Française, p. 87.

THE ONION FAIR OF MANTES-LA-JOLIE

This is one of the oldest fairs in France, dating to 1448. King Charles VII granted villagers permission to hold this fair once a year to thank them for their loyalty. They mainly sold onions and onion products at the fair. It still takes place today in November or December, and a large onion soup is prepared by the town's associations.

PANTRY GOODS

Rose petal jam from Provins

The rose petal jam made from the Provins rose variety (Rosa gallica) is translucent with a deep pink color. The current recipe, which is secret, calls for roses to be picked around mid-September. The petals are sorted and then cooked in water, sugar, and lemon. It is enjoyed as an accompaniment to Brie or foie gras.

PLACE OF ORIGIN

◉ *Provins (Seine-et-Marne)*

HISTORY

The city of Provins has been known throughout Europe since the eleventh century for its large, popular market fairs. The introduction of the rose in the region was thanks to Thibault IV, Count of Brie and Champagne, who brought the rose back from the Crusades. In the twelfth century, dried rose petals were shipped throughout Europe to flavor dishes and pastries. Rose-based confections became the town's specialty, including candies with dried rose petals, syrups, and the famous rose petal jam that was served in the early seventeenth century at the court of Louis XIV. Cultivation of the Provins rose almost disappeared during the Renaissance before being revived by some growing enthusiasts, including Bruno Clergeot, owner of La Roseraie de Provins.

🏛 PRODUCERS

Pâtisserie Gaufillier

◉ *2, rue Victor-Garnier, Provins (Seine-et-Marne)*

La Ronde des Abeilles

◉ *3, rue des Beaux-Arts, Provins (Seine-et-Marne)*

Barley sugar of the nuns of Moret-sur-Loing

This is a sugary treat with a sweet and delicate flavor, amber yellow, and translucent. It is in the shape of a small stick or slightly flattened and opaque hard candy. It is essentially sugar cooked in barley tea, but the real recipe is kept secret.

PLACE OF ORIGIN

◉ *Moret-sur-Loing and its surroundings (Seine-et-Marne)*

HISTORY

This is one of the oldest candies in France. Intended for orators, it was made by the Benedictines of the priory of Notre Dame des Anges from 1638 until 1782, when the nuns left the town to settle elsewhere. This popular confection was appreciated not only for its taste but also for its properties for relieving colds and sore throats. Napoléon I was a fan and encouraged the Sisters of Charity of Moret to resume production, which they did until 1970. The nuns eventually passed on the secret recipe to confectioner Jean Rousseau, who became its official owner in 1972. Rousseau's descendants continued the tradition until January 2012, when the recipe and the manufacturing monopoly were sold to the company Des Lis Chocolat. The local Loing Barley Sugar Brotherhood was established in 1997 with the motto: "Suck on barley sugar throughout life."

🏛 PRODUCER

Des Lis Chocolat

◉ *6, rue Louis-Blériot, Nemours; ZI du Rocher-Vert, Nemours,*

◉ *1, rue de Boissettes, Melun (Seine-et-Marne)*

Saffron from Gâtinais

SCIENTIFIC NAME

Crocus sativus (common saffron)

SEASON

📅 *Harvested in October and consumed year-round.*

PLACE OF ORIGIN

◉ *Gâtinais*

HISTORY

Starting in the eleventh century, saffron bulbs were brought into France near Boynes, in the Gâtinais, by the gentleman Geoffroy Porchaires on his return from the Crusades. He acquired them in Avignon. An edict of Louis XIV formalized the plant's cultivation in 1698, and the king declared his terroir to be the world's capital for saffron—with its incomparable aroma and taste—which remained so until the end of the nineteenth century; the depopulation of the countryside resulted in its decline around 1930. It was not until the late 1980s that it would be grown again as a crop in the region.

In 2017, Bien Élevées was the name given by four sisters to their project, which entailed growing saffron on Paris rooftops in the 5th arrondissement. The first saffron farm was established on the roof of the Arab World Institute, and four other buildings have since been the location for additional plantings. Saffron's popularity is now gaining new heights.

PRODUCERS

Ferme du Grand Balleau

 Route de Perreuse, Jouarre (Seine-et-Marne)

Hervé Viron

 45, rue Grande, Boulancourt (Seine-et-Marne)

Ferme Les Frères d'Armes

 2 ter, rue de la Mare, Saint-Escobille (Essonne)

Moutarde de Meaux Pommery

This is mustard made in the traditional way with slightly crushed whole seeds enhanced with a mixture of secret spices. The mustard is thick and a green-ocher to brown color. It is sold in stoneware pots sealed with red wax.

PLACE OF ORIGIN

 Nanteuil-lès-Meaux (Seine-et-Marne)

HISTORY

Paris and Dijon were already the two main centers of mustard production in France by the thirteenth century. At that time, there was no particular "moutarde de Meaux," since its production was a well-kept secret by the city's canons until 1760, when the recipe was entrusted to Pommery and other producers. The mustard gained its fame during the nineteenth century. The rich blend of herbs that flavors it makes it special: tarragon, coriander, cardamom, cinnamon, fennel, and others. By the beginning of the twentieth century, Pommery was the sole producer, but its special recipe had been lost. It was not until 1949 that the Chamois family, who took over the business under the name of Les Assaisonnements Briards, returned to the original recipe and packaged it in the distinctive stoneware pots. Today, the brand Moutarde de Meaux Pommery is sold worldwide.

A CURIOUS FACT

The word *mustard* derives from *must*, which refers to grape juice before fermentation. As defined by the monk Gauthier de Coincy in the thirteenth century, mustard is "a condiment prepared with crushed mustard seeds, added herbs, and diluted with must."

Vinegar from Lagny

This is vinegar made from beet alcohol and macerated with beech shavings in oak vats and, after fermentation, filtered and bottled. It can be flavored with plant extracts (tarragon, carrot, lingonberry . . .) or spices. It has a sweet-and-sour flavor and a watery and colorless appearance. If flavored, it takes on the color of the chosen aromatic.

PLACE OF ORIGIN

 Lagny-sur-Marne (Seine-et-Marne)

HISTORY

The Merovingian springs of the sixth and seventh centuries testify to rich wine terroir in the loop of the Seine downstream from Paris in the lower valley of the Oise and in the lower valley of the Marne, in Lagny. However, this beet alcohol vinegar was created thanks to the creation, in 1577, of the "twenty leagues" rule prohibiting the production of wine in Paris and its environs. The phylloxera crisis, which affected vineyards at the end of the nineteenth century, accelerated the vinegar's development. In 1865, Monsieur Mathon set up the Vinaigrerie du Lion in Lagny, which was sold in 1890 to the Chamois family, who also owned Moutarde de Meaux Pommery and used the vinegar in its production for years. In 2003, the company, which became Les Assaisonnements Briards, moved to Nanteuil-lès-Meaux, where descendants of the family continue production and now market the vinegar with the label *vinaigre d'alcool blanc Pommery* (Pommery white alcohol vinegar).

ÎLE-DE-FRANCE TERROIR

Honeys

From Paris to Gâtinais, Île-de-France is an abundant playground for bees.

Honeys from Paris

For the past twenty years, the hives of the capital have produced more honey than those of the fields surrounding the city.

Miel de Paris is an urban honey produced by bees foraging flowers in the city's private and public green spaces. Production is rather considerable, and a very pure honey is obtained thanks to the enormous diversity of area plants, the absence of chemicals, and more-constant temperatures. The result is a honey with an often fluid consistency and aromatic complexity specific to the terroir of the city, which has more than 250 different flower pollens. The honey will vary according to the harvest period. The nectar secreted by the flower is immediately foraged by the bee and therefore protected from city pollution.

HARVEST TIME
📅 *June to July and September*

PLACE OF ORIGIN
📍 *Paris, Seine-Saint-Denis and Hauts-de-Seine*

HISTORY
There were about thirteen hundred hives in Paris at the end of the nineteenth century. The supply of nectar was guaranteed considering the dynamic green belt surrounding the city. But Parisian beekeeping declined considerably the following century and became limited to the hives in Luxembourg Garden and some oratories. For the past twenty years, honey has once again been flowing, this time from Paris rooftops. From the Grand Palais to the Élysée Gardens and from the Opéra Garnier to the Musée d'Orsay, the capital has become a refuge for bees that impart the taste of the city into more than two thousand hives.

🏠 PRODUCERS

Zone Sensible
📍 *Urban farm of Saint-Denis 112, av. de Stalingrad, Saint-Denis (Seine-Saint-Denis)*

Olivier Darné is an urban beekeeper and visual artist. In 2003, he founded Parti Poétique, a collective of artists that "pollinate" the city and with whom he created, in 2018, the urban farm of Saint-Denis to develop the Zone Sensible project, conceived as a place of learning, sharing, and solidarity in a healthy and sustainable design. He created the Miel Béton brand of honey.

Un Apiculteur Près de Chez Vous
📍 *miel-paris.com*
Under this name, Rémy Vanbremeersch and Bruno Petit harvest Parisian honey produced by eighty-five hives located in the city's gardens, ranging from building rooftops to the Bois de Vincennes. It is sold in some markets.

Le Miel de Paris
📍 *lemieldeparis.com/lapiculteur-miel-paris*
Since 2009, beekeeper Audric de Campeau has been installing his hives on the rooftops of emblematic locations throughout the city, such as the Hôtel National des Invalides, Musée d'Orsay, École Militaire, Ministry of the Interior, Monnaie de Paris, Boucheron at Place Vendôme, Institut de France, and Le Cordon Bleu culinary school. Other honeys from emblematic locations are harvested by professional beekeepers and sold at the place of production, such as the shops of the Opéra Garnier and the Opéra Bastille for Miel de l'Opéra; specialized shops such as La Maison du Miel (24, rue Vignon, Paris 9th), or Apis Civi (4, rue de Suez, Paris 18th); at markets, such as those at Cours de Vincennes (Paris 12th) and Place des Fêtes (Paris 19th); and during annual events such as the Honey Festival in the Luxembourg Garden (Paris 6th) or Parc Georges-Brassens (Paris 15th).

Honey from Gâtinais

One of the most renowned wildflower honeys in France since the Middle Ages is produced in the heart of Gâtinais Natural Park.

This is a wildflower honey, clear to amber in color, with a velvety and creamy texture and a tendency to crystallize. This finely textured honey's flavor is subtle and delicate, with no bitterness.

HARVEST TIME
📅 *May to June*

PLACE OF ORIGIN
📍 *Parc Naturel Régional du Gâtinais (Seine-et-Marne and Essonne)*

HISTORY
The Gâtinais is a protected agricultural and forestry region. On this land, used in the past for livestock breeding and pastures, grows a multitude of plants such as alfalfa, clover, minette rose, and especially sainfoin, which gave honey the flavor that made it famous at the end of the eighteenth century, eventually becoming the most consumed honey in Paris. Despite the variation of flora and the evolution of crops toward more rapeseed, apple trees, and sunflower, the traditional honey from Gâtinais has maintained an excellent reputation.

🏠 PRODUCER

La Miellerie de Misery
📍 *Route de Misery, Vert-le-Petit (Essonne)*
Danielle, Didier, and Cédric Somson have been managing a collection of three hundred bee colonies since 1987. This company has an organic certification and produces honey-based recipes.

↪ SKIP TO
Urban Farms, p. 338.

CHEESES

Boursault

MILK
Cow, pasteurized

CHEESE FAMILY
Soft, bloomy rind; triple cream

AFFINAGE
2 weeks

PLACE OF ORIGIN
La Ferté-sous-Jouarre (Seine-et-Marne)

CHARACTERISTICS
A cylinder 3 inches (8 cm) in diameter and 1¾ inches (4.5 cm) thick. The paste is cream colored and melting and the rind is a pinkish white and very thin. The Pierre-Robert is a version 5 inches (13 cm) in diameter and 2 inches (5 cm) thick.

FLAVOR
Enriched with cream, this commercially made cheese has a delicate taste with notes of butter, yeast, and flowers.

HISTORY
Now produced in Mayenne, this cheese was created in the 1950s by the Boursault cousins in La Ferté-sous-Jouarre (Seine-et-Marne) to make use of excess cream and to enrich their cheeses. The cheese was a great success in the postwar period. Pierre-Robert was created in the 1970s by two friends, Pierre and Robert (the latter the son of the founder of the Rouzaire cheese dairy), near Melun, where it is still produced, with the idea of aging Brillat-Savarin cheese.

Brillat-Savarin
Protected Geographical Indication

MILK
Cow

CHEESE FAMILY
Soft, bloomy rind

AFFINAGE
3 days (fresh) to 2 weeks (aged)

PLACE OF ORIGIN
Seine-et-Marne

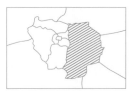

CHARACTERISTICS
A rindless cylinder when fresh, or a velvety white rind when aged. There are two formats: the small, measuring 2½ to 4 inches (6 to 10 cm) in diameter and 1 to 2½ inches (3 to 6 cm) thick, and 7 to 8 ounces (100 to 250 g); the large, measuring 4½ to 5½ inches (11 to 14 cm) in diameter and 1½ to 2¾ inches (4 to 7 cm) thick, and about 18 ounces (500 g). It has a creamy and melting texture.

FLAVOR
Tastes of milk and cream, slightly acidulous and salty when fresh. More fruity and woody when aged.

HISTORY
In the 1930s, Henry Androuët, a famous Parisian master cheesemaker, named this cheese in tribute to the famous gastronome Brillat-Savarin.

PRODUCER
Société Fromagère de la Brie
Barlonges, Saint-Rémy-de-la-Vanne (Seine-et-Marne)

Coulommiers

MILK
Cow

CHEESE FAMILY
Soft, bloomy rind

AFFINAGE
3 to 4 weeks

PLACE OF ORIGIN
Coulommiers (Seine-et-Marne)

CHARACTERISTICS
A disk 5 to 6 inches (13 to 15 cm) in diameter and 1 inch (3 cm) thick, weighing about 18 ounces (500 g). It has a thin bloomy rind. Its glossy straw-yellow paste is melting and soft.

FLAVOR
Mild tastes of milk and cream when fresh. Aromatic and mushroomy when aged.

HISTORY
The name of the cheese comes from the city of Coulommiers (Seine-et-Marne), birthplace of the Brie cheese family. It is sometimes called "Brie de Coulommiers" or "small, molded Brie." It owes its increased popularity to the Universal Exposition of 1878 and to its compact format that makes it more suitable than Brie for transporting.

PRODUCERS
La Fromagerie de Saint-Siméon
RD 66, Saint-Rémy-de-la-Vanne (Seine-et-Marne)

Ferme Sainte Colombe
28, rue Sainte-Colombe, Saint-Mars-Vieux-Maisons (Seine-et-Marne)

Délice de Saint-Cyr

MILK
Cow

CHEESE FAMILY
Soft, bloomy rind

AFFINAGE
3 to 4 weeks

PLACE OF ORIGIN
Saint-Cyr-sur-Morin (Seine-et-Marne)

CHARACTERISTICS
In the shape of a cylinder 4¾ to 5 inches (12 to 13 cm) in diameter and 1½ to 2 inches (4 to 5 cm) thick, weighing about 18 ounces (500 g). It has a white to yellow rind and cream-yellow paste with a creamy, buttery texture.

FLAVOR
Very mild with a light taste of butter and hazelnut.

HISTORY
This commercially produced triple-cream cheese, which takes its commercial name from the city of Saint-Cyr-sur-Morin (Seine-et-Marne), is a creation of Monsieur Boursault, who became famous for the cheese that bears his name. It is smaller than Boursault cheese. It is also sold under the names Saint-Antoine, Grand Vatel, Gratte-Paille, Jehan-Grogne, Jehan-de-Brie, Vignelait, Croupet 75, and Triple-Crème.

Explorateur

MILK

Cow, pasteurized

CHEESE FAMILY

Soft, bloomy rind; triple cream

AFFINAGE

🗓 *3 to 6 weeks*

PLACE OF ORIGIN

📍 *Saint-Siméon (Seine-et-Marne)*

CHARACTERISTICS

A cylinder 3 inches (8 cm) in diameter and 2¼ inches (6 cm) thick, with a thin white velvety rind and white crumbly paste.

FLAVOR

Very fatty, tasty, slightly tangy cheese.

HISTORY

This commercially produced cheese was invented in 1958 by Monsieur Duquesne in La Trétoire (Seine-et-Marne), and the trademark was registered in 1983. It may owe its name to the satellite *Explorer* that was launched the same year it was created, as pictured on its label, or perhaps to the trips across the Atlantic by the founder's daughter to sell the cheese.

🏭 **PRODUCER**

Société Fromagère de la Brie

📍 *Barlonges, Saint-Rémy-de-la-Vanne (Seine-et-Marne)*

Fontainebleau

MILK

Cow

PLACE OF ORIGIN

📍 *Fontainebleau (Seine-et-Marne)*

CHARACTERISTICS

White, smooth, and creamy, with a whipped top, often packed in a small gauze-lined jar.

🏭 **PRODUCERS**

Fromagerie Barthélémy-Goursat

📍 *92, rue Grande, Fontainebleau (Seine-et-Marne)*

📍 *51, rue de Grenelle, Paris 7th*

La Ferme des Sablons

📍 *19, rue des Sablons, Fontainebleau (Seine-et-Marne)*

Les Terroirs de France

📍 *41, rue des Sablons, Fontainebleau (Seine-et-Marne)*

↷ **SKIP TO**

The Fontainebleau, p. 288.

Mozzarella

MILK

Cow or buffalo

CHEESE FAMILY

Pulled-curd

AFFINAGE

Fresh cheese

PLACE OF ORIGIN

📍 *Paris and Yvelines*

CHARACTERISTICS

Off-white, stringy paste, firm when made from cow's milk. Porcelain white, thin, smooth, and resistant skin, melting paste when made from buffalo's milk.

FLAVOR

Soft, delicate, and subtly tart for cow's milk. Pronounced for buffalo's milk.

HISTORY

This cheese, originating from Campania, Italy, has been produced in Île-de-France since 2014. Artisans in the Paris region are producing local versions in accordance with traditional Italian recipes.

🏭 **PRODUCERS**

La Maison de la Mozzarella

📍 *15, rue Violet, Paris 15th*
Ciro and Vincenzo Rosa, two brothers from Naples, created the first Parisian factory in 2014 to produce mozzarella, using buffalo curd from Campania, Italy. They also manufacture burrata and scamorza.

Ottanta

📍 *2, rue Maryse-Bastié, Gazeran (Yvelines)*
In 2015, Sara Lacomba, originally from the Apulia region of Italy, produced the first organic and 100 percent local mozzarella, using cow's milk, just as they produce in Apulia. Ottanta is now based in Gazeran (Yvelines) and also manufactures burrata, scamorza, and stracciatella using organic milk produced by two farms in Val-d'Oise and Perche.

La Ferme des 4 Étoiles

📍 *La Petite Hogue, Auffargis (Yvelines)*
This cheese dairy was created in 2017 in the Chevreuse Valley (Yvelines) by Fabio Grossi from Naples. He produces mozzarella using cow's milk from small farms in his region and from buffalo's milk from the GIE Châtaigneraie dairy cooperative (Cantal). The dairy produces mozzarella, ricotta, burrata, and stracciatella.

Nanina

📍 *24, rue Basfroi, Paris 11th*
In 2017, Julien Carotenuto, originally from Naples, opened a factory producing mozzarella from buffalo's milk from the GIE Châtaigneraie dairy cooperative (Cantal). He also offers fresh ricotta.

Saint-Foin (or Saint-Jacques)

MILK

Cow, thermized

CHEESE FAMILY

Soft, bloomy rind

AFFINAGE

🗓 *2 to 4 weeks*

PLACE OF ORIGIN

📍 *La Boissière-École (Yvelines)*

CHARACTERISTICS

A cylinder, 5¼ ounces/150 g (small format) or 14 ounces/400 g (large format). Very delicate rind; ivory paste that is creamy, sometimes runny.

FLAVOR

Mild and fresh but can be stronger depending on the affinage. There is also an aged format with sage.

HISTORY

Similar to Coulommiers cheese, this farmstead cheese was created in the region where cheese-straining molds were produced in ancient Gaul. It is now called Saint-Jacques because of its proximity to the pilgrimage paths of the same name.

🏭 **PRODUCER**

La Ferme de la Tremblaye

📍 *Che. de la Tremblaye, La Boissière-École (Yvelines)*

Bries

This soft, bloomy-rind cheese made from raw cow's milk gets its name from the territory from where it originates. This is a large family of cheeses with two famous versions.

THE CHEESE OF KINGS, THE KING OF CHEESES

Seventh century. The Brie cheese tradition is born in the abbey of Notre Dame de Jouarre.

Around 880. Notker of St. Gallen, author of *Gesta Karoli Magni*, states that Charlemagne, a century earlier, requested, after tasting a bloomy-rind cheese, that the cheese be brought to him. Some historians identify this as Brie.

1217. The Countess of Champagne (at the time, the County of Brie was part of Champagne) sends to King Philip Augustus, for whom she had an affinity, "two hundred *galettes de Brie* [wheels of Brie]," which he distributed to his court.

1407. Charles d'Orléans is sent "twenty dozen cheeses from the *païs de Brie* [country of Brie]" to seduce the ladies of his court.

1791. An escaping Louis XVI is arrested in Varenne at a coaching house where he had stopped to have a slice of Brie.

1815. At the Congress of Vienna, during an international competition, Brie is unanimously recognized as the "king of cheeses."

OTHER BRIES

› **Brie de Montereau**, also called Brie de Ville-Saint-Jacques, 7 inches (18 cm) in diameter.

› **Brie de Nangis**, 8½ inches (22 cm) in diameter.

› **Brie de Provins**, trademark registered in 1979, 10½ to 11 inches (27 to 28 cm) in diameter.

› **Brie fermier (farmstead)**, size depending on the specific farm.

THE MATCHUP		
	BRIE DE MEAUX	**BRIE DE MELUN**
PRODUCTION	Seine-et-Marne, Marne, Meuse, Haute-Marne, Aube, Yonne, Loiret	Seine-et-Marne, Aube, Yonne
SHAPE	Flat wheel	Flat wheel
WEIGHT	2⅔–7¼ lb (2.6–3.3 kg)	3⅓–4¾ lb (1.5–2.2 kg)
SIZE	14–14½ in (36–37 cm) in diameter; 1–1⅛ in (2.5–3 cm) thick	10½ in (27 cm) in diameter; 1 in (3 cm) thick
AFFINAGE	4 to 8 weeks	5 to 12 weeks
MOLDING	With a Brie shovel	With a ladle
FAT CONTENT TO DRY CONTENT	45%	45%
AOC/AOP	1980/1992	1980/1992
VOLUME (2017)	6,318 tons	250 tons
RIND	Thin, white, fuzzy with red streaks or spots	Thin, white, with red-brown veining
PASTE	Ivory, supple, creamy	Yellowish, slightly gritty, elastic
TASTE	Delicate, elegant, fine. Mild, fruity, aromatic. Scents of butter, hazelnut, forest floor. Tangy and yogurtlike notes when younger.	Rustic, expressive, complex. Lactic flavor, slightly salty. Notes of cauliflower, mushrooms, and animallike scents when aged.
SEASON	Year-round	Year-round
PRODUCING FARM	Ferme des Trente Arpents, Favières (Seine-et-Marne)	Ferme de Juchy—1, route de Lizines, Lizines (Seine-et-Marne)

› **Brie noir de Nanteuil**, dried for several months resulting in a very strong taste; 12 inches (30 cm) in diameter.

› **Brie de Coulommiers**, also called "brie petit moule" (6 inches/15 cm in diameter). It was created to overcome problems with transporting the very large Brie formats.

› **Brie de Melun bleu**, 10½ to 11 inches (27 to 28 cm) in diameter, dusted with ash.

CURIOUS FACTS

› The **fougerus** was created in 1957 as homage to a cheese similar to Brie, made in the village of Chevru (Seine-et-Marne). It is partly covered with fern leaves.

› **In the eighteenth and nineteenth centuries**, Brie was found still made in pots. It had a runny paste that escaped from the cheese during aging and sold under the name of "cheese from Meaux."

› **Poetic Brie.** Charles d'Orléans mentioned it in a lyrical poem: "My sweetheart, I send to you / And carefully I chose / Delicious Brie de Meaux. / To tell you that I am unhappy / By your absence I am grieving / To the point of losing my craving. / And that's why I am sending it to you / What a sacrifice for me it will prove!" In 1646, the poet Saint-Amant composed "Les Goinfres," a realist gourmet poem, in which he exclaimed: "O God, what a precious thing to eat! / What a rare and delicious taste! / May its price be worth my impulse / to incarnate Saint Ambroise!"

› **Brie noir de Nanteuil**, nicknamed Brie *des moissons* or Brie *de vendanges* (Brie of good harvest). So called because it was served during harvesttime, as its firmer texture was considered better for tolerating the strong heat.

BRIE FARMERS

Since 2016, Camille and Nicolas Grymonprez have been raising Montbéliardes and Jersey cows and transforming their milk into Brie and Coulommiers as well as butter, faisselle cheese, and others. They offer farmstead, organic, and raw-milk cheeses.

La Ferme Sainte-Colombe

📍 *28, rue Sainte-Colombe, Saint-Mars-Vieux-Maisons (Seine-et-Marne)*

MEATS

Île-de-France lamb

This breed yields a meat that is firm and tender. The taste is pronounced due to sheep feeding on beet pulp, hay, and grain.

PLACE OF ORIGIN

📍 Maisons-Alfort (Val-de-Marne)

HISTORY
Sheep herds have been present in Île-de-France since ancient times. The people of Roman Lutecia appreciated their meat. In 1832, Charles-Auguste Yvart, professor at the veterinary school of Maisons-Alfort, crossed the Rambouillet merino with the Dishley. The result was a tasty meat, encouraging this crossbreeding to spread throughout the region. In 1922, the Dishley-Merino breed became the Île-de-France breed.

A CURIOUS FACT
Lambing takes place in November and December, so that the lamb is ready for sale by Easter, hence its other name, the "Passover lamb."

IN COOKING
Roasted, with flageolet beans.

PRODUCER
La Ferme de Filbois
📍 17, rue Grande, Aufferville (Seine-et-Marne)

↪ SKIP TO
Lamb Stew, p. 231.

Boudin noir from Paris

A casing filled with cooked fat, pig's blood, and onions, in equal parts. Slightly spicy, it can have cream or milk added. It is plump, blackish in color, and soft.

PLACE OF ORIGIN

📍 Ile-de-France

HISTORY
From the fourteenth century, many Parisian cookbooks described recipes for boudin noir (blood sausage). According to the *Code des usages de la charcuterie (Code of Usage for Charcuterie)*, the boudin de Paris, also called "boudin à l'oignon" (onion boudin), is the only one to use onions in equal parts with the other ingredients.

A CURIOUS FACT
Sold in *brasse* (long, undivided lengths) of 5 feet (1.50 m), and cut to order, it is also found in individual portions (5¼ ounces/150 g) or in minis.

IN COOKING
Eaten mostly in winter, panfried or poached, and accompanied by apples or mashed potatoes.

PRODUCERS
Ferme de Moneuse
📍 1, rue des Prés-de-Moneuse, Dagny (Seine-et-Marne)

Durand Traiteur
📍 2, rue d'Avron, Paris 20th

Maison Verot
📍 3, rue Notre-Dame-des-Champs, Paris 6th

Rabbit from Gâtinais

There is no breed specific to Gâtinais, but a tradition of rabbit breeding by small producers has been present there since the Middle Ages. The animals live in hutches or cages, where they are fed either hay and rabbit feed or—for the most virtuous breeders—beets, carrots, and wild herbs. The animals are slaughtered on the farm when about three months old.

PLACE OF ORIGIN

📍 Gâtinais

HISTORY
Archaeologists have uncovered rabbit-hunting activities in the southern sections of the Paris Basin as early as the Neolithic period. Breeding is attested in the Middle Ages, but the wild hare was long the preferred choice. At the beginning of the twentieth century, rabbit from Gâtinais began to earn a particularly good reputation and is now considered a quality farm-raised rabbit.

IN COOKING
Rabbit gibelotte, sautéed rabbit, and in casseroles.

PRODUCER
La Ferme de Filbois
📍 17, rue Grande, Aufferville (Seine-et-Marne)

↪ SKIP TO
Rabbit Stew, p. 297.

Garlic sausages from Paris

A cooked sausage made from lean and coarsely chopped pork fat, egg white, garlic, salt, pepper, and spices, contained in a casing 13⅓ to 14¾ inches (34 to 40 cm) long and 2 to 2⅓ inches (5 to 6 cm) in diameter. Pale pink in color, it remains soft, and the taste of garlic is present but subtle.

PLACE OF ORIGIN

📍 Throughout France

HISTORY
Sociologist and ethnologist Marcel Mauss considered, perhaps a little too unfairly, that "Celtic civilization is charcuterie and cheeses." Parisians have always consumed sausage. The first reference to a saucisson à l'ail (garlic sausage) is in 1760. Around 1890, reference appears in Joseph Favre's *Dictionnaire universel de cuisine* under the entry "saucisson de Paris."

IN COOKING
Simply sliced, with bread; or in hot dishes, such as sauerkraut.

PRODUCERS
Jean Dijols
📍 14, pl. de la Fontaine, Lagny-sur-Marne (Seine-et-Marne)

Arnaud Nicolas
RESTAURANT & BOUTIQUE
📍 46, av. de la Bourdonnais, Paris 7th
CHARCUTERIE
📍 125, rue Caulaincourt, Paris 18th

Jambon de Paris

Once considered "ordinary," this essential ingredient in the iconic jambon-beurre sandwich is now a traditional product that merits protection!

The name jambon de Paris is unfortunately not a protected designation, and the term is often wrongly used as a synonym for cooked ham or top-quality cooked ham. However, jambon de Paris has its own history and particular traits. Its preparation is also regulated by the charcuterie code. Traditionally, it is unrolled, parallelepiped-shaped, and about 11 pounds (5 kg). To make it, a pork leg is boned, defatted, then injected with an aromatic brine. The ham is placed in a mold and cooked in broth or steamed, with or without its rind. The ham cools for one or two days in a cold room before being unmolded and, sometimes, having its fat removed.

HISTORY

The French have loved ham since the Middle Ages, when the star was the ham of Mayence, a raw and smoked ham. Cooked ham, referred to as "ordinary," was less appreciated at the time.

IN THE FOURTEENTH CENTURY

A recipe very close to the current recipe for jambon de Paris appears in a treatise on home economics.

1793

The selling price of cooked ham appears in the Tableau du Maximum (an official inventory that set the maximum prices of edible goods in France in times of famine).

1869

In his *Livre des conserves*, Jules Gouffé describes an ordinary ham, salted, boiled, boneless, in a terrine with its rind underneath and chilled while pressed. The same

year, the jambon blanc de Paris appears in *Charcuterie ancienne et moderne, traité historique et pratique*, by the butcher Louis-François Dronne.

1873

In his novel *Le Ventre de Paris*, Émile Zola depicts jambon de Paris on the charcuterie counter of the beautiful Lisa: ". . . then, right and left, on boards, were breads of Italian cheeses and head cheese, and an ordinary ham of pale pink."

STARTING IN 1900

Jambon de Paris appears in several books and catalogs as boneless with its rind, and sometimes encased in a savory jelly.

1915

The increase in taxes on jambon de Paris makes it a luxury product, hence the need to highlight its origins.

IN COOKING

In the emblematic jambon-beurre sandwich, in a croque-monsieur, in a croissant au jambon (croissant with ham), in salade Parisienne, in feuilleté au jambon (flaky pastry with ham).

The Ham Fair

Starting in the Middle Ages, the Ham Fair has taken place every year on the forecourt of Notre Dame de Paris during Holy Week. In 1869, the fair was moved to boulevard Richard-Lenoir (Paris 11th) where scrap metal and secondhand dealers are found and thus was called the "Ham and Scrap Fair." It endured in this location until 1970 and is now held in Chatou.

⌒ **SKIP TO**
Le Jambon-Beurre, p. 48;
The Croque-Monsieur, p. 284.

A PRINCE OF PARIS

Located in the 11th arrondissement (166, rue de Charonne), Maison Doumbéa d'Yves Le Guel is the only producer in the capital to produce the Prince de Paris ham, which they have produced since 2005. The ham lives up to its name due to its superior quality, making it unique and highly appreciated. Le Geul's secret? The excellent French ingredients; the handmade method; the brine prepared according to a recipe using vegetables and spices; a slow, gentle cooking; and a longer-than-normal rest time before it's sold.

Maison Doumbéa
📍 *166, rue de Charonne, Paris 11th*

Poultry

There are two very different breeds of chicken from the Île-de-France region, both with excellent and highly prized flesh, and that at one time were experiencing their golden age but are now threatened by intensive breeding . . . Here's a match-up between these two former poultry stars.

Pâté de volaille from Houdan

The recipe for this traditional pâté en croûte (pâté in a flaky pastry crust) was developed by Victor Tasserie, a butcher in Houdan, in 1850. It was an oval pâté filled with meat of Houdan poultry, liver, jambon blanc (a lightly salted cooked ham), truffle, and foie gras. In the 1980s, the city's butchers revived this specialty, each customizing the traditional recipe, keeping poultry meat as the base (thin slices of meat, liver mousse, a light stuffing), eggs, a duxelles, and, sometimes, truffle or foie gras.

WHERE TO TRY PÂTÉ DE VOLAILLE?
Maison Verot
♀ 3, rue Notre-Dame-des-Champs, Paris 6th

TYPE OF POULTRY	GÂTINAIS CHICKEN	HOUDAN CHICKEN
QUALITY LABELS	Label Rouge (Red Label) Slow Food Ark of Taste PGI*	Label Rouge (Red Label) Slow Food Ark of Taste PGI*
PLACE OF ORIGIN	Gâtinais (north of Loiret, east of Yonne, south of Seine-et-Marne and southeast of Essonne)	Yvelines
PLUMAGE EYES BEAK COMB WATTLE CREST EARLOBE LEGS SIZE	White and thick Orange Pinkish white Simple, red, rather thick, 5–7 points No No Red Pink, 4 toes Medium (female: 5½–6½ lb/2.5–3 kg; male: 7½–8¾ lb/3.5–4 kg). A miniature breed exists.	Black, or black speckled with white Orange-red Short, pink Well-developed Double, leaf-shaped Domed Masked Mottled black-and-white, 5 toes Medium-small (female: max. 6 lb/2.5 kg; male: max. 6.5 lb/3 kg). A miniature breed exists but is very rare.
MEAT	White, delicate, abundant flesh	Dark flesh, very delicate, pronounced flavor
EGGS	Average egg layer, excellent brooder	Average egg layer, average brooder
HISTORY	Breed derived from the Gauloise, created in 1870 by the Count of Sachs. It made its first appearance in 1906 at the Salon de l'Aviculture.	Crested chickens have been appreciated since the twelfth century, and those from Houdan were being served during the reign of Louis XIII.
MOMENT OF GLORY	The interwar period: in 1935, the association bringing together breeders (professionals and amateurs) of this breed had 900 members.	In 1863, it was the French poultry par excellence, known as the "queen of ens," reserved for noble families. Between 1870 and 1914, its popularity and price reached new heights!
DECLINE	From 1940, its breeding declined in favor of breeds adapted to commercial practices. Since 1984, the breed has been classified by France's INRAE (National Research Institute for Agriculture, Food and the Environment) as a threatened breed.	After World War I, the breed disappeared. In the late 1930s, it started to be reintroduced. The delicacy of the breed makes it unsuitable for commercial use and thus prevents its wide availability.
FAN CLUBS	The Gâtinaise Club de France (GCF) was created in 2010 to protect the breed.	In 1906, the Houdan Club was founded to encourage and improve its breeding. Today, the Houdan-Faverolles-Mantes Club works to protect the three closest breeds. In 2016, the Confrérie Gastronomique de la Poule et du Pâté de Houdan (a brotherhood) was founded.
A CURIOUS FACT	In the eighteenth century, poultry à la gatinoise meant "semi-preserved," to keep longer.	Hens were recovered in the United States and England to reintroduce the species and have undergone genetic modifications, with less flesh and larger crests, but the quality of the meat has remained the same.
A BREEDER	Pierre-Nicolas Grisel, Orée de Milly farm, 36 bis, route de Fontainebleau, Milly-la-Forêt (Essonne)	Éric Sanceau, La Petite Hogue farm, Auffargis (Yvelines)

*The PGI regulates the production area, not the breed.

SPIRITS

Clacquesin

This is a liqueur made by distilling Norwegian pine buds and twenty-nine botanicals in alcohol. Originally at 28% ABV, Clacquesin is now 18% ABV. It is served as an aperitif or digestif, very chilled, straight, with an orange zest or with tonic water. It can also be enjoyed hot with milk or lemon or used as a base for cocktails.

PLACE OF ORIGIN

📍 Malakoff (Hauts-de-Seine)

HISTORY

This aperitif was invented around 1860 by Paul Clacquesin, an herbalist-pharmacist who took over his father-in-law's distillery located in Paris's 7th arrondissement. The liqueur experienced enormous success and received an award at the Universal Exposition of 1900. The company moved in 1903 to Malakoff to meet increased demand. Clacquesin was at the time one of the most consumed aperitifs in France and was even sold abroad. The outbreak of the war halted its production, however. Today, Yves Bataille, Paul Clacquesin's great-grandson, has taken over the company and oversees reviving the brand.

A CURIOUS FACT

Originally, this "hygienic tar" was reputed to treat lung infections. In the product's first ads, it was touted as "the healthiest aperitif!" The former factory in Malakoff, Espace Clacquesin, was classified as a historical monument in 2002 and is now used as an event space.

Noyau de Poissy

A digestif liqueur (after-dinner drink) made of brandy and an infusion of apricot kernels. There are two recipes: The oldest, Le Gobelet d'Argent, made via maceration with a strength at 25% ABV, is amber in color, due to the addition of caramel, and has a taste of sweet almond and orange blossom. The second, Le Sceau de Saint-Louis, made via distillation, is colorless and 40% ABV, with an intense almond taste and a hint of bitterness. The liqueur is intended to be consumed straight and shaken, in desserts, or in cocktails.

PLACE OF ORIGIN

📍 Poissy (Yvelines)

HISTORY

This is one of the oldest French liqueurs, dating to 1698. At the time, it was a family-owned production by an innkeeper from Poissy, Madame Suzanne, who served it to her customers. The family heirs exploited the secret recipe, and two families from the city claimed its paternity. In 1826, Alexandre Delporte manufactured the true Noyau de Poissy and was awarded with a silver cup, while the Chaumont Frères distillery, a little later, began selling Sceau de Saint-Louis and patented the recipe. Chaumont Frères was taken over in 1999 by the company Pagès Vedrenne, who today produces both recipes.

A CURIOUS FACT

The Noyau de Poissy distillery is today the only distillery with artisanal methods in Île-de-France. In recent years, it has produced the Liqueur de Paris at 18% ABV, from the seeds of sloe, a small wild berry.

Grand Marnier

A liqueur made from cognac and bitter orange peel, aged in oak barrels, orange-brown, with a syrupy texture and a 40% ABV. It is sold in a classic curvaceous bottle with a red cord sealed in red wax. It is served mainly as a digestif but also sometimes as an aperitif, with or without ice cubes. It is used in cocktails, desserts, or savory dishes.

PRODUCTION AREA

📍 Originally in Neauphle-le-Château (Yvelines)

HISTORY

It was created in 1880 by Louis-Alexandre Marnier-Lapostolle in the family distillery at Neauphle-le-Château. After moving to the commune of Cognac before the German invasion in 1870, the distillery returned to Île-de-France at the end of the war after acquiring a stock of cognac and started the production of Grand Marnier. In 2012, the distillery moved to Charente and the brand was bought in 2016 by the Italian company Campari.

A CURIOUS FACT

César Ritz, the founder of the Ritz Hotel, contributed his name to this liqueur, instead of the name "Curaçao Marnier" that the distiller had originally planned. Considered at the time a "liqueur for ladies," it was highly prized for its refined and sweet taste by very wealthy women who frequented social cafés. Auguste Escoffier made it the flagship ingredient in his famous recipe crêpes Suzette, and it is popular to add to cocktails (Grand Margarita, Red Lion, and many others). In his latest novel Anéantir (2022), where wines and spirits are veritable characters in his story, writer Michel Houellebecq declares that Grand Marnier is "an exceptional alcohol, and too ignored."

PARIS ADDRESS BOOK

Grocers and Produce Markets

Paris

ZINGAM
- 75, rue du Chemin-Vert, Paris 11th
- 51, rue de la Fontaine-au-Roi, Paris 11th
- 74, rue des Martyrs, Paris 18th

TERROIR D'AVENIR
- 7, rue du Nil, Paris 2nd
- 5, rue Paul-Bert, Paris 11th
- 84, rue Jean-Pierre-Timbaud, Paris 11th
- 123, rue des Dames, Paris 17th
{See also Île-de-France}

LES SEASONNIERS
- 10, rue Poissonnière, Paris 2nd
- 74, rue Marguerite-de-Rochechouart, Paris 9th
- 65, rue Jean-Pierre-Timbaud, Paris 11th
- 65, rue de Charenton, Paris 12th
- 32, rue Pernety, Paris 14th
- 100, rue d'Alésia, Paris 14th
- 64, rue Legendre, Paris 17th
- 77, rue Damrémont, Paris 18th
- 22, rue d'Orsel, Paris 18th
{See also Île-de-France}

LE PARI LOCAL
- 31, rue Chanzy, Paris 11th

HUMPHRIS
- 2, rue Milton, Paris 9th
- 74, rue des Poissonniers, Paris 18th

CAUSSES
- 99, rue Rambuteau, Paris 1st
- 222, rue Saint-Martin, Paris 3rd
- 55, rue Notre-Dame-de-Lorette, Paris 9th

AU BOUT DU CHAMP
- 35, rue Saint-Placide, Paris 6th
- 16, rue des Martyrs, Paris 9th
- 44, rue Oberkampf, Paris 11th
- 28, rue Daguerre, Paris 14th
- 98, rue Raymond-Losserand, Paris 14th
- 36, rue Lecourbe, Paris 15th
- 86, rue Cambronne, Paris 15th
- Gare Montparnasse, Paris 15th
- Drive fermier Porte de Champerret, Paris 17th
- 20, rue des Dames, Paris 17th
- 38, rue Lepic, Paris 18th
- 53, rue du Poteau, Paris 18th
- 118, rue Caulaincourt, Paris 18th
- 9, av. Secrétan, Paris 19th
- 140, rue de Belleville, Paris 20th
- 220, rue des Pyrénées, Paris 20th
{See also Île-de-France}

MIYAM
- 82, rue Beaubourg, Paris 3rd
- 161, rue du Faubourg-Saint-Antoine, Paris 11th
- 69, rue de la Convention, Paris 15th
- 11, rue du Poteau, Paris 18th

LA RÉCOLTE
- 43, rue Beaubourg, Paris 3rd
- 108, rue du Chemin-Vert, Paris 11th
- 111 bis, rue Faidherbe, Paris 11th
- 100, rue Chardon-Lagache, Paris 16th
- 18, blvd. des Batignolles, Paris 17th
- 162 bis, rue Ordener, Paris 18th

L'ÉPICERIE DES ENVIRONS
- 22, rue Ramey, Paris 18th

LES POIREAUX DE MARGUERITE
- 51, rue Saint Maur, Paris 11th
- 12, rue Alphonse-Baudin, Paris 11th
- 1 bis, rue Friant, Paris 14th

KILOGRAMME
- 10, rue de Meaux, Paris 19th
- 67, rue de Bagnolet, Paris 20th

RAYON
- 22, rue de Rivoli, Paris 4th
- 15, rue du Roi-de-Sicile, Paris 4th

LA PETITE CAGETTE
- 38–40, rue Popincourt, Paris 11th

Ô FERMIER
- 39, rue Mstislav Rostropovitch, Paris 17th

Île-de-France

JARDINS DE COURANCES
- 14, rue du Moulin, Courances (Essonne)

HERBIER DE MILLY
- 16, pl. du Marché, Milly-la-Forêt (Essonne)

LES SEASONNIERS
- 103, rue Louis-Rouquier, Levallois Perret (Hauts-de-Seine)

AU BOUT DU CHAMP
- 4, rue Camille-Pelletan, Levallois-Perret (Hauts-de-Seine)

BLETTE COMME CHOU
- 49, rue Royale, Saint-Mesmes (Seine-et-Marne)

TERROIR D'AVENIR
- 9, rue du Capitaine-Dreyfus, Montreuil (Seine–Saint-Denis)

BIOTOUTCOURT
- 8, che. des Patis, Cergy (Val-d'Oise) ⊛ ORGANIC

MARCHÉ DE CAROLINE
- Che. de Courcelles, Puiseux-Pontoise (Val-d'Oise)

FERMES DE GALLY
- 20, rue des Petits-Prés, Feucherolles (Yvelines)
- CD 7, rte. de Bailly, Saint-Cyr-l'École (Yvelines)
- 114, av. de Stalingrad, Saint Denis (Seine-Saint-Denis)

Producers

Farms

FABIEN LEGENDRE
- 9, rue de la Plaine, Merobert (Essonne) ⊛ ORGANIC

POTAGERS DU TÉLÉGRAPHE
- 10, che. du Larris, Étampes (Essonne) ⊛ ORGANIC

FERME DE COUARD
- 27, che. du Fay, Marcoussis (Essonne) ⊛ ORGANIC

FERME MARAÎCHAGE LES GRANDS PRÉS
- Rue de Vincelles, Boutigny (Seine-et-Marne) ⊛ ORGANIC

BIOLAB MARAÎCHAGE
- 10, rue de la Mairie, Châtenoy (Seine-et-Marne) ⊛ ORGANIC

CUEILLETTE DU PLESSIS
- RD 20, rte. de Lumigny, Lumigny-Nesles-Ormeaux (Seine-et-Marne) ⊛ ORGANIC

VILLAGE POTAGER
- 3300, rte. de Larchant, Saint-Pierre-lès-Nemours (Seine-et-Marne) ⊛ ORGANIC

C'TOUT BIO
- 34, che. des Voies, Cergy (Val-d'Oise) ⊛ ORGANIC

CHATELAIN MARAÎCHAGE
- 50, rte. de Roissy, Le Thillay (Val-d'Oise) ⊛ ORGANIC

LES PLAISIRS DU JARDIN
- 8, che. des Pâtis, Cergy (Val-d'Oise) ⊛ ORGANIC

SCEA BOURVEN
- 31, rue de Neuville, Cergy (Val-d'Oise) ⊛ ORGANIC

POTAGER DU ROI
- 10, rue du Maréchal-Joffre, Versailles (Yvelines)

BIO-FERME DE LOMMOYE
- 15, che. du Moulin, Lommoye (Yvelines) ⊛ ORGANIC

EARL BIO LÉGUMES FRANÇAIS
⚲ *Chemin du Fosse Turquant, Montesson (Yvelines)*
ⓐ ORGANIC

FERME DE LA HAYE
⚲ *Che. de la Ferme de la Haye, Les Mureaux (Yvelines)*
ⓐ ORGANIC

PETITE FERME AUFFERVILLOISE
⚲ *2, ham. de Morville, Aufferville (Seine-et-Marne)* ⓐ ORGANIC

THIERRY ET ÉLISE RIANT
⚲ *85, rue de Montesson, Carrières-sur-Seine (Yvelines)*

FERME DU CLOS D'ANCOIGNY
⚲ *D 74, Saint-Nom-la-Bretèche (Yvelines)*

Orchards

AUX CHAMPS SOISY
⚲ *Che. de la Padole, Champcueil (Essonne)* ⓐ ORGANIC

FERME CHAILLOTINE
⚲ *82, rte. de Paris, Chailly-en-Bière (Seine-et-Marne)*
ⓐ ORGANIC

CUEILLETTE DU PLESSIS
⚲ *Rue de la Cueillette, Chanteloup-en-Brie (Seine-et-Marne)* ⓐ ORGANIC

FERME DES MOËNES
⚲ *9, rue de Nemours, Ury (Seine-et-Marne)* ⓐ ORGANIC

Livestock farms

ENCLOS DES CHEVRETTES
⚲ *RD 148, Le Berceau, Villeneuve-sur-Auvers (Essonne)*

FERME DES SUEURS
⚲ *Rte. des Sueurs, Le Val-Saint-Germain (Essonne)*
ⓐ ORGANIC

FERME DE BEAUMONT
⚲ *Beaumont, Valpuiseaux (Essonne)* ⓐ ORGANIC

FERME DE MOIGNY
⚲ *3, Grande Rue, Moigny-sur-École (Essonne)* ⓐ ORGANIC

COCOBIO VIDELLOIS
⚲ *Che. de Varennes, Videlles (Essonne)* ⓐ ORGANIC

FERME DU PIGNON BLANC
⚲ *43, rue d'Étampes, Corbreuse (Essonne)* ⓐ ORGANIC

VOLAILLE PRUNAYSIENNE
⚲ *16, rue de la Vallée, Prunay-Sur-Essonne (Essonne)*
ⓐ ORGANIC

FERME DE LAVEAU
⚲ *Rte. de Châtenoy, D 403E1, Faÿ-lès-Nemours (Seine-et-Marne)* ⓐ ORGANIC

FERME DE LA NOUE
⚲ *Ld La Noue, La Celle-les-Bordes (Yvelines)* ⓐ ORGANIC

FERME DE L'ABONDANCE
⚲ *24, rue de Lorrez, Vaux-sur-Lunain (Seine-et-Marne)*
ⓐ ORGANIC

DOMAINE DE BEAULIEU
⚲ *Pécy (Seine-et-Marne)*

LES BERGERIES-FERME DE CHÂTENOY
⚲ *1 rue de la Mairie, Châtenoy (Seine-et-Marne)* ⓐ ORGANIC

FERME BIOLOGIQUE DE NORMANDIE
⚲ *18, rue des Capucines, Poissy (Yvelines)* ⓐ ORGANIC

FERME DE SAINT-CORENTIN
⚲ *Rosay (Yvelines)*

FERME D'ÉLEVAGE DE GRAND' MAISON
⚲ *Ham de Trottigny, rue Grand' Maison, Chevreuse (Yvelines)*

FERME DE JOUVENCE
⚲ *Rue de la Tremblaye, La Boissière-École (Yvelines)* ⓐ ORGANIC

Flour mills

FERME DE MONTGAZON
⚲ *Ham. de Montgazon, Courquetaine (Seine-et-Marne)* ⓐ ORGANIC

FERME DE GLOISE—LES BRIARDINES
⚲ *Vaudoy-en-Brie (Seine-et-Marne)*

MOULINS BOURGEOIS
⚲ *Rue du Moulin, Verdelot (Seine-et-Marne)* ⓐ ORGANIC

MOULIN DECOLLOGNE
⚲ *4, rue de l'Ancienne-Église, Précy-sur-Marne (Seine-et-Marne)* ⓐ ORGANIC

MOULIN DES GAUTHIERS (GILLES MATIGNON)
⚲ *Les Gauthiers, Château-Landon (Seine-et-Marne)*
ⓐ ORGANIC

MOULINS DE CHARS
⚲ *7, rue Dory, Chars (Val-d'Oise)*
ⓐ ORGANIC

MOULINS DE BRASSEUIL
⚲ *12, rue de la Vaucouleurs, Auffreville-Brasseuil (Yvelines)* ⓐ ORGANIC

MOULINS DE VERSAILLES
⚲ *18, rue des Chantiers, Versailles (Yvelines)*
ⓐ ORGANIC

Other producers & products to explore

CHAMPERCHÉ
⚲ *12, quai Saint-Exupéry, Paris 16th*
Herbs, chiles, microgreens.

ÉMILE ET UNE GRAINE—FERME DE FRÉMIGNY
⚲ *Soisy-sur-École (Essonne)*
Quinoa, lentils, chickpeas, mint from Milly.

FERME DU GRAND BALLEAU—TERRE DE BRIE
⚲ *Jouarre (Seine-et-Marne)*
ⓐ ORGANIC
Saffron, rhubarb.

DES PÂTES BRIARDES ÉPI C'EST TOUT !
⚲ *35, rue de l'Échelle, Marles-en-Brie (Seine-et-Marne)* ⓐ ORGANIC
Grains, livestock, housemade pasta.

HUILERIE AVERNOISE
⚲ *1, rte. de Théméricourt, Avernes (Val-d'Oise)*
Camelina oils, rapeseed, sunflower, carnations, wheat flour.

FERME LE LOUP RAVISSANT
⚲ *3, rte. de Richebourg Bazainville (Yvelines)*
Duck farmer and foie gras producer.

PISCICULTURE DE VILLETTE
⚲ *3, rue de Rosay, Villette (Yvelines)*
Trout.

HUILERIE PLAINE DE VERSAILLES
⚲ *Che du Clos-Poitou, La Couperie, Beynes (Yvelines)*
Rapeseed, sunflower, camelina, flax oils, pulses, flours.

On the Web

Direct local sales
→ Panier.biovor.com
ⓐ ORGANIC
→ Amap-idf.org
→ Marchesurleau.com

Fresh fruits and vegetables via SNCF
→ www.transilien.com

Local-Product Restaurants

LES COQS
⚲ *24, pl. du Marché, Milly-la-Forêt (Essonne). €€*
Fruits and vegetables from the Jardins de Courances, meat from La Ferme de L'Orée de Milly; Chef Emilien le Normand orders products less than 3 miles (5 km) from his restaurant.

RUCHE, AU DOMAINE LES BRUYÈRES
⚲ *251, av. de Neuville-Les-Pideaux, Gambais (Yvelines). €€*
In this former coaching house, Californian Cybele Idelot serves fruits and vegetables from her own vegetable garden to create inventive plant-based dishes.

LE DOYENNÉ
⚲ *5, rue Saint-Antoine, Saint-Vrain (Essonne). €€€*
In this farm-to-table restaurant and guesthouse, Australian chefs James Henry and Shaun Kelly cook within this historic site using products sourced on the estate that produces heirloom varieties of vegetables and animal breeds.

Leeks Vinaigrette

A star dish found in bouillons and bistros, leeks served in a vinaigrette sauce is a recipe for all seasons. —CHRISTINE DOUBLET

THE RECIPE

Season : Year-round
Difficulty ● ○ ○

SERVES 4

Salt

1 large "cuisse de poulet" shallot

2 tablespoons sherry vinegar

4 medium leeks

1 tablespoon Dijon mustard

3 to 4 tablespoons (45 to 60 ml) sunflower oil

Freshly ground black pepper

Chervil leaves or dill sprigs

Here is the classic recipe from brothers Paul Boudier and Albert Touton, chef-owners of the neighborhood bistro Le Maquis.*

Bring a pot of salted water to a boil. Chop the shallot, then combine it with 1 tablespoon of the vinegar and 1 pinch of salt to marinate it.

Remove the greens and roots from the leeks. Slice the leek whites lengthwise about 4 inches (10 cm), rinse the sections well, and blanch them for 10 to 15 minutes in the boiling salted water.

Prepare the vinaigrette: Whisk together the mustard and the remaining 1 tablespoon vinegar. Add the oil a little at a time while whisking constantly. Season with salt and pepper. Add the chopped shallot.

Let the leeks drain for 5 minutes. Trim the sections to even them up and arrange them on a serving plate. Pour the vinaigrette over the leeks while still hot. Let stand for at least 5 minutes. Serve, sprinkled with a few chervil leaves or dill sprigs.

*Le Maquis—53, rue des Cloÿs, Paris 18th.

THE TRUE HISTORY OF THE RECIPE

No one knows it! Neither Alexandre Dumas's *Grand dictionnaire de cuisine* nor Prosper Montagné's *Larousse gastronomique* devotes a single page to the recipe. Yet the recipe is ancient, dating to the Roman Apicius, who proposed in *L'art culinaire* (III, 10, 1) to season boiled leeks with oil, garum (a dried fish sauce), and pure wine. In France, it is only in some postwar books that the recipe makes an appearance.

MAY 5, 1948
The magazine *Claudine*, predecessor of *Elle* magazine, made one of the first mentions of it: "The white of the leek, seasoned with a vinaigrette or mayonnaise, makes a very nice salad."

1994
In his essay *La Belle Jardinière*, writer Éric Holder evokes "the France of Trenet, Pourrat, and Marcel Aymé, with his farmers and hardware stores, [and] the smell of leeks vinaigrette."

2018
Patrick Pécherot sets his novel *Hével* in postwar France: "We dived into the leeks vinaigrette when the bikers entered."

Produce sellers, Halles Centrales, 1925.

TOP
LET'S EAT PARIS!
ADDRESSES

Bouillon République
📍 *39, blvd. du Temple, Paris 3rd.* €

A Parisian neo-*bouillon* that concocts all the classics of French cuisine, including leeks impeccably dressed with vinaigrette.

Le Cadoret
📍 *1, rue Pradier, Paris 19th.* €€

A neighborhood watering hole that serves diners all day. The leeks are topped with a hard-boiled egg and dill vinaigrette.

Cuisine
📍 *50, rue Condorcet, Paris 9th.* €€

A little gem of an *izakaya*, where Franco-Japanese plates are raised to new heights . . . such as leeks with miso vinaigrette.

Les Arlots
📍 *136, rue du Faubourg-Poissonnière, Paris 10th.* €€

And last, but certainly not least, is this little gem that serves up spring leeks sprinkled with smoked herring.

"THE BEST THING IS TO FORGET THEM," according to chef Albert Touton about cooking leeks. For such a simple dish, there are many variations in cooking times among chefs:

4 minutes: La Cantine du Troquet

7 to 8 minutes: Le Bougainville, Caluche

10 minutes: Le Bon Saint Pourçain, Le Grand Pan, Le Cadoret

12 minutes: Bouillons Pigalle and République, Grande Brasserie, La Fontaine de Mars, Les Marches

15 minutes: Le Maquis, Les Arlots

20 minutes: À l'Épi d'Or

More than 60 minutes: Aux Bons Crus, Chez Michel

SKIP TO
Île-de-France Terroir, p. 20; Prosper Montagné, p. 53; Lutetia at the Table, p. 294.

Subterranean Breweries

During the nineteenth century, driven by the high prices for Parisian land, beer brewing took up residence in the city's hidden underground quarries. —ESTELLE LENARTOWICZ

Heads underground

The fine art of beer brewing was long a monopoly of abbey monks until Henry IV liberalized it. Beer then experienced considerable success in the nineteenth century, radically changing brewing and resulting in a fast proliferation of breweries. To serve their product at a lower price in the heart of Paris, beer brewers, many of whom arrived from Alsace at the end of the Franco-Prussian war in 1870, had the idea of establishing underground operations. This was not only a way to reduce the rent—especially since underground spaces had no doors or windows, which were heavily taxed at the time—but also a way to take advantage of the favorable conditions found underground for brewing, such as an ideal temperature and humidity and easy access to groundwater.

From quarries to breweries

Paris's former underground quarries were completely redeveloped to accommodate beer brewing and were transformed into veritable factories. Some were located on more than one level—a level for fermentation, and a level for storage—connected by steam elevators. Pillars reinforced the vaults, the floors were made of concrete and then tiled, and the walls were whitewashed to prevent mold. Finally, barrels were stored in concrete tanks with a wax coating to prevent scaling.

An end and a beginning

The two World Wars put an end to the golden age of underground beer brewing. The cellars were requisitioned to serve as shelters or to store military equipment. The effects of market concentration then led to a slow wave of closures. Imported by American GIs, soda competed with good old cervoise beer, whose production and distribution were also severely disrupted by the strikes of 1968. It was not until the 2010s that the trendy micro-breweries revived the tradition of Parisian beer brewing.

Beer under the cobblestones

Many of these underground breweries (aka brasseries) were established in the 13th and 14th arrondissements within old limestone quarries of these industrial and popular districts.

Rue Dareau (*Paris 14th*): The brasserie of the Dumesnil sons was established in 1880. Eight years earlier, their father Georges partnered with Louis Pasteur to create the first sterilized beer process. At the beginning of the twentieth century, the brasserie expanded to Ivry-sur-Seine.

Rue Sarrette and de la Voie-Verte (*now rue du Père-Corentin, Paris 14th*): Brasserie Gallia, whose emblem is a rooster, was renamed Nouvelle Gallia after its purchase in 1890 by the Alsatian J. J. Wohlhüter.

Rue de la Voie-Verte and de la Tombe-Issoire (*Paris 14th*): Brasserie l'Espérance, which became Filley, then Luxor in 1930.

Rue des Pyrénées (*Paris 20th*): Brasserie Karcher, near the square of the same name, was founded in 1891 and closed in 1968. At the end of the nineteenth century, about thirty underground brasseries supplied the taverns of the capital, supported outside the city by the legendary Brasserie Arcueil between 1865 and 1975 and that of Moulineaux in Issy beginning in 1875. Gruber in Melun opened in 1889 and closed in 1985.

TO SEE

This former brasserie-factory is open to the public once a year during Heritage Days (Journées du Patrimoine).

Cave de la Brasserie Dumesnil
📍 *Rue Georgette-Rostaing, Ivry-sur-Seine (Val-de-Marne)*

SKIP TO
Button Mushroom of Paris, p. 30; Microbreweries, p. 336.

Le Jambon-Beurre

Nicknamed the "Parisian," this baguette sandwich is *the* French snack par excellence. Enjoy one at the counter or on the go. — MINA SOUNDIRAM

Construction of the perfect "Parisian"

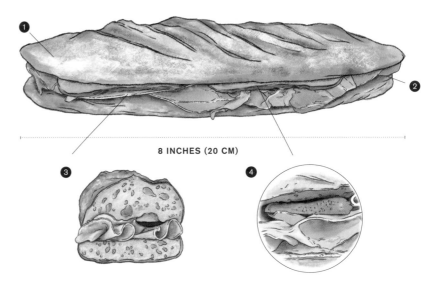

8 INCHES (20 CM)

❶ A crisp, golden baguette (preferably with crusty ends), 8 inches (20 cm) long, cut in half.

❷ Salted butter, spread on both halves of the baguette.

❸ Two thin slices of Prince de Paris ham (the thinner the better), making sure not to mash the slices between the bread halves.

❹ A cornichon, halved lengthwise.

For a perfect balance of freshness and crustiness, be sure to assemble the sandwich just before serving.

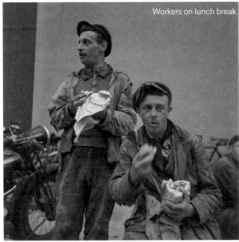

Workers on lunch break.

It all started with a sandwich

Pierre-Jean Grosley, in his work *Londres* (1770), states that the sandwich was the creation of John Montagu, Earl of Sandwich, in 1762, so that he could spend hours playing cards without interruption by eating slices of beef inserted between two slices of bread. During the 1830s, the idea became commonplace in France among the upper classes, according to poet Lord Byron. The sandwich was most likely consumed during the second half of the nineteenth century by the workers of Les Halles to *casser la croûte* (meaning "have a snack" in French, literally to "break the crust," an expression attested since 1871) and was composed of two slices of bread filled with lard or bacon. The sandwich became widespread in the 1930s, and around 1950, the baguette replaced the large bread slice, and ham, or pâté, with or without raw vegetables, joined the filling.

The jambon-beurre of chefs

Michelin-starred chefs often tackle street-food classics, and the jambon-beurre is no exception:

› As a soup by chef Éric Frechon at Le Bristol (Paris 8th), who offers a jambon-beurre soup with grilled bread crumbled on top. The soup tastes remarkably like the sandwich;

› In a checkerboard pattern by chef Yannick Alléno at Le Meurice (Paris 1st), who prepared it with a square of alternating cubes of butter and shredded ham, served with a piece of baguette.

In literature

Commissioner Maigret, the French detective in the novel series of the same name, snacks exclusively on jambon-beurre during lunch because he's overwhelmed with work—it's always the perfect meal when on the run!

In Numbers

› In 2017, out of 2.4 billion sandwiches sold in France, half were jambon-beurre.

› Modeled after the Big Mac Index and calculated by *The Economist*, management consulting firm Gira Conseil created the Jambon-Beurre Index to find out if the prices and sales of the sandwich reflect the exchange value of the euro.

› In France, the average price of the sandwich increased to €3.04 in 2021 according to Gira Conseil. In Paris, it is served up at €4 compared to €3.06 in Toulouse and €2.48 in Tulle.

SKIP TO Île-de-France Terroir, p. 20.

The Ritz

📍 *15, pl. Vendôme, Paris 1st*
Baguette: 11 inches (28 cm), housemade.
Ham: Prince de Paris.
Butter: with coarse-grain Meaux mustard, from the Coopérative d'Étrez-Foissiat dairy in Bourg-en-Bresse.
Add-ons: cornichons, 12-month Comté cheese, and coarse-grain Meaux mustard.

The Petit Vendôme

📍 *8, rue des Capucines, Paris 2nd*
Baguette: 8½ inches (22 cm), traditional.
Ham: French, cooked on the bone.
Butter: unsalted in block form from Bruel et Fils (Normandy).
Add-ons: cornichons.

Caractère de Cochon

📍 *42, rue Charlot, Paris 3rd*
Baguette: 8 inches (20 cm), traditional.
Ham: A choice between raw (noir de Bigorre) and cooked (Bleu-Blanc-Coeur), with Espelette pepper or bergamot.
Butter: unsalted in block form from Verneuil (Touraine-Berry).
Add-ons: cornichons and cheese of your choice (Saint-Nectaire, Ossau-Iraty, 8-month Comté cheese, or Manchego).

Brasserie Lazare Paris

📍 *Rue Intérieur, Paris 8th*
Baguette: 8 inches (20 cm), traditional.
Ham: Prince de Paris.
Butter: unsalted, from Maison Bordier (Brittany).

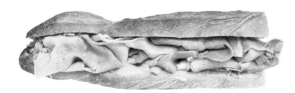

CheZaline

📍 *85, rue de la Roquette, Paris 11th*
Baguette: 8 inches (20 cm), traditional.
Ham: Prince de Paris.
Butter: lightly salted, from Maison Borniambuc (Normandy).

Le Favori

📍 *112, rue Saint-Maur, Paris 11th*
Baguette: 9¾ inches (25 cm), traditional.
Ham: French, cooked on the bone.
Butter: lightly salted, from Maison Bordier (Brittany).
Add-ons: cornichon slices.

Facades Save Face

The exteriors of these food establishments have retained their links to the past thanks to government protection. Here are some favorites. —MARIELLE GAUDRY

The important edifices of Paris (represented here are the "magasins de commerce," retail establishments) benefit from protection by the French government to guarantee their preservation. This protection also implies that the facades cannot be destroyed, moved, or modified without approval, due to their historical or artistic interest.

What is a historical monument?

During the Revolution, an instruction from 1790 charged the municipality of Paris with "drawing up the status and ensuring the conservation of monuments, churches, and establishments that have become national domains". However, this policy was only a guideline at the time. It was not until 1913 that the policy became a law and was enforced.

Two types of protection*

When a building is "classé" (classified), it has the highest level of protection. It is understood that "its conservation is, from the point of view of history or art, of public interest." When a building is "inscrit" (listed), it is "of sufficient historical or artistic interest to make its preservation desirable." In both cases, this protection may concern only certain parts of a building, its interior decor, roof, or facade.

*Source: Ministry of Culture.

↑ **CAFÉ-BAR LE ROYAL, PARIS 2ND**
Founded in 1910 under the name Pinzaronne Bar.
A wooden storefront and ceramic panels where lemons and oranges alternate with inscriptions from the vermouth company Martini and Rossi.
Listed, 1984

Change of purpose

There are many businesses whose initial purposes (bakery, cheese shop, restaurant, etc.) have changed but whose facades have been preserved: the horse butcher shop at the corner of rues Vieille-du-Temple and Roi-de-Sicile (Paris 4th) became a sock shop, the dairy-butter-and-eggs shop on rue Danielle-Casanova (Paris 1st) is now home to a coffee retailer, and the poissonerie (fish market) on rue de Seine (Paris 6th) has turned into Boissonnerie, a wine bistro.

↑ **RESTAURANT LE PETIT BOUILLON PHARAMOND, PARIS 1ST**
Founded in 1879 under the name À la Petite Normande.
On the facade are imitation Norman timber frames and glazed tiles representing a Norman native in festive costume.
Listed, 1989

↑ **PÂTISSERIE STOHRER, PARIS 2ND**
Founded in 1730.
Redecorated in 1864 by the painter Paul Baudry, its facade is wood paneling and a bas-relief is above the door.
Listed, 1984

↑ **RESTAURANT AU VIEUX PARIS D'ARCOLE, PARIS 4TH**
The building was constructed in 1512, and a wine bar opened here in 1723.
The metal railings and the storefront have a medieval look.
Listed, 1984

↑ **CHOCOLATERIE DEBAUVE & GALLAIS, PARIS 7TH**
The shop opened in 1817.
The front was designed by the architects Percier and Fontaine.
Listed, 1984

↑ **CONFISERIE À LA MÈRE DE FAMILLE, PARIS 9TH**
Founded in 1761. Panels of imitation sea green marble, copper letters gilded with gold leaf, late nineteenth century.
Listed, 1984

↑ **RESTAURANT AU ROCHER DE CANCALE, PARIS 2ND**
Founded on this site around 1846.
Nineteenth-century facades are wood paneled and varnished.
Listed, 1997

↑ **RESTAURANT CHEZ JULIEN, PARIS 4TH**
Founded in 1820 under the name Au Pigeon Blanc.
Cast-iron railings and panels under glass from 1900.
Listed, 1984

SKIP TO
The Invention of the Restaurant, p. 61; Art Nouveau or Art Deco?, p. 160.

The Flan Parisien

A comforting childhood memory for many Parisians, this pastry is an endless quest to find the right balance between crisp crust and creamy custard. —ANNE ETORRE

THE RECIPE

Season: year-round
Difficulty ● ● ○

SERVES 6 TO 8

12 ounces (350 g) Puff
Pastry (p. 58)

Custard filling

1 vanilla bean

3 cups (750 g) whole milk

1 cup plus 1 tablespoon
(250 g) heavy cream

3 large (60 g) egg yolks

3 large (150 g) eggs

1 cup plus 1 tablespoon
(210 g) sugar

2½ ounces (70 g) flan
powder

Equipment

One springform pan
measuring 9½ inches
(24 cm) in diameter and
1¾ inches (4.5 cm) tall

Stéphane Glacier,* MOF pastry chef, prefers puff
pastry to flaky pastry (which is most often used).
His golden rule: a flan must be enjoyed on the day
it is made, because it is at its best when fresh!

Line the pan with the puff pastry ❶.

Prepare the custard filling: Split the vanilla bean
lengthwise in half and scrape out the seeds using
the tip of a small knife. In a saucepan, heat the milk,
cream, vanilla seeds, and empty vanilla bean pod ❷.

In a bowl, whisk together the yolks, eggs, and sugar
until lightened in color. Whisk in the flan powder.
Pour half of the hot milk-cream mixture over the
egg mixture while whisking thoroughly. ❸ Pour
the mixture back into the saucepan. Bring to a boil,
then cook, while whisking, for 3 minutes. Remove
the vanilla bean pod. Pour the custard into the
prepared pan ❹.

Let cool, and refrigerate for 12 hours. The cream
will harden and develop a skin on top called a *crouter*.

Preheat the oven to 325°F (170°C) and bake for
about 1 hour, or until the top of the flan has dark
brown spots. Let cool and unmold.

*Pâtisseries et Gourmandises by Stéphane Glacier; 39, rue du
Général-Leclerc, Bois-Colombes (Hauts-de-Seine).

FROM *FLAON* TO *FLAN*

› From the Low Latin
flado, flan was first
called *flaon* in the
Middle Ages. These
were similar to galettes
or crêpes sold by street
vendors in Paris.

› The word *flan* appears
during the Renaissance,
but it refers to a kind of
cheese tart, cousin of
the *talmouse* or *dariole*.
Gradually, flan came to
mean an "egg cream"
to which fruits, prunes,
raisins, chicken livers,
or seafood was added.

› Around 1393, in *Le
Mesnagier de Paris*,
flanciaux succrés and
flaons de cresme are
mentioned.

› Its relatives: the Far
Breton, the *flognarde*
from Auvergne, and
the *fion* from Vendée.
Outside of France,
the *pastel de nata* in
Portugal and the
custard tart in England
are also relatives.

IS IT FLAN *PARISIEN*
OR FLAN *PÂTISSIER*?

A *flan pâtissier* is
distinguished from a
plain egg custard or
crème caramel by the
presence of a crust.
Chef Antonin Carême
was the first to mention
the *flan parisien* in *Le
Pâtissier royal parisien*
in 1815, but the dessert
seems identical to the
flan pâtissier. Since
this is the best-selling
dessert in Parisian
pastry shops and
bakeries, this could be
the origin of the term
parisien in the name.

TOP LET'S EAT PARIS! ADDRESSES

Jacques Genin
📍 *133, rue de Turenne,
Paris 3rd*
A perfect balance
between flaky pastry
and a vanilla flan filling.

Cyril Lignac
📍 *24, rue Paul-Bert,
Paris 11th +
6 additional locations*
Notes of caramel and a
barely perceptible thin
puff pastry crust.

Paris & Co
📍 *4, rue de la Convention,
Paris 15th + 4 bis, rue
des écoles, Paris 5th*
A delicate puff pastry
topped with a creamy
vanilla filling.

KL Pâtisserie
📍 *78, av. de Villiers,
Paris 17th*
A very light and thin puff
pastry crust and a nice
long finish of vanilla.

Nina Métayer
Ninametayer.com
An impeccable
shortcrust pastry is
filled with a tonka-bean
cream.

SKIP TO
Antonin Carême,
p. 156; The
Talmouse of
Saint-Denis, p. 159;
Portugal, p. 169;
Ladurée, p. 225.

Prosper Montagné (1865–1948)

A Mountain of Knowledge

In addition to being one of the most influential chefs of his time, Prosper Montagné (*mountain* in English) was one of the most prolific gastronomic authors. —CAMILLE MENNESSON

From pans to pen

Originally from Carcassonne, Prosper Montagné was passionate about painting and architecture, and he was encouraged by his father to cook. Recognizing that he had a talent for cooking, Montagné quickly joined the kitchens of grand hotels, including in Cauterets, then Monte-Carlo, and eventually Paris, where he took over as head of the kitchens of Le Pavillon d'Armenonville, Le Pavillon de Ledoyen, then the Grand Hôtel de Paris. During World War I, he provided soldiers on the front lines with hot meals from his mobile kitchens. He was awarded the Legion of Honor in 1922.

"After Carême, it was undoubtedly Prosper Montagné and Auguste Escoffier who had the greatest impact on French gastronomy, and that of the whole world."
—*Encyclopaedia Britannica*

The restaurant Montagné Traiteur.

Paris, a stage for his expertise . . .

"Cooking is my life," Montagné said. In all areas, Prosper Montagné spread his knowledge of gastronomy as . . .

› **A lecturer** on very diverse themes (from nutrition to techniques) particularly in Parisian salons, restaurants, and Galeries Lafayette in 1934.

› **General commissioner** of the Paris Culinary Expositions of 1908, 1909, and 1910.

› **Food inspector** of public assistance hospitals.

› **Contributor** to many Parisian newspapers and magazines, in which his columns were very popular, including *Excelsior* and *Femina*.

› **Editor-in-chief** of *Revue Culinaire*, created in 1920.

› **Author of numerous books:**
- *La Grande Cuisine illustrée*, in 1900;
- *Cuisine diététique*, in 1910;
- *La Bonne Chère pas cher ou les Repas sans viande*, in 1919;
- *Le Grand Livre de la cuisine*, in 1929;
- *Larousse Gastronomique*, in 1938.

. . . and his skills

RUE DE L'ÉCHELLE (PARIS 1ST)
At 5, rue de l'Échelle in Paris, there is a plaque commemorating Montagné Traiteur, the small restaurant with luxurious Louis-Philippe decor that Prosper Montagné opened in 1921. For nearly ten years, Montagné worked here and experienced immense success cooking from his stove top set up in the main dining room. The quality of the dishes served was excellent, including his famous papillote pomme de terre à la truffe (potato papillote with truffle), but the establishment's poor management forced it to close a decade later.

LA REINE PÉDAUQUE (PARIS 8TH)
In 1939, Montagné became a culinary advisor at the Rôtisserie de la Reine Pédauque in Paris where he served a "tournedos Saint-Germain" placed on thin toasts, garnished with tomatoes, new potatoes, and artichoke hearts filled with garden peas, and "foie gras Reine Pédauque"

surrounded by crushed ice and decorated with flowers, all following the sophisticated methods for cooking dear to the chef.

A CLUB IN HIS NAME, SINCE 1950
A defender of grand French cuisine, each year the *Club Prosper Montagné* awards the Prosper Montagné culinary prize, the oldest culinary competition in France. Less publicized than the prestigious MOF (Best Craftsman of France) competition, this is one of the most difficult and coveted competitions in the profession.

"The door opens, and the customer enters and immediately sees a majestic stove in front of which stood a cook more imposing in presence and appearance than any king in velvet robes. That's him! It's Prosper Montagné himself! He's dressed from head to toe in immaculate white, with glasses resting on his nose . . ."
—Pierre Andrieu and Curnonsky, *Les Fines Gueules de France*, Paris, Firmin Didot, 1935.

SKIP TO
Steak Tartare, p. 254; Fries Forever!, p. 142.

The Petite Neighborhood Groceries

Warm welcomes, late-night hours, and an infinite choice of staples, some of which have an exotic flair . . . Here is a decoding of *épiceries*, the neighborhood minimarkets.

—JACQUES BRUNEL AND MARIELLE GAUDRY

A changing landscape

Present in Paris since 1900, épiceries proliferated throughout Parisian neighborhoods after 1945 and reached their peak in the 1980s. For the last decade, however, these shops' numbers have been decreasing as they must compete with big-chain supermarkets that offer later and later hours, and because they have evolved very little during the last thirty years. New owners (often the nephews of former owners), however, have been transforming these shops, making them well-lit and tidy, and even offering delivery.

Unique and changing origins

Parisians have long affectionately referred to these shops as *l'arabe du coin* (the neighborhood Arab shop), and for good reason. As historian and journalist Patrick Girard has explained, the first generations of these shop owners belonged to Berber ethnic groups who were trade specialists, including Moroccans from the Souss region (south of the Agadir region) and Tunisians from the island of Djerba, a paradise for fresh produce markets and small start-up shops. But, increasingly, *épicerie* owners have become more diverse, representing other groups, such as the Turks, and particularly the Tamils, a minority group from northern Sri Lanka.

Alimentation Générale, on rue Claude-Bernard.

Au Marché de la Butte.

Filmography

Amélie (Jean-Pierre Jeunet, 2001), starring Audrey Tautou and Mathieu Kassovitz, was filmed in Montmartre. The film's heroine Amélie befriends the Arab clerk (Jamel Debbouze) of Parisian épicerie Collignon. You can visit this same shop today under its name Au Marché de la Butte.

Monsieur Ibrahim et les Fleurs du Coran (François Dupeyron, 2003), starring Isabelle Adjani and Omar Sharif. Sharif plays a Turkish grocer on rue Bleue (Paris 9th) who protects and guides a young Jewish boy.

Lahoussine

📍 *79, rue Marguerite-de-Rochechouart, Paris 9th*

Surrounded by minimarkets, this is probably one of the warmest welcoming épiceries in Pigalle (open for twenty-five years) that remains in business despite the changing landscape. The owner will tell you all about his collection of spirits between cups of thé à la menthe (mint tea).

FUN FEATURE
The shop's mural of shallots, the fake ivy and plastic lilacs that sprawl along the outside of the shop, and the green carpet that spills out onto the sidewalk.

Au Marché de la Butte

📍 *56, rue des Trois-Frères, Paris 18th*

Known to many as Épicerie Collignon, this shop, owned by Ismail and Myriam, Berbers from Agadir in Tunisia, is large and well stocked. Here you can enjoy anisette (anise-flavor liqueur) with the owners, who are considered pillars of the neighborhood.

FUN FEATURE
This épicerie has become a pilgrimage for fans of the movie *Amélie*.

Supérette des Martyrs

📍 *58, rue des Martyrs, Paris 9th*

Located in the center of a commercial hotspot, this épicerie has remained a constant throughout the years. You'll have to suck in your stomach to fit between all the display aisles as you browse and discover products such as halva, packets of chorba stew, and rose water.

FUN FEATURE
The owner uses a round mirror from the back room to know when customers enter the store.

Selim Orientale

📍 *63, blvd. Ornano, Paris 18th*

A veritable bazaar with an ocean of Middle Eastern products for sale, sometimes sold semi-wholesale: bâton salés (salted crunchy bread sticks), loukoums (Turkish delight), mouloukhia (Tunisian spinach), hibiscus syrup, mangoes, and more.

FUN FEATURE
Try Hamoud Cola (a caramel cola) and Gazouz (a soda) that are enjoyed in place of alcohol in the Maghreb region of north Africa.

Alimentation Générale

📍 *35, rue Claude-Bernard, Paris 5th*

Under a lacquered red clock, an old gentleman offers three thousand products in this tiny space, ranging from bananas from Martinique, fresh basil, spirits, drinking glasses, cassoulet, couscous, and more.

FUN FEATURE
The multicolored sign flashing under an enamel panel.

Au Petit Marché

📍 *114, blvd. du Montparnasse, Paris 14th*

A very clean shop open amid Montparnasse nights. Condoms, organic products, hookah tobacco, matzo, and pots of geraniums are among the many choices.

FUN FEATURE
The smiling and welcoming young bosses.

Eureka Market

📍 *44, rue Pernety, Paris 14th*

A flashy shop whose owners are Tamils. It offers staples as well as an influx of bazaar-type products from the Maghreb: raffia fans, cassava, plantains, and similar products. Speaking English is your best bet here.

FUN FEATURE
The small altar of Ganesh, the elephant god of commerce, located in the shop.

SKIP TO
The Maghreb, p. 176; When Hollywood Dines in Paris, p. 286.

A beacon in the night

These shops have in common:

› Extended hours

Most are open seven days a week in the morning and often close around 2 a.m. (5 a.m. in popular neighborhood night spots).

› A small footprint

Measuring anywhere from 190 to 430 square feet (18 to 40 sq m), where the maximum number of staple products are displayed, some crammed on displays fixed to the wall or hanging from the ceiling.

› A range of products

These shops sell a little bit of everything, from food (okra, fresh produce, dairy products, frozen foods, organic foods, etc.) to beverages (chilled cans, bottles of spirits in all sizes), hygiene products, candies, ice cream, toys, bandages, umbrellas, toilet paper, condoms, cat litter, phone chargers, light bulbs, and plug adapters—to name a few.

› Higher prices

Prices in these shops are between 1.25 and 1.5 times higher than at the nearby supermarkets, which are most often closed in the evening.

› Being a neighborhood fixture

These small shops are present almost everywhere and are often the beating heart of many neighborhoods. Here everyone shops, including the homeless, retirees, insomniacs, night owls . . . and the shops often deliver, accept credit cards for small purchases, extend credit to relatives, and sometimes provide minor services.

Au Petit Marché

ANGELINA

A gastronomic mecca and architectural jewel, this legendary salon de thé *serves the most famous hot chocolate in the world.* —**MORGANE MIZZON**

MAISON PARISIENNE
226, RUE DE RIVOLI, (1ST)

ANGELINA
Paris depuis 1903

120 years of history

In 1903, Anton Rumpelmayer, an Austrian confectioner who owned several successful shops in the south of France, decided to try his luck in Paris. He chose the very chic rue de Rivoli to establish his salon de thé (tearoom), which he entrusted to his son René, who named the place after his wife, Angelina.

A chocolate show

The undisputed star of the establishment is the "Africain." This hot chocolate is composed of three cocoas of African origin—from Niger, Ghana, and Ivory Coast—as well as whole milk and a touch of pastry cream. This precious blend then rests at 149°F (65°C) in the *chocolatière* before turning into a sublime, velvety cocoa served with a small pot of Chantilly cream.

Chanel number . . . 45

Coco Chanel, who worked in her studio next door on rue Cambon, often took breaks to enjoy a little something sweet. The fashion icon always sat at the same table here: number 45.

A rendezvous for stars

Located near the Opéra Garnier, the salon quickly attracted Paris's beau monde. Marcel Proust, connected to the owner, was a regular.
In the early 1980s, scenes from two French films were shot here: In Claude Zidi's *Inspecteur la Bavure* (1980), Michel Clément (Coluche) and his superior pursue their "protégé," journalist Marie-Anne Prossant (Dominique Lavanant). In Claude Pinoteau's *La Boum 2* (1982), Poupette (Denise Grey), the super granny, confides in her granddaughter Vic (Sophie Marceau) about her love life. Even today, many celebrities visit the establishment, including Laurent Voulzy, Monica Bellucci, and Kate Moss.

🔍 TO SEE

The architecture.
The work of Dutch architect Édouard-Jean Niermans, the tearoom brings together all the hallmarks of the Belle Époque period: a vaulted ceiling, molding, cornices, and beveled mirrors.

The ocher and azure blue frescoes by the French painter and designer Vincent Lorant-Heilbronn (1874–1912), who had worked on palaces, are a tribute to the Riviera, an area dear to founder Anton Rumpelmayer.

One thousand customers are served each Saturday in the salon de thé on rue de Rivoli.

🍴 TO TRY

The Mont Blanc:
the recipe for this classic dessert has not changed since 1903. It consists of a meringue covered with a layer of Chantilly cream and noodles of chestnut cream, which are supposed to evoke either Angelina's hair or the bob hairstyle, which was very fashionable at the time. The hotel sells an average of six hundred Mont Blancs per day in their only shop on rue de Rivoli.

The chocolate éclair:
from its cream filling to its glaze, this pastry is a true chocolaty achievement.

SKIP TO
Ladurée, p. 225;
Pastry Shops,
p. 312.

Île Flottante The Floating Island

A fluffy island of meringue floats on an ocean of custard in this flagship dessert with a complex genealogy. —SAMIR OURIAGHLI

THE RECIPE

Season : year-round
Difficulty ●●○

SERVES 6

For the crème anglaise (vanilla custard sauce)
(Make 6 hours ahead)
2 Bourbon-Madagascar vanilla beans
3¼ cups (800 ml) whole milk
⅔ cup (140 g) granulated sugar
8 large (160 g) egg yolks

For the meringue
8 large (240 g) egg whites
1 pinch fine salt
3 tablespoons superfine sugar

For the caramelized nuts
¼ cup (50 g) granulated sugar
1 teaspoon water
½ cup (50 g) chopped hazelnuts
½ cup (50 g) chopped almonds
½ cup (50 g) pecans
½ tablespoon butter

Equipment
Thermometer
6 ovenproof serving bowls
Fine-mesh strainer
Stand mixer

A glossy meringue, silky custard, and caramelized nuts . . . this version by Pierre Lecoutre, founder of L'Oseille,* makes everyone happy.

Prepare the crème anglaise: Split the vanilla beans lengthwise in half and scrape out the seeds using the tip of a knife. In a saucepan, bring the milk, empty vanilla bean pods, vanilla bean seeds, and ¼ cup (50 g) of the sugar to a simmer. Cover and let infuse for 20 minutes.

Whisk the egg yolks and remaining sugar together in a bowl until thickened and pale yellow in color. Slowly pour the hot milk into the yolk-sugar mixture while whisking constantly. Pour the mixture back into the saucepan, set it over very low heat, and stir using a spatula until the mixture coats the spatula (181°F/83°C). Strain and set aside.

Prepare the meringue: Preheat the oven to 300°F (150°C). In the bowl of a stand mixer fitted with the whisk attachment, beat the egg whites with the salt. When the whites begin to stiffen, slowly sprinkle in the sugar with the mixer running for several minutes until stiff peaks form. Divide the meringue among the ovenproof bowls using a spatula. Bake for 6 minutes.

Prepare the caramelized nuts: In a wide, shallow saucepan, heat the sugar and water until the mixture turns to a light amber caramel. Add the nuts to the pan and stir continuously over medium heat to completely coat them in the caramel. Thoroughly stir in the butter. Spread the coated nuts onto a sheet of parchment paper and let cool.

Add two ladles of custard to the cooled bowls with the meringues, making sure to pour the custard around the meringue and not on top of it. Push the meringues to the center of the bowls to float on top of the custard. Sprinkle with the caramelized nuts.

*3, rue Saint-Augustin, Paris 2nd.

Oeufs à la neige (*Le Livre de pâtisserie*, J. Gouffé, 1873).

OEUFS À LA NEIGE OR ÎLE FLOTTANTE?

There is often confusion between these two names for this dessert. Here is an explanation.

- **1651**
The first appearance of oeufs à la neige in *Le Cuisinier françois* by La Varenne (yolks beaten with butter and salt, heated over a fire, combined with beaten and sweetened egg whites).

- **1798**
The *Dictionnaire de l'Académie française* defines oeufs à la neige as: "eggs beaten in such a way that they resemble snow."

- **1806**
André Viard, in his *Cuisinier impérial*, proposes the current recipe for oeufs à la neige, adding orange blossom water instead of vanilla.

- **1886**
A recipe for île flottante (floating island) is published in the journal *Gil Blas* (a mousse of cooked apples incorporated in beaten egg whites and flavored with rose water or orange blossom water).

- **1890**
Madame Lebrasseur in *Ma cuisine* revisits Viard's recipe (beaten egg whites cooked in a caramelized mold

and then poured into a vanilla cream).

- **1903**
Auguste Escoffier publishes in *Le Guide culinaire* the recipe for île flottante composed of biscuit de Savoie (a light sponge cake) soaked with alcohol and covered with whipped cream and surrounded by a vanilla custard.

- **TODAY**
Some chefs distinguish the two recipes by baking the meringues in the oven in a water bath when making île flottante and in milk when making oeufs à la neige.

TOP LET'S EAT PARIS! ADDRESSES

La Poule au Pot
📍 *9, rue Vauvilliers, Paris 1st.* €€
Served with pink pralines and vanilla custard sauce.

Bouillon Pigalle
📍 *22, blvd. de Clichy, Paris 18th.* €
A quenelle of poached meringue floats on a custard sauce and is drizzled with caramel.

Le Coq & Fils
📍 *98, rue Lepic, Paris 18th.* €€
A meringue dome dusted with pink pralines, served with a vanilla sauce flavored with a very aromatic vanilla.

SKIP TO
Bistros, p. 352.

The Mille-Feuille

This grand classic pastry of "one thousand layers" is loved by all. —MARIELLE GAUDRY

THE RECIPE

Season : year-round
Difficulty ● ● ●

MAKES 1 POUND 9 OUNCES (700 G) OF PASTRY

½ cup minus 1 tablespoon (55 g) pastry flour or T45 flour

2½ cups (320 g) all-purpose flour or T55 flour, plus more for dusting

1 teaspoon (7 g) salt

½ cup (125 ml) water

½ teaspoon (2 g) white vinegar

6 tablespoons (85 g) butter, melted

10 ounces (280 g) unsalted cold butter, preferably AOP Poitou-Charentes or Isigny

Equipment
Stand mixer

JACQUES GENIN'S PUFF PASTRY*

This traditional recipe requires 10 hours of resting time for the dough. It is best to make it 48 hours in advance.

In the bowl of a stand mixer fitted with the dough hook, combine the pastry and all-purpose flours, the salt, water, and vinegar on medium speed. Incorporate the melted butter. Mix until a homogeneous dough is achieved. Cover in plastic wrap (this is called the *détrempe*) and refrigerate for 1 hour.

Remove the butter from the refrigerator and set aside to come to room temperature. Using a rolling pin, tap and shape the cold butter into a single 6-inch (15 cm) square measuring ⅓ inch (1 cm) thick ❶. Roll the détrempe into a rectangle measuring 8 inches wide by 19½ inches long (20 by 50 cm) ❷. Place the butter (called the *tourage*) in the center and fold the dough over the butter to cover it. Using your fingers, press the ends of the dough together to enclose the butter ❸.

Thoroughly dust a work surface with flour. Roll out the dough again into a rectangle measuring 8 inches wide by 19½ inches long (20 by 50 cm) ❹, then fold the upper third over to the center, then the lower third over that to make a "single turn." ❺ Turn the dough a quarter turn, cover in plastic wrap, and chill for 1 hour. Repeat these folding steps three more times, resting again for 1 hour between each turn.

When the last turn is made, chill for 4 hours so that each layer of butter (the *feuillets*, or sheets) firm up.

* 133, rue de Turenne, Paris 3rd.
27, rue de Varenne, Paris 7th.

CHANGING OVER TIME

The origins of the mille-feuille trace back to the seventeenth century when mentioned by François Pierre de La Varenne (*Le Cuisinier françois*, 1651). The recipe was perfected by Antonin Carême. However, this famous cake at the time did not include pastry cream or puff pastry. The mille-feuille we know today made its appearance at the pastry shop of Adolphe Seugnot on rue du Bac (Paris 7th) in 1867. Parisians lined up to buy his special treat.

DOES IT ACTUALLY HAVE A THOUSAND AND ONE LAYERS?

Well, no! Although *mille-feuille* in French means "a thousand layers," the pastry will have exactly 730 alternating layers of butter and dough if folded and turned correctly. The layers of butter are formed by the successive folds—called "turns"— and the pastry puffs into thin layers when baked. The cake is then composed into two or three layers of piped cream alternating with layers of the puffed pastry. François Pierre de La Varenne provided a detailed recipe in his work *Pâtissier françois* (1653). Antonin Carême later codified the number of turns.

WHICH PUFF PASTRY?
TWO POSSIBLE TECHNIQUES:

Traditional
The butter is wrapped in the *détrempe* (water + flour + salt + vinegar + butter) then undergoes five or six simple turns of folding.

Inverted
The détrempe is wrapped in beurre manié (butter + flour) and undergoes five rounds of folding.

Why choose the inverted version?
It dries out less quickly when baked, is more predictable, and its texture is lighter and crispier.

LEXICON
› In French, the word *mille-feuille* can mean infinite layers in regards to something complicated, such as: "An administrative or government mille-feuille . . ."
› In slang, especially as used by law enforcement, it's quite the opposite meaning, like saying "It's a piece of cake!"

TRUE TOURS DE FORCE
A mille-feuille isn't something you decide to whip up at the last minute. It requires an exacting technique. You must start with the lamination of the dough and butter. It should be perfectly cut and meticulously assembled. The lightness of the pastry cream is also a key to its success. It should be assembled at the last minute and enjoyed immediately.

THE RECIPE

Season : year-round
Difficulty ● ● ●

SERVES 6

For the puff pastry

1 pound 9 ounces (700 g)
Puff Pastry (opposite)

2 tablespoons
confectioners' sugar

For the diplomat cream

3 sheets gelatin, or
2 teaspoons powdered
gelatin

Scant 2 cups (480 ml)
heavy cream

1½ cups (350 ml) whole milk

1 vanilla bean

⅓ cup (50 g) brown sugar

5 tablespoons plus
1 teaspoon (50 g) cornstarch

1 tablespoon plus 1 teaspoon
(10 g) all-purpose flour

3 large (150 g) eggs

2 tablespoons unsalted butter

Equipment

Stand mixer

Pastry bag and 16 mm plain
pastry tube

2 metal rulers or pastry
bars, ⅓ inch (1 cm) thick

2 baking sheets

When this classic is created at the hands of pastry chef Nina Métayer, the result is peak creaminess.

Prepare the puff pastry: Preheat the oven to 300°F (150°C). Roll out the puff pastry into a rectangle measuring 24 by 15¾ inches (60 by 40 cm). Place the dough on a parchment paper–lined baking sheet. Place the two rulers on both sides and place another baking sheet on top. Place heavy, heatproof weights (such as a heavy baking dish) on top. Bake for 45 minutes.

Remove the top baking sheet. Lightly dust the puff pastry with the confectioners' sugar and bake for another 20 minutes at 320°F (160°C). Remove the puff pastry from the oven (it should be a light golden color) and let it cool on a rack.

Cut into three equal parts ❶ while still warm. Move to a cooling rack.

Prepare the diplomat cream: Soak the gelatin sheets in a bowl of ice water. (If using powdered gelatin, sprinkle it over 3 tablespoons of cold water and stir to moisten it; let soften for 5 minutes.) Heat ¾ cup (180 ml) of the cream, all the milk, and the split and scraped vanilla bean in a

saucepan set over low heat. In a bowl, combine all the dry ingredients. Add the eggs and whisk to thoroughly combine.

Slowly add the milk mixture to the egg and flour mixture, whisking continually, then return everything to the saucepan over low heat, and continue to whisk for 5 minutes. Squeeze the water from the gelatin sheets and add them to the pan (or add the softened powdered gelatin, if using); stir to dissolve the gelatin. Add the butter. Blend using an immersion blender. Cover the cream by gently pressing plastic wrap onto its surface. Refrigerate for 1 hour.

Beat the remaining cold cream using an electric mixer. Using a silicone spatula, fold the beaten cream into the cooled pastry cream. Refrigerate for 20 minutes.

Assemble: Place the cream in the pastry bag fitted with the plain pastry tube and pipe rows of the diplomat cream down the length of one of the puff pastry rectangles ❷. Place a second puff pastry rectangle on top ❸ and pipe the cream again in rows. Place the third puff pastry rectangle on top to complete the mille-feuille.

SKIP TO
Antonin Carême,
p. 156; Pastry
Shops, p. 312.

SKIP TO
Antonin Carême, p. 156; Pastry Shops, p. 312.

TOP · LET'S EAT PARIS! · ADDRESSES

Jacques Genin
📍 *133, rue de Turenne, Paris 3rd + 1 other location*
A nice balance between airy cream and crispy puff pastry.

Hugo & Victor
📍 *40, blvd. Raspail, Paris 7th*
Perfectly structured with a crispy, caramelized puff pastry. A nice texture of two creams (crème légère, which is pastry cream lightened with whipped cream, and chocolate ganache) and Bourbon Madagascar vanilla.

Sébastien Gaudard
📍 *22, rue des Martyrs, Paris 9th + 1 other location*
A great classic. An all-butter puff pastry encases a silky cream.

Gilles Marchal
📍 *9, rue Ravignan, Paris 18th*
A caramelized puff pastry triumph. A light and airy Bourbon Madagascar–vanilla pastry cream.

A DIFFERENT WAY
Cédric Grolet
📍 *35, av. de l'Opéra, Paris 2nd*
A balanced composition using phyllo dough, substituting for puff pastry, and an intense vanilla cream.

THE INVENTION OF THE RESTAURANT

The term *restaurant* is one of the most common French words in the world but, paradoxically, few people know it's a French invention. From the first establishments around the Palais-Royal in Paris in the early 1760s to the golden age of the *pavillons* on the Champs-Élysées, let's revisit these roots of Parisian gastronomy.

—FRANÇOIS-RÉGIS GAUDRY

The time of the auberges

From the Middle Ages to the eighteenth century, the capital's inns and taverns had a dismal reputation: unrefined peasant-style soups, flavorless breads, adulterated wines, water sourced directly from the Seine—all served at a fixed time of day. To eat, you had to accept what the inns offered at the times it was offered . . . Brillat-Savarin testifies to this in his work *The Physiology of Taste* (1825): "Around 1770 . . . , foreigners had very few resources as regards to good food, so that those, who did not have the pleasure of being invited to some opulent patrician house, left the great city without knowing the resources and delights of Parisian cuisine."

Roze, the first restaurateur

• 1765

Mathurin Roze de Chantoiseau (often referred to as "Champ d'Oiseau") was a crazy idealist thirsty for recognition. He establishes the first restaurant on rue des Poulies (today the beginning of rue du Louvre in the 1st arrondissement). For a reasonable fee, customers, seated at marble pedestal tables, can order broth, fresh eggs, and chicken in a salt crust. This is a revolutionary idea.

• 1766

Roze de Chantoiseau joins forces with Sieur Pontaillé to move his establishment to the Hôtel d'Aligre on rue Saint-Honoré (Paris 1st).

• 1769

Chantoiseau publishes an almanac about commerce in Paris in which he praises his own restaurant: "Roze, the first restaurateur" is recommended for his delicate and beneficial broths. These "yellow pages," an idea before their time, highlight other locations that opened in the wake of Roze, where broths were served along with other "healthy" choices such as creams, vermicelli or rice soups, macaroni, jams, and compotes. Among these new establishments, Jean-François Vacossin, "the second restaurateur," located at rue de Grenelle, opened with his motto borrowed from the Gospel (according to Saint Matthew): "*Venite ad me, omnes qui stomacho laboristis, et ego vos restaurabo*" (Come to me, all ye who are hungry, and I will restore you.")

• 1777

The *Almanach Dauphin* mentions the word *restaurant* to designate this type of "establishment for health" with "principles of cleanliness, decency, and integrity."

A small revolution

"The custom of these houses, which are very well arranged, is not to provide food as at a table d'hôte, but at any time of the day, by dishes, and at fixed prices." This is how Roze de Chantoiseau described the new codes of restaurants.

› **Service throughout the day.** Restaurants were organized to ensure this flexibility: broths were kept warm in a bain-marie, eggs were cooked when ordered, and fruit was freshly cut . . .

› **A fee-based card.** The expression "à la carte" service became commonplace in the 1770s. This card set the price of each dish, unlike inns and taverns that imposed a menu and announced the amount due only at the end of the meal. At the end of the meal in a restaurant, the customer paid the "pay card." This was considered *l'addition* (the bill).

› **An individual table.** The noisy and rough promiscuity of inns, which were considered unsanitary, was fading in favor of privacy and comfort conducive to healthy digestion. The restaurant became a kind of "publicly private place"—and ladies were admitted.

A new healthy diet

During the Enlightenment, the philosophical debate took aim at earthly foods. Voltaire, the unrepentant pleasure seeker who loved "turkeys with truffles from Ferney," went up against Rousseau, the leader of food renunciation and follower of vegetarianism and nutrition. Vincent La Chapelle promoted a nouvelle cuisine in *Le Cuisinier moderne* (1735). François Marin, in *Les Dons de Comus ou les délices de la table* (1739), provided a recipe for digestible and reconstituted broth called "quintessence or *restaurant*":

"Take a well-tinned and very clean saucepan, place in the bottom a few slices of onions with a little beef marrow; fill your pan with slices of veal rolls . . . ; put on the slices a few strips of healthy and well-defatted ham, and then some peels of parsnips and carrots. Have a healthy hen killed at once and well cleaned outside and inside; cut it at the limbs and crush them; Put them hot in your saucepan. . . . Observe that to get two pints of this quintessence, it takes only four pounds of veal, and four ounces of ham with the hen. . . . Seal the pan well, and put it on a good fire first. . . . When your meat is done, put your pan on a moderate fire for three-quarters of an hour, and let it sweat continuously."

Diderot at the Restaurant

In 1767, in a letter to Sophie Volland, the philosopher Diderot recounted his happy experience at the restaurateur's: "It is served a little expensively, but at the time you want. The beautiful hostess never comes to chat with the *restauré*, as she is too honest and too decent for that. . . . We eat alone, each at his own little cabinet where one's attention may wander."

← Scene in an inn. Engraving, end of eighteenth century.

THE PALAIS-ROYAL, A RENDEZVOUS FOR PALATES

With its arcades and garden, the Palais-Royal is today a quiet haven, but between the eighteenth and nineteenth centuries, it was the gastronomic epicenter of Europe. —FRANÇOIS-RÉGIS GAUDRY

La promenade publique au Palais-Royal, 1792, by Philibert Louis Debucourt.

BŒUF À LA MODE.

① BEAUVILLIERS, THE GREAT RESTAURATEUR

Antoine Beauvilliers (1754–1817) was the greatest restaurateur of his time.

HIS CAREER: As a former private chef of the Count of Provence (the future Louis XVIII), Beauvilliers set up his business in 1782 and opened La Grande Taverne de Londres at 26, rue de Richelieu. He then opened, on the eve of the Revolution, an establishment in his name, under the Palais-Royal arcades.

HIS TALENT: Like a general, he would walk among the diners with his sword at his side. He had a prodigious memory and would recognize customers he served twenty years ago. He also spoke several languages . . .

HIS WORK: In 1814, he published *L'Art du cuisinier*, a book of essential recipes, and collaborated with Antonin Carême in editing *La Cuisine ordinaire* (1848).

Chronology

- **1628**
  Richelieu builds the Palais-Cardinal, a sumptuous residence.

- **1633**
  The palace is renamed Palais-Royal and offered to King Louis XIII.

- **1780**
  The Duke d'Orléans renovates the palace, employing architect Victor Louis. He builds 3 galleries, 180 arcades, and 60 rental buildings.

- **1815**
  The heyday of the Palais-Royal: its galleries house 15 restaurants, 20 cafés, and 18 gambling houses.

- **1836**
  Closure of the gambling houses and beginning of the decline of the surrounding restaurants.

② LE GRAND VÉFOUR: THE SOLE SURVIVOR!

Carved woodwork, Louis XVI–style garlands, mirrors, red velvet benches, Empire frescoes with Pompeian themes . . . This neoclassical jewel located on the site of the Café de Chartres (see opposite) was founded in 1820 by Jean Véfour. In 1859, Le Grand Véfour took over its neighbor Véry. In 1947, it was bought by Louis Vaudable, the owner of Maxim's, who sold it a year later to chef Raymond Oliver, a chef from Gascony who attracted the attention of the literary and artistic crowds (including Colette, Cocteau, Guitry, Pagnol, and others) and was eventually awarded three Michelin stars in 1953. Today, the restaurant is owned by Savoyard chef Guy Martin, who was awarded three stars in 2000.

📍 *17, rue de Beaujolais, Paris 1st*

③ MÉOT, THE CHEF OF THE REVOLUTION

Starting in 1789, many figures of the nobility and aristocracy went into exile abroad or were arrested—and many were guillotined. Several cooks and masters, who worked in their service, thus set up their own businesses. Among them was Méot, the former officer of the Duke d'Orléans, who opened his own restaurant on May 26, 1791, on rue des Bons-Enfants. The incredible space had a golden peristyle, a salon decorated with mirrors, a boudoir decorated with arabesques, and ceilings representing the works of Hercules. It is said that, in one of the salons, a bathtub was filled with champagne in which a customer could be massaged by skilled women. The constitution of 1793 was drawn up in one of these salons. Robespierre, Danton, and Saint-Just were spotted here during the Reign of Terror. The execution of Marie-Antoinette was even celebrated here on October 16, 1793.

Famous addresses

These establishments have all disappeared, but during their peak they attracted gourmets from all over Europe.

④ VÉRY

The Véry brothers, farmers from Lorraine, purchased three galleries on rue de Beaujolais in 1790 to open an opulent restaurant. They sent their menu in a sealed envelope to encourage their wealthy customers to come and taste their steaks with anchovy butter.

⑤ LES TROIS FRÈRES PROVENÇAUX

Maneille, Barthélemy, and Simon, brothers-in-law from the banks of the Durance, set up their tables in 1798 in the Beaujolais gallery. Customers could try olives stuffed with capers and anchovies, wild duck and eggplant, and white nougat from Marseille . . .

⑥ LE BOEUF À LA MODE

Founded in 1792 on rue de Valois, this restaurant, identifiable by its large logo, was famous for its beef à la mode recipe: a meat stew with bacon, cognac, red wine, onions, garlic, and carrots. It closed in 1936.

⑦ LE CAFÉ DE FOY

Founded in 1749 by Monsieur De Foy, a former officer, on rue de Richelieu. Perched on a table, Camille Desmoulins harangued the crowd on July 12, 1789, and gave the signal for the insurrection that led to the storming of the Bastille.

⑧ LE CAFÉ DE CHARTRES

This establishment opened in 1784 by Monsieur Aubertot in three arcades of the Beaujolais gallery. This was a place of debate that attracted Murat, the Duke de Berry, Brillat-Savarin, and Grimod de La Reynière.

Maison Corcellet.

⑨ L'ÉPICERIE CORCELLET

In L'Almanach des gourmands (1803), Grimod de La Reynière raved about several "nutritional institutions" in the Palais-Royal galleries: Hyrment, Chevet, and, the best known, Corcellet, built in 1787 by Jean-Pierre Corcellet at 104, rue de Valois. "The most beautiful shop for comestibles at the Palais-Royal and even in Paris," known for the goose liver pâtés from Strasbourg, mortadella from Lyon . . . the name Corcellet would shine until the end of the 1980s.

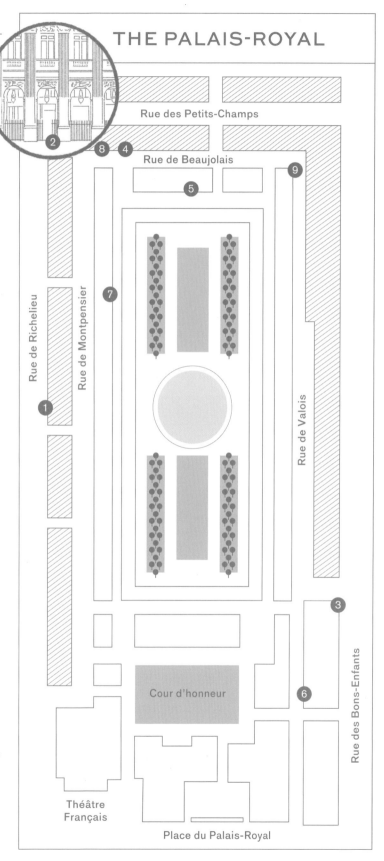

THE PALAIS-ROYAL

63

AROUND THE GRANDS BOULEVARDS

With their wide sidewalks lined with elegant boutiques and theaters, the boulevards of northern Paris became, in the 1830s, the rallying point of Parisian gastronomy. However, almost none of these establishments have survived.

—FRANÇOIS-RÉGIS GAUDRY

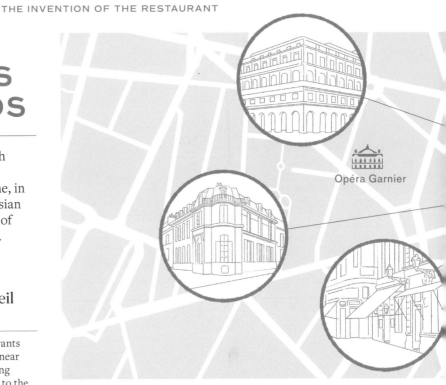

Opéra Garnier

The Regulars

BOULEVARDIERS
Regular customers of theaters, gambling houses, cafés, and restaurants of the Grands Boulevards.

LIONS
Young male upstarts adorned with a flower in their lapel who would stroll the boulevards for a taste of worldliness. The feminine form of the word referred to elegant female fortune hunters.

VAUTOURS DE L'AGIOTAGE
The nickname of the people of the nearby Bourse commodities exchange.

COCOTTES
Sex workers who lived off payment for their services but were not registered with the police, as was required at the time.

DEMIMONDAINES
These were somewhere between mistresses and high-end sex workers, kept by rich Parisians. Also called courtesans or *grandes horizontales*.

The Montorgueil District

Famous restaurants began opening near Les Halles during their migration to the northern sections of the capital.

CHAMPEAUX
Opened around 1800 at the corner of rue Vivienne and rue des Filles-Saint-Thomas, this was a businessman's restaurant where patrons would enjoy steaks and chicken while making deals.

AU ROCHER DE CANCALE
A cabaret doubling as a shellfish shop, founded in 1805 by Alexis Balaine at the corner of rues Montorgueil and Mandar.

PHILIPPE
Located on rue Montorgueil, this was "the largest restaurant of the Second Empire" according to historian Jean-Paul Aron, and experienced fame from 1864 and the arrival of Pascal, the former chef of the Jockey Club, renowned for his matelote (fish stew), turtle soup, venison chops with pepper, and rum puddings.

In front of Café Frascati, rue de Richelieu, Paris.

Inside Café Frascati.

Boulevard des Italiens

This was the boulevard with the largest concentration of restaurants during the nineteenth century. It was referred to as "Boulevard de Gand," then just "Le Boulevard."

① LE CAFÉ HARDY
Founded at 20, boulevard des Italiens. Madame Hardy invented, under the Directory, the "lunch by fork," served under a large cloche that included kidneys, chops, papillotes, stuffed andouilles, fish . . . all waiting to be pricked and picked up with a large fork, at the customer's request, and placed on a grill.

Became
LA MAISON DORÉE
In 1841, Verdier, owner of Le Café Hardy, renamed it Maison Dorée because of its windows decorated with large gilded balconies. The restaurant welcomed many personalities, including Alexandre Dumas, who would arrive to visit chef Casimir Moisson, creator of what was considered the best bouillabaisse in Paris. Flaubert set Frédéric Moreau's dinner here in his *L'Éducation sentimentale* (1869). The story of this illustrious establishment ended in 1902.

② LE CAFÉ ANGLAIS
Opened in 1802 at 13, boulevard des Italiens. The restaurant had a white facade, understated decor, and was divided into twenty-two salons and private stalls. Dukes, princes, and the wealthy would meet here. Some would dine in the restaurant's cellar, which contained nearly two hundred thousand flasks and was equipped with a small track that would transport the bottles to the table. Adolphe Dugléré was the restaurant's emblematic leader. Balzac's Marsay and Lucien dined here in *Illusions perdues*, while Zola made *Nana*'s heroine stand out here.

③ LE CAFÉ DE PARIS
Located on the ground floor of the Hôtel de Brancas at 24, boulevard des Italiens. Lady Yarmouth, Marquise de Herford, opened her restaurant on July 15, 1822. It was decorated with high ceilings, frescoes, benches with red velvet backrests, and diamond-shaped window tiles trimmed in muslin. Balzac evoked the cutlets with sauce soubise, and Brillat-Savarin loved the pheasants with truffles à la Sainte-Alliance.

④ LE CAFÉ RICHE
Located at the corner of rue Le Peletier, this restaurant was opened in 1791 by a Monsieur Riche. In 1847, Louis Bignon acquired it and had the decor renovated to include a marble staircase, bronze banister, onyx panels, and Aubusson rugs. Here Offenbach, Flaubert, Ferdinand de Lesseps, Jules Ferry, Gambetta, among others, would arrive. The restaurant competed with Le Café Hardy with its mussel soup and its famous sauce Riche. A saying attributed to Jean-Jacques-Régis Cambacérès, Duke of Parma, circulated among the boulevards: "You have to be very rich to dine at Hardy's and very *hardi* [bold] to dine at Riche's." The restaurant closed in 1916.

⑤ AU PETIT RICHE
Louis Bignon founded Au Petit Riche in 1854 at 25, rue Le Peletier for less fortunate clients. After a fire in 1873, the restaurant was resurrected in 1880 by a man named Besnard who made it an anteroom for Loire specialties and wines. The decor has survived today and is made up of small adjoining rooms, crimson banquettes, gleaming brass, dark woodwork, and engraved mirrors.

⑥ FRASCATI
Founded in 1789 at the corner of boulevard Montmartre and rue de Richelieu under the name Jardins de Frascati. An ice cream vendor from Naples named Garchi bought it in 1792 and renamed it Café Frascati. He turned it into a gambling house, restaurant, and pastry shop renowned for its ice cream. In *La Comédie humaine*, Balzac quoted Garchi more than a dozen times.

⑦ TORTONI
Opened in 1803 at 22, boulevard des Italiens, it was one of the most fashionable places in the capital from 1830 to 1848. Musset described it in 1840: "The boulevard does not begin to stir until noon. Then the dandies arrive. They enter Tortoni through the back door since the steps are invaded by the barbarians, that is to say, the people of La Bourse."*

*Musset, *Le Boulevard de Gand*, 1837.

⑧ PETER'S
Opened in the 1860s by Pierre Fraysse, inventor of the dish *l'homard à l'américaine* at 24, passage des Princes. It had sumptuous salons with columns and palm trees inspired by the Alhambra in Granada. The restaurant eventually became Noël Peter's.

Boulevard du Temple

LE CADRAN-BLEU
This beer hall opened in 1773 at the corner of rue Charlot and became, in the early nineteenth century, a posh restaurant.

LE CAFÉ TURC
Located opposite Le Cadran-Bleu, this musical café was unique because of its garden, illuminated by Bengal lights and pyrotechnics. The entire literary circle paraded through there, including Hugo, Goncourt, Vigny, Sainte-Beuve, and Musset.

LOVE IS SERVED

The *cabinet particulier* was a small, private, and partitioned room within a restaurant. During the nineteenth century, it was a place of secrecy, declarations of love, and debauchery. —FRANÇOIS-RÉGIS GAUDRY

Lunch in a cabinet particulier.

The origin of the cabinet particulier

Featured in the design of the first restaurants, these private small rooms were not originally intended for a romantic or libertine purpose. The first restaurateurs in the 1760s created private rooms in their establishments for modest women who did not want to expose themselves to scrutiny by others and for men who needed to meet privately for political purposes. It was not until the end of the eighteenth century, however, when restaurants were established at the Palais-Royal, that cabinets particuliers lent themselves to romantic rendezvous. "Honest and good-natured women would never be caught here. These were private rooms where you can dine or sup with an elegant lady who was invited; These spaces for two or four are always very expensive."

Mayeur de Saint-Paul, *Tableau du nouveau Palais-Royal*, 1788.

Cabinet particulier: a joyful supper with students and shopgirls in 1830.

Dining pleasures at Lapérouse

Lapérouse is one of the few restaurants where you can, today, immerse yourself in the seductive atmosphere of a cabinet particulier. Behind the facade of an eighteenth-century mansion, this establishment, opened by Jules Lapérouse around 1850, was known worldwide for its poulet docteur (chicken with liver sauce), langoustines gratin, and its fourteen private upstairs salons decorated with framed paintings, moldings, and precious rugs. Under the Second Empire, a playful society flocked here in search of libertine pleasures. It is said that a hidden staircase (some mentioned a secret underground!) discreetly led men of power to their courtesans. On the mirrors of some cabinets, enigmatic graffiti is still visible. Women here would be inclined to scratch the diamonds they were offered to verify their authenticity.

📍 *51, quai des Grands-Augustins, Paris 5th*

A secret supper!

To escape the gossip spread by the boulevardiers, seekers of these surreptitious suppers would take care to arrive separately at the meeting place and rely on the discretion of the boss and the staff. In *La Vie parisienne* (1866), Offenbach, Meilhac, and Halévy formulated the code for the perfect cabinet particulier boy. Here is an extract:

"If sometimes, on the arm of an actress, an important man slips in, close your eyes! Let's not embarrass the lovers, close your eyes!"

Bel-Ami at Le Café Riche

Guy de Maupassant created, in the cabinets particuliers at Le Café Riche, a gallant dinner between Madame de Marelle and Bel-Ami.

"He was led into a small restaurant lounge, covered in red, and the only window opening onto the boulevard. . . . Ostend oysters arrived, small and plump, like small earlobes enclosed in shells, melting between the palate and the tongue, as well as salty sweets. Then, after the soup, a trout was served as pink as a maiden's flesh. . . . And when the first entrée didn't arrive, they drank a sip of Champagne from time to time while nibbling on crusts torn off the backs of round buns. And the thought of love, slow and invasive, entered them, gradually intoxicated their souls, like clear wine, falling drop by drop down their throats, warming their blood and arousing their spirits."

THE DAYS OF THE BRASSERIES

These were the first places where beer was sold, but during the nineteenth and twentieth centuries under the impetus of Alsatian entrepreneurs, the brasseries became a richly adorned Parisian institution.

—FRANÇOIS-RÉGIS GAUDRY

Origins

The brasserie appeared in the mid-nineteenth century. This was a simple pub for the masses, devoted to the consumption of beer. Brasseries experienced high growth in 1860 due to the phylloxera crisis, which raised the price of wine. In brasseries, patrons could indulge in rustic German foods: cabbage, sausage, and pretzels. Louis Andler, a German immigrant, was the pioneer of this concept and in 1847 opened his namesake brasserie. In a setting of whitewashed walls and rustic oak benches, Courbet, Baudelaire, Nerval, Vallès, and Proudhon would arrive to reinvent the world while emptying beer glasses and devouring sauerkraut. Many other brasseries soon opened their doors: Brasserie des Martyrs near Notre-Dame-de-Lorette; Hoffmann, at Place de l'Observatoire; and Brasserie Glasser in the heart of the Latin Quarter.

The Alsatian sector

Driven to Paris by France's defeat by Prussia, a few enterprising Alsatians refined the concept of the brasserie during the 1870s: Brasseries Zimmer, Wepler, and Bofinger were all the rage and are still popular today. Frédéric Bofinger was the pioneer of the tap thanks to a beer pump that carefully filled glasses with a cold beverage topped with foam. The invention of pasteurization, which made it possible to produce a stable drink, gave a boost to the production of Alsatian beer during a tense political context with Germany. Alsatian brasseries multiplied. In 1880, Léonard Lipp moved to boulevard Saint-Germain. Terminus Nord, opposite the Gare du Nord, and Chez Jenny, in the République district, were Alsatian hot spots.

↑ Caricature of Gustave Courbet by André Gill, *La Lune*, 1867.

A brasserie of women

As early as 1867, the *brasserie à femmes* appeared, which were a new generation of establishments where the newest, beautifully golden beer, made of a fermented base, was served by flirtatious women, often of foreign origin, dressed in provocative bathing outfits and extravagant costumes. A male audience of artists and students would let loose at Brasserie de l'Espérance, Brasserie des Nanas, Brasserie des Odalisques, and Le Temple de Venus . . . whose advertisements were displayed on walls around the capital.

Temples of decor

Once despised, often infamous, the brasserie took a new turn starting at the end of the nineteenth century and became a privileged showcase for decorative arts. Louis Mollard, from Savoy, started the movement in 1895 in front of the Saint-Lazare station by embellishing his establishment with mosaic ceilings, Sarreguemine faience panels, and a teak counter, now classified as historical monuments. This was followed by the generation of art nouveau establishments during the Belle Époque and art deco decor during the interwar period.

FROM THE MADELEINE TO THE CHAMPS-ÉLYSÉES

Paris entered the twentieth century as the world's capital by hosting the Universal Exposition of 1900. Its gourmand geography thus changed: Place de la Madeleine and the Champs-Élysées became the gastronomic epicenter of the City of Light. —FRANÇOIS-RÉGIS GAUDRY

"J'accuse . . . !" at Le Café Durand

Just opposite Larue, on the other side of Place de la Madeleine, is a forgotten café. But it was here that Émile Zola wrote his letter "J'accuse!" published on January 13, 1898, in the newspaper *L'Aurore*. It is also in these kitchens where chef Joseph Voiron, around 1860, is said to have invented Mornay sauce.

Caviar at Prunier

Alfred Prunier opened a restaurant at 9, rue Duphot, in 1875. This maison served oysters and caviar to the beau monde of the Belle Époque. Émile, Alfred's son, became a pioneer in 1921 of the production of French caviar in Aquitaine. In 1992, Goumard, a fish restaurant, moved to the location of Prunier.

Anglomania at Weber

Opened on rue Royale in 1865, this popular restaurant was one of the Parisian showcases of English specialties, which were very fashionable at the time. You could enjoy York ham, Welsh rabbit, and Cambridge sausages! Here Léon Daudet and Paul Déroulède would sit out on the terrace.

With knives drawn

As a link between the Grands Boulevards and the Champs-Élysées, Place de la Madeleine was home to several grand restaurants starting at the end of the nineteenth century. Two in particular competed with each other.

LUCAS-CARTON

📍 *9, pl. de la Madeleine, Paris 8th*

Menu.

A LITTLE HISTORY
In 1732, Englishman Robert Lucas founded an English tavern. In 1890, a man named Scaliet bought the establishment and began extensive renovations in 1902. In 1925, Francis Carton bought Lucas and added his name to it.

THE DECOR
In the purest art nouveau style, this establishment contains woodwork by Majorelle and bronze sconces by Planel. There are salons upstairs.

3 MICHELIN STARS
Earned from 1985 to 2005, under the direction of Alain Senderens.

MAIN DISHES
Potage Germiny, lobster Newburg, lamb noisettes Madeleine, served until the 1950s; canard Apicius (duck), lobster with vanilla, and foie gras au choux (foie gras rolled in cabbage) under chef Alain Senderens.

FAMOUS CUSTOMERS
A few names have filtered through, but the political world of the Belle Époque accessed it by a hidden entrance intended for discreet meetings.

LARUE

📍 *3, pl. de la Madeleine; and 27, rue Royale, Paris 8th*

Menu.

A LITTLE HISTORY
In 1886, a cook named Larue opened a restaurant. Chef Édouard Nignon bought it in 1908. It was taken over by Célestin Duplat in 1919 before closing its doors in 1954.

THE DECOR
Red and gold, with velvet banquettes, pink lampshades, felted cabinets particuliers located upstairs.

3 MICHELIN STARS
Earned from 1933 to 1939, under the direction of Célestin Duplat.

MAIN DISHES
Turtle consommé Claire, sole fillets in a flaky crust, Polignac lamb mignonnettes, poulardes Lyonnaise, artichoke hearts from Nantes, and others.

FAMOUS CUSTOMERS
All the Third Republic (Freycinet, Grévy, Clemenceau, Briand . . .), and Proust. From 1927, the Club des Cent, founded by Louis Forest, met here.

LES PAVILLONS

Starting in the nineteenth century during the Belle Époque, the Avenue des Champs-Élysées was home to spectacularly designed pavilions where a part of Parisian gastronomy unfolded. —FRANÇOIS-RÉGIS GAUDRY

① PAVILLON LEDOYEN
♀ *8, av. Dutuit, Paris 8th*

At the site of an inn called Ledoyen and run by Antoine-Nicolas Doyen starting in 1791, this establishment moved in 1848 to its current location.

An anecdote: This was the filming location of Jacques Besnard's *Grand Restaurant* (1966) and Robert Altman's *Ready to Wear* (1994).

Notable chefs: Ghislaine Arabian, Christian Le Squer, Yannick Alléno (current owner).

② PAVILLON ÉLYSÉE
♀ *10, av. des Champs-Élysées, Paris 8th*

In 1898, Monsieur Paillard, owner of a large restaurant on the Grands Boulevards, commissioned from architect Albert Ballu for the Universal Exposition of 1900 a small, refined establishment in neo–Louis XV style, flanked by a turret. Named Le Petit Paillard, it is now a city event venue.

An anecdote: Gaston Lenôtre bought it in 1984 and named it Élysée Lenôtre.

Notable chefs: Gaston Lenôtre, Thierry Marx.

③ LE LAURENT
♀ *41, av. Gabriel, Paris 8th*

Successor to Le Café du Cirque built by Jacques Hittorff in 1842. It has salmon pink facade decorated with pilasters, capitals, and Pompeian-style columns. In 1860, Monsieur Laurent took it over.

An anecdote: The open ceiling was decorated with nude dancers by the painter Touchagues. He eventually repainted them dressed due to pressure by outraged customers.

Notable chefs: René Lasserre, Michel Roth, Jean-Louis Nomicos.

An anecdote: This has become a meeting place for business and politics. Martin Bouygues, Vincent Bolloré, and Nicolas Sarkozy are seen here regularly.

Notable chefs: Alain Pégouret, Justin Schmitt, Mathieu Pacaud.

④ LASSERRE
♀ *17, av. Franklin-D.-Roosevelt, Paris 8th*

The Basco-Béarnais restaurateur René Lasserre learned his trade in Paris and set up his own business in 1942 in a dilapidated bistro built for the 1937 Universal Exposition. It expanded in 1951 and was awarded three Michelin stars in 1962.

⑤ LA GRANDE CASCADE
♀ *Carr. de Longchamp, Paris 16th*

Built in 1900 for the Universal Exposition, this pavilion displays a retro-metro style that has remained intact.

An anecdote: The restaurant has maintained one Michelin star since 1965.

Notable chefs: Jean-Louis Nomicos, Jean Sabine, Frédéric Robert.

⑥ LE PRÉ CATELAN
♀ *Bois de Boulogne, Paris 16th*

In 1905, Guillaume Tronchet built a vast pavilion combining Empire, Louis XV, and Louis XVI styles.

An anecdote: Under the Fourth Republic, the prime minister Antoine Pinay living nearby regularly visited here and inquired with the owner about everything happening in Paris.

Notable chefs: Gaston Lenôtre, Frédéric Anton.

THE PARISIAN BOUILLON

Parisian *bouillons* continue to flourish thanks to a few establishments that remain, vestiges of a bygone era, and the concept has become somewhat trendy again. But what exactly is this nineteenth-century Parisian institution? —LOÏC BIENASSIS

DUVAL: THE FIRST BOUILLON

The now defunct Dutch Trading Company (created in 1828, dissolved in 1854) may have paved the way, but it was Baptiste-Adolphe Duval who is commonly considered the founding father of Paris's modern bouillon restaurant. On June 3, 1855, Duval, a butcher located on rue Coquillière, after initial attempts for which there is little documentation, opened a large establishment at 6, rue Montesquieu. To do so, he renovated a vast hall built in 1830. It was an elegant building with iron and cast-iron architecture. This was a new type of establishment where more than five hundred people could be served simultaneously. The risk paid off, and Duval's adventure began.

A SUCCESS STORY

1867
The limited liability company Établissements Duval is founded. Eleven years later, in 1878, the company will oversee sixteen locations. That year, counting the temporary restaurant at the Universal Exposition, Duval's bouillons served 5.3 million meals.

1870
It is presumed that after his death, Duval's wife, Anne-Ernestine, took over and managed the company that had now become a small Parisian empire including butchers, a bakery, a laundry, a seltzer water factory, and wine cellars, creating many ways to control both quality and price of raw materials needed for the eating establishments.

1882
Alexandre, Duval's son, takes over the management of the company and is made a Knight of the Legion of Honor in 1900.

THE DUVAL SYSTEM

VALUE FOR THE MONEY

The restaurants served bourgeois cuisine in portions adapted to an individual eater and at moderate prices, and the assurance of quality meat. At Duval's, who was a butcher by training, beef was the foundation of the basic offerings: broth, of course, but also plain beef, stuffed beef, ribs, steaks, etc.

HYGIENE

The cleanliness of these restaurants, with their white marble tables and lack of tablecloths, was unanimously praised.

ORGANIZATION OF THE SERVICE

At the entrance, a controller handed the customer a printed card containing the food and drinks with their prices. The customer would sit down, and the server would check off his or her choices on the menu, which was handed to one of the cashiers when the customer was leaving. The cashier would tally the bill, take the payment, and stamp the card, which was given back to the controller when the customer left.

These three traits were the basis of modernity that inspired the growth of these new types of restaurants and became keys to their success.

THE DUVAL SERVER
Women took the role of servers, and the emblematic "Duval server" became recognizable by their (winter) uniforms consisting of a black merino dress, a white apron, and a white tulle cap.

Bouillon Duval in Parc Champs-de-Mars.

ESTABLISHMENTS FOR THE POOR?

We often imagine the bouillon as a restaurant intended for the less fortunate masses, but this is not necessarily true, as the clientele is first and foremost the upper working class (the best paid workers), the middle class, and the lower middle class. In 1865, an English observer claimed, with exaggeration, that Parisian society shunned Bignon or Café Anglais, which were luxurious establishments, to dine at Duval's. The fixed-price menu, in addition to the items à la carte, was not austere. One of these menus, dating from 1884, listed foie gras terrine, Astrakhan caviar, and oysters from Courseulles . . .

THE DECLINE

During the Belle Époque, the Duval company became less and less profitable. When Alexandre Duval died in 1922, the company was in bad shape. Félix Potin bought the restaurant in 1925, but it gradually disappeared. The time of the bouillons was over. Everything that made them original had become commonplace; "modernity" was no longer their prerogative, and many other establishments offered these same features, brasseries in particular. The term *bouillon* as an eating establishment had been stripped of its prestige and meaning . . . until today, as Paris is now witnessing their rebirth.

In the arts

> *Une serveuse au restaurant Duval*, by Auguste Renoir, circa 1875.

> *La Caissière du bouillon Duval*, by Aristide Bruant and Émile Duhem, 1879.
> *La Bonne de chez Duval*, an operetta by Anthony Mars, Hippolyte Raymond, and Robert Planquette, 1892.
> In *Les Beaux Quartiers* (1936), Louis Aragon tells the story of the young medical student Edmond Barbentane, from his daily eating place at Chartier Bouillon to the chic restaurants of the Bois de Boulogne.

---

400 Bouillons in Paris in 1893

The term *bouillon* was eventually used as a generality to describe small, popular restaurants with ill-defined traits, and other bouillons were sometimes modest in size, having been inspired by Duval's methods. On the other hand, some "creameries" could serve essentially only broths yet not refer to themselves as a bouillon!

Bouillon Duval, 1889.

BOUILLON CHARTIER

Bouillon Chartier, located on rue du Faubourg-Montmartre, is the only Chartier establishment that Parisians associate with a bouillon. The history of brothers Frédéric and Camille Chartier and their establishments is, however, little known. This is due to their business model, which was very different from Duval's. They would create a restaurant, then sell it, sometimes having managed it for a while and sometimes not. The establishment would keep the name Bouillon Chartier as a guarantee of quality to attract regulars.

A CHANGING WORLD

Following their success on the Grands Boulevards, the Chartier brothers opened about twenty bouillons.

STILL OPEN

Bouillon Chartier Montparnasse
Classified decor.
⚲ *59, blvd. du Montparnasse, Paris 6th*

NEW

Bouillon Chartier Gare de l'Est
Opened in 2022.
⚲ *5, rue du 8-Mai-1945, Paris 10th*

CHANGED THEIR NAMES

Vagenende: this is the former Bouillon Chartier Odéon. Classified decor.
⚲ *142, blvd. Saint-Germain, Paris 6th*

Le Bouillon Julien: This is the former Grandon-Fournier restaurant, bought in 1905 by the Chartier brothers, with a sublime art nouveau decor. Serving classics such as leeks vinaigrette and beef broth, the restaurant has had the same motto since its opening: "Here everything is beautiful, good, and cheap."
⚲ *16, rue du Faubourg-Saint-Denis, Paris 10th*

Le Bouillon Racine became a separate restaurant but maintained the sign "Grand Bouillon Camille Chartier." Classified decor.
⚲ *3, rue Racine, Paris 6th*

THE BOUILLON RENAISSANCE

Brothers Pierre and Guillaume Moussié opened their first bouillon in 2017, offering three hundred seats, and serving 1,500 meals a day with uninterrupted service from noon to midnight. The secret of the endless lines? Serving classics of French cuisine, all homemade, and at low prices. In 2021, Bouillon République opened with four hundred seats and always the same offerings: world champion oeuf mayonnaise, celery remoulade, and drinks served in sizes from a quarter liter to a Jeroboam.

Bouillon Pigalle
⚲ *22, blvd. de Clichy, Paris 18th*

Bouillon République
⚲ *39, blvd. du Temple, Paris 3rd*

SKIP TO
Bouillon Chartier, p. 210; The Pot-au-Feu, p. 272.

LES GUINGUETTES

These suburban cabarets, often located on the banks of rivers, flourished in the eighteenth and nineteenth centuries. On their menu was wine, hearty food, and popular recreation.

—JACQUES BRUNEL

What Is a Guinguette?

Created in Paris, the *guinguette* was a wine bar serving food and offering an extended green space that patrons could enjoy. Customers could often dance and enjoy leisure activities. What's the origin of the name? There are two theories:

› *ginguet*, which meant a slightly sour wine, a *piquette* (cheap wine);

› from the verb *ginguer* or *giguer* ("frolicking," or "jumping" in the fourteenth and fifteenth centuries), which is related to the French *gigoter* (move about) and which could derive its origin from the *gigue* (a musical instrument).

Advertising poster, 1888–1894.

A long history

SEVENTEENTH AND EIGHTEENTH CENTURIES

Guinguettes first referred to small, country pieds-à-terre before eventually referring to, beginning in the eighteenth century, establishments outside the city limits (the current Grands Boulevards) where the businesses could escape taxes levied on the importation of wines into Paris. Guinguettes, which served meals to workers, abounded in the working-class districts of Petite Pologne (near Gare Saint-Lazare train station), Porcherons (near rue des Martyrs), and Courtille (Belleville).

AROUND THE TIME OF THE REVOLUTION

In 1788, the government built a barrier that included the guinguettes as part of Paris, making them subject to taxation. This led to widespread fraudulent schemes to avoid the tax, including transporting the wine through buried pipes, throwing wine bottles over the barrier, and even transporting wine by hot air balloons. On July 11, 12, and 13, 1789, the owners and customers of the guinguettes, helped by winegrowers and wine merchants, stormed the barriers and burned them down. The next day, the Bastille was stormed.

NINETEENTH CENTURY AND THE BELLE ÉPOQUE

Continuing to flourish in Montmartre, guinguettes were moved outside of the fortifications to Montrouge and Bagnolet. Canoeing, originating in England, was becoming a popular sport and offered a new attraction along riverbanks. Every Sunday, Parisians would arrive by train by the hundreds for these activities.

On the Seine: Guinguettes proliferated in Chatou (Maison Fournaise), Bougival (Bal des Canotiers), Suresnes (La Belle Cycliste, served by a small cable car . . .), Croissy (La Grenouillère), and Rueil-Malmaison (Chez Giquel) . . .

On the Oise: Auvers, L'Isle-Adam . . . The clientele was seasonal, bringing together bourgeois boaters, who could come to be seen, and families out canoeing for enjoyment. The French quenched their thirst with aperitifs and local wines, played, danced, and flirted among the foliage . . .

TWENTIETH CENTURY

After the Great War, the rise of left-wing ideals valued the popular spirit. Excited by all the new dances (the tango, the Charleston, etc.), the guinguettes would see writers and artists arrive incognito. The introduction of paid leave by the Popular Front announced the imminent end of the guinguettes, however. After 1950, the guingettes would bring together an elderly clientele with greasers from the working-class suburbs. Ten years later, a ban on swimming in the rivers around Paris dealt guingettes the fatal blow.

On the plate

A meal at a guinguette was inexpensive, and they offered a hearty menu for the masses, serving finger foods to locavores, including fish (eels, carp, pike, small goatfish, etc.) supplied by local fishermen and locally hunted rabbit and game.

A typical menu

Pork, asparagus vinaigrette, deviled eggs

Fried gudgeons with fries, moules marinières, wild rabbit, eel stew, carp, crayfish, gudgeons simmered in white wine from Suresnes or piccolo from Argenteuil, salted beef, frogs' legs

Brie and Cantal cheeses

Gaufres [waffles], *strawberry whipped cream, and glace plombières* [a fruit-based ice cream].

In the glass

White wines from Île-de-France

Montmartre, Suresnes, Argenteuil, Courbevoie . . .

Popular aperitifs

Anisette, Byrrh, Dubonnet, Picon-bière, absinthe downed with sugar dissolved through a perforated spoon . . .

SKIP TO
La Closerie des Lilas, p. 112; Outdoor Cafés, p. 368.

Le Déjeuner des Canotiers, Manet, 1880–1881.

Guinguette on the banks of the Marne, mid-twentieth century.

In music

In the eighteenth century, people danced in guinguettes to the sound of the violin, hurdy-gurdy, and clarinet. A few decades later, Italian emigration brought the accordion, then the Auvergnats their musette. After 1918, real orchestras were introduced. Among the stars of the "piano with suspenders" were Tony Murena, Jo Privat, Aimable, and Yvette Horner, the queen of the accordion, with her vermilion hair. After World War II, jazz and rock and roll arrived.

In paintings

Since the time of Watteau, countryside festivals have been a subject for painters. Attracted by the shimmer of the rivers, impressionists haunted the guinguettes at the end of the nineteenth century, creating— especially in Chatou— some of their most famous paintings:
- *Le Déjeuner des Canotiers* (1880–1881) by Renoir, sketched on the balcony of Maison Fournaise.
- *La Grenouillère* (1869) by Renoir, and *Bain à La Grenouillère* (1869) by Monet.
- *Le Déjeuner sur l'herbe* (1863) by Manet.

In movies

Guinguettes attracted documentary filmmakers such as Marcel Carné (*Nogent, Eldorado du dimanche*, 1929) and Philippe Pinson (*La Marne, une rivière de chansons*, 2002), but above all offered their setting for the intrigues of *L'Atalante* (Jean Vigo, 1934), *La Belle Équipe* (Julien Duvivier, 1936), *Casque d'or* (Jacques Becker, 1952), and *Guinguette* (Jean Delannoy, 1959).

"In the floating establishments, there was a laughing and screaming crowd. . . . In the open space between the tables, dominating the ordinary public of the place, was a battalion of rowdy boaters with their companions in short flannel skirts." —Guy de Maupassant, *La Femme de Paul*, 1881

THE RECIPE

Season: spring and summer
Difficulty ● ○ ○

This is a typical fried dish in a guinguette on the banks of the Marne and Seine.

SERVES 6

1⅓ pounds (600 g) small river fish (gudgeons, sea bream, bleak, roach)

2 cups (500 ml) milk

1 teaspoon salt

¾ cup (100 g) all-purpose flour

4 cups (1 L) vegetable oil, for frying

Salt and freshly ground black pepper

½ bunch parsley

1 lemon

Soak the fish for 1 hour in a bowl with the milk and salt.

Drain, blot dry with a paper towel, and thoroughly dust the fish with the flour, gently shaking off any excess.

In a large saucepan, bring the oil to a boil and add the fish. Once the fish are crisp and browned, move to a rack to drain and blot with paper towels.

Season with salt and pepper. Enjoy hot with chopped parsley and a squeeze of lemon.

Oysters with Les Halles Sauce

Oysters are the pearl of Parisian gastronomy and are present on platters of some of the most famous brasseries. —SACHA LOMNITZ

THE RECIPE

Season: fall and winter
Difficulty ● ○ ○

SERVES 4

For the sauce
2 to 3 shallots
1 lemon
Scant ⅔ cup (150 ml) red wine vinegar
1 large pinch finely crushed or coarsely ground pepper

2 dozen oysters

Les Halles sauce was created by the oystermen of the famous Les Halles wholesale market, which closed in 1969. It is an essential accompaniment to oysters and many seafood dishes, even if modern-day gourmets may shun it for masking the taste of the shellfish.

To make the sauce: Using a knife, chop the shallots very finely and place them in a medium bowl. Drizzle a few drops of lemon juice on them. Add the vinegar and season with pepper.

Stir well to combine. Set aside for 4 to 5 hours to marinate, stirring two or three times during this time.

Present the sauce on the side so that each person can add the sauce to the oysters to their liking.

Le Déjeuner d'oytres by Jean-François de Troy, 1735.

EVEN THE PARISII . . .

Considered a delicacy since ancient times, the European flat oyster *Ostrea edulis* comes from natural deposits, particularly on the Normandy coast. In Lutetia, the Parisii (the Gallic tribe that lived on the lands now occupied by Paris) enjoyed them often, as revealed by archaeological excavations in the Luxembourg Garden and at rue Pierre-et-Marie-Curie. Unlike Parisians today, the Gallo-Romans most often consumed oysters cooked, without concern for freshness.

A TOP ADDRESS

In the nineteenth century, Alexis Balaine opened Au Rocher de Cancale, which became the hot spot for savoring oysters.

BELLY UP TO THE OYSTER BAR!

From Brasserie Lipp to La Coupole to Le Dôme to Le Procope—oysters are a top menu item in the capital's historic brasseries, but not just these establishments!

Paris has no less than 250 restaurants serving what the Romans called *callibléphare*, the "beautiful eyelid," and they are a top item on the menus of nearly thirty of these establishments.

" . . . two dozen of the expensive flat, faintly coppery marennes . . . picking them from their bowl of crushed ice on the silver plate, watching their unbelievably delicate brown edges react and cringe as I squeezed lemon juice on them and separated the holding muscle from the shell and lifted them to chew them carefully."

—Ernest Hemingway, *A Moveable Feast*, 1964.

SKIP TO
Au Rocher de Cancale, p. 223;
Paris: A Moveable Feast, p. 244;
Lutetia at the Table, p. 294.

Chestnuts, Hot Chestnuts!

When temperatures drop, chestnut vendors appear on Paris street corners and at metro exits. Prepared on the spot, these tasty and convenient snacks, grilled over hot coals, have warmed passersby since the Middle Ages.

—ESTELLE LENARTOWICZ

Advertising postcard, Paris, 1900s.

Who are the vendors?

The first chestnut vendors arrived in Paris from Lyon during the twelfth century, dressed as monks. Setting up near the Palais-Royal, they attracted crowds with their cries and costumes. The following decades, poor and out-of-work peasants from Limousin, Auvergne, and Savoy came to the city hoping to earn a few pennies when chestnut season began. Since these times, the popularity of hot chestnuts purchased on the street corner has lived on. The only changes have been the origins of the vendors, most of whom arrived from France's provinces until the twentieth century. After 1917, many were Russian, while others from north Africa arrived after World War II. Today, many are from India, Pakistan, and Africa.

How much for chestnuts?

The market sets the prices for the chestnuts, with the price of a cone of chestnuts varying according to the popularity of the neighborhood. A cone costs about €5 in front of the Louvre, Sacré Coeur, or around the Eiffel Tower, but €2 or €3 in Barbès or Belleville, where the vendors—who, on good days, pocket about €50—may also negotiate their prices when encouraged by a customer.

Why are they so popular?

Commercially produced sweets didn't appear until the nineteenth century and were for a long time seasonal: cherries or raspberries in summer, apples in spring, chestnuts in autumn! Children love the chestnuts, attracted by their wonderful aroma and the crackling of the embers. Roasted chestnuts have held up against the competition with other snacks, as they are popular for their low cost, festive touch during cold months, and nutritional value.

Hot chestnut vendor, Paris, 1942.

Hot chestnut vendor, Paris, 2014.

How are they sold?

IN THE NINETEENTH CENTURY

Some chestnut vendors were equipped with a handcart, while others had a storefront with a designated location in front of a department store or tourist site.

IN THE 1920s

A salesman near the Eiffel Tower caused a sensation by using a roaster in the shape of a locomotive. The idea was soon adopted by fairground workers throughout France.

IN 1960

A man named Georges Cefalas, a famous chestnut vendor located at 53, rue de Rivoli, had the honor of being part of a report that aired on France's national television. His stand was decorated with paintings that, as an accomplished artist, he would paint in his studio after his day's work.

TODAY

The most resourceful chestnut vendors use a simple portable brazier with a large skillet set on top. They use a small shopping cart to store the coals, chestnuts—typically from Portugal, Italy, and Spain and purchased in Belleville in 22-pound (10 kg) bags—and sheets of newspaper, folded into cones with their hands, which are usually rough from the cold and from the blade of the knife they use to slit the chestnuts across the top before roasting them.

What are the risks?

Under French law, unlicensed selling is punishable by six months imprisonment and a fine of €3,750. The equipment must therefore be light and mobile enough to be packed up and moved quickly when police officers are lurking nearby. Because many vendors arrive from foreign countries, they do not always have the correct immigration papers in order. As a consequence, they most often receive a warning and seizure of their equipment.

SKIP TO
Street Food in the Middle Ages, p. 108.

Colette (1873–1954)

A Citizen of the Palais-Royal

This writer from Burgundy made Paris her gastronomic playground.

—STÉPHANE SOLIER

Le Grand Véfour, Colette's hangout

During the 1940s and 1950s, French author Sidonie-Gabrielle Colette (known simply as Colette) and playwright Jean Cocteau, self-proclaimed "citizens of the Palais-Royal," found themselves sitting next to each other at their regular tables at Le Grand Véfour. In 1948, chef Raymond Oliver, who took over Le Grand Véfour, offered dishes from his native southwest France, as well as forgotten recipes (fish terrine Taillevent, sweetbreads with verjus, pigeon Prince Rainier III stuffed with truffles, and foie gras in cognac)—all to please Colette! Soon the chef and writer became romantically involved. Oliver composed her favorite dishes that he named after her, and he sent a sedan chair to her when she became immobilized from polyarthritis.

Paris in all directions

In "J'aime être gourmande" (her column for *Marie-Claire*) on January 27, 1939, Colette discusses her favorite spots in Paris.

"In the mild weather last November, I still found a few St. George's mushrooms in the fields of the **Bois de Boulogne**. With their bare looking suede-skin tops that can be eaten on the spot, how delicate they are!"

"My dear **first arrondissement** is full of unpretentious gastronomic treasures. The ragout of mutton is immutable, equal to nothing else, topped with a sauce cooked neither too short nor too long. Cassoulet gratiné, in its small individual tureens; this sort of vault, half underground, continually turns out crêpes; pigs' feet and sheep's feet compete with one another in their succulence. . . ."

"**Saint-Denis and Saint-Martin** favor beautiful thick sole and spit-roasted chicken licked by high flames."

"**La Villette** has its marvelous meats, its thick, quasi-cubic 'châteaux,' which you, dear brothers, must seek, from time to time, after days and nights of hard work."

"**Montmartre** adulterated, Montmartre itself is not without its honest resources, but the wines that we drink there do not ripen on the vineyard on the hill . . ."

Colette and her husband, Maurice Goudeket (left). Restaurant Le Grand Véfour, Paris, June 1946.

"A mainstay, thanks to the privilege of fragile things that last longer than rock, Le Véfour, with its Louis XVI ceiling and Directory coasters . . . , would be the Caffè Florian of this village that is Paris, a village where leisure plays a considerable role. It is impossible to love Paris without going on pilgrimage to this exquisite wreck among great storms."

—Colette, *Le Bicentenaire du Grand Véfour*, 1949

"I refuse the help of the champignon de Paris, which dampens juices without real profit. I banish it from hunter's chicken, sautéed rabbit, veal fillet, which it turns even more pallid. But I smile when it appears alone, naked and rosy pink, ready to be sautéed in an impeccable butter, or grilled, or eaten raw, moistened with oil and lemon."

—"J'aime être gourmande," *Marie-Claire*, January 27, 1939

HER GO-TOS AT LE GRAND VÉFOUR

› Salmon koulibiac

› Lièvre (hare) *à la royale* prepared to order: "A successful lièvre à la royale does not taste like garlic. Sacrificed to a collective glory, reduced to consumption in an instant, the sixty cloves of garlic, unrecognizable, are nevertheless present, indistinguishable, a caryatid that supports a subtle and climbing flora of garden spices."

Prisons et Paradis, 1932

SKIP TO
Île-de-France
Terroir, p. 20.

From Cattle Farms to Dairies

It's hard to imagine the streets of Paris filled with cattle, but Paris was once the center for milk production and processing.

—PIERRE COULON*

Cowshed, Paris, nineteenth century.

Dairy Guillemot, rue de Montmorency, Paris 3rd, early twentieth century.

Outdoor dairy, in the Bois de Vincennes, early twentieth century.

New cardboard milk packaging, 1952.

❶ Parisian cowsheds

Dairy animals have been bred in Paris since the Middle Ages, inspiring the names of many streets and districts (Île aux Vaches, Pré-Saint-Germain . . .). Though goats and donkeys roamed the city's streets and were milked on demand in front of customers, cows were housed in cowsheds. The animals were bought at the La Villette markets and housed in stalls where they were fed straw, cabbage leaves, and cooked potatoes. Managing dairy cattle was a substantial business, with nearly 16,000 gallons (70,000 L) of milk produced in Paris each day during the nineteenth century.

❷ The rise of dairy farms

At the end of the nineteenth century, the profession became more organized, and dairies were created. They flourished in all the city's arrondissements, and Île-de-France milk was made available for sale. Dairies belonged to merchants or commercial manufacturers.

❸ A daily back-and-forth

With Paris's expansion, animals were eventually moved to the suburbs. In 1950, there were three cowsheds, including the Montsouris farm (Paris 14th), which were all closed years later. Milkmaids took over the operations. They would leave the farms in the suburbs early in the morning and come by cart into Paris to sell the milk, which was not sold chilled and was often skimmed or mixed with water.

❹ The milk carton revolution

After World War II, several factors contributed to the disappearance of dairies. The invention of the sterilized milk carton and household refrigerators, in addition to a government ordinance prohibiting the sale of bulk milk, caused the closure of dairies one by one. Milk would now keep longer and was no longer a food that you had to purchase every day. In the 2020s, dairies in Paris and its suburbs started making a comeback. In addition to milk, these dairies also sell cheese and yogurt.

TOP LET'S EAT PARIS! ADDRESSES

*Laiterie de Paris
📍 74, rue des Poissonniers, Paris 18th
Artisanal cheesemaker by Pierre Coulon (the author of this page), located in the Goutte-d'Or district.

Laiterie de la Chapelle
📍 72, rue Philippe-de-Girard, Paris 18th
In this ultralocal dairy, Paul Zindy makes cheeses, cream, yogurts, and desserts using organic raw milk from Vexin, collected 22 miles (35 km) from Paris.

Fromaville
📍 10, rue des Bateliers, Saint-Ouen (Seine-Saint-Denis)
Near the Saint-Ouen flea market, Xavier Hugol-Gential has opened a locavore urban dairy where he makes organic cheeses and yogurts with raw milk produced less than 62 miles (100 km) away.

SKIP TO
The Fontainebleau, p. 288; Cheese Shops, p. 320.

The Thousand-Year Saga of Île-de-France Wines

Wine has existed in the Paris region since before the time of Clovis I, and winemaking accompanied the expansion of the Church and the city until it disappeared around fourteen hundred years later. The twenty-first century, however, has experienced a much-heralded rebirth of Paris's winemaking industry.

—BENOIST SIMMAT

A thousand years of wine-growing activities in Île-de-France

EPOCH 1

From the ninth century: the time of the abbeys

Main monasteries or wine-producing establishments:

01 ABBEY OF SAINT-DENIS
02 ABBEY OF SAINT-GERMAIN-DES-PRÉS
03 VILLA DE RUEIL
04 ABBEY OF SAINTE-GENEVIÈVE

EPOCH 2

From the thirteenth century: the time of vins françois

Surrounding Paris, the villages or neighborhoods where there were vineyards:

01 CHÂTILLON
02 BAGNEUX
03 FONTENAY
04 VANVES
05 ISSY
06 CLAMART
07 MONTROUGE
08 CLIGNANCOURT
09 MONTMARTRE
10 LA COURTILLE
11 MONTREUIL
12 PICPUS
13 CHARONNE
14 SAVIES (BELLEVILLE)
15 LA CHAPELLE
16 CHAILLOT
17 AUTEUIL
18 MEUDON
19 SAINT-CLOUD
20 SURESNES
21 RUEIL
22 NANTERRE
23 VAUGIRARD
24 SCEAUX
25 IVRY
26 VITRY
27 THIAIS
28 ARGENTEUIL
29 MONTMORENCY

EPOCH 3

From the sixteenth century: the time of the Île-de-France communes

Vineyards farther away from Paris or farther away from Île-de-France:

01 MANTES
02 MEULAN
03 ANDRÉSY
04 BEAUVAIS
05 POISSY
06 PLEIVIERS (PITHIVIERS)
07 CHARTRES
08 CLERMONT-EN-BEAUVAISIS
09 SENLIS
10 COMPIÈGNE
11 MORET
12 ESTAMPES
13 MEAUX
14 LAON
15 SOISSONS
16 CHÂTEAU-THIERRY
17 PALAISEAU
18 NOGENT-SUR-MARNE
19 THORIGNY
20 DAMPMART
21 VILLEVAUDÉ

EPOCH 4

From the twentieth century: the time of Parisian micro-vineyards

Those in Paris, or very close to Paris, that resisted the eradication of Île-de-France vineyards:

01 CLOS-MONTMARTRE
02 BERCY (JARDIN YITZHAK-RABIN)
03 VINES OF PARIS-BAGATELLE
04 CLOS DES ARÈNES DE LUTÈCE
05 BUTTE BERGEYRE
06 CLOS DE BELLEVILLE
07 VINES OF PARC GEORGES-BRASSENS
08 CHEMIN DES VIGNES (ISSY-LES-MOULINEAUX)
09 CLOS DE RUEIL-BUZENVAL (RUEIL-MALMAISON)
10 VINES OF PARC DU SAUSSET (AULNAY-SOUS-BOIS)

EPOCH 5

From the twenty-first century: the time of the resurgence of Île-de-France vineyards

The "PGI" labels in 2021:

01 VINES OF SURESNES
02 DOMAINE BOIS BRILLANT (GUÉRARD)
03 DOMAINE MAGALYVAL (MELZ-SUR-SEINE, JEAN-MICHEL BOURGOIN)
04 DOMAINE LA BOUCHE DU ROI (DAVRON).

Other encouraging areas:

05 LE CLOS FEROUT (LE HEAULME, BRUNO LAFONT)
06 WINES OF COTEAUX DE SAINT-PRIX

Source: Roger Dion, *Histoire de la vigne et du vin en France*, Flammarion, 1990.

Lutetia, the vineyard of the north

According to ancient sources (Diodorus, Pliny, Columella), the Gauls enjoyed wine as far back as the first century BCE. For the most part, however, wine was imported into what is now France from the Mediterranean shores and the Rhône and Garonne Valleys. Archaeological excavations attest to the first traces of Île-de-France vines (Boran-sur-Oise) in the second century CE. The discovery of local amphorae and grape press production confirms that wine-making activity was in full operation and very organized by the Gauls between the second and third centuries.

The year 276 CE was a significant milestone for the young Gallo-Roman viticulture industry. Soon after coming to power in Rome, the new emperor Probus authorized the planting of vines *Gallis omnibus* ("for all the Gauls"). Vines were planted in the Seine valley, the last of the wine-growing regions in the northern sections of a country where wine grapes had already conquered the Rhône, Bordeaux, and the future Burgundy regions. The reputation of the wines in what would become the city of Paris proliferated, so much so that in 358 CE, the wines received acclaim from emperor Julian the Apostate:

"I was then in winter quarters near my dear Lutetia . . . Good vines grow there."

—Julian, *Mispogon*

The abbey of Saint-Denis, the first wine-growing power

Under Charlemagne (early ninth century), the monks of Saint-Denis formed one of the region's most active communities of *vignerons* (winegrowers). They made a modest wine from their nearby lands, intended for the masses and for consumption at the monastery. The abbey also had excellent acreage on the side of the Argenteuil and Montmorency massifs (the term *terroir* was not used at this time) and on the current slopes of Nanterre and Saint-Germain-en-Laye. The *muids** (a French term for "cask") were exchanged during the great fair of Saint-Denis, which began every October ninth. Founded by Dagobert, this was the primary wine market in Île-de-France. The abbey's wine production stood up to Norman incursions and claims by tax authorities. The cellars of Saint-Denis were considered, at the time, as "inexhaustible," according to historical geographer Roger Dion.

*Former unit of measurement, equivalent to one barrel, or 73 gallons (278 L), for wine.

The apogee of *vins françois* under Saint Louis

In the Middle Ages, grapevines surrounded Paris and penetrated even into the suburbs. From Clamart to Montmartre to Rueil to Montreuil, Parisian vineyards were, at the time, called *vins françois* (or in modern French spelling, *vins français*, French wines) to distinguish them from those of Auxerre or Burgundy. The kings of France owned vineyards and produced cuvées. From the time of Saint Louis to Philip IV, the area of what is today Montagne Sainte-Geneviève provided most of the royal supply. Since the time of Philippe Auguste, Parisian wines were protected against "foreign" wines (from neighboring regions), which were forbidden to unload on the river ports of the Seine. Moreover, the local market could not absorb the large quantity of wine from Parisian production, so the wine was exported to Flanders and England. The wine's reputation, therefore, became firmly established. The most famous wines, such as the distant wines of Mantes or Meulan, or the nearest wines of Argenteuil, were "the worthiest . . . to quench the thirst of the king of France."*

La Bataille des vins, poem by Henri d'Andeli (1224).

Tastes and grape varieties in the thirteenth century

Fromentel, Morillon, Gouais . . . These now unknown grape varieties were at the time the most famous in the northern part of France in the thirteenth century, according to legal documents.* Fromentel, the most expensive, produced the best white wines in the Paris region. The neighboring Champagne region would eventually use this variety under the name Fromenteau (or Pinot Gris). Morillon, a variety of Pinot, produced a delicate red wine for which bards celebrated its brilliance in song. Gouais was a productive plant that produced good, fruity wines that Parisians called *gros noir*.

In the late Middle Ages, wealthy customers preferred white wines, but these wines were nothing like today's clear, modern vintages. Just as reds were often light in color, even pink, white wines were called "clarets," because they were tinged with gray. At the time, enology as a study did not exist, and the enormous production of wine in the Paris Basin often mixed grape varieties, and sometimes colors.

Coutumes de Beauvaisis, Phillipe de Beamanoir (fin XIIIᵉ siecle).

GUILLAUME BUDÉ, THE HERALD OF PARIS WINES

After the Hundred Years' War, Guillaume Budé, a humanist and protégé of François I, became the herald of Parisian merchants to compete with the wines of Beaune and Reims that had achieved preeminence. Budé undertook the task of improving the reputation of "French" wines, more particularly the vineyards of western Paris (Coteaux de Vanves, Puteaux, Issy, Saint-Cloud, and Meudon).

The death of the Parisian wine-growing region

The *guinguettes*, railway, and phylloxera led to the near total extinction of Parisian vineyards at the end of the nineteenth century. One hundred years earlier, Parisian wine growing had become the largest in France (124,000 acres/50,000 ha) and intended to supply the enormous market demand of the *guinguettes*, the public drinking establishments that were flourishing around the capital at the end of the Ancien Régime. The quality vines of the west disappeared in favor of lowland vineyards fertilized with the urban sediment from the capital, which lent the wines an impure taste. The advent of the railway in the mid-nineteenth century provided Parisian workers with a delicious substitute product, however: wines from the south. And when the aphid pest phylloxera reached Île-de-France, the high-yielding vines disappeared one after the other and were not replanted, except for a few community vines.

150 DOMAINS IN THE TWENTY-FIRST CENTURY

Many wine estates that remain in the Paris region are simply city curiosities (the vineyards of Montmartre, Belleville, and Bercy, for example) or suburban curiosities (the vineyards of Argenteuil, Rueil, Clamart . . .). Their production is very small, except for the historic vineyard of Suresnes, which officially sells up to 1,300 gallons (5,000 L) of table wine per year. Today, several dozen estates exist: Bois Brillant, Magalyval, La Bouche du Roi, and Clos Ferout, to name a few. Their goal is to revive quality wines produced on these forgotten but excellent terroirs of the region, which are composed of sand and silt and clay-limestone with a high pH.

PATRICE BERSAC, FATHER OF PGI-LABELED ÎLE-DE-FRANCE WINES

The long campaign by Patrice Bersac, a lover of Île-de-France wines, ended at the beginning of May 2021. As of this date and thanks to Bersac's efforts, several wineries are now able to market their cuvées in France and Europe under the PGI label "Île-de-France." Bersac fought a long fight against government bureaucracy that stated that, since Île-de-France vineyards officially "disappeared" a century ago, commercial wine estates were prohibited in the Paris region! After a first meeting in a bistro on rue de Charonne in 1999, Bersac, a former engineer, worked to eliminate this absurd law. He became president of the new Syndicat des Vignerons d'Île-de-France (Syvif) and campaigned for a deliberately broad set of specifications: seventy-three grape varieties authorized in ten departments, which was a rebirth for the former largest vineyard in France.

SKIP TO
The Adventures of Bercy, p. 302; Les Guinguettes, p. 72; Renowned Wine Cellars, p. 376.

4 recommended cuvées

DOMAINE LA BOUCHE DU ROI

Cuvée Le Grand Lever, Chenin

12, rue Saint-Jacques, Davron (Yvelines)

CLOS DU PAS SAINT-MAURICE

Cuvée "Classique," Chardonnay

4, rue du Passage-Saint-Maurice, Suresnes (Hauts-de-Seine)

DOMAINE DU BOIS BRILLANT

Cuvée Blanche, Chardonnay, Pinot Gris

30, rue de la Brosse, Le Charnoy, Guérard (Val-de-Marne)

CLOS MONTMARTRE

Cuvée des Lumières, about twenty grape varieties

Rue des Saules, Paris 18th

MAXIM'S

Maxim's reached gastronomic heights during the Belle Époque as the rendezvous for socialites.
—FRANÇOIS-RÉGIS GAUDRY

Maxim's opened in 1893 in the location of the famous Italian ice cream shop Imoda.

A temple of art nouveau

In February 1899, the architect-designer Louis Marnez was engaged to create the establishment's art nouveau decor. The greatest artists of the time—Gallé, Guimard, Majorelle, Prouvé, Mucha, and others—were brought together to create a cozy cocoon filled with mahogany, laminated and copper ornaments, beveled mirrors, and murals. The decor, which bears the marks of the École de Nancy, a group of art nouveau artisans and designers, has been classified as a historical monument since 1979.

Sacred Gaillard

In 1893, Maxime Gaillard joined forces with Georges Everard and opened a café–ice cream shop called "Maxim's et Georg's" at 3, rue Royale (Paris 8th). This modest bistro, intended for coach drivers of the time, became the rendezvous of the golden youth of Paris under direction of Arnold de Contades and Irma de Montigny. Gaillard surrounded himself with big names in the restaurant industry, including chef Henri Chauveau (formerly of Café Anglais) as well as Eugène Cornuché (formerly of Durand) who had served front of house in various establishments and, on Gaillard's death in 1895, took over the management.

Maxim's owners

- **1893**
Maxime Gaillard and Georges Everard
- **1895**
Henri Chauveau and Eugène Cornuché
- **1931**
Octave Vaudable
- **1942**
Louis Vaudable
- **1981**
Pierre Cardin
- **2020**
Rodrigo Basilicati-Cardin, great-nephew and heir of Pierre Cardin

"Maxim's is an actor in and a mirror of Parisian life."

—Pierre Cardin, 2011

Maxim's chefs

- **1893**
Henri Chauveau
- **1920**
Louis Barthe
- **1953**
Earns three Michelin stars.
- **1955**
Alex Humbert
- **1975**
Michel Menant
- **1978**
Maxim's is no longer included in the Michelin Guide at the request of Louis Vaudable.
- **2009**
Olivier Guyon
- **2021**
Nicolas Castelet

The culinary repertoire

1953–1977: This period represents nearly a quarter of a century during which Maxim's was at the top of the gastronomic world, crowned with three Michelin stars. Alex Humbert, who had been chef for twenty years, was particularly responsible for the gastronomic style of the restaurant. In his book *Maxim's* (1958), Jean Mauduit recalls this period:

"You are spoiled for choice, and everything to meet your requests is possible, from an everyday steak to a flambéed woodcock, from the grape-fruit to the Edward VII lamb saddle studded with foie gras, and from the sole Albert—a classic, just like the chef, and irreproachable, just like the chef—to the *homard en uniforme de chasseur* [lobster]."

Other Maxim's signature dishes:

LE POTAGE BILIBI

A mussel soup created by chef Louis Barthe in Normandy and then "imported" to Maxim's.

LA SELLE D'AGNEAU BELLE OTERO

A boneless lamb's saddle, stuffed with a duxelles of mushrooms, truffles, and foie gras.

LES CRÊPES VEUVE JOYEUSE

Sweet wheat-flour crêpes topped with a lemon soufflé.

Woody Allen.

John Travolta.

Society life

DECEMBER 1897
Edmond Rostand celebrates the triumph of *Cyrano*.

1907–1914
Roland Garros, Louis Blériot, Ettore Bugatti, André Citroën, Louis Renault, and others frequent the establishment. This is the era of sportsmen and captains of industry.

1920s
Tristan Bernard, Jean Cocteau, Georges Feydeau, Sacha Guitry, Marcel Proust, Mistinguett, Yvonne Printemps, and Paul Poiret make Maxim's a place to be seen.

JUNE 1940
During the German occupation, Hermann Göring was a regular.

1958
Maria Callas discovers the restaurant. Seduced by it, she returns at least once a month and asks for the "red table," which was the table of the Duke of Windsor.

1970s
Brigitte Bardot causes a scandal by entering the restaurant barefoot.

1980s
This is the era of designer Pierre Cardin, the new owner. Arielle Dombasle, Margaux Hemingway, Mick Jagger, Caroline de Monaco, Diana Ross, and John Travolta are among the regulars.

In film

Several films include scenes shot in this monument to Parisian life:

1958
Gigi by Vincente Minnelli

1958
Bonjour tristesse by Otto Preminger

1967
La Nuit des généraux by Anatole Litvak

1976
Le Chasseur de chez Maxim's by Claude Vital

2009
Chéri by Stephen Frears

2011
Midnight in Paris by Woody Allen

2013
Des gens qui s'embrassent by Danièle Thompson

The scenes of Sem

Poster artist, illustrator, and caricaturist Georges Goursat, known simply as Sem, was a pillar of social life in Belle Époque Paris. His wry personality and unique style of muted colors and crisp black lines hit the right notes in the press and advertising of the time. Maxim's was his favorite playground. The personalities and vanity of the world's greatest characters who paraded through the famous restaurant were an inexhaustible source of inspiration. His drawings amazed Jean Cocteau, who said of his work: "It's beautiful, like any art where hard work and spontaneity meet."

TO SEE

The glass ceiling
Overlooking the dining room, the glass ceiling displays flowers, fruits, orange, and lemon leaves in a baked enamel finish.

The poppy seed stained glass
Representing poppies growing along a riverbank, it's a nod to the use of drugs by high society.

TO TRY

Chicken with sauce Périgueux, beef Wellington, Grand Marnier soufflé, Saint-Pierre fillet with herb butter and green asparagus . . .

> "The only time Paris will be damned is when Maxim's disappears."
> —Jean Cocteau, 1944

SKIP TO
The Soufflé, p. 102; Art Nouveau or Art Deco?, p. 160.

The Balzac Eating Guide

Through his novels and his writings about his peregrinations through the capital, let's get a taste of the sometimes acidic, sometimes sweet, pen of Balzac's gastronomic analysis. —STÉPHANE SOLIER

![Y]	*Balzac liked*
![YY]	*Balzac liked a lot*
![YYY]	*Balzac loved madly*

Les Halles

A popular neighborhood where the favorite restaurant of this author of La Comédie humaine *stands out in the firmament.*

Au Rocher de Cancale ۩۩۩

◦ *59, rue Montorgueil, Paris 2nd*

(Alexis Balaine, 1802–1815, then Pierre-Frédéric Borel, 1815–1845)

Classic seafood dishes, high-end (30 percent of its savory dishes are fish and shellfish based).
"To find Paris again! Do you know what it is, oh, Parisians! It is to find again, not the cuisine of *Au Rocher de Cancale*, as Borel guards it for the gourmets who know how to appreciate it, for that is to be met with only in the rue Montorgueil, but a service which recalls it! (*Honorine*, 1843; Translation by William Walton, George Barrie & Sons, publishers, 1897, page 6.)

ON THE MENU: Oysters from Normandy, Brittany (Cancale), Marennes, and Ostend, turtle soup, truffled fillet, plum-pudding with chipolata, vol-au-vent with cream . . .

PRICE: between 100 and 500 francs per head.

Left Bank

The neighborhood of the young, of thinkers, students, and dreamers.

Restaurant Flicoteaux ۩

◦ *Corner of the Place de la Sorbonne and rue Neuve-de-Richelieu, Paris 5th*

Honest cuisine for students and artists in search of glory.

"The name of Flicoteaux is engraved on many memories. Few indeed were the students who lived in the Latin Quarter . . . and did not frequent that temple sacred to hunger and impecuniosity. . . . This establishment consists of two rooms arranged in long squares, narrow and low, . . . both furnished with tables from some abbey refectory. . . . Few Parisian restaurants offer such a beautiful spectacle. There you find only youth and hope, which poverty gaily endured. (*Illusions perdues*, 1843; partial translation by Zachary R. Townsend and other authors.)

ON THE MENU: All-you-can-eat bread, mutton chops, beef or horse meat, potatoes, cooked prunes . . .

PRICE: 18 sous for three courses with a small carafe of wine or a bottle of beer, 22 sous with a bottle of wine.

Maison Vauquer ۩

◦ *Rue Neuve-Sainte-Geneviève, between the Latin Quarter and Faubourg Saint-Marceau, Paris 5th (run by Madame Vauquer, with "fat Sylvie" as the cook)*

A middle-class boarding house for men and women, young people, and the elderly. Accommodating leftovers.

"This room, entirely in panel walls, . . . is surrounded with dirty sideboards. . . . In one corner is a box with numbered pigeon-holes used to keep the napkins, wine-stained and greasy, of each guest. The whole room is a depository of worthless pieces of furniture. . . , a long table covered with oilcloth . . . , broken chairs. . . . In a word, here is poverty without relieving sentiment. (*Le Père Goriot*, 1842; excerpt from the translation by Katharine Prescott Wormeley, Robert Brothers Publishers, Boston, 1894. p. 8.)

ON THE MENU: Haricots de mouton [similar to a cassoulet] with potatoes, cooked pears.

PRICE: 30 francs per month.

The boulevards

The very best in gastronomic dining starting in the 1830s.

Le Cadran-Bleu 🍴🍴

📍 *27, blvd. du Temple, Paris 3rd*

Classic dishes, luxurious

"The boulevards were then [in 1800] only a first-class royal route that led to pleasurable activities, and we know this is what Le Cadran-Bleu was! . . . The famous Cadran-Bleu does not have a window or a floor that are of equal aplomb." (*Histoire et physiologie des boulevards de Paris,* 1845.)

ON THE MENU: Mushrooms on toast, champagne.

PRICE: 50 francs per head; lunch for delivery.

À la Flotte du Commerce 🍴

📍 *271, rue Saint-Denis, Paris 10th*

Regional dishes.

"It is in the bar of Le Havre that the painter wanted to depict to us. . . . Rush, friends of good food . . . enter the salons of La Flotte, where you can travel, sitting conveniently, from Bordeaux to Auvergne, from Burgundy to Spain; Bacchus will save you from the rigors of Neptune. (*Petit Dictionnaire critique et anecdotique des enseignes de Paris,* 1826.)

PRICES AND DISHES NOT SPECIFIED

Café de Paris 🍴🍴

📍 *24, blvd. des Italiens, Paris 9th*

Classic dishes, luxurious.

This "temple of elegance," which displays true "Parisianism," has existed since 1822. The cuisine is spectacular but forbidden to night owls. "A very delicate meal and very well understood." (*La Peau de chagrin,* 1831.)

ON THE MENU: Various appetizers, oysters from Ostend, chops à la soubise, chicken Marengo, lobster mayonnaise, mushrooms on toast.

PRICE: "And I thought it was a joke when I saw the number of gold coins that the menu required." (*Les Comédiens sans le savoir,* 1846.)

Le Boeuf à la Mode 🍴
📍 *8, rue de Valois, Paris 1st*

Provençal Cuisine.

"From Schalls [sic], a hat adorns an ox that the . . . restaurateur thought he would call à la mode; Some, fooled by the pun, wanted to try the food, but they found it a little too salty. (*Petit Dictionnaire critique et anecdotique des enseignes de Paris,* 1826.)

ON THE MENU: Colorful cuisine from the Provence region.

PRICE: High.

Au Veau qui Tète (Lelong et fils) 🍴

📍 *Rue de la Vrillière, pl. du Châtelet, Paris 1st*

Traditional cuisine.

"By a very strange oddity, suckling calves are the famous wood hedgehog mushrooms. Although the sign announces a compassionate feeding, the menu puts at a high price the appetizing items of this restaurateur. . . . A warning to gourmands without money." (*Petit Dictionnaire critique et anecdotique des enseignes de Paris,* 1826.)

ON THE MENU: sheep's feet.

PRICE: High.

SKIP TO Grimod de la Reynière, p. 222.

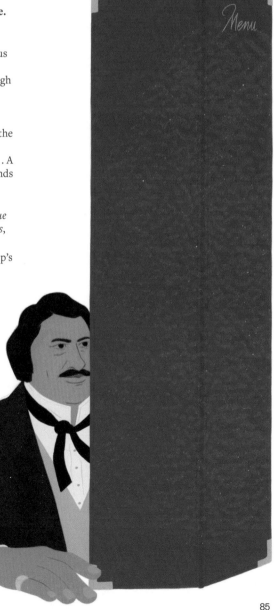

Other notable addresses

Le restaurant Deffieux (*Histoire et physiologie des boulevards de Paris,* 1845), **Le Café du Jardin Turc** (*Les Employés ou la Femme supérieure,* 1838), **le Café Anglais** (*Béatrix,* 1839; *Le Père Goriot,* 1842; *Illusions perdues,* 1843), **Hurbain** (*Illusions perdues,* 1843), **Katcomb** (*Les Employés ou la Femme supérieure,* 1838), **Grignon** (*Gobseck,* 1830), **Les Frères provençaux** (*Le Lys dans la vallée,* 1836), **le Café Riche** (*La Muse du département,* 1837), **Le Café Tortoni** (*Béatrix,* 1839), **Le Café Hardy, Le Véfour, Les Cafés de Foy, Corazza, Lamblin, de Valois** . . . *Traiteurs* **Chevet** (*César Birotteau,* 1837; *Illusions perdues,* 1843), and **La Maison d'Or** (*La Cousine Bette,* 1846).

Sèvres: The Tableware of Grand Tables

As a conservator of unrivaled French technique and heritage, this Île-de-France manufacturer has been crafting prestigious tableware for more than 260 years. —MARIE-LAURE FRÉCHET

Origin

- **1740**
  Founding in Vincennes of a studio for making soft-paste porcelain.
- **1756**
  Madame de Pompadour, a patron and customer of the tableware, moves Sèvres near her château in Bellevue.
- **1759**
  Achieves royal affiliation.
- **1768**
  Discovery of the first deposit of kaolin near Limoges, an essential material in the manufacture of hard-paste porcelain.
- **1800–1847**
  The porcelain flourishes under the influence of its director, Alexandre Brongniart, a specialist in mineralogy.
- **1824**
  Opening of the Museum of Ceramics.
- **1876**
  The move of the factory and museum to a Parc de Saint-Cloud, where the manufacturer is located today.

Sèvres today

The 130 Sèvres ceramicists produce several thousand pieces a year. Twenty-five percent of porcelain production is ordered by the major entities of the State, and the other portion is sold in the manufacturer's galleries in Sèvres (2, place de la Manufacture) and Paris (4, place André-Malraux). The establishment is listed as a Living Heritage Company.

Sèvres's grand tableware collections

1758
DUPLESSIS AUX OISEAUX
Commissioned by Louis XV, it has scalloped edges and is decorated with birds in the style of the engravings of naturalist Buffon's *Histoire naturelle*. It is still used during official receptions at the Élysée presidential residence.

1770
DU BARRY
Commissioned by Madame du Barry for her music pavilion in Louveciennes (Yvelines), this tableware is decorated with small vases and garlands of flowers with the monogram *DB* in the center.

1824–1832
DÉPARTEMENTS
The sites and monuments of the departments of France are represented on each of the one hundred plates in this collection commissioned for the Ministry of Foreign Affairs.

1832
PETITES VUES DE FRANCE
Commissioned by Louis-Philippe after he was installed at the Tuileries Palace, this tableware's design is composed of a frieze of golden palms on an agate blue background.

Bleu de Sèvres

This deep blue, created around 1778, is made from cobalt oxide fired over a large fire. By modifying the modeling technique, the nuances of the design can be changed:
> a thin layer: agate blue.
> a thick layer: granite blue.
> three layers with intermediate drying: bleu de Sèvres.

At the presidents' tables

All the heads of state of the Fifth Republic, apart from François Hollande, placed orders with the manufacturer. The Macrons' tableware was inspired by an outline of the Élysée from 1913 and cut into three hundred circles that form the plates' motif. The collection has fifteen hundred pieces and remains the property of the manufacturer.

Parts of a Plate

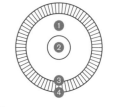

1. **Well**
   Bottom of the plate
2. **Umbilic**
   Center of the plate
3. **Lip**
   Curved part that connects the rim and well
4. **Rim**
   Edge of the plate

SKIP TO
The Goldsmiths Who Set Our Tables, p. 232; Tableware Dealers, p. 378.

Peas à la Française

Prepared as soon as possible after harvesting, this "king of spring" vegetable needs only proper cooking, a few fresh herbs, and a touch of fat to make it a delicious dish.

—MANON FLEURY

THE RECIPE

Season : spring to summer **Difficulty** ● ○ ○

SERVES 4

2¼ pounds (1 kg) fresh peas in their pods
½ bunch sorrel
4 spring onions
Olive oil

1 bunch chervil
1 bunch flat-leaf parsley
Fleur de sel sea salt
Freshly ground black pepper

Chef Manon Fleury offers a cold version of this dish in which olive oil replaces butter. Sorrel adds acidity to the vinaigrette.

Shell the peas. Trim the sorrel, reserving the leaves and stems. Clean the onions, cut off the green portion, and set aside. Cut the onion whites into quarters.

Place the peas and onion whites in a sauté pan set over low heat and drizzle with olive oil. Add a bouquet garni made of chervil (½ bunch), parsley (½ bunch), and a few sorrel leaves . Add just enough water to cover the vegetables, season with salt, and add 2 tablespoons of olive oil. Cook for about 5 minutes, covered. Taste to check the doneness; the peas should remain somewhat firm. Drain.

For the sauce, chop the reserved onion greens, the sorrel stems, and the remaining ½ bunch of chervil and parsley. Add these to a small bowl and add 2 tablespoons of olive oil. Season with a pinch of sea salt and pepper.

Chop the remaining sorrel leaves ❷. Spoon the pea mixture into a bowl. Add the fresh herb sauce and the chopped sorrel ❸.

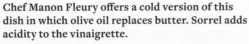

Taste and adjust the seasoning, if necessary. Serve.

THE SUN KING'S GREEN PEARLS

Originally from Central Asia and cultivated since antiquity around the Mediterranean Basin, peas, commonly eaten dried, were brought back fresh from a trip to Italy by the chef of the Comtesse de Soissons in 1660. Louis XIV loved them and introduced them into French gastronomy by ordering that they be grown in Versailles. Expensive and reserved for the Court, they were democratized in the nineteenth century once preserving was possible. Their cultivation developed in the Paris region at the beginning of the twentieth century when winegrowers, impacted by phylloxera, had to find an alternative to wine grapes.

À LA FRANÇAISE

It was Auguste Escoffier who proposed a version of peas *à la française* that we know today. It was prepared as a vegetarian dish using butter, spring onions, and a lettuce heart. The secret to mastering them is steaming.

Combine 2¼ pounds (1 kg) freshly shelled peas, 12 small spring onions, 2 teaspoons salt, 2 tablespoons sugar, and a bouquet garni of parsley and chervil. Set aside to keep chilled. To cook, add 3 tablespoons water to a saucepan and cook the pea mixture gently, covered. Just before serving, remove the bouquet garni and stir in 9 tablespoons (125 g) butter, off the heat. For serving, quarter a lettuce heart and place the pieces on top of the peas.

> **"Peas are without a doubt the best of all the vegetables to be eaten in Paris."**
>
> —Grimod de la Reynière, *Le Gastronome français*, 1828

TOP — LET'S EAT PARIS! — ADDRESSES

Aux Lyonnais
📍 *32, rue Saint-Marc, Paris 2nd.* €€
Chef Marie-Victorine Manoa serves vegetables grown by truck farmer Erwan Humbert (Essonne) and cooks classic recipes to perfection.

Dupin
📍 *11, rue Dupin, Paris 6th.* €€
Risk-taker chef Nathan Helo serves "peas *almost à la française*" by adding pieces of smoked eel from locally sourced fish.

SKIP TO
Paris in the Soup, p. 266; The Royal Vegetable Garden, p. 274.

FRANCE'S REGIONS IN PARIS

Parisian gastronomy was built on the fertile soils of its sedimentary basin and has been nourished over the centuries by resources and talented cooks from the country's beautiful provinces. From Alsatian brasseries to Auvergne cafés and from the *bouchons* of Lyon to Breton *crêperies*, here is a gourmet guide to all of France found in Paris. —AIMIE BLANCHARD, THOMAS DARCOS, FRANÇOIS-RÉGIS GAUDRY, PIERRICK JÉGU, CHARLES PATIN O'COOHOON, MARILOU PETRICOLA

LA CONQUÊTE DE LA CAPITALE PAR LES PROVINCES DE FRANCE

Normandie 89.200
Champagne 55.700
Auvergne 212.400
Ile de France 141.000
Provence 21.500
Dauphiné 13.400
Corse 7.700
Bourgogne 113.500
Savoie 22.500
Berry Anjou & Touraine 72.700
Lyonnais 24.500
Poitou et Charentes 53.300
Nord 104.400
Brie et Sologne 60.600
Languedoc 37.600
Pyrénées 34.700
Alsace et Lorraine 88.300
Gascogne 43.000
Bretagne 145.500

D'où proviennent et comment se répartissent les Parisiens de France.

Source: *Almanach*, Hachette, 1932.

AUVERGNE

In 1850, the Auvergnats fled an agricultural crisis and settled around Bastille, eventually spreading, little by little, throughout the eastern sections of Paris. They became water carriers for public baths, coppersmiths, knife grinders, and tinsmiths. These difficult and thankless jobs caused them to become pariahs in the capital. After the Second Empire, the Auvergnats ran brasseries, where they also sold and delivered coal. The people were nicknamed the bougnats,

a diminutive form of charbonnier (coalman) and auvergnat or charbouniat.

Before 1939, Paris had twenty-five hundred "wine and coal" cafés, which disappeared after World War II. The Auvergnats took up managing bars, tobacco shops, restaurants, and hotels such as Le Café de Flore, Les Deux Magots, and La Rotonde. With more than eighty thousand Auvergnats in the city, Paris is sometimes called "the fifth department of Auvergne"!

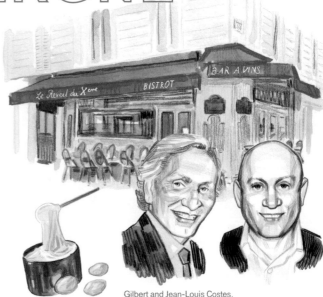
Gilbert and Jean-Louis Costes.

Well-known personalities

AVEYRON

Alexandre Cammas
Journalist and founder, in 1999, of Le Fooding.

Roger Cazes
Famous owner of Brasserie Lipp (Paris 6th), starting in 1955.

Gilbert and Jean-Louis Costes
These two brothers own a hotel and restaurant empire, including Hôtel Costes and Le Café Marly (Paris 1st).

Christophe Joulie
Businessman at the head of fourteen restaurants in Paris, including Bouillon Chartier (Paris 9th, 10th, 15th).

Cyril Lignac
Chef and TV presenter, originating from Rodez.

Henri Richard
In 1938, he bought Maison Richard, a coffee, wine, and beverage distributor.

Léon and Maria Tafanel
Founders of a beverage distribution company.

CANTAL

Olivier Bertrand
Founder in 1997 of the Bertrand group (La Coupole, Le Procope, Angelina, and others), the second largest French restaurant group.

Richard, Pierre, and Guillaume Moussié
Siblings at the head of Brasserie Barbès, Bouillon Pigalle, and Bouillon République (Paris 3rd, 9th, 18th).

Christian Valette
Livestock breeder and restaurateur (La Maison de l'Aubrac, Paris 8th), popularizing meats from Aveyron in Paris.

PUY-DE-DÔME

David Rathgeber
Chef of restaurant L'Assiette (Paris 14th), from Clermont-Ferrand.

Louis Vaudable
Emblematic head of Maxim's (Paris 8th) in 1932.

Recommended addresses

GROCERIES

Au Petit Bar
♥ 7, rue du Mont Thabor, Paris 1st. €
Auvergne sausage, salt pork with lentils . . . Originating from Lozère, Marie Dalle has been at the helm here since 1966.

Greffeuille Aveyron Paris
♥ 120, rue Saint-Denis, Paris 2nd
Founded in 2014 by Bernard Greffeuille, this establishment

specializes in suckling lamb, nursed by its mother.

Tribolet au Boeuf Cantal
♥ 54, rue Montorgueil, Paris 2nd
Alain Tribolet's butcher shop offers a selection of Cantal and Aveyron meats.

À la Ville de Rodez
♥ 22, rue Vieille-du-Temple, Paris 4th
Since 1920, this market has been dedicated to Rouergue products: Salers cheese, aged for fifteen months; chestnut boudin noir (blood sausage).

Mas Rouget
♥ 3, rue des Martyrs, Paris 9th + 2 other locations
Offers charcuterie products from the Auvergne terroir.

Côte2boeuf
♥ 8, rue des Moines, Paris 17th
Grocer, butcher, charcuterie, cheese—an ode to Auvergne products.

RESTAURANTS

L'Ambassade d'Auvergne
♥ 22, rue du Grenier-Saint-Lazare, Paris 3rd. €€
Opened in 1966, the establishment was taken over by Didier Desert in 2015.

On the menu are Salers and Aubrac beef, veal from Ségala, aligot, and Auvergne wines.

La Ferrandaise
♥ 8, rue de Vaugirard, Paris 6th. €
Gilles Lamiot founded this restaurant in 2005, where he serves veal blanquette and cuts of beef from the Ferrandaise cattle breed.

La Maison de l'Aubrac
♥ 37, rue du Marbeuf, Paris 8th. €€
In direct connection with the family farm, Christian Valette has been offering Aubrac beef since 1997 in choices of rib eye, sirloin, aged prime rib, etc.

Le Réveil du 10ème
♥ 35, rue du Château-d'Eau, Paris 10th. €€
Serving Saint-Nectaire, Salers, Cantal charcuterie, Aubrac beef. This is a true Parisian watering hole with an Auvergne accent.

BRITTANY

Starting in 1865, after the opening of the Paris–Brest train line, many Bretons settled in Paris to flee difficult conditions in the countryside. The majority of those who arrived settled in Montparnasse. Considered social outcasts, the uprooted Bretons quickly became disillusioned; many women were recruited into prostitution, and the men were subjected to exhausting jobs, such as digging the metro subway lines. Despite this, the Bretons were committed to "their" Montparnasse and managed to make a home for themselves. Many eventually opened the first crêperies, such as Ti Jos (30, rue Delambre, Paris 14th), which has been serving galettes and crêpes since 1937. Starting in the 1960s, the revival of regionalism led to a second wave of establishments opened by the Bretons. Today, along the streets flanking Montparnasse Tower, close to the Bretagne Cinéma, it is impossible to walk just a few yards without stumbling upon a crêperie, passing the Bretagne Cinéma, or spotting the white-and-black background of the Gwen ha Du, the famous Brittany flag.

Thierry Breton

Well-known personalities

Christophe Adam
This famous pastry chef from Finistère, the land of butter, enjoys spending time at his shop L'Éclair de Génie (Paris 2nd), dedicated solely to the éclair—and he offers one filled with a salted-butter caramel.

Thierry Breton
This chef from Fougères (Ille-et-Vilaine) manages La Pointe du Grouin (Paris 10th), where the menu includes his famous barnacles.

Gwenaëlle Cadoret
From a family of oyster farmers in Finistère, she cofounded Le Bistrot Paul Bert and L'Écailler du Bistrot (Paris 11th).

Jean Imbert
The top toque of the restaurant at the Plaza Athénée luxury hotel, this Costarmoricain (from Côte d'Amor, a department in Brittany) has achieved many accolades at this Landerneau-influenced monument of Parisian gastronomy.

Stéphane Jégo
This ultra-energetic chef of L'Ami Jean (Paris 7th), a native of Lorient (Morbihan), never forgets his beginnings, reflected in his legendary riz au lait (rice pudding), salted-butter caramel, and langoustines and lobsters.

Arnaud Larher
This Finistérien (from Finistère) and MOF (Best Craftsman of France) is the king of all things sweet. He created a box of chocolates called "Ma Bretagne."

Georges Larnicol
This MOF (Best Craftsman of France) chef from Bigouden sells his fabulous kouign-amanns, cakes, and confections throughout Paris.

Christian Le Squer
From Plouhinec (Morbihan), this amazing chef moved to the George V hotel (Paris 8th), where he brilliantly revisits the buckwheat galette.

Gaël Orieux
A native of Finistère, this chef is a lover of seafood and sustainable cooking, which he represents in his restaurant Auguste (Paris 7th).

Recommended addresses

GROCERY

Épices Roellinger
📍 *51, bis rue Saint Anne, Paris 2nd*
Mustard made from seaweed and cider vinegar, orange thyme from Brittany's Emerald Coast, curry corsair. These are just some of the products offered by Olivier Roellinger and his daughter Mathilde.

RESTAURANTS

Breizh Café
📍 *1, rue de l'Odéon, Paris 6th + 8 locations.* €€
A cross between Brittany and Tokyo, Bertrand Larcher's nine modern crêperies continue to delight with classic galettes and Japanese-inspired creations.

Tanguy
📍 *15, rue de l'Échiquier, Paris 10th.* €
Gwilherm Tanguy creates organic buckwheat galettes just like around the Baud commune of Brittany: thin and crispy.

Krügen
📍 *4, rue du Général-Renault, Paris 11th.* €
You can enjoy crispy buckwheat or wheat crêpes and an impeccable galette-saucisse (hot sausage wrapped in a crêpe) made with pork from Brittany.

La Crêperie de Josselin
📍 *67, rue du Montparnasse, Paris 14th.* €
This is an institution, with its burnished-wood setting and iconic galettes, such as the bretonne with sausage and cheese.

Brutus
📍 *26, rue de la Gaîté, Paris 14th.* €
📍 *99, rue des Dames, Paris 17th.* €
This contemporary crêperie appeals to both cider and crêpe fans with its organic artisan ciders and irreproachable galettes.

La Cantine Bretonne
📍 *22 bis, rue de l'Ourcq, Paris 19th.* €
With a string of organic buckwheat galette offerings (including grilled artisanal cooked ham, grated Emmental and Comté cheeses, and fried egg), this place is a slice of Finistère, located just near the canal. The establishment is also a market for Breton foods.

ALSACE

Pierre Hermé

As a result of the war with Prussia, France lost three departments in 1871 to German forces, and Alsace-Moselle became Elsaß-Lothringen. Consequently, many Alsatians made their way to Paris, a move facilitated by the Strasbourg–Paris train line. Alsatian families (Wepler, Zimmer, Dreher Bofinger, and others) set up brasseries and beer breweries. At the end of the two World Wars, Alsatians had established roots in the capital, and Paris became an El Dorado when low-pay workers from other regions arrived and frequented their establishments. Many Alsatian brasseries have historically been located around the Gare du Nord and Gare de l'Est and have been transformed by time and by their owners.

Well-known personalities

Jean-Paul Bucher

Originally from Molsheim (Bas-Rhin), Bucher founded the Flo restaurant group in 1968. His son Mathieu runs Maison Bucher, which operates Le Murat (Paris 16th) and Gallopin (Paris 2nd).

Claire Heitzler

Born in Niedermorschwihr (Haut-Rhin), she was crowned pastry chef of the year by *Le Chef* magazine in 2012 and by *Gault & Millau* in 2013.

Pierre Hermé

A native of Colmar (Haut-Rhin), he was voted best pastry chef in the world by the World's 50 Best in 2016.

Robert Jenny

In 1932, this Colmarien founded Chez Jenny, the emblematic Alsatian brasserie of République, which was replaced by Bouillon République (Paris 3rd).

Léonard Lipp

He and his wife, Pétronille, opened what would become Brasserie Lipp in 1880.

Recommended addresses

GROCERY

Schmid Traiteur

📍 *76, blvd. de Strasbourg, Paris 10th*

Located outside Gare de l'Est since 1904, this establishment is a veritable embassy of Alsatian products: beer from Brasserie Perle, artisanal sausages, organic raw Alsatian cabbage, and an impressive collection of excellent sauerkraut.

BAKERIES

Boulangerie Raoul Maeder

📍 *111, blvd. Haussmann, Paris 8th*

Baker Raoul Maeder has earned a solid reputation for his Alsatian specialties: pretzels, savory and sweet kugelhopf, and Linzer torte. His bread was served at the Élysée presidential residence.

Boulangerie Vandermeersch

📍 *278, av. Daumesnil, Paris 12th*

A native of Normandy, Stéphane Vandermeersch has become a specialist in puff pastry at his bakery, which dates to the nineteenth century. He also makes an exemplary kugelhopf.

RESTAURANTS

Zimmer

📍 *1, pl. du Châtelet, Paris 1st. €€*

Zimmer is an institution. Within these walls is where the world-renowned Tour de France bike race was imagined. Sarah Bernhardt, Guillaume Apollinaire, and Igor Stravinsky were regulars. Redecorated in 2000 by Jacques Garcia, this café serves sauerkraut among its Alsatian offerings.

Bofinger

📍 *5–7, rue de la Bastille, Paris 4th. €€*

Founded in 1864 by Frédéric Bofinger, the pioneer of beer on tap, this institution and its historic decor—including a stained-glass dome and brass railings—has maintained its Alsatian accent: soupe à l'oignon (onion soup) with Muenster cheese, mussels in Riesling, and a large selection of sauerkraut are among the selections.

L'Alsace

📍 *39, av. des Champs-Élysées, Paris 8th. €€*

Located on the Champs-Élysées since 1968, this establishment, which remains open through lunch, showcases its regional repertoire with flammekueches, sauerkraut, and an impressive wine list.

Floderer

📍 *7, cours des Petites-Écuries, Paris 10th. €€*

Referred to as "the most Alsatian of Parisian brasseries," here guests can enjoy a Strasbourg sauerkraut (cumin sausage, Frankfurt sausage, and bacon) surrounded in wood-paneled decor.

Café Mirabelle

📍 *16, rue La Vacquerie, Paris 11th. €*

In her bistro-tearoom, chef Marion Goettlé whips up what is probably the best flammekueches in Paris (organic onions, lardons from Alsace, farmstead Muenster).

Zeyer

📍 *62, rue d'Alésia, Paris 14th. €€*

Amid a decor by Russian-born French decorator Slavik, this independent brasserie serves the classics of Alsatian cuisine and sauerkraut all day long.

THE SOUTHWEST

Historically considered a place of refuge, this region experiences a lower number of people who move to the French capital. The TGV (the country's high-speed train) permits a healthy back-and-forth between the region and Île-de-France without causing a significant uprooting of the region's population.

Well-known personalities

GERS

Michel Sarran

This two-star chef from Gers has created locations in Paris dedicated to the croque-monsieur.

LANDES

Hélène Darroze

The multi-Michelin-starred chef heads up two Parisian locations: Marsan (Paris 6th) and Jòia (Paris 2nd).

Julien Duboué

This Landes chef has opened many concepts in Paris, including B.O.U.L.O.M. (Paris 18th).

Alain Dutournier

Nicknamed the Cyrano of the kitchen, this starred chef offers cuisine inspired by his native Gascony.

Michel Guérard

He opened Le Pot-au-Feu in Asnières-sur-Seine (Hauts-de-Seine) in 1965 before settling in Eugénie-les-Bains (Landes), where he obtained three Michelin stars in 1977. He is a native of Val-d'Oise.

TARN-ET-GARONNE

Christian Constant

Born in Montauban, Constant led an exceptional crew when he was chef at the Hôtel de Crillon in 1988.

PYRÉNÉES-ATLANTIQUES

Yves Camdeborde

A Palois (from Pau) and trained by Christian Constant, he opened La Régalade (Paris 14th) in 1992, the first Parisian bistronomy concept.

Alain Ducasse

A native of Orthez, Ducasse trained with Michel Guérard in the Landes and became the most Michelin-starred chef in the world in 2018.

Recommended addresses

GROCERIES

Valette

- *186, rue de Rivoli, Paris 1st*
- *16, rue Daguerre, Paris 14th*
- *48 bis, rue d'Auteuil, Paris 16th*
- *218, rue des Pyrénées, Paris 20th*

This family food market, founded in 1920 in the Périgord, perpetuates a unique expertise for foie gras, black truffles, and other specialties.

Maison Tête

- *20, rue Cadet, Paris 9th*

This Gascon shop offers products for sale, such as spreads and homemade preserves from the southwest, and a café, open throughout the day.

Comptoir Corrézeien

- *8, rue des Volontaires, Paris 15th*

Since 1986, this shop offers truffles, foie gras, and mushrooms, according to the season.

L'Amour du Terroir

- *248, rue de la Convention, Paris 15th*

This shop showcases southwest terroir with off-the-shelf products and rotisserie and other dine-in or takeout selections.

RESTAURANTS

A Noste

- *6 bis, rue du Quatre-Septembre, Paris 2nd. €€*

Taken over by chef Guy Martin, this restaurant,

Hélène Darroze

whose name means "Chez Nous" in Gascon patois, offers up twenty-six tapas from starters to desserts on its tall communal tables.

Jòia

- *39, rue des Jeûneurs, Paris 2nd. €€*

A nod to the Landes and Béarn, chef Hélène Darroze draws her inspiration from these areas, offering foie gras terrine, poulet jaune (superior quality chicken) from Landes, and suckling veal chops.

La Cantine du Troquet

- *79, rue du Cherche-Midi, Paris 6th. €€*
- *101, rue de l'Ouest, Paris 14th*
- *89, rue Daguerre, Paris 14th*
- *53, blvd. de Grenelle, Paris 15th*
- *7, av. des Savoies, Rungis*

Here chef Christian Etchebest offers the best of the southwest, including razor clams à la plancha and boudin noir Parmentier (blood sausage).

La Fontaine de Mars

- *129, rue Saint-Dominique, Paris 7th. €€€*

Managed by Christiane Boudon, this bistro-brasserie offers a tour of the southwest. Chef Pierre Saugrain has been delighting customers here since 1992 with his specialty

poulet aux morilles (chicken with morels).

Au Trou Gascon

- *40, rue Taine, Paris 12th. €€€*

Alain Dutournier founded this Gascon stronghold in 1973. Here customers enjoy high-quality salted meats, exemplary cassoulet, and a cellar of more than a thousand labels, including a rare collection from Bas-Armagnacs.

Aux Produits du Sud-Ouest

- *21–23, rue d'Odessa, Paris 14th. €€*

Since 1986, this restaurant-charcuterie-boutique offers a veritable anthology of regional specialties to enjoy on the spot or for takeout.

Il Était une Oie Dans le Sud-Ouest

- *8, rue Gustave-Flaubert, Paris 17th. €€*

This establishment highlights the products of its terroir: baba flambéed in Armagnac at the table, duck breast, young rooster en cocotte, confit of farmstead duck, and potatoes Sarladaise.

BASQUE COUNTRY

This region's population in Paris numbers only around five thousand, and yet Basque gastronomy has carved out an important place in the capital. The young people from the region who arrived in Paris in the 1960s settled around the La Maison Basque, rue Duban (Paris 16th), and today in Saint-Ouen in the northern suburbs, but establishments featuring pintxos (appetizers similar to tapas), tapas, Iberian pork, and chipirons (squid) are scattered throughout the capital. Bon appétit, or as they say in Basque, on egin!

Well-known personalities

Inaki Aizpitarte

This self-taught chef from the Basque country arrived in Paris at the age of twenty-seven. He heads restaurant Le Châteaubriand (Paris 11th) and the tapas bar Le Dauphin (Paris 11th).

Gabriel Biscay

Born in Biarritz, this MOF (Best Craftsman of France) has worked for prestigious restaurants, such as Prunier (Paris 8th, 16th), Royal Monceau (Paris 8th), and the Ritz (Paris 1st).

René Lasserre

Born in Bayonne in 1912 and died in 2006, he was the founder and chef of Lasserre (Paris 8th), awarded three Michelin stars from 1962 to 2001.

Recommended addresses

GROCERIES

L'Atelier du Chocolat

📍 109, rue Saint-Antoine, Paris 4th
📍 107, rue du Havre, Paris 9th
📍 44, rue du Commerce, Paris 15th

Founded in Bayonne in 1951 by the Andrieu family of artisan chocolatiers who have since opened shops all over France.

Pierre Oteiza

📍 18, blvd. Saint-Michel, Paris 6th
📍 13, rue Vignon, Paris 8th
Behind its green storefront, a wide choice of charcuterie hangs from the ceiling, and the shelves hold many tins of confit and foie gras. You can also order a house-made sandwich here.

Maison Pariès

📍 9, rue Saint-Placide, Paris 6th
Gâteaux Basques, macarons by Mouchou, Kanouga (the soft chocolate-flavored caramel that made the shop famous), and other sweet delights are on sale in this Parisian outpost opened in 1895 in Bayonne.

RESTAURANTS

Amatxi

📍 20, rue du Général-Guilhem, Paris 11th. €€
Behind its large windows is an old-fashioned bar with tiles from the seventies and zinc and Formica tables designed by the father-and-son duo Perez. Shared plates of Basque "grandmother" (amatxi in Basque) cuisine are created by chef Minwou Choi. You can wash it all down with a natural wine.

Auberge Etchegorry

📍 41, rue de Croulebarbe, Paris 13th. €€
This former cabaret of Madame Grégoire (the sign still adorns the red facade adorned with greenery) offers an ode to Basque cuisine in a rustic setting. On the menu are stuffed chipirons (squid) and duck confit, followed up with gâteau Basque for dessert.

Inaki Aizpitarte

Le Volant Basque

📍 13, rue Béatrix-Dussane, Paris 15th. €€
A wide choice of offal and meat dishes including traditional axoa de veau (veal stew) from the Labourd region, and sheep's-milk cheese with Itxassou black cherry preserves to finish.

La Kontxa

📍 8, quai Saint-Exupéry, Paris 16th. €€
After running roadside restaurants, the Dumant family turned to the southwest with a location in the heart of Trinquet Village and featuring pintxos (similar to tapas) and quality cuts of meat, including the 2¼-pound (1 kg) prime rib. Before or after dinner, patrons can play Basque pelota on the huge terrace.

TAPAS BARS

Osaba

📍 29, rue Saint-Placide, Paris 6th. €
Meaning "uncle" in Basque. This fine-foods market and tapas bar delights with cheese boards, charcuterie, and pintxos (similar to tapas), to be washed down with a glass of Irouléguy wine or sangria.

Hiru

📍 14, rue Duc, Paris 18th. €€
Hiru means "three" in Basque and "noon" in Japanese, a nod to the Basque origins and memories from Japan of the two cofounders Alexandre Lacroix and Antoine Micoin. On the menu? Iberian ham croquettes, slow-cooked pork, and eggplant caviar.

CORSICA

Augustin Grisoni

Their image in Paris has often been reduced to the stereotype of hoodlums around Pigalle and the mafia controlling the gambling circles, but the population of Corsicans in Île-de-France represents more than half of the million or so Corsicans who have settled in continental France. The peak of this immigration to Paris and its region occurred between 1870 and 1914. Many islanders settled in the 5th arrondissement, whose former mayor Jean Tiberi was of Corsican descent.

Well-known personalities

Florent Ciccoli

Cofounder of popular bars Au Passage (Paris 11th), Bones (Paris 11th), and Les Pères Populaires (Paris 20th), this son of French Algerians from Ajaccio directs high-end establishments on the bistronomy scene, including Jones (Paris 11th), Cheval d'Or (Paris 19th), Café du Coin (Paris 11th), and Recoin (Paris 11th).

Augustin Grisoni

Son of hoteliers-restaurateurs in Calacuccia, he founded Casa Corsa, rue Mazarine (Paris 6th), in 1997 then La Villa Corse in 2001 (Paris 15th), the first chic brasserie dedicated to Corsican cuisine.

Jean-Jacques Raffiani

This Corsican native of Vivario opened Vivario in the Maubert district (Paris 5th) in 1979. It was the first Corsican restaurant in the capital and a meeting point for famous French personalities such as Gainsbourg, Hallyday, Dutronc, and Jean Tiberi. He also opened La Main d'Or (Paris 11th) in 1992, which became an institution, but is now closed.

Recommended addresses

GROCERIES

À l'Heure du Vin

♀ *46, rue Sainte-Anne, Paris 2nd*
More than three hundred selections of Corsican wines and dozens of products from the island, including charcuterie, canistrelli (a cookie), honey, and jams are available in Bruno Geoffroy's *cave à manger* (eat-in wine shop).

U Spuntinu

♀ *21, rue des Mathurins, Paris 9th*
Founded in 1982, Jean-Philippe Ceccaldi's marble storefront delivers a wide choice of cheeses, charcuterie, honeys, jams, chestnut products, and prepared dishes. At lunch, it's time for a *spuntinu* (snack), with choices of several sandwiches with typical Corsican ingredients.

Missià

♀ *38, rue Marguerite-de-Rochechouart, Paris 9th*
This is a contemporary Corsican food market but very much dedicated to traditions: farmstead brocciu, AOP porcu nustrale charcuterie, figatellu sausage (when in season), chestnut flour, liqueurs, jams, and original wines.

RESTAURANTS

À la Main

♀ *31, rue Saint-Sauveur, Paris 2nd. €€*
This wine bar and tasting counter offers a Mediterranean meal based on excellent products: porcu nustrale charcuterie, organic veal from Galeria, all with the choice of washing it down with the finest Corsican vintages.

Chez Rosito

♀ *4, rue du Pas-de-la-Mule, Paris 3rd. €*
Since 1997, the Ajaccian Marie-Paule Fenocchi and her husband, Franck Merton, have served the Corsican family repertoire including storzapretti, polpette di carne, figatellu-pulenda, and pastizzu.

L'Alivi

♀ *27, rue du Roi-de-Sicile, Paris 4th. €€*
This bistro has set the standard for Corsican cuisine in the Marais since 1996, from the Cap Corse Mattei aperitif to sweet chestnut moelleux (cake) to AOP charcuterie from Dumè Cesari in Cozzano.

U Mulinu

♀ *28, blvd. de l'Hôpital, Paris 5th. €€*
Serving veal sausage by Jacques Abbatucci, porcu nustrale charcuterie by Castagniccia, and Cervione hazelnut moelleux (cake), this charming bistro by Jean-Marc Pieri and his cousin Frédéric Keller-Pieri offers the best in Corsica ingredients.

Le Papacionu

♀ *7, rue Cadet, Paris 9th. €*
An outpost of the famous location in Ajaccio, this pizzeria offers crispy-soft *pizzzzz* with tomato sauce simmered with herbs from the maquis and Corsican terroir toppings.

Chez Minnà

♀ *20, rue d'Hauteville, Paris 10th. €*
This modern café, the bistronomy version of *cucina corsa*, offers cannelloni with brocciu, arancini (rice balls) with Corsican cheese and prisuttu, and fiadone (a crustless cheesecake).

A Cursita

♀ *255, rue du Faubourg-Saint-Antoine, Paris 11th. €*
Formerly at La Main d'Or, François Guerrini revisits this establishment's specialty: roasted cabri (kid) with herbs from the maquis. The brocciu and mint omelet and fiadone (a crustless cheesecake) are sure to please. Cheeses and charcuterie arrive directly from the owner's village of Albertacce in the Niolo.

LYON

There have been no historic waves of immigration from Lyon to Paris, but continual exchanges of people between the two cities have occurred since the opening of the TGV high-speed train line in 1981.

Well-known personalities

Gérard Besson

Originally from Bresse (Ain), Besson, an MOF (Best Craftsman of France), has held two Michelin stars for twenty-five years at his location on rue du Coq-Héron (Paris 1st).

Georges Dumas

This chef from Lyon manned the kitchens of Lasserre (Paris 8th) in the 1960s.

Yves Labrousse

This native of Lyon worked for fifteen years alongside Raymond Oliver at Le Grand Véfour (Paris 1st) before becoming the head chef in 1984.

Recommended addresses

GROCERIES

Giraudet

📍 *6, rue du Pas-de-la-Mule, Paris 3rd*
📍 *16, rue Mabillon, Paris 6th*
Founded in 1910, this authentic establishment from Bresse has sold its popular products, including organic ravioli with Comté, artisanal quenelles shaped by hand using a spoon, and seasonal sauces and soups, since 2011.

Chocolats Bernachon

📍 *127, rue de Sèvres, Paris 6th*
The famous master chocolatier from Lyon set up his first boutique in Paris in 2019. Here you can find his entire collection of chocolate bars, spreads, and bonbons.

RESTAURANTS

Le Petit Mâchon

📍 *158, rue Saint-Honoré, Paris 1st. €*
A top *bouchon* (a restaurant that serves hearty traditional Lyonnaise cuisine) and the specialties to go with it, like andouillette Beaujolaise and quenelles with sauce Nantua.

Aux Lyonnais

📍 *32, rue Saint-Marc, Paris 2nd. €€*
Marie-Victorine Manoa makes all the Lyonnaise specialties—including cervelle de canut (a Lyonnaise cheese spread) and saucisson brioché—in this bistro from 1890, taken over in 2002 by Alain Ducasse.

L'Opportun

📍 *62, blvd. Edgar-Quinet, Paris 14th. €*
This bouchon is managed by Morgane Alzérat, and the classics of this "capital of the Gauls"—tablier de sapeur (fried breaded tripe), saucisson chaud (sausage), veal andouillette—all rub shoulders with bistro classics.

La Cuisinière Lyonnaise

📍 *37, rue Saint-Ferdinand, Paris 17th. €€*
Salade Lyonnaise, pike quenelles, aged Saint-Marcelli—here is found a complete Lyonnaise repertoire, headed by MOF (Best Craftsman of France) chef Stéphane Gaborieau.

THE ALPS

In the nineteenth century, Savoyard immigrants collected items for Hôtel Drouot (Paris 9th), the world's oldest auction house, where they had the job of collecting, storing, and carrying objects into the auction rooms. They were known as the cols rouges *(red collars) of the Hôtel Drouot. Many also became oyster openers, working behind the ice counters in brasseries. They returned to their home region when the "white gold" (snow) transformed their region into a tourist destination; today, there are only about twenty thousand in the city.*

Well-known personalities

Julien Dumas

This chef of the Saint James (Paris 16th) is from Grenoble (Isère).

Guy Martin

Originally from Bourg-Saint-Maurice (Savoie), he is the chef-owner of Le Grand Véfour (Paris 1st).

Michel Rostang

Born in Pont-de-Beauvoisin (Isère), this Michelin-starred chef continues, along with his daughters, the tradition of cooking for over six generations.

Guy Savoy

This chef has earned three Michelin stars at Hôtel de la Monnaie (Paris 6th). He grew up in Bourgoin-Jallieu (Isère).

Recommended addresses

GROCERY

La Laiterie Gilbert

📍 *1, rue de Vintimille, Paris 9th*
📍 *36, rue Popincourt, Paris 11th*
📍 *72, rue de Montreuil, Paris 11th*
📍 *104, rue d'Alésia, Paris 14th*
This dairy, founded in Grenoble in 1948, has made a name for itself by offering cheeses from the region as its specialty. There are also fine food products and wine.

RESTAURANTS

Pain Vin Fromages

📍 *3, rue Geoffroy-l'Angevin, Paris 4th. €€*
Located in the heart of the Marais, this establishment offers cheese platters and charcuterie with fondues and raclettes.

Le Chalet Savoyard

📍 *58, rue de Charonne, Paris 11th. €€*
Copious tartiflettes (a potato, cheese, lardons, and onion gratin), a half raclette dripping directly onto potatoes and fondues for all tastes.

Les Fondus de la Raclette

📍 *209, blvd. Raspail, Paris 14th. €€*
Savoyard products certified PGI to enjoy in raclette and fondue, or to cook yourself on grills in the center of the table, in a chalet-style restaurant.

PROVENCE

Three friends who came to Paris from the Durance region created, in 1786, the first Provençal restaurant in Paris: Les Trois Frères Provençaux. Since then, their products and dishes have been a bright spot in the city's culinary scene and have contributed to the fame of southern specialties.

Well-known personalities

Frédéric Duca
This Marseille chef, who has worked in the kitchens of Hélène Darroze and Gérald Passedat, officiates over his own location, Rooster (Paris 17th).

Flora Mikula
This chef from Nîmes, trained by Alain Passard, opened several locations in Paris before becoming a culinary consultant.

Alain Pégouret
Originally from Cannes, he spent time in the kitchens of Joël Robuchon and Christian Constant and is chef-owner of Sergent Recruteur (Paris 4th).

Julia Sedefdjian
Born in Nice, she is the youngest chef to have obtained one Michelin star, at just twenty-one years old. Her restaurant Baieta (Paris 5th) also achieved a star in 2019.

Alain Senderens
Born in Hyères in 1939 and died in 2017, he was the three-starred chef of Lucas-Carton (Paris 8th) before buying the restaurant and renaming it Senderens until 2013.

Recommended addresses

GROCERY

Cicéron

◉ *8, rue de Poissy, Paris 5th.*
This fine-foods and gourmet to-go shop operated by chef Julia Sedefdjian, from Nice, showcases the chickpea.

RESTAURANTS

Chez Janou

◉ *2, rue Roger-Verlomme, Paris 3rd.* €€
Bright plates and a menu offering eighty pastis help you explore this famed aperitif of southern France.

Brasserie Cézanne

◉ *45, av. Kléber, Paris 16th.* €€
A friendly atmosphere and Provençal-inspired dishes.

Chez Jacky

◉ *69, rue du Faubourg-Saint-Denis, Paris 10th.* €
This is Marseille in all its glory: wood-fired pizzas, baked sardines, aioli, Provençal-style roast chicken, and homemade frites (fries).

STREET FOOD

Bagnard

◉ *7, rue Saint-Augustin, Paris 2nd.* €

◉ *58, rue de Saintonge, Paris 3rd*
Chef Yoni Saada's celebration of pan bagnat (a sandwich consisting of tuna, hard-boiled egg, greens, vegetables, and olive oil), made in a dozen delicious and hearty ways.

BURGUNDY

With the Dukes of Burgundy in Paris since the Middle Ages, the links between the capital and France's Burgundy region have always been strong. The Burgundian community brought its share of simmering dishes and great bottles to Paris.

Well-known personalities

Raymond Berthillon
Originally from the department of Yonne, a master ice cream maker and founder of the eponymous shop (Paris 4th).

Marguerite Boucicaut
Born in Verjux (Saône-et-Loire) in 1816, she was the owner of the Hôtel Lutetia (Paris 6th) and cofounded the department store Le Bon Marché.

Adeline Grattard
Born in Dijon (Côte d'Or), this chef trained with Pascal Barbot and heads his starred restaurant Yam'Tcha (Paris 1st).

Jean-Nicolas Marguery
Born in Dijon in 1834, he was the chef and owner of the restaurant Le Marguery (Paris 10th), frequented by the political world. The Delaville Café that replaced it has retained some of the decor.

Recommended addresses

WINE BAR

La Cave des Climats

◉ *35, rue de Verneuil, Paris 7th.* €€
Offering 3,500 bottles onsite and another 28,200 in its cellars, this impressive collection of Burgundian wines is by Caroline Colin and Denis Jamet. Guests can enjoy offerings on-site or as takeout.

RESTAURANTS

Au Bourguignon du Marais

◉ *52, rue François-Miron, Paris 4th.* €€
Offering regional specialties, including the essentials jambon persillé and beef bourguignon, but above all, a 100 percent Burgundian wine list.

Bourgogne Sud

◉ *14, rue de Clichy, Paris 9th.* €€
Beef bourguignon, oeuf meurette, and salade Mâconnaise are served in this brasserie that also presents Lyonnaise specialties. The long wine list highlights Burgundy vineyards and Beaujolais.

NORD

Having most often arrived for professional reasons, 104,000 inhabitants from France's north region lived in Paris in 1932, the third largest region in France. A reverse wave of emigration from Paris to northern France, particularly to Lille, has been taking place since the early 2000s.

Well-known personality

Ghislaine Arabian

Born in Croix (Nord), this chef obtained two Michelin stars at the Pavillon Ledoyen (Paris 8th) between 1992 and 1998. In 2007, she took over the restaurant Les Petites Sorcières (Paris 14th).

Recommended addresses

GROCERIES

Méert

📍 *16, rue Elzévir, Paris 3rd*
The gaufre de Lille (an oblong filled waffle cookie) was created in Lille in 1849 and contributed to this establishment's success. You can also try them at a location in the heart of the Marais. Recommended: the traditional vanilla filling.

Les Merveilleux de Fred

📍 *29, rue de l'Annonciation, Paris 16th + 10 locations*
The Merveilleux cake that Frédéric Vaucamps created in the 1980s in Lille has become widely established around the world and in Paris. It consists of a meringue covered with chocolate whipped cream and chocolate shavings.

RESTAURANT

Le Galibot

📍 *17, rue Paul-Lelong, Paris 2nd. €*
From delicious Welsh dishes to Flemish carbonades, flamiches, and good beers from Nord are served up in this typical *estaminet* (small café) with exposed brick walls, echoing the redbrick houses of Nord-Pas-de-Calais.

NORMANDY

The first arrivals of the Normans date to the sieges of Paris by the Vikings in 845. After the development of the train lines from Saint-Lazare station, these two regions have had a favorable relationship. In 1906, the writer Louis Auguste Salles founded the cultural group Les Normands de Paris, which used to meet at Le Petit Bouillon Pharamond.

Well-known personalities

Éric Fréchon

Originally from Le Tréport (Seine-Maritime), he is the three-Michelin-starred chef of Épicure, the restaurant at Le Bristol hotel (Paris 8th), and Lazare (Paris 8th) located at Saint-Lazare train station.

Rodolphe Paquin

This chef from Angerville-Bailleul (Seine-Maritime), previously at the Hôtel de Crillon, took over Le Repaire de Cartouche (Paris 11th) in 1997.

Christophe Saintagne

From Caen (Manche), this former chef of Le Meurice is now at the head of his restaurant Papillon (Paris 17th).

David Toutain

He is a native of Orne and the two-Michelin-starred chef of his eponymous restaurant (Paris 7th).

Recommended addresses

RESTAURANT

Petit Bouillon Pharamond

📍 *24, rue de la Grande-Truanderie, Paris 1st. €*
Although the establishment became a *bouillon* in 2019, it continues to serve tripes à la mode de Caen (a beef tripe dish, on the menu since 1832) as well as whelks from Normandy and leeks from La Manche, seasoned with a vinaigrette à la pommée (apple balsamic).

The Feast of Fake Foods

In 1878, the prefect of police created the Paris Municipal Laboratory. The goal? Allow citizens to have foodstuffs analyzed because adding dyes, chemical substitutes, and additives to foods to fool the consumer was common. —BRUNO FULIGNI

Red-dyed pâté

The Municipal Laboratory targeted Parisian butchers who reduced costs by incorporating only a minimum amount of pork in their pâtés. Since pork is composed of fat, the ingredient can be made to look more appetizing by coloring it, using blood in the best cases, but often with the help of fuchsine, an artificial dye used in tattoos.

Gooseberry jelly with tartaric acid

Because it's expensive when it contains real fruit, gooseberry jelly could be just a simple gelling agent colored with beet juice and flavored with syrup. A pharmacist developed a more dangerous substitute using kelp jelly for texture, hollyhocks for color, and tartaric acid with added glucose for flavor.

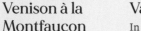

Venison à la Montfaucon

In the 1830s, the prefect of police Gisquet closed the cesspool at Montfaucon where the city dumped, but also used, the carrion from the capital: dogs, cats, and even deer fetuses. Much of these scraps were served to the less aware as well-made venison. This atrocity is reminiscent of the rue des Marmousets affair during the fifteenth century when two men were charged with making pâtés . . . from human flesh.

Vaseline pastries

In a circular dated July 10, 1885, on the topic of hydrocarbons used in food, the prefects were alerted to "the use, in certain pastries, to replace butter or fat, of a product under the names vaseline, *pétroléine*, or *neutraline*, and which is extracted from the heavy oils of petroleum." (Adolphe Gronfier, *Dictionnaire de la racaille: le manuscrit secret d'un commissaire parisien au XIX siècle*, 2010).

Borax-and-brain milk

Milkmen would sometimes cut milk using water, and sometimes taken from gutters. The milk obtained was bland and too liquid, so they would correct its texture by adding starch, cooked white carrots, and sometimes the serum, or brains, of ground-up animals. So that the contaminated milk would keep longer, the crooks would add a pinch of baking soda and a few drops of formalin or ammonia, or even a touch of borax, which today is used as a household cleaner.

Leaded-plaster bread

Bread was at one time deliberately partially baked so that it retained moisture and was thus denser. Some bakers increased the weight by adding chalk, plaster of paris, or alabaster. To give a nice appearance to the crust, bakers would add a little alum, copper sulfate, or magnesium carbonate, and voilà! As if this wasn't enough, bread would often be baked using wood coated with lead-based paint, salvaged from demolition sites.

Truffles with iron perchloride

According to a status report by Professor Girard, director of the laboratory from 1878 to 1911, "truffles are sometimes replaced by potato slices blackened with iron perchloride solution and tannin."

SKIP TO Macabre Legends and Tales from the Table, p. 131.

Félix Potin (1820–1871)

The King of the Épicerie

This farmer's son, born in Arpajon in the Essonne, turned his *épicerie* (small neighborhood grocery store) into an empire, thanks to his innate sense for selling and his revolutionary methods.

—CAMILLE MENNESSON

"Félix Potin, Your Go-To Store!"

To remedy the dishonest image of the nineteenth-century shop owner and to restore trust, Félix Potin established rules for his store:

Display fixed prices: this was a new concept and a guarantee of transparency and fairness.

Sell at a loss: he sold the most common products often at cost, or even sometimes a loss, making his profit off luxury products.

Spoil with choice: at Potin, you could find everything from canned goods to household products.

From field to plate

With a goal of profit and better prices, yet without ever neglecting quality, Félix Potin limited the middleman. The arrival of the railway made this task easier. In 1861, not far from La Villette, he built a factory to stock and then make his own products (lump sugar, chocolate, canned items, distilled liquor). A second factory opened in 1881 in Pantin and he also purchased land and vineyards. Operating as a producer, processor, and distributor, he mastered the supply chain from A to Z and was the first to develop a store brand.

The Félix Potin building, rue de Rennes, Paris 6th, circa 1900.

A Félix Potin store and employees, Paris, circa 1900.

Two birds with one stone

As early as 1860, Félix Potin set up a delivery service using cars branded with his name. Delivery—and advertising—guaranteed! From 1898 to 1922, his company sold chocolate bars containing portraits shot by renowned photographers, which customers could collect.

A rapidly changing Paris

The end of the monarchy, the First and Second Empires, and the Industrial Revolution in Paris posed challenges for Félix Potin and Aristide Boucicaut (founder of Le Bon Marché). The emergence of large stores, changes due to a fallen nobility, and an aristocracy in full bloom reflected new buying habits.

Potin evidence still visible today

› **The "poivrière,"** the neo-baroque headquarters, at 103, boulevard de Sébastopol (Paris 2nd).
› **The "bouchon de champagne,"** the art nouveau grocery at 140, rue de Rennes (Paris 6th).
› **The factory**, at 63, rue Archereau (Paris 19th).

CHRONOLOGY

1836
Arrives in Paris where he becomes a clerk at a grocery at 6, rue du Rocher (Paris 8th).

1844
Opening of his first grocery at 28, rue Neuve-Coquenard (now rue Rodier, Paris 9th).

1850
The shop moves to 6, rue du Rocher (Paris 8th).

1860
Appearance of the "Félix Potin" sign at 103, boulevard de Sébastopol (Paris 2nd).

1864
Opening of a second store, at 47, boulevard Malesherbes (Paris 17th), with a tearoom and English products.

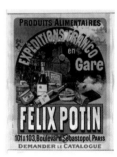

Advertising poster, 1888.

The beginning of the end

Potin died in 1871, leaving behind the largest grocery in Paris. In 1886, the trademark "Félix Potin" was registered and remained under control of the family until 1927. Both World Wars and strained family relations led to the sale of the company in 1958.

SKIP TO
Gainsbourg at the Table, p. 264; Delicatessens, p. 326.

The Cheese Naan

Despite its name, this specialty bread with cheese doesn't originate from India. Paris can boast as its birthplace. —FRANÇOIS-RÉGIS GAUDRY

THE RECIPE

Season : year-round
Difficulty ●●○

MAKES 1 DOZEN NAANS

4 cups (500 g) all-purpose or T55 flour, plus more for dusting

½ cup (125 g) whole natural Bulgarian yogurt

3 tablespoons sunflower oil

1 teaspoon brown sugar

1 teaspoon fine salt

2½ teaspoons or 1 packet active dry yeast

Scant 1 cup (220 ml) cold water

1 container Laughing Cow cheese

2 tablespoons ghee (clarified butter) or butter

Equipment

Food processor

Crêpe pan or small nonstick pan

1 transparent lid

If you don't have a tandoor oven at home, a good skillet will do the trick. Here is a perfect version inspired by a recipe by Bernard Laurance, itself inspired by India-born cookbook author Sandra Salmandjee.

Place the flour, yogurt, oil, brown sugar, salt, yeast, and water into the bowl of a food processor fitted with the bread (kneading) blade. Process for 10 minutes. Transfer the dough to a bowl and cover it with a cloth. Set aside in a warm spot to rise for 1½ to 2 hours; it should double in volume.

Scrape the dough out onto a floured work surface and flatten it to expel air. Divide it into 10 portions. Spread one of the dough portions out with a rolling pin to make a small disk ❶.

Place 2 segments of Laughing Cow cheese in the center and spread them using a knife ❷. Fold the dough toward the center to cover the cheese. Pinch the dough closed to ensure the cheese stays in the center and does not leak out.

Place the pan over high heat. When the pan is hot, place the first naans in the pan, without adding any fat. Cover with a transparent lid to monitor the cooking. The naans will swell and bubble ❸. Cook on each side. Once done, brush with ghee and serve.

Opening of Annapurna restaurant in 1967.

TERMINOLOGY

NAAN

An Indo-Pakistani flatbread made from flour, baked on the hot wall of a tandoor (a terra-cotta oven).

PANEER NAAN

Naan common to northern India, topped with paneer, a homemade cheese made from drained curds.

CHEESE NAAN

A Gallicized version of paneer naan, filled with a spreadable Gruyère-type cheese.

WHO INVENTED IT?

TWO THEORIES

Most likely André Risser, the Alsatian who discovered Indian gastronomy in London and opened the first Indian Restaurant in Paris, Annapurna, in 1967 at 32, rue de Berri (Paris 8th). To attract Parisians, he developed the naan filled with Laughing Cow cheese.

› **Kirane Grover Gupta,** a cook from Bombay, opened the restaurant Indra at 10, rue du Commandant-Rivière (Paris 8th) with her husband in 1976. They offered paneer naan à la carte, which was not popular with customers. They tried several cheese brands and finally chose Laughing Cow in 1978.

TOP · LET'S EAT PARIS! · ADDRESSES

Annapurna
📍 32, rue de Berri, Paris 8th
The classic naan, puffed and buttery.

Sheezan
📍 84, rue du Faubourg-Saint-Denis, Paris 10th
Renowned for its garlic cheese naan.

New Jawad Longchamp
📍 30, rue de Longchamp, Paris 16th
This successful Indian establishment offers an excellent cheese naan.

Kirane's
📍 85, av. des Ternes, Paris 17th
📍 20, rue du Débarcadère, Paris 17th
The naan with Laughing Cow, by Kirane Grover Gupta. A honey version is available at Kavéri, in Asnières-sur-Seine (Hauts-de-Seine).

SKIP TO
India, p. 195.

Not the Same Lemonade!

A tangy drink gives birth to a profession, creating an effervescent period in the capital's history. —JACQUES BRUNEL

The saga of the limonadier

› **Originally,** the profession of *limonadier* included the treatment of all fruits. In his memoirs, Sieur Audiger portrays how, installed at Place du Palais-Royal, he delighted Louis XIV and his court for twelve years with jams, liqueurs, hippocras (mulled wine), and iced waters to drink. His colleagues also offered liqueurs (ratafias) and eventually tea, chocolate, and coffee.

› **In 1676,** in order to sanctify their profession, which competed with vinegar makers and apothecary-grocers, limonadiers joined forces with distillers to form a corporation. Open at night, their shops welcomed (according to the police in 1685) "thieves, tricksters, and other corrupt and contemptable sorts." They leaned against vats where street vendors would fill their cans that they would drink in the streets.

› **In 1725,** the four hundred limonadiers of Paris were part of everyday life in the city, sometimes achieving unique successes. The limonadier of King Louis XV, Sieur Lefèvre, bought in 1766 an urban mansion to house a restaurant that would become famous: the future Lapérouse.

› **At the beginning of the nineteenth century**—with the considerable increase of coffee sales—the term *cafetier* replaced *limonadier* or *vinaigrier*. The term *limonadier* was used until the Revolution to refer to the owner of a drinking establishment.

Lemonade, in the literal sense

Since the Middle Ages, the Jewish community in Cairo enjoyed sweetened lemon juice, which they called qatarmizat. In Europe, some Italian historians claim that lemonade originated in Paris. It was invented in the ninth century by King Louis

A limonadier's oufit, late seventeenth to early eighteenth centuries.

the Pious's cupbearer, or probably around 1630, by the makers of fruit waters. In 1654, the cook La Varenne published the recipe: lots of lemon juice, water, sugar, and sliced lemon. This citrusy water was called lemonade. At the end of the eighteenth century, with the discovery of carbonated water and carbonation methods, lemonade evolved: it was enlivened by adding fizziness.

The female limonadiers of the Palais-Royal

Madame Romain, known as the Belle Limonadière of the Palais-Royal.

› **Madame Romain,** known as the Belle Limonadière, was a figure of the Palais-Royal, the most Parisian of places during the 1800s. Owner of the Café des Mille Colonnes (so named for its mirrors that reflect its thirty columns), at 36, galerie Montpensier, she sat at the cash register on a gilded throne because she was, it is said, "the most beautiful woman in Paris." Quoted by Balzac in *César Birotteau*, the memory of "La Belle Limonadière" would haunt Paris until the middle of the century.

› **Charlotte Reynier Bourette,** known as the Muse Limonadière, welcomed poets and philosophers in her café L'Allemand on rue Croix-des-Petits-Champs (Paris 1st). The author of the play *La Coquette punie* (1769), she knew how to make verses shine:

Of the people of our state, at her counter, the true merit is to be accurate; To examine, morning and night, the recipe she yields; To welcome the good clientele; To let chat the scholars; And as my taste is to write, the credits I carefully note, And often occupy myself with reading The books in which they are shown.

—Joseph de La Porte, *Histoire littéraire des femmes françaises*, 1769

SKIP TO
Chestnuts, Hot Chestnuts!, p. 75; Odd Food Jobs, p. 239.

The Soufflé

It puffs like a chef's hat and is as light as a cloud. Let's shine the spotlight on this inflated specialty. —MARIELLE GAUDRY

THE RECIPE

Season : year-round
Difficulty ● ● ○

SERVES 4

For the Mornay sauce

2 tablespoons unsalted butter

4 tablespoons (30 g) all-purpose flour

1 cup (250 ml) milk

Salt and freshly ground black pepper

¾ cup (80 g) grated Comté cheese

3 large (60 g) egg yolks

For preparing the molds

1 tablespoon butter

1 tablespoon flour

For the egg whites

5 large (180 g) egg whites

1 pinch of salt

1 pinch of Espelette pepper

1 pinch of ground nutmeg

Equipment

Stand mixer

4 round soufflé molds, 3 inches (8 cm) in diameter

Jean-Marie Vétier, chef at Auberge Bressane,* makes this recipe for soufflé au Comté, served in individual portions.

Make the Mornay sauce: Melt the butter in a saucepan and add the flour (this makes a roux). Cook over medium heat for 2 minutes without letting the roux brown. In a separate saucepan, bring the milk to a boil. Pour the hot milk over the roux and stir for 3 to 4 minutes. Season with salt and pepper and add the cheese. Transfer the mixture to the bowl of the stand mixer fitted with the paddle attachment and beat on medium speed until cooled. Beat in the egg yolks one at a time. Reduce the mixer speed and beat until completely cooled. Grease the molds by spreading a thin layer of butter on the inside bottom and sides and dust completely with flour. Tap out any excess flour.

Make the egg whites and bake the soufflés: Beat the egg whites with the pinch of salt to stiff peaks. Carefully incorporate the egg whites into the Mornay sauce. Gently incorporate the pepper and nutmeg. Divide the batter among the four bowls and smooth the tops. Bake for 15 to 20 minutes, or until very puffed and browned on top. Serve immediately.

*Auberge Bressane—16, av. de la Motte-Picquet, Paris 7th.

A PARISIAN LEGEND

› **Between 1722 and 1814:** Several cooks (François Massialot, André Viard, Antoine Beauvilliers) developed the ancestor of the soufflé, which was prepared salty or sweet.

› **1839:** Antonin Carême invents an iced sweet soufflé in honor of Baron James de Rothschild, made with pastry cream and candied fruits.

› **1873:** Alexandre Dumas lists a dozen recipes for the soufflé in his *Grand dictionnaire de cuisine.*

DEFINITION

"Soufflés are made of the chosen base ingredient (fish, meat, etc.) that has been puréed, bound together with egg yolks off the heat, seasoned, and into which is incorporated beaten egg whites to ensure swelling during cooking in a moderate oven."—*Dictionnaire de l'Académie des gastronomes,* 1962

Louis de Funès in *Le Grand Restaurant* by Jacques Besnard, 1966.

"MUSKATNUSS, HERR MÜLLER!"

In *Le Grand Restaurant,* M. Septime (Louis de Funès), manager of an establishment on the Champs-Élysées, is summoned to give the recipe for potato soufflé to a table occupied by the divisional commissioner (Bernard Blier) and his Italian and German colleagues. He states the ingredients in German while a shadow theater draws on him a wig and a mustache resembling Hitler.

TOP · LET'S EAT PARIS! · ADDRESSES

Le Soufflé

📍 *36, rue du Mont-Thabor, Paris 1st.* €€
The cheese soufflé has been the specialty here since 1961, along with its Henri IV version served with a chicken and mushroom sauce.

Champeaux

📍 *12, pas de la Canopée, Paris 1st.* €€
An inverted cheese soufflé is featured as the menu's top choice, followed by a sweet seasonal fruit version.

Le Récamier

📍 *4, rue Juliette-Récamier, Paris 7th.* €€
Offering seven savory recipes (with snails, salmon, and other bases) and as many sweet options (chocolate, Grand Marnier, etc.).

Le Pantruche

📍 *3, rue Victor-Massé, Paris 9th.* €€
The Grand Marnier and salted-butter caramel soufflés are this Parisian bistro's signature desserts.

SKIP TO
Édouard Nignon, p. 124; Antonin Carême, p. 156.

Trucks Pull Up to the Table

In Paris and within Île-de-France, several food establishments offer all guests affordable and hearty dishes originally intended for driving professionals. —ESTELLE LENARTOWICZ

Relais routiers (truck stop diners) over time

> **1934**: Parisian François de Saulieu de la Chomonerie, motivated by the working conditions of truck drivers, creates a newsletter titled *Les Routiers*. Starting in 1937, this *guide rouge* (red guide) lists locations serving simple and hearty meals at moderate prices.

> **1960s**: under the reign of the automobile, the *relais* increase and gain popularity, thanks especially to famous customers including Brigitte Bardot, Jeanne Moreau, and Michel Sardou.

> **2014**: for its 80th anniversary, the guide publishes a special edition for the public. The best of the one thousand or so establishments presented are stamped with a "pan," which acts as a kind of "road badge" of honor.

Map labels:
LE COQ CHANTANT · LA MARMITE · VAL D'OISE · LE MOUFLON D'OR · LES ROUTIERS · YVELINES · PARIS · AU BON ACCUEIL · AUX ROUTIERS · NATIONALE 4 · SEINE-ET-MARNE · LA MANDOLINE · HÔTEL DE LA GARE · ESSONNE · AU PASSÉ RETROUVÉ · LE PETIT PÉRICHOIS

Paris inset: PARIS · LES ROUTIERS · CHEZ LÉON · LES MARCHES · AUX BONS CRUS

LES ROUTIERS

"Feed drivers respectably and be respectful of them."

This is the motto of the one thousand restaurants that comply with AQP regulations (Association of Quality Weighing) in France—good hospitality, impeccable quality, and a fair price. Throughout the year, volunteer inspectors and retired food-loving truck drivers take to the roads to ensure compliance with their charter and to highlight the best locations.

TRUCK STOPS IN PARIS

These locations re-create the "on-the-road" ambience in the capital—but at Parisian prices.

1 AUX BONS CRUS
◦ *54, rue Godefroy-Cavaignac, Paris 11th*

2 LES MARCHES
◦ *5, rue de la Manutention, Paris 16th*

In the heart of the 11th arrondissement and near the Eiffel Tower, these two diners, owned by the Dumant family (Auberge Bressane, Aux Crus de Bourgogne), offer careful cuisine served on red tablecloths that includes stuffed rolls topped with a tomato sauce, curly endive and bacon salad, steak au poivre, and matchstick fries.

3 LES ROUTIERS
◦ *50 bis, rue Marx-Dormoy, Paris 18th*

A diner at heart with a rustic atmosphere, serving endives, kidneys, calf's liver with parsley, and couscous.

4 CHEZ LÉON
◦ *5, rue de l'Isly, Paris 8th*

With its 1950s decor, this has been a family establishment for three generations, serving up roast chicken, roast beef, and a hamburger patty topped with fried egg.

TRUCK STOPS IN ÎLE-DE-FRANCE

Here is an overview of roadside restaurants and their specialties.

5 LE COQ CHANTANT
◦ *D1017, Survilliers (Val d'Oise)*

Portuguese-style roast chicken and moules frites (mussels with fries) are always in season.

6 NATIONALE 4
◦ *av. Louis Renault, ZAC du Val-Bréon, Châtres (Seine-et-Marne)*

A large relais with sixties decor and American drive-in style. Serves up a house-made hamburger and sauced dishes.

7 LE PETIT PÉRICHOIS
◦ *606 RD rond-point de la Brosse, La Brosse-Montceaux (Seine-et-Marne)*

A family business since 1989. Specialties include tête de veau (veal head) with sauce gribiche, pork cheek with spices and honey.

8 LE MOUFLON D'OR
◦ *62, av. de Verdun, RN 3, Trilport (Seine-et-Marne)*

Couscous, the house specialty, is served in a rustic setting.

9 LA MANDOLINE
◦ *Blvd. d'Italie, ZA Paris Sud 1, Lieusaint (Seine-et-Marne)*

Grilled items and sandwiches, served any time.

10 HÔTEL DE LA GARE
◦ *45, av. du Maréchal-Foch, Nangis (Seine-et-Marne)*

A hotel-restaurant. Specialties include calf's head, homemade terrine, beef bourguignon.

11 AUX ROUTIERS
◦ *100, rte. de Fleury, Viry-Châtillon (Essonne)*

The Castilho family regales with Franco-Portuguese specialties served in this large establishment.

12 AU PASSÉ RETROUVÉ
◦ *1, blvd. du Gouverneur-Félix-Eboué, Milly-la-Forêt (Essonne)*

Here it's grilled red meats and fresh fries.

13 AU BON ACCUEIL
◦ *RN 13, Chaufour-lès-Bonnières (Yvelines)*

On the menu are lobster fricassee, leg of lamb with honey, grilled turbot, and Saint-Jacques scallops with citrus.

14 LA MARMITE
◦ *1, rte. de Meulan, Limay (Yvelines)*

Calf's head, couscous, and Portuguese cassoulet are the house specialties.

The Baguette:
A History and Survey

How did this long white loaf, native to the capital, become part of
Parisian daily life and the symbol of France? —LOÏC BIENASSIS

The first white bread, August 24, 1944.

The Parisian tradition of long loaves

1767
Paul-Jacques Malouin states, in *Description et details des arts du meunier, du vermicelier et du boulenger,* "In the past, we made more round breads than long breads, but today it's the opposite, because we like the crust better." Elongated but massive breads, such as the 4-pound (1.8 kg) bread measuring 21 to 24 inches (54 to 60 cm) long, were the most popular in Paris.

1834
According to S. Vaury in the *Guide du boulanger indiquant les moyens à prendre pour bien fabriquer le pain,* the shape of luxury breads varies infinitely. It lists many elongated breads, but generally short ones. Vaury speaks of flat flute shapes, 8 inches (20 cm) long, pointed at the end, and scored with a small knife on top. These notches, called *grignes* today, are one of the traits of the baguette.

1858
The sociologist Frédéric Le Play counts seventy kinds of Parisian fancy breads of various shapes and sizes, the price of which was liberally set. The "wine merchant" bread was 43 inches (1.10 m) long, weighing 2¼ pounds (1 kg). It was likely there were loaves whose proportions were close to those of today's baguette.

1874
In an article on bread consumption in Paris, the economist Armand Husson writes: "The Parisian consumer's taste for delicate bread is not only about bread made using the most beautiful flours; consumers also require the luxury of elongated or flat bread, offering larger surfaces for an appealing crust."

The evolution of the baguette

LATE NINETEENTH CENTURY
Various technical developments have made the baguette as we know it now: the use of pure, very white flour, obtained by grinding by cylinder rather than the grinding wheel, and the use of "direct" fermentation—i.e., without the need for any preparation of the ferment—thanks to the use of dry yeast diluted in the water used to make the bread.

1904
The first known occurrence of the term *baguette* in *Manuel du boulanger et de pâtisserie-boulangère* by Étienne Favrais. The author mentions in particular "so-called baguettes of 200 grams [7 ounces]." A plate presents two baguettes, one without scores, and the other "cut," whose "length varies according to the weight and taste of the customer."

INTERWAR PERIOD
The term *baguette* becomes commonplace, but a certain lack of standard still reigns. Baguettes were loaves of 100, 300, or even 700 grams (3½, 11, 25 ounces), as appears in *Le Blé, la Farine et le Pain* (1935) by Dr. Alfred Gottschalk.

SEPTEMBER 1956
The section "Retail prices in Paris and the Paris agglomeration" of the very formal *Bulletin mensuel de statistique* includes the *pain baguette* of 300 grams (11 ounces). At this time, the baguette officially becomes a staple of Parisian food. The conquest of the baguette in other parts of France will happen gradually. According to a 1972 study, the baguette represents:

→ 59% of bread purchased in Paris.

→ 72% in Marseille.

→ 60% in Saint-Étienne.

→ 67% in the countryside around Bouches-du-Rhône.

Other POVs

Starting in the nineteenth century in other countries, the (justified) rapprochement between France and long loaves was forged. This cliché developed oversees was already established when baguettes finally became common in Paris. Among the many examples is an article published in the *San Francisco Examiner* in June 1928: "*These picturesque long sticks of bread that every traveler associates with the Paris scene.*"

The baguette in Hollywood

As early as the 1930s, the baguette made notable appearances in American films celebrating the City of Light:

› In the opening scene of *Love Me Tonight* (Rouben Mamoulian, 1932), Maurice Chevalier sings a hymn to Paris ("That's the Song of Paree") while passing a baker loaded with long loaves.

› In the famous restaurant scene in *Ninotchka* (Ernst Lubitsch, 1939), Greta Garbo learns to laugh with baguettes in the background.

› The baguette plays an extra in *An American in Paris* (Vincente Minnelli, 1951), *Gigot* (Gene Kelly, 1962), and *Irma La Douce* (Billy Wilder, 1963).

Mirror effect

The French will eventually embrace this stereotype, especially starting during the second half of the 1960s.

Here are a few examples:

- **1952**

  Willy Ronis, *Le Petit Parisien*. This photograph illustrates the story of a Parisian who, after fifteen years in New York, returns to his hometown and highlights its uniqueness: "Among all these unique things was of course the large Parisian bread," writes Ronis. The loaf of bread was almost as big as the little boy who carried it under his arm.

- **1972**

  Sempé draws a man walking his dog, standing on the terrace of a café. He speaks to a gentleman, beret on his head, cigarette butt hanging from his lips, baguette under his arm, and says in a worrisome tone: "We are becoming more and more Americanized . . ."

- **1975**

  Claude Sarraute, in a paper entitled "Des Français d'opérette" (*Le Monde*), is aggravated by a television report devoted to a small provincial town. "The Frenchman as we see him abroad. The Frenchman at the bistro, the Frenchman at the market, his beret tipped to one side, and his hand on his heart, the Frenchman laughing and imbibing. The baguette and the Beaujolais."

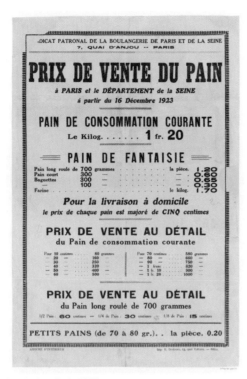

Bread prices, Paris, 1923.

Boulangerie Lavenir, 103, rue du Faubourg-du-Temple, Paris 3rd.

Manuel du boulanger et de pâtisserie-boulangère by E. Favrais, 1904.

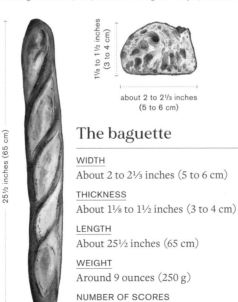

1⅛ to 1½ inches (3 to 4 cm)

about 2 to 2⅓ inches (5 to 6 cm)

25½ inches (65 cm)

The baguette

WIDTH
About 2 to 2⅓ inches (5 to 6 cm)

THICKNESS
About 1⅛ to 1½ inches (3 to 4 cm)

LENGTH
About 25½ inches (65 cm)

WEIGHT
Around 9 ounces (250 g)

NUMBER OF SCORES
5

Crumbling myths

There are a few crazy—and poorly supported—theories regarding the origin of the baguette, which is claimed to have been invented:

› by the bakers of Napoléon I to facilitate the transport of bread in the vests of soldiers' uniforms.

› by the Viennese, who introduced it to Paris.

› at the request of Fulgence Bienvenüe, the "father" of the Paris metro, to create a bread that was easy to break apart without using a knife, thus avoiding introducing such "weapons" into the metro and initiating bloody fights between workers.

Birth of the traditional baguette

In the 1980s, many voices were raised against the supremacy of a white-flour baguette that was undercooked, tasteless, and lacking crispness. Thus, the baguette came to embody an artisanal know-how specific to France. In 1993, a law stipulated that, to be sold under the name "pain de tradition française," a bread must never have been frozen, nor contain additives. The law's text is not specific to the baguette but, for the consumer, this was the birth of the *baguette tradition*.

SKIP TO
Paris Loves Bread, p. 158; Bakeries, p. 308.

THE BEST "BAGUETTES TRADITION" IN PARIS

 Tout autour du pain

📍 *134, rue de Turenne, Paris 3rd*

Ingredients: T65 flour from Moulins Bourgeois (Seine-et-Marne), yeast, water, salt.
Fermentation: 24 hours.
Texture and taste: tight crumb, a light crispiness with a nice flavor of grains.

 Boulangerie de la Tour

📍 *2, rue du Cardinal-Lemoine, Paris 5th*

Ingredients: T65 flour from Moulins Familiales (Île-de-France), liquid starter, yeast, water, untreated sea salt from Camargue.
Fermentation: 20 hours.
Texture and taste: off-white and dense crumb. Crisp with a slight acidity.

 Des Gâteaux et du Pain

📍 *89, rue du Bac, Paris 7th*
📍 *63, blvd. Pasteur, Paris 15th*

Ingredients: organic T65 flour from Moulins Viron (Eure-et-Loir), yeast, water, sea salt from Noirmoutier.
Fermentation: 48 hours minimum.
Texture and taste: soft crumb, perfectly honeycombed, slightly caramelized crust.

 Maison Louvard

📍 *11, rue de Châteaudun, Paris 9th*

Ingredients: T65 "French tradition" flour from Moulin Paul Dupuis (Seine-Maritime), liquid starter, yeast, water, sea salt from Guérande.
Fermentation: 24 hours.
Texture and taste: white and light crumb, crispy crust with nicely executed scores.

 Union Boulangerie

📍 *2, rue Bleue, Paris 9th*

Ingredients: T65 Label Rouge (Red Label) flour from Moulins de Chars (Val-d'Oise), liquid starter, yeast, water, sea salt from Guérande.
Fermentation: 15 to 18 hours.
Texture and taste: dense, but well-leavened crumb, thin and crispy crust, slight acidity.

 Farine&O

📍 *153, rue du Faubourg-Saint-Antoine, Paris 11th + 3 locations*

Ingredients: T65 "French tradition" flour Label Rouge (Red Label) from Moulins Bourgeois (Seine-et-Marne), liquid starter, yeast, water, salt.
Fermentation: 15 to 24 hours.
Texture and taste: honeycombed crumb, a good crispiness, the touch of salt makes the difference.

 Graine

📍 *54, rue Oberkampf, Paris 11th*

Ingredients: T65 Label Rouge (Red Label) flour from Moulins Foricher (Val-d'Oise), liquid starter, yeast, water, sea salt from Camargue.
Fermentation: 12 to 24 hours.
Texture and taste: airy crumb with a beautiful texture and crispiness.

 La Pâtisserie Cyril Lignac

📍 *24, rue Paul-Bert, Paris 11th + 2 locations*

Ingredients: T55 "French tradition" flour from Moulins Viron (Eure-et-Loir), yeast, water, salt.
Fermentation: 24 to 72 hours.
Texture and taste: dense and off-white crumb. Crust with beautiful scores.

 Utopie

📍 *20, rue Jean-Pierre-Timbaud, Paris 11th*

Ingredients: T65 flour from Moulins de Chars (Val-d'Oise), liquid starter, water, salt.
Fermentation: 24 to 48 hours.
Texture and taste: off-white crumb, beautiful mastery of baking for a subtle crispiness.

 Léonie

📍 *15, av. de Trudaine, Paris 9th*
📍 *96, rue de Lévis, Paris 17th*

Ingredients: T55 "French tradition" flour from Moulins Viron (Eure-et-Loir), liquid starter, yeast, water, sea salt from Guérande.
Fermentation: 72 hours.
Texture and taste: very light crumb thanks to a well-developed honeycomb. Crisp crust with a slight caramelized taste.

 The French Bastards

📍 *35, pl. Saint-Ferdinand, Paris 17th + 2 locations*

Ingredients: T55 CRC Label Rouge (Red Label) flour from Moulin Paul Dupuis (Seine-Maritime), liquid starter, water, salt.
Fermentation: 48 hours.
Texture and taste: light crumb, beautiful texture, caramelized crust with a good baked flavor.

 Les Saveurs de Pierre Demours, Maison Julien

📍 *13, rue Pierre-Demours, Paris 17th*

Ingredients: organic T80 flour from Moulins Familiales (Île-de-France), liquid starter, yeast, water, salt.
Fermentation: 12 hours.
Texture and taste: honeycombed crumb and crisp baguette.

 Maison Lohézic

📍 *143, rue de Courcelles, Paris 17th*

Ingredients: gluten-free T55 and T65 flour from Moulins Bourgeois (Seine-et-Marne), liquid sourdough starter, yeast, water, sea salt from the Midi.
Fermentation: 24 to 48 hours.
Texture and taste: off-white crumb, beautiful crisp crust with nicely pointed ends.

 Pain pain

📍 *88, rue des Martyrs, Paris 18th*

Ingredients: gluten-free T65 "French tradition" flour from Moulins Bourgeois (Seine-et-Marne), yeast, water, salt.
Fermentation: 12 to 24 hours.
Texture and taste: long and thin baguette with a beautiful honeycomb and good crispness.

 Benoît Castel

📍 *150, rue de Ménilmontant, Paris 20th + 2 locations*

Ingredients: organic T65 "French tradition" flour from Moulins Bourgeois (Seine-et-Marne), liquid starter, yeast, water, salt.
Fermentation: 12 hours.
Texture and taste: good honeycomb, soft crumb, crisp crust.

 Boulangerie Au 140

📍 *140, rue de Belleville, Paris 20th*

Ingredients: T65 flour from Moulins Bourgeois (Seine-et-Marne), stiff starter, yeast, water, sea salt from Guérande.
Fermentation: 24 hours.
Texture and taste: beautifully honeycombed crumb, a slight acidity and good crust.

 Chez Meunier

📍 *2, rue Charles-Graindorge, Bagnolet (Seine-Saint-Denis) + 10 locations*

Ingredients: organic T60 flour from Moulins Bourgeois (Seine-et-Marne), stiff starter, water, sea salt from Guérande.
Fermentation: 24 hours.
Texture and taste: honeycombed crumb, crisp crust lightly caramelized from baking.

Street Food in the Middle Ages

For food on the go, the Parisian from the thirteenth to fifteenth centuries was spoiled with choices. Here is a short tour of the "fast-food restaurants" of the time. —LOÏC BIENASSIS

Parisians at the end of the Middle Ages bought food from butchers, roasters, chicken coops, vinegar-sauce-mustard makers, fishmongers, scrap-food dealers, and various food traders. But some craftsmen were favored more than others.

The oubloyeurs

Their specialty, the oublie (a type of wafer), was a light pastry baked between two irons that were placed into a fire. It was difficult to determine the difference between the large oublies, the "on-the-go" oublies, and those for supplication, which were a heavier and thicker sort of waffle.

The boulangers

There were different kinds of bread among the *talemeliers*, who were the ancestors of *boulangers* (bakers), a name that would be imposed during the fifteenth century:
› **Fouaces:** white breads enriched with eggs and/or butter that were quite expensive.
› **Échaudé** (pastries poached, then baked) or **flamiches** (flat cakes with fromage blanc), which were more affordable.
› **Meat and fish pâtés.**

The pâtissiers

The pastry chef (*pâtissier*) was the perfect purveyor for "fast food." There was a wide range of baked dough preparations: meat and fish pâtés, tarts, veal and pork hand pies, flans, talmouses (a pastry shell with cheese), échaudés, ratons (small tarts made with fromage blanc), casse-museaux (a very moist and crumbly cake), and more.

Crier of Paris: the pastry chef.

The little pâtés of Paris

Cookbooks continue the recipe for these little pâtés, the perfect example of handheld foods.

"Take from the loin the center, and make soft cuts, and chopped fat on top. And to make the sauce, bake well some pain noir [brown loaf], and then soak in verjus and vinegar and pass through a muslin cloth, and the spices that belong are: ginger, cloves, long pepper, grains of paradise, nutmeg, by equal portion, except that the clove overcomes the other spices; and let the sauce be boiled in a pan of iron, and, when the pâté is cooked, take the fat . . . and, therefore, put the sauce in it, and boil . . . in the oven."

—Taillevent, *Viandier*, fifteenth century

The criers of Paris

Among the countless peddlers in Paris during the Middle Ages, there were some specialized merchants who sometimes had a mobile oven and whose shouts filled the narrow streets of the city. Starting from the thirteenth century, songs passed down these cries through generations:

"I have cherries, or verjus. And the juice of leeks. And there are eggs, now hot leek pâtés there are, hot cakes."

—Guillaume de La Villeneuve, *Crieries de Paris*, circa 1265

SKIP TO
Chestnuts, Hot Chestnuts!, p. 75; The Pâté Pantin, p. 127; The Kebab, p. 134, The Talmouse of Saint-Denis, p. 159.

> ## Oublies
>
> There is no recipe for oublies from the Middle Ages. This one, a condensed version, dates from the early seventeenth century.
>
> "For oublies, a fine flour soaked in water, wine, eggs, sugar, or honey. They are to be cooked between two hot irons, but before removing them, they are all folded hot on a round iron. Some *levain* [starter] can be added to it."
>
> —Étienne Servrain and Jean Antoine Huguetan, *Trésor de santé ou ménage de la vie humaine*, 1607
>
>
>
> Round iron to make oublies.

Oublies seller.

LE RELAIS DE VENISE

This meat-centric bistro became one of the best restaurant success stories in Paris.
— FRANÇOIS-RÉGIS GAUDRY

MAISON PARISIENNE
271, BLVD. PEREIRE,
17TH ARR.

THE RECIPE FOR THE "MYSTERY" SAUCE

Season: year-round
Difficulty ● ○ ○

SERVES 2

2 shallots
4 stems fresh thyme
2 stems rosemary
2 sprigs parsley
4 sprigs chervil
4 sprigs tarragon
5 tablespoons (70 g) unsalted butter

Salt and freshly ground black pepper
1 teaspoon crème fraîche
1 teaspoon Dijon mustard
Freshly squeezed lemon juice from ¼ lemon
2 teaspoons water
Grilled meats, for serving

Equipment
Blender

Fat, umami, and a delicate seasoning is why this sauce is so addictive. The recipe is a carefully kept secret by the family and is often believed to contain chicken liver. This version—without chicken liver—is a true success.

Chop the shallots. Wash all the herbs. Remove the leaves from the thyme and rosemary stems. Place the thyme and rosemary leaves, chopped shallots, and remaining herbs in a saucepan with the butter over low heat. Season with salt and pepper and cook for 5 minutes; the mixture should only become translucent, not browned.

In a bowl, combine the crème fraîche and mustard. Pour the mixture into the saucepan. Add the lemon juice and water. Stir to combine. Adjust the seasoning, if needed, and keep warm. Serve over grilled meats.

A little history

In 1959, Paul Gineste de Saurs, a winemaker, sought to diversify his business. After a friend revealed the secret of a particularly successful sauce, de Saurs opened a restaurant in Porte Maillot with a unique formula: steak frites (steak and fries) and a walnut salad, all at a moderate price. The original name, emphasizing "entrecôte" (steak), remains above the restaurant.

THE FOUNDER'S THREE CHILDREN:

› **Hélène** participated in the openings of Le Relais de Venise in London, Mexico City, and New York.

› **Marie-Paule** founded Le Relais de l'Entrecôte in Geneva in 1982, then three in Paris and one in Zurich.

› **Henri** created L'Entrecôte in Toulouse in 1962 and opened restaurants in Bordeaux, Montpellier, Nantes, Lyon, and Barcelona.

All the establishments in these three groups are based on the same concept, and they still belong to the same family.

Le Relais de Venise®

The 3 hallmarks

THE FAMOUS STEAK FRITES

This dish has remained unchanged since 1959. It is composed of **a contre-filet of beef (strip loin)**, 6⅓ ounces (180 g), served precut, the customer chooses their level of doneness; **a secret khaki green-colored sauce**; **shoestring fries**, peeled and cut by hand, about 1 pound (450 g) per person; **a green salad with walnuts**.

THE DESSERTS

Chocolate profiteroles, fruit tarts, and vacherins (a meringue dessert) are the bestsellers.

THE SERVERS

Smiling and impeccably dressed female servers in a black dress, apron, and white collar. They serve (and re-serve) meat and fries on silver trays set on candle warmers.

Locations

Open every day of the year at 11:30 a.m. and 7 p.m. (except Good Friday, Christmas, and New Year's Day), no reservation required.

Le Relais de Venise
Steak frites menu: €28
📍 *271, blvd. Pereire, Paris 17th*

La Baguette du Relais
serves the famous *steak frites* and its sauce on a baguette bun.
📍 *10, rue des Archives, Paris 4th*

Le Relais de l'Entrecôte is based on the same formula as Le Relais de Venise.
Steak frites menu: €27.50
📍 *101, blvd. du Montparnasse, Paris 6th*
📍 *20, rue Saint-Benoît, Paris 6th*
📍 *15, rue Marbeuf, Paris 8th*

La Tête de Veau
Calf's Head

This is what happens when a guillotined king gives birth to a bistro classic: the tête de veau. —SACHA LOMNITZ

THE RECIPE

Season: fall to winter
Difficulty ● ● ○

SERVES 6

1 flattened, boneless, and very white calf's head, rolled with the tongue

1 lemon

1 calf's brain

For the aromatics

(These should be abundant, with plenty of pepper.)

3 carrots

3 leeks

2 heads garlic

5 stalks celery

1 bunch flat-leaf parsley

4 onions, studded with a few cloves

White and black peppercorns

A mixture of 3½ tablespoons lemon juice, 1¼ cups (300 ml) water, 1¼ cups (150 g) all-purpose flour

Coarse salt

For the filling

3 carrots

2 leeks

10 potatoes

Wine vinegar

Salt and black peppercorns

1 bouquet garni (thyme, bay leaf)

Sauce ravigote

7 ounces (200 g) capers

7 ounces (200 g) cornichons

12 hard-boiled eggs

4 cups (1 L) peanut oil

2 cups (500 ml) sherry vinegar

4 shallots

3½ ounces (100 g) flat-leaf parsley

3½ ounces (100 g) chives

Jean-Pierre Vigato's recipe for tête de veau made waves at restaurant Apicius. Today, it is served at Disciples,* the establishment he owns with chef Romain Dubuisson.

Cut the calf's head in half ❶ and immerse it in a large pot of cold water. Cover and bring to a boil. Reduce to a simmer and let cook for 5 minutes. Drain and rinse. Discard the water.

Rub the entire surface of the head with the flat side of a lemon half. Using a knife, remove all parts of the head that are too fatty and those with small bumps along the cheeks. Remove the string, and cut the head into pieces measuring about 3 by 2 inches (8 by 5 cm).

Place all the pieces of the head and the tongue in a pot filled with water and bring to a boil; skim off any impurities, if necessary. Add the aromatics and the lemon-water-flour mixture, which will allow the head to remain white ❷. Cover with a cloth and cook for about 1½ hours at a simmer. After 1 hour, taste a piece of the meat to check the doneness; the head should not be too firm or too soft.

Once cooked, set the meat aside, covered in a little broth. Reserve the rest of the broth.

Make the filling: Peel and cook the carrots, leeks, and potatoes in the reserved broth.

Prepare the calf's brain: Soak the brain for 1 hour in ice water. "Peel" the brain ❸ by removing all the membranes that contain blood. Immerse the brain in a pot of cold water with a little wine vinegar, salt, peppercorns, and the bouquet garni. Bring to a boil. As soon as the brain rises to the surface, take it out using a slotted spoon or skimmer and set aside on a cloth to drain.

Make the sauce ravigote: Roughly chop the capers and cornichons. Chop the hard-boiled eggs into large pieces, to maintain some texture. Add the oil ❹, sherry vinegar, and the chopped shallots, parsley, and chives. Stir well to combine.

Carefully arrange all the elements on a large serving platter, keeping the sauce and brains separate.

*Disciples—136, blvd. Murat, Paris 16th.

JANUARY TWENTY-FIRST IS FOR TÊTE DE VEAU!

On January 21, 1793, King Louis XVI was beheaded at the Place de la Révolution, now the Place de la Concorde, in Paris. This event marked the end of the absolute monarchy by divine right. A year later, the pamphleteer Romeau invited all citizens to celebrate this day around a pig's head since Louis XVI was often caricatured as a pig-king.

For reasons unknown, the calf's head replaced the pig's head in 1848 with the formation of the Second Republic. Flaubert documented the origin of this in a dialogue in his novel *L'Éducation sentimentale* (1869) in which he explains that this tradition was borrowed from a custom of the English who, since 1649, had celebrated the beheading of their King Charles I (January 30) by serving a calf's head, the symbol of the king.

FROM NORTH TO SOUTH OF PARIS

Today, on January 21, when those nostalgic for the monarchy celebrate a mass in the Basilica of the Kings of France in Saint-Denis, you can assert your soul as a sansculotte by joining a group of cheerful sorts who enjoy calf's head just nearby. To enjoy it on any other day, note the banquets and celebrations program of the Rungis-Paris Brotherhood of the Calf's Head (Confrérie des Vitellicéphalophages).

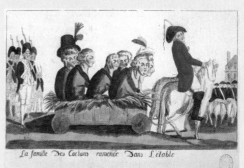

La famille Des Cochons ramenée Dans L'étable

The family of pigs brought back to the stable (caricature of the return of the royal family to Paris after the escape to Varennes).

PARIGOT, TÊTE DE VEAU!

At the end of the nineteenth century, the Parisian, considered a vulgar and grouchy city dweller who often jabbered in slang, became known as a "Parigot" (silent *t*) by the people of France's provinces, to rhyme with *veau* (veal) and its *tête* (head), a morsel considered of little value to the butcher! President Jacques Chirac, a Parigot living in the capital's chic districts, constantly praised the merits of the tête de veau.

SKIP TO
Les Halles: The Belly of Paris, p. 113.

TIPS AND VARIATIONS*

Cook the calf's head cut into pieces with the whole tongue, vegetables, bouquet garni, grilled onion studded with cloves, coarse salt, and peppercorns. Accompany the calf's head with a mustardy and vinegary mayonnaise-based sauce to which finely chopped shallots and chives have been added.

*Marc Lomnitz, restaurateur and author of this page.

TOP
LET'S EAT PARIS!
ADDRESSES

Le Mesturet
⚲ *77, rue de Richelieu, Paris 2nd.* €€
Alain Fontaine's bistro offers tête de veau rolled with the tongue with the breaded brains and a sauce gribiche.

Vaudeville
⚲ *29, rue Vivienne, Paris 2nd.* €€
The legendary brasserie near the Bourse serves "vaudeville-style" tête de veau (a secret recipe) with a sauce gribiche and cooked vegetables.

La Ravigote
⚲ *36, rue Mathurin Regnier, Paris 15th.* €€
The tongue, cheek, and hide are cooked in broth and served with a sauce ravigote and cooked vegetables.

Au Veau Qui Tète
⚲ *2, rue de l'Aubrac, Rungis (Val-de-Marne).* €€
Located in the tripe market pavilion, this institution in Rungis serves, from midnight to 4 p.m., a rolled head with a sauce ravigote.

LA CLOSERIE DES LILAS

A former refuge for writers and the broken souls of the Left Bank, this historic establishment on boulevard du Montparnasse impresses with its bucolic terrace and retro interior. —ESTELLE LENARTOWICZ

MAISON PARISIENNE
171, BLVD. DU
MONTPARNASSE,
6TH ARR.

La Closerie des Lilas

⊙ TO SEE

The incredible curves of the mosaic floor, which lead to the art deco restrooms with mahogany doors, flower-shaped chandeliers, and flamboyantly colored glazed tiles.

The piano bar, with whiskey bottles lit from the back and the Hemingway plaque on the counter. It was at La Closerie that the writer wrote *The Sun Also Rises* (1926).

The bright red leather banquettes and the graphically patterned windows at which Alfred Jarry shot a revolver (a blank) one evening before declaring, in the direction of a young woman: "Now that the ice is broken, let's talk!"

🍴 TO TRY

Seafood, with an impressive selection of oyster platters.

The classic and well-executed **leeks vinaigrette, steak tartare-frites, and pike quenelles.**

The abundant menu of house **cocktails.**

Headed to the ball

Located on the gardens of a former Carthusian monastery on rue d'Enfer, this now-famous restaurant was initially just a modest *guinguette*, serving as a stop for travelers on the road to Orléans. In the nineteenth century, François Bullier, the owner of a brasserie on the opposite side of the boulevard, used it to host the before-and-after gatherings of his Bullier ball, a not-to-be-missed rendezvous of the dancing Parisian smart set. The thousand feet of lilacs (*lilas*) he planted there, and the title of a successful play at the time—*La Closerie des genêts* by Frédéric Soulié—inspired the name of the café, founded in 1847.

Inside/Outside

Retro elegance reigns in its interior, and its exterior charm is thanks to its countryside-like terrace where the tall arbor—replaced by a large veranda—enticed strollers to stop under the shade of the plane trees. It was a touch of green cut off from the hustle and bustle of the boulevard—La Closerie calms and inspires.

A respite for the literary world

› Painters were well represented here, thanks to Ingres, Monet, Renoir, Modigliani, Picasso, and Sonia and Robert Delaunay who would arrive, but it was the literary world that, above all others, camped out on its leather banquettes, including Zola, Verlaine, Apollinaire, Jarry, the Goncourt brothers, Breton, Sartre, and Aragon.
› At the beginning of the twentieth century, poet Paul Fort organized his "literary Tuesdays" here between two chess games with Lenin, another regular. The English, including Samuel Beckett, and the American intelligentsia also liked to imbibe here. It was on this terrace where F. Scott Fitzgerald had Henry Miller read the manuscript of *The Great Gatsby.*
› Since 2007, the Prix de la Closerie des Lilas, whose jury is all women, awards a literary prize each year to a female French-language novelist.

SKIP TO
Paris: A Moveable Feast, p. 244; The Taste of the Prix Goncourt, p. 248; Microbreweries, p. 336.

The History of the Belly of the Capital

Created from the need to replace the medieval markets of Palu and Grève, Les Halles de Paris continues to evolve to this day.

—STÉPHANE SOLIER

Detail of the map of Paris, called Truschet et Hoyau, circa 1550.

Pillers des Halles, rue de la Tonnellerie, Charles Marville, 1851.

L'Assassinat de Baltard, Jean-Claude Gautrand, 1971.

TWELFTH–EIGHTEENTH CENTURIES: BIRTH AND EVOLUTION

AROUND 1135

On the site of the current Les Halles district, Louis VI (Louis the Fat) drains the Paris marshes. He sets up, at the crossroads of three major traffic cross points—Saint-Denis, Montmartre, and Saint-Honoré—an open-air market called Champeaux.

1181–1183

Philippe Auguste brings the market of Saint-Ladre from the northern suburbs to the market area. Two wooden buildings are erected for clothiers and weavers, and the covered and enclosed market takes the name of "Halles" (from the Low Franconian *halla*, meaning "vast covered site"). In 1190, the first food shops are established here.

THIRTEENTH CENTURY

Saint Louis enlarges Les Halles with three buildings, two of which, in 1269, are dedicated to fish. He sets up "selling jurors" (what would become "agents"), "unloading jurors" (the future *forts* of Les Halles), "prud'hommes jurors" (the veterinarians), and authorized the common people to sell retail around Les Halles.

1543–1572

Francis I and his son Henry II create a vast square surrounded by columned buildings according to an organized plan. Shopping at the markets becomes a daily routine, regulated to avoid famine, and leads to a market of breads, cheeses, eggs, and butter.

EIGHTEENTH CENTURY: THE REVOLUTION OF LES HALLES

1763

The Halle au Blé (wheat exchange) is built.

1776

Turgot replaces the "selling jurors" with official intermediaries, the *facteurs*.

1788

A large herb and vegetable market is created on the site of the Holy Innocents' Cemetery.

NINETEENTH CENTURY: MODERNIZATION

Napoléon I established slaughterhouses on the outskirts of the city and undertook a cohesive reorganization of the covered markets by building a central hall in 1811, but his defeat delayed the project.

1818

The meat market hall is transferred to the new market of Prouvaires on the outskirts of Les Halles.

1822–1823

A fish market and a butter, egg, and cheese market are created.

1841–1854

Several projects to redevelop Les Halles were proposed, but it was the architect Baltard whose design was chosen in 1848. Under the impetus of Napoléon III, Baltard changed his original plan for stone buildings to iron and cast iron.

1857–1874

The first pavilions were opened and inaugurated by the emperor in 1857, with the others following in 1858, 1860, 1869, and 1874, and the last two in 1936. In 1896, a law, which was valid until 1953, regulated the market of Les Halles: wholesale and retail markets, authorized agents, private or auction sales, and Le Carreau (an open-air market) reserved for farmers and growers.

TWENTIETH CENTURY: THE TIME OF THE MOVE

1900–1949

Fruit and vegetables sold at Les Halles increase from 17,000 to 678,000 tons. In 1919, the retail trade was removed.

1950s

As traffic difficulties worsen, the decision to move Les Halles resulted in the new location in Rungis (Val-de-Marne) in 1959.

FEBRUARY 28– MARCH 2, 1969

What is described as the "move of the century" of Les Halles de Paris takes place.

1970–1973

Les Halles structures are demolished.

END OF TWENTIETH– BEGINNING OF TWENTY-FIRST CENTURIES: POST LES HALLES

1979

The Forum des Halles, by architect Claude Vasconi, is opened.

1980s

The Forum, improved by the addition of an RER station, becomes a shopping and leisure hub.

2016

The new Forum, enhanced by the Canopy by Patrick Berger and Jacques Anziutti, is inaugurated.

SKIP TO
Markets, p. 12; Covered Markets, p. 339.

The Kitchens of Les Halles

Not just a market, Les Halles was surrounded by kitchens that served the workers and patrons of Les Halles.

A nourishing heart

Les Halles had to meet the appetites of the five thousand workers of all kinds who had been working there since 1 a.m., not to mention the customers who walked the aisles. Dozens of restaurants and cafés in the neighborhood, open twenty-four hours a day, satisfied their cravings.

They fed our writers . . .

CHEZ BARATTE

📍 *8–10, rue Berger* CLOSED

"The custom is to ask for Ostend oysters with a small stew of shallots chopped in vinegar and peppered, which are lightly sprinkled on the oysters. Then there is the onion soup, which is executed admirably at Les Halles, and on which the aged, grated Parmesan is sprinkled."

—Gérard de Nerval, *La Bohème galante*, 1852

LE CABARET CORINTHE

📍 *Rue Mondétour* CLOSED

"Hucheloup invented an excellent thing that was only eaten at home, it was stuffed carp that he called carpe au gras."

—Victor Hugo, *Les Misérables*, 1862

A BRASSERIE IN LES HALLES

"They found a taxi to Les Halles, dined in a brasserie open all night. . . . Together they enjoyed a royal sauerkraut, with artisanal Montbéliard sausages."

—Michel Houellebecq, *Les Particules élémentaires*, 1998

. . . and our imaginations

LE COCHON À L'OREILLE

📍 *15, rue Montmartre* OPEN

Beautiful meat dishes or a gratin in a lively decor of Les Halles dating to 1914, decorated with ceramic-tile murals hand-painted by Boulenger.

L'ESCARGOT MONTORGUEIL

📍 *38, rue Montorgueil* OPEN

Opened in 1832 and taken over in 1919 by André Terrail (La Tour d'Argent), the restaurant serves up the aphrodisiac virtues of these gastropods, in a listed Second Empire setting.

LE PETIT BOUILLON PHARAMOND

📍 *24, rue de la Grande-Truanderie* OPEN

This large half-timbered Norman-style building combines the beauty of art nouveau decor, in part designed by Picard, with the serving of Caen-style tripe.

LA TOUR DE MONTLHÉRY–CHEZ DENISE

📍 *5, rue des Prouvaires* OPEN

Visitors can admire the Belle Époque cash register on the counter and the old coffee machine. Hearty plates and leeks vinaigrette, pot-au-feu, haricot du mouton (diced lamb ragout).

LA POULE AU POT

📍 *9, rue Vauvilliers* OPEN

Founded in 1935, this popular night-owl bistro was taken over by Jean-François and Élodie Piège in 2018. Original items include the bar, the stone walls, and the golden mosaic columns.

AND ALSO

Au Chien Qui Fume
📍 *33, rue du Pont-Neuf*
Le Louchébem
📍 *31, rue Berger, corner 10, rue des Prouvaires*
Au Père Tranquille
📍 *16, rue Pierre-Lescot*
À La Cloche des Halles
📍 *28, rue Coquillière*
Au Pied de Cochon
📍 *6, rue Coquillière*

They devour themselves on the big screen

VOICI LE TEMPS DES ASSASSINS, JEAN DUVIVIER (1956)

Immerse yourself in the steaming pots of André Chatelin's (Jean Gabin) bistro Au Rendez-vous des Innocents, in the heart of Les Halles. On the menu: pickled herring and potato salad with sauce gribiche.

PARIS BLUES, MARTIN RITT (1961)

A scene at the neighborhood bar, Les Halles at night, where the couple Eddie and Connie (Sidney Poitier and Diahann Carroll) fight with the strings of Gruyère cheese in the onion soup.

IRMA LA DOUCE, BILLY WILDER (1963)

During the tribulations of Nestor Patou (Jack Lemmon) in which the ingenuous police officer assigned to Les Halles is in love with the beautiful and lively Irma la Douce (Shirley MacLaine), the bistro of Moustache (Lou Jacobi) serves its not-to-be-missed and delightful onion soups for only fifteen francs.

Robert Doisneau, *Le Bouillon de la rue Tiquetonne*, 1953.

Detail of the murals from Cochon à l'Oreille, Maison Boulenger (ceramists), circa 1914.

Jean Gabin (André Chatelin) and his bistro in Les Halles in Jean Duvivier's *Voici le temps des assassins* (1956).

SKIP TO
When Hollywood Dines in Paris, p. 286.

Small Trades and Lifestyle

Baltard's Les Halles evoked nonstop activity, an abundance of goods, and a multitude of small trades, some of which were quite unusual.

Forts des Halles, anonymous postcard, circa 1900.

Henri Lomnitz at the wholesale meats pavilion, 1958.

In Les Halles

In Les Halles

› *Facteurs* (who became "agents" in 1896 or "wholesalers-brokers" in 1960) were approved by the prefecture of police, charged by the producer to sell privately or by auction, and established the official price of meat, fruit, fish, butter, poultry, and game.

› *Forts* or *musclés* (**strong bearers**) were recruited through a competition by the prefecture of police and identifiable by their medal with the coat of arms of the City of Paris, their large blue canvas smocks, and their yellow leather hat. They were paid by the tonnage and would unload cars, transport goods to stalls, and control traffic flow. They were helped by porters and occasional *renforts* (reinforcements).

› *Les dames de la Halle* (**market women of Les Halles**) were a group of female merchants who spoke in a colorful language. Among them, the president, or queen, of Les Halles, responsible for welcoming heads of state or sovereigns during official visits to the market.

FISH PAVILION

› *Maquilleurs de poisson* (**fish makeup artists**) fraudulently represented merchandise (by coloring the gills, replacing the eyes, etc.).

› *Croque-morts* (**undertakers**) would immerse dying oysters in a saltwater basin with algae to revive them.

BUTTER, EGG, CHEESE PAVILION

› *Flaireurs* (**sniffers**) would oversee sanitary control of foodstuffs thanks to their developed sense of smell.

› *Fruitiers* would use a probe and taste butter, for quality control, which they would then spit out on a bed of straw. These pieces were recovered, melted, and resold to *traiteurs* (prepared-foods vendors) to use for their fried foods.

PUBLIC BREAD AND FRUIT PAVILION

› *Boulangers en vieux* (**recycling bakers**) would make bread from croutons collected from the city's schools.

› *Marchands de viandes cuites* (**cooked meat merchants**) or *bijoutiers* would use leftovers from high-end restaurants to compose and sell as "bijoux," or plates of leftovers.

In the cellars of Les Halles

› *Lotisseurs-gaveurs* would force-feed young pigeons.

› *Bombeurs* would flatten the ducks' keel to make them plump.

› *Cabocheurs* or *pourfendeurs* would remove brains from the heads of sheep they would break down.

› *Compteurs-mireurs* would count eggs, weigh them, and examine them with candles to check their condition.

› *Soutireurs* would knead and shape butter.

Around Les Halles

› *Marchands au petit tas* or *terrassiers* would sell small piles of vegetables for pot-au-feu around pavilions 6 to 8, after the departure of

Gaveuses de pigeons.

Les caves des Halles centrales (retail), Auguste-André Lançon, circa 1869.

the merchants from Le Carreau (the open-air market) at 8 a.m.

› *Tasseurs* would help truck farmers unload their cargo at night and arrange vegetables in well-aligned piles or pyramids.

› *Marchands d'arlequins* (**scrap vendors**), distinct from the *bijoutiers* (see above), would sell a hodgepodge meal using the leftovers from bourgeois tables or restaurants.

› *Marchands de soupe* (**soup vendors**) would warm passersby with soup prepared and eaten on-site, in bowls provided by the cook, then collected and used again.

SKIP TO
Odd Food Jobs,
p. 239.

At Les Halles with Zola

In *Le Ventre de Paris* (*The Belly of Paris*), published in 1873, author Émile Zola was fascinated by this "Babylon of metal," and painted an exciting, odorous, and noisy picture of everyday life within the pavilions.

Follow the guide: Les Halles step-by-step

On his return to Paris after years of confinement, the hero in *Le Ventre de Paris*, Florent, realizes that a new district, Les Halles, has emerged. He takes a job there, and the author thus proceeds to meticulously describe the Les Halles pavilions, each dedicated to a type of food. An entire world exists inside the pavilions, but also outside of them at Le Carreau des Halles, located on the side of the Saint-Eustache church, for the lowlier vendors.

With 350 shops each, the 10 pavilions built by Baltard between 1854 and 1874 rested on large, vaulted cellars and were lit by gas and supplied with water.

Two other pavilions (1 and 2), planned by Baltard, were built in 1936 in a semicircular arrangement around the Bourse de commerce. These were after Zola's time.

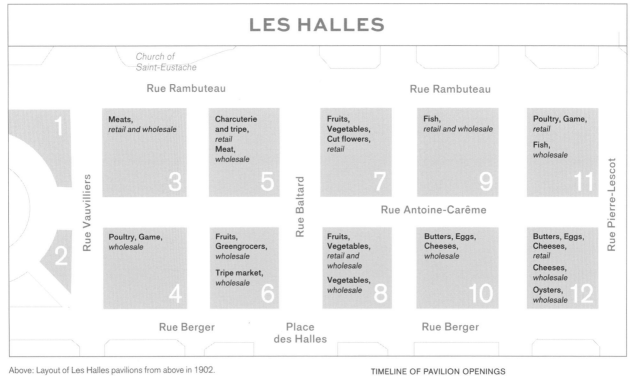

LES HALLES

Church of Saint-Eustache

Rue Rambuteau — Rue Rambuteau

1

3 Meats, *retail and wholesale*

5 Charcuterie and tripe, *retail* Meat, *wholesale*

7 Fruits, Vegetables, Cut flowers, *retail*

9 Fish, *retail and wholesale*

11 Poultry, Game, *retail* Fish, *wholesale*

Rue Vauvilliers

Rue Baltard

Rue Antoine-Carême

Rue Pierre-Lescot

2

4 Poultry, Game, *wholesale*

6 Fruits, Greengrocers, *wholesale* Tripe market, *wholesale*

8 Fruits, Vegetables, *retail and wholesale* Vegetables, *wholesale*

10 Butters, Eggs, Cheeses, *wholesale*

12 Butters, Eggs, Cheeses, *retail* Cheeses, *wholesale* Oysters, *wholesale*

Rue Berger — Place des Halles — Rue Berger

Above: Layout of Les Halles pavilions from above in 1902.
Below: Sketch of Les Halles in 1863.

TIMELINE OF PAVILION OPENINGS

1853 PAVILION 5 (rebuilt in 1869)	1866 PAVILION 4
1857 PAVILIONS 9, 11, AND 12	1874 PAVILION 6
1858 PAVILIONS 7, 8, AND 10	1936 PAVILIONS 1 AND 2
1860 PAVILION 3	

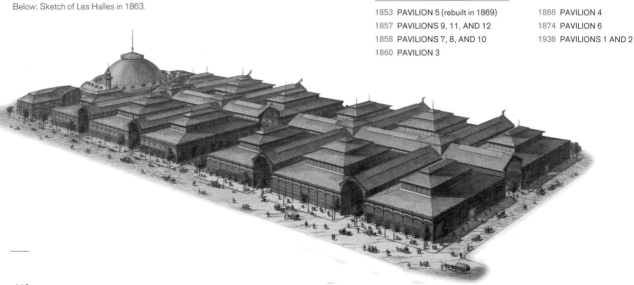

LE CARREAU DES HALLES

"It was a sea. . . . The torrent grew, the vegetables were flooding the cobblestones. . . . The greens, the lettuces, the escaroles, the chicory, open and fertile still with soil, exposed their radiating hearts; the bunches of spinach, the bunches of sorrel, the bunches of artichokes, the heaps of beans and peas, the stacks of romaines, bound with a strand of straw, sang the whole range of green . . . Claude . . . found 'these scoundrels of vegetables' extravagant, mad, sublime. And he maintained that they had not died, that pulled up from the day before, they waited for the next day's sun to bid him adieu on the cobblestone of Les Halles."

NO. 3: THE MEAT PAVILION

"Other trucks unloaded whole calves, swaddled with a tablecloth, lying all along, like children, in large baskets that only let in the four stumps, spread and bleeding. There were also whole sheep, beef sections, thighs, shoulders. The butchers, with large white aprons, marked the meat with a stamp, carved it, weighed it, hung it on the auction bars; while, with his face glued to the gates, he looked at those rows of hanging bodies, the red oxen and sheep, the paler calves."

NO. 4: POULTRY AND GAME PAVILION

"Along the narrow aisles, the women, sitting, plumed.

Rays of sunshine fell between the raised tents, feathers flew under the fingers, like dancing snow, in the fiery air, in the golden dust of the rays. Cries, a whole trail of offers and touches, followed Florent. 'A beautiful duck, sir? . . . Come and see me . . . I have some lovely fat chickens . . .'"

NO. 5: THE MEAT AND TRIPE PAVILION

"He walked to the square of the tripe market, among the heads and feet of pale calves, the tripe neatly rolled into bundles in boxes, the brains delicately arranged on flat baskets, the livers bleeding, the purple kidneys."

NO. 8: THE FRUIT AND VEGETABLE PAVILION

"Behind, along the shelves, were lines of melons, cantaloupes stitched with patches, truck farmers with gray guipures . . . On the shelf, the beautiful fruits, delicately adorned in baskets, had the roundness of cheeks that hide faces of beautiful children half-revealed under a curtain of leaves; peaches especially, the blushing Montreuils, thin-skinned and fair like girls of the North, and the peaches of the South, yellow and burned, having the tan of the girls of Provence."

NO. 9: THE FISH PAVILION

"They unloaded, they released the flood, in the closed enclosures. . . . , and even on the sidewalks. There was, along the

Victor Gabriel Gilbert, *Le Carreau des Halles*, 1880.

square, piles of small nets, a continuous arrival of crates and baskets, stacked bags of mussels letting gullies of water flow. . . . When the large baskets were spread out, Florent believed that a school of fish had just washed up there, on this cobblestone. . . . There were red mullets, with exquisite flesh, red illuminated cyprinids, crates of whiting with opal reflections, baskets of smelt, small clean baskets, pretty as baskets of strawberries, which let out a powerful smell. . . ."

NO. 10: THE BUTTER, EGGS, CHEESE PAVILION

"Around them, the cheeses stunk. On the two shelves of the shop, at the back, were huge lumps of butter . . . Under the display table, of red marble veined with gray, baskets of eggs lent a whiteness of chalk. . . . But it was mostly on the table that the cheeses piled up. There, beside the

Merchants of the fruit and vegetable pavilion.

loaves of butter by the pound, in perry leaves, opened a giant Cantal, as if split with an axe; Then came a Chester, the color of gold, a Gruyère, like a wheel fallen from some barbarian chariot, Holland, round as severed heads, smeared with dried blood. . . . A Parmesan cheese,

in the middle of this weightiness of cooked paste, added its hint of strong odor. Three Bries, on round boards, had the melancholy of extinct moons. . . . The Roqueforts, too, under crystal bells, took on a princely appearance, marbled and fat faces, veined with blue and yellow."

SKIP TO
Île-de-France Terroir, p. 20.

Rungis, the Market of Markets

To remove the clutter from the center of Paris, Les Halles moved to Rungis, selected for its proximity to the capital and offering the MIN (National Interest Market), a framework for wholesale foods that aims to promote the country's exceptional know-how.

Continually evolving

During its 50-year history, the Rungis market has constantly modernized to comply with health requirements, adapt to the needs of professionals, and resist the expansion of mass distribution and online commerce. Recent years have witnessed the creation of the organic farming pavilion (2016), the intermediation of GAFAs (the tech industry), and the founding of the university campus of the Rungis Academy (2020).

And next? The developers want to extend the market to the north (the Agoralim project) within the 1,730 acres (700 ha) of the Triangle de Gonesse near Le Bourget and Roissy airports to create an agroecological vegetable production center and partner with the Port of Abu Dhabi to create an agricultural logistics hub.

IN THE LIMELIGHT
The market has been the backdrop in many films: *La Bûche* by Danièle Thompson (1999), *Paris* by Cédric Klapisch (2008), *The Chef* by Daniel Cohen (2012).

The advantages of the MIN in Rungis

A MARKET SERVICING MARKETS
Rungis maintains a network of local markets, particularly in Paris and Île-de-France.

A MARKET WITH NATIONAL AND INTERNATIONAL DIMENSIONS
Initially designed to supply Paris and its region, Rungis has expanded its reach. Producers from France and around the world send products to the market every day.

A SHOWCASE OF ALL TERROIRS
The MIN offers diversity of France's various terroirs, from the country's four hundred cheeses to French-raised poultry to trout from the Pyrénées to Île-de-France watercress from Méréville to the yellow onion of Vertus.

A PLACE OF CONVIVIALITY
Every day, transactions are wrapped up at the café or in one of the eighteen restaurants in the market.

SUSTAINABLE WASTE MANAGEMENT
Tons of unsalable or unsold products are either transformed into compost or used for other purposes. Spoiled packaging and products are incinerated to provide heating for the market and Orly airport.

IN NUMBERS
FRUITS AND VEGETABLES
9 sales pavilions

1 square for Île-de-France producers

MEAT PRODUCTS
1 butcher's pavilion

2 pork pavilions

1 poultry and game pavilion

1 tripe pavilion

FRESH CATCH
1 sales pavilion

1 subsidiary pavilion

DAIRY PRODUCTS AND GASTRONOMY
7 pavilions (2 dairy pavilions, 4 traiteur [prepared foods] pavilions, 1 organic pavilion)

HORTICULTURE AND DECORATION SECTOR

TOP · LET'S EAT PARIS! · ADDRESSES

IN THE MIN
La Cantine du troquet
📍 *1, av. des Savoies, PLA 376, Rungis (Val-de-Marne)*
A small eatery with a southwest accent that delights customers from 5:30 a.m. to 3:30 p.m. in the heart of the market.

Au Veau qui tète
📍 *2, rue de l'Aubrac, Rungis (Val-de-Marne)*
Between midnight and 4:30 p.m., this is the hangout for offal lovers in the tripe pavilion.

AROUND THE MIN
La Grange des Halles
📍 *28, rue Notre-Dame, Rungis (Val-de-Marne)*
An authentic bistro of chef Alexis Leiber, which cooks up dishes using fresh products from the markets of Rungis.

SKIP TO
The "Fifth Quarter" of Paris, p. 221.

The Vol-au-Vent

Although considered an invention of Antonin Carême, the stuffed puff pastry, whose name translates to "flight in the wind," has taken many forms. —THOMAS DARCOS

THE RECIPE

Season: fall to winter
Difficulty ● ● ●

SERVES 4

For the puff pastry shells
1 recipe Puff Pastry (p. 58)

For the spinach-béchamel mixture
3 tablespoons unsalted butter
¼ cup (30 g) all-purpose flour
1 cup (250 ml) milk
1 cup (250 ml) crème fraîche

Salt and freshly ground black pepper
⅔ teaspoon freshly grated nutmeg
1 pinch of ground Espelette pepper
Scant ½ cup (100 ml) heavy cream
14 ounces (400 g) baby spinach

For the filling
1 pound 2 ounces (500 g) sweetbreads
4 free-range chicken breasts
A few tablespoons unsalted butter, for sautéing
1 clove garlic

A few sprigs thyme
1⅔ cups (400 ml) chicken broth
9 ounces (250 g) white button mushrooms
Scant 1 cup (200 ml) whipping cream (preferably 35% fat)
A few sprigs chervil, for garnishing
1½ ounces (40 g) black truffle

Equipment
1 round 3-inch (8 cm) cookie cutter
1 round 4-inch (10 cm) cookie cutter

Board depicting pastry cases ("croustades"), p. 58, *Le Livre de pâtisserie* by Jules Gouffé (1873).

This is a splendid vol-au-vent with sweetbreads, free-range chicken, and black truffles by Jean Sévègnes.*

Make the puff pastry shells: Preheat the oven to 365°F (185°C). Roll out the puff pastry to a large circle ¹⁄₁₀ inch (2 mm) thick. Cut out eight circles using the 4-inch (10 cm) cookie cutter. Set aside four of the circles for the bottoms of the vol-au-vent and cut out rings from the remaining four circles using the 3-inch (8 cm) cookie cutter. Moisten the bottom circles with a little water, and place the dough rings on top, flush with the edges. Transfer to a baking sheet and bake for 17 minutes, or until browned and puffed.

Make the spinach-béchamel mixture: Melt the butter in a saucepan. Add the flour. Add the milk and crème fraîche and stir over low heat until thickened. Season with salt and black pepper. Add the nutmeg, Espelette pepper, and cream.

Sauté the spinach in a skillet until wilted. Let cool, then add the cooked spinach to the béchamel and combine.

Make the filling: Place the sweetbreads in ice water for 1 hour. Transfer them to a saucepan, cover with cold water,

and bring to a boil. Reduce the heat and simmer for 5 minutes. Peel the membrane from the sweetbreads by immersing them in ice water. Set aside, wrapped in a cloth.

Cut the chicken breasts into thick slices. In a skillet over medium heat, sauté in butter; remove and set aside. Add the sweetbreads to the pan and brown in butter with the garlic clove and a few sprigs of thyme. Deglaze the pan with the chicken broth and add the chicken. Clean the mushrooms and chop them. In a separate pan, sauté them in butter, then add them to the pan with the meats. Simmer over low heat for 20 minutes.

Beat the whipping cream and set aside in the refrigerator.

Assemble: Place a puff pastry on each of four plates. Cut out the center of the puff pastry (making a sort of "container") and spoon the spinach-béchamel mixture into the shell. Bake for 5 minutes at 350°F (180°C).

Cook the sauce to reduce it so that it thickens and coats the sweetbreads and chicken.

Spoon the sweetbreads, chicken, and mushrooms into the vol-au-vent shells. Combine the whipped cream with the remaining sauce in the pan and fill the shells with a little bit of the lightened sauce. Spoon the remaining sauce around the shells on the plate. Finish by garnishing with chervil sprigs and slices of black truffle.

*Café des Ministries—83, rue de l'Université, Paris 7th.

FIRST MENTIONS

1742
François Marin, in *Suite des Dons de Comus: Volume III*, mentions a cake that "vole au vent" (flies in the wind), made of puff pastry, in a triangular or diamond shape.

1800
The Paris elite flocks to Méot, a famous restaurant where the vol-au-vent is served, described as "receptacles" filled with rooster's comb and milt.

1812
In *Le Cuisinier impérial*, André Viard describes a petit vol-au-vent garni (a small, filled vol-au-vent) and a vol-au-vent de macédoine (vol-au-vent with diced mixed vegetables) as puff pastries filled with vegetables, served as a starter.

1815
Antonin Carême perfected the recipe and presented dozens of variations, using fruits and meats, in *Le Pâtissier royal*.

WHAT ABOUT "LA BOUCHÉE A LA REINE"?
In the mid-eighteenth century, a vol-au-vent was served to Queen Marie Leszczynska. Thus, the description *la bouchée à la reine* (queen's morsel) was born.

TOP ADDRESSES
LET'S EAT PARIS!

Maison Verot
⚲ *3, rue Notre-Dame-des-Champs, Paris 6th + 2 locations*
Offers a family-size version topped with lobster, sweetbreads, morels, and rooster's comb.

Le 110 de Taillevent
⚲ *195, rue du Faubourg-Saint-Honoré, Paris 8th. €€*
The vol-au-vent à la financière combines rooster's comb, rooster's kidneys, and roasted langoustines.

SKIP TO
The Invention of the Restaurant, p. 61; Antonin Carême, p. 156.

The Paris-Brest

Its accepted birthplace is Maisons-Laffitte, yet it's one of the most famous pastries of Paris. —LOÏC BIENASSIS

LE DÉPART DE LA COURSE PARIS-BREST
(Devant le PETIT JOURNAL)

Start of the Paris-Brest race, 1891.

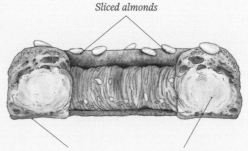
Sliced almonds

Choux pastry   Praline cream

THE ORIGINS OF THE PARIS-BREST

The Durand pastry shop in Maisons-Laffitte claims its invention. Founder Louis Durand is said to have created this cake in 1910 in the shape of a bicycle wheel and gave it its name in homage to the Paris-Brest-Paris bicycle race, whose first year was in 1891. In 1930, Paul Durand (the son) attempted to file a patent. However, the effort was in vain, as recipes could no longer be patented.

COMPOSITION

The oldest published recipe seems to date to the first edition of *L'Art culinaire moderne du célèbre cuisinier* by Henri-Paul Pellaprat, in 1936.

"Make a crown in choux pastry the width of two fingers, put it on an unbuttered metal sheet. Brown the top and sprinkle with sliced almonds. Lightly sprinkle with sugar and bake hot enough to start then moderate so that the dough becomes a little dry. When the crown is cooled, open it and fill it with a fine praline pastry cream with a little butter added. Sprinkle the top with confectioners' sugar."

In the mid-1930s, the "Paris-Brest" of the restaurant Chapon Fin (avenue Malakoff) combined choux pastry, whipped cream, and almonds. In 1975, the book *Faire votre pâtisserie* by Lenôtre suggested three fillings:

- the "classic": a pastry cream enriched with powdered praline and softened butter.
- a Chiboust cream.
- a crème pâtisserère allégée, a whipped cream added in.

PARIS-BREST IN THE MOVIES

Jean-Marie Poiré's *Les Anges gardiens* (1995) includes a hilarious scene involving a Paris-Brest: Struggling with his inattentive guardian angel, priest Hervé Tarain (Christian Clavier) has lunch in a small Brussels restaurant with the owner Antoine Carco (Gérard Depardieu) who has set aside the last Paris-Brest from the pastry case and has gone to make a phone call. Meanwhile, the priest feels his demons tempting him toward the delicious pastry, which he unintentionally messes up and has to devour to hide his mistake.

TOP
LET'S EAT PARIS!
ADDRESSES

Philippe Conticini
📍 *31, rue Notre-Dame-de-Nazareth, Paris 3rd + 2 locations*
Intense hazelnut praline, creamy texture, caramelized and crispy nuts.

La Grande Épicerie
📍 *38, rue de Sèvres, Paris 7th*
A praline cream hides a second disk of choux pastry topped with hazelnut praline. As a bonus, the top has a craquelin topping with added chopped nuts and delicate chocolate shavings.

Maison Louvard
📍 *11, rue de Châteaudun, Paris 9th*
This lightly dusted disk houses a very generous praline, a light buttercream, and a crispy insert.

Maison Durand
📍 *9, av. de Longueil, Maisons-Laffitte (Yvelines)*
The so-called original version: soft choux pastry, filled with a light praline cream, and sprinkled with sliced almonds.

Nina Métayer
Delicatisserie.com
A crown of very light choux pastry, a bitter praline, and a lightly sweetened diplomat cream.

THE RECIPE

Season: year-round
Difficulty ● ● ●

SERVES 8

For the choux pastry

3 tablespoons unsalted butter

Scant ½ cup (100 ml) whole milk

3 tablespoons grapeseed oil

⅓ teaspoon salt

Scant ½ cup (100 ml) water

1 cup (125 g) all-purpose flour

3 large (150 g) eggs, beaten

For the craquelin topping

¼ cup (60 g) turbinado sugar

3 tablespoons unsalted butter

½ cup (60 g) all-purpose flour

1 large (30 g) egg white

For the hazelnut praline

¼ cup plus 2 tablespoons (80 g) sugar

1¼ cups (160 g) hazelnuts

1 pinch of fleur de sel sea salt

For the diplomat cream

1 sheet gelatin, or ⅔ teaspoon powdered gelatin

Scant 1 cup (200 ml) whole milk

3 large (60 g) egg yolks

3 tablespoons sugar

1 tablespoon plus 1 teaspoon all-purpose flour

2 teaspoons cornstarch

Scant 1 cup (200 ml) whipping cream (30% fat), cold

For the decoration

3 tablespoons confectioners' sugar

¾ cup (100 g) caramelized hazelnuts

15 toasted hazelnuts

Equipment

Stand mixer

Food processor

Pastry bags

16 mm plain piping tip

10 mm star piping tip

SKIP TO
The Chouquette and Its Cousins, p. 278;
Pastry Shops, p. 312.

Liberally adapted from the recipe by pastry chef Yann Couvreur,* this Paris-Brest promises both lightness and crispness.

Make the choux pastry: In a saucepan, add the butter, milk, oil, salt, and water and bring to a boil. Add the flour all at once. Stir the dough over medium heat for 5 minutes until dry (it will no longer stick to the sides of the pan) ❶. Transfer the dough to the bowl of the stand mixer fitted with the paddle attachment and mix on low speed until the steam disappears. Add the eggs in a stream until the dough closes slowly behind the spatula as the spatula moves along the bottom of the pan. Scrape the dough into a pastry bag fitted with the plain piping tip.

Preheat the oven to 325°F (170°C). Pipe a ring of choux pastry about 8 inches (20 cm) in diameter on a silicone baking mat–lined baking sheet ❷.

Make the craquelin topping: Place the ingredients in the bowl of the stand mixer fitted with the paddle attachment and mix to obtain a homogeneous mixture. Spread the mixture between two sheets of parchment paper to a thickness of ¹⁄₁₀ inch (2 mm) and place in the refrigerator. Cut out a ring 8 inches (20 cm) in diameter and 1 inch (3 cm) wide. Place on top of the choux pastry, then bake for 50 minutes.

Make the hazelnut praline: In a saucepan, heat the sugar until it turns dark amber in color. Pour the caramel onto a baking sheet lined with a silicone baking mat and let cool. Break the caramel into pieces and process in the food processor with the hazelnuts and sea salt until a smooth paste is achieved.

Make the diplomat cream: Soak the gelatin sheet in a small bowl of cold

water. If using powdered gelatin, sprinkle it over 1 tablespoon of cold water and stir to moisten it; let soften for 5 minutes. Bring the milk to a simmer. In a bowl, combine the yolks, sugar, flour, and cornstarch and pour half the hot milk into the yolk mixture while stirring continuously. Pour the entire mixture back into the pan. Cook, stirring for 2 minutes once it starts to boil. Transfer the warm pastry cream to a container. Squeeze the water from the gelatin sheet and add it to the warm pastry cream (or add the softened powdered gelatin, if using); stir to dissolve the gelatin.

In the bowl of the stand mixer, beat the cold whipping cream.

Combine half the praline with the pastry cream, then fold in the whipped cream using a spatula. Set aside in a cool place.

Compose: Using a serrated knife, cut the choux pastry disk horizontally in half and place a little of the remaining praline on the bottom ring (the base).

Scrape the diplomat cream into a pastry bag fitted with the star piping tip and pipe the cream into the bottom ring ❸. Add some more praline and close with the second choux pastry disk, pressing down only enough to set the top disk.

Dust with confectioners' sugar and sprinkle with caramelized and toasted hazelnut pieces.

*Yann Couvreur Pâtisserie—137, av. Parmentier, Paris 10th + 4 locations.

① THONET

② DRUCKER

③ BAUMANN

④ GATTI

⑤ COSTES

Capital Chairs

Some of Paris's iconic chairs can still be spotted indoors or on terraces today, while others have become emblems of a bygone era—but all are intimately linked to the history of the capital's cafés and restaurants.

—SYLVIE WOLFF

⑥ TOLIX

⑦ FERMOB

① The Thonet No. 14

Creation date › 1859

A LITTLE HISTORY
Made up of just six pieces, ten screws, and two nuts, this bestseller is a model of ingenuity and simplicity. Between 1859 and 1910, nearly fifty million copies and variations were sold. Its visionary creator from the Rhine region was cabinetmaker Michael Thonet, who invented, long before IKEA, furniture that would come available as a kit to meet the high demand for cafés, accommodating thirty-six chairs in a single box measuring 35 cubic feet (1 cu m). Renamed No. 214 in the 1960s, it is now available with a solid backrest and an enlarged seat, in a cane or plywood version, upholstered in leather or fabric.

DISTINCT SIGNATURE
A brass plaque with the name of the establishment affixed to the back of the backrest.

WHERE CAN YOU TAKE A SEAT?
Brasserie Balzar (Paris 5th), Bouillon Julien (Paris 10th).

② The Drucker

Creation date › 1885

A LITTLE HISTORY
After modest beginnings in a small studio workshop on rue des Pyrénées (Paris 20th), this chair, handwoven in rattan and vegetable-fiber polyamide, caught the attention of brasseries such as La Coupole and Le Flore. The arrival of Chinese models in the 1980s jeopardized this family-owned business. Thus, in 2006, the buyer Bruno Dubois restored all its luster by taking inspiration from the company archives. Labeled a Living Heritage Company since 2008, this flagship furniture manufacturer still handcrafts more than fifteen thousand chairs per year, styled in an incredible variety of shapes and colors, inspiring collaborations.

DISTINCT SIGNATURE
A brass plate nailed to the bottom of the backrest.

WHERE CAN YOU TAKE A SEAT?
La Closerie des Lilas (Paris 6th), Brasserie Bofinger (Paris 4th), La Coupole (Paris 14th).

③ The Baumann

Creation date › 1901

A LITTLE HISTORY
Its story began when Émile Baumann from Switzerland moved to Colombier-Fontaine (Doubs) to build a factory for children's curved-back chairs. Two years later, his son Walter Baumann successfully launched dozens of models for hotels, offices, and brasseries. From the 1940s, chair No. 43—originally with three vertical bars and a curved back—became a fixture in many Parisian bars before being replaced in the 1960s by two models: the Dove, in molded and curved plywood with an opening in the back at the base, and the Mouette, in beech with a rounded back with an inset large oval in the shape of a bottle opener inspired by the Scandinavian style.

DISTINCT SIGNATURE
A company logo stamped under the seat and branded with a red iron on current models.

WHERE CAN YOU TAKE A SEAT?
Au Petit Riche (Paris 9th).

④ The Gatti

Creation date › 1920

A LITTLE HISTORY
This rattan model, woven in Rilsan (a vegetal and durable polyamide fiber produced from castor beans), took over the terraces of the brasseries of the Grands Boulevards starting in the 1980s, before conquering chic hotels and restaurants. The company was first founded by Italian immigrant Joseph Gatti, then taken over by the Maugrion family in 1992, and now managed, since 2019, by Alexis Dyèvre, who has continued the hand braiding in his workshops in Seine-et-Marne and Spain. Available in about thirty shapes and colors, these chairs have been manufactured identically for a century and can be restored if necessary.

DISTINCT SIGNATURE
The signature under the seat is not consistent, that's the problem.

WHERE CAN YOU TAKE A SEAT?
Le Dôme (Paris 14th), Au Père Tranquille (Paris 1st), Le Tourville (Paris 7th), the Carette tearooms (Paris 3rd, 16th, and 18th).

⑤ The Costes

Creation date › 1984

A LITTLE HISTORY
Designed by Philippe Starck at the beginning of the 1980s for the Costes des Halles café, this tripod chair caused a sensation until the café's closure in 1994. The chair is balanced on three legs to reduce floor space and facilitate the circulation of servers. It comprises a steel tube base and an arched beech plywood backrest. It has been manufactured since its creation by Driade in several finishes: mahogany, gray oak, bamboo, and others.

DISTINCT SIGNATURE
The label "Aleph" engraved under the seat.

WHERE CAN YOU TAKE A SEAT?
You can't. You can only see it in the art collection at Centre Georges-Pompidou, where it was installed in 1993.

SKIP TO
La Closerie des Lilas, p. 112; Café de Flore or Les Deux Magots?, p. 256; Brasseries, p. 356.

THEY KNEW HAPPY DAYS

⑥ The Chair A by Tolix

Creation date › 1927

This chair, made of galvanized steel and created by the young visionary Xavier Pauchard, had an incredible journey. Long-lasting, stackable, and above all stainless, this model, still made in Autun in Saône-et-Loire, was acclaimed for half a century by cafés. The chair enjoyed fame on the ocean liner *Normandie*, at the Universal Exposition of 1937, and even in the collections of the Vitra Design Museum in Germany, the MoMA in New York, and Centre Georges-Pompidou. Considered too heavy, restaurants gradually abandoned the chair to fade into one of the emblems of industrial design.

⑦ The Bistro Chair by Fermob

Creation date › 1889

Created in the nineteenth century to fill the terraces of the *guinguettes* on the banks of the Marne, this folding model was an immediate success with lemonade vendors who could escape taxes for having a permanent terrace. Although Fermob, located in the Ain department, still manufactures this chair in beech slats, a metal version has largely taken over. The Bistro is now available in twenty-four snazzy colors, and more than two hundred thousand are sold yearly.

Édouard Nignon (1865–1934)

The Society Cook

Admirer of Antonin Carême, contemporary of Auguste Escoffier, and culinary author, this chef was one of the most important of the twentieth century. —**CHARLES PATIN O'COOHOON**

Serving the state

After organizing banquets for Tsar Nicholas II in Moscow, Édouard Nignon managed the kitchens of the great gala dinners at the Élysée Palace and became the "chef de bouche" for US President Wilson during his stays in Paris.

"Going from table to table, suggesting a sole, proposing a partridge, describing a dessert, watching everything, salting this, sweetening that, he can say that he had all Paris at his table."

—Sacha Guitry in the preface of *Éloge de la cuisine française* by Édouard Nignon

Menu of restaurant Larue, 1915.

Fashionable Paris rushes to Larue

With Octave Vaudable, future owner of Maxim's, Nignon purchased restaurant Larue, located at the corner of rue Royale and Place de la Madeleine, from the Duke d'Uzès. Anatole France, Edmond Rostand, and Aristide Briand were regulars. The establishment brought together the most beautiful clientele in the world. Artists, ministers, and kings savored Houdan chicken on a spit stuffed with ortolans, fresh peas Dame Simonne, and the famous soufflé. Léon Daudet wrote at the time: "The people whose job is to do nothing were there, and usually very occupied." The restaurant took in 1.6 million francs per year. In 1921, Nignon sold the restaurant to his nephew Célestin Duplat.

Expert blade and gifted pen

In 1919, he published fifteen hundred copies of a masterpiece of culinary literature, *L'Heptaméron des gourmets*, which combines recipes and literary texts by some of the greatest Parisian poets such as Henri de Régnier and Guillaume Apollinaire. In 1921, he retired to Brittany where he wrote *Les Plaisirs de la table* (1926), followed by *Éloges de la cuisine française* (1933).

HIS PARIS CAREER

Born in Nantes into a family of eight children to a father who was a day laborer and a mother who was a seamstress, Édouard Nignon entered the kitchen at the age of nine at Cambronne, a restaurant in Nantes, before setting off to conquer Paris.

- **1880**
  Begins at prepared-foods vendor Potel et Chabot (16th)
- **1884**
  Begins at Maison Dorée (9th)
- **1885**
  Commis at Café Anglais (2nd)
- **1885**
  Chef de partie at Café de la Paix (9th)
- **1887**
  Saucier at Voisin (1st)
- **1889**
  Chef entremétier at Noël Peter's at the Universal Exposition
- **1890**
  Chef rôtisseur at Lapérouse (6th)
- **1891**
  Chef des cuisines at Marivaux (2nd)
- **1891**
  Chef de cuisine at Barbote (10th)

The country's taste buds

After the death of his son Marcel-Édouard in 1916 during the Battle of Somme, he founded an orphanage of restaurateurs, café owners, cooks, and hoteliers in Sannois (Val-d'Oise).

SKIP TO
The Invention of the Restaurant, p. 61; The Soufflé, p. 102; Antonin Carême, p. 156.

LE TRAIN BLEU

With the majestic nave of the Gare de Lyon as a setting, Le Train Bleu revives luxury rail travel in an opulent grand restaurant from the Belle Époque. —LOÏC BALLET

MAISON PARISIENNE
PLACE LOUIS-ARMAND,
12TH ARR.

GARE DE LYON - PARIS — Le Buffet

TO SEE

The old counter and its cash register

Just outside the kitchens, these items have not moved since the restaurant's opening. This observation point allowed the cashier to draw up the checks of each of the tables without missing a thing.

The decorative frescoes

These represent all of the most beautiful destinations served by the Paris-Lyon-Méditerranée (PLM) company painted on the ceilings 26 feet (8 m) high. The greatest painters of the time participated in creating these forty-one legendary scenes.

The bellhop

This old-fashioned character welcomes visitors in song. They accompany guests to the table, carry suitcases, and share anecdotes and historical information about the restaurant.

TO TRY

The leg of lamb

The restaurant serves about twenty every day. It is carved in the dining room on the famous slicing cart. This jewel of silversmithing by Maison Christofle, which was very fashionable at the end of the nineteenth century, is estimated to be worth several tens of thousands of euros.

The baba

Served with rum arranged with citrus fruits and sweetened by vanilla whipped cream.

The crêpe suzette

Invented at the other end of the train line, near Monaco, by Auguste Escoffier. The dessert is flambéed with Grand Marnier in front of guests.

SKIP TO
Art Nouveau or Art Deco?, p. 160; When Hollywood Dines in Paris, p. 286; Brasseries, p. 356.

A tribute to transportation

The name "Le Train Bleu" was adopted in 1963. This was the nickname of the all-blue luxury train of the Compagnie des Wagons-Lits that linked the capital to the Mediterranean in 1922. The blue color paid tribute to the brilliant cyan of the landscapes of the Côte d'Azur and the Côte Bleue, then served by the Paris–Ventimiglia train line.

All in first class

This grandiose stop, originally named "Le Buffet de la Gare," was built in 1900 during the Universal Exposition to dazzle the fifty million visitors expected to come to the City of Light. The popular architect of the time Marius Toudoire was commissioned, along with twenty-seven renowned painters, to create the monumental murals. The restaurant quickly attracted Paris high society and the greatest artists, such as Sarah Bernhardt, Alain Delon, Brigitte Bardot, Coco Chanel, and Salvador Dalí.

Let's roll!

Luc Besson chose Le Train Bleu as the backdrop for a classic scene in his feature film *Nikita* (1990). In this scene, an Anne Parillaud and Tchéky Karyo rendezvous at table number 10 ends in a shoot-out. Scenes from other films were shot on location here: *Place Vendôme* by Nicole Garcia (1998), *Filles uniques* by Pierre Jolivet (2003), and *Mr. Bean's Holiday* by Steve Bendelack (2007).

The Royal Kitchens of the Conciergerie

The Conciergerie is a former medieval royal palace that became Marie Antoinette's prison. It has Paris's oldest preserved kitchens. Let's take a tour. —BRUNO LAURIOUX

Kitchens of the Middle Ages

Of remarkable Gothic architecture, and though long attributed to Saint Louis, the kitchens of the Conciergerie were built in the fourteenth century, probably during the reign of John the Good. They were located near the Grande-Salle (Great Hall), one of the largest halls in the west spanning approximately 19,000 square feet (1,785 sq m). Official meals were held in the Conciergerie, which was then the palace of the kings of France on the Île de la Cité.

The common kitchens

› With their 21-foot (6.5 m) ceilings and an area covering 3,100 square feet (289 sq m), the kitchens' imposing dimensions were intended principally for food preparation for the servants and officers of the king, which included several hundred people daily. These were the so-called "common" kitchens.
› At each corner of the square room measuring 55 by 55 feet (17 by 17 m) is a fireplace, probably designated for preparing dishes that compose a medieval meal: soups, roasts, desserts. Historians believe that the kings' kitchens were above this room on a second floor, which is now gone.

Illustrious meals

After 1360, King Charles V preferred to stay in the Louvre, the Hôtel Saint-Pol, or the Château de Vincennes rather than in the old Palais de la Cité, where he had experienced difficult times. For special occasions, however, the palace's Grande-Salle was used, as this was the only room that could accommodate nearly one thousand guests. From this point forward, the common kitchens, much larger than the kitchens reserved for the king, were used. Such was the case in 1378 during the reception for Emperor Charles IV, under the leadership of the royal head chef, the illustrious Taillevent.

The Grand-Salle.

THE ÎLE DE LA CITÉ . . . FOR GOURMANDS

Since antiquity, the old district in the center of the Île de la Cité has offered Parisians choices to satisfy their gustatory cravings.

› Starting in the fifth century, at the end of the Petit Pont was Paris's first market, the **marché Palu** ❶ (from the Latin *palus*, meaning marsh) set up on unpaved and muddy ground. This market provided the king and the bishop with vegetables and precious products up to the twelfth century. The market was then moved to the Les Halles district, but a "new market" emerged in the sixteenth century on the Île de la Cité, located a little farther west and offering a fish market and butcher.

› The central district (around the current rue de la Cité) was designated, during the Middle Ages, for food trades:

❷ **Rue de la Juiverie.** With its wheat market (until the sixteenth century), this was the street for bakers.

❸ **Rue des Oubloyers** (then rue de la Licorne). Oublies (a type of wafer) were made here, especially for religious festivals.

❹ **Rue aux Fèves.** Occupied by many vegetable merchants.

❺ **Rue du Four-Basset.** Located near the church of Saint-Germain-le-Vieux, an oven owned by the monastery of Saint-Éloi was used for bread baking.

Many cabarets offered their services here (wine, cervoise beer, prostitutes), such as La Bouteille d'Or and the very famous Cabaret de la Pomme de Pin ❻, where Villon sang and which was later frequented by Boileau, Molière, and Racine.

SKIP TO Street Food in the Middle Ages, p. 108; Taillevent, p. 129; Lutetia at the Table, p. 294.

The Pâté Pantin

Originating in the Paris region, this warm, flaky pie enclosing a pâté is the French-cuisine archetype in charcuterie. —**FRANÇOIS-RÉGIS GAUDRY**

THE RECIPE

Season: fall to winter
Difficulty ● ● ●

SERVES 6

For the dough

8½ tablespoons (120 g) unsalted butter

½ cup (125 ml) lukewarm water

2¼ cups (270 g) all-purpose flour

1 teaspoon salt

1 large (20 g) egg yolk

For the filling

7¾ ounces (220 g) pork liver

3¾ ounces (110 g) pork shoulder

3¾ ounces (110 g) veal shoulder

2⅛ ounces (60 g) white button mushrooms

⅓ ounce (10 g) dried porcini mushrooms

4½ ounces (130 g) bard or hard fat

2½ ounces (70 g) cooked foie gras

1⅓ teaspoons salt

1 teaspoon freshly ground black pepper

1 tablespoon plus 1 teaspoon Armagnac

Scant ½ cup (100 ml) heavy cream

For the savory jelly

⅔ cup (150 ml) chicken or beef broth

2 sheets gelatin, or 1⅓ teaspoons powdered gelatin

Equipment

Meat grinder with a 7 mm plate

At Le Repaire de Cartouche,* Rodolphe Paquin is the king of pâté pantin.

The day before, make the dough: Melt the butter and add the water. Place the mixture into a bowl with the flour and salt. Knead until you achieve a homogeneous dough. Chill in the refrigerator for 12 hours.

The same day, make the filling: In the meat grinder fitted with the 7 mm plate, grind the liver, half the pork shoulder, half the veal, the white button and porcini mushrooms, and half the bard fat and place in a large bowl. Cut the remaining half of each ingredient and the foie gras into ⅓-inch (1 cm) cubes and add to the bowl. Season with the salt and pepper. Add the Armagnac then the cream. Stir everything together to combine. Refrigerate for 1 hour.

Preheat the oven to 425°F (220°C). Roll the dough into two disks ⅓ inch (1 cm) thick. Cut out a disk measuring 8½ inches (22 cm) in diameter and a second measuring 9½ inches (24 cm); the larger disk will serve as a top for the pâté. Transfer the smaller disk to a baking sheet and spoon the filling into the center, spreading it out evenly to about 1 inch (3 cm) from the edge. Brush the edges of the dough disk with some of the egg yolk. Place the second dough disk on top of the filling. Press the edges of the dough disks together to seal them. Brush the top with the remaining egg yolk, and cut a small hole out of the center of the top to create a steam vent. Using the tip of a knife, score a decorative pattern in the dough. Let stand for 20 minutes in a cool place.

Bake for 45 minutes. Set aside in a cool spot for 24 hours.

The next day, make the savory jelly: Warm the broth. Soak the gelatin sheets in cold water until softened. Add the gelatin sheets to the warm broth and stir to dissolve. (If using powdered gelatin, sprinkle it over the warm broth and let sit for 5 minutes to soften; stir the gelatin, ensuring it is fully melted in the broth.) Once the broth has cooled, pour it into the pâté and set aside for 2 hours to cool.

*8, blvd. des Filles-du-Calvaire, Paris 11th.

THE ORIGIN

The recipe is thought to have originated in Pantin. One theory states the proximity of this town (now part of Seine-Saint-Denis) to the slaughterhouses of La Villette gave rise to the tradition.

The slaughterhouses of La Villette in Paris, circa 1900.

THE REPUTATION

The pâtés of Pantin have been popular since the middle of the eighteenth century. The chemist Cadet de Gassicourt mentions them in 1809 in his inventory of French culinary specialties (*Cours gastronomique*).

THE RECIPE

Little is known about its original shape and composition. In *Le Pâtissier moderne* (1856), Louis Bailleux described "petits pâtés Pantin," which were oval and filled with veal and pork. But in *Larousse ménager* (1926), they are rectangular.

THE TECHNIQUE

In culinary literature of the nineteenth century, pantins made with larks and partridges are mentioned, so it seems that from "pâté de Pantin" came the expression "pâté Pantin," to refer to any pâté baked in a flaky crust without using a mold.

TOP · LET'S EAT PARIS! · ADDRESSES

Maison Verot

📍 *3, rue Notre-Dame-des-Champs, Paris 6th* + 2 locations. €€.

Baked either rectangular or round and the filling changes with the season.

Lenôtre

📍 *44, rue d'Auteuil, Paris 16th* + 9 locations. €€

Rectangular or elongated with various fillings.

Arnaud Nicolas

📍 *46, av. de la Bourdonnais, Paris 7th*

📍 *125, rue Caulaincourt, Paris 18th.* €€

Small individual hot pâtés with fillings made with pork belly, caramelized onions, and port.

SKIP TO
Charcutier-Caterers, p. 318.

The Parisian Crêpe

To the shock of many Bretons, who make their traditional crêpes with buckwheat flour, the Parisian crêpe, including savory versions, is made with wheat flour.

—AIMIE BLANCHARD

Young boys eating crêpes, Paris, 1933.

THE RECIPE

Season: fall to winter
Difficulty ● ○ ○

**SERVES 4 (AS A MAIN DISH)
OR 6 (AS A HOT APPETIZER)**

For the crêpe batter

1¼ cups (150 g) all-purpose flour

1 teaspoon neutral-flavored oil

3 to 4 large (150 g) eggs

1½ cups (350 ml) milk

3 tablespoons unsalted butter, plus more for greasing

¼ cup plus 2 teaspoons (70 ml) beer

1 pinch of freshly grated nutmeg

Salt

For the béchamel

2 cups (250 ml) milk

¼ cup (30 g) all-purpose flour

1½ tablespoons unsalted butter

Salt and freshly ground black pepper

2 large (40 g) egg yolks

1 tablespoon crème fraîche

For the filling

5¼ ounces (150 g) jambon blanc (slightly salted cooked ham)

1⅓ cups (5¼ ounces/150 g) grated Gruyère cheese

Equipment

Strainer

Baked ham and cheese crêpes are a classic among Parisian families. Here is a recipe inspired by *l'Art et magie de la cuisine* (1955), by Raymond Oliver.

Make the crêpe batter: Place the flour in a bowl and make a well in the center. Add the oil and 3 eggs, which should absorb all the flour; add an additional egg if the flour is not completely absorbed. Warm the milk. Add the butter to the milk to begin melting it. Add the beer and nutmeg. Season with salt. Stir to thoroughly combine; if there are lumps, strain the mixture. Refrigerate for 1 hour.

In a hot pan with no added fat, add a small ladle of the batter and swirl the pan to spread the batter in a thin layer. When the crêpe can be detached from the pan and is golden on one side, flip it, and cook for a few seconds. Repeat these steps with the remaining batter.

Make the béchamel: Heat the milk over medium-low heat. Add the flour and butter to a saucepan. Pour in the hot milk, and whisk until smooth and creamy. Season with salt and pepper. In a saucepan over low heat, combine the egg yolks and crème fraîche. Add in part of the milk mixture, whisk well, then incorporate the remaining mixture. Set aside.

Make the filling: Chop the ham. In a bowl, add the ham and a scant cup (3½ ounces/100 g) of the Gruyère cheese and two-thirds of the béchamel.

Spoon 1 spoonful of the mixture onto each crêpe, roll up the crêpe, and transfer them to a baking dish greased with butter. Cover the crêpes with a spoonful of the remaining béchamel and sprinkle the remaining grated cheese on top. Place the dish under the broiler at 350°F (180°C) for 7 to 10 minutes, or until the cheese is browned and bubbling.

A THOUSAND-YEAR-OLD RECIPE

Around 1393, the guidebook *Mesnagier de Paris* codified a recipe very similar to the modern crêpe, made of wheat flour, eggs, water, wine, and salt. The recipe involves pouring the batter into a greased pan, starting in the center, and "swirling it all around the pan" (a method still used today), then sprinkling the crêpe with sugar once placed on a serving plate.

THE RISE OF THE CRÊPE

Over the last thirty years in Paris, a new era of the crêpe has emerged. From one end of the capital to the other, fast-food stalls have sprung up like mushrooms, capitalizing on the success of the Breton *crêperies* and offering both sweet and savory wheat-flour crêpes. In Brittany, only sweet crêpes are made with wheat flour, whereas savory galettes are made with buckwheat flour.

A TOUR OF PARIS

The success of Parisian crêpes is due to their low price and the number of food stands that offer them. High-quality ingredients are not always part of the equation, however, but when the craving strikes, head to:

Food stalls in parks and on boulevards

⚲ *The Carrousel kiosk at the foot of the Eiffel Tower.*

⚲ *The Bastille kiosk.*

The windows of Parisian brasseries

⚲ *L'Avant-Comptoir— 3, car. de l'Odeon, Paris 6th.*

Street food stalls

⚲ *36, 64, and 68 rue Mouffetard, Paris 5th.*

Open-air stalls

⚲ *Tabac de la Fontaine— 42, rue Saint-Séverin, Paris 5th.*

Urban fast-food style crêperies

⚲ *Mardi—137, rue Montmartre, Paris 2nd.*

And also

⚲ *On the lawn of Reuilly (Bois de Vincennes).*

⚲ *At the Foire du Trône, Paris 12th.*

SKIP TO
Brittany, p. 90.

Funerary headstone of Guillaume Tirel (image taken from the collections of Jérôme Pichon and Georges Vaire, Paris, Techener, 1892).

Taillevent (1310–1395)

The King's Cook

Born Guillaume Tirel, Taillevent was the first chef to leave his name in the history of French cuisine, and it was in Paris that he practiced an art codified in the collection *Le Viandier*.

—BRUNO LAURIOUX

70 years in the kitchens of the Kings of France

> Around the age of ten or fifteen, Guillaume Tirel began working in the kitchens of one of France's queens, where he went by the nickname Taillevent.

> His career in the kitchen led him eventually to the top post. He was a *queux* (cook) in 1346 and the top queux thirty years later. He served at least three kings of the Valois dynasty: Philip VI, Charles V, and Charles VI.

> Serving for Charles VI, he was given the important position of first squire, overseeing supplies and managing cooks to whom he regularly distributed their most precious tools—their knives. By this time, he was over eighty years old.

A cuisine as brilliant as the throne of France

Taillevent prepared several official meals offered by the King of France, Charles V, to his uncle, the German Emperor Charles IV in January 1378. The menus attest to cuisine with bright colors (red, green, pink, purple). The most striking are the golden yellows that matched perfectly with the precious tableware that Charles V accumulated and the blue, a symbolic color of the Capetian dynasty, abundantly present in the room's decor.

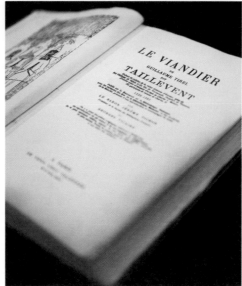

Le Viandier, 1892 edition.

A culinary bestseller

Taillevent is generally credited with a medieval collection of recipes entitled *Le Viandier*, which he, at best, revised and corrected since a version of the work existed before he was born. The success of his work spread his name far beyond the court. The cuisine that he described, which was fundamentally Parisian, thus became known throughout France. Through *Le Viandier* are witnessed the first styles of what is considered French gastronomy, incorporating at the time aromatic flavors of exotic spices, as evidenced by the camelina sauce recipe, a preparation so popular merchants sold it ready-made.

CAMELINA SAUCE RECIPE
"Grind ginger, cinnamon in abundance, cloves, grains (of paradise), and long pepper for those who desire it. Then pour it over bread soaked in vinegar heat everything gently and salt it thoroughly."

Taillevent, a member of the Parisian elite, is represented on his tomb in Saint-Germain-en-Laye dressed in his sergeant-at-arms armor with a shield bearing a coat of arms depicting . . . three cooking pots.

IN A FEW DATES

1326
"Enfant de cuisine" (kitchen boy) for Queen Jeanne d'Évreux, wife of Charles IV (the Fair).

1362
The Dauphin Charles gave him one hundred gold francs to buy a house in Paris to be "closer to him."

1378
Organization of the sumptuous banquet of the Epiphany offered to Emperor Charles IV at the Palais de la Cité.

1392
Pierre Buffaut buys a manuscript in Paris of *Viandier Taillevent maître-queux du Roi.*

Taillevent literature

The poet and rogue François Villon made Taillevent a character of French literature in 1461 with these lines from his ironic poem *Le Grand Testament*:

"So I consulted Taillevent

In the chapter on fricassees,

From beginning to end, upside down and right side up,

Which does not discuss it at bottom or top."

SKIP TO
Street Food in the Middle Ages, p. 108; The Royal Kitchens of the Conciergerie, p. 126.

129

A P'tit Noir, Please

Here is a short history of Paris's past with the *p'tit noir,* the very Parisian pick-me-up.
—MARCELLE RATAFIA AND ALICE BOSIO

Difficult beginnings

Introduced in Paris in 1657, coffee gained prestige through an Ottoman Empire ambassador, Suleiman Aga, who, in 1669, arrived in Paris after a tense political scandal in Versailles at the court of Louis XIV. After being sent away, Aga introduced Parisian society to a Turkish-style coffee drink, serving it in settings worthy of scenes from *The Arabian Nights.* This enchanting extravagance was introduced to King Louis XIV who brought it to his court. The popularity of all things from the Ottoman Empire prompted the monarch to commission a comedy-ballet from writer Molière and composer Lully. The plot was to be "A ridiculous Turkish ballet," famous for its "March of the Ceremony of the Turks"! The Sun King would eventually grow his own coffee beans in the greenhouses of Versailles.

Café Tortoni, boulevard des Italiens, 1877.

Women and cafés

Unaccompanied women were forbidden to enter cafés. They would have to gulp down their cups at the door of the cafés or enjoy an ice cream while sitting in their carriages. This inequality brought about the trend at the end of the eighteenth century of garden cafés, such as the famous Café Turc on boulevard du Temple (Paris 2nd), or the café-terraces of the Grands Boulevards, in particular the famous Café Tortoni.

The Sicilian of the Odéon

Parisian coffee owes its rise in popularity to a Sicilian who arrived in the city in 1670: Francesco Procopio Dei Coltelli, known as Procope, began as an assistant to an Armenian who was selling coffee at the Saint-Germain Fair. In 1686, Procope opened a café with his namesake, Café de Procope, serving the tropical elixir. He also sold ice cream and even installed a *jeu de paume* (an early outdoor variant of tennis) to attract the likes of Diderot and Rousseau. This approach marked the end of the cabaret-style cafés and the beginning of a more literary-style establishment where the intelligentsia arrived for conversation.

Perco ti amo

Coffee was becoming more popular among the masses and was often inadvertently burned. Café Génin on rue Vavin (Paris 6th) installed its first coffee machine in 1857, signaling a bright future for the p'tit noir.

The coffee machine, 1856.

The arrival of Cafés Richard

In 1955, André Richard, descendant of the founder of Maison Richard, started roasting coffee in Asnières (Hauts-de-Seine). The establishment grew and was conquering Parisian cafés starting in 1964.

THE INVENTOR OF THE COFFEE MAKER?

This was none other than Monseigneur de Belloy, Archbishop of Paris. In 1801, he was the first to develop a system for drip coffee.

The second wave

As early as 1960, Verlet—a roaster founded in 1880 at 256, rue Saint-Honoré (Paris 1st)—responded to the industrialization of coffee by offering better-quality coffee. This movement was followed, in the 1970s, by Starbucks in the United States.

The third wave

The 2000s are synonymous with a new wave of micro-roasters from the Anglo-Saxon world. This era has made specialty coffees a triumph in which the origin of the beans is more carefully chosen than ever before, the roasting is more precise, and the barista has been elevated to the rank of artist. Coffee shops dedicated to these specialty coffees have been opening in Paris since 2010.

SKIP TO
Le Procope, p. 281; Ice Cream Shops, p. 332; Coffee Roasters, p. 372.

A lexicon for the coffee bar

P'TIT NOIR
Literally a "little black." This is the most Parisian way to order an espresso at the counter.

GRAND CRÈME
Literally a "large cream," but this is indeed a café au lait (coffee with milk), made with half espresso, half milk. The grand crème was revered in a French song and during the New Wave film movement of the 1950s.

NOISETTE
A Paris-style macchiato, the name comes from the noisette (hazelnut) color that results from adding just a dash of milk to soften the character of a p'tit noir.

PETIT BOSSU
Now a bygone drink, this coffee once referred to the café-calva (coffee combined with apple brandy from Normandy) that was popular among early-morning risers.

Macabre Legends and Tales from the Table

In Paris, it's not just steaks that are served up a little bloody—some legendary stories are, too. —MARCELLE RATAFIA

The assassin with the fork

Father Gourier was a very wealthy customer of Le Grand Véfour and Tortoni in the nineteenth century. A sophisticated sadist, he would invite poor students to dinner, not so much for their good company as to stuff them until they died. While this sad sire boasted about bringing about death, a circus actor got wind of the killing spree. The actor braved dining with this "assassin with a fork" for three years, slipping away discreetly each time to administer the cure of castor oil to purge himself while his executioner continued to gorge himself at the table. Depending on the version of the story told, it was either eventually a trout or foie gras that caused the demise of this twisted gastronome.

The all-night buffet for two

It is recounted that during the Second Empire, two customers of the Café Anglais resolved to end their quarrel over dinner. The first service began at six o'clock, with chickens, stews, and slow-cooked dishes that followed one after the other until midnight—a caloric late-night supper if ever there was one. The night ended with a supper consisting of a roast, crayfish, salade Russe, and foie gras. As the new day dawned and the witnesses to this affair had fallen asleep, they awoke again to see the duelists fighting around a "frugal" lunch of oysters and grilled meats. When noon arrived, the most satiated slipped under the table. The unfortunate man left the scene on a stretcher while his opponent continued to eat.

A bad server

A server named Loufiat killed his girlfriend one day. *Loufiat*, therefore, became a term used by the anti-alcohol leagues to refer to someone who condemned drinkers to death. Although the word *loufiat* actually derives from the slang *loufdingue* (a weird man), the term is still used in brasseries today to refer to servers!

The hot pâtés of Notre Dame

Legend has it that in 1387, a dog was barking for several days and nights in front of a baker's shop on rue des Marmousets (now rue Chanoinesse), arousing suspicion from the neighborhood—and leading to the baker's confession: The local barber gave a haircut each week to a German student who was a clerk at Notre Dame de Paris. When the barber accidentally shaved the student a little too close, the barber finished the job by chopping the student up for pâté. (The poor dog, calling in vain for his young German master, may have saved others from the same fate.) The bakery, located near Notre Dame, supplied food to the nuns. After realizing they had enjoyed cannibalistic pâtés, they traveled to beg for the pope's absolution to avoid being excommunicated.

SKIP TO
The Feast of Fake Foods, p. 98.

TOUR D'ARGENT

Many legends surround this most famous of Parisian restaurants. Here is the true story from its pressed duck to its legendary wine cellar.

—LOÏC BIENASSIS

« UNIQUE A PARIS ». - Pour y déjeuner ou dîner

RESTAURANT DE LA TOUR D'ARGENT "FRÉDÉRIC"
Le plus ancien restaurant de Paris 1582
15, Quai de la Tournelle - PARIS (V°) - Téléphone Odéon 23-32

Le numéro de votre canard 500205
(depuis 1890)

Frédéric préparant son célèbre Canard
LA TOUR D'ARGENT
CLAUDE TERRAIL

A place of legend(s)

There have been several Parisian establishments bearing the name "Tour d'Argent" throughout history, the term being common for a place of distinction. This has led to the many legends entailing the current Tour d'Argent:

› **King Henry III** witnesses Italian travelers using a fork here and adopted its use.

› **Louis XIV** visited the establishment with his court.

› **Cardinal Richelieu** and his nephew, the Duke of Richelieu, were regulars and had their favorite dishes.

The wine cellar

Since the time of André Terrail, the Tour d'Argent wine cellar, perhaps one of the most beautiful in the world, is one of the jewels of the establishment. More than three hundred thousand bottles are stored here, and the wine list is a tome of three hundred pages weighing almost 16 pounds (7 kg). On the evening of June 14, 1940, Claude Terrail bricked up part of the wine cellar before the Germans entered Paris, painting the wall with lime, to hide the most prestigious bottles.

The era of Delair

› **In the eighteenth century,** an inn, located on the same site, had a sign that displayed "À la Tour d'Argent."

› **In 1885,** its consecration as a stronghold of Parisian gastronomy is thanks to Frédéric Delair, known as "Monsieur Frédéric," the maître d' who worked in some of the most prestigious establishments in the capital.

› **As early as January 1886,** a journalist from *Le Figaro* testified to the new status of the place. The article described how all those whose careers were struggling could be found here: deputies, ministers, prefects, magistrates. These misfortunates would arrive to console themselves "by feeding their hopes with sole Cardinale and beignets Tour d'Argent, the restaurant's two masterpieces."

› **From about 1890,** the restaurant became famous for its pressed duck—the canard, or caneton, Tour d'Argent. Each duck served is numbered.

TOUR D'ARGENT
PARIS

The Terrail dynasty

● **APRIL 1911**
The death of Frédéric Delair and the arrival of André Terrail, who renovated the establishment but maintained its same ambience.

● **MAY 1912**
The thirty-five thousandth duck is served.

● **INTERWAR PERIOD**
Becomes one of the rendezvous of the elite of Paris and the world.

● **1929**
The one hundred thousandth duck is served.

● **1933**
Awarded three Michelin stars.

● **1936**
Opening of a terrace on the sixth floor. This terrace is eventually enclosed and becomes the heart of the establishment.

● **1947**
Claude Terrail succeeds his father.

● **2003**
The millionth duck is served.

● **2006**
André Terrail, of the same family, takes over as head of this noble institution.

● **2022**
The restaurant closes for nine months for major renovations.

The artist of the Tour d'Argent duck

Excerpt from an obituary for Frédéric Delair, as a tribute to this artist of the pressed duck:

"Frédéric only made a set number of pressed ducks each night. The care he put into this delicate preparation forbade him, he said, to repeat this effort too often. It was therefore necessary, so to speak, to order the ducks in advance, and the customers waited patiently forty, fifty minutes, even an hour, for their turn to come. Frédéric would set up his press, his little glass divider with a kind of priestly allure, then, with a famous gesture, moistening his thumb, index, and middle finger of his left hand with wine, he passed a live flame from one lamp to the other lamp of his portable stove."

—"Frédéric," *Excelsior*, April 13, 1911

SKIP TO
Renowned Wine Cellars, p. 376; To See and to Drink, p. 282.

Beef Bourguignon

It may come as an offense to some natives of Burgundy, but their emblematic beef dish was created from the boarders of their region—in Paris.

—FRANÇOIS-RÉGIS GAUDRY

THE RECIPE

Season: year-round
Difficulty ●●○

SERVES 4

2 carrots

1 yellow onion

5 tablespoons (70 g) unsalted butter

2¼ pounds (1 kg) beef stew meat (such as chuck, cheek, or short rib), cut into about 2-inch (5 cm) cubes

4½ ounces (125 g) salted pork belly, stripped of its rind and cut into lardons

2 cloves garlic, peeled and crushed

Salt

¼ cup (30 g) all-purpose flour

5¼ ounces (150 g) small button mushrooms

20 small white onions or spring onions

1 bottle (750 ml) Burgundy red wine

3 cups (750 ml) chicken broth

1 bouquet garni (fresh thyme, celery stalk, bay leaf, parsley)

Tagliatelle noodles or steamed potatoes, for serving

This recipe is the slightly modified version of the boeuf bourguignon served by Roxane and Jean Sévègnes.*

Peel and wash the carrots. Peel the yellow onion. Cut the carrots and yellow onion into rounds.

In a pan, melt 3 tablespoons (50 g) of the butter and brown the pieces of beef on all sides.

Remove the beef pieces from the pan. Add the lardons to the pan and cook to brown them. When browned, add the sliced carrots and onions and the garlic cloves. Cook, while stirring, just until the vegetables begin to sweat; do not let them brown.

Place the pieces of beef back into the pan, season with salt, and add the remaining butter. Sprinkle the mixture with a little flour and let it cook over medium heat for 5 minutes to "toast" the flour, stirring continuously.

Add the mushrooms and small white onions and sauté for 5 minutes, stirring frequently. Add the wine, let cook to reduce by half, and add just enough of the chicken broth to cover the meat. Add the bouquet garni. Cook gently for about 2 hours.

When the beef pieces are cooked, remove the bouquet garni. Check the consistency of the sauce. Reduce if necessary, removing the meat to do so. The sauce should be slightly thickened and shiny. Serve immediately with tagliatelle noodles or steamed potatoes.

*Café des Ministères—83, rue de l'Université, Paris 7th.

Auguste Colombié.

GENEALOGY

Although this red-wine-simmered beef specialty was inspired by the Burgundian terroir, it was codified in Paris, after evolving from many variations.

"À la Bourgogne"
In the eighteenth century, Joseph Menon cooked carp, lamprey, and skate "à la Bourgogne" by integrating Burgundy wine.

"À la bourguignonne" and "à la bourguignotte"
In the nineteenth century, this expression implied the presence of red wine. In 1835, Antonin Carême mentions a sauce "à la bourguignotte" based on Volnay wine.

"Boeuf bourguignon"
First mentioned in 1867 in Pierre Larousse's *Grand Dictionnaire universel*. The chef Auguste Colombié codified the recipe in the magazine *Le Monde moderne* (1898).

"Madame Pardon had prepared a beef bourguignon as only she could, and this dish . . . substantial and refined, was worth the price of conversation."

—Georges Simenon, *Maigret et le tueur*, 1969.

TOP LET'S EAT PARIS! ADDRESSES

Aux Crus de Bourgogne
📍 *3, rue de Bachaumont, Paris 2nd.* €€
Beef chuck cooked at low temperature in red wine from the opened bottles, served in a casserole dish.

Café des Musées
📍 *49, rue de Turenne, Paris 3rd.* €€
Beef chuck and Burgundy wine; simmered for five hours, served in a casserole dish with mashed potatoes.

Au Bourguignon du Marais
📍 *52, rue François-Miron, Paris 4th.* €
Beef chuck and Burgundy wine; served in a casserole dish with new potatoes.

Le Cabanon de la Butte
📍 *6, rue Lamarck, Paris 18th.* €
Beef chuck and red wine; served in individual casserole dishes, to be enjoyed with mashed potatoes.

SKIP TO
Antonin Carême, p. 156; Chef-Driven Restaurants, p. 348.

The Kebab

It was a star dish in the capital's surrounding regions before infiltrating the city. The kebab now reigns as a popular Parisian food. —JORDAN MOILIM

From a Turkish dish to a German sandwich

• MIDDLE AGES
Legends say Ottoman soldiers used their swords to grill pieces of meat.

• 1830
To facilitate cutting, a man named Amid Oustaz has the idea to add the meat to a vertical spindle rather than use horizontal skewers.

• 1867
This vertical cooking method is adopted by (and the idea claimed by) Iskender, a cook from Bursa, in northwestern Anatolia (Turkey).

• 1971
Mehmet Aygün, a Turkish immigrant, is a worker in a small snack bar in a Berlin train station where he serves grilled meat. He has the idea of placing strips of mutton meat inside a pita, the traditional Mediterranean round bread. He shares the idea of this sandwich, called a kebap in Germany, with his compatriots, including Kadir Nurman and Nevzat Salim.

A Turkish name

The etymology of the sandwich comes directly from the Turkish *döner*, which means "turning," and *kebab*, "grilled food."

A suburban hit

In the world of rap, references in songs to this favorite late-night sandwich are numerous. The kebab created a culture and identity specific to the suburbs before becoming popular and trendy in the city.

Gaining momentum

In the gastronomic version, in Anthony Marciano's film *Les Gamins* (2013), during a dinner at a restaurant, Gilbert (Alain Chabat) and Irène (Elisa Sednaoui) order a burger and a kebab, respectively.

The server repeats: "Slice of beef in layers" and "sautéed lamb and Turkish galette."

467
The number of kebab establishments registered in Paris in 2017.

The kebab family, 4 schools

❶ THE DÖNER KEBAB
In a pita or pide bread, the meat (usually lamb and/or poultry) is cut on a vertical spit. This is the most classic version.

❷ THE DÜRÜM
This is the bread that is used in a kebab, which lends it its name. Literally, *dürüm* means "roll up" in Turkish. It is composed of wheat flour salted and panfried. It is sometimes referred to as yufka.

❸ THE BERLINOIS (BERLINER)
Served in a pita that has been split open, composed of meat, many grilled vegetables, and feta. Derived from the city of Berlin, kebap food stalls have been growing in number in Paris in recent years.

❹ THE ISKENDER
This is the kebab served on a plate, as it is traditionally served in restaurants in Bursa, Turkey.

Traits of the Parisian version

THE NICKNAME
Only in Paris is the kebab called a "grec" (Greek). The confusion dates to the interwar period and the arrival of the first Greek immigrants in the Latin Quarter. Some of them served "gyros" (meaning "to turn" in Greek) in a pita with a white sauce (tzatziki).

THE FILLING
In the 1990s, the most popular version of the sandwich throughout Paris's districts became a cultural icon. Order a salade-tomate-oignon (lettuce-tomato-onion) and you could feast for less than ten francs (the currency at the time), including a drink and fries.

THE SAUCE
Simply a white sauce made of yogurt, garlic, and mint. In Paris, it's often kicked up with harissa.

SKIP TO
Paris, A Cosmopolitan City, p. 164.

THE BEST KEBABS IN PARIS

Grillé

📍 *15, rue Saint-Augustin, Paris 2nd + 2 locations*
Type: Turkish.
Bread: homemade organic flat spelt bread cooked while you wait.
Meat: suckling veal on a spit by Hugo Desnoyer; cooking time and marinade proprietary.
Filling: lettuce, tomato, onion, napa cabbage, herbs.
Sauce: horseradish.

B. Bell Broche

📍 *74, rue de Turbigo, Paris 3rd*
Type: French.
Bread: house-made, between a baguette and a kebab.
Meat: suckling veal and smoked turkey on a spit; cooking time and marinade proprietary.
Filling: iceberg lettuce, tomato, red onion.
Sauce: honey mustard.

Casse-Croûte Grec

📍 *4, rue de l'École-Polytechnique, Paris 5th*
Type: gyros.
Bread: Greek pita.
Meat: veal and turkey on a spit; cooking time and marinade proprietary.
Filling: red cabbage, white cabbage, lettuce, tomato, onion.
Sauces: tzatziki, house-made harissa.

Ozlem

📍 *57, rue des Petites-Écuries, Paris 10th*
Type: Turkish.
Bread: house-made flatbread.
Meat: veal and turkey on a spit; marinated twenty-four to forty-eight hours, proprietary recipe.
Filling: iceberg salad, sumac onion.
Sauce: spicy.

Sürpriz

📍 *28, blvd. Saint-Denis, Paris 10th*
📍 *110, rue Oberkampf, Paris 11th*
Type: Berliner.
Bread: house-made pita, buttered with house-made butter.
Meat: chicken on a spit and peppers; marinated for thirty minutes, proprietary recipe.
Filling: eggplant, grilled zucchini and carrot, romaine lettuce, cabbage, herbs, red onion, cucumber, tomato, feta, paprika.
Sauces: spicy, garlic, and yogurt.

Antalya

📍 *19, rue Pernety, Paris 14th*
Type: Turkish.
Bread: house-made pita.
Meat: veal on a spit; marinated twenty-four hours, proprietary recipe.
Filling: lettuce, tomato, onion.
Sauces: house-made white, harissa.

Gemüse

📍 *61, rue Ramey, Paris 18th*
Type: Berliner.
Bread: traditional sesame pita.
Meat: chicken on a spit; marinated twenty-four hours, proprietary recipe.
Filling: lettuce, tomato, onion, grilled vegetables (zucchini, eggplant, pepper, carrot), herbs, fresh cheese, lemon juice.
Sauces: white, red harissa.

Buffet Dost

📍 *92, rue d'Avron, Paris 20th*
Type: Turkish.
Bread: house-made pita.
Meat: veal and turkey on a spit; cooking time and marinade proprietary.
Filling: lettuce, tomato, onion.
Sauces: house-made white, harissa.

O Dürüm

📍 *32, blvd. Jean-Jaurès, Saint-Ouen (Seine-Saint-Denis)*
Type: Berliner.
Bread: house-made pita.
Meat: veal on a spit; cooking time and marinade proprietary.
Filling: lettuce, tomato, onion, feta, pomegranate seeds.
Sauces: house-made white, harissa.

Poilâne, a Family History

For three generations, this family has baked up its emblematic sourdough loaf in wood-fired ovens for the delight of the capital. —MARIE-LAURE FRÉCHET

Pierre Poilâne in front of the shop on 8, rue du Cherche-Midi.

Family profile

- **PIERRE LÉON POILÂNE (1909–1993)**
A baker from Normandy, Pierre Poilâne moved to Paris and opened his bakery in 1932 at 8, rue du Cherche-Midi (Paris 6th). Refusing to give in to the postwar trend of white bread, he sold a brown-loaf sourdough made with stone-ground flour. He supplied bistros and restaurants, where a sign was displayed that read: "*Ici, Pain Poilâne* [Here, Pain Poilâne], made with sourdough, baked in a wood-fired oven and made with flour ground on millstones."

- **LIONEL POILÂNE (1945–2002)**
The son of Pierre Léon, Lionel began his apprenticeship at the age of fourteen, trained by his father, whom he succeeded in the business. In 1974, he registered the Poilâne brand and was committed to its development, particularly abroad. In the 1980s, he built a factory in Bièvres (Essonne), where several tons of bread are still produced every day. Throughout his career and his writings, he remains the ardent defender of "good bread," contrary to industrial standards.

- **MAX POILÂNE**
The son of Pierre Léon and brother of Lionel, he founded the company Max Poilâne in 1976. This was the beginning of a long legal battle between the two brothers and their heirs, relating to the use of the surname. His son Julien was also a baker in Lyon.

- **APOLLONIA POILÂNE**
Daughter of Lionel, she took over the reins of the company at the age of eighteen when her father died in 2002. She continued in the same spirit of Poilâne and developed the family business alongside her sister Athena, including the creation of an eating space, the Comptoir Poilâne, and the launch of a corn bread.

DISTRIBUTION OF SALES TODAY

20% from 5 boutiques in Paris and 1 in London

80% from retailers and restaurateurs

Lionel Poilâne and his wife, Irena.

Apollonia Poilâne.

The bakery's bestsellers

MICHE POILÂNE: a round bread weighing about 4 pounds (1.9 kg), with a thick crust and brown crumb, baked in a wood-fired oven, marked with the *P* for "Poilâne."

PUNITION: sablés baked in a wood-fired oven.

TARTE AUX POMMES (APPLE TART): apple wedges sprinkled with brown sugar over which puff pastry is folded.

> **SHOP ADDRESSES**
> ♦ *38, rue Debelleyme, Paris 3rd*
> ♦ *8, rue du Cherche-Midi, Paris 6th*
> ♦ *49, blvd. de Grenelle, Paris 15th*
> ♦ *39, rue de Lévis, Paris 17th*
> ♦ *83, rue de Crimée, Paris 19th*

SKIP TO
Paris Loves Bread, p. 158; Bakeries, p. 308.

THE RECIPE FOR "CROQUE POILÂNE"

Season: year-round **Difficulty** ●○○

SERVES 2

For the béchamel

1 tablespoon unsalted butter

2 tablespoons all-purpose flour

Freshly ground black pepper

Scant ⅔ cup (150 ml) milk

½ cup (60 g) half-and-half mixture of grated Cantal and Gruyère cheeses

2 large slices of Poilâne wheat pain au levain

2 large slices (50 g each) jambon blanc

The Poilâne family shares their original recipe for the croque-monsieur Poilâne.

Make the béchamel: In a medium saucepan, melt the butter over low heat. Add the flour and a pinch of pepper. Stir with a whisk for several minutes until smooth. Gently add the milk, whisking until the mixture thickens. Remove from the heat and let cool.

Preheat the oven to 350°F (180°C). Cut the bread slices in half. Spread half of the béchamel on one side of the four bread slices.

On two slices of bread, spread half the grated cheese mixture on the béchamel and top with one slice of ham. Cover with the remaining slices of bread.

Spread the remaining béchamel on top of each sandwich and sprinkle the tops with the remaining grated cheese.

Bake for 12 to 15 minutes, or until the cheese on top is melted and browned. Serve with a green salad on the side, if desired.

Dalí's Bread

In 1971, Lionel Poilâne made furniture out of bread for Salvador Dalí, the surrealist genius who was in love with Paris.
— JACQUES BRUNEL

Salvador Dalí and the painter Georges Mathieu at the Paris Fair, 1958.

Dalí in Paris

• **FROM THE LATE 1950s**
He has his suite (number 102, now named after him) at Le Meurice hotel. At parties, he likes to dress up as a monarch, wearing a crown.

• **1960s–1970s**
He organizes social dinners in Paris where great chefs make over-the-top recipes for him, such as Swan and Toothbrush Tart, and "spoutniks astiqués d'asticots statistiques" (with snails and frogs).

Dalí, bread's friend

› **A religious food,** whose color and elasticity evoke human flesh, bread is at the center of his erotic-nutritive obsessions, a symbol of life that he paints in a basket, in human form, or even crucified. He styles a Parisian baguette into the bust of a woman and dons a Catalan triangle-shaped bread on his head, evoking a bullfighter's cap.

› **In 1945** Dalí painted a portrait of Gala whose crossed arms "resemble the interlacing of a bread basket, and her breast the crust of bread."

› **On May 12, 1958** with the painter Georges Mathieu, he strolled around the Paris Fair carrying "trium-phallically" a 40-foot (12 m) long baton, escorted by masked bakers with fake mustaches.

› **On November 18, 1956,** in Montmartre for the release of a study for *Don Quixote*, which he sketched, he used bread dipped in ink to create a drawing in public.

Salvador Dalí and Lionel Poilâne, 1971.

His collaboration with Poilâne

In 1971, at age twenty-one, Lionel Poilâne, son of the founder of the Poilâne bakery, was approached by Salvador Dalí. The painter wanted to offer Gala, his partner, a room made of bread under the pretext of determining whether there were mice at Le Meurice where he lived. After discussion, they narrowed down the pieces to an eighteenth-century Spanish sideboard, a chandelier, candlesticks, a four-poster bed, and a birdcage, which the imprisoned occupant would have to peck through to achieve freedom. "Dalí also asked me for a television," says Lionel Poilâne, "but that would have created electrical problems."

THE SIDEBOARD
Made of unleavened bread, the 5-foot-high (1.65 m) furniture piece was separated into assembled elements, each taking two and a half hours to bake. After baking, the all-bread sideboard (except for its metal hinges) weighed between 110 and 177 pounds (50 and 55 kg), depending on the room's humidity level. Upon delivery of the masterpiece at Le Meurice, Dalí exclaimed: "We are experiencing a historical moment! . . . . I think we can extract treasures of cybernetic information from it!"

THE CHANDELIER
The light had six arms, candle cups, and lamp sockets, and was decorated with edible rosettes. This was the only object from the room that outlived its creator, and it is displayed today on the ceiling of Poilâne. In 2004, to celebrate Dalí's one hundredth birthday, the Maison Poilâne's bakers re-created the four-poster bed, sideboard, and chandelier, which were auctioned off and the proceeds donated to help the homeless.

SKIP TO
La Coupole, p. 296.

The four-poster bed and dressers made of bread, 2004.

Restaurants of the Eiffel Tower

Standing at 410 feet (125 m) tall, these eateries have a view over Paris's landscape like no other. It's an achievement within an achievement. — JACQUES BRUNEL AND EZEKIEL ZÉRAH

Did Eiffel have steel teeth?

Perhaps Gustave Eiffel, a native of Burgundy, was a gourmand. Maybe he was as equally skilled in handling metal cutlery, bottle openers, and escargot tongs as he was at engineering his metalwork marvels. He lunched at L'Improviste, a bistro near his studio, and he included a space for a kitchen in the 1,080-square-foot (100 sq m) apartment he occupied at the top of the Eiffel Tower.

A waistline too thin

French poet Paul Verlaine found the Eiffel Tower too thin, describing it as a "skeletal belfry." It was perhaps a good counterpoint, therefore, that opposite the tower in 1889, stood an "obese" building, the Trocadéro Palace, a neo-Byzantine inflated-looking structure resembling a larded turkey with its "drumsticks" raised to the sky. So perhaps a tower resembling a roasting spit set across from it made sense!

Restaurants on the first level, 1889.

1889 Built for dining pleasure

During the Universal Exposition of 1889, two million visitors ascended the newly opened tower to get a taste of a bit of vertigo. On the first floor were rows of four wooden pavilions. Each pavilion could feed five hundred guests (their kitchens and cellars were suspended under the platform). These four pavilions were made up of **an Anglo-American bar-restaurant** between the west and south pillars; **a Russian restaurant** between the east and north pillars; **a bar called "Flamand"** (although the name means "Flemish," it was dedicated to Alsatian specialties, with servers wearing folkloric dresses, lending a theatrical feel); and **the French restaurant** run by Brébant, equipped with private lounges and opening onto the Champ-de-Mars grassy lawn that extends behind the tower.

The restaurant dining room, circa 1900.

1937 A clean plate

Set up on the Champ-de-Mars, the Universal Exposition of 1937 forced the city to address the renovation of the Eiffel Tower, equipping it with modern lighting. The four restaurants on the first floor were demolished, and two were built in their place. The chicest of the two establishments was En Plein Ciel. It was adorned with art deco crystal chandeliers, and its banquet hall offered an extrawide panorama of the Trocadéro.

The restaurant dining room on the second floor, mid-twentieth century.

1965–1971 The tower puts its best foot forward

In 1965, chef André Pignarre regaled the actors of *Is Paris burning?* (Simone Signoret, Orson Welles, Kirk Douglas, Jean-Louis Trintignant, Michel Piccoli, Alain Delon, Jean-Paul Belmondo) with smoked salmon Grand Palais, timbale of lobster Rivoli, lamb saddle Champs-Élysées, gratin Dauphine, and petits fours Luxembourg.

The following year, in 1966, chef Pignarre was succeeded by Roger Gross, who promoted the French regions with poularde haute mère (quartered whole chicken) cooked in cognac and crème fraîche. He embellished the decor with statues, Venetian chandeliers, and lamps in the shape of the Eiffel Tower.

In 1971, a new change occurred: the first floor now housed a brasserie and two restaurants: Le Paris (reception rooms) and Le Trocadéro.

1983–2009 The Slavik years

FIRST FLOOR

The renovation in 1983 removed everything from the past and started from the ground up, creating a new brasserie, La Belle France, and a bistro, Le Parisien. Sixteen years later, they merged into a large brasserie, Altitude 95 (referring to the height of the first floor). Entrusted to Slavik, the premier Parisian designer at the time, and architect Jean-Jacques Loup, the brasserie's vast metal space with railings and revolving seats evoked the cabin of an airship sailing through the air.

SECOND FLOOR

The tower's second floor was converted in 1983 to house a gourmet restaurant, Le Jules Verne, with a private elevator. Slavik reinterpreted the Eiffel Tower with black-and-white decor, matching porcelain, a cubist moucharaby, and even a grand piano. MOF and starred chef Louis Grondard innovated cleverly (such as kidney with bacon and mustard seed) and was awarded a Michelin star. He was succeeded by Alain Reix, an inventive seafood chef (sea bass with artichokes with Saint-Émilion sauce, or scallops breaded with orange peel) who prepared the presidential dinner between Jacques Chirac and Hu Jintao in 2004.

2007–2019 The reign of Ducasse

In 2006, the Alain Ducasse group modernized the tower's restaurants. Architect Patrick Jouin initiated a major face-lift for the tower.

FIRST FLOOR: the Altitude 95 brasserie—renamed 58 Tour Eiffel—no longer copied the exterior architecture of the tower but was inspired by it: carbon-fiber armchairs in the colors of the tower, woven cane–back chairs, and a floating staircase. The materials were weighed to the nearest gram weight, lightening the structure by 8 tons.

SECOND FLOOR: within a mythical setting, the new Le Jules Verne played the poetic allusion—"Rue de Paris la Nuit" ceiling lights, window seats, pixelated luminous screens. Both spectacular and sober, Patrick Jouin's decor gave the impression of floating in air.

THE SMALL KITCHEN (480 SQUARE FEET/45 SQ M): there is a commissary under the Champ-de-Mars where food is cleaned and prepped before being taken up to the kitchens.

Michelin-starred chef Pascal Féraud never failed to dazzle, such as with his souffléd potatoes cut in the shape of the Eiffel Tower. In 2017, however, it was Alain Ducasse himself who oversaw the dinner prepared for Donald Trump.

SINCE 2020 Anton at the top

Despite Alain Ducasse's resistance, the management of the restaurants on the Eiffel Tower transferred, in 2019, to the Sodexo group, allied with two great chefs.

FIRST FLOOR: out with the loud metal decor: Renamed Madame Brasserie, the ex–58 Tour Eiffel was designed by Ramy Fischler in natural earth tones in a style of a Mesopotamian temple. With the installation of ultracomfortable furniture and extralarge bay windows, the kitchen is led by Michelin-starred Thierry Marx, who combines modernity with the past: hake seared with artichokes, pork spare rib Cantal with carrots and quinoa . . .

SECOND FLOOR: redesigned by Aline Asmar from Amman, the new Le Jules Verne plays with ethereal white and Dior gray, and occasional zebra stripes with tinges of gold. The most beautiful features are provided by Frédéric Anton, with three Michelin stars, whose delicate dishes (langoustine ravioli with Parmesan cream and truffle jelly, artichoke pepper à la romaine, curry and juice of saffron milk cap mushroom) resemble constructivist paintings.

The Iron Lady's technical challenges

› Apart from erosion, the Eiffel Tower's greatest enemy is fire, which its iron structure would not tolerate. **Consequence:** the brasserie and restaurant do not use gas appliances; only electricity is allowed.
› Le Jules Verne has the smallest gourmet kitchen in Paris. **Consequence:** a meticulous organization is required to plan the back-and-forth necessary between the commissary kitchens hidden under the Champ-de-Mars, 330 feet (100 m) from the tower and service elevator.

A potpourri of styles

❶ **Wicker restaurant chair** with backrest in the shape of an inverted Eiffel Tower, 1900.

❷ **Chair with braided metal back** from Le Jules Verne, registered in the Mobilier National, Slavik, 1983.

❸ **Armchair with wheels,** metallic and riveted, from Le Jules Verne and Altitude 95, Slavik, 1983.

❹ **Rectangular steel table** from Altitude 95, using the same bolts as the Eiffel Tower, Slavik, 1983.

❺ **"Rues de Paris" lighting** by Patrick Jouin for Le Jules Verne, 2000s.

❻ **Charger plate** "Structure," a tribute to the metallic interlacing of the tower, designed by Pierre Tachon for Le Jules Verne, 2000s.

❼ **Chocolate nut,** crispy praline, and hazelnut ice cream from Manufacture Alain Ducasse for Le Jules Verne, 2000s.

In the movies

In the film *Dangerously Yours* (1985), James Bond (Roger Moore) meets Achille Aubergine (Jean Rougerie), who is killed by May Day (Grace Jones) during the meal at the restaurant on the second floor of the Eiffel Tower.

SKIP TO Art Nouveau or Art Deco?, p. 160.

The Rum Baba

Instantly recognizable, this boozy pastry is held in high regard in Paris's hall of fame of pastries. —JEAN-PHILIPPE MARSAN

THE RECIPE

Season: year-round
Difficulty ● ● ●

SERVES 6

For the baba dough

1½ cups (180 g) pastry flour or T45 flour

1 tablespoon plus 2 teaspoons superfine sugar

⅔ teaspoon fine salt

⅓ ounce (10 g) fresh yeast

½ tablespoon milk

2 large (100 g) eggs

4 tablespoons (60 g) unsalted butter, at room temperature + 2 teaspoons for greasing

For the vanilla Chantilly cream

½ vanilla bean

1¼ cups (300 ml) heavy whipping cream

3 tablespoons confectioners' sugar

For the syrup

2¼ cups (520 g) water

1 cup plus 2 tablespoons (230 g) superfine sugar

Zest of 1 lemon

Zest of 1 orange

1 vanilla bean

½ cup (125 ml) rum

Equipment

Stand mixer

One 6-inch (16 cm) kugelhopf mold

This home cook's recipe is adapted from the legendary version by Cyril Lignac.*

Make the baba dough: In the bowl of a stand mixer fitted with the dough hook, combine the flour, sugar, and salt. Dissolve the yeast in the milk and add it to the flour mixture. Knead on low speed (speed 1). Using a fork, briefly whisk together the eggs and slowly stream them into the mixer while on low speed. Knead until the dough detaches from the sides of the bowl.

Once a smooth dough is achieved, incorporate the butter in three additions. Knead the dough at speed 3 until a small piece of dough stretched using your fingers creates a very thin membrane that light will shine through without breaking. Set aside the dough for 45 minutes in a warm spot to rise.

Preheat the oven to 350°F (180°C). Place the dough in a pan greased with butter, large enough so that the dough fills the pan just two-thirds full. Set aside again for 30 minutes to rise. Bake for 20 minutes.

Make the vanilla Chantilly cream: Split the vanilla bean lengthwise in half and scrape out the seeds using the tip of a knife and set aside. In the clean bowl of the stand mixer fitted with the whisk attachment, beat the cream to stiff peaks. Stir in the vanilla seeds. Fold in the confectioners' sugar to stabilize the cream. Keep chilled in the refrigerator.

Make the syrup: In a saucepan, bring the water and sugar to a boil. Add the grated lemon and orange zests, then the seeds and empty pod of the split and scraped vanilla bean. Cover and let infuse for 30 minutes over low heat. Stir in the rum. Keep warm.

Assemble: Dip the baba in the hot syrup and set aside on a rack to drain. When cooled, use a piping bag to top the center of the cake with Chantilly cream.

*La Pâtisserie Cyril Lignac—24, rue Paul-Bert, Paris 11th + 4 locations.

Baba mold (*Le Livre de pâtisserie*, J. Gouffé, 1873).

FROM POLAND TO PARIS

Created in Poland in the sixteenth century, the baba, according to legend, arrived in the region of Lorraine with the exiled king Stanislas Leszczynski. At that time, the baba was simply a round cake made from brioche, topped with raisins, and flavored with saffron. Another legend tells that the monarch was a gourmet with fragile teeth and asked his pastry chef Nicolas Stohrer to dip his baba in tokay, the famous Polish wine, to make the cake softer. Starting in 1820, Parisian pastry chefs began soaking the baba with alcohol, rum especially, an approach attributed to Stohrer.

BABA OR SAVARIN?

Today, these refer to the same cake, yet the savarin has its own history. In their pastry shop on Place de la Bourse around 1845, the Julien brothers created a cake similar to a baba but in the shape of a crown (ring). It was named after the famous gastronome Brillat-Savarin.

TOP LET'S EAT PARIS! ADDRESSES

SHOPS

Maison Stohrer

📍 *51, rue Montorgueil, Paris 2nd*

Offers an authentic traditional baba with or without Chantilly cream.

Pain de Sucre

📍 *14, rue Rambuteau, Paris 3rd*

Filled with a creamy Madagascar vanilla mousseline cream and soaked in vanilla syrup, citrus zest, and dark rum.

Sébastien Gaudard

📍 *22, rue des Martyrs, Paris 9th*

This baba's honeycombed and spongy dough shimmers from the syrup made with an agricultural rum syrup from the West Indies.

RESTAURANTS

Oui Mon Général!

📍 *14, rue du Général-Bertrand, Paris 7th*

This fabulous and generously soaked baba stands out with its three different dark rums.

Maison Fournaise

📍 *Ile des Impressionnistes, Chatou (Yvelines)*

In this restaurant on the banks of the Seine where Renoir painted *Le Déjeuner des canotiers*, the chef serves a massively huge warmed baba with vanilla cream and citrus zest.

SKIP TO
Chez l'Ami Louis, p. 218.

HARRY'S NEW YORK BAR

Hemingway was a regular, and the Bloody Mary was born here. This American-style bar is one of the most emblematic in the capital. —**CHARLES PATIN O'COOHOON**

MAISON PARISIENNE
5, RUE DAUNOU,
2ND ARR.

Straw Vote, November 1960.

From New York to Paris

This temple of the cocktail, hailing from the United States, opened on November 23, 1911, Thanksgiving Day. After finishing his career in Europe, jockey Tod Sloan had a bar dismantled on Manhattan's Seventh Avenue and opened it at 5, rue Daunou. To run the bar, he called on Harry MacElhone, a Scottish bartender from Dundee, who took it over a few years later. The New York Bar was thus christened Harry's New York Bar.

A mecca for Americans

Ernest Hemingway would down up to twenty whiskey sours in one visit before returning to work at his hotel.
Francis Scott Fitzgerald, Gertrude Stein, and part of the Lost Generation bellied up to the bar here.
George Gershwin composed some of the melodies of his symphonic work *An American in Paris* here, directed by Vincente Minnelli in the film of the same name.
Dwight D. Eisenhower would take some time out here before becoming the thirty-fourth president of the United States.

Sank roo doe noo

In 1924, Harry MacElhone published the following message in the *New York Herald Tribune*: "Just tell the taxi driver 'sank roo doe noo,' and get ready for the worst." This is the phonetic pronunciation of 5, rue Daunou, the bar's address. Learning this phrase would allow English speakers passing through Paris to make it to the bar. How clever!

The Straw Vote

This is a mock vote open to all adult Americans residing in Paris. The vote begins one month before the official announcement of the US presidential election. The results are displayed in white paint on the mirror behind the counter. During its history, the Straw Vote has been wrong three times: in 1976, when Jimmy Carter was elected; in 2004, when George W. Bush was reelected; and in 2018, when Donald Trump became president.

US customs

In 1919, Harry's was the first bar in France to serve Coca-Cola. A few years later, in 1933, Harry bought a hot dog machine at the Chicago World's Fair. Harry's Bar became the first establishment to bring hot dogs to France.

TO SEE

The impressive collection of university pennants from Yale, Princeton, Oberlin, Harvard.
University coats of arms hanging on the mahogany walls.
The piano bar being played in the Downstairs Room.
The skilled bartenders in their white aprons.

TO DRINK

An impressive collection of whiskeys (350 labels).

A string of cocktails, some of them legendary, created at Harry's Bar:

1921
THE BLOODY MARY
Vodka, tomato juice, lemon juice, Tabasco, salt, and pepper

1923
THE WHITE LADY
Gin, triple sec, lime juice

1931
THE SIDE CAR
Cognac, triple sec, lemon juice

1960
THE BLUE LAGOON
Vodka, blue curaçao, lemon juice

SKIP TO
Paris: A Moveable Feast, p. 244; Cocktail Bars, p. 374.

Fries Forever!

Fries (frites) are a Parisian invention—a popular dish of the people. The Belgians also deserve credit for their notoriety. —**MARIE-LAURE FRÉCHET**

The origins

The story begins on the banks of the Seine, in Paris. At a dinner he offered to Louis XVI in 1785, pharmacist Antoine-Agustin Parmentier highlighted the potato. From the end of the eighteenth century, the street vendors of Pont-Neuf fried them in a pot of fat, similar to when making fitters. From that time and until the end of the nineteenth century, the "pomme Pont-Neuf" was cut into strips; today, it refers to classic fries.

> "It's Parisian, this flavor of fries."

—Louis-Ferdinand Céline, *Voyage au bout de la nuit*, 1932

From stand to cup

In 1838, a German fair vendor, Frederik Krieger, known as Monsieur Fritz, opened his fried potatoes stand at the fair in Liège. He learned his cooking technique for the potatoes in a restaurant in Montmartre. In 1852, he founded a popular tasting parlor and offered "cornet de frites" (fries in a paper cone). Fritz died at age forty-six, but his widow continued and expanded his business and maintained the reputation of fries, which everyone enjoyed starting at the beginning of the twentieth century in both Belgium and France.

> **"Fried potatoes are one of the most spiritual creations of the Parisian genius."**

—Curnonsky, 1927

Add Some Oil!

The first fries were cooked in lard. Monsieur Fritz used clarified butter, later replaced by beef or horse fat for reasons of economy, a tradition that continues in Belgium and northern France, and which gives fries an incomparable flavor. Today, primarily sunflower or peanut oil is used.

Paris Vécu. — La Marchande de Frites

Fry vendor, circa 1900.

LE DOYEN DE LA FRITURE

Fritz.

Parisian-style

Should it be Belgian-style or Parisian-style? Since the nineteenth century, the birthplace of the fry has been debated. Is it possible the great Baudelaire gave us the key to the mystery? His friend Georges Barral, who guided him on his gourmet tours in Brussels in 1864, seemed rather categorical: "No sooner had we finished than they put in the center of the table a large earthenware bowl, all overflowing with fried potatoes, blond, crisp, and tender at the same time. A masterpiece of frying, rare in Belgium. They are exquisite, said Baudelaire, crunching them slowly, after having taken them one by one, delicately with the fingers: a classic method mentioned by Brillat-Savarin. Moreover, it is an essentially Parisian gesture, as fried potatoes are a Parisian invention. It was the French outcasts of 1851 who introduced them to Brussels."

—Georges Barral, *Cinq journées avec Charles Baudelaire à Bruxelles* [1864], Éditions du Paquebot, Paris

The expanding potato

Under the impetus of French chefs, the fried potato became a classier food. In Auguste Escoffier's *Le Guide Culinaire*, there are many recipes and techniques for frying a potato. Variations include pomme croquette (cylinders of fried potatoes mixed with yolk), pomme dauphine (croquettes of puréed potatoes and choux pastry, fried), pomme duchesse (cooked potatoes puréed with egg yolk and butter and shaped or piped and baked), and pomme gaufrette (waffled fries).

SKIP TO Le Relais de Venise, p. 109; Chez l'Ami Louis, p. 218.

THE BEST FRIES IN PARIS

To go

Label'ge Frite

⚲ *169, rue Montmartre, Paris 2nd*
Variety: Bintje
Cut: matchstick
Cooking: fried twice, in beef fat

Frenchie To Go

⚲ *9, rue du Nil, Paris 2nd*
Variety: Bintje
Cut: matchstick
Cooking: fried twice, in sunflower oil

Le Camion Qui Fume

⚲ *6, rue Grégoire-de-Tours, Paris 6th*
⚲ *66, rue Oberkampf, Paris 11th*
⚲ *132, av. de France, Paris 13th*
Variety: Bintje
Cut: thick
Cooking: fried twice, in sunflower oil

In restaurants

La Bourse et La Vie

⚲ *12, rue Vivienne, Paris 2nd*
Variety: Agria
Cut: thick
Cooking: fried three times, in sunflower oil

L'Ami Louis

⚲ *32, rue du Vertbois, Paris 3rd*
Variety: Agria
Cut: straw (cut by knife or machine)
Cooking: fried once, in sunflower oil

Les Marches

⚲ *5, rue de la Manutention, Paris 16th*
Variety: Voyager or Agria
Cut: matchstick
Cooking: fried twice, in sunflower oil

Chez Nenesse

⚲ *17, rue de Saintonge, Paris 3rd*
Variety: Bintje or Agria
Cut: matchstick
Cooking: fried twice, in peanut oil

L'Évasion

⚲ *7, pl. Saint-Augustin, Paris 8th*
Variety: Samba
Cut: matchstick
Cooking: fried twice, in sunflower oil

Le Coq & Fils

⚲ *98, rue Lepic, Paris 18th*
Variety: Agria
Cut: thick
Cooking: fried twice, in sunflower oil

Bouillon Pigalle/ Bouillon République

⚲ *39, blvd. du Temple, Paris 3rd*
⚲ *22, blvd. de Clichy, Paris 18th*
Variety: Agria
Cut: matchstick
Cooking: fried twice, in sunflower oil

Bien Élevé/Bien Ficelé

⚲ *47, rue Richer, Paris 9th*
⚲ *51, blvd. Voltaire, Paris 11th*
Variety: Agria
Cut: matchstick
Cooking: fried twice, in beef fat

Chez Pradel

⚲ *168, rue Ordener, Paris 18th*
Variety: Agria
Cut: thick
Cooking: fried twice, in vegetable oil (rapeseed, sunflower)

How to Fry

Whether deep-fried or baked in the oven, the potato endures all methods of cooking in Paris. Here is a recipe manual for fries. —BENOÎT NICOLAS, COOKING PROFESSOR, MOF (BEST CRAFTSMAN OF FRANCE) 2015

DEEP FRIED

Fries

Season: year-round
Difficulty ● ○ ○

SERVES 4

4½ pounds (2 kg) Bintje potatoes
2 quarts (2 L) sunflower oil
Salt

The secret to good fries? Twice frying, according to cook Suzy Palatine, who has achieved an unrivaled expertise when it comes to making fries.

Peel the potatoes and wash them ❶. Cut them into ⅓-inch-thick (1 cm) sticks using a knife or fry cutter ❷. Dry them twice using a cloth, then a third time using a paper towel.

In a deep pan, heat the oil to 338°F (170°C).

Fry the potatoes for 7 minutes. Remove them from the oil, let drain ❸, and cool for 20 minutes.

Place the fries back in the oil, heated to 338°F (170°C), for an additional 7 minutes. Drain, and season with salt before serving. Serve hot.

IT'S ALL IN THE VARIETY!

· **Choose a potato that is** starchy, for a soft interior once fried; of a late variety, harvested at maturity; large and regular in size.
· **The most popular:** the Bintje. Also very popular: Agria, Jelly, and Samba.
· **Attention:** starting from harvesttime in early autumn, the starch level of the potato is transformed into glucose as time passes and causes a deeper coloration of the fries.

"Bûche" (very thick cut)
¾ inch (2 cm) in size

"Pont-Neuf" (thick cut)
⅓ inch (1 cm) in size

"Allumette" (matchstick)
Just less than ¼ inch (5 mm) in size

"Paille" (straw)
About ⅛ inch (2.5 mm) in size

Wedge fries

Season: year-round **Difficulty** ● ○ ○

SERVES 4

3⅓ pounds (1.5 kg) Bintje potatoes
2 quarts (2 L) sunflower oil
Salt

Peel and wash the potatoes.

Cut them into thick slices ❶.

Cut the slices into wedges about ¼ inch
(5 to 6 mm) thick ❷.

Rinse. Dry.

Fry at 320°F (160°C) for about 10 minutes,
without browning. Drain ❸.

Fry at 350°F (180°C) until golden. Drain, and
season with salt.

A LITTLE HISTORY

Referred to in French as pomme coin due rue *(street-corner fries), these fries are a specialty of Fouquet's (Paris 8th), which always has them on the menu and serves 330 pounds (150 kg) each day. The name refers to the location of the restaurant—on a street corner of rue des Champs-Élysées—but also to its cut: at a right angle and with a curved side. This size was originally created to make use of the trimmings resulting from shaping rounded potatoes.*

Pomme soufflée (puffed potatoes)

Season: year-round **Difficulty** ● ● ●

SERVES 4

6½ pounds (3 kg) Agria potatoes
2 quarts (2 L) sunflower oil
Salt

Equipment

Mandoline
1½-inch (4 cm) cookie cutter
Thermometer

Peel and wash the potatoes. Using a mandoline
(or very sharp knife), slice them to ⅛ inch (3 mm)
thick ❶ then cut out circles of 1½ inches (4 cm)
from the center using the cookie cutter ❷.

In a saucepan or deep fryer, fry the slices at 284°F
(140°C), stirring to help the potatoes puff.

As soon as the slices begin to puff, immerse them
in oil heated to 350°F (180°C), until pale golden ❸.
Drain, and season with salt.

A LITTLE HISTORY

The result of a train that happened to arrive ten minutes later than expected at the Saint-Germain-en-Laye train station in Yvelines. When the delay was announced, the cook, who had planned to fry the potatoes, took the potatoes out of their oil, placed them into a colander to drain, then requested they be fried again when the train arrived. They went from cold fries to puffed fries.

Pomme Chatouillard
(spiralized fries)

Season: year-round **Difficulty** ● ● ●

SERVES 4

6½ pounds (3 kg) Agria potatoes
2 quarts (2 L) sunflower oil
Salt

Equipment
1 potato spiraler
1 plain piping tip with a diameter of ¾ inch (2 cm)
1 trussing needle

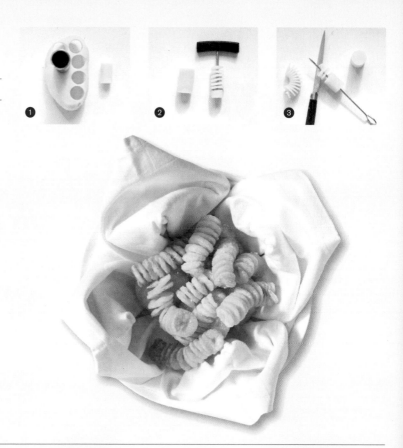

Peel and wash the potatoes. Use the potato spiraler to cut the forms or cut them out into tube shapes using the piping tip ❶. Pierce the ends of the tubes with the needle all the way through ❷.

Using a small sharp knife, spiral cut the potatoes ⅛ inch thick (3 mm) to obtain a ribbon ❸. Briefly fry at 284°F (140°C), stirring until blistered but not browned. When the potato begins to puff, fry them in oil at 350°F (180°C) to puff and brown them. Drain, and season with salt.

A LITTLE HISTORY
According to Prosper Montagné, the name comes from "an old practitioner, excellent roaster, and the most skillful produce merchant."

Pomme dauphine

Season: year-round **Difficulty** ● ● ○

SERVES 4

2½ tablespoons unsalted butter
½ cup (125 ml) water
½ cup (65 g) all-purpose flour
2 large (100 g) eggs
1½ pounds (700 g) Pomme Duchesse mixture (see recipe opposite)
2 quarts (2 L) sunflower oil
Salt

Equipment
2 tablespoons, for shaping

Make a choux pastry: In a saucepan, bring the butter and water to a boil ❶. Add the flour all at once and stir to make a smooth dough. Heat for 5 minutes over medium heat while stirring ❷. Add the eggs one at a time, stirring until incorporated.

Add the pomme duchesse mixture and stir to combine. Dip two spoons in oil to grease. Scoop out a tablespoon of the batter and use the two spoons to shape into an oval ❸. Fry in oil heated to 338°F (170°C). Once puffed and browned, remove from the oil and set aside to drain. Season with salt.

A LITTLE HISTORY
"Dauphine" refers to the wife of the dauphin. The first occurrence of this term was in 1830 in a sweet dessert made with cooked apples.

Pomme duchesse

Season: year-round **Difficulty** ● ● ○

SERVES 4

1¾ pounds (800 g) Bintje potatoes
5½ tablespoons (80 g) unsalted butter
5 large (100 g) egg yolks
Nutmeg
Salt and freshly ground black pepper

Equipment
1 pastry bag
1 fluted piping tip
Fine-mesh strainer

If needed, cut the pastry bag to fit the piping tip. Peel and wash the potatoes. Cut them into even pieces. Cook them in boiling water just until softened. Drain.

Mash the cooked potatoes into a purée and press them through a fine-mesh strainer to obtain a fine texture. Add the butter, egg yolks, and nutmeg and stir to combine. Season with salt and pepper. While still warm, transfer the mixture to the pastry bag fitted with the pastry tube. Pipe according to the desired shape. Bake at 350°F (180°C) until lightly browned on top.

A LITTLE HISTORY
Created by Auguste Escoffier in his 1907 Le Guide Culinaire. *Its shape is reminiscent of a small brioche bun with the rounded head.*

Pomme Anna

Season: year-round **Difficulty** ● ● ●

SERVES 4

6½ pounds (3 kg) Agria potatoes
Salt and freshly ground black pepper
7 ounces (200 g) clarified butter

Equipment
Mandoline
1 (1⅛-in/3 cm) cookie cutter
1 pomme Anna mold (or round cake pan)
1 parchment paper circle, cut to fit the inside bottom of the mold or pan

Peel and wash the potatoes. Using the mandoline, slice the potatoes into ¹⁄₁₀-inch-thick (2 mm) rounds. Using the cookie cutter, cut out circles from the center of the rounds. Season with salt and pepper and sauté in the butter until softened.

In the bottom of the mold lined with parchment paper, arrange the potato circles in a rosette pattern (overlapping the circles until the pan is fully covered in layers). Pick up the mold and tamp it lightly on the work surface to help press the potato layers down a little more firmly. Bake at 350°F (180°C), covered, for 30 minutes, then continuing baking uncovered until nicely golden. Unmold onto a cooling rack.

A LITTLE HISTORY
A creation of Adolphe Dugléré, chef at Café Anglais, which he dedicated to Anna Deslions, a famous courtesan, by whom Émile Zola was inspired for his novel Nana.

Pomme Maxim's

Season: year-round **Difficulty** ● ○ ○

SERVES 4

3⅓ pounds (1.5 kg) Agria potatoes
Salt and freshly ground black pepper
1 ounce (30 g) clarified butter

Equipment
Mandoline
1 (1⅛-in/3 cm) cookie cutter
4 tartlet molds

Peel and wash the potatoes. Using the mandoline, slice the potatoes into rounds about ¹⁄₂₀-inch-thick (1.5 mm). Using the cookie cutter, cut out circles from the center of the rounds; do not rinse them. Season with salt and pepper.

Briefly sauté the potatoes in the butter to soften them. Arrange the potatoes in a rosette pattern in the molds. Make a second layer in a rosette pattern in the opposite direction.

Drizzle with the clarified butter and bake at 350°F (180°C) until golden. Unmold, and let drain.

A LITTLE HISTORY
This potato dish was created in the kitchens of Maxim's, probably during the era of chef Louis Barthe.

BLANCHED / PANFRIED

Pomme Parisienne

Season: year-round **Difficulty** ● ○ ○

SERVES 4

4½ pounds (2 kg) Bintje potatoes
Scant ¼ cup (50 ml) sunflower oil
1 tablespoon unsalted butter
Salt

Equipment
1 melon baller

Peel and wash the potatoes. Scoop out balls from the potatoes using the melon baller. Blanch the balls in boiling water for 5 minutes. Drain, and let dry. To finish cooking, sauté the balls in hot oil until uniformly golden. Add the fresh butter to finish cooking. Drain, and season with salt.

A LITTLE HISTORY
The name comes from the utensil used to shape it: a cuillère à pomme Parisienne *in French (melon baller). There is no specific size, as it varies according to each utensil.*

Urbain Dubois (1818–1901)

Tsar of the Stove

Before inventing veal Orloff, a popular dish in Russia, this Provençal was a star at the stoves in some of the best Parisian restaurants.

—JACQUES BRUNEL

With the Russians

In 1855, he began working for Alexei Fyodorovich Orlov, ambassador of Tsar Nicholas I. He went into exile in Russia to serve the royal family. After, he went frequently to the court of Berlin to head the kitchens there, alternating with Émile Bernard. From his travels, he collected surprising recipes, such as pattes d'ours à la russe and pâtés à la choucroute. He was passionate about the visual aspect of a dish, adding to his repertoire appetizers on silver pedestals, wedding cakes, complex skewers, and tiered desserts. He would eventually promote service "à la russe" (Russian-style service), a stylish forebear of plated service where dishes were sequentially released from the kitchen and portioned out at a sideboard in the dining room before being served to each guest.

The virtuoso

› As a young man, he worked in his uncle's (Jean Dubois) restaurant in Trets (near Aix-en-Provence). Discipline there was strict.

› After a brief stay in Cannes, he went to Paris and completed his apprenticeship with Louis Haas in the kitchens of the Rothschild family.

› Ingenious and insightful, he worked his way into the most important establishments: alongside Chiboust in his shop, at Café Tortoni, at Café Anglais (working under Dugléré), and at Le Rocher de Cancale, where chef Langlais, the creator of sole Normande, headed the kitchen.

The writer

From 1856 to 1894, he penned many detailed and abundantly illustrated treatises:

› *La Cuisine classique: études pratiques, raisonnées et démonstratives de l'école française appliquée au service à la russe* (coauthored with Émile Bernard, cook of Napoléon III)

› *Cuisine de tous les pays. Étude cosmopolites*

› *Cuisine artistique. Étude de l'école moderne*

› *École des cuisinières. Nouvelle cuisine bourgeoise, pour la ville et pour la campagne*

› *La Cuisine d'aujourd'hui*

As well as two books on the art of sweet creations:

› *Grand livre des pâtissiers et confiseurs*

› *La Pâtisserie d'aujourd'hui. École des jeunes pâtissiers*

His work was considered a link between that of Antonin Carême and Auguste Escoffier.

THE RECIPE FOR VEAL ORLOV

Season: year-round
Difficulty ●●○

SERVES 6

2¼ pounds (1 kg) round of veal or lower rack of veal, split and flattened

Salt and freshly ground black pepper

20 slices bacon

7 ounces (200 g) grated Emmental cheese

Unsalted butter

1 cup (250 ml) veal stock

Equipment
Kitchen string
Aluminum foil

Arrange the veal flat on a work surface and season it with salt and pepper. Arrange two layers of bacon and Emmental on top. Fold over the edges of the meat, then roll the meat up tightly. Tie to secure it using the kitchen string.

Preheat the oven to 400°F (200°C). In a Dutch oven, sear the roast over high heat on each side in about ½ tablespoon of butter. Baste with the cooking juices, then add the veal stock. Cover and bake for 1 hour 10 minutes; the internal temperature should be about 154°F (68°C) in the center. Wrap the roast in foil and let stand for 20 minutes. Serve with the cooking juices poured over the top.

Model of a tiered stand, *Grand livre des pâtissiers et des confiseurs*, Urbain Dubois.

The Mystery of Veal Orloff

Some attribute this very famous recipe to Léonor Cheval, chef of Café Tortoni, where Prince Orlov often came to dine. But most consider Urbain Dubois to be its creator. The original recipe, which combines wine-braised veal with mushrooms, truffles, soubise, and Mornay sauces, has little to do with the butcher's "veal Orloff," a sliced roast topped with slices of bacon and cheese. It is more like its Russian version. French chefs often make it with the best part of the veal: the saddle. There are many variations: demi-deuil (styled with black and white ingredients), with pears, with cheddar, etc.

SKIP TO
The Invention of the Restaurant, p. 61; Antonin Carême, p. 156.

Counters That Count

When it's time for a p'tit noir (an espresso) or a glass of wine, standing up at one of the many beautiful "zincs" (counters, though not necessarily made of zinc) in the capital is a very Parisian approach. Here is a selection of several eye-catching bar tops. —CAMILLE MENNESSON

Zinc = bar top

As early as 1873, in *Le Ventre de Paris* (*The Belly of Paris*), Émile Zola mentions a *zinc* as a counter in bars and cafés at which customers were served standing:

"Sometimes the noise became so loud that Rose, with her languidness, pouring for a beautiful lady at the counter, turned her head worriedly. 'Oh well! Thank you' . . . the lady said, resting the glass on the zinc, wiping her mouth with the back of her hand."

NOT WHAT'S IN A NAME

Although referred to as "zinc," the bar tops are most often composed of tin and lead, a material that is much more malleable and easier to maintain.

SKIP TO
Cocktail Bars, p. 374.

LA JAJA
📍 *56, rue d'Argout, Paris 2nd*

OPENING DATE
2010

BAR TOP LENGTH
14 feet (4.20 m)

MATERIALS
Brass; oak

LE PROGRÈS
📍 *1, rue de Bretagne, Paris 3rd*

OPENING DATE
Twentieth century, renovated in 1998

BAR TOP LENGTH
20 feet (6 m)

MATERIALS
Tin and lead; oak

LE VOLTIGEUR
📍 *45, rue des Francs-Bourgeois, Paris 4th*

OPENING DATE
1930s

BAR TOP LENGTH
18 feet (5.50 m)

MATERIALS
Copper; mica and mosaic

AU CHIEN QUI FUME
📍 *19, blvd. du Montparnasse, Paris 6th*

OPENING DATE
1930s

BAR TOP LENGTH
33 feet (10 m)

MATERIALS
Tin and lead; beech

LE BISTROT DU PEINTRE
📍 *16, av. Ledru-Rollin, Paris 11th*

OPENING DATE
1902, renovated in 2012

BAR TOP LENGTH
18 feet (5.50 m)

MATERIALS
Tin and lead; wood

LE CYRANO
📍 *3, rue Biot, Paris 17th*

OPENING DATE
1914

BAR TOP LENGTH
13 feet (4 m)

MATERIALS
Granite; wood

And Then Came Bistronomy

At the dawn of the 2000s, the fate of Parisian bistros was saved thanks to the leadership of young chefs who rallied toward a new movement. This is how a simple word came to mean an entirely new genre of restaurant. —EMMANUEL RUBIN

Three milestone dates

LATE 1980s

The bistro, the pinnacle of the Parisian landscape, was an exhausted, overserved genre, lost among clichéd recipes and postcard decor. Bored with Nouvelle Cuisine, which had become a caricature of itself, and after decades of good and loyal service, some star chefs (Guy Savoy, Michel Rostang, Gérard Cagna, and others) began opening "bistro-style" outposts of their grand restaurants (Bistrot de l'Étoile, closed; Bistrot d'à Côté Flaubert, Paris 17th; Le Christine, Paris 6th).

1990s

A wave of young chefs, trained in multistarred restaurants and opulent hotels, opened bold new establishments in unexpected locations. These eateries offered plates executed with great skill yet with simpler service and at moderate prices. Among them were Yves Camdeborde (La Régalade, Paris 14th), Thierry Faucher (L'Os à Moelle, Paris 15th), and Éric Frechon (La Verrière, Paris 19th). *Le Figaroscope* described the genre as "neo-bistro" or "gourmet bistro."

2000s

Pioneered by chef Yves Camdeborde, the concept welcomes a tribe of young free-spirited, militant, and creative chefs, led by Inaki Aizpitarte (La Famille, Paris 18th, then Le Chateaubriand, Paris 11th), Grégory Marchand (Frenchie, Paris 2nd), Bertrand Grébaut (Septime, Paris 11th), and Sven Chartier (Saturne, Paris 2nd). The *Le Fooding* movement coins the term *bistronomy*, as a combination of the two schools of cooking styles.

The story behind the name

One morning in November 2004, in a Parisian brasserie, four years after its creation, the jury of the fledgling *Le Fooding* met to decide on the awards for best restaurants of the year. When deciding upon one of these new-style bistros, each member mulled over the decision to find the most striking appellation to categorize the winner. *Bistroy? Bistrotteur? Post-bistro?* Words were fused and re-fused to find a description. Suddenly, in a flash of brilliance, food writer Sébastien Demorand let out a thunderous announcement: "I've got it . . . best *bistronomique*!" Silence fell across the room, followed by a sudden roar from the group. The term was adopted unanimously. It quickly became one of the leading categories for *Le Fooding* columnists. The lucky winner was announced: Mon Vieil Ami, a "bistronomique" that opened on Île Saint-Louis (Paris 4th) in the spring of 2004 by the former Alsatian three-Michelin-starred Antoine Westermann.

SKIP TO
Chef-Driven
Restaurants,
p. 348.

Bistronomy in 6 Iconic Dishes

› Terrine de Compagne by Stéphane Jégo's

L'Ami Jean
⚲ 27, rue Malar, Paris 7th. €€€

› Fillets de maquereaux confits, rémoulade de céler by David Rathgeber

L'Assiette
⚲ 181, rue du Château, Paris 14th. €€

› Cervelle Meunière by Raquel Carena

Le Baratin
⚲ 3, rue Jouye-Rouve, Paris 20th. €€€

› Couteaux à la Plancha by Christian Etchebest

La Cantine du Troquet
⚲ 101, rue de l'Ouest, Paris 14th + 4 locations. €

› Côte de Veau de Corrèze by Benoît Gauthier

Le Grand Pan
⚲ 20, rue Rosenwald, Paris 15th. €€

› Riz au Lait by Bruno Doucet

La Régalade
⚲ 106, rue Saint-Honoré, Paris 1st. €€

A PORTMANTEAU

May 28, 2015, was the consecration date. Ten years after its creation, *bistronomy* was an official entry in the dictionary *Le Petit Larousse illustré 2016*. The definition is as follows: "feminine noun (from *bistro* and *gastronomy*). Refined and inventive cuisine, gastronomic, but served in a simple, nonstarred restaurant (bistro, café, or brasserie)."

What we owe it

Bistronomy has gently shaken up the order of the meal as well as introduced new terminology in the French restaurant industry by inventing, accompanying, or imposing trends that have become, over the last twenty years, new approaches to dining, adopted by many prestigious restaurants. Here are ten.

· NATURAL, LIVING, AND BIODYNAMIC WINES ❶.

· SIGNATURE COCKTAILS.

· REFILLS OF DISTILLED WATER.

· THE SINGLE MENU AND THE "CARTE BLANCHE" MENU ❷.

· THE NO-TABLECLOTH TABLE ❸.

· THE ARTISAN'S KNIFE, INCLUDING THE FAMOUS PERCEVAL 9.47 ❹.

· THE KITCHEN THAT OPENS TO THE DINING ROOM ❺.

· SOURCED AND TRACED INGREDIENTS ❻.

· LOCAVORE FOCUSED.

· THE "SLASH" DESCRIPTION OF A DISH: SUCH AS "ENDIVE/MUSTARD/TROUT EGGS" OR "POLLACK/CABBAGE/TURMERIC/HAZELNUTS" ❼.

Pizza Conquers Paris

Parisians are among the biggest consumers of pizza in France, and yet, the first Parisian pizzeria didn't open until the 1950s. Here is a chronology of an illustrious saga. —ALESSANDRA PIERINI

Philippo, making his pizzas in the window, Paris, October 1960.

Bartolo (right) and Ginette Memola (left) taste the restaurant's first pizza.

Pizzeria Cotti, Paris, 1950s.

1950
Chez Bartolo, the first pizzeria, opens at 7, rue des Canettes (Paris 6th).

1955
Pizzeria Odessa (Paris 14th) is founded by a Frenchman nicknamed "Cotti."

1956
After opening in 1948 with Sicilian and Neopolitian owners, Palurino is transformed into a pizzeria.

1962
While the gigantic Pizza Hut and Domino's Pizza chains were established in the United States, brothers Max and André Sfez, Italian Jews from Tunisia, open the first location of the Pizza Pino empire in the Latin Quarter. Another legendary location opens on rue Mabillon (Paris 6th): Da Pietro.

1968
Pizza Pino ennobles itself and opens on the Champs-Élysées (Paris 8th) in a location measuring 8,600 square feet (800 sq m) and becomes the first chain of pizzerias in Paris.

1970
With other former employees of Chez Bartolo, Alfredo Petrone opens pizzeria Positano in Saint-Germain-des-Prés (Paris 6th).

1987
The American chain Pizza Hut, established in the United States in 1958, opens its first location near the Opéra Garnier.

1989
Domino's Pizza, the home-delivery chain, first opens in Montpellier then arrives in Paris.

1993
Despite the establishment of large chains, independent pizzerias make up the majority of the Parisian market. This is the year Pizza Santa Lucia (Paris 6th) was founded by the Esposito family, who will open the Neapolitan Bistrot (Paris 8th) in 1998.

2008
Julien Cohen elevates pizza with Pizza Chic (Paris 6th), a popular Italian restaurant.

2014
Gennaro Nasti, a Neapolitan *pizzaiolo*, launches his "signature" pizza in Paris. After the success of Popine (Paris 20th), he opens Bijou (Paris 18th) in 2016, where he offers "gourmet" pizzas, costing up to forty euros.

2015
The Italian restaurant group Big Mamma, cofounded by Victor Lugger and Tigrane Seydoux, opens its first location, East Mamma (Paris 11th). The concept starts with dazzling success and has eight establishments in Paris.

2018
Two first Parisian pizzerias are labeled VPN (Vera Pizza Napoletana, which certifies know-how respecting pure Neapolitan tradition): Motorino (Paris 17th) and Guillaume Grasso (Paris 15th). Since 2022, only Guillaume Grasso's now bears this title.

2020
Giuseppe Cutraro, selected as pizza world champion in 2020 and European champion in 2021, chooses Paris to open his three locations: Peppe (Paris 20th), Casa di Peppe (Paris 5th), and Peppe Martyrs (Paris 9th).

SKIP TO
Italy, p. 166.

THE BEST PIZZAS IN PARIS

⌀ DIAMETER • ✣ DOUGH • ● TOPPINGS • ● OVEN • NEAPOLITAN: soft crust, puffed edges • ROMAN: thin, crunchy, and moist crust

Dalmata

📍 *8, rue Tiquetonne, Paris 2nd*
PUGLIA MIA

Neapolitan ⌀ 12 inches (30 cm) ✣ Petra flour, fresh yeast; fermentation 36 hours. ● Pesto, fior di latte, Datterini tomatoes, stracciatella, pine nuts ● Wood-burning

Daroco

📍 *6, rue Vivienne, Paris 2nd*
📍 *3, pl. Clément-Ader, Paris 16th*
FORMAGGISSIMA

Neapolitan ⌀ 12.2 inches (31 cm) ✣ Caputo whole-meal flour, yeast; fermentation 48 hours ● Fior di latte, Gorgonzola, ricotta, scamorza, Parmesan ● Wood-burning

Peppe Pizzeria and Casa di Peppe

📍 *222, rue Saint-Jacques, Paris 5th + 2 locations*
CAMPIONE DEL MONDO

Neapolitan ⌀ 12.2–13 inches (31–33 cm) ✣ Italian flour, fresh yeast; fermentation 36 hours ● Yellow tomatoes, cured ham, provolone, buffalo mozzarella, almonds, fig jam ● Gas

Pizza Chic

📍 *13, rue de Mézières, Paris 6th*
PIZZA CHIC

Romaine ⌀ 12 inches (30 cm) ✣ 5 flours, fresh yeast; fermentation 5 days ● Lardo di Colonnata, rosemary ● Wood-burning

Pizzou

📍 *28, rue de Douai, Paris 9th*
📍 *14, rue de Cotte, Paris 12th*
RÉGINE

Roman-Neapolitan ⌀ 12 inches (30 cm) ✣ Flours: Grands Moulins de Paris and Moulin Decollogne, yeast; fermentation 48–72 hours ● Tomatoes, jambon blanc (cooked ham), fior di latte, button mushrooms ● Gas

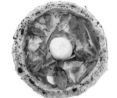

Alto Chalice

📍 *4, rue de Parma, Paris 9th*
📍 *2, rue Louise-Michel, Choisy-le-Roi (Val-de-Marne)*
CALICE ALTO

Neapolitan ⌀ 12 inches (30 cm) ✣ Petra flour, sourdough; fermentation 72 hours ● Tomatoes, buffalo mozzarella, burrata, Parma ham, Parmesan ● Gas and wood-burning

Faggio

📍 *72, rue de Rochechouart, Paris 9th*
📍 *16, pas. des Panoramas, Paris 2nd*
PIZZA MOITIÉ/MOITIÉ

Roman-Neapolitan ⌀ 13 inches (33 cm) ✣ Molino Grassi flours, yeast; fermentation 72 hours ● San Marzano tomatoes, anchovies Sangiolaro, fior di latte, Parmesan, Grana Padano, Taggiasche olives ● Wood-burning

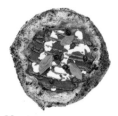

Big Mamma

📍 *East Mamma—133, rue du Faubourg-Saint-Antoine, Paris 11th + 6 locations*
NEYMAR BURRATA

Neapolitan ⌀ 12.2–13 inches (31–33 cm) ✣ Proprietary flour, fresh yeast; fermentation 48 hours ● San Marzano tomatoes, capers, Taggiasche olives, burrata ● Wood-burning

Fratelli Castellano

📍 *43, rue Fondary, Paris 15th*
CASTELLANO'S

Neapolitan ⌀ 12.6 inches (32 cm) ✣ Abruzzo flour, sourdough; fermentation 48–72 hours ● Tomatoes, fior di latte from Agerola, Parma ham, arugula ● Electric

Guillaume Grasso

📍 *45, rue Brancion, Paris 15th*
MARGHERITA

Neapolitan ⌀ 12 inches (30 cm) ✣ Italian flour, fresh yeast; fermentation 12 hours ● Italian tomatoes, fior di latte, Grana Padano, basil ● Wood-burning

Tripletta

📍 *88, bd. de Belleville, Paris 20th + 4 locations*
TRIPLETTA

Neapolitan ⌀ 12 inches (30 cm) ✣ Italian flours, fresh yeast; fermentation 48 hours ● San Marzano Tomatoes, Grana Padano, fior di latte d'Agerola, spianata calabra, green peppers, n'duja di Spilinga ● Wood-burning and gas

Atelier Pizza

📍 *11, all. Louis-Tillet, Saint-Germain-lès-Corbeil (Essonne)*
SARDENAIRA

Slow-fermentation Roman ⌀ 13 inches (33 cm) ✣ Petra flour, fresh yeast; fermentation 3–6 days ● Tomatoes from Emilia-Romagna, anchovies from Cetara, Taggiasche olives, onions ● Wood-burning

FOUQUET'S

A bright red awning, perfect Haussmann-style lines: this emblem of Parisian power and opulence has a turbulent history. —ESTELLE LENARTOWICZ

MAISON PARISIENNE
99, AVENUE DES CHAMPS-ÉLYSÉES, 8TH ARR.

The terrace of Fouquet's in 1969.

C. Deneuve, Y. Montand, K. Novak, and G. Depardieu after the Césars, January 31, 1981.

The founding father

In 1899, *limonadier* Louis Fouquet bought The Criterion tavern and renamed it Criterion-Fouquet's Bar. Renowned for the quality of its long drinks (an alcoholic mixed drink with a relatively large volume), the establishment became the headquarters for French and international pilots and aviators. In 1906, Brazilian Alberto Santos-Dumont celebrated his success here of the very first motorized free flight in an airship.

Celebrating cinema

Starting in the 1920s, the bar became a high-end brasserie where the world's great personalities would congregate, especially radio personalities (the FM studios were close by) and the artistic world of Paris's 7th arrondissement: Gene Kelly, Jean Gabin, Colette, Arletty, Josephine Baker, and Édith Piaf were frequently here, followed in the 1950s by the directors and actors of the New Wave and the writers Romain Gary and Joseph Kessel. Since the 1970s, the place has hosted the gala meals of the Césars and Molières.

External threats

The establishment faced threats in 1988 of being transformed into a shopping mall, but famous clientele mobilized to save it. With the support of Jack Lang, the building and brasserie were registered landmarks in 1990 and included on the list of historical monuments. The establishment was bought by the Barrière group and renovated in 2017, but it was set on fire during a demonstration by the Gilets Jaunes (Yellow Vests), a grassroots protest movement, in March 2019. The institution reopened four months later, on July 14.

Fouquet's

May 6, 2007

On the evening of his victory in the presidential election, Nicolas Sarkozy dines at Fouquet's. On the menu by MOF chef Jean-Yves Leuranguer:

- FOIE GRAS ON TOASTS
- RISOTTO WITH ARTICHOKE AND SHRIMP
- RISOTTO WITH TRUFFLES
- PIÈCE MONTÉE OF PUFFED RICE AND ROSE SABLÉS

The incomparable Pierre Ducroux

Chef Pierre Ducroux officiated over the kitchens here for forty-two years, until 1998. Under his leadership, nearly two hundred covers were served each day, and eighty dishes were on the menu, more than half of which were fish, including whole cooked turbot and sole au champagne. The Paris elites delighted in veal blanquette and duck aiguillette with lime and pineapples with pepper.

TO SEE

The portraits of aviators on the walls in the Escadrille bar.
The plaques of the former favorite tables of Édith Piaf, Charles Aznavour, and Jean Gabin.
The collection of silver napkin rings, engraved with the names of regulars (including Johnny Hallyday and Charles Aznavour).

TO TRY

The onion gratinée, served à la carte for more than fifty years.

The famous tartare, in traditional version or in Fouquet's style, revisited by Pierre Gagnaire, with bluefin tuna, smoked herring, and Beaufort, glace de foie gras de canard, drizzled with a shot of red currant tomatoes.

SKIP TO
Colette, p. 76; The Onion Soup of Les Halles, p. 204; Gabin, the Boss from Pantruche, p. 238; Steak Tartare, p. 254.

The Financier

Tender on the inside, crispy and golden on the outside, these small ingot-shaped cakes, made with ground almonds and browned butter, earned their reputation in the capital's former business district. —CHARLOTTE LANGRAND

THE RECIPE

Season: year-round
Difficulty ● ○ ○

MAKES 16 FINANCIERS

13 tablespoons (180 g) unsalted butter

1½ cups (100 g) almond flour

¾ cup (100 g) all-purpose flour

1⅛ cups (220 g) superfine sugar

½ vanilla bean or 1 teaspoon pure vanilla extract

6 medium (180 g) egg whites

Equipment

Stand mixer

Pastry bag

2 financier molds measuring 1 by 3 by ⅔ inch (3 by 8 by 1.5 cm)

Deliciously rich, this financier by Benoît Castel* is ready in a flash and is gobbled up just as quickly.

Preheat the oven to 320°F (160°C).

In a saucepan, heat the butter until the solids have dropped to the bottom of the pan and browned (beurre noisette) ❶.

In the bowl of a stand mixer fitted with the whisk attachment, mix together the almond and all-purpose flours and sugar. Split the vanilla bean lengthwise in half and scrape out the seeds with the tip of a knife. Add the egg whites and vanilla seeds (or the 1 teaspoon of vanilla extract) to the flour mixture, mixing well after each addition. Incorporate the browned butter ❷.

Pipe the dough into the ungreased financier molds ❸. Bake for 24 minutes, or until golden brown.

VARIATION

Flavor the batter with 3½ ounces (100 g) of pistachio paste and push 2 raspberries into the raw batter after piping it into the molds.

*Benoît Castel—150, rue de Ménilmontant, Paris 20th.

FROM NANCY TO PARIS

In the seventeenth century, the sisters of the convent of the Visitation de Nancy, who sought a way to use their leftover egg whites, invented this cake, baked into an oval, and called it visitandine. During the Renaissance, the cake fell into oblivion.

AT THE BOURSE

Around 1890, pastry chef Lasne, located near the Bourse (the Paris stock exchange), revived the recipe. He sought to delight the hurried Bourse workers (the *financiers*) with a cake that was easily carried and eaten on the go. He used browned butter in his recipe.

FEEDING THE FINANCIERS

Paris's Vivienne district was transformed in the mid-nineteenth century with the opening of the Bourse and the Tribunal de Commerce. This created an environment ripe for food establishments:
> Café Gobillard, opened in the eighteenth century.
> Champeaux, a restaurant founded in 1800, served as the meeting place for the *coulissiers* (unofficial brokers), who would meet in its white-and-gold salon.
> The restaurants La Sole Marguery and La Maison Dorée were located on the surrounding boulevards.

THE CLASSICS

Blé Sucré
◉ 7, rue Antoine-Vollon, Paris 12th
Roasted almonds and crunchy crust—2 ounces (55 g).

Lenôtre
◉ 44, rue d'Auteuil, Paris 16th + 9 locations
Intense almond flavor, moist texture—1½ ounces (40 g).

Stohrer
◉ 51, rue Montorgueil, Paris 2nd
Subtle almond and butter flavor. In the shape of a mini loaf—2½ ounces (70 g).

THE CREATIVE

Yann Couvreur
◉ 137, av. Parmentier, Paris 10th + 2 locations
Almond, intense vanilla, and a hint of fleur de sel sea salt—1 ounce (25 g).

Hugo & Victor
◉ 40, blvd. Raspail, Paris 7th
Note of fresh grapefruit—1¼ ounces (35 g).

SKIP TO
The Talmouse of Saint-Denis, p. 159; The Niflette of Provins, p. 295.

155

Antonin Carême (1783–1833)

The Architect of Taste

He was a pioneer of pastry, a genius of gastronomy, but forgotten by history. Marie-Antoine (known as Antonin) Carême transported the prestige of Parisian and French cuisine far beyond national borders. —MARIE-PIERRE REY

A Parisian journey

RUE DU BAC
Born in 1783.

PORTE DU MAINE
Around 1793, trains as a kitchen hand.

RUE SAINT-HONORÉ
First steps in pastry at Ducrest.

RUE VIVIENNE
In 1796, perfects his techniques at pâtisserie Bailly.

RUE RICHELIEU
In 1800, discovers the topic of architecture at the "Imperial" Library.

RUE DE GRENELLE
In 1800, he becomes head pastry assistant under the orders of Jean Avice, pastry chef of Foreign Minister Talleyrand, at the Hôtel de Galliffet.

RUE DES PETITS-CHAMPS
Begins working at pâtisserie Gendron in 1803.

RUE DE LA PAIX
1808–1813, opening of his only pâtisserie.

RUES GRENELLE, ANJOU, VARENNE, SAINT-FLORENTIN
1803–1814, perfects his culinary techniques in the kitchens of the various palaces of Talleyrand and other dignitaries of the Empire (Galliffet, Créqui, Matignon, Saint-Florentin, Élysée Palace).

RUE LAFFITTE
In 1823, after a career in Europe, he enters in the service of banker James de Rothschild in his private mansion, a veritable "reception factory."

RUE NEUVE-SAINT-ROCH
In 1833, dies young, at the age of forty-nine.

Anecdotes

› Tsar Alexander I, as a sign of esteem and in recognition of his talent, offered Carême a large diamond ring, which he proudly wore.

› In 2001, the Antonin Carême Literary Prize for Gastronomy was created.

› Carême was the troubling protagonist of the detective novel *Le Cuisinier de Talleyrand* by Jean-Christophe Duchon-Doris (2006).

› His notoriety was such that, at his death, his brain was dissected, in keeping with the trends in phrenology, to unravel the mystery of his talent. His skull is now part of the collections of the Musée de l'Homme (Museum of Man) in Paris.

"The fine arts are five in number, namely: painting, sculpture, poetry, music, and architecture—whose main branch is pastry."

—Antonin Carême, *Le Pâtissier pittoresque*, 1815

HIS WORK

- **1815**
  Le Pâtissier royal parisien
- **1815**
  Le Pâtissier pittoresque
- **1822**
  Le Maître d'hôtel français
- **1828**
  Le Cuisinier parisien
- **1828**
  L'Art de la cuisine française au xixe siècle.

The Family Kitchen, 1906.

Cook-writer

Antonin Carême endowed French cuisine with a methodical culinary system, codifying recipes and specific proportions and methods. His five-volume encyclopedic collection, *L'Art de la cuisine française au xixe siècle*, was translated worldwide and was responsible for disseminating recipes, know-how, and an entire vocabulary that is still used in international culinary jargon today. He included in his books the drawings of his prodigious creations and sought to broaden his audience by addressing not only professionals and gourmets but also, in an unprecedented way, everyday Parisiennes, whom he wanted to make ambassadors of haute cuisine.

An artist-artisan

Here are some of Carême's artistic masterpieces, which were quickly adopted by his contemporaries.

❶ THE CROQUEMBOUCHE

Inspired by ancient architecture, it was a tall structure, sometimes more than a meter high, in columns, similar to Greek temples, Egyptian pyramids, and Chinese pagodas.

❷ THE TOQUE

Invented in Vienna during his stay in 1821, it was a hat, "lined with a cardboard circle," which lent a prouder look to cooks than the flattened white cap previously worn. The toque became an international symbol of excellence and culinary professionalism.

❸ THE CHARLOTTE

Inspired by an English dessert, this molded dessert is made of ladyfinger sponges, which he invented, surrounded by a whipped fromage blanc and flavored with vanilla.

THE ART OF LAMINATION

A dough is beaten and aerated to become a "mille-feuille with flaky layers in twelve turns."

❹ VOL-AU-VENT

Inspired by the tourte du vent from François Marin's *Dons de Comus* (1739) and the gâteau vol-au-vent from Briand's *Dictionnaire des aliments* (1750), this revision of the very old charcuterie-based pastries systematized the use of puff pastry, making it lighter.

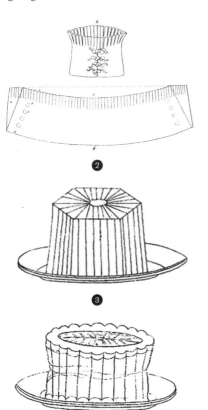

Carême's Guidelines

A cuisine must delight both the eyes and the taste buds, with harmony among dishes and tableware (crockery, glassware, and silverware).

Cuisine should be local and seasonal, without abusing game or red meat, for dietary reasons.

Cooking must have short cooking times to preserve food's firmness and natural flavors.

There should be a moderate use of spices.

There is a need to adjust recipes to one's budget, which heralds bourgeois cuisine.

There should be defense and promotion of the profession of cook, for its recognition and wages.

The cook of Europe's elites

A tireless promoter of French culinary art, Carême resonated throughout Europe with this national cuisine. He cooked in the service of:

> **Talleyrand,** one of the most influential dignitaries of the time.

> **Empress Marie-Louise of Austria,** second wife of Napoléon I.

> **Caroline Bonaparte and Joachim Murat,** queen and king of Naples.

> **Emperor Francis I of Austria,** father of the empress of the French, Marie-Louise.

> **Alexander I,** tsar of Russia.

> **George IV,** future king of the United Kingdom and Hanover.

> **Lord Charles Stewart,** ambassador to Vienna.

> **James de Rothschild,** the banker, and his wife, Betty.

A diplomatic cuisine

After Napoléon's defeat, France had to salvage something for itself at the Congress of Vienna (1814–1815). Napoléon's trump card: the cunning Talleyrand, the "lame devil," and his cook Carême. French pots would stun the greats of Europe in diplomatic efforts and save the nation's prestige.

SKIP TO
The Mille-Feuille, p. 58; Talleyrand vs. Cambacérès, p. 247; The Chouquette and Its Cousins, p. 278.

Paris Loves Bread

Parisians have always loved to break into a finer loaf than other parts of France. —MARIE-LAURE FRÉCHET

PAIN MOLLET OR PAIN À LA REINE

This pain au lait (milk bread) has been made since the sixteenth century using fine white flour, salt, milk, and brewer's yeast—rare ingredients at the time. The bread was called "mollet" because its crumb was supple, or "à la reine" because Catherine de Médicis was a fan. Parisian bakers could make these provided they were not displayed in the window, as a gros pain (large-format bread) was regulated by weight and price.

PAIN RÉGENCE

This resulted from another trend for another sovereign. Under the regency of Philippe d'Orléans, this small bread was dipped in coffee. It was shaped into balls, often stuck together in twos. The shape inspired the more contemporary version of the "pain régence" of the Oise: a string of five balls of yeast buns, but made without milk.

PAIN DE GONESSE

Quality water, flour mills, and generations of bakery workers who mastered flour bolting shaped the reputation of the commune of Gonesse as far back as the seventeenth century. This is evidenced today by the city's coat of arms, which depicts a sheaf of wheat. For a long time, bakers in Gonesse supplied Parisian markets with bread, since Paris lacked ovens (and therefore breads) at the time.

PAIN VIENNOIS

Moving to Paris in 1839, Auguste Zang opened the first Viennese bakery there, radically transforming the way bread was sold. Pain viennois was also called pain à l'empereur (emperor's bread). It was first a small round bun made with milk and soft-wheat flour. After 1956, it took the form of a baguette with a brioche crumb and a shiny crust with several scores on top.

A "Parisian" is also . . .

. . . the name of the cabinet where the baker places the dough to rise on wooden supports or stainless-steel grids. A liftable or removable door allows the cabinet to be closed. A baguette is sometimes referred to as a pain parisien.

A battle of yeast

The Parisian pain mollet stirred jealousy among the bakers of Gonesse, who denounced it in Parliament. On August 30, 1668, the use of brewer's yeast was suspended, and twelve doctors and other bigwigs were consulted. The medical panel opposed what was referred to as "this ugly foam." The bigwigs noted, however, that if yeast "was so detrimental to health . . . that the gentlemen of the faculty of medicine . . . probably would not expect so many people of high quality . . . to have eaten this bread for so long." Among them, Guy Poquelin, Molière's relative, who accustomed to disagreements with doctors, may have written this opinion, which tipped the scales in yeast's favor. In 1670, yeast was again allowed.

(Source: *Journal encyclopédique ou universel*, January 1, 1783).

THE RECIPE PAIN VIENNOIS (VIENNESE BREAD)

A bakery classic, modified for home bakers.

Season: year-round   **Difficulty** ● ● ●

MAKES 4 SMALL BAGUETTES

1 cup (250 ml) milk

1⅔ teaspoons (10 g) salt

½ ounce (15 g) fresh yeast

3 tablespoons (40 g) sugar

4 cups (500 g) pastry flour or T45 flour, plus more for dusting

5 tablespoons (70 g) unsalted butter, diced and at room temperature

1 cup (200 g) chocolate chips (optional)

1 large (50 g) egg, lightly beaten

In the bowl of a stand mixer fitted with the dough hook, add the milk, salt, crumbled yeast, sugar, and flour. Knead for 5 minutes on the lowest speed (speed 1), then for 6 minutes at speed 2. Add the butter and knead on speed 1 until incorporated. Add the chocolate chips, if using.

Turn the dough out onto a floured work surface and shape it into a ball, cover, and let stand for 1 hour at room temperature.

On a floured work surface, divide the dough in half and shape each dough half into a ball. Let stand for 15 minutes, covered with a clean cloth.

Shape each dough ball into a small baguette (an elongated log). Place them on a baking sheet lined with parchment paper and brush them with some of the beaten egg. Set aside for 20 minutes in a cool place.

Brush the dough again with the egg, then slash the top on the diagonal using a baker's lame. Let stand for 1½ hours at room temperature.

Set a baking sheet in the oven and preheat the oven to 350°F (180°C). Place the baguettes with the parchment paper on the hot baking sheet and bake for 15 minutes.

SKIP TO
Poilâne, a Family History, p. 136; Bakeries, p. 308.

The Talmouse of Saint-Denis

This is the ancestor of Parisian street food. It consists of a triangle of dough (today, puff pastry is used) filled with cheese—and there is also a sweet version.
—VALENTINE OUDARD

THE RECIPE

Season: winter
Difficulty ● ○ ○

SERVES 4

10½ ounces (300 g)
Puff Pastry (p. 58)

5¼ ounces (150 g)
Emmental cheese

1 tablespoon unsalted butter

3 tablespoons all-purpose flour

Just over ¾ cup (200 ml) milk

Salt and freshly ground black pepper

Nutmeg

1 large (20 g) egg yolk

Before evolving into a sweet treat, this flaky triangle was composed of a creamy Mornay sauce. If you can't find it in a sweet or savory version in shops around Île-de-France, you can make it at home.

Roll the puff pastry out to ⅛ to ¼ inch thick (4 to 5 mm) and cut it into squares. Cut the squares in half into triangles measuring 5 inches (12 cm) on each side ❶. Set aside.

Grate the cheese.

Add the butter and flour to a saucepan set over medium heat and cook (this makes a roux), stirring with a spatula, for 2 to 3 minutes. Add the milk while continuously stirring, and cook for 5 to 10 minutes, or until the mixture thickens. Season with salt and pepper. Add a little nutmeg. Add the grated cheese and stir to combine off the heat.

Brush the puff pastry triangles with the egg yolk and divide the cheese mixture among the centers of each triangle. Pick up the corners of the dough and pinch them together to partially enclose the filling ❷.

Preheat the oven to 425°F (220°C). Place the talmouse on a baking sheet lined with a silicone baking mat and bake for 15 minutes. Serve very hot.

Des patez, des talmouses toutes chaudes, François Boucher, sevententh century.

THE ORIGIN OF THE NAME

› From Arabic *talimūsa* (pastry or cake) from the Semitic root *ṭlm*, to flatten and fold the dough to fill it.

› From the medieval name of the baker, the *talmelier* (from the Low Franconian *tarewamelo*, wheat flour).

› From the Provençal *taler* (to bruise) and *mouse* (face or muzzle), the *talmouse* was also referred to as a *casse-museau* (literally "muzzle-breaker"), designating a blow or a slap.

A LITTLE HISTORY

› **Very popular in the Middle Ages,** this on-the-go street food appears in the first Parisian culinary works, *Le Ménagier de Paris* and *Le Viandier* (fourteenth century).

› **Its place of origin** seems to be the city of Saint-Denis, as attested by many literary and historical sources, even though some historians believe it was created on rue Saint-Denis in Paris.

› **At the beginning of the nineteenth century,** Antonin Carême worked

with the recipe and proposed a flaky variation. He worked for Madame de Bagration and brought the talmouse into the great Parisian salons. It consisted of rolled-out puff pastry filled with Neufchâtel cheese, sugar, whipped cream, or frangipane.

› **Today,** the talmouse of Saint-Denis exists in a savory version, which is a mixture of puff pastry and choux pastry, with béchamel or with spinach or mushrooms incorporated.

IN TEXTS

The talmouse was a celebrated treat by Musset, Balzac, and Dumas.

"Bernerette took from her pocket a talmouse, which she had taken while passing through Saint-Denis, and offered it so graciously to Gérard that he kissed her hand to thank her."
—Alfred de Musset, *Frédéric et Bernerette,* 1840

"Pizza is a kind of talmouse, like we do in Saint-Denis."
—Alexandre Dumas, *Le Corricolo,* 1841

"We entered Saint-Denis where Pierrotin stopped at the door of the innkeeper who sells the famous talmouses."
—Balzac, *Un début dans la vie,* 1842

SKIP TO
The Balzac Eating Guide, p. 84; Street Food in the Middle Ages, p. 108; Antonin Carême, p. 156.

❶

❷

Art Nouveau or Art Deco?

Let's not confuse these two styles. Art nouveau is the oldest, in style for only twenty years, while art deco continues to inspire.

—JACQUES BRUNEL

ART NOUVEAU
A return to nature

ART DECO
A reformed future

	ART NOUVEAU — A return to nature	ART DECO — A reformed future
DESCRIPTION	Phasing out at the end of the nineteenth century, art nouveau came about around 1890 and died out twenty years later. Also known as "1900s style" or "Belle Époque," it was started in Brussels by Victor Horta and conquered the world with Antoni Gaudí, Gustav Klimt, and Louis Tiffany. In France, it was showcased by the architect Hector Guimard, the glassmaker René Lalique, and the brilliant artisans of the École de Nancy school: the cabinetmaker Louis Majorelle and the glassmakers Émile Gallé and Antonin Daum. Reactionary in its lyricism and its inspirations (Gothic fairy tales and the picturesque), modernist in its boldness and techniques (wrought iron, painted glass), it was nevertheless very modern in its ambition, which was to change the city into a forest, hence these sinuous decorations of brambles and water lilies, naiads, and large birds, entangled in a subtle disorder to form a total universe.	After World War I, geometric sobriety and stylized forms defined the new world. Preceded by modernism, the art deco style took hold after 1920 in New York (the Chrysler Building) and Paris (Auguste Perret, Le Corbusier). Eventually adopted by all in the artistic world (the goldsmith Puiforcat, decorators Jacques-Émile Ruhlmann, Pierre Chareau, and Jules Leleu, and painter Tamara de Lempicka), this new style, also called "Roaring Twenties," celebrated industrial materials (concrete, Bakelite), the poetry of machines, the simple forms of cubism, but also comfort, height, and speed. The style was ostentatious, displaying shiny metals, lacquers, and precious woods to create a total universe similar to what was done with art nouveau.
AESTHETIC	Naturalistic, organic, fantastical	Geometric, rhythmic, majestic
MOOD	Playful, poetic, nostalgic	Optimistic, collective, conquering
LIGHTING	Individual dimmed lamps, false glass roofs	Frosted glass ceiling lights, columns of light
COLORS	Aquatic, dusty, muted	Beige, black, gold, silver
IMAGES OF WOMEN	Opulent, pompous, pastoral	Slim, sporty, powerful
PLANT MOTIFS	Stems, zigzagged roots, organic forms	Roses, sunflowers, garlands
WALL TILES	Large tiles	Pointillist mosaics
FAVORITE MATERIALS	Ironwork, stained glass	Chrome, Bakelite, moleskin, faceted glass
FAVORITE WOODS	Walnut, cherry, mahogany	Ebony, rosewood, stained maple
TILING	Floral, animal	Geometric, kinetic
FONT	Winding, medieval inspired	Rounded, geometric

Masterpieces

Le Printemps, ceramic panel in the Beefbar

📍 *5, rue Marbeuf, Paris 8th*

Listed as a historical monument, this nymph scattering maple seeds evokes both Botticelli and Japan.

CREATOR: Jules Wielhorski, a painter of Polish origin who also decorated the Villa Primavera, in Cap-d'Ail.

① Verrière, at Printemps Haussmann

📍 *64, blvd. Haussmann, Paris 9th*

Dating to 1923, this cathedral dome (3,185 glass fragments) in the shape of an expanded umbrella is a late witness to art nouveau, tinted with all the colors of the sky, leaves, tulips, and heraldic motifs.

CREATORS: Eugène Brière, an emblematic glassmaker of the Belle Époque, and most notably Gustave Eiffel.

② "Nymph" wall lights, at Lucas-Carton

📍 *9, pl. de la Madeleine, Paris 8th*

These gilded bronze sconces show, in bust form, a smiling young woman, adorned with flowers.

CREATOR: Maison Planel.

③ Ceramic walls at Brasserie Lipp

📍 *151, blvd. Saint-Germain, Paris 6th*

Reflected by mirrors, a jungle of bamboo, banana, and fig trees under a covering of macaws.

CREATOR: Léon Fargue, A Parisian ceramist, father of the great poet Léon-Paul Fargue.

Aquarium, at Goumard

📍 *9, rue Duphot, Paris 1st*

Of all sizes, multicolored cut-glass fish swim in the open air in the light coming from the windows. It's a fairy-tale scene.

CREATOR: René Lalique, a stunning glassmaker who defined the era.

Restaurant-museums

Brasserie Mollard

📍 *115, rue Saint-Lazare, Paris 8th*

In shades of sea green, royal blue, and gold, a vast room under a glass roof displays tile landscapes and pastoral scenes. A palace of illusions (a classée space) of rare finesse.

CREATOR: Édouard-Jean Niermans, the architect of the Folies Bergères (Paris 9th) and the Hôtel Negresco in Nice.

Maxim's

📍 *3, rue Royale, Paris 8th*

This coquettish boudoir, which became a chic restaurant, brought together the cream of the crop of art nouveau for its woodwork facade and its interior bijou space invaded by lianas, dragonflies, and butterflies painted on glass, carved in wood, or cast in copper. On the first floor is a private museum that exhibits other masterpieces from 1900.

CREATORS: Émile Gallé, who revolutionized glasswork; Hector Guimard, creator of the metro entrances from 1900; Jean Prouvé, who would become a highly successful architect; Léon Sonnier, seascapes painter.

④ Bouillon Julien

📍 *16, rue du Faubourg-Saint-Denis, Paris 10th*

A space increased by mirrors, this magical forest where nymphs and peacocks frolic is the most amazing (classée) art nouveau setting in Paris.

CREATORS: Hippolyte Boulenger (floral tiles), Louis Majorelle (Cuban mahogany bar), Charles Buffet (glass ceiling), Louis Trézel (glass panels designed by Alfons Mucha).

⑤ Bouillon Chartier Montparnasse

📍 *59, blvd. du Montparnasse, Paris 6th*

A beautiful *bouillon* of the period, under a glass ceiling, with art nouveau sconces and ceramic flowered pergolas on the wall.

CREATOR: Louis Trézel, the great glassmaker of the 1900s.

Le Cochon à l'Oreille

📍 *15, rue Montmartre, Paris 1st*

The classée decor of this restaurant assertively reproduces the proliferation of Les Halles in 1914.

CREATOR: Hippolyte Boulenger, the great ceramist of the Belle Époque and creator of the tiles of the Paris metro.

Le Petit Bouillon Pharamond

📍 *24, rue de la Grande-Truanderie, Paris 1st*

This temple to tripe, which opened in 1879, was a bistro in Les Halles that would become the Normandy Pavilion for the Universal Exposition in 1900. Its art nouveau decor is classée, thanks to its Chinese glass paste panels and rich mirrored salons, where Clemenceau and Mitterrand were regulars.

CREATOR: unknown.

Masterpieces

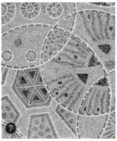

❻ Ruhlmann staircase, at Drouant

📍 16–18, rue Gaillon, Paris 2nd

The iconic staircase with floral motifs is the last vestige of a decoration designed by Ruhlmann.
CREATOR: Jacques-Émile Ruhlmann designed many of the most beautiful pieces of art deco furniture, decorating the Élysée presidential residence, the ocean liner *Île-de-France*, and the former Musée des Colonies.

Restaurant-museums

❾ La Coupole

📍 102, blvd. du Montparnasse, Paris 14th

All the intelligentsia of the Roaring Twenties would imbibe in this huge brasserie (now a historical monument), whose twenty-seven pillars bore frescoes by Henri Matisse, Fernand Léger, Moïse Kisling, Ossip Zadkine, Othon Friesz, and others. The art deco style is also illustrated by extraordinary tiles, imposing moldings, and ceiling lights, and the menu's cubist script.
CREATORS: the architects Barillet and Lebouc; the Solvet brothers, who were decorators for restaurants.

❼ Exterior mosaic, Prunier

📍 16, av. Victor Hugo, Paris 16th

Listed as a historical monument (classée), this mosaic covers the entire facade of this seafood house. A careful examination between the bubbles makes it possible to distinguish fish, sea urchins, and starfish.
CREATOR: Auguste Labouret, the doyen of stained glass and ultraluminous mosaics.

❽ Bar at the hotel Provinces Opéra

📍 36, rue de l'Échiquier, Paris 10th

This crenellated bar with floral motifs is the centerpiece (classée) of a breathtaking decor of woodwork from 1925, which keeps a foot in art nouveau.
CREATOR: Joël Robert.

Prunier

📍 16, av. Victor-Hugo, Paris 16th

The most beautiful restaurant in Paris? In this art deco setting, everything can be admired: from the acid-etched windows to the Carrara marble bar to the gilded wood bas-relief to the ceiling lights worthy of Chareau. Upstairs is perhaps the most beautiful room decorated by Jacques Grange.
CREATORS: architect Louis-Hippolyte Boileau; sculptor Gaston Le Bourgeois; glass engraver Paul Binet; draftsman Léon Carrière; designer Alexey Brodovich; mosaicist Auguste Labouret; painter Mathurin Méheut.

Postscripts

Extended by the styles of the 1950s, then by the revival of the 1980s (Philippe Starck, Andrée Putman), the art deco style, simple and chic, never ceases to inspire.

❿ Le Wepler

📍 14, pl. de Clichy, Paris 18th

The 1930 chandeliers, the moleskin banquettes, and the windows engraved with the W logo remind us that this gathering place for painters (Utrillo, Picasso, Modigliani) was very active in the interwar period, but the current art deco decor, dated 2009 and 2011, is contemporary.

Le Zéphyr

📍 1, rue du Jourdain, Paris 20th

Due to modifications, this neighborhood café has been reinventing itself for twenty years as a temple of art deco.

Brasserie Lutetia

📍 43, blvd. Raspail, Paris 6th

Recently redecorated in white and black in the art deco ocean-liner style.

Le Boeuf sur le Toit

📍 34, rue du Colisée, Paris 8th

Frequented by Picasso, Diaghilev, and the Cocteau gang, this effervescent temple of the Roaring Twenties has changed locations three times. Dating to 1941, if not much later, its superb art deco decor is not original.

⓫ Noto

📍 252 bis, rue du Faubourg-Saint-Honoré, Paris 8th

Decorated in the Italian style, the restaurant of the Salle Pleyel retains its original art deco character: glimmering walnut, marble, and brass.

The ocean-liner style

The ocean liners of the time were guardians of the transatlantic links and symbolized modernity, prestige, and power. As sort of cathedrals of the ocean, the *Île-de-France* and *Normandy* were showcases of France, where the best decorators were assembled. Their stately and luxurious style, combining rare woods and precious metals, inspired the decor of restaurants of the time.

⑫ Foyer du Théâtre de Chaillot

◍ *1, pl. du Trocadéro, Paris 16th*

Available for private events on request, this pharaonic space built in 1937 is simply breathtaking, with its Raymond Subes sconces.
CREATORS: the architect Jean Niermans, son of Édouard-Jean and cocreator of the Palais de Chaillot; Fauve painter Othon Friesz; ironworker Raymond Subes; decorator Louis Süe.

Vin et Marée

◍ *165, rue Saint-Honoré, Paris 1st*

This tribute to the *Normandy* includes engraved and gilded mirrors on drawings by Jean Dupas, and especially the extraordinary gilded lacquer panel, *Le Char de l'Aurore*, whose final version adorned the famous ocean liner.
CREATORS: Jean Dunand, master lacquerer and exceptional coppersmith from the Swiss watchmaking industry who decorated the former Musée des Colonies; painter Jean Dupas, with a decorative style marked by surrealism; Jacques Champigneulle, master glassmaker.

Relais Plaza

◍ *21, av. Montaigne, Paris 8th*

Inspired in 1936 by the first-class-passenger dining room on the *Normandy*, this classée decor, tastefully renovated, remains a fine example of the ocean-liner style: a well-lit ceiling, a giant chandelier, ultralarge mirrors framed in sycamore, and a long curved bar, all under a fresco that resonates with the gold lacquer panels of the *Normandy* smoking room by Jean Dunand.
CREATOR: Saqui (fresco).

⑬ ⑭ ⑮ Vaudeville

◍ *29, rue Vivienne, Paris 2nd*

Columns of light, etched windows, stained-glass windows, and woodwork: the 1927 decor of this brasserie is reminiscent of the grand salon of the *Île-de-France*.
CREATOR: unknown.

SKIP TO
The Days of the Brasseries, p. 67; Maxim's, p. 82; Brasseries, p. 356; Seafood Spots, p. 364.

PARIS, A COSMOPOLITAN CITY

From the Japanese establishments around the Opéra district to the African luncheonettes of the 10th arrondissement to the Iranian food shops on rue des Entrepreneurs and to the Chinese restaurants of Belleville, the capital is a vast cosmopolitan scene that offers multiple culinary journeys that cross the globe within easy reach by metro. Here is a road map across 64 countries and 413 locations within the capital.

2 SPAIN
Seine-Saint-Denis

CÔTE D'IVOIRE, CAMEROON, NIGER, SENEGAL, ETHIOPIA, SOUTH AFRICA

19

RUSSIA 15

18ᵉ

MAGHREB 18

7
GERMANY

17ᵉ

9ᵉ

31 INDIA

35 BRAZIL
36 CHILE

24 AFGHANIS

POLAND 10

INDIA 31

35

TURKEY 17

19

INDIA 31

10

PASSAGE BRADY

15 RUSSIA

8ᵉ

5

SCOTLAND

ITALY

4

1

28 JAPAN

2ᵉ

35 BRAZIL

35 BRAZIL

ARGEN

3ᵉ 8 SWITZERLA

CHINA

27

RU

UNITED STATES

33

ENGLAND

1ᵉʳ ITALY

1

22

22

4ᵉ

7ᵉ

JEWISH COMMUNITY

ROMANIA

12 22

16

22

34 ARGENTINA

18 ALGERIA
Yvelines, Val-d'Oise

16ᵉ

15
RUSSIA

23 IRAN

29 KOREA

6ᵉ

CHINA

34

ARGENTINA

27

LEBANON

25 TIBET, CHINA
SCOTLAND

21 5

6

IRELAND

11 HUNGARY

5ᵉ

2

15 RUSSIA

15ᵉ

3
PORTUGAL

27 CHINA

1.20

30 26

THAILAND

14ᵉ

VIETNAM LAOS CAMBODIA

14 ARMENIA
Val-de-Marne

7
GERMANY

13ᵉ

LEGEND

→ Historic migration flow

36 CHILE
Essonne,
Seine-et-Marne

13 GEO
Esso

Map labels:

18 ALGERIA
Val-d'Oise

32 WEST INDIES
Seine-Saint-Denis,
Val-d'Oise

20 MALI
Seine–Saint-Denis

7 GERMANY

18 ALGERIA
Seine-et-Marne

19e

ERMANY
MAGHREB
7 18
16
27

HINA

20e

MBIA
11e

BELGIUM

MANY

12e

3 PORTUGAL
Val-de-Marne

14 ARMENIA
Val-de-Marne

2 WEST INDIES
Val-de-Marne

7 GERMANY
Seine-et-Marne

---

① Italy
Middle Ages
Rue des Lombards
(Paris 1st, 4th)
1840–1890
Grands Boulevards (Paris 2nd, 9th, 10th)
And also: from Gare de Lyon to Bastille (Paris 12th), Val-de-Marne, and Seine-Saint-Denis

② Spain
Late nineteenth century
La Plaine Saint-Denis around the impasse and the passage Boise district called "Little Spain"
And also: Les Halles district (Paris 1st), Montmartre (Paris 18th)

③ Portugal
1945–1972
Parc du Plateau in Champigny-sur-Marne (Val-de-Marne) called "the Portuguese village of Champigny," Plaisance district (Paris 14th)
And also: Nanterre (Hauts-de-Seine), Seine-Saint-Denis, Val-de-Marne, Massy (Essonne), Pontault-Combault (Seine-et-Marne)

④ England
1814–1860
Faubourg Saint-Germain (Paris 7th), Faubourg Saint-Honoré (Paris 8th)
And also: Saint-Germain-en-Laye (Yvelines)

⑤ Scotland
Early nineteenth century
Scottish Church of Paris (17, rue Bayard, Paris 8th), Collège des Écossais (65, rue du Cardinal-Lemoine, Paris 5th)

⑥ Ireland
Early nineteenth century
Rue des Irlandais (Paris 5th)

⑦ Germany
1835
Seine-et-Marne, av. Jean-Jaurès (Paris 19th), and rue de la Chaussée-d'Antin (Paris 9th)
1850
Place d'Italie (Paris 13th), Faubourg Saint-Antoine (Paris 11th and 12th), Batignolles (Paris 17th), and Belleville (Paris 20th)
And also: Yvelines

⑧ Switzerland
Twentieth century
Haute-Marne and Paris

⑨ Belgium
1860
The districts of La Roquette and Sainte-Marguerite (Paris 11th), Picpus (Paris 12th), Charonne (Paris 20th), and Faubourg Saint-Antoine (Paris 11th)

⑩ Poland
Twentieth century
Around the current Gare Saint-Lazare (Paris 8th)

district called "Little Poland" and around Batignolles (Paris 17th)
And also: Champeaux cemetery in Montmorency (Val-d'Oise), Batignolles school (5, blvd. des Batignolles, Paris 17th), Church of Notre-Dame-de-l'Assomption (263, rue Saint-Honoré, Paris 1st)

⑪ Hungary
Late nineteenth century
Latin Quarter (Paris 5th)

⑫ Romania
Early nineteenth century
Odéon district (Paris 6th)

⑬ Georgia
1920s
Château de Leuville-sur-Orge (Essonne)

⑭ Armenia
1915
Alfortville (Val-de-Marne) called "Little Armenia"
And also: Issy-les-Moulineaux, Val-d'Oise, Hauts-de-Seine, Val-de-Marne

⑮ Russia
Early 1920s
The districts of Grenelle (Paris 15th), Grandes-Carrières and Clignancourt (Paris 18th), Auteuil (Paris 16th), Church of Saint-Alexandre-Nevsky (Paris 8th), and rue de la Roquette (Paris 11th)

⑯ Greece
1923
Belleville (Paris 20th)
Early 1950s
Saint-Michel district (Paris 5th and 6th)

⑰ Turkey and Kurdish Cuisine
1950s
Between Porte Saint-Denis, the end of Faubourg Saint-Denis and the adjacent streets to Faubourg Poissonnière (Paris 9th and 10th)

⑱ Maghreb
1950s
Goutte-d'Or districts (Paris 18th), Ménilmontant and Belleville (Paris 20th)
And also: 19th and 20th arr.
Algeria
Trappes and Mantes-la-Jolie (Yvelines), Cergy and Sarcelles (Val-d'Oise), Meaux (Seine-et-Marne)

⑲ Côte d'Ivoire, Cameroon, Niger, Senegal, Ethiopia, South Africa
1960s–1970s
Goutte-d'Or (Paris 18th) and Château-d'Eau (Paris 10th) districts
And also: north of butte Montmartre (Paris 18th), west of the 13th arr., north of Buttes-Chaumont (Paris 19th), north of the 17th arr., Charenton-le-Pont

(Val-de-Marne), Issy-les-Moulineaux (Hauts-de-Seine), Montreuil and Pantin (Seine-Saint-Denis)

⑳ Mali
1960s
Montreuil, Seine-Saint-Denis

㉑ Lebanon
Late nineteenth–early twentieth centuries
Maronite Church of Notre-Dame-du-Liban (Paris 5th)
And also: 15th and 16th arr.

㉒ Jewish Cuisines
First century
Church of Saint-Julien-le-Pauvre (Paris 5th)
Tenth–eleventh centuries
Rue de la Harpe, between rue de la Huchette and rue Saint-Séverin (Paris 4th)
Twelfth century
Rue de la Cité, quai de la Corse, and rue de Lutèce (Paris 4th)
End of twelfth century
The streets of Moussy, Renard, Saint-Merri, de la Tacherie, and Petit-Pont (Paris 4th)
Starting in the thirteenth century
Marais (Paris 3rd and 4th)
And also: the east of Buttes-Chaumont to the Canal de l'Ourcq (Paris 19th)

㉓ Iran
Second half of the nineteenth century, 1930s, then 1979
Rue des Entrepreneurs, Beaugrenelle (Paris 15th)
And also: La Défense (Hauts-de-Seine), Créteil (Val-de-Marne)

㉔ Afghanistan
1980s
Around the Gare du Nord and Gare de l'Est (Paris 10th)

㉕ Tibet, China
1960s
Around the Pantheon (Paris 5th)

㉖ Vietnam, Laos, Cambodia
1975
Les Olympiades sector (av. d'Ivry and de Choisy, blvd. Massena, Paris 13th)
And also: Val-de-Marne

㉗ China
1914
Latin Quarter (Paris 5th), Arts et Métiers (Paris 3rd), between the passages Raguinot and Brunoy and the rue de Chalon (Paris 12th)
Since the mid-1970s
13th arr.
Since 1980–1985
Belleville
And also: Aubervilliers (Seine-Saint-Denis), rue Nationale south of Boulogne-Billancourt

(Hauts-de-Seine), Cormeilles-en-Parisis (Val-d'Oise)

㉘ Japan
1970s–1980s
Rue Sainte-Anne, Pyramide (Paris 1st, 2nd) and Opéra (Paris 9th) districts
And also: 15th and 16th arr., Boulogne-Billancourt (Hauts-de-Seine), Val-d'Oise

㉙ Korea
1950s–1970s
Beaugrenelle, blvd. de Lourmel, rue Lecourbe (Paris 15th)

㉚ Thailand
1975
Les Olympiades sector (av. d'Ivry and de Choisy, blvd. Massena, Paris 13th)
And also: Val-de-Marne

㉛ India
1960s
Rue Clauzel (Paris 9th)
1983
Passage Brady, rue du Faubourg-Saint-Denis (Paris 10th)
Late 1990s
Rue du Faubourg-Saint-Denis, between La Chapelle and Gare du Nord (Paris 18th), known as "Little India"
And also: La Courneuve (Seine-Saint-Denis)

㉜ West Indies
1950s
Sarcelles (Val-d'Oise) and Seine-Saint-Denis
Since 1969
Créteil (Val-de-Marne)

㉝ United States
1946–1954
Place des États-Unis (Paris 16th) and 7th arr.
And also: 15th arr., Yvelines and Hauts-de-Seine

㉞ Argentina
Late nineteenth century
5th, 11th, and 16th arr.

㉟ Brazil
Early twentieth century
Rue de Turbigo (Paris 3rd), Montholon (Paris 10th), Richer (Paris 3rd), and avenue de l'Opéra (Paris 1st and 2nd)

㊱ Chile
Since 1973
Massy and Bièvres (Essonne), Melun (Seine-et-Marne), rue de Trévise (Paris 9th)

㊲ Colombia
Since the mid-1990s
Chemin-Vert district (Paris 11th) called "Little Bogotá"

Italy

The cuisine of "France's cousins"—the second largest foreign community in the capital—has thrilled Parisians for ages.

—ALESSANDRA PIERINI*

SINCE THE MIDDLE AGES

Since the Middle Ages, artists, craftsmen, shopkeepers, and, especially, Lombard bankers have settled en masse in the eponymous street (Paris 4th), which has since become one of the most commercial streets in Paris. In the sixteenth century, Italian cuisine arrived to France's court thanks to translated cookbooks.

FROM THE CAFÉ . . .

Under the Ancien Régime, the opening of new café–ice cream parlors by Italians attracted Parisian intellectuals: the Boulevard des Italiens saw the birth of Café Frascati (1792) and the famous Café Tortoni (1804). Around 1880, after Italian unification, the migratory wave accompanied the opening of food shops.

. . . TO THE RESTAURANT

In 1920, Paris had twenty-eight Italian café-restaurants, including fifteen around the Grands Boulevards and, among them, the famous Poccardi, where Apollinaire celebrated his wedding in 1918. Since 1944, immigration has slowed, but Paris continues to attract Italians seeking cultural and professional experiences. Today, almost fifty thousand Italians live in Île-de-France and own more than seven hundred businesses, most of them in the food sector.

*Culinary author and founder of the transalpine wine cellar-grocery, with shelves filled from floor to ceiling with finely sourced treasures.
♀ RAP—4, rue Fléchier, Paris 9th

THE PIONEER

Davoli
♀ 34, rue Cler, Paris 7th
This shop offering prepared foods and grocery items has been handed down from father to son for four generations. The shop was founded in 1913 on rue de Passy by Francesco Cella from Genoa. His son-in-law, Rino Davoli, took over in 1936 and began manufacturing the charcuterie on premises before moving, in 1962, to the current location. In 2021, the Davoli family sold the boutique to Thierry Pélissier, who continues its excellence.

RESTAURANTS

Mori Venice Bar
♀ 27, rue Vivienne, Paris 2nd. €€
With chandeliers and a counter in Murano glass, this refined location was opened in 2005 by Massimo Mori, also owner of the Emporio Armani Caffè, serving up a cuisine with Venetian accents: sarde in saor (sardines with escabeche), sea bass carpaccio, spider crab, risi e bisi (pea risotto), with particular attention to ingredients and terroir.

Caffè Stern
♀ 47, pas. des Panoramas, Paris 2nd. €€
In 2014, the Michelin-starred Alajmo brothers opened this elegant trattoria with the appearance of a Venetian café in the location of the Stern engraving studios. On the menu: potato cappuccino alla bolognese, calf's liver alla veneziana with polenta, and an irresistible pistachio ice cream.

Racines
♀ 8, pas. des Panoramas, Paris 2nd. €€
Under its air of a Parisian bistro, this establishment of Sarde Simone Tondo offers home-style cuisine with, depending on the season, osso buco, melanzane alla parmigiana (eggplant Parmesan), and lasagna verde.

Epoca
♀ 17, rue Oudinot, Paris 7th. €€€
Of Calabrian chef Denny Imbroisi's four restaurants, this is the most Italian. A trattoria in the spirit of art deco: intense colors and mosaic on the floor where, since 2017, he delivers all the classics, from tagliatelle Bolognese to Jewish artichokes to beef carpaccio and cacio e pepe (pasta with cheese and pepper).

Il Carpaccio
♀ 37, av. Hoche, Paris 8th. €€€€
Located in the Royal Monceau hotel, this Michelin-starred restaurant is managed by chefs Oliver Piras and Alessandra Del Favero. In a comfortable and cozy room in the chic of a winter garden, diners enjoy tidy, modern, and welcoming high-end cuisine. The signature dish: paccheri alla Vittorio (pasta with tomato and Parmesan), named after the three-star restaurant in Bergamo by chefs Enrico and Roberto Cerea, who oversee them.

Il Ristorante Niko Romito
♀ 30, av. George-V, Paris 8th. €€€
The three-star chef Niko Romito offers, in the luxurious setting of the Bulgari hotel, all the family classics of Italian and regional cuisine with a fresh and refined interpretation. Among his signature dishes: cotoletta di vitello alla milanese (Milanese-style veal chop), ricotta and spinach tortelli (large ravioli) with sage butter, spaghetti with tomato sauce.

Pastore
♀ 26, rue Bergère, Paris 9th. €€
The Sicilian chef Lorenzo Sciabica directs the kitchen hidden underneath this neo-trattoria with a calm elegance. In the dining room, Emma Hayes pours excellently sourced wines. Essential Italian dishes are offered along with more modern proposals, such as gnocchi with seafood, broccoli and ink bread crumbs, and paccheri with asparagus, onions of Tropea, and guanciale (pork cheek).

Osteria Chez Marius

📍 *11, rue de Chabrol,
Paris 10th. €€*

Opposite the Saint-
Quentin market, this
establishment is halfway
between an osteria and
a Parisian bistro sporting
checkered tablecloths.
In the kitchen, Venetian
Dimitri Gris whips up
classics (vitello tonnato,
pasta al pomodoro,
Venetian-style veal liver)
in the middle of a neo-
bistro ambience. There
is a very nice selection of
natural wines.

Osteria Ferrara

📍 *7, rue du Dahomey,
Paris 11th. €€*

Since 2008 in his Caffè
dei Cioppi, Fabrizio
Ferrara is a benchmark
for Italian cuisine. In a
bistro atmosphere from
yesteryear, this Sicilian
chef serves the classics
of northern Italy, where
he trained, as gourmet
dishes without fuss.

Tempilenti

📍 *13, rue Gerbier,
Paris 11th. €€*

In this tiny single-story
structure near Père-
Lachaise cemetery,
Francesca Feniello and
Silvia Giorgione create
seasonal family cuisine
with emblematic dishes

from different regions:
Venetian sardines,
puntarella salad, vitello
tonnato (veal with tuna),
and ravioli. Small-
production transalpine
wines are offered.

Il Bacaro

📍 *9, rue Auguste-Laurent,
Paris 11th. €€*

In Venice, its name
means a wine bar, but in
Paris, a Venetian-Friulian
trattoria where chef
Eleonora Zuliani serves
her typical northeast
Italian specialties: baccalà
mantecato (Venetian-
style cod brandade),
musetto (cooked pork
sausage), cjalsons (half-
moon ravioli), and squid
ink risotto.

Passerini

📍 *65, rue Traversière,
Paris 12th. €€€*

The Roman chef
Giovanni Passerini,
with an obsession for
searching the right
ingredients, employing
perfect cooking methods,
and adhering to great
techniques, revisits
dishes of the *cucina
povera* in a modern and
refined version: Roman
tripe, veal meatballs,
and fresh pasta from
his adjoining *pastificio*
(pasta-making studio).

Ristorantino
Shardana

📍 *134, rue du Théâtre,
Paris 15th. €€€*

All of Sardinia is
represented in this
authentic location and
its small room of twenty
seats: culurgiones (large
ravioli with potato),
squid in fregulas,
seadas (cheese and
honey cake), and all the
classics of Sardinian
cuisine executed by chef
Salvatore Ticca.

Dilia

📍 *1, rue d'Eupatoria,
Paris 20th. €€€*

In this tiny restaurant
with a terrace, Michele
Farnesi formulates
creative and market-
inspired dishes. This
chef of Tuscan origin
offers a very personal
cuisine, presented in a
tasting menu that makes
an impression: zucchini
linguine, mussels,
lovage, and baccalà (cod)
tortellini.

GROCERIES

Latte Cisternino

📍 *17, rue Geoffroy-Saint-
Hilaire, Paris 5th*

📍 *37, rue Godot-de-
Mauroy, Paris 9th*

📍 *46, rue du Faubourg-
Poissonnière, Paris 10th*

📍 *108, rue Saint-Maur,
Paris 11th*

It is first and foremost an
old-fashioned creamery
whose specialties are
fresh products that arrive
once a week directly from
Italy: ricotta, mozzarella,
burrata, scamorza, and
other specialties from the
south.

La Tête dans Les
Olives

📍 *2, rue Sainte-Marthe,
Paris 10th*

📍 *54, rue du Couédic,
Paris 14th*

A 100 percent Sicilian
grocery where Cédric
Casanova, a Franco-
Italian, offers a very keen
selection of olive oils,
used in the best kitchens
throughout the capital.
Great wines can also be
enjoyed on its fixed-price
menu reserved for a
small number of guests.

Paisano

📍 *159, rue Saint-Maur,
Paris 11th*

An Italian couple, Davide
Moschini and Federica
Rella, select and import
the best food products
from Italy: farmstead
mozzarella, Menaica
anchovies, cinta senese
charcuterie, alpine
cheeses, tomatoes and
vegetables preserved in
oil, artisan wines.

Raffinati

📍 *74 ter, rue de
Clignancourt, Paris 18th*

A fine-foods shop, cheese
cave, and charcuterie
designed by Nicola
Balestra, a passionate
gourmet from Apulia. You
can enjoy the essentials
on the spot or for takeout
as well as more limited
creations using products
from small producers, and
an excellent coffee.

ICE CREAM SHOP

Pozzetto

📍 *16, rue Vieille-du-
Temple, Paris 4th*

📍 *39, rue du Roi-de-Sicile,
Paris 4th*

Generous artisanal ice
creams with the taste
of the seasons . . . the
historic Italian *glacier* of
Paris.

SEE ALSO
Pizza Conquers Paris, p. 152.

Spain

Paris has always been an attractive destination for Spaniards. More than 300,000 arrived in the 1980s and now number 38,200 in Île-de-France.

—AÏTOR ALFONSO

A CENTURY OF IMMIGRATION

Artists of the 1900s, political refugees fleeing Francoism in the late 1930s, and immigrant laborers in the 1960s—this diaspora brought with it rich and invigorating foods: tortillas, fried foods, garlicky and leguminous pork stews.

TAPAS

A typical Spanish tradition has conquered the French capital: tapas, these small share plates that adapt so well to modern ways of dining.

THE PIONEER

At Ramona's

📍 17, rue Ramponeau, Paris 20th. €

In this small restaurant in Belleville, Ramona's odds and ends seem to have been here since the end of the last century. On the walls are kitsch trinkets, and à la carte are classics of the Spanish comida at popular prices: tortilla (with onion), Galician octopus, fried chipirons, fresh anchovies, patatas bravas, crème Catalan.

RESTAURANT

Galerna

📍 7, rue du Cher, Paris 20th. €€

In a place with a Parisian look, the Navarrese Iñigo Ruiz Rituerto skillfully cooks kokotxas (hake necks) with piquillos, paella arancini, pluma iberico on the barbecue, and octopus with mojo picón sauce (a condiment made with Canarian pepper).

TAPAS

Le Dauphin

📍 131, av. Parmentier, Paris 11th. €€€

Iñaki Aizpitarte sets out tapas at this marble-clad dining bar designed by architect Rem Koolhaas. There are very creative share plates of perfect croquetas with jamón, gildas as in San Sebastián (olive pincho, anchovies and guindillas in vinegar), changurro (dish with spider crab), and tocinillo de cielo (flan with egg yolks).

Amagat

📍 23, villa Riberolle, Paris 20th. €€

This trendy restaurant tucked away at the end of an alley replays Barcelona's countertop classics. At Amagat (meaning "hidden" in Catalan) are boquerones (anchovies) in vinegar, grilled prawns carabineros, boles de picolat (Catalan mince dumplings), bombas (pork croquettes) with aioli sauce, bunyetes (chocolate fritters), and natural wines from Catalonia.

GROCERIES

Bellota Bellota

📍 18, rue Jean-Nicot, Paris 7th

📍 11, rue Clément-Marot, Paris 8th

📍 27, rue Yves-Kermen, Boulogne-Billancourt (Hauts-de-Seine)

Bellota is an acorn in Spanish, the noble food of the Iberian pig that gives its flesh its unique nutty taste. Bellota Bellota gives pride of place to the great PDOs: hams from Jabugo, Guijuelo, Los Pedroches, and Dehesa de Extremadura, sliced by hand. In addition, there is a house-made gazpacho and other refined Spanish products.

Fogón Ultramarinos

📍 38, rue de Verneuil, Paris 7th

After being awarded a Michelin star for his restaurant, Alberto Herraiz honors Spanish paellas in his shop. Versions of squid ink, vegetables, or a banda are assembled for takeout to finish cooking at home. There are also house-made tapas and exceptional products from the peninsula.

La Vendimia d'Espange

📍 2, rue Hégésippe-Moreau, Paris 18th

📍 8, allée de la Fontaine-des-Tournelles, Saint-Mard (Seine-et-Marne)

In their traditional shop, Nonata and Senen Fente Diaz offer basic Spanish necessities. On the shelves are bomba rice, soft and hard turrón, PDO Manchego cheese, Galician wines, Asturian cider . . . all at friendly prices.

Maison Aitana

📍 144, av. de la République, Montrouge (Hauts-de-Seine)

maisonaitana.com

Carlos Gutiérrez sources the very top Iberian products: exceptional meats and premium pork, matured with care, such as blonde de Galicia, lomo, and Iberian chorizo from Bellota, jamón pata negra Cinco Jotas, and anchovies from Cantabria.

Portugal

Well established in Paris, the country of fado *has a cuisine with a strong temperament.*
—XAVIER VAN KERREBROUCK

World War I kicked off significant Portuguese migration. In the 1960s, many fled poverty, increasing the Portuguese population in the Paris region by sevenfold and making Paris and its suburbs the third largest Portuguese-settled city in the world, after Lisbon and Porto.

THE PIONEER

Restaurant Saudade
⚲ *34, rue des Bourdonnais, Paris 1st. €€*
Since 1979, Maria de Fatima has manned the kitchen and Fernando Moura the dining room, delighting customers with Portuguese specialties such as fried sardines, cod fritters, roast pork with clams, marinated kid, suckling pig, and pudim molotov (typical flan).

RESTAURANTS

Comme à Lisbonne/ Tasca
⚲ *37, rue du Roi-de-Sicile, Paris 4th. €€*
The address with two concepts: a café serving one of the best pasteis (flan pâtissier) in Paris and galão (an espresso and milk-foam drink) and a Portuguese wine bar where you can taste the tosta mista (croque-monsieur) and sip a vinho verde (wine from the north of Portugal).

Nossa Churrasqueira
⚲ *147, blvd. de Charonne, Paris 11th. €€*
⚲ *1, rue de l'École-Polytechnique, Paris 5th. €€*
Try the chouriço (spicy sausage) flambéed at the table, and grilled chickens from Susa Silva and Romeo Azevedo.

Les Comptoirs de Lisbonne
⚲ *14, rue Faidherbe, Paris 11th. €€*
Here you can enjoy grilled octopus à la plancha and a beef picanha with feijãos (black beans), in a restaurant with a family atmosphere.

Sapinho
⚲ *85, rue Lamarck, Paris 18th. €€*
The latest opened location, and the trendiest, is in Montmartre. Rafael Dos Santos and Maria (his mother) cook bulhão pato (cockles marinières), octopus, bolinhos de bacalhau (cod fritters), and bacalhau à brás (cod, potatoes, onions, scrambled eggs).

Pedra Alta
⚲ *6, av. du Général-Leclerc, Boulogne-Billancourt (Hauts-de-Seine). €€*
Customers elbow their way into this large brasserie that dishes up Portuguese classics in generous proportions.

PASTRY SHOPS

Don Antónia Pastelaria
⚲ *8, rue de la Grange-aux-Belles, Paris 10th*
A lunch counter and pastry shop serving cod fritters, fabulous pastéis de nata, and bolas de Berlim where you can eat on-site near the Canal Saint-Martin, or even take with you a little piece of Portugal thanks to its boutique section.

Pastelaria Belém
⚲ *47, rue Boursault, Paris 17th*
There are a few tables where you can enjoy squid, chouriço (chorizo), bifanas (pork sandwich), and on the sweet side, coconut pasteis, chocolate almonds, or bolas de Berlim (beignets filled with pastry cream).

GROCERIES

Antepasto
⚲ *84, rue du Chemin-Vert, Paris 11th*
Salads at lunch, pasteis for snacks, wine, olives, beautiful cheese and charcuterie boards for an aperitif, to enjoy on-site or as takeout. Also jarred items and oil from small Portuguese producers.

Queijaria Nacional
⚲ *96, blvd. des Batignolles, Paris 17th*
A shop offering a wide variety of cheeses, charcuterie, packaged food, and pastries.

There are a few tables downstairs or on the terrace for lunch on the premises.

Paris–Porto
⚲ *100, rue des Martyrs, Paris 18th*
A fine-foods shop opened by two Portuguese sisters, who sell specialties directly from Portugal and pastries to taste on the few tables, along with coffee.

WINE SELLER

Portologia
⚲ *42, rue Chapon, Paris 3rd*
This port merchant (Porto and Douro wines), with two hundred labels of wines from small producers, is a wine cellar, wine bar, and tasting room.

The British Isles

Between brunch and happy hour, the capital often takes on a British accent. Here is an overview of British establishments.

—CHARLES PATIN O'COOHOON

Great Britain

In the mid-nineteenth century, many British nationals settled in Paris and lived around the Saint-Honoré and Saint-Germain-des-Prés districts. With the influx of Anglo-Saxon students in the 1990s, English-style pubs also flourished. Today, the community brings together 18,600 Britons throughout Île-de-France.

THE PIONEER

Willi's Wine Bar (England)

📍 *13, rue des Petits-Champs, Paris 1st.* €€

Since 1980, Mark Williamson has turned this British bastion into a bistro of taste doubling as a temple of wine in Paris, immortalized by a legendary collection of posters.

RESTAURANTS

Juveniles (Scotland)

📍 *47, rue de Richelieu, Paris 1st.* €€

Since March 1987, the Scotsman Tim Johnston, joined by his daughter Margaux and her husband, Romain Rondeau, has been delighting with a bistro menu: langoustines from Scotland, London cheeses from Neal's Yard Dairy, and a very serious wine bar.

L'Entente (England)

📍 *13, rue Monsigny, Paris 2nd.* €€

In this British outpost, the London dandy Oliver Woodhead serves the best of Anglo-Saxon cuisine: pudding pie, sausage, and cheeses from Paxton & Whitfield, the monarchy's official supplier.

PUBS

The Auld Alliance (Scotland)

📍 *80, rue François-Miron, Paris 4th.* €

This pure Scottish pub serves more than one hundred whiskeys and some very fine pints such as from Orkney Brewery to sip around a haggis or homemade fish-and-chips in front of the eight screens that broadcast live sports events.

Sir Winston (England)

📍 *5, rue de Presbourg, Paris 16th.* €€

This is one of the oldest English pubs in the capital. In 2020, the pub, located at the foot of Charles de Gualle Étoile, took a "return from India" direction with curried Scotch eggs, fish-and-chips, and tandoori chicken.

BARS

Bar Anglais at Hôtel Regina (England)

📍 *2, pl. des Pyramides, Paris 1st.* €€€

Named after Queen Victoria, the Hôtel Regina features a jewel of Victorian decor. Between the varnished oak woodwork and the garnet velvet armchairs, you can enjoy a whiskey from a menu that has about forty labels.

Cambridge Public House (England)

📍 *8, rue de Poitou, Paris 3rd.* €

In a British decor with woodwork, curtains, and old-school paintings, the duo Hyacinthe Lescoët and Greg Inder shake cocktails made from artisanal spirits that they serve with small plates of English fare.

PASTRY SHOP

Rose Bakery (England)

📍 *46, rue des Martyrs, Paris 9th*

📍 *1, rue de Navarin, Paris 9th*

📍 *Tearoom at Le Bon Marché, 24, rue de Sèvres, Paris 7th*

Since 2002, the couple Rose and Jean-Charles Carrarini have sanctified breakfast and lunch with scones, crumbles, pies, salads, and carrot cakes. They now offer a takeout counter, a grocery, and a tearoom.

WINE SELLER

La Maison du Whisky (Scotland)

📍 *20, rue d'Anjou, Paris 8th*

In the 1960s, this establishment was the first to import single malts from Scotland to France. Today, this temple of whisky stocks in its shop more than twenty-two hundred labels, with a space dedicated to Islay and the Lab, a tasting and training laboratory.

Ireland

Accustomed to celebrating St. Patrick's Day every year on March 17, the taste of Ireland intersects in the capital's only Irish restaurant and in many pubs.

RESTAURANT

Molly's

📍 *91, rue de Charenton, Paris 12th.* €

This Irish enterprise offers cheeses imported directly from the island (Cashel Blue, Killeen), local organic salmon, and a shoulder of lamb braised in beer. The restaurant offers a nice and rare selection of Irish gins.

PUB

The Green Goose

📍 *19, rue des Boulets, Paris 11th.* €

Behind its green facade within its wood interior, this pub distills Irish liquors and craft beers, offered up with Scotch eggs, Irish whiskey, chicken pâtés, and organic salmon rillettes.

Oliver Woodhead, manager of L'Entente (Paris 2nd).

Scandinavia

There aren't many Scandinavian establishments in Paris, but those that do exist are ever popular. —ELVIRA MASSON

In its current geographical context, the region of Scandinavia includes Sweden, Norway, and Denmark. By extension, Finland and sometimes Iceland are often included. This group is referred to as the Nordic countries. Among the pioneering locations in Paris were La Petite Sirène de Copenhague (Paris 9th), though the business is now closed.

THE PIONEER

Flora Danica (Denmark)

📍 *142, av. des Champs-Élysées, Paris 8th.* €€

A legendary address on the Champs-Élysées, it is the pride of all Scandinavians, not just the Danes. On the ground floor, the "Scandi brewery" Flora Danica offers a nice choice of well-sourced salmon products, including gravlax and tartare.

RESTAURANT

Lilla Krogen (Sweden)

📍 *1, pl. de Mareil, Saint-Germain-en-Laye (Yvelines).* €€

An adorable location just a ten-minute walk from the exit of the RER Saint-Germain-en-Laye that offers Swedish classics in a "bistronomy" fashion. The Skagen toast is perfect, the varmrökt lax (homemade hot smoked salmon pavé) is impeccable, and its dill-lemon cream and honungsmarinerad fläsksida (pork belly with honey) and potato salad are typical of this simple and everyday cuisine that Sweden enthusiastically produces.

CAFÉS

Café Fika (Sweden)

📍 *11, rue Payenne, Paris 3rd.* €

Fika? This is the name for the coffee and snack break that Swedish workers take. Set up in the heart of the Swedish Institute, this café plays somewhat the role of a gourmet embassy at any time of the day: smørrebrød, herring with dill, smoked fish, pastries.

Café Maa (Finland)

📍 *60, rue des Écoles, Paris 5th.* €

The place is beautiful, with its heavy wooden front door and heavily influenced Alvar Aalto decor. The Finnish Institute is an exciting meeting and exhibition venue, and its Café Maa is a marvel: you can drink coffees from the Frukt Coffee Roasters workshops in Turku, Finland, while feasting on korvapuustit (cinnamon buns), rye bread toasts, or karjalanpiirakat (Karelian pies).

Le Café Suédois (Sweden)

📍 *20, rue de Martignac, Paris 7th.* €

Anna and Maria left the Swedish Institute in the Marais in autumn 2021 to set up their café in another private mansion: the Hôtel de Vogüé, in the 7th arrondissement. Their simple and fresh cuisine lost nothing in the move: savory pies, soups, and salads of the day, and above all, Maria's divine cakes.

GROCERY

Affären (Sweden)

📍 *80, rue de Saussure, Paris 17th*

This boutique-grocery by Agneta Kossovski who is, like many Swedes, very good at baking. Her kanell and kardamom bullar are delicious, especially when enjoyed still lukewarm. Ask if she has homemade köttbullar (meatballs) in the freezer (in a plastic bag, closed with a colored ribbon)—they are famous.

CANDY SHOP

Käramell (Sweden)

📍 *15, rue des Martyrs, Paris 9th*

Godis in Swedish means "sweets." Bonbon shops are everywhere in Sweden, and in all the Scandinavian countries, which are major consumers of commercial sugar. Lena Rosen has managed to make Käramell a stop where people come to raid salta lakrits (salted licorice), gele hallån båtar (small raspberry boats), and bilar (car-shaped sweets, the all-time bestseller among Swedish confections).

Western Europe

The cuisine of France's Western European neighbors—though not well represented in the capital—offers a rich, diverse, and too-little-known culinary heritage.
—MARILOU PETRICOLA

Germany

With only eighteen thousand nationals in Île-de-France, Germany is represented with very few establishments.

RESTAURANT

Le Stube

📍 *31, rue de Richelieu, Paris 1st. €€*

In their red-hued shop, Franco-German couple Gerhard Weber and Sylvie Blum serve traditional currywurst, grilled sausage sprinkled with curry, impeccable sauerkraut, and delicious apple strudel to enjoy on wooden tables.

STREET FOOD

Sürpriz

📍 *28, blvd. Saint-Denis, Paris 10th. €*

📍 *110, rue Oberkampf, Paris 11th. €*

A real kebab, just like in Berlin. Döner (Turkish pide bread) or dürüm (Turkish galette) topped with a delicious marinated chicken, or the vegetarian version.

Le Wunderbär

📍 *16, rue Beaurepaire, Paris 10th. €*

Delicious würste served roasted or with water, curry, cheese, or homemade sauce accompanied by a large plate of fries and drizzled with German beer. Available all day on one of the large wooden shareable tables. And for dessert? Apfelstrudel (apple strudel).

BAKERIES

House of 3 Brothers

📍 *25, rue de Lancry, Paris 10th*

This pastry shop, run by Mirko Schmitt in memory of his childhood with his two brothers, offers cakes inspired by the traditional recipes of their grandmother and great-aunt. A soft gingerbread, the famous käsekuchen (cake made of fromage blanc), or the katzi, with chocolate and hazelnuts. At lunch, salads, savory tarts, and soups are offered.

Kaffeehaus

📍 *11, rue Poncelet, Paris 17th*

Behind the glass case can be found huge German cakes: Black Forest, apple strudel, Sachertorte, which can be enjoyed on premises. There are also some savory dishes to enjoy: sauerkraut, koulibiac or sausage, as well as a selection of German breads, such as vollkornbrot, a multigrain brown loaf.

GROCERY

Der Tante Emma Laden

📍 *Marché de la Porte-Saint-Martin—31–33, rue du Château-d'Eau, Paris 10th*

These iconic boutiques, present throughout Germany until the 1970s and traditionally run by elderly women, exist in Paris. You can find everything in these temples of German products: charcuterie, cheese, bratwurst, beers, Verpoorten Eierlikör (an egg liqueur), and Toffifee (chocolate, hazelnut, and caramel sweets).

Switzerland

More than 28,422 Swiss nationals are registered with the consulate with an address in Île-de-France.

RESTAURANT

Tradiswiss

📍 *81, blvd. Raspail, Paris 6th. €€*

The rendezvous spot for enjoying fondue, raclette, or röstis in a warm mountain chalet setting. To end a meal, the must-have double-cream meringue.

Austria

Considering the Viennese croissant and Marie-Antoinette's "brioche," Austria is known in Paris for its sweet locations.

PASTRY SHOP

Pâtisserie Viennoise

📍 *8, rue de l'École-de-Médecine, Paris 6th*

Opened in 1928, this pastry shop has hardly changed: yellow walls, tightly packed tables, and delicious pastries. Sachertorte, a chocolate cake with apricot jam; kifli, a croissant rolled with walnuts or poppy seeds; and Viennese chocolate with plenty of Chantilly cream.

Belgium

Some ninety thousand Belgians live in Paris as of 2022, and this number is constantly growing.

STREET FOOD

Label'ge Frite— Le Roi des Frites

📍 *169, rue Montmartre, Paris 2nd. €*

The only real frites shop in Paris. Here all the codes are respected: Bintje variety and double cooking in beef fat. Crispy on the outside and melting on the inside.

Le Comptoir Belge

📍 *58, rue des Martyrs, Paris 9th. €*

📍 *1, rue de Passy, Paris 16th. €*

📍 *1, rue Pierre-Lescot, Paris 1st. €*

A food counter with real waffles from Liège, from the plain to the Belgian, filled with chocolate (Belgian), covered with homemade whipped cream and broken pieces of speculoos cookies.

Eastern Europe and Russia

The French capital has its share of foods with an Eastern European flair. From the Urals to Georgia, here is an overview.

—ESTELLE LENARTOWICZ AND AIMIE BLANCHARD

Poland

Due to World War II and the Soviet era, thousands of Poles made Paris their second home, numbering today about eight thousand. Many enjoyed meals at La Crypte, a restaurant located under the Church of the Assumption (Paris 16th).

BAKERY

La Boutique Jaune by Sacha Finkelsztajn

📍 *27, rue des Rosiers, Paris 4th*

In the heart of the Marais, this Jewish shop dating to the late nineteenth century offers Linzer torte, apple strudel, and even Hungarian cheeses.

GROCERY

Comme en Pologne

📍 *9, rue Hégésippe-Moreau, Paris 17th*

Locals shop here to stock up on canned food, fresh twarog cheese, salt pickles, kabanos (long thin, smoked pork sausages), horseradish, and pierogis with cabbage or cheese. There is also a selection of beers and vodkas.

Hungary

This Slavic cuisine, rare in Paris, is marked by the flavors of spices, especially paprika.

RESTAURANT

Le Paprika

📍 *28, av. Trudaine, Paris 9th. €*

Since 1995, this establishment has been at the top of Hungarian cuisine in Paris, offering charcuterie, körözött (sheep's-milk cheese with paprika and herbs), fillet of beef with morels, and cherry strudel.

Romania

With sixty-six hundred Romanian immigrants in 2019, this community is booming in Paris.

RESTAURANT

Ibrik Kitchen

📍 *Ibrik Kitchen: 9, rue de Mulhouse, Paris 2nd. €€*

📍 *Ibrik Café: 43, rue Laffite, Paris 9th. €*

In the middle of the neighborhood of Sentier, Ecaterina Paraschiv has set up a restaurant dedicated to the Balkans with barbecue of smoked kidneys, octopus confit, polenta with sage, and papanași (sweet beignets).

GROCERY

Épicerie Nicolae

📍 *5, rue de Latran, Paris 5th*

Right in front of the Church of the Holy Archangels you will find preserves, cheeses, charcuterie, meats, and Romanian wines at affordable prices.

Georgia

Leuville-sur-Orge (Essonne), whose chateau housed the Georgian government in exile in 1922, is the historic stronghold of this community.

RESTAURANTS

Pirosmani

📍 *6, rue Boutebrie, Paris 5th. €*

Named after the Georgian painter Pirosmani, the kitchen here prepares khatchapuris (bread filled with cheese), chakapouli (lamb with coriander and tarragon), and khartcho soup with mutton broth, all to be washed down with Georgian spirits.

Colchide

📍 *97, rue des Poissonniers, Paris 18th. €*

📍 *79, rue des Martyrs, Paris 18th. €*

📍 *Wine shop: 87, rue des Poissonniers, Paris 18th*

This Georgian bistro offers delicious khachapuris, ragouts and slow-cooked specialties with herbal notes, and a selection of Georgian orange wines.

La Bicyclette

📍 *5, rue de Chaumont, Paris 19th. €*

Fusion cuisine is made in this neighborhood bistro where chef Slavica Marmakovic and Bertrand Disset harmonize house-made tarama, chakapuli (stew), cabbage stuffed with pig's head and feet, and natural wines.

Armenia

The genocide of 1915 pushed the Armenians from Turkey to an international diaspora, where some settled in France in Issy-les-Moulineaux (Hauts-de-Seine).

RESTAURANT

La Maison de la Culture Arménienne

📍 *17, rue Bleue, Paris 9th. €*

This business has no storefront, just a gate that you will have to pass through before crossing a courtyard to climb a few stairs to savor juicy khinkalis with beef (ravioli that are enjoyed by first sucking up the broth inside with the first bite), stuffed eggplant, and khachapuris (cheese breads).

Russia

Paris had fifty-eight hundred Russian immigrants in 2019. Since the arrival of the first wave of refugees in 1917, the district of Saint-Alexandre-Nevsky Cathedral (Paris 8th) is their historic center.

RESTAURANTS

La Cantine des Tsars

📍 *21, rue du Roule, Paris 1st. €*

This restaurant, run by Elisa Bedrossian, serves up her specialty pelmenis (meat ravioli), typical of the Urals.

À La Ville de Petrograd

📍 *13, rue Daru, Paris 8th. €€*

Founded in 1924 and renovated in 2020, this restaurant gives pride of place to traditional Russian dishes: pirozhkis (stuffed brioche bread), Baeri caviar, and makovnik (rolled bread with poppy seeds).

Le Zakouski

📍 *127, rue du Château, Paris 14th. €€*

Here the menu lists beef stroganoff and homemade blinis with herring, all to be enjoyed with an iced vodka (literally "small water" in Russian).

Chez Mademoiselle

📍 *21, rue Mademoiselle, Paris 15th. €€*

Kazakh, Russian, and Ukrainian specialties: borscht, beef stroganoff, pelmenis (meat ravioli), and Georgian wine or vodka. (A little sister to the restaurant, La Table des Russes, opened in the 16th.)

GROCERY

Prestige

📍 *16, rue Lecourbe, Paris 15th*

This shop offers charcuterie, preserves, spirits, confections, and traditional homemade dishes.

LA CANTINE DES TSARS

Greece

Rich in sun-kissed ingredients, the Mediterranean cuisine of Greece is well represented in the capital.

—JORDAN MOILIM

THE FIRST WAVES

Although immigration to France intensified at the end of World War II, the Greek diaspora has been present in Paris since the nineteenth century.

BELLEVILLE TO SAINT-MICHEL

Having first settled in Belleville, the Greek community soon filled the district of Saint-Michel, making famous the folkloric breaking of plates, reminiscent of the rituals of Athenian tables.

RENEWAL

Greek cuisine is now spread throughout the capital, far from the typical touristy areas where they were traditionally located.

THE PIONEER

Mavrommátis

📍 *42, rue Daubenton, Paris 5th.* €€€

A historic establishment founded by the benchmark for Greek cuisine in Paris: Andréas Mavrommátis. Opened since 1978, he achieved a Michelin star in 2018, forty years after the opening of his first grocery.

RESTAURANTS

Tzeferakos

📍 *24, rue Monge, Paris 5th.* €

In this family-style lunch counter in the Mouffetard district, patrons sit elbow to elbow to enjoy excellent stewed

dishes: beef dumplings, stuffed squid, and an incomparable semolina cake for something sweet, all washed down with cold Mythos beer.

Kafé Jean

📍 *9, rue de Trévise, Paris 9th.* €

A tempting Franco-Greek menu in an especially cozy and tidy setting. A multitude of delicious mezzedes are available: tarama, keftedes, ktipiti, hummus, feta saganaki, accompanied by a glass of Greek retsina wine.

Grand Café d'Athènes

📍 *74, rue du Faubourg-Saint-Denis, Paris 10th.* €€

A nice bistro run by Chloé Monchalin and Benjamin Rousselet. Everything is impeccable: tarama with smoked cod eggs, orzo risotto, and, not to be passed up, one of the most beautiful Greek natural wine lists.

Etsi

📍 *23, rue Eugène-Carrière, Paris 18th.* €€

Since 2017, Mikaela Liaroutsos has been reciting the high mass of mezes in her tavern in blue-and-white tones: tender grilled octopus, halloumi fritters (goat's-milk and sheep's-milk cheeses), and unmatched baklavas.

STREET FOOD

Filakia

📍 *9, rue Mandar, Paris 2nd.* €

Faithful to its big brother, Le Grand Café d'Athènes, this spot attracts the cool kids and connoisseurs who come to enjoy gyros of farmstead pork

on-the-go or delectable little zucchini fritters with mint to dip cheerfully in an always successfully executed tzatziki.

Casse-Croûte Grec

📍 *4, rue de l'École-Polytechnique, Paris 5th.* €

A notice to all Greek food lovers: this is one of the best sandwiches in the capital. A cousin to the kebab, the gyros here are exemplary. A house-made spit grilled over a flame and enhanced with veal and turkey, hot pita, a garlicky tzatziki, house-made hot sauce, a lot of oregano, and some raw vegetables.

CATERER

Evi Evane

📍 *20, rue Saint-Placide, Paris 6th*

📍 *49, rue Condorcet, Paris 9th*

Maria and Dina Nikolaou serve as ambassadors of Hellenic cuisine in

their restaurant on rue Guisarde (Paris 6th) as well as in their grocery stores where the great classics are perfectly executed: first-rate tarama or insanely good moussaka, to enjoy on-site or as takeout.

GROCERY

Profil Grec

📍 *109, rue de Belleville, Paris 19th*

Since 2009, Alexandros Rallis has proclaimed his love of Greece. On the shelves are some of the best products Greece has to offer: a prodigious feta and olive oil, oregano . . . all direct from the producers.

Turkey and Kurdish Cuisine

At the crossroads of Asian, Eastern European, and Mediterranean influences, this culinary repertoire of Ottoman origin is represented in all its diversity. —JORDAN MOILIM

Turkey

Paris's 10th arrondissement has been nicknamed "Little Turkey" since the massive influx of Turkish workers in the early 1970s, resulting from demands from France for foreign workers as well as the result of the political crisis in Turkey. Around Porte Saint-Denis, a veritable village sprung up with its share of grocers, butchers, restaurants, and even hairdressers who landed directly from Asia Minor, where can be found some three hundred thousand nationals.

THE PIONEER

Pizza Grill Istanbul

📍 *66, rue du Faubourg-Saint-Denis, Paris 10th. €€*

All kinds of dishes have passed over the flames here since 1989: lamb and eggplant caviar, chicken and tomato sauce, and the must-have juicy adana beef kebabs, served with a fine pita prepared in a flash.

RESTAURANTS

Sizin

📍 *47, rue Saint-Georges, Paris 9th. €€*

Classics are revisited here in this cozy setting: muhammara (spicy walnut puree with feta), tarama, grilled skewers. Special mention goes to the mantis, ravioli stuffed with ground meat covered with cream. There are four locations in Paris.

Derya

📍 *16, rue du Faubourg-Saint-Denis, Paris 10th. €€*

This family affair has been delighting gourmets continuously from 11 a.m. to midnight since the 2000s with cig köfte (spicy dumplings of raw meat with bulgur) and kadaif (crisp strands of phyllo with pistachio).

Le Janissaire

📍 *22–24, allée Vivaldi, Paris 12th. €€*

A stone's throw from Nation, this spot is like stepping into Istanbul: white tablecloths, logoed plates, homemade warm bread, and à la carte: real white tarama, eight-hour shoulder of lamb, and the timeless moussaka.

Elma & Nar

📍 *45, av. Secrétan, Paris 19th. €*

Located next to the Halle Secrétan covered market, "Pomme & Grenade" offers a real pasha brunch: fried eggs with sucuk (beef sausage, beyaz peynir) and simit, a wheel-shaped bread beset with sesame.

STREET FOOD

Pidè Paris

📍 *48, rue du Faubourg-Saint-Denis, Paris 10th. €*

Young Turk owners in the 10th arrondissement offer pidè, a thin pizza in the shape of a boat and topped with kasar, a soft cow's-milk cheese, and pastirma, slices of dried beef with cumin.

Adana

📍 *197, rue de Crimée, Paris 19th. €*

Here hungry visitors will enjoy an authentic Turkish kebab. House-made veal on a spit made every day, that frolics on the plate in a creamy and sour white sauce, all drizzled with ayran, the famous salty milky drink.

GROCERY

Épicerie du Faubourg

📍 *22–24, rue du Faubourg-Saint-Denis, Paris 10th*

Here specialized products can be found, such as yufkas, sheets of pasta used for börek, and feta peynir, the Turkish cousin of Greek cheese. A must try are the homemade breads topped with feta or potato and onion.

Kurdish cuisine

In the 1990s, the conflict between the Kurdish Workers' Party and Turkey led to Kurdish immigration. Originally from Iran, Turkey, Iraq, and Syria, this ethnic group is concentrated around the Kurdish Institute (10th), which houses the largest library of Kurdish books in the world.

RESTAURANTS

Avesta

📍 *5, rue d'Enghien, Paris 10th. €*

A show takes place in the window with the making of gözleme. On a Turkish billig, thick crêpes are shaped and stuffed with a choice of mint-parsley-feta or a mixture of onion and slightly spicy potato.

Anatolia Village

📍 *74, rue du Château-d'Eau, Paris 10th. €*

In the Kurdish tavern of Egun Celik, you can enjoy lahmacun on the go and cooked in a flash. These are very thin disks of dough filled with peppers, ground meat, and onions. Also not to be missed is the tavuk sis, generous pieces of grilled chicken cooked with smoked eggplant caviar, all topped with yogurt.

STREET FOOD

Urfa Dürüm

📍 *58, rue du Faubourg-Saint-Denis, Paris 10th. €*

Food lovers rush here to taste the dürüm, the cousin of the kebab, with a fine house-made pita in which is inserted a grilled skewer (lamb liver, chicken, beef), raw vegetables, sumac, a squeeze of lemon, and a dash of olive oil.

SEE ALSO
The Kebab, p. 134.

The Maghreb

Algeria, Morocco, Tunisia (aka the Maghreb) are the winning trio from North Africa that has been unveiling its spicy flavors and pastries in Paris since the postwar period. —NADIA HAMAM

THE ALGERIAN LINK

Due to colonial history and geographical proximity, people from Algeria constitute the first immigrant community in Île-de-France with nearly 295,000 people, followed by Morocco (233,000) and Tunisia (112,000).

FROM BOUGNATS TO KABYLES

At the end of the 1950s, the Auvergne coffee shops ceded certain addresses in eastern Paris to the Kabyles, workers from Algeria, who opened establishments to immigrants in need of housing . . . and the flavors from home.

NORTH OF PARIS

The districts of Belleville and Ménilmontant, followed by the famous Goutte-d'Or (Barbès) district, remain epicenters of North African culture. Parisian gourmets take advantage of it.

Abdel Alaoui, founder of Yemma (Paris 11th).

THE PIONEER

La Mascotte (Algeria)

📍 *174, rue de Crimée, Paris 19th. €*

All the hits of Berber cuisine are offered up in this modest and authentic location run by the same family since the 1950s. Osban kabyle (semolina dumplings) are made every Sunday.

RESTAURANTS

Majouja (Algeria)

📍 *43, rue Laffitte, Paris 9th. €*

To discover flavors from the Kabyle side, try the amekfoul (couscous) with beans and peas, topped with a hard-boiled egg. Also the uncommon dish rechta, Algerian pasta all finely steamed then drizzled with a white broth, with turnips and cinnamon, served with chicken.

Tounsia (Tunisia)

📍 *55, rue de Paradis, Paris 10th. €*

Within a modern and invigorating decor, two sisters from Sfax cook serious classics from home: shakshouka (panfried peppers topped with an egg), aromatic chorba, not to mention the Tunisia's street-food hits (chapati, tabuna, mlawi).

Yemma (Morocco)

📍 *119, rue du Chemin-Vert, Paris 11th. €*

A scent of Morocco floats around colorful kemias (zaalouk, mechouia, carrots with cumin) and tagines. Those in a hurry will scoop up a filled cake, a brik pastry, or a stuffed msemen (flatbread). Sip on a ginger jasmine tea.

BerbèrHygge (Kabylian-Scandinavian)

📍 *7, rue de Wattignies, Paris 12th. €*

Here Kabylian-Scandinavian fusion is dared! In a calm ambience, you can enjoy semolinas made from whole wheat or barley and rolled by hand, lamb couscous, and tikourbabines (semolina balls flavored with mint).

Le Petit Bleu (Tunisia)

📍 *23, rue Muller, Paris 18th. €*

In the heart of Montmartre are found spices, harissa, and orange blossom, direct from Tunisia. Tajines borrow influences from their Moroccan cousin. Kafteji (minced fried vegetables completed with a fried egg), mloukhiya (stew made from nalta jute leaves), and slata mechouia (salad of grilled peppers and tomatoes) made to order.

L'Atlantide (Algeria)

📍 *7, av. Laumière, Paris 19th. €€*

In a total Kabyle look, stuffed sardines, bourekas (savory pastry), and pastillas waltz around amekfoul and couscous. An original creation is the tagine with lamb, fig, and date flambéed with bukha (fig brandy).

La cantine de Ménilmontant (Algeria)

📍 *6, rue des Maronites, Paris 20th. €*

This establishment well represents the spirit of the Kabyle Belleville of the 1960s. Loubia (white bean soup), berkoukes (large-grain couscous, vegetables, and meat), and tikourbabine (semolina balls flavored with mint and spices, served with calf's foot or tripe). Sardines are grilled up on Fridays.

Chez Tante Farida (Algeria)

📍 *13, rue de Bagnolet, Paris 20th.* €€

In a simple corridor wedged between a counter and a few tables, Mrs. Farida cooks with pride the Algerian cuisine inherited from her mother and grandmother: Kabyle galettes, filled mhajebs (semolina flatbreads), and fresh homemade plates of the day (harira, house-made brik) in a vibrant atmosphere.

Sidi Bou Said (Tunisia)

📍 *69, av. Jean-Jaurès, Aubervilliers (Seine-Saint-Denis).* €

Located close to the metro, this establishment's ocean-blue storefront, oyster bar, and no-fuss atmosphere serving up high-quality family-style and working-class Tunisian food lights up the neighborhood.

STREET FOOD

Tabouna, Tunisian terroir (Tunisia)

📍 *2, rue Moret, Paris 11th.* €

Featured is the famous Tunisian sandwich made in tabuna bread, but also typical plates and a dish of the day. A location for 100 percent Tunisian products.

BAKERY

La Bague de Kenza (Algeria)

📍 *173, rue du Faubourg-Saint-Antoine, Paris 11th*

📍 *106, rue Saint-Maur, Paris 11th*

📍 *233, rue de la Convention, Paris 15th*

The classics of Algerian baked goods in the window catch the attention. Breads (kesra, matloo, khoubz eddar), brioches (the famous mouna), beignets (sfendj), and the baghrir (semolina pancakes riddled with holes, traditional or reinvented). Enjoy a quick latte or a mint tea.

PASTRY SHOPS

Laouz (Algeria)

📍 *136, rue Saint-Honoré, Paris 1st*

📍 *111, rue Mouffetard, Paris 5th*

📍 *20, rue Dauphine, Paris 6th*

📍 *61, av. du Général-Leclerc, Paris 14th*

📍 *23, rue Poncelet, Paris 17th*

Algerian confections delicately sweetened are available in traditional or contemporary versions, flavored with yuzu, matcha, or poppy seed. Gluten-free and egg-free alternatives are available.

Masmoudi (Tunisia)

📍 *106, blvd. Saint-Germain, Paris 6th*

The little cakes of this famous pastry shop founded in 1972 in Sfax are dizzying in their beauty, diversity, and gustatory finesse. It's difficult to choose.

Tipana

📍 *2, rue Clément, Paris 6th*

Soft brioches, éclairs, macarons . . . Halfway between French and pastries from the East, Dima Al Husseini's creations combine flavors from the Maghreb (rose, pistachio, dates . . .) and Europe (praline, raspberry . . .).

Diamande (Algeria)

📍 *4, rue Sedaine, Paris 11th*

Flowery, fruity, spicy, chocolate, and even gluten-free, the mini-creations flirt between France and Algeria, between cakes and bonbons. Stuffed pastries with violet, apricot makrout, pear-pistachio baklava—it's a gourmet journey.

Maison Gazelle (Morocco)

📍 *2, rue Jean-Macé, Paris 11th*

Rose, lemon, cardamom, Piedmont hazelnuts . . . Delicate fragrances and sourced almond flour lend a unique identity to these gazelle horns (a crescent-shaped cookie) that summon the splendor of Maghreb weddings.

GROCERY

Le P'tit Souk

📍 *86, rue Patay, Paris 13th*

Mountains of spices, platters of Algerian desserts, all the breads of the Maghreb, and ingredients for cooking reside here. This is a veritable Ali Baba's den.

MARKET

Les Délices de Biskra (Algeria)

📍 *Rue Gabriel-Péri, Saint-Denis (Seine-Saint-Denis)*

Since 2004, Djamila Hadji has been regaling regulars with her Algerian classics. Visit the Saint-Denis market on Tuesday, Friday, and Sunday mornings.

SEE ALSO
Couscous, p. 298.

Sub-Saharan Africa

African flavors abound in the capital. In addition to the French-speaking countries of West Africa, Ethiopia, known for its great culinary diversity, is also well represented. —JORDAN MOILIM

FROM THE 1960s

Mainly settling in Île-de-France, immigration from sub-Saharan Africa began in the very early 1960s, first as part of a temporary labor migration project called *tournant*, then in the 1970s due to the drought in the Sahel and the search for a better future.

HEAD FOR NORTH PARIS

In Paris, the African population is concentrated around two iconic metro stations, Château-Rouge and Château-d'Eau, but is even more generally established in the 18th, 19th, and 20th arrondissements, which host neighborhoods with a strong identity around an extraordinary mix of African cultures. The city's suburban areas such as Charenton-le-Pont, Issy-les-Moulineaux, Ivry-sur-Seine, Montreuil, and Pantin are also home to large African communities. Here are excellent options when exploring and feeling a little hungry.

Alexandre Bella Ola, chef of Moussa l'Africain (Paris 1st).

THE PIONEER

Moussa l'Africain (Cameroon)

📍 *21, rue Pierre-Lescot, Paris 1st.* €€

The location of the shining example of African cuisine in Paris: Alexandre Bella Ola, along with his wife, Vicky, has been representing their Cameroonian culture for more than twenty years. The "hit" of the house is the DG chicken, standing for *directeur général*, a marinated and grilled chicken, accompanied by plantains, bell peppers, and beans.

RESTAURANTS

Waalo (Mauritania)

📍 *9, rue d'Alexandrie, Paris 2nd.* €

At the helm of this new lunch counter in the Sentier is Harouna Sow, a Mauritanian chef who has worked in the kitchens of Refugee Food. He revisits the great classics with his own touch, such as a dressed-up maafe with fennel, or the famous acras (fritters), offered in a veggie version with a yam-based batter.

Le Djoliba (Senegal)

📍 *6, rue Blondel, Paris 3rd.* €

An address for connoisseurs. In the narrow rue Blondel, lovers of thieboudienne flock to taste this one-pot fish and tomato rice dish, which owes its glowing color to the broth in which it's cooked. A hearty and remarkable plate for barely ten euros.

BMK—Paris Bamako (Mali)

📍 *14, rue de la Fidélité, Paris 10th.* €€
📍 *40, rue Jean-Pierre-Timbaud, Paris 11th.* €€

Founded by two talented Malians, Fousseyni and Abdoulaye Djikine, this African destination for food sources its products directly from the country, such as their amazing peanut paste produced by their aunt. Add a Charolais steak, some fried plantains, and you have one of the best maafe in Paris. Equally gratifying is their second location in the 11th, BMK-Folie-Bamako.

Oh Africa (Cameroon)

📍 *6, rue de Paradis, Paris 10th.* €

As good for simmering maafe as for listening to playlists, Hervé Aboya has been lighting up the place for five years. At lunch, an unbeatable formula is available: for just about ten euros, a generous portion of coconut chicken with the bonus of a bissap, hibiscus juice.

L'Étoile d'Afrique (West Africa)

📍 *69, blvd. de Strasbourg, Paris 10th.* €

A good destination close to the Gare de l'Est. In this lunch counter, full of regulars, you can savor the mastered great classics: acheke (cassava

couscous) perfectly accompanies the chicken yassa and its famous sauce made from olives, mustard, and lemon.

La Reine de Saba (Ethiopia)

📍 78, rue Jean-Pierre-Timbaud, Paris 11th. €€

In this Ethiopian tiny space, share the injera, a famous tangy cake made from teff flour (a seed similar to millet) garnished with preparations of your choice such as chicken stew, slow-cooked lentils, braised cabbage, and spinach with a touch of lemon.

Waly-Fay (West Africa)

📍 6, rue Godefroy-Cavaignac, Paris 11th. €€

Opened in the 2000s, this was one of the first new generation locations to give pride of place to the African culinary repertoire. In this loftlike establishment, you can taste an authentic ndolé:

a Cameroonian dish of green leaves (similar to spinach) simmered with shrimp and peanut.

Le Kompressor (Côte d'Ivoire)

📍 72, rue du Ruisseau, Paris 18th. €

In the depths of the 18th arrondissement, this place takes its name from a famous nightclub-restaurant in Abidjan. On the turntables, owner Amidou offers real Ivorian cuisine, to eat on the cheap. Hits: sauce gombo and sauce claire made with oxtail, smoked chicken, and a little tripe.

Les Saveurs d'Alberto (Cameroon)

📍 12, rue Adolphe-Mille, Paris 19th. €

A stone's throw from La Villette, the famous Alberto Ketaze has forged a reputation thanks to his honey-mango chicken that he has been serving up every day for eight years. On-site, the dishes

cost only €9.50, for which students of the neighborhood are aware.

Itegue Taitu (Ethiopia)

📍 66, rue Armand-Carrel, Paris 19th. €€

This restaurant, named after the empress of Ethiopia, offers a royal formula: every day for lunchtime, it's mainly an all-you-can-eat vegetarian buffet to enjoy with injera, an iconic cake made from teff flour.

Ohinéné (Côte d'Ivoire)

📍 14, rue de la Chine, Paris 20th. €€

Édith Ohinéné worked for a long time in the family restaurant before moving to Paris. Here she creates the best of her cultural heritage with, for example, a divine kedjenou, a specialty of meat stewed in a house-made broth served with the famous acheke (cassava couscous). For tripe lovers, the tripe soup is worth a visit.

STREET FOOD

New Soul Food— Le Maquis (West Africa)

📍 177, quai de Valmy, Paris 10th. €

In their words, the meal of this food truck would be "afro-disiac." Here customers savor braised chicken kicked up with a choice of Caribbean curry or Penja pepper. Another bit of good news: a second location has recently opened up in the 10th, at quai de Valmy.

GROCERIES

Au Marché de la Côte d'Ivoire

📍 66, rue de Doudeauville, Paris 18th

The best African grocery in Paris. Opened in 1994 by his parents, Yohann Abbé took over the business with great success by offering only the best sourced products from Abidjan. On the shelves: fresh produce (plantains, yams, okra), but also little

gems not typically found elsewhere: exceptional shea butter, hibiscus flower, dried shrimp powder.

Le Livreur du Bled

📍 46, rue des Poissonniers, Paris 18th

Building on its success, this online grocery has settled in the 18th arrondissement. Via the Internet or in the shop, the best of African products can be found: Cameroonian peanuts, soursop leaves, and even saka saka, cassava leaves you can cook like spinach.

MARKET

Barbès Market

📍 60, blvd. de la Chapelle, Paris 18th

A food market held under the Barbès elevated metro station, bringing together all the aromas and flavors of the continent.

Cuisines of the Levant

The cuisine of the Levant (Mashreq in Arabic) refers to that which is traditionally prepared in the countries bordering the eastern coast of the Mediterranean Sea: Syria, Lebanon, Palestine, Jordan, and Kuwait.
—ANTOINE TÉZENAS DU MONTCEL

Through its historical links with the Levant and its tradition of welcoming populations affected by conflicts, France has a significant Levantine diaspora. More than two hundred and fifty thousand Lebanese live in France, including a significant portion in the Paris region. Sometimes unfairly reduced to a few little-varied mezes or too-fatty shawarma, Levantine cuisine in Paris offers a completely different image. Driven by talented and dynamic chefs, this cuisine is now resolutely modern and full of creativity while keeping a strong link to its culinary tradition.

THE PIONEER

Les Cèdres du Liban (Lebanon)

♀ *5, av. du Maine, Paris 15th. €€*

At the helm, since 1973, of this venerable establishment located near the Montparnasse train station, the El Hakim family offers traditional and timeless Lebanese cuisine: traditional mezes and kebabs, as well as Asian-influenced sweets.

RESTAURANTS

Liza (Lebanon)

♀ *14, rue de la Banque, Paris 2nd. €€€*

In a refined setting, Liza and Ziad Asseily have offered since 2005 a benchmark Lebanese cuisine between traditional and contemporary. On weekends, a huge brunch is served with the famous mouloukhieh (made from nalta jute, rice, and chicken).

Qasti (Lebanon)

♀ *205, rue Saint-Martin, Paris 3rd. €€*

This is one of the Parisian addresses of the three-starred, high-energy chef Alan Geeam. Everything is executed with precision and generosity: from feta-mint turnovers to lamb confit (kharouf) in casserole served with freekeh (a green-kernel whole grain) smoked with spices. There is a clever selection of Lebanese wines.

Al Ajami (Lebanon)

♀ *58, rue François 1er, Paris 8th. €€€*

A few steps from the Champs-Élysées, Al Ajami offers authentic and well-mastered gourmet cuisine in an elegant setting. A favorite for the unctuous frakeh or kebbeh nayyeh, a typical dish from southern Lebanon (raw meat with bulgur accompanied by onions and spices).

Tawlet (Lebanon)

♀ *2, rue de la Fontaine-au-Roi, Paris 11th. €€*

Between his cooking at his restaurant and his grocery, Kamal Mouzawak pays tribute, as in Beirut, to the cuisine of the terroirs and to grandmothers. Every day of the week, a region of Lebanon is honored.

Chef Elias Fares (Lebanon)

♀ *54, rue de la Convention, Paris 15th. €*

Lovers of raw meats will enjoy savoring all the offerings: a melting kibbeh nayyeh (ground lamb fillet) embellished with an explosive garlic cream, or kibdeh (lamb liver with spicy onions). Not to be missed is the juicy and tasty shish taouk (marinated chicken).

Le Bois Le Vent (Lebanon)

♀ *59, rue de Boulainvilliers, Paris 16th. €€*

Since 1994, the Abi Khalil family has been offering abundant and appetizing family-style cuisine in a setting with old-fashioned charm. Across the street, the gourmet to-go area offers sandwiches and Asian-influenced mezes for takeout.

Rimal (Lebanon)

♀ *94, blvd. Malesherbes, Paris 17th. €€€*

A veritable institution with a solid reputation, Rimal offers a perfect setting to discover the great classics of Lebanese cuisine through the forty mezes, grilled items, and fish.

Tintamarre (Lebanon)

♀ *80, av. Jean-Jaurès, Paris 19th. €€*

Gabrielle Beck skillfully reinvents the old-fashioned cuisine of her jeddo (grandfather), such as tasty Halloumi croquettes or a simple pork shawarma. If your wallet allows it, dare a rare bottle of Obeideh, an ancient old Lebanese grape variety, from Domaine Sept.

STREET FOOD

Ayadi Gourmet (Syria)

♀ *17, rue Frédéric-Sauton, Paris 5th. €€*

In an Asian atmosphere of kitsch, you can taste a wide range of fatteh, a traditional Mashreq dish, created by chef Ghena Al Barazi, with white mulberry juice. The prepared foods menu offers a wide selection of delicate Syrian dishes.

Kamal Mouzawak, founder of Tawlet (Paris 11th).

Ya Bayté by Hébé (Lebanon)

📍 *1, rue des Grands-Degrés, Paris 5th.* €

With a view of Notre Dame, Ya Bayté offers authentic Lebanese street food. On the menu, traditional meze (tabbouleh, hummus, or batata harra), but above all a wide choice of excellent grilled meats (mashewe) of lamb, beef, or chicken—all to enjoy just as in Beirut.

Chez le Libanais (Lebanon)

📍 *35, rue Saint-André-des-Arts, Paris 6th.* €

In this snack bar located in Saint-Germain-des-Prés, succulently moist man'ouche (Lebanese flatbreads) are cooked on an authentic *saj*, a domed convex griddle. There is something for everyone here, with za'atar, chicken liver, or cod.

La Sajerie (Lebanon)

📍 *20, rue d'Abbeville, Paris 9th.* €

In this small shop near Rochechouart are found creative man'ouche. Typically made with rice flour, these flatbreads are fresh and tasty. They also work very well for takeout.

Le Daily Syrien (Syria)

📍 *12, rue des Petites-Écuries, Paris 10th.* €

Not far from its veggie and prepared-foods locations on Rue du Faubourg-Saint-Denis, this bistro offers a wide range of house-made Eastern dishes that will delight meze lovers. Everything is prepared to order, such as falafel or fresh and crispy rikakats (cheese rolls).

Nemesis (Lebanon)

📍 *37, rue Laugier, Paris 17th.* €

Enjoy, on the go, in a resolutely modern decor, mouthwatering man'ouche with za'atar, as well as modernized kebab or falafel sandwiches, accompanied by colorful and original sauces.

ICE CREAM SHOPS

Bashir (Lebanon)

📍 *58, rue Rambuteau, Paris 3rd*

The specialty of the house is achta ice cream, made from milk, cream, and orange blossom, covered with pistachios.

Bältis (Lebanon)

📍 *27, rue Saint-Antoine, Paris 4th*

This Lebanese artisan ice cream maker offers organic sorbets, varied and rich in fruit. The chocolate-arak-raisins or achta–cotton candy ice cream specialties are original and delightful.

PASTRY SHOP

Maison Aleph

📍 *20, rue de la Verrerie, Paris 4th*

Tucked into the heart of the Marais is Myriam Sabet's pastry shop with Levantine influences. It's difficult to resist the "flower of milk" orange blossom-mastic-pistachio ice cream or the nests made from kadaïf noodles (angel hair) filled with different flavors from the East (cardamom, citron, Damascus rose, and sumac).

GROCERY-CATERERS

Mouneh (Lebanon)

📍 *32, blvd. Saint-Michel, Paris 6th*

Once inside, visitors are transported to a Lebanese village grocer, a veritable Capernaum, offering all sorts of Eastern products: Aleppo soaps, Palestinian za'atar, markouk (bread as thin as parchment paper), or several Lebanese confections, such as Cheque peppermint chewing gum.

Les Délices d'Orient (Lebanon)

📍 *52, av. Émile-Zola, Paris 15th*

More than a small convenience shop, this is a supermarket that has become the rallying point for the homesick Lebanese diaspora. There is absolutely everything, including fresh fruits and vegetables shipped directly from Beirut.

Les mots et le ciel (Lebanon)

📍 *81, rue Olivier-de-Serres, Paris 15th*

In his eat-in shop, virtuoso Karim Haïdar delights palates while introducing the essence of Lebanese cuisine and the art of mouneh (a food preservation technique employed to get through harsh winters). Its gourmet takeout menu is remarkable (from the impressive maaloubit batenjen to the succulent katayef to its hummus enhanced with squid ink).

Jewish Cuisines

Judaism has enriched the world through its own unique cultural traits in literature, music, and visual arts, and most certainly through a vibrant cuisine that has been influenced by the various migrations of the Jewish people. —**ANNABELLE SCHACHMES**

THE DIFFERENT JEWISH CUISINES

› Sephardic cuisine, derived from the Maghreb, is the best known.

› Ladino or Judeo-Spanish cuisine, from the Mediterranean Basin and the southern Balkans, with Persian influences.

› Ashkenazi cuisine (the majority in Paris in the 1980s, and which could be enjoyed at Goldenberg, a restaurant now closed), hailing from Eastern Europe and the northern Balkans.

› Today, it is mainly Israeli cuisine that is enlivening Paris's culinary scene, with its rich flavors of a true Middle Eastern terroir and all the influences of different Jewish cultures.

THE PIONEERS

L'As du Fallafel

📍 *34, rue des Rosiers, Paris 4th. €*

From the falafel (a fried chickpea patty or ball) to the sabich (pita stuffed with grilled eggplant and egg) to the schnitzel (breaded chicken cutlet) to the endless lines and the elbow-to-elbow tables, everything is iconic in this restaurant, which opened in 1979. The sandwiches are exactly like those found in Israel, both in aesthetics and flavor.

La Boule Rouge

📍 *1, rue de la Boule-Rouge, Paris 9th. €€*

Couscous loubia, ganaouia or pkaïla (with beans, okra, or stewed meat), and kemias have filled the tables since 1976. Those hungry come just as much for the slightly old-fashioned atmosphere as for the offerings. Enrico Macias has become a fixture here.

Chez Bob de Tunis

📍 *10, rue Richer, Paris 9th. €*

A shop unchanged since opening, offering the best banatages (potato croquettes), brik doughs, fricassees, and Tunisian snacks in the capital. The unlikely decoration combining cans of tuna and yellowed photos has been the same for forty years, and this is what gives the place its charm.

RESTAURANTS

Shabour/Tekés

📍 *Shabour—19, rue Saint-Sauveur, Paris 2nd. €€€*
📍 *Tekés—4 bis, rue Saint-Sauveur, Paris 2nd. €€*

Shabour means "broken" in Hebrew, and it must be said that chef Assaf Granit breaks the codes of Mediterranean cuisine here. Not far from here is Tekés, the chef's other location, a true celebration of nature where plants are honored in all their forms, colors, and textures.

Salatim/Maafim

📍 *Salatim—15, rue des Jeûneurs, Paris 2nd. €€*
📍 *Maafim—5, rue des Forges, Paris 2nd. €€*

Coming from great establishments, chef Yariv Berreby offers family-style cuisine, such as his mother's fabulous schnitzels. Not far from Salatim is Maafim, where the chef also offers a bakery counter for eating in or for takeout.

Adar

📍 *Restaurant—49, pas. des Panoramas, Paris 2nd. €€*
📍 *Caterer—11, rue Faidherbe, Paris 11th.*

Tamir Namias infuses his cuisine with the flavors of his native Israel. These bistronomy-style dishes reflect his career in France with exceptional technique, cleverly reinvented with new Israeli flavors.

Chiche

📍 *29 bis, rue du Château-d'Eau, Paris 10th. €€*

A little taste of Israeli seaside can be found in this lunch spot–café with generous plates of hummus enlivened with eggplant or ground meat, but also the majadra

TRAITEUR

bowl (a bowl of rice, lentils, and butternut with za'atar), shakshuka, labneh, or borekas, with the choice to wash it all down with house-made lemonade.

Chez René et Gabin

⚲ *92, blvd. de Belleville, Paris 20th. €*

This restaurant serves simple cuisine that strictly respects Tunisian flavors and traditions. In addition to the complete-meal essentials, and fricassees and laablabi (chickpea soup) offered every day, traditional dishes are offered à la carte such as mloukhia (a dish based on ground nalta jute) on Thursdays or batata bel'ham (potato stew with cumin) on Tuesdays.

STREET FOOD

Janet By Homer

⚲ *13, rue Rambuteau, Paris 4th. €*

Tradition and a respect for history are the hallmarks of Janet, including the very essence of smoked meat sandwiches from the Ashkenazi Jewish diaspora, which have

immigrated to the United States. The pickles and sauces are house made. The best bread is sourced to match the original taste of these sandwiches.

Miznon

⚲ *22, rue des Écouffes, Paris 4th. €*
⚲ *3, rue de la Grange-Batelière, Paris 9th. €*
⚲ *37, quai de Valmy, Paris 10th. €*

Chef Eyal Shani has achieved the feat of making his restaurant the star of Israeli "soul food." A mix of street food (sandwiches are served in pita) and ready-made meals (beef bourguignon or sautéed mushrooms), everything is infinitely precise, generous, and perfectly seasoned.

Dizen

⚲ *27, rue Pierre-Fontaine, Paris 9th. €*

Dizen offers an "enhanced" version of an iconic Israeli street food sandwich, the sabich. Pieces of breaded and fried eggplant, house-made mango amba sauce, and pita imported from Israel—nothing has been left to chance to

transform this street-food specialty into a three-star sandwich.

BAKERIES

Florence Kahn

⚲ *24, rue des Écouffes, Paris 4th*

On the shelves are challah and babkas as well as Ashkenazi specialties, such as strudel. The specialty? The pletzel, a round brioche flatbread topped with cooked onions, bearing the ancient name of the legendary Marais district in which the bakery is located.

Babka Zana

⚲ *65, rue Condorcet, Paris 9th*
⚲ *8, rue du Pas-de-la-Mule, Paris 4th*

Building on the success of the first shop on rue Condorcet, Emmanuel and Sarah Murat opened this coffee shop where you can grab a bite throughout the day. Choose from myriad offerings for breakfast, brunch, lunch, or a snack, and enjoy the star choice: the babka, which can be enjoyed eaten on the spot or bagged up for takeout.

GROCERY CATERERS

Pich Pich

⚲ *28, rue d'Enghien, Paris 10th*

People come here for the borekas (savory pastry), eggplant caviar, citrus artichoke hearts, and other essential recipes by Régine, grandmother of the founder, Julie Sadaka, and whose portrait sits behind the counter. Pich Pich is one of the very few Parisian restaurants to offer classics of Ladino Jewish cuisine (Sephardic Mediterranean cuisine).

Boker

⚲ *1, rue Saint-Ambroise, Paris 11th*

Antalya (beef simmered with spices), Sidi Bou Saïd (tuna in oil, preserved lemon, and olives), or Jaffa (feta, pecorino, ricotta, mint): so many city names to define the flavors of borekas, a Mediterranean street food specialty consisting of triangular puff pastries filled with tasty things. Choose from savory or sweet options, to eat in or for takeout.

BUTCHERS

Boucherie Norbert

⚲ *7, rue des Écouffes, Paris 4th*

An unchanged vestige in a rapidly changing district, this butcher shop remains a must-see on rue des Rosiers. In addition to the kosher meat and the lively character of Henri, the master of the house, there is pastrami, "gendarmes" (small smoked sausages), and charcuterie made every day in the kitchens located just a few steps from the shop.

Michel Kalifa— Maison David

⚲ *6, rue des Ecouffes, Paris 4th*

Taken over in 1975 by Michel Kalifa, the shop offers exceptional pastrami among other Ashkenazi specialties.

Iran and Iraq

These two border countries share many common flavors inherited from the Persian empire.

—FRANÇOIS-RÉGIS GAUDRY AND CHARLES PATIN O'COOHOON

Koukou (Paris 15th).

Iran

After the fall of the Shah of Iran in 1979, some Iranians settled in the brand-new buildings of the Front de Seine in the 15th arrondissement, making the district a true Persian haunt. Since then, a network of grocers and restaurants has sprung up along the artery at the end of the Beaugrenelle shopping center on rue des Entrepreneurs. Today, the community has 25,000 nationals.

THE PIONEER

Mazeh

📍 *55 and 65, rue des Entrepreneurs, Paris 15th. €*

Subtitled *Les saveurs persanes* (Persian flavors), this establishment has been shining since 1984. Today, Shayan and Sam Tavassoli continue the family adventure with ache (lamb soup) and kotlet (a potato and meat galette). At number 55, they opened Mazeh Bah Bah, a street-food extension.

RESTAURANTS

Shabestan

📍 *5, rue du Commandant-Rivière, Paris 8th. €*
📍 *98, blvd. de Grenelle, Paris 15th*

On the Champs-Élysées or the Left Bank: there are two locations for trying the great classics of Iranian cuisine, including slow-cooked stews (ghormeh polo) and marinated skewers.

Koukou

📍 *59, rue des Entrepreneurs, Paris 15th. €*

The impressive blue ceramic tandoor oven at the entrance sets the tone here: delicious variations of minced lamb skewers (makhssousse) and polo (a delicate saffron rice).

Restaurant Cheminée

📍 *60 bis, rue des Entrepreneurs, Paris 15th. €€*

Marinated grilled meats, kebabs, gheimeh bademjan (veal sautéed with eggplant and split peas), and a choice menu of sweet items: faloudeh shirazi (rose and lime sorbet) and baklava made in-house.

Tiam—Chez Darius

📍 *81, rue du Théâtre, Paris 15th. €€*

Tiam? This means "welcome" in Persian. This family-style establishment serves several simmering classics: dolmeh bademjan (stuffed eggplant) or fesenjān, a walnut chicken drizzled with a pomegranate juice sauce.

À Table

📍 *92, rue de la Réunion, Paris 20th. €*

Shirine polo (rice with carrots and grilled onions), sholeh zard (saffron rice cake), and the all-you-can-eat buffet created by chef Catherine Massoudi offers an amazing value for the money.

TEAROOM

Sohan Café

📍 *30, blvd. de la Chapelle, Paris 18th*

This hybrid space plays the role of restaurant (saffron rice), tearoom (black tea served with samovar, griotte syrup), concept stores (Persian decoration), and cultural gathering space.

PASTRY SHOP

Shirinkam

📍 *4, rue Lobineau, Paris 6th*

Under the covered market of Saint-Germain, the charismatic Esmaeil Rezaei whips up the entire repertoire of Persian pastry: all with almond paste and Isfahan rose water, a saffron and pistachio roulade, and a flaky pastry with honey and nan khamei.

ICE CREAM SHOP

Bastani

📍 *36, rue de Clignancourt, Paris 18th*

Serving lightly sweetened artisanal ice creams with flavors from afar: black lemon, date, raw pistachio or tamarind, and the specialty of the house, rose and saffron.

GROCERIES

Eskan

📍 *62 bis, rue des Entrepreneurs, Paris 15th*

Since 1990, this small shop has been serving the best products from Iraq: Akbari pistachios directly from Iran, candied fruits, nougat, torchi (pickled vegetables).

Sépide

📍 *62 ter, rue des Entrepreneurs, Paris 15th*

Spices, freshly pressed Shiraz pomegranate juice, dried fish from the Caspian Sea, curdled milk, limou omani (dried black lemon). This shop owned by Mr. Ali is a gold mine.

Iraq

Since 2014 and the second Iraqi civil war, France has welcomed several thousand Iraqi nationals, mainly of Christian faith. Their cuisine is at the crossroads of Persian, Levantine, and Turkish influences.

RESTAURANT

Bistro Baghdad

📍 *17, rue du Colisée, Paris 8th. €€*

This cuisine hailing from the border of Iran and Turkey offers eggplant caviar, bourak (small rolls of puff pastry with meat or cheese), and kibbeh (with spiced ground meat and grain).

Central Asia

This vast region of the Asian continent is rich in culinary traditions.
— MARILOU PETRICOLA

Tibet, China

Although Tibetan nationals number just barely a few thousand in Paris, their cuisine is nevertheless well represented in the city. They have historically settled around the Pantheon starting in the 1960s.

THE PIONEER

Tashi Delek

9 *4, rue des Fossés-Saint-Jacques, Paris 5th.* €

Since 1988, this must-see location in the Latin Quarter has been offering traditional Tibetan cuisine in a sober and elegant setting: nemangthang soups with five lentils, essential momos (beef or vegetarian steamed ravioli), or dresil, a dessert made from sweetened rice with butter, honey, raisins, cashews, and yogurt.

RESTAURANTS

Lhassa and Pema Thang

9 *13, rue de la Montagne-Sainte-Geneviève, Paris 5th.* €

These two restaurants, opened just a door apart from each other in the early 1990s, have a welcoming and pleasant setting. They specialize in steamed momos, fried ravioli, and dishes based on barley flour: in spinach soup, with cheese from the dri (female yak), in dumplings, and even sweetened for dessert.

Tibet Peace House

9 *54, rue d'Aubervilliers, Paris 19th.* €

Of the three Tibetan restaurants on the street, this establishment's specialty is plump tingmo (braided Tibetan steamed bread), large plates of pork noodles in sauce, and tongue-on-fire mapo tofu. You'll find a warm welcome and good prices here.

Afghanistan

Arriving in France in the 1980s, the community first settled around the Gare du Nord and Gare de l'Est.

THE PIONEER

Kootchi

9 *40, rue du Cardinal-Lemoine, Paris 5th.* €

A haunt for students and regulars of the neighborhood, this family-style restaurant opened in 1996 offering an unbeatable fixed-price lunch menu of Afghan soup, kofta challow (meatballs in sauce accompanied by rice), and ferni, the traditional pistachio, cardamom, and rose-water flan for dessert.

RESTAURANTS

Kabul Kitchen

9 *2, rue Saint-Sauveur, Paris 2nd.* €

On the few tables inside or on the terrace, Fatima Bourahla, supported by Ali and Shayan, two Afghan refugees, serves kabuli rice with carrot, cardamom, raisins, and cumin; Afghan rice and vegetable sandwiches; and korma beef.

Khana

9 *69, rue Saint-Louis-en-l'Ile, Paris 4th.* €

Both a chic and warm restaurant and tearoom, the restaurant serves a khana salad generous with coriander, mantus, and ashaks, steamed ravioli, and skewers of leg of lamb and tikka kabob.

Buzkashi

9 *7, rue des Dames, Paris 17th.* €€

Under the neon sign of this restaurant, whose name means "goat dragging" in Afghan, a warm room with benches covered with carpets and cushions awaits customers. Sitting on the floor cross-legged, savor Madame Azizan's plates, the borani (grilled eggplant slices and tomato sauce), or the confit leg of lamb with sautéed rice with nuts.

Uzbekistan

The history of Uzbek gastronomy is very recent in Paris. The first restaurant, now closed, opened in 2005.

RESTAURANT

Bukhara Treviso

9 *37, rue de Trévise, Paris 9th.* €€

Bright orange walls covered with plates and carpets surrounding generously filled plates: the traditional plov (stew with or without meat served with rice, carrots, chickpeas, and spices) or hanums, Uzbek lasagna with beef, and steamed potatoes.

Vietnam, Laos, Cambodia

France is home to the second largest immigrant population of Vietnamese in the world, second only to the United States. —**DEBORAH PHAM**

FROM 1887 TO 1954

Established in France since the beginning of the colonization of Indochina, the Vietnamese community was recruited during the two World Wars to participate in France's war effort.

SINCE 1975

A new wave of migration occurred at the time of the fall of Saigon, when people from Vietnam, Laos, and Cambodia decided to flee the dictatorships of their respective countries. They were called "boat people" because their journey was made aboard precarious and overcrowded boats that were frequently shipwrecked. They settled mainly in the Val-de-Marne and in the 13th arrondissement of the capital, around the triangle formed by Avenue d'Ivry, Avenue de Choisy, and Boulevard Masséna.

TODAY

The cuisine of these three countries is intermingled in the restaurants of the capital with very similar specialties such as crispy chicken, caramel pork, and egg rolls.

THE PIONEER

Chez Tan Dinh (Vietnam)

📍 *60, rue de Verneuil, Paris 7th.* €€€

Welcome to the oldest Vietnamese restaurant in Paris. The former hangout of artists such as Serge Gainsbourg and Marguerite Duras, this location opened in 1968 and offers refined cuisine such as the famous Vietnamese dumplings with smoked goose or its sea bream with confit ginger. A great wine lover and the manager Robert Vifian will gladly offer suggestions.

RESTAURANTS

Ha Noï 1988 (Vietnam)

📍 *72, quai des Orfèvres, Paris 1st.* €€

This beautiful location on the side of the Île de la Cité has the reputation of serving one of the best phos of the capital. The restaurant has been awarded by the Association of Vietnamese Culinary Culture for its famous pho, which simmers for at least eight hours.

Song Heng (Vietnam)

📍 *3, rue Volta, Paris 3rd.* €

This institution in the Marais combines simplicity with a hyper-effective menu. On the menu, pho and bo bun served large or extra large.

Foyer Vietnam (Vietnam)

80, rue Monge, Paris 5th. €

This nonprofit eatery serves traditional Vietnamese specialties such as pork ribs five ways and caramel pork. The service is provided by volunteers and students, and the profits are donated to associations.

Hanoï Corner (Vietnam)

7, rue Blanche, Paris 9th. €

Halfway between a lunch counter and coffee shop, this establishment offers a simple but thought-out menu: banh mi and bo bun are among a nice selection of pastries, including the chiffon cake with pandan and the banana-coconut tart, to enjoy with a homemade soda made with cacao, or a true Vietnamese coffee.

Ngoc Xuyen Saïgon (Vietnam)

4, rue Caillaux, Paris 13th. €

Visit for the phenomenal crab soup on Thursday (only!), but also for the pho served with pig's feet and spiced with fresh pepper. For dessert, a selection

of traditional sweets is served in the three colors of the French flag.

Pho Bom (Vietnam)

71, av. de Choisy, Paris 13th. €€

Students and families line up every day in front of the restaurant for its nems, phos, bo bun, or bun cha Hanoi, vermicelli with Hanoi style-grilled pork.

Pho Tai (Vietnam)

13, rue Philibert-Lucot, Paris 13th. €€

In this tucked-away location in the 13th arrondissement, one of the best crispy chickens is available, as well as superb banh cuon (ravioli topped with ground pork and black mushrooms) and a special and generous shrimp and chicken rice.

Pho Bida Viet Nam (Vietnam)

36–38, rue Nationale, Paris 13th. €

On the esplanade of Les Olympiades hides one of the best eateries in Paris. You can eat a delicious bo bun that comes in a dozen different variations. Special mention for the one with grilled pork and egg rolls.

STREET FOOD

Banh Mi (Vietnam)

81, rue de Turbigo, Paris 3rd. €

Although it is possible to enjoy a bo bun on the micro-terrace on rue de Turbigo, chef Angela is especially worth a visit for her banh mi. The sandwiches come in meat-centric versions (chicken, beef, or caramel pork), but also vegetarian, to flavor (or not!) with Maggi seasonings.

Nonette (Vietnam)

71, rue Jean-Pierre-Timbaud, Paris 11th. €

The little sister to The Hood (a Singaporean restaurant on the same street, see p. 196), this shop gives pride of place to banh mi, the famous Vietnamese sandwich. Here everything is homemade: pickles, chicken liver mousse, as well as all the charcuterie that make up the dac biet served in a baguette spread with AOP butter.

Coupi Bar (Vietnam)

48, av. de la Porte-d'Ivry, Paris 13th. €

This spot at the Porte d'Ivry is invaded by students. The super-popular address revisits Vietnamese classics, offering banh mi, bao, and Asian-style tacos topped with pork, beef, or tofu.

GROCERIES

Thanh Binh Jeune

18, rue Lagrange, Paris 5th

In this supermarket, you can find products not only from Vietnam but also Laos, Cambodia, and Thailand. Nuoc-mam, hoisin sauce, oyster sauce, and shrimp paste—in short, all the essential ingredients to cook the recipes of southeast Asia.

Tang Frères

48, av. d'Ivry, Paris 13th

163, blvd. de Stalingrad, Vitry-sur-Seine (Val-de-Marne)

210, av. du Général-Leclerc, Pantin (Seine-Saint-Denis)

15, cours des Deux-Parcs, Noisiel (Seine-et-Marne)

8, rue Nicolas-Appert, Lognes (Seine-et-Marne)

1, pl. de la Marne, Bussy-Saint-Georges (Seine-et-Marne)

Launched in 1981 by Bou and Bounmy Rattanavan, this iconic supermarket on avenue d'Ivry quickly expanded throughout Île-de-France. There is a wide selection of products from Asia.

China

The presence of Chinese cuisine in Paris reflects the successive waves of immigration since the beginning of the twentieth century. —HANDA CHENG

CHINATOWN DISTRICTS

The first locations, most of which are closed today, were established in the Latin Quarter and Arts et Métiers districts, the oldest Chinatown in Paris. The settlement in the 13th arrondissement of Paris's Chinese populations has grown since the 1970s. Most are from the southern China (Guangdong), hence the strong historical presence of Cantonese restaurants.

CATERERS

Starting in the 1980s, it was the Chinese from Wenzhou, a city in southeastern China, who began to emigrate en masse. The explosion of Chinese caterers in Paris dates from this time. This population is now the primary Chinese community in Paris, with one hundred fifty thousand people out of the two hundred fifty thousand living in Île-de-France.

THE NEW WAVE

The early 2010s marked the rebirth of Chinese cuisine in Paris, with a more varied, more regional offering, which was accompanied by a gradual uptick in quality offerings.

THE PIONEER

Empire Céleste
📍 *5, rue Royer-Collard, Paris 5th. €*
Opened in 1900, this is the oldest Chinese restaurant in Paris still in operation. Regulars come for the dumplings, served on Sundays only.

RESTAURANTS

Xiao Long Kan (Szechuan)
📍 *8, rue Saint-Marc, Paris 2nd. €€*
One of the safe bets in Paris for fondue Chinoise (hotpot). The idea is that everyone gathers around a pot of hot broth placed in the center of the table with plenty of ingredients for sharing (meat, vegetables, tofu, noodles), all ready to cook in the broth and dip in sauces.

Royal China (Guangdong)
📍 *85, rue Beaubourg, Paris 3rd. €*
This is a temple of dim sum at a low price. Cheung fun, a roll of rice with char siu pork, is a must. The more adventurous will try the chicken feet with black beans, also delicious.

A casual eatery, and crowded on weekends.

Imperial Treasure (Guangdong and Shanghai)
📍 *44, rue de Bassano, Paris 8th. €€€€*
One of the few Chinese gourmet restaurants in the capital. In a majestic setting, there are signature dishes from Guangzhou and Shanghai. Not to mention the best Peking duck in Paris, in three courses, as tradition dictates.

Délice de Condorcet (Tianjin)
📍 *10, rue Condorcet, Paris 9th. €*
The manager, from Tianjin, offers up favorite dishes from northern China: noodles and dumplings, made all in-house and whose colors come from the various vegetable juices used in the recipe. A curiosity for the eyes—and a pleasure for the taste buds.

Muqam (Xinjiang)
📍 *36, rue de Trévise, Paris 9th. €*
This institution offers Uyghur specialties (northwest China). The

lamb skewers with cumin, the house-made noodle dishes, and the emblematic dapanji—a chicken dish simmered with potatoes, peppers, and a dozen spices—are the main attractions.

La Taverne de Zhao (Shaanxi)
📍 *49, rue des Vinaigriers, Paris 10th. €*
Opened in 2011 near the Canal Saint-Martin, this first location of the Zhao group takes you on a journey to northern China. Among the dishes to discover are momo, a round bun filled with simmered pork, or liang pi, noodles served cold with sesame sauce.

Chez Ravioli Chen Chen (Tianjin)
📍 *5, av. Philippe-Auguste, Paris 11th. €*
A neighborhood boui-boui run by a lovely couple from Tianjin, southeast of Beijing. Popular are the dumplings, the bao zi (meat-filled buns) of course, and also small cold starters such as black mushroom salad. All at a good price.

Hibao (Szechuan)

📍 28, rue de Malte,
Paris 11th. €

The chef is originally from Chengdu, so this small neighborhood restaurant is attractive for its Szechuan specialties. Not to be missed: the Chongqing noodles or the dumpling with spicy oil.

Grand Bol Belleville (Zhejiang)

📍 7, rue de la Présentation, Paris 11th. €€

Zhejiang cuisine and seafood are honored here. The menu is original, with dishes not found elsewhere: sautéed crab with sticky rice (a delight!) or the amazing pyramid-shaped ceinture de porc (pork). Without a doubt the best place in Belleville.

Les Délices de Yunnan (Yunnan)

📍 128, rue de Tolbiac, Paris 13th. €

A destination for discovering the specialties of Yunnan, a huge province bordering Myanmar and little known in Paris. The traditional "noodles that cross the bridge" are an experience worth trying. Not to mention a pu-erh tea, native to the region.

Shang Palace (Guangdong)

📍 10, av. d'Iéna, Paris 16th. €€€€

Found in the Shangri-La hotel, this is the only Chinese Michelin-starred restaurant in France. Since 2015, chef Samuel Lee has been offering refined cuisine, mainly Cantonese, with some great Chinese classics, including Peking duck in three courses.

Xiang Piao Piao (Beijing)

📍 4, rue Davy, Paris 17th. €

In a corner of Paris lacking in quality Chinese cuisine, this small neighborhood eatery is a delight for locals. Their dumplings (grilled or steamed) are very popular, but the cold starters are also worth the detour.

Pavillon aux Pivoines (Szechuan)

📍 21, rue des Couronnes, Paris 20th. €

The huge dining room has a certain vintage charm. Liney, one of the daughters of the Zhao family, is in charge here and offers a short menu with dishes served on attractive plates, such as the twice-cooked pork, a great Szechuan classic.

TEAROOM

T'xuan

📍 56, rue La Fayette, Paris 9th

Its name in Chinese means "sweet pavilion." It is one of the first places in Paris to combine a salon de thé (tearoom) and Chinese desserts. You can enjoy a mille-feuille of crêpes with durian or a shaved-ice with red beans in a traditional and refined decor.

CATERERS

Best Tofu

📍 9, blvd. de la Villette, Paris 10th

Paris's entire Chinese community comes here for the tofu: plain, flavored, or fried, the choices abound. It is possible to order typical breakfast dishes: douhua tofu, sticky rice with broth, or the classic baozi.

Ang Traiteur

📍 73, av. d'Ivry, Paris 13th

People come from far and wide to find happiness in this very popular rotisserie, open since 1986 in the 13th arrondissement. Some talk about the best Cantonese Peking duck in Paris, others swear by the crispy pork. Crowds are heavy on Sundays.

GROCERY

Les Halles de l'Asie "Super Store"

📍 19, rue de Belleville, Paris 19th

Among the many Chinese supermarkets in Belleville, this is the best supplied with spices, sauces, and other dry goods. Although the outside does not look like much, you have to go upstairs to discover a true treasure trove.

Japan

Listed as an Intangible Cultural Heritage by UNESCO, Japanese cuisine has found a true culinary playground in Paris. — CHIHIRO MASUI

THE FIRST SIGNS

In 1954, Takumi Isao, a twenty-year-old Japanese man, arrived in Paris. Four years later, he opened Takaraya near the Pantheon, the first Japanese restaurant in France and Europe. Takaraya expanded, moved, and became Takara in 1963. Even though, at the time, the French were horrified at the idea of eating raw fish, today, sushi has found its place as one of the favored cuisines in the city.

RUE SAINTE-ANNE

With the popularization of air travel in the 1970s, the Hôtel du Louvre, Place du Palais-Royal, became *the* hotel of choice for Japanese tourists. The Banque de Tokyo reopened its Paris branch in 1962 on rue du Quatre-Septembre that formed an axis point with rue Sainte-Anne. The first Japanese grocery, Kioko, moved to rue des Petits-Champs in 1972. Paris's Japanese community has the particularity of having nationals who never apply for French citizenship. The community now numbers forty thousand people in Paris.

ONE RESTAURANT, ONE CUISINE

Japanese cuisine can be divided into four main groups:
1. the cuisine of the nobles, kaiseki-ryori, originally from Kyoto, a former imperial city.
2. the cuisine of the people, the most popular (sushi, yakitori).
3. cuisine from China that is still called "Chinese" in Japan, even though it now has mostly Japanese influences (ramen, gyoza).
4. Western cuisine, called yōshoku (curry rice, tonkatsu).

Only since the 2010s has Paris seen the appearance of Japanese restaurants serving styles other than sushi and yakitori.

Takuya Watanabe, chef of the restaurant Jin (Paris 1st).

THE PIONEER

Takara

📍 *14, rue Molière, Paris 1st. €€*

Founded in 1958. This restaurant has an atmosphere of a bygone Japan. Serving mainly sushi but also sukiyaki (a beef hotpot style, once served in the first Japanese restaurants in Paris but now rare in the city), donburi, and tonkatsu.

RESTAURANTS

Enyaa

📍 *37, rue de Montpensier, Paris 1st. €€€*

This place has three features that lend it originality: first, the presence of a kaiseki-ryori chef, a Japanese gourmet cuisine whose origins date back to the time of tea ceremonies, coming straight from Kyoto. Second, food and wine pairings that alternate Champagnes and sake. And finally, an unusual location in old Paris, with a Japanese-style counter where the chef officiates and an old stone room modestly decorated with French and Japanese bottles.

Toyo

📍 *17, rue Jules-Chaplain, Paris 6th. €€€*

For a long time, the private chef of the couturier Kenzo, Toyomitsu Nakayama, was the first Japanese chef to open an intimate signature restaurant, bringing Japanese touches to a French-inspired cuisine. Among the signature dishes: bouillabaisse curry, fusing flavors of the French seafood soup dish with Japanese curry, as well as Toyo-style paella, based on takikomi gohan, a Japanese classic revisited using Breton products. A large counter allows you to sit and watch the chefs perform their duties with precision.

Aida

📍 *1, rue Pierre-Leroux, Paris 7th. €€€*

The first gourmet Parisian restaurant specializing in Japanese teppanyaki and where chef Aida quickly obtained his first Michelin star. Here you'll find simple but clever dishes expertly prepared before your eyes at a counter that seats eight, as well as a list of selected wines

and sake. A traditional private lounge is available for bookings.

Yamaya

📍 *62, rue de Babylone, Paris 7th. €*

All of Yamaya's staff, starting with manager Chika, are considered shifu (skilled person). This is evidenced by the service, which is buzzing and attentive, and by the menu, which offers four or five donburi, accompanied by miso soup. Large bowls of rice or soba noodles are topped with balanced and healthy ingredients and a profusion of vegetables.

Okuda

📍 *7, rue de la Trémoille, Paris 8th. €€€*

This is the Parisian restaurant of chef Tooru Okuda, a starred chef in Tokyo. The interior is all in hinoki (cypress) wood from Japan, assembled by fifteen carpenters from Japan. It serves typical gourmet kaiseki cuisine.

NOMIYA AND IZAKAYA

Kanadé

⚲ 8, rue de Ventadour, Paris 1st. €

A stone's throw from Ryô, Kanadé is the other location in Paris's Japanese district not to be missed. The menu has the mood of a nomiya (drinking bar) or a Tokyo izakaya (sake bar) with several sunomono (vinegar dishes), family-style sushi (natto maki, grilled salmon skin), kakuni (stewed pork belly), and yamakake (grated yam and bluefin tuna).

Ryō

⚲ 7, rue des Moulins, Paris 1st. €€

Chief Toyofumi Ozuru is an elder of Kinugawa, a Japanese institution in the rue Saint-Honoré district. The restaurant's menu consists mainly of varied, plump, and well-constituted sushi, but on the board, typical Japanese dishes such as nasu-dengaku (eggplant with sweet miso), persimmon-furai (breaded oysters), or the "amberjack cheek," which is actually kama (yellowtail collar) are what regulars flock here for—by 9, it's all gone.

Zakuro

⚲ 4, rue de Port-Mahon, Paris 2nd. €€

A small restaurant, opened by Atsuko Sakamoto and her son Go Sato. Atsuko is a former Japanese actress. Go Sato is a cook, born in France. They offer a family-style cuisine, such as curry rice, oden, and kinpira gobo, sometimes whipped up with a new twist, such as the delicious tuna karate served with an anchovy sauce and the incredibly light soufflé cheesecake. There is a selection of sakes from all over Japan, with the map of Japan marking the origins.

SUSHI

Jin

⚲ 6, rue de la Sourdière, Paris 1st. €€€

Often cited as the best sushi in Paris, Jin masters fish from France's Breton and Mediterranean terroir in the purest Japanese tradition, the result of ten years of study of French merroir (flavors from the sea) by chef Takuya Watanabe. A counter seats eight per service, no table.

Oinari

⚲ 34, rue La Bruyère, Paris 9th. €

Inari-sushi, an offering to foxes, messengers of the god Inari, is a slice of sweet and salty fried tofu, filled with vinegar rice. The Inari-sushi here is made in accordance with the rules of the art. À la carte offerings are bentos and udon for lunch and small Japanese tapas in the evening.

Yushin

⚲ 77, rue Chauveau, Neuilly-sur-Seine (Hauts-de-Seine). €€€

In this peaceful corner of Neuilly, chef Shuhei Yamashita opened his first restaurant in January 2022. At lunch are offered a beautiful shokado bento (an entire menu served in a partitioned lacquered box). Dinner options include a sushi menu with gourmet starters followed by quality sushi. For dessert, there are the best omogashi (tea ceremony pastries) in the capital, made by Manabu Shiraishi, sake sommelier, wagashi artisan, and tea master, who prepares matcha at your table. Ask for the four-seat counter in front of the chef.

STREET FOOD

Kodawari Tsukiji

⚲ 12, rue de Richelieu, Paris 1st. €

Japanese nationals living in Paris appreciate Kodawari Tsukiji for its original ramen. The decor is reminiscent of Tokyo's legendary Tsukiji Fish Market, and the ramen in its fish-based broth stands out from the common ramen made from the bones of pork and chicken.

Bento&Go!

⚲ 18, rue Notre-Dame-de-Nazareth, Paris 3rd. €

⚲ 3, rue Sauval, Paris 1st. €

Chef Go Tachibana, trained in French cuisine at the prestigious Tsuji school, has found his calling for serving typical bentos, such as karaage chicken (fried chicken), grilled salmon, or tofu steak for a veggie version. Chef Go's bentos are not far from the old Japanese adage: "Eat thirty different foods at each meal"!

ONE RESTAURANT, ONE SPECIALTY

› UNAGI

Nodaïwa

⚲ 272, rue Saint-Honoré, Paris 1st. €€

The Parisian branch of the Tokyo restaurant founded under the shogun Tokugawa Ienari (1787–1837) specializing in unagi. The sweet and salty lacquered eel in the Tokyo tradition is grilled over a fire and served in a box on a bed of rice. You can also enjoy fresh eel starters.

› RAMEN

Kotteri Ramen Naritake

⚲ 31, rue des Petits-Champs, Paris 1st. €

The Parisian outpost of a chain of six restaurants in Japan created in 1996, this temple to ramen (kotteri means "thick and heavy" in Japanese) shapes it in the style of the province of Chiba, where it originated, with a salty, thick, and fatty soup, acclaimed by lovers of popular ramen.

› RAMEN

Ippudo Ramen

📍 *3 Parisian locations including the first, Ippudo Saint-Germain—14, rue Grégoire-de-Tours, Paris 6th.* €

This global chain, founded in 1985 in Fukuoka on the island of Kyushu, serves ramen in the style of Hakata (the former name of Fukuoka) and enhances its tonkotsu soup with pork bones.

› TEMPURA

Tenzen

📍 *8, rue de l'Échelle, Paris 1st.* €€€

Located in the basement of restaurant Zen, this establishment is dedicated to tempura, served here in a chic and elegant Japanese cypress-wood setting. Don't expect popular tempuras, which are often just crispy beignets with more batter than product. Instead, offered here are eight choices for lunch and ten for dinner: shrimp, taro, nori seaweed, yam, beans, corn—depending on the season—all coated in a straight dough batter that is light and delicate in the pure style of Kyoto, fried in cottonseed oil imported from Japan. To end a meal, choose ten-don (a bowl of rice topped with a tempura of vegetables) or ten-chazuké (a bowl of rice with tempura and green tea).

› UDON

Kunitoraya Udon Bistro

📍 *41, rue de Richelieu, Paris 1st.* €€

The first udon noodle restaurant to open in Paris (taken over by Udon Jubey of the Kintaro group), Kunitoraya was for a long time the only establishment to offer these large white wheat noodles from Sanuki, Shikoku Island, the smallest of Japan's four main islands. Hot or cold udon, donburi (a large bowl of filled rice), and small dishes for nibbling.

Sanukiya

📍 *9, rue d'Argenteuil, Paris 1st.* €

A rather classic location offering cold or hot noodles for dipping in a broth, with traditional options such as kitsune udon filled with fried and seasoned sliced tofu, or udon curry, in a Japanese curry soup.

› SOBA

Yen

📍 *22, rue Saint-Benoît, Paris 6th.* €€

A soba noodle restaurant with a chic atmosphere. Soba is the popular thin noodle from East Japan, made from a mixture of buckwheat and wheat flours. Here soba are prepared according to the rules of the art by a master soba craftsman. Served hot in broth, or cold, to dip in full-bodied, fresh broth, with or without an addition, such as tempura or duck. Several typical appetizers are offered: soba-miso or natural silk tofu.

› KUSHI-AGE

Shu

📍 *8, rue Suger, Paris 6th.* €€

A specialty originating in Osaka, kushi-age is a breaded skewer. To access the restaurant requires you to bend a little to take a steep staircase to end up in one of its two rooms. The large period beams and old stones from the heart of ancient Paris offer an elegant contrast to the typical Japanese menu that begins with small fresh starters. Next follows about fifteen dishes threaded onto wooden skewers and coated with a delicate breading, including whole shrimp, stuffed shiitake mushrooms, and rolled beef slices.

PASTRY SHOPS

Toraya

📍 *10, rue Saint-Florentin, Paris 1st*

Serving the imperial household in Kyoto since 1586, Toraya expanded to Tokyo with its first boutique in 1869. The Paris location, opened in 1980, remains, to this day, the only traditional Japanese pastry shop. The kakigori, crushed ice with matcha toppings and sweet azuki beans, served in the salon, deserves special mention.

Tomo

📍 *11, rue Chabanais, Paris 2nd*

📍 *16, rue Grégoire-de-Tours, Paris 6th*

A pastry shop and tearoom whose specialty is dorayaki, traditionally azuki bean paste sandwiched between two small golden "pancakes." Here the choice can be the traditional version or a Franco-Japanese version, such as the Paris-Kyoto, inspired by the iconic pastry Paris-Brest, or dorayaki baba with Japanese whisky. There are also omogashi, all-Japanese seasonal cakes served especially during tea ceremonies. There is only one savory dish served year-round: a generous omurice (omelette + rice) with Japanese curry.

Maison du Mochi

📍 *120, rue de Turenne, Paris 3rd*

📍 *39, rue du Cherche-Midi, Paris 6th*

Daifuku mochi is a popular home-style pastry, made from a dough using sticky rice flour, traditionally filled with a sweet mashed azuki bean. Mathilda Motte fell in love with it and developed her French-Japanese mochi, smaller than a traditional daifuku mochi, less sticky, and not very sweet. Some favorites? Black sesame, yuzu, matcha, and seasonal fruit.

GROCERIES

Nishikidôri Paris

📍 *6, rue Villedo, Paris 1st*

Chef Olivier Derenne is the son of a financier and grandson of a livestock dealer who sold his last horses in Japan, and now explores producers all throughout his native country in search of the best products: artisanal soy sauce, aged more than thirty years (not even to be found on the shelves even in Japan), miso with unusual flavors, and several brands of yuzu-kosho, the yuzu and chile condiment typical of the island of Kyushu.

Workshop Issé

📍 *11, rue Saint-Augustin, Paris 2nd*

Toshiro Kuroda was the first bridge between Japanese cuisine and Parisian gastronomy. By founding Workshop Issé—a grocery and place of discovery as well as a culinary laboratory—he introduced the great chefs to previously unknown ingredients while allowing all his customers to taste selected Japanese sake. Since his death in 2017, his wife has taken over the shop, and there are still select ingredients as well as a selection of sake from establishments at least two hundred years old.

Kioko

📍 *46, rue des Petits-Champs, Paris 2nd*

The first Japanese grocery in Paris. You can find a little bit of everything here, including fresh, frozen, dried, and instant products as well as cooking tools, crockery, and kitchen utensils either produced in Europe or imported from Japan or elsewhere.

Ogata

📍 *16, rue Debelleyme, Paris 3rd*

As a creator of a line ranging from clothing to cooking to tea to pastry, Shinichiro Ogata is a visionary designer. Ogata Paris is a clever marriage of old Paris and a certain Japanese neoclassicism. It functions as a gallery, shop, restaurant (upstairs), tearoom, and fragrance workshop in the basement. Ogata is an immersive and aesthetic experience of today's Japan.

Jugetsudo

📍 *95, rue de Seine, Paris 6th*

Since its founding in 1854, Maruyama has been the main supplier of sushiya nori seaweed to the Tokyo area. Its branch specializing in tea is called Jugetsudo, and it opened the Parisian shop in 2008, selling Japanese teas, dishes, and accessories.

Kim Kwang-Loc, chef of the restaurant Mandoobar (Paris 8th).

Korea

The "Land of Morning Calm" has a cuisine that is flavorful, spicy, and with options for both vegetable and meat lovers.

—SUN AND THÉOPHILE ROUX

Since the liberation of South Korea in 1945, the Korean community in France has seen its population grow from about thirty nationals in the 1950s to about fifteen thousand today. Seventy percent are located in Île-de-France and mainly in the 15th arrondissement of Paris. The first Korean restaurants opened in Paris in the 1970s. Today there are about one hundred.

THE PIONEER

Han Lim

📍 6, rue Blainville, Paris 5th. €

First named Maison de la Corée (Korea House) when it opened in 1981, this family-run restaurant continues traditional Korean cuisine with a warm welcome and authentic and moderately spicy dishes. Specialties include: seolleongtang (beef-bone soup), bulgogi (marinated and grilled pork or beef), jajangmyeon (noodles with fermented black soy sauce paste, onions, zucchini, and potatoes), and garlic fried chicken.

RESTAURANTS

Soon Grill

📍 78, rue des Tournelles, Paris 3rd. €€

📍 10, rue du Commandant-Rivière, Paris 8th. €€

Arguably the best Korean barbecue restaurant in Paris, offering a wide choice of grilled meats including Iberian pork, aged beef, and Kobe beef, accompanied by banchans served in brass dishes.

Mandoobar

📍 7, rue d'Edinburgh, Paris 8th. €

Steam wisps upward from the bamboo baskets in the open kitchen.

Here is minimalist decor, refined cuisine, and abundant flavors. You can savor mandu (Korean dumplings), meat and fish tartars flavored with Korean herbs.

Jong-no Samgyetang

📍 23, blvd. de Port-Royal, Paris 13th. €

The specialty of the house? Samgyetang, a spring chicken stuffed with sticky rice, cooked in a broth of ginseng, garlic, ginger, and jujube. Other dishes will take you on a journey through the different regions of Korea.

Hanzan

📍 11, rue Beaugrenelle, Paris 15th. €

A Korean luncheonette with the true taste of Korea. Perfect for a drink (han zan in Korean) accompanied by traditional dishes such as braised pig's feet, pork and kimchi sauté, or seafood and tofu stew.

Woo Jung

📍 8, blvd. Delessert, Paris 16th. €€

A favorite table of Korean personalities passing through Paris for thirty years, Woojung has maintained consistency and authenticity in cooking. You can savor classic Korean dishes with great wines.

CAFÉ

+82 Paris

📍 11 bis, rue Vauquelin, Paris 5th

There are sweet treats in Korea to enjoy with tea or coffee. This small Korean café is the temple of bingsu, a mountain of crushed ice covered with condensed milk, sesame powder, and red beans or seasonal fruits.

GROCERY

Ace Mart

📍 63, rue Sainte-Anne, Paris 2nd

📍 134, rue de Tolbiac, Paris 13th

📍 43, rue Saint-Augustin, Paris 2nd

📍 71 bis, rue Saint-Charles, Paris 15th

Since 1998, the shop on rue Sainte-Anne has been a delight for Koreans. There are many products: rice, noodles, fresh vegetables, tofu, kimchi. For meat and banchans (traditional pickles), just cross the street.

Thailand

Soul-satisfying, spicy, and aromatic, Thai cuisine is also one of the most charismatic.

—JEAN-PIERRE MONTANAY

The first Thai nationals landed in Paris in the early 1970s. They are a minority compared to their Vietnamese and Cambodian neighbors fleeing a communist regime. It was during this time that the first Parisian Thai restaurants opened.

THE PIONEER

Chieng Mai

📍 *12, rue Frédéric-Sauton, Paris 5th.* €€

Created in 1973, this old-fashioned location is one of the oldest Thai restaurants in Paris, serving up cuisine with traditional character and some very typical dishes, including a crispy rice salad with fermented pork. Not to be missed: the excellent rice sautéed with Thai sausage.

RESTAURANTS

Yo

📍 *10, rue de Port-Mahon, Paris 2nd.* €€

An elegant spot in a cozy setting that offers a Franco-Thai hybrid cuisine. A must: the melting and subtly fragrant beef cheek curry.

Le Chef Thaï

📍 *59, rue des Gravilliers, Paris 3rd.* €

Generous portions of pad Thai to enjoy in a trendy atmosphere. Well-balanced tom kha kai soup in galangal and warm pork salad full of flavors.

Tamarind

📍 *33, rue François-Miron, Paris 4th.* €€

A refined establishment that has delighted a clientele of regulars since 2008. Enjoy fried shrimp coated in taro, dumplings with green curry, and a spicy pomelo salad. The signature dish: the melting lamb knuckle cooked in red panang curry sauce.

The Crying Tiger

📍 *72, rue du Cherche-Midi, Paris 6th.* €€

A chic address popular with tourists. At the marble bar of this vintage bistro, you can enjoy addictive pork sausages with lemongrass, a chicken mikati that holds its own, and, for dessert, pearls of tapioca, banana, and coconut milk with an original pandanus (a tropical plant) ice cream.

Villa Thaï

📍 *23, blvd. de la Tour-Maubourg, Paris 7th.* €€

In this beautiful room surrounded with woodwork, a tasty classic cuisine is served including impeccable fried shrimp cakes and delicate amok, fish with coconut sauce steamed in a banana leaf.

Makham Thaï

📍 *11, rue de Montyon, Paris 9th.* €€

An elegant place that offers good surprises: chicken papillotes marinated and steamed in pandanus leaves, or grilled eggplant in sesame oil. Alongside the classic curries, the grilled bass fillet with lemongrass in banana leaf is a great choice.

Baan Issan

📍 *12, rue Véronèse, Paris 13th.* €€

In the midst of photos and antique Thai artifacts, savor an invigorating salad of pineapple with shrimp, and fish cakes with well-made peanut sauce. The red duck curry rocks with its homemade curry paste, and the rice sautéed with crab remains a reference.

Krung Thep Mahanakorn

📍 *61, rue de Belleville, Paris 19th.* €

A historic address in Belleville since 1983, with its traditional wooden tables. The menu is a rich offering of some treasures, including its dynamite banana flower salad and molting crabs with garlic and pepper.

Lao Siam (Thailand and Laos)

📍 *49, rue de Belleville, Paris 19th.* €€

Here the upper crust of the Parisian *food* scene can be found, and for good reason: this Bellevilloise institution showcases Thai and Laotian specialties, from grilled rice salad with herbs and nem chua to Laotian sausage to free-range chicken wings sautéed with grilled garlic and green pepper.

STREET FOOD

Street Bangkok, 6 locations/ 3 concepts

› *Thai Market*

📍 *73, rue de Seine, Paris 6th.* €

📍 *3, rue Eugène-Varlin, Paris 10th.* €

📍 *13, rue de la Roquette, Paris 11th.* €

📍 *49, rue Ernest-Renan, Ivry (Val-de-Marne).* €

› *Fry temple*

📍 *71, rue du Faubourg-Poissonnière, Paris 10th.* €

📍 *49, rue Ernest-Renan, Ivry (Val-de-Marne).* €

› *Roast Club*

📍 *112, rue Saint-Denis, Paris 2nd.* €

📍 *28, rue de Douai, Paris 9th.* €

Between rotisserie (with the choice of Peking duck and pork, and crispy pork) and a frying temple, Street Bangkok offers a varied panorama of Thai cuisine. The must-have: the pad see ew, large sautéed rice noodles.

Original Thai Food

📍 *18, rue de Moscou, Paris 8th.* €

A small, quaint restaurant that serves an original and delicious duck simmered with herbs.

GROCERY

Sulamee Thaï

📍 *60, blvd. Voltaire, Paris 11th*

This pocket-size shop offers directly imported or homemade Thai specialties, such as chile noodles with fish sauce or fermented fish noodles. There are all kinds of soy sauces, ready-to-use curry pastes, and bags of galangal, lemongrass, and dried Thai basil.

Annapurna (Paris 8th).

India

Restaurants clad in carved doors, red wall coverings, and incense: Paris's Indian culinary scene has been enriched over the past twenty years by both traditional eateries and trendy spots.

— BEENA PARADIN MIGOTTO

For a long time, Yugaraj, now closed, was an institution, being the first restaurant to position itself on a gastronomic niche with local French ingredients. Indian migrants arrived in France in the 1970s from former French trading posts, particularly from Puducherry, joined by Pakistanis and Mauritians, then Sri Lankans and Bangladeshis starting in the 1980s. The community now numbers more than seventy thousand people in Île-de-France. The first food shops were set up on rue Clauzel side (Paris 9th) in the 1960s. During the 1980s, diaspora entrepreneurs opened shops and restaurants along rue du Faubourg-Saint-Denis in the Passage Brady (Paris 10th), turning this district into what came to be known as "Little India."

THE PIONEER

Annapurna

📍 *32, rue de Berri, Paris 8th. €€*

Opened in 1967, this restaurant claims to be the first Indian restaurant in the capital. Its founder, André Risser, had the idea of filling naan, traditional bread of northern India, with cheese, to attract French palates.

RESTAURANTS

Jugaad

📍 *16, rue Favart, Paris 2nd. €€*

For this second location from chef Manoj Sharma, delicious dishes and a cocktail bar await, the winning combination of London Indian cuisine, which arrived in Paris in 2021. The open kitchen with two large tandoor ovens provides a real show.

Desi Road

📍 *14, rue Dauphine, Paris 6th. €€*

Open since 2015, the restaurant offers the capital a refreshing perspective by combining chic decoration by Stéphanie de Saint-Simon with the authentic cuisine of chef Manoj Sharma.

Dishny

📍 *25, rue Cail, Paris 10th. €*
📍 *212, rue du Faubourg-Saint-Denis, Paris 10th. €*

Founded in the early 1990s by Papa Dishny, this institution offers a hearty biryani, the festive dish.

Krishna Bhavan

📍 *24, rue Cail, Paris 10th. €*
📍 *25, rue Galande, Paris 5th. €*

This vegetarian eatery showcases simple and authentic southern Indian food. There is notably poori, deep-fried unleavened bread, traditionally served with a chickpea curry.

Muniyandi Vilas

📍 *207, rue du Faubourg-Saint-Denis, Paris 10th. €*

You can admire the cook in the window shaping, with great dexterity, parottas (the flaky flatbread from southern India), the house specialty.

Saravanaa Bhavan

📍 *170, rue du Faubourg-Saint-Denis, Paris 10th. €*

This franchise of a chain of vegetarian restaurants in southern India serves authentic and good food. You can eat dosas, very popular filled crêpes, or uthappams, savory, thick pancakes.

Kirane's

📍 *85, av. des Ternes, Paris 17th. €€*
📍 *20, rue du Débarcadère, Paris 17th*

Tandoor cuisine, carved decorations, and Ganesh galore, this institution, operated by chef Kirane Gupta, has everything you would expect from an Indian restaurant.

GROCERY

VS.CO Cash & Carry

📍 *197, rue du Faubourg-Saint-Denis, Paris 10th*

Located in the heart of the Indian district, this grocery store compiles absolutely everything to cook Indian food: from pappadums to exotic fresh vegetables and fruits to spices.

Southeast Asia and Oceania

From Malaysia to Australia, these cuisines half a world away from France have both Asian and Western influences.

—SUN AND THÉOPHILE ROUX, MARILOU PETRICOLA

Indonesia, Malaysia, and Singapore

Even though French nationals are numerous in Indonesia, Malaysia, and Singapore, these communities are poorly represented in France. Their population is estimated at about five thousand people.

THE PIONEER

Indonesia

📍 *12, rue de Vaugirard, Paris 6th. €€*

With its bamboo-lined walls, masks, and a percussion ensemble, this restaurant has been transporting its clientele to Indonesia since 1982. Among the options are gado-gado salad with peanut sauce, nasi goreng, and beef rendang.

RESTAURANTS

Jakarta Bali

📍 *9, rue Vauvilliers, Paris 1st. €€*

A refined atmosphere, Indonesian decor, and typical dishes, such as gado-gado, nasi goreng, rendang, and mie ayam.

The Hood

📍 *80, rue Jean-Pierre-Timbaud, Paris 11th. €€*

A former bazaar converted into a café, The Hood brings together the dishes from Singaporean food courts: nasi lemak (national dish made from rice), laksa (noodle soup with coconut milk), chicken rice (poached chicken and fragrant rice).

GROCERY

Maison de l'Indonésie

📍 *5, rue Jean-Zay, Paris 14th*

This shop is a gastronomic embassy. In addition to the spices for purchase, you can taste the specialty of the day while sipping coffee.

Philippines

This exotic and little-known cuisine has only two restaurants in Paris.

RESTAURANTS

Bobi—Filipino Food

📍 *17, rue Oberkampf, Paris 11th. €€*

This all-blue and wooden small eatery serves the classics in generous portions. On the menu are cheese sticks; adobo, the national dish; and kare-kare, beef with peanut sauce and vegetables.

Reyna

📍 *41, rue de Montreuil, Paris 11th. €*

Within the pale pink walls of this bistro, chef Erica Paredes cooks her origins with an astonishing modernity: sisig (a minced pig's head with calemensi, the citrus fruit) or kare, eggplant with peanut sauce.

Taiwan, China

Taiwanese cuisine has managed to carve out a small place in Paris.

RESTAURANTS

Chez Ajia

📍 *4, rue du Roi-de-Sicile, Paris 4th. €€*

Lo bah bang (pork belly confit), gua bao (filled steamed buns), hei tang gao (brown sugar steamed cake)—all classics served in this white wooden cabin.

Bopome

📍 *48, rue de Lancry, Paris 10th. €*

The specialty is Taiwanese crêpes topped with marinated beef, egg, or pork, or raw vegetables.

Australia

The cuisine from down under has a few locations in the capital.

BRUNCH

Hardware Société

📍 *10, rue Lamarck, Paris 18th. €€*

This coffee shop twists the classics: pain perdu with lemon, thyme, and strawberry syrup, scrambled eggs, and cauliflower beignets. Veggie and gluten-free options are plentiful.

Creole Cuisines

Often used to designate a mixed language, the term Creole also evokes a cuisine that draws its influences from the West Indies to Réunion.

—JORDAN MOILIM

LATE NINETEENTH CENTURY

The easier access to colonial food and the hosting of Universal Expositions in France highlighted the cuisines across the French Empire, which infiltrated the culinary repertoire of Parisians through household magazines, such as *Le Cordon bleu* and *Le Pot-au-feu*.

END OF WORLD WAR II

The departmentalization allowed the arrival of many Domiens (inhabitants of the DOM-TOM, France's overseas territories and departments) into Paris, who took on the adventures of the city.

STARTING IN 1955

Arriving by the thousands, encouraged by the policy of the Bumidom, the office responsible for the immigration of Creole populations into France.

TODAY

More than two hundred thousand Creoles reside in Île-de-France, and some of them have opened delightful places.

THE PIONEER

La Créole

📍 *122, blvd. du Montparnasse, Paris 14th.* €€

This spot, which resembles a colonial house, has been enlivening the neighborhood since 1956. You can taste almost all the Creole classics: cod chiquetaille, braised fish, or goat colombo.

RESTAURANTS

Le Babylon bis

📍 *34, rue Tiquetonne, Paris 2nd.* €

Celebrities, partygoers, and taxi drivers rub shoulders in this iconic place open all night. They enjoy chicken colombo and order rounds of hot accras.

Jah Jah By Le Tricycle

📍 *11, rue des Petites-Écuries, Paris 10th.* €

Coralie Jouhier and Daqui Gomis ignite veggie cuisine with their joyful and delicious Afro-Caribbean eatery. Barbecue cauliflower wings will make you forget chicken nuggets forever.

Le Maloya

📍 *59 bis, rue de Lancry, Paris 10th.* €€

In this small eatery that proudly bears the name of the Réunion dance, Marie-Claude Lui-Van-Sheng cooks one of the best sausage rougails in Paris using house-made charcuterie escorted by the trio rice-grains-peppers. To drink: the famous Dodo beer.

Caffé Creole

📍 *62, blvd. Beaumarchais, Paris 11th.* €€

It is impossible to miss this remarkable Creole storefront case. Here the braised chicken is generously drizzled with sauce chien (chile, vinegar, lime, and other ingredients), and you never leave without tasting one of the fifty rums offered.

Spécialités Antillaises Ménilmontant

📍 *14–16, blvd. de Belleville, Paris 20th.* €

The historic headquarters of the West Indians in Paris. Since 1960, this twenty-table restaurant-caterer has served up the flavors of Creole boudin, gratin of christophines, in the style of Réunion, and an avocado-cod well-spiced mixture, aptly named férose (fierce).

STREET FOOD

Banm Bokit

📍 *20, rue Barbanègre, Paris 19th.* €

Here they pay tribute to the star of Guadeloupean street food: the bokit, a sandwich made from fried bread filled most often with cod, but there is a red meat version.

GROCERY

Christian de Montaguère

📍 *20, rue de l'Abbé-Grégoire, Paris 6th*

This is an essential stop for cooking Creole food. Christian de Montaguère's grocery takes you on the rum route with nearly fifteen hundred products: chile noodles, achar, and even flavored syrups made of cooked cane juice that is often flavored with coconut sorbets.

United States

Americans love Paris and vice versa. Uncle Sam's kitchen is firmly established in the capital.

—CATHLEEN CLARITY

Thomas Jefferson said, "Every man has two countries: his homeland and France." Today, France welcomes 2.5 million American tourists each year and more than 100,000 permanent expatriates, including 14,000 in Île-de-France. And to our delight, a good number of them have opened indulgent establishments.

THE PIONEERS

Joe Allen

📍 30, rue Pierre-Lescot, Paris 1st. €€

Created in 1972, in the heart of Les Halles, this establishment transports you directly to Manhattan with its checkered tablecloths and dim lights. You can enjoy, among other things, an excellent "Joe Allen" burger, bagels worthy of a good deli, and a great pork rib with barbecue sauce.

Harry's New York Bar

📍 5, rue Daunou, Paris 2nd. €€

Opened in 1911, this legendary cocktail bar was also the first to sell Coca-Cola (1919) and make hot dogs in France.

RESTAURANTS

Ellsworth

📍 34, rue de Richelieu, Paris 1st. €€

This is the second restaurant of the duo Braden Perkins and Laura Adrian after Verjus. In this elegant and wood-clad decor, the chef offers three starters and three entrées that vary according to the season and his inspiration, but there is always the famous fried chicken, cucumber pickles, and lait ribot (a traditional fermented milk) sauce.

Montecito

📍 27–29, blvd. des Capucines, Paris 2nd. €€

For a good dose of "Cali vibes," head to Montecito located on the ground floor of the Kimpton Hotel in the Opéra district. Chef Nicolas Pastot, assisted by Carrie Solomon, offers a menu full of specialties including a langoustine tostada, a T-bone asada, and one of the best cioppinos (fish stew) outside of San Francisco.

Coffee Parisien

📍 4, rue Princesse, Paris 6th. €€

📍 7, rue Gustave-Courbet, Paris 16th. €€

📍 46, rue de Sablonville, Neuilly-sur-Seine (Hauts-de-Seine). €€

Founded in 1990 in Saint-Germain-des-Prés, this American bistro is one of the only restaurants where you can enjoy a brunch worthy of the name all day long: juicy burgers served with hash browns and one of the best Caesar salads in the capital.

Ralph's

📍 173, blvd. Saint-Germain, Paris 6th. €€€

Behind its air of a private club with a magnificent tree-lined terrace, the spot serves several American standards, such as the seared NY steak and the New England–style crusted cod, a fish served on a large shell, and clam chowder.

Bob's Juice Bar

📍 15, rue Lucien-Sampaix, Paris 10th. €

📍 Bob's Bake Shop 12, esp. Nathalie-Sarraute, Paris 18th. €

📍 Bob's Café MK2 Bibliothèque, 128–162, av. de France, Paris 13th. €

You can read "Juice Bar" in big letters on the facade, so the location is unmistakable. Chef and founder Marc Grossman offers freshly squeezed organic juices, protein smoothies, Brooklyn-style iced coffee, a grilled hummus-eggplant bagel, and a Bob's bowl with roasted vegetables, guacamole, and brown rice.

Holybelly

- 5, rue Lucien-Sampaix, Paris 10th. €€
- 19, rue Lucien-Sampaix, Paris 10th. €€

Open since 2013, Holybelly delights us with sweet or savory pancakes, probably the best in Paris, poached eggs with Parmesan sauce flanked by bacon from Perche (Normandy), and good coffee served in a large mug. Be aware of lines.

Keïli

- 106, rue Amelot, Paris 11th. €

In her small coffee shop a stone's throw from the Cirque d'Hiver, Caleigh Megless-Schmidt creates a healthy, colorful, and ultrafresh cuisine with several vegan options: homemade granola bowl, coconut curry with roasted chickpeas, and gluten-free dark chocolate–tahini cookies.

STREET FOOD

Homer Lobster

- 21, rue Rambuteau, Paris 4th. €€
- 15, rue de l'Ancienne-Comédie, Paris 6th. €€
- 106, av. Victor-Hugo, Paris 16th. €€

To feast on street food as found in Maine, head to Homer Lobster. Enjoy the famous Connecticut lobster roll made using Breton lobster, mayonnaise, hot lemon butter, and a secret herb mixture, all on a toasted and buttered brioche bun.

Janet by Homer

- 13, rue Rambuteau, Paris 4th. €

For those nostalgic for a good Jewish New York deli, Janet offers a variation of corned beef sandwiches on a brioche and rye buttered bun. The must-have? The Langer's, a nod to the Reuben sandwich, consisting of slices of corned beef, sauerkraut, and coleslaw with house-made Russian dressing and melted cheese.

Schwartz's Hot Dog

- 15, rue des Archives, Paris 4th. €
- 54, rue du Faubourg-Poissonnière, Paris 10th. €
- 122, av. Victor-Hugo, Paris 16th. €

A must on the list for hot dog lovers. Go for the classic ketchup, mustard, and fried onions or the "trop choux," topped with sauerkraut, mustard, and relish.

Le Camion Qui Fume

- 6, rue Grégoire-de-Tours, Paris 6th. €
- 66, rue Oberkampf, Paris 11th. €
- LeCamionQuiFume.com

A shining example of a food truck since 2011. Proof that a restaurant doesn't have to be fixed between four walls to offer amazing fare: the bacon cheeseburger, the bleu à la fourme d'Ambert (blue cheese), and the barbecue with onion rings have lost nothing from being on the move.

BARBECUE

Flesh

- 25, rue de Douai, Paris 9th. €€
- 23, rue Louis-Blanc, Paris 10th. €€

A good barbecue cooked low and slow. Here almost everything is smoked and grilled: eight-hour smoked pork ribs, rib steaks, free-range chicken, and a good selection of vegetables and garlic fries (fried three times).

Melt

- 74, rue de la Folie-Méricourt, Paris 11th. €€
- 103, rue Cambronne, Paris 15th. €€
- 83, rue Legendre, Paris 17th. €€

It was the meeting of duo Jean Ganizate and Paul Loiseleur with Jeffrey Howard, pitmaster of the famous Pecan Lodge in Texas, that triggered everything. Here is a real Texas barbecue with its house-made marinade and its special cooking that gives the meats an unmatched taste. The brisket, the pulled pork, the spareribs, maple bacon—absolutely everything is here.

BAKERY

Boneshaker Donuts & Coffee

- 86, rue d'Aboukir, Paris 2nd

The offering here is of one track: the vegan donut, which comes in many flavors: the OG (Original Glazed), the Boneshaker cream-filled with vanilla pastry cream and choco-cardamom glaze, and the Fluffernutter filled with peanut-butter pastry cream and marshmallow icing.

GROCERY

In Good We Trust

- 67, rue Quincampoix, Paris 3rd

Want Pop-Tarts or Lucky Charms cereal while in Paris? The shop offers a nice selection of American snacks, but there is also a large selection of artisanal products: lemon and avocado aïoli from Stonewall Kitchen, organic apple cider vinegar from Bragg, or the indispensable seafood spice blend Old Bay.

SEE ALSO
The Burger, p. 208.

Latin America

There are many interesting Latin American restaurants in Paris, especially from countries with a strong culinary heritage, such as Brazil, Mexico, Argentina, and Peru.

—HUGO DE SAINT-PHALLE, SUN AND THÉOPHILE ROUX

Argentina

The ties between Argentina and France have run deep since Argentina achieved independence in 1816. Argentina's love of France has its roots in the ideals of the Enlightenment, embodied by the *libertador* José de San Martín. The regular influx of French migrants in Argentina from the late nineteenth century until the Algerian War favored the intensity of exchanges between the two countries in many areas. There are now seven thousand Argentines in Paris. The carnivore restaurant El Palenque (Paris 5th), now closed, waved the Argentine flag in the capital for many years before others took over.

THE PIONEER

Anahi

 49, rue Volta, Paris 3rd. €€€

Resuming operations in 2017 after many changes, this Argentinian restaurant has remained an unmissable carnivorous

event since 1985. Riccardo Giraudi (Beefbar) is now watching over the establishment's direction and has entrusted the menu to Mauro Colagreco. Chimichurri sauces, cebolla, and criolla haute couture top the cuts of seared Angus and Wagyu beef.

RESTAURANTS

Caminito

 46, rue de Cléry, Paris 2nd. €€

Offering a nice terrace in the middle of the Sentier neighborhood and a good atmosphere in this bistro from the Barrio Norte group (Palermo and La Recoleta in the 17th). The menu fuses everything: beef tacos, grilled octopus, and caponata or rib steak rounds for two.

Volver

 18, rue Dauphine, Paris 6th. €€
 34, rue Keller, Paris 11th. €€

The historic haunt of Paris-Saint-Germain football players, Argentine or otherwise. Carlos Muguruza's restaurant is not a fancy

place. Empanadas of good quality rub shoulders with rib eye steak and Black Angus strip loin.

Loco

 31 bis, rue du Faubourg-Montmartre, Paris 9th. €€

At any time of the day, customers can enjoy grilled beef or purchase them vacuum-packed in the shop on the ground floor. There is also an interesting selection of Argentine wines.

Biondi

 118, rue Amelot, Paris 11th. €€

Although named after one of Argentina's greatest comedians, this bistro takes its food seriously. In a glamorous setting, bife de lomo (fillet) and multiple pieces of beef flame-seared dominate the plates. The less carnivorous also have a choice: fried red mullet, monkfish à la plancha. There is a nice wine list.

Unico

 15, rue Paul-Bert, Paris 11th. €€
 10, rue Amélie, Paris 7th. €€

An old butcher shop with pop decor. Under the orange seventies hanging lights, the meat-filled program focuses on beautiful pieces of Argentine meat grilled over coals. Empanadas and flan dulce de leche also set the tone.

Fulano

 15, rue Boinod, Paris 18th. €

On-site or for takeout, empanadas are the feature offering of this neighborhood eatery that also operates as a small shop. Ground onions-raisins-beef, chicken-leeks-peppers, dulce de leche: whether offered as savory or sweet, there is no shortage of combinations for the empanadas. Also try the alfajores cookies.

Onoto

 8, rue Cavallotti, Paris 18th. €€

Below the Montmartre cemetery, set on a peaceful street with a pleasant terrace, this spot invites a relaxing pause. With a Quilmes cerveza in hand, you can savor delicious empanadas to the sound of Latin music, or choose generously filled small sandwiches, or bife de chorizo, served with a salad and garlic confit.

GROCERY

Carnar

 23, rue de la Comète, Paris 7th

This shop offers large cuts of vacuum-packed Argentine beef for professionals and individuals. In addition to local beers and wines, the place is worth a visit for its beautiful selection of yerba maté leaves, the base of the famous South American herbal tea.

Bolivia

Three thousand Bolivians live in Paris, a community whose gastronomic heritage remains underrepresented here.

RESTAURANT

Tambo

 21, rue Godefroy-Cavaignac, Paris 11th. €€

Everything smells fresh and house-made in this welcoming lunch counter that crosses Bolivia and Peru. Like empanadas, their Argentine cousins, Bolivian salteñas are stuffed with meat. House-made bread for the chicharron sandwich (crispy pork) and generous portions in the bowls that bring together Peruvian rice, choclo corn, and marinated chicken.

Brazil

There has been trade between Brazil and France for four hundred years. During the Getúlio Vargas dictatorship in Brazil, artists, intellectuals, and activists representing the Brazilian elite settled in Paris. After the departure of the Vargas regime, immigration was due largely to reasons of economics. There are now an estimated twelve thousand Brazilians in the Paris region.

THE PIONEER

O Corcovado

 152, rue du Château, Paris 14th. €€

Since 2006, this small restaurant has been promoting family-style cooking. Caipirinha with passion fruit and beignets as a starter. As a main course, try moqueca (fish stew with coconut milk), bobó de camarão (coconut shrimp and cassava purée), and grilled meats.

RESTAURANTS

Pitanga

 11, rue Jean-Jacques-Rousseau, Paris 1st. €€

In this loftlike space, Brazilian-born chef Alexandre Furtado represents his native country in tapas, with coxinhas (chicken croquettes), ceviche, and bistronomy-style dishes.

Itacoa

 185, rue Saint-Denis, Paris 2nd. €€

This is a nod to Itacoatiara Beach, the beach in Rio where Brazilian chef Rafael Gomez grew up. The restaurant serves a pão de queijo (cheese bun) or a pão com chouriço (chorizo roll) as well as a solomillo iberico (Iberico pork tenderloin with salmorejo cashew sauce), among a menu of many influences.

Oka

 1, rue Berthollet, Paris 5th. €€€

Oka means "house" in the Tupi-Guarani language. From the open kitchen of his home, Michelin-starred Brazilian chef Raphael Rego sails between France and Brazil with lobster and maracuja, scallops and couve (Brazilian cabbage), and some flavors drawn from the Amazon such as castanha do Pará, the Brazil nut.

Sabor Da Roça

 50, rue Daubenton, Paris 5th. €

This is a small, family restaurant in a pedestrian street close to rue Mouffetard, where an authentic and generous cuisine is cooked up. Coxinhas, fritters of ground meat, are a great starter, and feijoada or moqueca are good for the main. For dessert, choose either the guava pâte de fruit or the crème caramel.

La Bahianaise

 85 bis, blvd. de Magenta, Paris 10th. €

This is a journey through Brazil from the Saint-Quentin market. This small, welcoming restaurant serves delicious Bahian cuisine. Every week, there is a new dish on the fixed menu and a choice of starters and desserts. On weekends, it's feijoada (black bean stew) to enjoy.

Brasileirinho

📍 129, rue Legendre, Paris 17th. €€

With its decor in the colors of Brazil, the view of the Guanabara Bay, and the live bossa concerts on weekends, the atmosphere is perfectly set for a Brazilian cultural immersion. As a starter, you can enjoy the assortment of Ronaldinho beignets, traditional dishes, and grilled meats.

Carajas

📍 24, rue des Trois-Frères, Paris 18th. €€

In this colorful Brazilian luncheonette with a local playlist, you can enjoy cheese rolls with a passion fruit cocktail. Traditional dishes, such as picanha and moqueca de camarão, are available.

GROCERY

Brésil Market

📍 43, rue Volta, Paris 3rd

A small shop with a good variety of Brazilian products: grilled cheese, meat for making feijoada, Brahma beer, Guarana soda, and everything necessary to make pão de queijo, small cheese rolls—and traditional Bon o Bon for the gourmands.

Chile

Since the closure of Tierra del Fuego (Paris 10th), there are only two representatives of Chilean cuisine in Paris.

RESTAURANTS

El Camino

📍 16, rue Guillaume-Bertrand, Paris 11th. €

Take note of this family-style restaurant. Pastel de choclo (a sort of corn Parmentier) and hot dog completo evoke a rustic element while the remaining menu explores Latin America and beyond with, especially, a good chili con carne.

Amor y Pan

📍 80, rue François-Arago, Montreuil (Seine-Saint-Denis). €

Cazuelas (Chilean osso buco: chicken and vegetables), charquican beef stew, and many sandwiches make up the selections in this friendly location.

Colombia

Political relations between France and Colombia have run deep since the eighteenth century, when the future liberator Simón Bolívar (a metro is dedicated to him) was raised in the Rousseauist spirit. Dynamic cultural, economic, and gastronomic ties unite the two countries.

RESTAURANTS

El Sol y la Luna

📍 31, rue Saint-Jacques, Paris 5th. €€

A colorful setting for this restaurant in the Latin Quarter, with a chandelier of Corona bottles. The menu oscillates among guacamole, empanadas, and burritos. Prices have increased, but the plates are of a generous portion.

Bazurto

📍 5, rue de l'Ancienne-Comédie, Paris 6th. €€

At the helm of this brand is Colombian chef Juan Arbelaez. The place has two faces: on the ground floor are found a festive spirit and plates to share (tacos, empanadas, grilled octopus, etc.), with a more classic restaurant space upstairs, focused around a tasting menu.

El Juanchito

📍 69, rue de la Folie-Regnault, Paris 11th. €

A real star! Under the Colombian flag attached to the ceiling, prices are moderate on a menu that focuses on essentials, including bandeja paisa, a hearty specialty with plantain, rice, ground beef, crispy pork belly, sausage, avocado, and fried egg.

CAFE

Espeletia Café

📍 52, rue Davy, Paris 17th

Happy are the neighbors of this little café, named after an endemic Andean plant. Smiling and passionate, the owner recommends the coffee beans that he roasts himself, to enjoy at the counter or to take away, ground or whole.

GROCERY

Léandrés

📍 78, rue de Maubeuge, Paris 9th

There is a lot of charm in this feel-good haunt run by a Franco-Colombian couple. Freshly roasted coffee can be enjoyed in a dozen forms, accompanied by sweet and savory snacks. Taste the agua de panela—very refreshing.

Ecuador

Ecuadorians have been in France since the 1970s and now number four thousand in Paris.

RESTAURANT

Ayahuma

📍 74, rue Léon-Frot, Paris 11th. €€

Kindness and a smile are handed out for free in this small, colorful bistro, opened in 2019 by an Ecuadorian couple. She attends to the dining room while he serves from the kitchen. On order? Beef hearts sautéed with peppers, Iberian pork loin, large sucio corn kernels, plantains.

Mexico

Although relations between Mexico and France were troubled during the nineteenth century, the exchanges have since been tempered, and Mexican immigration in France has increased in recent years. Widely popularized by American pop culture, Mexican cuisine has developed in a "haute cuisine" fashion since the end of the twentieth century, recognized as an Intangible Cultural Heritage by UNESCO in 2010.

RESTAURANTS

Candelaria

📍 52, rue de Saintonge, Paris 3rd. €

On one side, this is a micro-taqueria where customers wolf down, among other things, excellent tacos. On the other side, it's a well-hidden cocktail bar reminiscent of a speakeasy. Divine beverages and a fireside ambience were created by the Quixotic Projects team.

Anahuacalli

📍 30, rue des Bernardins, Paris 5th. €€

With tablecloths and shimmering colors, this location transforms small plates into large ones and serves a nice classic cuisine including a mole poblano, an emblematic recipe not easy to find in Paris. Twenty-seven ingredients, including six different peppers, make up the sauce that accompanies the chicken breast.

Luz Verde

📍 *24, rue Henry-Monnier, Paris 9th. €€*

Alexis Delassaux is one of the architects of the resurgence of Mexican cuisine in Paris. He offers fresh and colorful dishes, including excellent ceviches. A location for takeout was opened just across the street.

STREET FOOD

El Nopal

📍 *5, rue Duperré, Paris 9th. €*

📍 *3, rue Eugène-Varlin, Paris 10th. €*

These are two good spots to stop for a break while wandering the city by foot, located in Pigalle or near Canal Saint-Martin. The taco trio offers three different meats (pork, beef, chicken).

Distrito Francès

📍 *10, rue du Faubourg-Saint-Martin, Paris 10th. €*

📍 *25, rue du Pont-aux-Choux, Paris 3rd. €*

A good place to sip with friends on mezcal, pisco, or tequila cocktails, served by the glass or pitcher. Choose from various tacos prepared to order, generous burritos, and authentic dishes such as fried relleno pepper stuffed with cheese.

Café Chilango

📍 *82, rue de la Folie-Méricourt, Paris 11th. €*

Mexican street food is on the menu at this establishment opened in 2014. There are plentiful small plates, including excellent quesadillas with a side of guacamole or refried beans and, of course, tacos. For margaritas, choose tequila or mezcal.

Paraguay

A very small community (about seven hundred nationals) has been present in Paris since the 1950s.

RESTAURANT

Passion Guarani

📍 *21, rue Alexandre-Dumas, Paris 11th. €€*

The only Paraguayan restaurant in Paris seats guests around a large wooden central table. The welcome is warm and the menu is essentially meat based but served with typical dishes such as green tallarines, a kind of fresh, spinach tagliatelle.

Peru

Since the 1990s, Peru has been one of the most represented Latin American countries on the Parisian gastronomic scene with a wide variety of establishments to choose from, including cantoche (snack bars) to large concepts.

THE PIONEER

El Picaflor

📍 *9, rue Lacépède, Paris 5th. €€*

Opened in 1994, this restaurant is one of the emblems of Peruvian cuisine. In addition to classic ceviche, tiradito and lomo saltado can be found, but less common dishes are among the choices, too, such as rocoto, a rather spicy Peruvian red pepper, stuffed with pork and olives, served with potatoes au gratin.

RESTAURANTS

La Cevicheria

📍 *14, rue Bachaumont, Paris 2nd. €€*

📍 *16, av. Niel, Paris 17th. €*

An establishment that serves up several types of ceviches. Tiger's milk marinade and nikkei sauce bathe fresh sea bream, tuna, and salmon while beef or bonito are served tataki—quickly seared over high heat and rare in the center.

Inka

📍 *13, blvd. du Temple, Paris 3rd. €€*

The menu at the restaurant at hotel 1K Paris is a trip through Latin America. Offering nikkei cuisine (a style between Peruvian and Japanese), the restaurant's options include maki served as ceviches, the catch of the day with Colombian sudado sauce, and sautéed hangar steak. Set up behind the kitchens, the mezcaleria serves solid cocktails while in front of the hotel, the taqueria El Vecino sets a relaxed mood.

Candela II

📍 *32, rue de la Folie-Regnault, Paris 11th. €€*

Don't be fooled by the simplicity of the room. This family-run location serves typical Peruvian cuisine, priced right. On the menu are all the classics (tamal, ceviches, arroz con mariscos, lomo saltado . . .), all simple but good.

Mi Perú

📍 *7, rue Rondelet, Paris 12th. €€*

This family-style restaurant brings together connoisseurs for lunch and dinner around good ceviches, tamales (pork or chicken wrapped around cornmeal and cooked in a banana leaf), and other papas a la huancaína, potatoes in a kind of spicy mayonnaise.

El Pulpo

📍 *85, rue Lamarck, Paris 18th. €€*

It's a good sign when the restaurant is always full of regulars chatting in Spanish. This place has a menu of the day at a friendly price. Causa, ceviche, and chicharron are part of a lineup of dishes rarely offered elsewhere, including sopa de mote, a soup made from corn and beef tripe.

Uruguay

Uruguayan cuisine only recently arrived in Paris, with the opening of the first restaurant in 2016.

RESTAURANT

Comptoir Montevideo

📍 *44, rue Coquillière, Paris 1st. €€*

This is the first Uruguayan restaurant in Paris! The menu, in addition to grilled meats, offers gourmet tapas including empanadas with smoked sausage and chorizo and a crispy corn tortilla, topped with pulled beef stewed in red wine.

Venezuela

About three thousand Venezuelans live in Paris, a number that has been growing since the Venezuela's economic and political crisis of 2015.

RESTAURANTS

Aji Dulce

📍 *19, rue Notre-Dame-de-Lorette, Paris 9th. €*

The green counter in this snack bar catches the eye from the other side of the street. To order on-site or for takeout, try a dozen arepas (filled cornmeal breads) and tequeños (fried sticks of dough with melted queso blanco in the center).

Bululu Arepera

📍 *20, rue de la Fontaine-du-But, Paris 18th. €*

This small, casual diner, whose name means "joyful disorder," specializes in arepas. Made to order, they are eaten over a bowl to catch any part of the steaming filling that may tumble out while you're eating them. The pabellón is particularly delicious, made with plantain, pulled beef, black beans, and cheese.

The Onion Soup of Les Halles

Enjoyed by night workers, bourgeois night owls, and merrymakers, this gratinéed onion soup was an emblematic dish of the Belly of Paris. —JACQUES BRUNEL

THE RECIPE

Season: year-round
Difficulty ●○○

SERVES 4

1¾ pounds (800 g) yellow onions

5½ tablespoons (80 g) unsalted butter

6¾ cups (1.6 L) water

⅓ cup (40 g) all-purpose flour

Salt

4 slices pain de campagne (rustic bread made with rye), not too thick

1 cup (120 g) grated Emmental or Comté cheese

Freshly ground black pepper

Equipment

Individual oven-safe soup crocks (ideally lion's head tureens)

GRATINÉED CHEESE
SLICE OF BREAD
BROTH

Here is our classic recipe with the right balance between thick broth, well-soaked bread, and stretchy cheese.

Peel and finely slice the onions **1**. In a saucepan with a thick bottom, add the onions, butter, and a scant ½ cup (100 ml) of the water. Cover, and cook over low heat for 35 to 40 minutes, stirring three or four times. Add the flour **2**, stir, and cook until the onions are lightly browned (without browning them too much to avoid making them bitter.) Boil the remaining water and add it to the pan. Let simmer for 15 minutes. Season with salt.

Preheat the oven broiler.

Divide the soup among the crocks **3**. Place a slice of bread on top of the broth, sprinkle with the grated cheese, and broil immediately (do not wait before placing them in the oven, as the bread may break down into the broth).

Broil until the cheese is browned on top. Serve immediately.

VARIATION

For an even tastier broth, the boiling water can be replaced with chicken or beef stock.

Onions on display at Les Halles de Paris, late nineteenth–early twentieth centuries.

A UNIVERSAL DISH

Onion soup is present in many of France's regions. The Parisian version is distinguished by a slice of bread covered with Gruyère or Emmental cheese. By placing the soup under the broiler, the cheese thickens and keeps the broth warm.

1852
Poet and author Gérard de Nerval mentions "the onion soup, which is executed admirably in Les Halles, and to which those who are of a refined lot add grated Parmesan" (*Les Nuits d'octobre*, 1852).

1886
The writer Paul Mahalin discovers, at the Grand Comptoir, an onion soup "whose cheese stretches like a cable."

ONIONS FOR STRENGTH

The auctions of Les Halles started around 4 a.m., so the bistros of Les Halles stayed open all night to provide food for the workers. Too expensive for many, onion soup was the dish enjoyed by the "*forts*"

(the strongmen acting as loaders and carriers) as well as the police and butchers. Aristocrats and bourgeois revelers also enjoyed the soup, reputed to cure a hangover.

TOP LET'S EAT PARIS! ADDRESSES

La Poule au Pot
📍 *9, rue Vauvilliers, Paris 1st.* €€€
Yellow onions, Madeira, beef broth, sourdough bread, Emmental and Beaufort cheeses.

Au Pied de Cochon
📍 *6, rue Coquillière, Paris 1st.* €€
Yellow onions, beef consommé, traditional baguette, grated Emmental cheese.

📍 **Le Petit Vendôme**
8, rue des Capucines, 2nd. €€
Roscoff onions, beef and veal broth, baguette tradition, twelve-month Comté cheese.

SKIP TO
Île-de-France Terroir, p. 20; Les Halles: The Belly of Paris, p. 113; Paris in the Soup, p. 266.

Caviar Dynasties

These two companies have made Paris one of the strongholds in the world of caviar.

—CHARLES PATIN O'COOHOON

PETROSSIAN

FONDÉ À PARIS EN 1920

Parent company:
📍 *18, blvd. de la Tour-Maubourg, Paris 7th*
Founded: 1920
Enduring: for three generations

The tin since 1920: a ship with red sails crosses the waves of the Caspian Sea in front of a radiant sun.

Armen Petrossian.

HISTORY

The Petrossian brothers, Melkum (an architect) and Mouchegh (an attorney) left Russia for Paris to flee the anti-Armenian pogroms of the Caucasus. There they opened a fine-foods shop dedicated to Caspian seafood. The Petrossian caviar company soon became the first to market caviar. In 2008, when sturgeon supplies decreased, the Convention on International Trade in Endangered Species of Wild Fauna and Flora (CITES) banned sturgeon fishing. Consequently, fish farms soon flourished, and caviar supplies arrived from France, Germany, and China. Armen Petrossian succeeded his father, Mouchegh, in 1992 before handing over the reins to his son Mikael in 2019.

PRODUCT RANGE

› Baeri Baika, from the sturgeon *Acipenser baerii*
› Sevruga, from the sturgeon *Acipenser stellatus*
› Ossetra, from the sturgeon *Acipenser gueldenstaedtii*
› Daurenki, from the crossbreeding of the sturgeons *Huso dauricus* and *Acipenser schrenckii*
› Beluga, from the sturgeon *Huso huso*

THE RARE GEM

The Beluga Special Reserve. Large grains, varying from light gray to deep gray, with a very mild texture and an amazing persistence. Observed price in 2022: €12,800 per kg.

SPECIAL CREATIONS

The famous tin in a 22-pound (10 kg) format with fleur de caviar, a dried caviar that grinds like pepper.

DINING

Located on the sidewalk opposite the shop, the Petrossian restaurant delights with Russian-inspired cuisine.
📍 *13, blvd. de la Tour-Maubourg, Paris 7th + 2 locations*

Kaviari
PARIS

Parent company:
📍 *13, rue de l'Arsenal, Paris 4th*
Founded: 2001
Enduring: for two generations

The tin since 2019: a curled up golden sturgeon on a midnight-blue background.

Jacques Nebot.

HISTORY

Jacques Nebot has been involved in caviar since the 1970s and quickly became an authority among Iranian operators. In 1981, he created the caviar house Astara, specializing in black gold from the Caspian Sea. In 1985, he opened his restaurant, Le Coin du Caviar, near Bastille. Along with Raphaël Bouchez in 2001—who oversaw caviar at Hédiard—he founded Kaviari. His daughter, Karin Nebot, joined them in 2009 as CEO. Since then, the company has been working with farms in Italy, France, and China.

PRODUCT RANGE

› Transmontanus, from the sturgeon *Acipenser transmontanus*
› French Baeri, from the sturgeon *Acipenser baerii*
› Oscietra, from the sturgeon *Acipenser gueldenstaedtii*
› Kristal, from the crossbreeding of the sturgeons *Acipenser schrenckii* and *Huso dauricus*
› Beluga, from the sturgeon *Huso huso*

THE RARE GEM

The Beluga Imperial, large elephant-gray grains with a melting texture, buttery and delicate notes, and an incredibly long finish. Observed price in 2022: €9,500 per kg.

SPECIAL CREATIONS

The En-K, a small format (½ oz/15 g) that makes the caviar experience accessible.

DINING

In 2020, Kaviari created the Delikatessen Kaviari brand, a combination of fine-foods seafood shop and a restaurant.
📍 *116, rue de la Convention, Paris 15th + 5 locations*

SKIP TO
Eastern Europe and Russia, p. 173; Delicatessens, p. 326.

The Saint-Honoré

This crown of puff pastry bejeweled with small, caramelized choux puffs filled with vanilla cream has majestically occupied the repertoire of dessert lovers for nearly two centuries. —JEAN-PHILIPPE MARSAN

Pâtisserie Chiboust, circa 1850.

THE BEGINNINGS OF THE "SAINT-HO"...

The Saint-Honoré made its first appearance in the window of the Chiboust pastry shop on rue Saint-Honoré in 1846. Created by Auguste Jullien, the dessert at the time was simply a crown of brioche topped with small balls of brioche and all filled with pastry cream. Jullien, also a clever marketer, had the brilliant idea to christen the dessert the "Saint-Honoré" in reference to the patron saint of pastry chefs. But, much more practically, this was the name of the street where the Chiboust pastry shop was located

(Paris 1st). It was a stroke of genius.

FIVE TEXTURES IN ONE BITE

Although the dessert's puff pastry base has endured through the centuries, the Chiboust cream filling (a mixture of pastry cream and Italian meringue) has stepped aside for diplomat cream (a mixture of pastry cream, whipped cream, and gelatin) flavored with vanilla. An eloquently piped Chantilly cream decoration and small choux puffs filled with cream and delicately caramelized complete the look.

IT TOOK SIX HANDS

Three chefs innovated this now-timeless Parisian dessert before it became an icon. When Auguste Jullien left Chiboust, he reinvented the Saint-Honoré, along with his brother, by replacing the brioche base, first with pâte brisée (a flaky pastry with perhaps sugar and egg), then with pâte feuilletée (puff pastry, or a laminated dough). Desiring to refine it further, they swapped the brioche balls for choux puffs, whose tops he lightly caramelized. Chiboust wanted to lighten the filling. After many tests, he innovated by using a vanilla pastry cream lightened with the addition of an Italian meringue, giving birth to what is today referred to as Chiboust cream.

Tip

The look of the piped Chantilly cream decoration is characteristic of the Saint-Honoré cake. The decoration is made using a pastry bag fitted with a "Saint-Honoré" piping tip, which has a special notched or beveled shape. To practice, pastry chefs fill their pastry bags with shaving cream—much cheaper than making a cream!

THE BEST SAINT-HONORÉS IN PARIS

Individual formats

Hugo et Victor

📍 40, blvd. Raspail, Paris 7th

The pastry: puff pastry, well baked.
The choux: small, caramelized.
The creams: Bourbon vanilla crème légère, vanilla Chantilly cream.

KL Pâtisserie

📍 78, av. de Villiers, Paris 17th

The pastry: puff pastry, delicate.
The choux: small, caramelized.
The creams: salted butter caramel, vanilla Chantilly cream.

The French Bastards

📍 35, pl. Saint-Ferdinand, Paris 17th + 2 locations

The pastry: sweet, with hazelnut.
The choux: plump, caramelized.
The creams: creamy vanilla, vanilla Chantilly cream.

Large formats

Carl Marletti

📍 51, rue Censier, Paris 5th

The pastry: puff pastry, crisp.
The choux: medium, caramelized.
The creams: a silky Chiboust, vanilla Chantilly cream.

Jean-François Foucher

📍 10, rue Madeleine Michelis, Neuilly-sur-Seine (Hauts-de-Seine)

The pastry: puff pastry, caramelized.
The choux: plump, beautiful craquelin top.
The creams: fluffy diplomat cream with Madagascar vanilla, Chantilly cream with crème Normande (a custard with Calvados).

La Délicatisserie

📍 Delicatisserie.com

The pastry: puff pastry, crisp.
The choux: plump, caramelized.
The creams: vanilla diplomat cream, tonka bean.

THE RECIPE

Season: year-round
Difficulty ● ● ●

SERVES 6

For the puff pastry

All-purpose flour, for dusting

14 ounces (400 g) Puff
Pastry (p. 58)

For the choux pastry

¼ cup (60 ml) water

¼ cup (60 ml) whole milk

3 tablespoons (50 g)
unsalted butter

1 teaspoon (5 g) granulated
sugar

⅛ teaspoon (1 g) salt

⅔ cup (75 g) all-purpose
flour

2 large (100 g) eggs

For the pastry cream

1 cup (250 ml) milk

⅓ cup (80 g) whipping
cream (ideally 30% fat)

1 vanilla bean

2 large (40 g) egg yolks

¼ cup (50 g) granulated
sugar

¼ cup (30 g) cornstarch

For the caramel

½ cup plus 2 tablespoons
(125 g) sugar

5 tablespoons (75 ml) water

3 tablespoons glucose
syrup or corn syrup

For the Chantilly cream

1 vanilla bean

1⅓ cups (330 ml) whipping
cream (ideally 30% fat), well
chilled

½ cup plus 2 tablespoons
(65 g) confectioners' sugar

Equipment

Pie weights

Pastry bags

Saint-Honoré piping tip

Plain ⅓-inch (10 mm)
piping tip

This recipe by Jacques Genin* is perfectly balanced.

Make the puff pastry: Preheat the oven to 300°F (150°C) convection heat. Dust the work surface and top of the dough with flour. Roll out the dough into a rectangle measuring 9¾ by 12 inches (25 by 30 cm) and ¹⁄₁₀ inch (2 mm) thick ❶.

Place the dough on a baking sheet lined with parchment paper. Place a second baking sheet on top and add the pie weights. Bake for about 35 minutes. Remove the top baking sheet and bake again for 15 minutes, until golden. Set aside on a rack to cool.

Make the choux pastry: Preheat the oven to 350°F (180°C) (not convection). Line a baking sheet with parchment paper.

Place the water, milk, butter, granulated sugar, and salt in a saucepan over low heat until the butter has melted and the mixture begins to boil. Off the heat, stir in the flour all at once and stir continuously until the dough detaches from the sides of the pan. Transfer the dough to the bowl of a stand mixer fitted with the paddle attachment and mix for several minutes on medium speed until cooled.

Lightly beat the eggs and add them in a slow stream to the bowl while mixing, until the dough becomes homogeneous; the dough is ready when a gap created by dragging the spatula through it slowly closes.

While the dough is still warm, scrape it into a pastry bag fitted with the plain piping tip and pipe small rounds about 1 inch (3 cm) in diameter on the prepared baking sheet. Bake for 20 minutes, or until the rounds are puffed and golden.

Make the pastry cream: In a saucepan set over medium-high heat, bring the milk and cream to a boil. Split the vanilla bean lengthwise in half and scrape out the seeds using the tip of a knife; set aside. Place the yolks, granulated sugar, cornstarch, and vanilla bean seeds and empty pod in a saucepan. Stir in half of the hot milk-cream mixture, then pour all the contents back into the saucepan with the remaining milk-cream mixture. Cook for 5 minutes over medium heat. Transfer to a bowl, gently press plastic wrap onto the surface, and refrigerate to cool completely.

Make the caramel: Add the sugar, water, and syrup to a saucepan and cook over low heat until it turns to a caramel. Dip each choux puff in the caramel, then set aside until completely cooled ❷ ❸.

Make the chantilly cream: Split the vanilla bean lengthwise in half and scrape out the seeds using the tip of a knife; set aside. In the bowl of a stand mixer fitted with the whisk attachment, beat the cream with the vanilla seeds on medium speed. Sprinkle in the confectioners' sugar and beat to stiff peaks. Transfer the cream to a pastry bag fitted with the Saint-Honoré piping tip.

Assemble: Using a pastry bag, fill the choux puffs with the pastry cream.

Using a serrated bread knife, cut out a rectangle measuring 8 by 10 inches (20 by 25 cm) from the puff pastry. Line the short edges of the rectangle with choux puffs and add two rows of equally spaced choux puffs in the center. Using a pastry bag, fill in the empty space between the rows with pastry cream, then cover with piped Chantilly cream.

* 📍 *133, rue de Turenne, Paris 3rd.*
📍 *27, rue de Varenne, Paris 7th.*

SKIP TO
The Chouquette
and Its Cousins,
p. 278; Pastry
Shops, p. 312.

The Burger

Created in the nineteenth century in the United States thanks to the influence of German immigrants, the burger has been ennobled in Paris. Here is a quick chronology.

—CHARLES PATIN O'COOHOON

1961
On May 31, Jacques Borel, an agro-food industrialist opens Wimpy, the first burger joint in France on rue du Quatre-Septembre (Paris 1st).

1972
Opening in Créteil (Val-de-Marne) of the first McDonald's in France (contrary to what the American food giant claims—for licensing reasons— of the opening in Strasbourg in 1979).

1980
Burger King opens its first restaurant in France on the Champs-Élysées (Paris 8th).

1988
Opening on the Champs-Élysées of the most profitable McDonald's in the world.

1997
Burger King closes its thirty-nine France locations.

1998
McDonald's moves to 119, rue Saint-Lazare (Paris 8th) in the space of the former restaurant Au Roi de La Bière in a building built in 1892.

2001
Filming in Aubervilliers (Seine-Saint-Denis) of the first season of Burger Quiz, the game show hosted by Alain Chabat.

2008
"Mr. Burger," created by Yannick Alléno the three-Michelin-starred chef at Le Meurice (Paris 1st), is voted best burger in the world by the *New York Times*.

2011
Californian Kristin Frederick parks her "Le Camion Qui Fume," the first Parisian food truck, at Place de la Madeleine (Paris 8th), Porte Maillot (Paris 16th), and Point Éphémère (Paris 10th).

2012
Steve Burggraf, Alexandre Auriac, and Guillaume Pagliano open Big Fernand, the first French burger chain (which now has sixty-one restaurants) on rue du Faubourg-Poissonnière (Paris 10th).

2015
At the head of Siseng (Paris 10th), Stéphane Siseng launches the first bao burger, where steamed buns replace the typical bun.

2016
Five Guys, the American hamburger chain, opens its first restaurant in Bercy Village (Paris 12th).

2016
The launch of the Coupe de France du Burger (France Burger Cup) at the Sandwich & Snack Show at Porte de Versailles (Paris 15th).

2017
Sales of the hamburger exceed those of the iconic French sandwich-on-the-go, the jambon-beurre, for the first time.

2018
At Echo (Paris 2nd), Matthias Gloppe opens the first Smashburger from the United States. The very flattened beef patty is crisp and juicy.

2020
Stéphanie Le Quellec, two-Michelin-starred chef at La Scène (Paris 8th), creates a home burger kit for takeout during the COVID-19 lockdown.

2022
Alain Ducasse opens Burgal (Paris 11th), a kiosk dedicated to vegan burgers.

In Quentin Tarantino's film *Pulp Fiction* (1994), Vincent Vega (John Travolta) and Jules Winnfield (Samuel L. Jackson) philosophize about the name of burgers in Paris:
"And you know what they call a Quarter Pounder with cheese in Paris?"
"They don't call it a Quarter Pounder with cheese?"
"No, they got the metric system there, they wouldn't know what the fuck a Quarter Pounder is."
"What do they call it?"
"They call it a Royale with Cheese."
"A Royale with Cheese. . . . What do they call a Big Mac?"
"A Big Mac's a Big Mac, but they call it 'Le Big Mac.'"
" 'Le Big Mac' . . . Ha ha ha ha ha ha ha! What do they call a Whopper?"
"I don't know, I didn't go into a Burger King."

SKIP TO
Le Jambon-Beurre, p. 48.

THE BEST BURGERS IN PARIS

Blend
📍 *44, rue d'Argout, Paris 2nd + 4 locations*

BACON CHEESY

Bun: potato bun by MOF chef Frédéric Lalos.
Patty: 4½ ounces (125 g), Angus beef, 12% fat, ground twice on-site.
Cheese: 18-month Somerset cheddar.
Toppings: beechwood smoked bacon, house-made ketchup, fried onions, house-made zucchini pickles, iceberg lettuce.

Echo
📍 *95, rue d'Aboukir, Paris 2nd*

DOUBLE ECHO SMASH BURGER

Bun: potato bun by Martin's Potato Rolls.
Patty: double × 2½ ounces (75 g), French meat, 10% fat, ground on-site.
Cheese: cheddar.
Toppings: tomatoes, iceberg lettuce, white onions, mini-cucumber pickles, secret sauce.

Le Camion Qui Fume
📍 *6, rue Grégoire-de-Tours, Paris 6th*
📍 *66, rue Oberkampf, Paris 11th*
📍 *5, rue François Mitterrand, Ivry-sur-Seine*

CHEESEBURGER

Bun: potato bun by Bread Shop.
Patty: 4½ ounces (130 g), Norman beef, 20% fat.
Cheese: 9-month red cheddar.
Toppings: ketchup, mustard, pickles.

Dumbo
📍 *64, rue Jean-Baptiste-Pigalle, Paris 9th*
📍 *14, rue des Petites-Écuries, Paris 10th*

CHEESEBURGER

Bun: artisanal potato bun.
Patty: double × 2⅓ ounces (65 g), Montbéliarde beef, 25% fat.
Cheese: cheddar.
Toppings: house-made cucumber dill pickles, raw onions, ketchup, American mustard.

PNY
📍 *50, rue du Faubourg-Saint-Denis, Paris 10th + 7 locations*

VINTAGE CHEESEBURGER

Bun: artisanal brioche bread.
Patty: 4¾ ounces (135 g), Black Angus, Angus, or Salers beef, 15% fat, ground on-site.
Cheese: 16- to 18-month Somerset cheddar.
Toppings: iceberg lettuce, ketchup, mustard, pickles.

Sold Out
📍 *2, rue Lucien-Sampaix, Paris 10th*

CHEESEBURGER

Bun: potato bun by Bread Shop.
Patty: 4 ounces (115 g), Limousin beef, 15 to 20% fat, ground on-site.
Cheese: 9-month Somerset cheddar.
Toppings: red onions, Noa cucumber pickles, house-made sauce.

Baby Love Burger
📍 *63, rue Saint-Maur, Paris 11th*

SIMPLE

Bun: artisanal potato bun.
Patty: 4½ ounces (120 g), Montbéliarde beef, 20% fat, ground on-site.
Cheese: English cheddar.
Toppings: onions, cucumber pickles in white balsamic vinegar, iceberg lettuce, house-made sauce.

Garnett
📍 *85, rue Cardinet, Paris 17th*

CHEESEBURGER

Bun: potato bun by Rachel's.
Patty: 3½ ounces (100 g), Black Angus beef, ground on-site.
Cheese: English cheddar.
Toppings: gem lettuce, red onions, pickles, tomatoes, ketchup, American mustard.

Le Ruisseau
📍 *65, rue du Ruisseau, Paris 18th + 3 locations*

CHEESEBURGER

Bun: house-made brioche bread.
Patty: 3¾ ounces (110 g), Limousin beef, 10% fat, ground on-site.
Cheese: English cheddar.
Toppings: American mustard, ketchup, chopped red onions, pickles.

BOUILLON CHARTIER

It is one of the last bouillons in Paris still thriving, a living testament to a daring entrepreneurial adventure. —JACQUES BRUNEL

MAISON PARISIENNE
7, RUE DU FAUBOURG-
MONTMARTRE, 9TH ARR.

BOUILLON CHARTiER

A cult following

– The student Edmond Barbentane, the hero of the book *Les Beaux Quartiers* (1936) by Louis Aragon, was a regular.
– Humoristic singer Fernandel sang about seducing a woman named Félicie here. Since then, the fried pig's foot has been called the "Félicie."
– In movies, Chartier has been the backdrop in *La Passante du Sans-Souci* (Jacques Ruffio, 1982), *La Chose publique* (Mathieu Amalric, 2003), and *Un long dimanche de fiançailles* (*A Very Long Engagement*), by Jean-Pierre Jeunet, 2004.

TO TRY

Serving 365 days a year from 11:30 a.m. to midnight and without a reservation, all for a bill less than twenty euros.

The oeuf mayonnaise at two euros: three hard-boiled egg halves and a house-made mayonnaise with a coating consistency.

The bestsellers: celery remoulade, free-range chicken with fresh-made frites, the "Félicie" (pig's foot), tête de veau (calf's head) with sauce gribiche, and rum baba.

The tripoux de la maison Savy et la saucisse au couteau (sheep tripe and thick sausage): Savy is in northern France, the opposite direction from the Auvergne origins of Christophe Joulie, the new owner since 2006.

TO SEE

The numbered wooden lockers: the napkins for regulars were stored in them.

The fresco: created in 1929 by Germont to pay off his credit at the restaurant and to be able to enjoy a table for several more weeks.

The waitstaff: Servers dressed in black vests can stack six filled plates on their arms, serving eighteen hundred meals a day, or twenty-five hundred on peak days. The order is written on the tablecloth, just as the bill. The wait between courses rarely takes more than five minutes.

SKIP TO

The Parisian Bouillon, p. 70; Art Nouveau or Art Deco?, p. 160; Celery Remoulade, p. 246.

The Founders

Two butcher brothers from Orgeval (Yvelines), Frédéric and Camille Chartier—sons of a wheel repairman with a predestined name (*chartier* meaning *charretier*, or cart driver)—were indignant about the poor quality of working-class meals offered in Paris and dreamed of offering low-cost, nourishing meals by waitstaff in a luxury setting, improving upon the concept of a *bouillon* launched by Alexandre Duval in 1860.

Year zero

In 1896, the two brothers opened their first bouillon on rue du Faubourg-Montmartre, where coach drivers, delivery men, and bank employees made up the clientele. The bouillon overlooked the street, but the entrance was through the courtyard of the building. The second courtyard became the bouillon's dining room.

THE ROOM

Measuring 20 feet (6 m) high, 82 feet (25 m) long, and equipped with a mezzanine, the dining room evoked a luxurious train-station café of the Belle Époque. The decor was rather art nouveau, with a revolving door, expansive mirrors, stucco medallions, bubble-shade lamps, and copper hat racks. In the center stood an enormous wood-burning stove. Guests would pay for the meal in advance at the register, where they were given tokens corresponding to the chosen dishes. A clock prompted them not to linger.

THE DISHES

Originally, a choice of about fifty dishes was a mark of true luxury as most restaurants that served cheap fare offered only one. The worker here was treated as a bourgeois.

The Opéra

With its chocolate ganache enhanced with coffee notes, whether square or a rectangle, this dessert hits a high note on the Parisian pastry stage. —VALENTINE OUDARD

THE RECIPE

Season: fall to winter
Difficulty ● ● ●

SERVES 8

For the Joconde sponge

1 cup (125 g) almond flour
¼ cup (33 g) all-purpose flour
1¼ cups (125 g) confectioners' sugar
3 large (150 g) eggs
3 large (90 g) egg whites
1 tablespoon plus 2 teaspoons (20 g) granulated sugar
1½ tablespoons (25 g) unsalted butter, melted

For the coffee soaking syrup

Scant ¼ cup (50 ml) water
¼ cup plus 1½ tablespoons (70 g) granulated sugar
4 brewed espresso coffees

For the coffee buttercream

¼ cup plus 2 tablespoons (75 g) granulated sugar
1 tablespoon plus 1 teaspoon (20 ml) water
½ vanilla bean
1 large (50 g) egg
1 large (20 g) egg yolk
11 tablespoons (160 g) unsalted butter, at room temperature
2 teaspoons (10 g) coffee extract

For the chocolate ganache

¼ cup (60 g) whole milk
1 tablespoon plus 1 teaspoon (20 g) heavy cream
¾ cup (100 g) 72% cacao dark chocolate
1½ tablespoons (25 g) unsalted butter

For the chocolate glaze

7 ounces (200 g) dark chocolate
2 tablespoons (30 g) grapeseed oil

Equipment

1 square pastry frame 6 by 6 inches (15 by 15 cm) and 1 inch (2.5 cm) high
2 baking sheets 12 by 12 inches (30 by 30 cm)
Stand mixer
Pastry brush
Silicone baking mat

Maison Dalloyau has created a version of this sweet symphony.

Make the Joconde sponge: Preheat the oven to 375°F (190°C). Using a stand mixer fitted with the paddle attachment, beat together the almond and all-purpose flours, confectioners' sugar, and whole eggs. In a separate clean bowl, begin beating the egg whites to stiff peaks while sprinkling in the granulated sugar. Add the melted butter to the bowl with the flour mixture then carefully incorporate the beaten egg whites. Spread the batter out to a thickness of ¼ inch (5 mm) on two baking sheets, each lined with a silicone baking mat and bake for 10 minutes, or until pale golden. Unmold the cakes immediately to cool on a rack.

Make the coffee soak: In a saucepan over medium-high heat, boil the water and granulated sugar together and add the espressos.

Make the coffee buttercream: Heat the granulated sugar and water to 255°F (124°C). Split the vanilla bean lengthwise in half and scrape out the seeds using the tip of a knife; set aside. Place the egg, egg yolk, and vanilla bean seeds in a stand mixer fitted with the whisk attachment. With the mixer on the highest speed, drizzle the hot syrup into the bowl; the mixture should triple in volume. On medium speed, incorporate the butter in pieces and add the coffee extract.

Make the chocolate ganache: In a saucepan, heat the milk and cream. Place the chocolate in a pan and pour the hot mixture over the chocolate and vigorously stir to blend until smooth and creamy. At 95°F (35°C), add the butter and stir thoroughly using a silicone spatula until the mixture is smooth and shiny.

Assemble: Cut the two sponges in half. Place one of the sponge layers into the bottom of the pastry frame. Using a pastry brush, soak the sponge with some of the coffee syrup. Spoon a layer of buttercream (about 4 ounces/115 g) on top of the sponge cake and spread it out evenly. Repeat the process with a second layer of cake, coffee soak, and buttercream. Pour the warm chocolate ganache on top, then place the third sponge layer on top followed by another layer of the buttercream in the same quantity. Discard the fourth layer or repurpose for another recipe. Smooth the top and refrigerate for 1 hour. Remove the frame and set the cake aside to come to room temperature.

Make the chocolate glaze: Combine the chocolate and oil and warm them to 95°F (35°C). Cover the top of the cake with the glaze; set aside until set. Slice and serve.

Stohrer
📍 51, rue Montorgueil, Paris 2nd
The slight bitterness of the coffee plays well with the sweetness of the entire ensemble.

Lenôtre
📍 44, rue d'Auteuil, Paris 16th + 9 locations
An intense taste of chocolate steps aside to introduce subtle coffee aromas.

Dalloyau
📍 101, rue du Faubourg-Saint-Honoré, Paris 8th
Well harmonized, the thin chocolate layer dissolves on the tongue.

Pain Pain
📍 88, rue des Martyrs, Paris 18th
A cast of Joconde sponge, intense ganache, coffee cream, and crackly chocolate coating.

AN INTERLUDE

Cinq Sens
📍 114, rue Saint-Charles, Paris 15th
An espresso gelée replaces the chocolate ganache layer and a whipped ganache replaces the coffee buttercream.

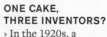

ONE CAKE, THREE INVENTORS?

› In the 1920s, a Monsieur Riss created a version he called the "Clichy," which was sold until 2018.
› In 1955, Cyriaque Gavillon, pastry chef at Dalloyau, created a cake with exposed layers and many flavors that could be enjoyed in one bite. Gavillon's wife, Andrée, named the cake L'Opéra, perhaps because of its shape, reminiscent of the opera stage, or to pay tribute to the dancers of the Opéra who were regular customers.
› In 1960, Gaston Lenôtre created his own version.
› In 1988, the origin of the cake was officially attributed to pastry house Dalloyau.

Plants along the Pavement

Buttes-Chaumont, Vincennes, Boulogne, and
Saint-Cloud are four Parisian parks ideal for picking
wild herbs and flowers. —CHRISTOPHE DE HODY*

Bois de
Boulogne

Les buttes
Chaumont

Parc de
Saint-Cloud

Bois de
Vincennes

The golden rules for picking plants

- Identify the plant using all five senses and with 100 percent certainty of what's being picked.

- Avoid polluted places and diseased or damaged plants.

- Clean all plants or cook them.

- Never collect rare species or plants in protected areas.

- Always leave the largest and best plants behind.

- Pick gently and avoid pulling out the roots.

- Pick only what is absolutely needed and never take more than a third of any patch.

- Avoid wasting what was harvested.

PLANT-HARVESTING GUIDELINES

- Ask for the owner's permission before picking on private land.

- In French public forests, picking is free up to 5 liters (just over a gallon, or the equivalent of a small, full basket).

- On public land, picking is free for those who live in the community.

- Picking in nature reserves is regulated and generally prohibited.

- There are lists of protected species (whose collection is prohibited) at national, regional, and departmental levels. These lists are unique to each country. For France, the information can be found on the website of the National Inventory of Natural Heritage (https://inpn.mnhn.fr).

*Herbalist and botanist, founder of LeCheminDeLaNature.com.

Wild garlic, bear garlic

Allium ursinum L.

SEASON
Mid-February to mid-May.

HARVESTING AREAS
Herbaceous undergrowth, boarders of cool and moist wooded areas.

DESCRIPTION
A perennial that grows in carpet patches with a garliclike scent. Semi-cylindrical stem, hairless leaves that are oval and lance shaped, shiny on top and dull on the underside. It has white flowers forming an umbel that looks like an upturned umbrella.

IN COOKING
Fully edible plant with a pronounced garlic taste. The leaves and flower buds have a crunch. The bulbs have a slightly milder flavor. Can be eaten raw in salad, pesto, mayonnaise; with fromage frais; and added to compound butter. Add to savory pies, quiches, and soups.

NUTRIENTS
Magnesium, sodium, calcium, potassium, and vitamin C.

Garlic mustard

Alliaria petiolata (M.Bieb.) Cavara & Grande

SEASON
Year-round, before flowering (when it's less bitter).

HARVESTING AREAS
Very common up to an altitude of 3,300 feet (1,000 m). Grows voluntarily in cultivated areas, cool and semi-shaded places, and in the undergrowth, along paths and hedges, and among crops.

DESCRIPTION
Ranges from 1½ to just over 3 feet (40 to 100 cm), upright, with a few hairs soft to the touch. Round stem, rather rounded leaves at the base of the plant, with long stalk and triangular leaves. The white flower has four cross petals. Two-year growth cycle: the seed germinates, the leaves appear in year 1 followed by the flowers and fruits in year 2.

IN COOKING
From the cabbage family, but its leaves have the smell and taste of garlic. When cooked, they lose this taste. The best use is raw, such as in a pesto.

NUTRIENTS
Vitamin C and E, beta-carotene, calcium, and iron.

English oak

Quercus robur L.

SEASON
September to November (when the acorns are on the ground).

HARVESTING AREAS
Woods, forests with tall trees (hornbeam, beech, sessile oak), wilderness areas, hedges, and embankments.

DESCRIPTION
Large tree 100 to 130 feet (30 to 40 m) tall and 20 to 23 feet (6 to 7 m) in circumference. Smooth bark, shiny, silvery gray, cracks over time to become dark brown, thick and rough in mature trees. Leaves are lobed shaped, typical of oaks. Acorns are its nuts, often grown in pairs.

IN COOKING
The acorn nuts are edible once cooked. Their harshness and astringency disappear after three to eight cooking times (fifteen to twenty minutes each), depending on the acorns. The taste is very pronounced and slightly astringent. Used in puréed soups, porridges, vegetable pâtés, or added into flour.

NUTRIENTS
Carbohydrates, fats, proteins, and vitamin B.

Ground ivy

Glechoma hederacea L.

SEASON
Year-round.

HARVESTING AREAS
Cool to moist soils, meadows, forest boarders, hedge boarders, paths, full light or partial shade.

DESCRIPTION
Perennial plant 4 to 12 inches (10 to 30 cm) in height, with creeping aerial stems, forming leafy almost year-round colonies. Green leaves tinged with yellow, slightly hairy, aromatic, they emit a smell of lemon and menthol when crinkled.

IN COOKING
A very aromatic plant, slightly minty, even lemony, with notes of humus and an animal-like flavor. Its slight bitterness disappears once cooked. Goes very well with mushrooms. The leaves have a strong taste and are used raw in salads or to flavor desserts, pestos, and sauces.

NUTRIENTS
Vitamin C.

Dog rose

Rosa canina L.

SEASON
Late September to late winter

HARVESTING AREAS
Hedges, forest boarders, and open woods.

DESCRIPTION
Shrub 3 to 16 feet (1 to 5 m) tall with branching trunks, bushy, loses its leaves in fall. The branches have curved prickles. The stipules at the base of the leaves (small leaves, inserted in pairs) are toothed. The flowers are pale pink to whitish with a pleasant smell. Rose hips are a red, oval, smooth, and shiny accessory fruit.

IN COOKING
Rose hips have a tart taste and are edible if they are red. Used raw or cooked, puréed, or in sauce. Remove any hairs that may irritate.

NUTRIENTS
Calcium, potassium, carotenoids, and vitamin C.

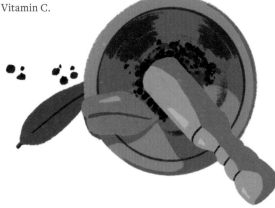

Shrubby blackberry

Rubus fruticosus Aggr.

SEASON
August to October.

HARVESTING AREAS
Glades, woods, hedges, wilderness areas, forest boarders. Shade or sun.

DESCRIPTION
Subshrub 1 to 8 feet (0.3 to 2.5 m), invasive, with leaves that fall in autumn or are semi-evergreen and thorny. Stems with hairless leaves, with curved prickles and formed by three or five leaflets that spread out from a common point. The stalk and central veins of the leaf have small prickles. The inflorescence is a cluster of white or pink flowers.

IN COOKING
The plant is almost entirely edible. The fruits, blackberries, are black and shiny when ripe and sweet and tangy. Consumed raw in fruit salads, juices, and sorbets. Cooked in tarts or jams. The flowers smell and taste like rose; the stems are crunchy. When raw, the shoots have a flavor close to butter, but when cooked, they reveal a blackberry flavor.

NUTRIENTS
Manganese, vitamins E, K₁, and C.

Dandelion

Taraxacum spp.

SEASON
Year-round (optimally in March).

HARVESTING AREAS
Meadows, pastures, roadsides, in sun or partial shade.

DESCRIPTION
A plant that is often hairless and with a white latex, 2 inches to 1½ feet (5 to 40 cm), without a stem. It has typical leaves that are triangular and in the shape of a "lion's tooth" (*dent de lion* in French) and arranged in a "rosette" along the ground. The "flower" of the dandelion is a group of small yellow inflorescences.

IN COOKING
It's a fully edible plant. When raw, dandelion has a certain bitterness that goes away when cooked. The cooked leaves are very soft. The flowers, even when consumed raw, are not very bitter. The cooked roots have a flavor close to Jerusalem artichoke. When raw, the leaves are eaten in salads. They can be cooked in soups, omelets, or vegetable pâtés. The roots can be panfried or roasted to substitute for coffee.

NUTRIENTS
Vitamins K₁, A, C, E, iron, and potassium.

Black elderberry

Sambucus nigra L.

SEASON
July to September.

HARVESTING AREAS
Thickets, woods, hedges, banks, wilderness areas, near populated areas.

DESCRIPTION
A shrub with spreading branches. The branches are covered with many bumps. The leaves are made up of five to seven toothed leaflets. When crinkled, they have an unpleasant musky smell. The fruits are small spherical berries that are black and full of a dark purple juice when ripe.

IN COOKING
When raw they are toxic. When cooked in jams, jellies, or spicy sweet-and-sour sauces (chutney), the fruits have a tangy flavor of red fruits that are very slightly sweet. The flowers have a taste close to lychee. They are cooked in beignets, syrups, and added to beverages.

NUTRIENTS
Potassium, calcium, vitamins B₂, B₉, and C.

Stinging nettle

Urtica dioica L.

SEASON
Spring and early autumn (young shoots), preferably before flowering.

HARVESTING AREAS
Uncultivated soils (ditches, clearings, wilderness areas, etc.).

DESCRIPTION
A perennial 5 to 7 feet (1.5 to 2 m), dark green, covered with rough stinging hairs and grows in beds. Green or burgundy square stem. Flowers are inconspicuous and somewhat green.

IN COOKING
When fresh, the young raw leaves are rendered harmless by several soakings in lemon water and have a taste close to cucumber. After drying, they have a flavor close to seaweed. The leaves are eaten raw in salads, herb juices, gazpacho, or pesto, or cooked to enrich fillings, tarts, and gratins.

NUTRIENTS
Vitamin C and E, calcium, iron, potassium, and magnesium.

Littleleaf linden

Tilia cordata Mill.

SEASON
April to July.

HARVESTING AREAS
Woods and forests in deep, low-acid, semi-shaded soil.

DESCRIPTION
A large tree (66 to 100 feet/20 to 30 m), rounded and uniform, that loses its leaves in fall. The bark is gray-green, smooth and shiny, not very thick. In older plants, it becomes gray-brown and develops long cracks. The leaves are green and heart shaped with fine-toothed edges.

IN COOKING
All linden trees are edible. Raw leaves are eaten in salads. They have little taste but a melt-in-the-mouth consistency thanks to the molecules they contain, called mucilage.

NUTRIENTS
Laxative properties.

SKIP TO
Île-de-France Terroir, p. 20; Paris in the Soup, p. 266.

Claude Jolly, also known as Claude Lebey
(1923–2017)

A Gastronomic Tour Guide

Growing up in Paris's chic neighborhoods, Claude Lebey lived seemingly a thousand lives as an industrialist, gastronome, publisher, producer, food critic, and visionary. —VINCENT BRENOT

The Parisian publisher

In the 1970s, he published, along with Robert Laffont, the legendary collection *Les recettes originales de*, bringing together the greatest names, including Alain Chapel, Joël Robuchon, Pierre Gagnaire, Alain Senderens. He also published *Michel Guérard's Cuisine minceur*, by Michel Guérard, translated into thirteen languages with more than a million copies in print. For nearly forty years, he was one of the most prolific gastronomic publishers.

The Lebey Guide

In 1987, Claude Jolly launched *Le Guide Lebey*, a review reference for Parisian restaurants and bistros. He was the first to integrate the description and date of the last meal eaten in the noted establishment. He dined at nearly five hundred Parisian restaurants and bistros each year to establish these guides, which are still referenced today. *Le Guide Lebey des restaurants de Paris et sa banlieue* was sold in 2011 to two partners, Gérald de Roquemaurel and Pierre-Yves Chupin.

"Eat little, but eat fat. Only fat has flavor."

His chefs and artisans

› **Yannick Alléno,** for sauces.
› **Alain Senderens,** for food and wine pairings.
› **Yves Camdeborde,** for the bistro revival.
› **Jean-Luc Poujauran,** the baker who made individual breads for him encapsulating a beautiful truffle.
› **Pierre Gagnaire,** for everything else . . .

The club goer

1966
Membership in the Club des Cent.

1981
Creation of the Club des Croqueurs de chocolat (Chocolate Eaters).

1987
Creation of the Amateurs de cigares de Havane (Havana Cigar Lovers Club).

1990
Creation of the Club des Amis des Bistrots (Friends of Bistros).

1999
Creation of l'Association pour la sauvegarde de l'oeuf mayonnaise (Association for Safeguarding the Oeuf Mayonnaise).

HIS HISTORIC MOMENT

In 1975, Valéry Giscard d'Estaing awarded the Legion of Honor to Paul Bocuse. For lunch, Bocuse's VGE soup (vegetables and black truffles), created for the occasion, and canard Claude Jolly (duck) by Michel Guérard, were served.

His food obsessions

› **Oeuf mayonnaise** from Parisian bistros.
› **Joël Thiébault's vegetables** from the market on avenue du Président-Wilson (Paris 16th).
› **The club sandwiches** of the luxury-hotel restaurants (*palaces*) located on the Right Bank.
› **The ganaches** of Robert Linxe.
› **Peking duck** from Chez Vong (Paris 1st).
› **Picard Surgelé's délice aux amandes** (with an old tawny port).
› **Caviar** from Kaviari.
› **Parisian gnocchi** from Lillo (Paris 16th).

CHRONOLOGY

1942
Involvement in the Resistance.

1968
First steps as a food critic (*Adam*, *Paris-Match*, *L'Express*, *Gault & Millau*).

1974
Producer of the show *La Grande Cocotte* on TF1, presented by Michel Guérard.

1975
Beginning of his career in publishing (Éditions Robert Laffont and Albin Michel).

1987
Creation of *Les Guides Lebey*.

1990–2012
Involvement in *L'Inventaire du patrimoine culinaire de la France*, a twenty-two-volume series documenting the culinary traditions of France's provinces and territories.

SKIP TO
Caviar Dynasties, p. 205; Parisian Gnocchi, p. 235; Egg with Mayo, p. 262.

Through Doisneau's Eyes

Over the course of his travels and his culinary friendships, the famous photographer playfully depicted the belly of Paris. —MARIELLE GAUDRY

Robert Doisneau

Born in Gentilly (Val-de-Marne) in 1912, died in Montrouge (Hauts-de-Seine) in 1994.

Self-portrait, Villejuif, 1949.

A "fisherman of images"

"I walked tirelessly on the cobblestones and asphalt of Paris, crisscrossing the city in all directions, for half a century."

After World War II, Doisneau focused on the commoners of Paris, capturing moments of happiness in everyday life. This "patient passerby" photographed workers, street vendors, and barflies at all hours and with profound human expression, depicting scenes that reveal striking truths within the context of food.

Sandwich vendor at the door of a café in the Les Halles district, 1960, Paris.

Old man looking at a calf's head hanging from the display of a butcher shop in the Les Halles district of Paris in 1949.

The Two Roberts

French journalist and poet Robert Giraud* and Robert Doisneau told the story of the clochard life in postwar Paris, its bistros, streets, and nighttime underground of wine and drink through their words and photography. These two Roberts maintained a solid (and fluid) friendship, which began at the counter of a *bistro-tabac* (*a bistro that sells tobacco*) where they were regulars among a cheerful lot that included the Prévert brothers and musician and actor Maurice Baquet.

"Funny for a bar manager, you think! and look! Boutanches [old bottles] *loaded in front, behind, left, right, on the ground, on the sides, he can keep the pace and go the distance. Watching the water in his sink that a leaking tap could overflow, he dips his glasses in it that he rinses and fills on request, with seemingly little effort. Curious, these wine barrels that he occasionally pampers with a casual cloth. Imagine a large glass as thick as a crystal ashtray and possessing, like him, a powerful magnifying power, giving the impression of having a comfortable ration of fuel oil when in fact there is none."*

*Robert Giraud, *Le Vin des rues*, preface by Robert Doisneau, Paris, Éditions Denoël, 1955.

SKIP TO
The History of the Belly of the Capital, p. 113.

Forts [strongmen] of Les Halles taking a break at the café Cartalade, 23, rue des Halles, Paris, 1953.

CHEZ L'AMI LOUIS

A bistro as iconic as it is mysterious, L'Ami Louis is the friend some love to hate.
—FRANÇOIS-RÉGIS GAUDRY

MAISON PARISIENNE
32, RUE DU VERTBOIS,
3RD ARR.

Antoine Magnin.

32 CHEZ L'AMI LOUIS 32

Legendary bistro

With its dark wood facade and its gingham curtains, this sixty-seat hidden bistro on a quiet street near Place de la République is one of the most famous in the city. And yet the bistro discreetly welcomes some of the world's greatest personalities.

5 key dates

- **1924**
  Chef Louis Pedeboscq from Gers opens his bistro.
- **1936**
  Antoine Magnin, Swiss chef at La Tour d'Argent, becomes chef de cuisine and soon becomes a partner in the business, then owner in 1952.
- **1978**
  Louis Gadby becomes its director and charismatic figurehead.
- **1985**
  Antoine Magnin leaves and the restaurant is bought by the Ludéric group (still the owner today) with Louis Gadby.
- **2000**
  Louis Gadby retires but continues to watch over the bistro.

You either love it or hate it

L'Ami Louis doesn't just have friends. It is the "worst restaurant in the world," according to A. A. Gill, the famous British food critic, in *Vanity Fair* in 2011. The article attacked the bistro for its gargantuan dishes and sky-high prices, such as the three (huge) slices of foie gras as a starter: €70. In 1963, the *Guide Julliard* quoted the fresh duck liver with grapes copiously served for the modest sum of nineteen francs (a fortune at that time).

The wine cellar

The cellar contains all the important vintages, between fourteen thousand and nineteen thousand bottles, of which ten thousand are opened every year. L'Ami Louis has relationships with the greatest producers: Jean-Louis Chave, Clos Rougeard, and Romanée-Conti, to name a few.

President Chirac and his wife at dinner with the Clintons, June 16, 1999.

The *ami* of American celebrities

> **Art Buchwald,** a famous American journalist stationed in Paris in the postwar period, wrote several columns that introduced the restaurant to Hollywood and the world of American politics and business.
> On June 16, 1999, **Jacques Chirac**, a regular, accompanied by his wife, Bernadette, dined with the Clintons. **Bill Clinton** has returned eleven times since then.
> American stars **Johnny Depp** and **Tim Burton** asked for the table under the clock.
> In the early 2000s, **Francis Ford Coppola** invited the restaurant crew to come and cook at his house for ten days. His daughter, Sofia, was a regular.

The famous poulet frites

Farmstead chicken from Burgundy is roasted to order in goose fat, served whole, accompanied by the gâteau de pommes de terre (a baked terrine of potato) Béarnaise or their impressive mountain of shoestring fries. Price in 2022: €118.

Inspired sneakers

In 2015, Nike and Fragment Design created a limited-edition sneaker whose gray-and-white checkered pattern was inspired by the pattern of the restaurant's floor, one of the favorites of Hiroshi Fujiwara, founder of the Fragment label. The Nike Hyperchase Geometric is available for €135.

🔍 TO SEE

The waiters (only men) in white suits and black ties.

Coatracks fixed 7 feet (2 m) from the floor, where Louis Gadby skillfully throws customers' jackets.

🍴 TO TRY

The baba soaked in more than just rum, poured generously at the table.

Snails: a plate of twelve large.

The bread, almost a whole baguette, served cut, toasted, and accompanied by a block of butter.

SKIP TO
Fries Forever!, p. 142;
Bistros, p. 352.

Herring Recipes

Abundant and cheap, *Clupea harengus* fished in the Atlantic lands in Parisian bistros. —CHARLES PATIN O'COOHOON

HARENG PORTIÈRE (HERRING WITH MUSTARD)

Season: winter
Difficulty ●○○

SERVES 4

⅔ cup (75 g) all-purpose flour

4 fresh herrings (9 ounces/250 g each)

9 tablespoons (125 g) unsalted butter, cubed and chilled

2 tablespoons mustard

Salt and freshly ground black pepper

Fresh herring is prepared with mustard in this favorite dish of Parisian portières (doormen).

Flour the herring with a little more than ⅓ cup (50 g) of the flour. Fry them in a tablespoon of butter over medium heat for 5 minutes on each side.

Make a roux: In a saucepan set over low heat, combine 1½ tablespoons (25 g) of the butter and the remaining flour. Off the heat, stir in the mustard and remaining butter. Season with salt and pepper. Spoon the sauce over the herrings.

HARENG POMME À L'HUILE (HERRING IN OIL WITH POTATOES)

Season: year-round
Difficulty ●○○

SERVES 4

8 smoked herring fillets

2 carrots

2 white onions

1 teaspoon coriander seeds

1 teaspoon cumin seeds

2 cups (500 ml) grapeseed oil

1¾ pounds (800 g) Roseval potatoes or similar waxy potato

Salt

1 tablespoon white wine

¼ bunch chives

Freshly ground black pepper

Starting in the nineteenth century in Paris, herring could be found cooked in oil and served with potatoes.

Cut the herring fillets on an angle into ¾-inch (2 cm) pieces. Peel and slice the carrots. Peel the onions, slice them, and separate them into rings.

In a lidded container, place the herring, carrots, onions, and coriander and cumin seeds. Add the oil, close the container, and refrigerate overnight to marinate.

The next day, cook the unpeeled potatoes for 25 minutes in boiling salted water. Peel the cooked potatoes and slice them into ⅔-inch (1.5 cm) rounds. Drizzle with the white wine. Season with salt and pepper and let cool.

In a serving dish, arrange the potatoes, herring (drained after removing from the marinade; reserve the marinade), carrots, and onion rings. Drizzle with some of the marinade, sprinkle with chives, and serve.

Herring merchant, late nineteenth century.

SAINT HARENC, THE GLORIOUS MARTYR

This joyful sermon from the fifteenth century humorously tells of the martyrdom of a herring from the time it is caught to when it's plated up in Paris.

"In Dieppe was his hanged body. | There came a stunned yurongue, | Around midnight, by candlelight | Who carried him to the tavern | On the grill he was put to roast | And then the gourmand without fail | Ate him bones and all | The others upon horses | led them where, in Paris | . . . | in barrels of salt | Such there were who burned him | All alive, of which it was a great pity for which never was made such an outrage | . . . | For he was put in smoke | Hanged as a thief | And next eaten with watercress | In vinegar and mustard | . . . | this saint of whom we speak | Was put with onions."

THE HERRING BANDWAGON

Because it was easy to preserve, herring was one of the first kinds of seafood to be consumed by the populations of the north. The arrival of the Vikings on the French coast increased the fishing and consumption of herring (which at the time was abundant). In the eighteenth century, herring became a currency of exchange. In Paris, they even paid for barrels of wine with it.

Le Rubis
⚲ 14, rue Léopold-Bellan, Paris 2nd. €
This bistro serves hareng pomme à l'huile in excellent quality oil, lending it a silky and melting texture.

Flora Danica
⚲ 142, av. des Champs-Élysées, Paris 8th. €€
This legendary Danish brasserie offers a variation of herring with dill, curry, and spices.

Bar à Hareng
Present at various Parisian food markets since 2009, this establishment cooks herring in all its forms: smoked, in salads, rollmops, etc.
For more information, see *Facebook.com/baraharengs*.

SKIP TO
Fries Forever!, p. 142 ; Bistros, p. 352; Seafood Spots, p. 364.

Tastes and Distastes

Shot in the heart of Paris in 1973, *La Grande Bouffe* was one of the most scandalous films in the history of French cinema. This is a behind-the-scenes look at a Parisian movie that became a permanent restaurant.

—LAURENT DELMAS

An Italian-Parisian plot

In this satirical film about the decadence of the bourgeoisie, Italian writer and director Marco Ferreri tells the tale of suicide by overeating of four friends, played by Michel Piccoli, Philippe Noiret, Marcello Mastroianni, and Ugo Tognazzi. The movie takes place in a hôtel particulier (a private urban home) located at 68, rue Boileau, in the 16th arrondissement, a location that was demolished shortly after the film's release.

The origins of the film

Director Bertrand Tavernier recounts that in the 1970s, Ferreri, musician Philippe Sarde, and his brother Alain, a producer, would meet for copious lunches at Brasserie Prunier. "They were always afraid of missing out and would order dishes nonstop." One day, their lunch continued into dinner at the brothers' home, where comedian Ugo Tognazzi was also present. They soon invited over prostitutes. When Marco Ferreri woke up, he realized their day of debauchery and excess would be the perfect setup for a movie.

Luxury treatment

The production company entrusted the famous luxury French foods company Fauchon with providing the food each day during filming. "Quality food," said Philippe Noiret in an interview, who remembered the delivery trucks arriving in a convoy each morning. In April 1973, as noted on the film's scheduling sheet, the shooting began each day with a delivery of the following:

ACCESSORIES AND FOODS READY AT 8 O'CLOCK

- 3 roast turkeys
- 5 kilos of bread
- 1 kilo of caviar
- 6 bottles of Bordeaux
- 1 croquembouche
- Tomato sauce
- Chestnut purée
- Polenta
- 6 duck livers
- Cut of beef
- 10 brioches
- 1 bottle of blackcurrant syrup
- 3 strawberry pies
- 1 bunch of bananas
- 1 liter of Chantilly cream
- 1 pot of flageolet beans
- Chocolate mousse

Well equipped

Ferreri frequently sought culinary advice from Giuseppe Maffioli, an Italian actor, writer, and gastronome who appeared in the film. French chef Jacques Quelennec assisted him. The film's unprecedented and monstrous undertaking required such gastronomic and culinary talents to accomplish.

Playing It Up?

Many years after the film was released, Michel Piccoli somewhat downplayed the orgiastic scope of the film: "We cheated a lot! We ate less than it appeared. Ferreri often took only one take. The quantities of food were eventually reduced!" The fact remains that the film shot multiple scenes of a friendly competition mingling oyster eating, a dome of Saint-Pierre in foie gras, various mousses and pâtés, and a huge pair of pink gelatin breasts among other delicacies.

SKIP TO
When Hollywood Dines in Paris, p. 286.

The "Fifth Quarter" of Paris

The capital likes to spill its guts! Here is an overview of Paris's "fifth quarter" tradition, from head to tail.

—NICOLAS D'ESTIENNE D'ORVES

The Parisian tripe merchant of the lower classes

Gervaise, the heroine in *L'Assommoir*, exhausts herself at work while her husband, Coupeau, and his former lover Lantier lead the good life at her expense, revealing the preferred spots for offal for special occasions among the Parisian proletariat of the nineteenth century:

"They went, at Grande-Rue des Batignolles, to eat Caen-style tripe, which was served to them on small hot burners. . . . Rue des Martyrs, Les Lilas had tête de veau [calf's head] as a specialty; while, on chaussée Clignancourt, the restaurants Lion d'Or and Les Deux Marronniers made them sautéed kidneys that made them lick their lips." —Émile Zola, *L'Assommoir*, 1877

The Offal Academy

In Paris, a secretive and gourmet brotherhood has been meeting since the mid-1980s and challenges chefs to step up their game when it comes to preparing tripe. The brotherhood hosts two historic summits: a lunch of fish offal at Michel Rostang, Paris 17th (monkfish bladder, whole cod head, etc.), and another of horse offal, previously at the now-closed Le Taxi Jaune in the Marais (horse brain fritters, foal heart, etc.).

Saint Anthony's temptation.

What a dish

Although not specifically a Parisian tripe preparation, the *"tentation de Saint Anthony"* (Saint Anthony's temptation), whose name pays tribute to the patron saint of butchers, is a one-of-a-kind dish: Breaded pig's ear, tail, snout, and foot, served with fries and a Béarnaise sauce. It's a real slap in the face to any animal lover! Au Pied de Cochon has served it to die-hard meat lovers since 1947, an impressive span of time (6, rue Coquillière, Paris 1st).

Places of the past

These bygone tripe sellers will be missed. RIP the Lyonnaise tripe entrées at Moissonnier, rue des Fossés-Saint-Bernard (5th); the tripe at Chez Grenouille, rue Blanche (9th); the snout and testicles at Ribouldingue, rue Saint-Julien-le-Pauvre (5th); the fried breaded tripe at l'Auberge Pyrénées Cévennes (when Françoise was there), rue de la Folie-Méricourt (11th).

Tripe in 5 dates

- **1096**
  The first tripe seller opens at Châtelet.
- **1292**
  The profession of *tripier* (tripe merchant) is listed for the first time in the Paris tax register.
- **1830**
  The tripiers have the right to sell veal offal, until that time reserved exclusively for butchers.
- **1853–1874**
  Creation of the Baltard tripe pavilions.
- **1973**
  The Parisian tripiers move to Rungis to a 30,000-square-foot (2,800 sq m) pavilion.

TOP
LET'S EAT PARIS!
ADDRESSES

FROM THE FOOD STALL . . .

Triperie Vadorin
176, *rue Lecourbe, Paris 15th*
As a worthy successor to Maurice Vadorin, Proba Sivasamboo runs the last tripe stall in Paris and supplies the capital's starred restaurants.

. . . TO THE TABLE

Au Veau Qut Tête
2, *rue de l'Aubrac, Rungis.* €€
The restaurant at the tripe pavilions in Rungis.

Aux Lyonnais
32, *rue Saint-Marc, Paris 2nd.* €€
This chef-driven bouchon (a Lyonnaise easy-style bistro) cooks the fifth quarter from ears (pork) to brains (veal).

Chez Marcel
7, *rue Stanislas, Paris 6th.* €€€
Andouillettes, tripe, brains, calf's head, pig's ears . . . Pierre Cheucle celebrates the fifth quarter in all its forms.

Le Beaucé
43, *rue Richer, Paris 9th.* €€
From the cervelle (brains) meunière to the crispy sweetbreads, Marius Bénard has made offal a signature dish of his bistro.

Let's not confuse . . .

Red offal, which is pure and untouched (liver, kidney, tongue, brains, sweetbread, cheek, etc.) with white offal, which has been scalded, stiffened, or precooked (rumen, reticulum, foot, head, etc.).

SKIP TO
Les Halles: The Belly of Paris, p. 113.

Alexandre Balthazar Laurent Grimod de la Reynière (1758–1837)

The Father of Gourmands

This eccentric jack-of-all-trades was Paris's first gastronomic critic.

—CAROLINE POULAIN

"We will then, in Paris, make some *nutritive walks*, and stop with complacency in the most interesting stores that arouse the appetite with their assortments and reasonable prices."

—*Almanach des gourmands*, 1804, 3rd ed., preface

MASTER CRAYFISH
Grimod was born with deformed hands, a handicap that seems to have influenced his personality. Much was written to describe the deformity—stumps, webbed hands, claws, and talons—and he referred to himself in a self-mocking way as "Master Crayfish."

"This little book has become the *Handbook of Gourmands*, the delight of the people of the world, and it has even found favor in the eyes of abstinent persons. This was probably the most difficult praise for it to achieve."

—*Almanach des gourmands*, 1807, foreword

Les Rêves d'un Gourmand.

Almanach des gourmands, sixth year.

The *Almanach des gourmands*

With this book, Grimod launched the genre of food, although the book was available only between the years 1803 to 1812. The text contains much more than just reviews, as a large part of it is dedicated to chronicling seasonal products, gastronomic thoughts, and recipes.

"**The village of Montreuil, near Paris, is in possession of sending us the best peaches eaten in France and probably in Europe. . . . La Mignonne is the first peach that appears in Paris, usually at the end of July; but the one known as the Téton de Vénus, which ripens near the end of August, is rightly regarded as the best of all.**"

—*Almanach des gourmands*, 1806

THE GENUS OF THE ALMANAC
Almanacs, in the form of a calendar, provided much in the way of practical information to their readers. They made up a very popular genre of publications in the eighteenth and nineteenth centuries, were published in large quantity, and focused on various themes.

Eating in good company

As part of his almanac, Grimod organized 465 meetings of *"jurys dégustateurs"* (tasting juries). These gourmands met at his home on rue des Champs-Élysées where they tasted samples sent by Parisian restaurateurs, pastry chefs, and other food artisans, one after the other, in the order of the services specific to that time, as shown on the menus printed for the occasion. Starting at seven o'clock and for five hours, the guests would discuss the quality of the anonymously presented items. They would then cast a vote before sending their observations to the restaurateurs in the form of a certificate to be displayed in the window.

"Starting from the Porte Saint-Honoré and going up the street of this name, we will begin by greeting No. 55, occupied by Monsieur Benaud, a still little-known pastry chef but who instead deserves to be, considering the extreme lightness of his *biscuit de Savoie*, the finish of his meringues, and the delicacy of his petits-fours."

—*Almanach des gourmands*, 1804, 3rd ed.

Almanach des gourmands, third year.
Séance d'un Jury de Gourmands dégustateurs.

The *Manuel des amphitryons*

After the almanac, Grimod's best-known work was the *Manuel des amphitryons* which, after the Revolution, was intended to "reteach the new *amphitryons* (hosts) and their guests the fine art of savoir-vivre." It included topics on the history of dining, a treatise on meat carving, a labeling system for seasonal menus, and points on etiquette.

Manuel des amphitryons, frontispiece.

"We will restrict ourselves to saying that for fish vendors, for example, it becomes impossible to note trusted shops, because such a person who served you well yesterday may not do so tomorrow. This is why, still full of the memory and smell of a certain head of cod sold on October 27, 1809, by Madame George in one of her oldest practices, we will be careful to bring it to someone's attention tomorrow as a possible pitfall. Good faith is not the virtue of these ladies."

—*Almanach des gourmands*, 1810

Grimod, the Eccentric

His first supper that made headlines occurred in 1783 and reflected his taste for the dramatic. He invited guests with a funeral invitation to sit around a coffin draped in black and discover a series of macabre rituals throughout the meal. This is just one example of his eccentricity, which was also reflected in his clothing choices, his relationships, and his aversion to his parents' good place in society.

Au Rocher de Cancale

This was one of the restaurants that Grimod and high Parisian society loved. Located at the corner of rues Montorgueil and Mandar, Au Rocher de Cancale was renowned for the best oysters, the best seafood, and the best poultry in the capital, as well as its "hot pâté with quail and Malaga wine, worthy of the table of the gods."

SKIP TO Peas à la Française, p. 87; Nicolas Appert, p. 240.

The Parisian Taste for Wine

Paris is not only a mecca for satisfying hunger, but also for satisfying thirst. —ANTOINE GERBELLE

SKIP TO
The Thousand-Year Saga of Île-de-France Wines, p. 78; Renowned Wine Cellars, p. 376.

When the capital dictates trends

Bistros and restaurants have always had a large influence on which regions or appellations are most available throughout the capital.

- **1950s**
  › The Grands Boulevards lean toward Muscadet.
  › Les Halles bistros push Beaujolais.
  › *Bougnats* (coalman/barkeepers) serve Marcillac wines.

- **1970s**
  › Brasseries close to train stations and theaters have a penchant for the reds from the Loire (Chinon) and Saumur-Champigny.
  › Southwest-inspired restaurants go for Cahors under President Pompidou.

- **1980s–1990s**
  › Pizzerias, just as throughout the world, uncork (usually bad) Chianti.
  › Bistros in the east and north sections of Paris promote natural wines.

- **2000s**
  › Bistronomy advocates "everything except Bordeaux": natural wines from Jura, Champagne, Corsica, Beaujolais, Languedoc, Italy, Slovenia, Georgia; natural sparkling wines (*pét' nat'*); and orange wines.

Poster for Beaujolais Nouveau, 1989.

Advertising poster for Nicolas, 1931.

Wine in bottles

"The story begins at the time when wine was drunk on the spot in cabarets or wine shops. If you wanted to consume wine at home, you had to go to a wine merchant or the producer to buy a barrel!" Louis Nicolas, after observing this, invented a concept that revolutionized consumption and trade: bottled wine. Opened in 1822, Maison Nicolas's main boutique was located at 53, rue Sainte-Anne (Paris 2nd), with three warehouses in the capital. The concept of providing quality wines at a reasonable price established the company's reputation. Today, the Nicolas brand has 312 stores in Île-de-France, including 170 in Paris (out of more than 498 in France).

Bordeaux bashing

Whether done for good or bad reasons, the criticism of wines from the Gironde department, which encompasses Bordeaux, was perceived in the early 2000s as faddish snobbery, practiced by some "*bobo*" (a term to describe bourgeois/bohemian ideals) wine merchants and natural wine bars in east Paris. The indictment of the wines was serious: The wines are "too expensive, too haughty, too woody, too rigid, too uniform, and too technical." However, young consumers have changed their approach to red and white wines, which the region of Bordeaux did not anticipate. Low-intervention wines ("natural" wines) were the new star. This ecologically committed wine is organic, biodynamic, and vinified without sulfur.

LADURÉE

From its beginnings as a small bakery to its achievement as the global emblem of the macaron, this Parisian enterprise has a unique history. — **MORGANE MIZZON**

MAISON PARISIENNE
16, RUE ROYALE,
8TH ARR.

Originally, a boulangerie

In 1862, Louis Ernest Ladurée opened a boulangerie at 16, rue Royale (Paris 1st) in La Madeleine, a business district with luxury shops. Soon after, he added a counter for pastries. In 1871, following a fire, the establishment was renovated by the famous painter and poster artist Jules Chéret, who gave it the look we know today. It became one of the first Parisian salons de thé. The Holder family bought the establishment in 1993 and opened the Champs-Élysées salon and boutique in 1997 before selling the business in 2021 to Stéphane Courbit. The group now has 106 stores worldwide, from the Palace of Versailles to Kyoto in Japan.

TO SEE

The ceiling by Jules Chéret: he was inspired by the Sistine Chapel and the Opéra Garnier to paint a sea of clouds with frolicking cherubs.

The pastry angel: in addition to its wings, this cherub holds a baker's peel. The challenge is to find him in the middle of all his chubby friends.

TO TRY

Macarons: apart from the iconic ones (vanilla, chocolate, and pistachio), the boutiques offer 120 flavors, including the famous Ispahan (rose, raspberry, lychee).

The Parisian flan: a light puff pastry crust filled with a firm cream generously flavored with vanilla.

Some Leading Pastry Chefs

PIERRE HERMÉ
(1996–1998)
Over just two years, he made his mark at Ladurée, notably by creating one of his iconic macarons: the Ispahan.

CLAIRE HEITZLER
(2016–2018)
She modernized and lightened the maison's creations, such as the Mont Blanc, which she embellished with mandarin orange.

JULIEN ALVAREZ
(since 2021)
Awarded World Pastry Champion in 2011, he brings his personal touches by favoring ethically and locally sourced products.

A family history

Louis Ernest Ladurée, miller and baker–pastry chef, born in 1836, opens the establishment's historic boutique.

Ernest Ladurée (son of Louis Ernest) and his wife, Jeanne Souchard, aware that women of the time lacked places to meet in public, created one of the first Parisian salons de thé (tearooms).

Isabelle Ladurée (daughter of Ernest) took over the management of the maison in 1933 upon the death of her father.

Pierre Desfontaines (Louis Ernest's second cousin) took over the business in 1944 and created, in 1960, the macaron as we know it today.

In the movies

Released in 2006, Sofia Coppola's film *Marie Antoinette* is a love letter to Ladurée: pastel colors and pyramids of macarons flood the Palace of Versailles. The only problem is that Marie-Antoinette did not have the opportunity to taste macarons as they didn't come into existence until two centuries after her reign.

SKIP TO
The Macaron, p. 242;
Pastry Shops, p. 312.

Holy Croissant!

As the emblem of Parisian bakeries, the croissant has a history steeped in legends. —MARIE-LAURE FRÉCHET

August Zang's Viennese bakery, 92, rue de Richelieu, Paris 2nd, circa 1840.

The symbol of French breakfast

In the eighteenth century, bourgeois and aristocratic families, upon waking, indulged in "breakfast in a cup," which was coffee or drinking chocolate. The working classes, however, indulged in a hearty meal of soup, or soup and bread, to face their laborious day. Observers of the time (French men of letters Antoine Caillot and Louis-Sébastien Mercier) noted the inclination of the Parisian population to purchase invigorating café au lait from street vendors. The croissant was not introduced into bourgeois breakfasts until the beginning of the twentieth century, as revealed by the habits of Marcel Proust and his characters in *In Search of Lost Time*. The commercial production of pastries in the mid-twentieth century and the popularity of the urban lifestyle elevated the croissant to one of the emblems of French breakfast.

The ancestors

The Egyptians, Assyrians, and Persians made crescent-shaped loaves to glorify their gods. The Ottoman Empire adopted this shape as its emblem before this type of pastry spread throughout the Mediterranean. The origins of today's croissant, the kipferl, in the shape of a crescent, began in the thirteenth century in central and eastern Europe, and also from a later time in Austria, as the Hörnchen (small horn).

The legend

In 1683, during the siege of Vienna by the Turks, the bakers alerted the town to an attack, which was thus repelled. As thanks, Leopold I, Archduke of Austria, granted them privileges. To commemorate the event, the bakers created a pastry in the shape of an Ottoman crescent. Queen Marie Antoinette, from Austria, made the pastry fashionable.

The croissant jambon (croissant with ham)

This savory croissant rivals the croque monsieur. It is traditionally filled with jambon de Paris (ham), cheese, and béchamel.

Its Parisian history

As evidenced by the notation of a Parisian pastry chef who delivered *"quarente gasteaulx en croissans"* (forty cakes as a crescent) for the banquet of Catherine de' Médicis in 1549, crescent-shaped cakes had existed in Paris before the seventeenth century. But it was in 1838 or 1839 that the Austrian August Zang opened the first Viennese bake shop in the capital. The chroniclers of the time praised the quality of his breads and specialties, such as the kipferl, in the shape of a crescent, although made of brioche. Its success was immediate, and the term *croissant* entered the dictionary: *Littré* (1863) then *Larousse* (1869). Armand Husson mentioned, in *Les Consommations de Paris* (1875), "croissants for coffee" among the delicacies of bakeries in 1875, and Joseph Favre noted "heaps of croissants" in storefronts in his *Dictionnaire universel de cuisine pratique* from 1894.

Poster of the café Au Clairon de Plaisance (14th), late nineteenth century.

BUTTER OR ORDINARY

Modern croissants containing more butter cost more. In the 1970s, a less-pricey margarine-based croissant appeared. These were distinguished by their shape: curved for "ordinary" (made with margarine), or straight for "all-butter." But this is a generality, not a requirement. Today, croissants of both types are found in either shape.

"I remember a street in Paris where there were three competing bakers. The first had inscribed on its window 'the best croissant in France,' the second 'the best croissant in Europe,' the third 'the best croissant in the world.' I have a friend who also set up a bakery on the same street. He hit the jackpot. On his window, he wrote 'the best croissant on the street.'"

—Jean Yanne, On n'arrêt pas la connerie, 2014

SKIP TO
Paris Loves Bread, p. 158; Bakeries, p. 308.

THE BEST CROISSANTS IN PARIS

Cédric Grolet Opéra

◈ 35, av. de l'Opéra, Paris 2nd
Appearance: uniform layers.
Interior: perfect honeycomb.
Taste: balanced, slightly caramelized.

Maison Louvard

◈ 11, rue de Châteaudun, Paris 9th
Appearance: rustic.
Interior: dense, with a slight crispiness.
Taste: round and delicate due to the milk starter.

Union Boulangerie

◈ 2, rue Bleue, Paris 9th
Appearance: rounded and regular.
Interior: very honeycombed.
Taste: buttery.

Carton Paris

◈ 6, blvd. de Denain, Paris 10th
Appearance: striped lamination, caramelized crust.
Interior: honeycombed.
Taste: buttery.

Liberté

◈ 39, rue des Vinaigriers, Paris 10th + 4 locations
Appearance: light golden.
Interior: honeycombed.
Taste: balanced.

Sain Boulangerie

◈ 15, rue Marie-et-Louise, Paris 10th
Appearance: layers, slightly overbaked.
Interior: airy, imperfect honeycomb.
Taste: buttery, sourdough note.

Paris & Co

◈ 4, rue de la Convention, Paris 15th
◈ 4 bis, rue des Écoles, Paris 5th
Appearance: caramelized and shiny lamination.
Interior: honeycombed.
Taste: nice and buttery.

Boulangerie Baptiste

◈ 17, rue des Moines, Paris 17th
Appearance: puffed and shiny.
Interior: very honeycombed.
Taste: slight brioche note.

Boulangerie Milligramme

◈ 3–5, rue du Plateau, Paris 19th
Appearance: rustic.
Interior: dense.
Taste: notes of sourdough.

Boulangerie au 140

◈ 140, rue de Belleville, Paris 20th
Appearance: rounded and glossy lamination.
Interior: fluffy.
Taste: caramelized notes.

Grégory Pailliette

◈ 121, av. de Paris, Saint-Mandé (Val-de-Marne)
Appearance: colored lamination.
Interior: airy.
Taste: slightly saline.

Boulangerie Fred

◈ 8, av. du Château, Vincennes (Val-de-Marne)
Appearance: rounded.
Interior: dense.
Taste: buttery.

The Croissant

Recipes date back to the late nineteenth century, with many iterations in existence today.

THE AUTHENTIC PARISIAN CROISSANT

In 1895, *Le Journal des confiseurs-pâtissiers* published the first recipe for a laminated croissant. The dough was turned twice, then shaped into a ball. The croissants were then shaped making an oval of dough rolled onto itself.

The recipe for the original French croissant dates to the 1930s. The dough was more hydrated, less buttery, less yeasted, and either not sweetened at all or sweetened very little, compared to today's croissants.

Special mention goes to Jacky Delplanque for his "true" croissant that he makes in his bakery La Pétrifontaine in Pierrefonds (Oise).

THE CROISSANT TODAY

Starting in the 1960s and 1970s, the French croissant was enriched with sugar and butter. The amount of yeast used also increased. Since the 1990s, the tremendous industrialization of pastries and the addition of additives and flavor enhancers to compensate for freezing have contributed to the loss of flavor of an authentic croissant, which is pending an official label certifying "French tradition croissant" similar to the decree for bread.

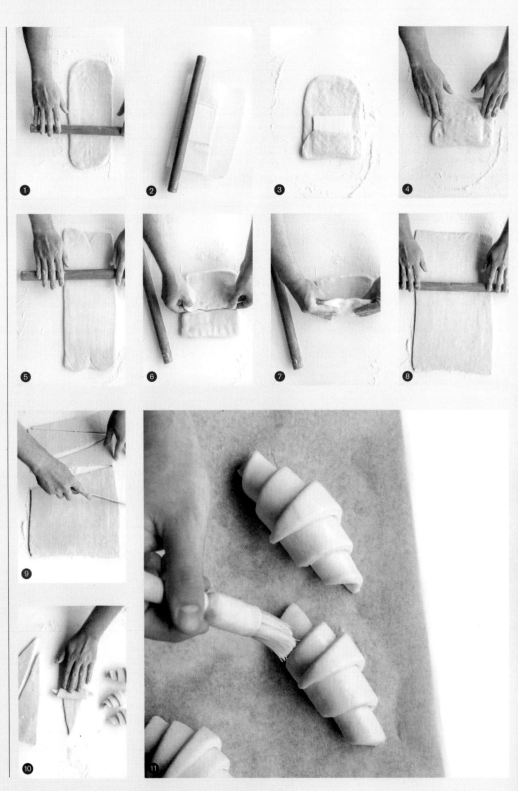

THE RECIPE

Season: year-round **Difficulty** ● ● ●

MAKES 8 CROISSANTS

For the détrempe dough

⅔ cup (80 g) high-protein all-purpose or T65 flour, plus more for dusting

⅔ cup (80 g) soft-wheat flour or pastry flour or T45 flour

2 tablespoons (30 ml) whole milk, cold

1 tablespoon (15 g) sugar

1 teaspoon (5 g) unsalted butter

1 teaspoon (6 g) fresh yeast

1 pinch of salt

Scant ¼ cup (50 ml) water, very cold

For the beurre de tourage (roll-in butter)

6½ tablespoons (90 g) unsalted butter or dry tourage butter (high-fat unsalted butter) in a square, cold

For the glazing

1 large (50 g) egg, lightly beaten

Using her nineteenth-century mixer, baker Florence Abelin* fashions an impeccable croissant that can be made at home. Take out your rolling pins!

Make the détrempe dough: In the bowl of a stand mixer fitted with the dough hook, place the flours, milk, sugar, butter, yeast, salt, and water. Turn the mixer speed to low speed (speed 1), then increase to speed 2 and knead for 15 minutes, or until the dough detaches from the sides of the bowl. Cover, and let stand for 20 minutes at room temperature.

On a floured work surface, roll out the dough to a rectangle measuring 12 by 8 inches (30 by 20 cm) and about ⅓ to 1 inch (1 to 2 cm) thick ❶. Wrap the dough in plastic wrap and refrigerate overnight.

Make the tourage butter: The next day, place the butter square inside a folded sheet of parchment paper. Using a nontapered rolling pin, pound the butter to soften it, turning it frequently. With the butter square still wrapped in the parchment paper, roll it out into a rectangle measuring 8 by 6 inches (20 by 15 cm) and ⅓ inch (1 cm) thick ❷.

Remove the détrempe dough from the refrigerator and set it aside to reach room temperature. Place the tourage butter in the middle of the dough, without handling the butter too much. Fold the bottom one-fourth and the top one-fourth of the dough over the butter square, bringing the dough together edge to edge in the center without overlapping it ❸. Gently press the edges together with your fingertips to seal the butter in completely ❹.

Turn the butter-dough package over seam side down and roll it out starting from the center to the edges to over a length of 24 inches (60 cm) ❺. When the package has been rolled out to half this length, turn it seam side up and continue.

Make a double turn: fold one-fourth of the dough from each end in toward the center without letting the edges overlap ❻. Seal the edges together by gently pressing with your fingertips. Fold the dough

package in half (to close like a book) ❼. Slightly flatten the dough with the rolling pin and turn the dough package one quarter turn so the folded edge is on the left side (like a book). Roll it out starting from the center to the outside edges to over a length of 24 inches (60 cm) without increasing its width. Fold it to make a second double turn and place it in the freezer for 45 minutes.

Make the croissants: Remove the dough from the freezer. Make another double turn, then roll the dough to a thickness of 1⅓ inch (3.5 cm) to make a rectangle 15¾ by 9¾ inches (40 by 25 cm) ❽. Cut out 8 croissants (long triangles), making them equal size ❾. Relax the dough by slightly pulling on it from the pointed end with your hands to stretch it.

Roll up the croissants without tightening them ❿ and place them staggered on a parchment paper–lined baking sheet. Brush the croissants with the beaten egg ⓫, then set them aside to rise in a warm place (always below 80°F/27°C to prevent the butter from leaking out), covered, for 2 hours. When the croissants have risen, preheat the oven to 325°F (170°C) convection heat. Brush them again with the beaten egg, and bake for 16 minutes, lowering the position of the baking sheet in the oven and reducing the temperature if they begin to brown too quickly. Set aside on a rack to cool.

*Boulangerie Milligramme,
3–5 rue du Plateau, Paris 19th.

> **"I took a second croissant. She preferred toast with jam and butter. It is true that France is divided. There are those who prefer toast and those who prefer croissants."**
>
> —Émile Ajar/Romain Gary,
> *L'Angoisse du roi Salomon,*
> 1979

The Club des Cent
Club of One Hundred

Every Thursday for more than a century, members of this secret society have celebrated their love of gastronomy together around the dinner table. —ESTELLE LENARTOWICZ

Banquet of the Club des Cent, Paris, 1923.

A rolling affair

Founded in 1912 by motorists of upper-crust circles, members would share their best food-centric addresses they discovered along France's roadways. At the time, travelers who were lucky enough to afford travel by car around the country struggled to find quality lodging and food establishments.

Menu of the forty-sixth dinner at Maxim's.

Gastro-diplomacy

Since the club's beginnings, its sophisticated patriots have worked to defend French excellence on the international stage, especially on the eve of the Great War against their German rivals. The tradition endured during the conflict, becoming a discreet club for promoting French gastronomy within society's upper echelons. The club worked toward inclusion of the "French gastronomic meal" on UNESCO's Intangible Cultural Heritage list.

At the table of one hundred

Some of its big bosses: Martin Bouygues, Patrick Ricard, Robert Peugeot, and Éric Frachon.

Some of its aristocrats: Jean de Luxembourg, Éric de Rothschild, Albert II of Monaco.

Personalities from the press and arts and letters: Erik Orsenna, Philippe Bouvard, Claude Imbert, Nicolas d'Estienne d'Orves, Bernard Pivot, Pierre Arditi, Guillaume Gallienne.

Politicians: Jean-Pierre Raffarin, Xavier Darcos.

Food critics and Michelin-starred chefs (who are exempt from the entrance exams): Curnonsky, Henri Gault, Christian Millau, Paul Bocuse, Joël Robuchon, Alain Ducasse, Bernard Pacaud, and Jean-Pierre Vigato.

Becoming a member

❶ IT'S A BOYS CLUB
Women are not officially excluded and can therefore, in principle, apply. Yet this has never happened, except in the 1930s, when one woman did apply who would have been the club's only-ever female member.

❷ CO-OPTATION
Sponsorship of two club members is required to apply. The jury also ensures, as much as possible, the diversity in ages and professional backgrounds of its members.

❸ "LE GRAND ORAL"
This is an essential, and feared, oral exam for membership. The test consists of being "cooked" by a jury of eighteen members responsible for testing both food and wine knowledge and the qualities of manners and conversation of the candidate. "A tribunal of the Inquisition!"

according to Bernard Pivot, admitted in 1993. On average, nine out of ten candidates are rejected.

Past questions asked during "le grand O"

Do you prefer Bordeaux or Burgundy? What is the difference between a gourmet meal and a gourmand meal? Which bean should I choose to make a haricot de mouton? What is ziste? What wine should you serve with asparagus? Which poet of the early twentieth century was very adept at preparing tête de veau?

❹ THE TRAINEE PERIOD
This lasts until a membership becomes available.

❺ INDUCTION
Each "centiste" gets a membership number at the end of their trainee period. Except in unusual cases (such as absenteeism, as was the case with Christian Clavier), membership is for life.

Club des Cent

21, Rue Montmartre – (1ᵉ Arrᵗ)
Tél : Gut. 52-47

Thursday lunch

Each Thursday from 12:40 to 2:30 p.m. the group sits down for a ritual lunch in a restaurant in the capital or one of the surrounding suburbs. A member, called the "brigadier," is chosen, in turn, to select the menu and wines. At the end of the meal, a previously selected member is chosen to present a "fair and witty" critic of the meal. Each year, the benevolent members choose the most brilliant among them to be rewarded with a prize for Critic and Presentation.

SKIP TO
Maxim's, p. 82;
Curnonsky, p. 276.

Navarin d'Agneau
Lamb Stew

A tasty dish with a not-so-distant name. —SACHA LOMNITZ

THE RECIPE

Season: spring to summer
Difficulty ●○○

SERVES 6

2 large yellow onions

5 tomatoes

3½ pounds (1.5 kg) lamb (shoulder, neck, top rib)

Olive oil, for sautéing

Salt and freshly ground black pepper

1 tablespoon flour

3 cups (750 ml) vegetable broth, warmed

1 bouquet garni

12 cloves garlic, peeled

4 carrots (or 8 spring carrots)

4 turnips (or 8 spring turnips)

4 potatoes (preferably Charlotte variety)

This is a no-fuss, family-style recipe that is even better with the season's first vegetables.

Peel and slice the onions. Immerse the tomatoes for 1 minute in a pot of boiling water. Remove the tomato skins and cut the flesh into pieces. Set aside.

Cut the lamb into 1½-inch (4 cm) cubes. Brown them in olive oil in a skillet. Season with salt and pepper.

In a saucepan, sauté the sliced onions in a little olive oil. Add the browned meat. Sprinkle with the flour and stir to evenly distribute the flour. Add the hot broth. Add the tomatoes, bouquet garni, and garlic. Simmer for about 2 hours over low heat, uncovered.

Peel the carrots, turnips, and potatoes and cut them into medium-size pieces. Place them in the pan on top of the pieces of meat 30 minutes before the end of the cooking time. Check for doneness (the meat should be tender), and adjust the seasoning, if necessary.

Arrange the pieces of meat in a serving dish. Spoon the vegetables around the meat. Top with some of the cooking liquid and serve.

The fresh produce grocers' square, Les Halles, Paris, circa 1900.

NOT FROM NAVARRE, OR GREECE, BUT PARIS!

The introduction of the term *navarin* in gastronomy most likely traces to Antonin Carême in his work *L'Art de la cuisine française au xixᵉ siècle* (*The Art of French Cuisine in the Nineteenth Century*) from 1828. This term referred to the Bay of Navarino in Greece, which was the scene of a naval battle six years earlier and referred to recipes cooked in Champagne.

In Parisian casual eateries, *navarin* was a slang word for the turnip used in stews. For rather pretentious reasons, the stew would be described in a more swanky way as à la Navarin and in an even more snobby way as plat d'agneau aux navets (lamb with turnips).

"The slice of veal cushion, lying pale on its bed of sorrel, and the dubious navarin [the extras] wait for them at the local brasserie."

—Colette, *Music-hall*, 1913

THE TURNIP

Turnips (*Brassica rapa*) were a root vegetable consumed daily by Parisians until the potato made its appearance. Once demoted in the French diet to a commodity for the poor and to be eaten only in times of scarcity, the turnip today figures prominently in the capital's food market stalls. A turnip soup from Freneuse (Yvelines) was served to the 150 heads of state who gathered in Paris in 2015 on the occasion of COP 21, the world climate conference.

SKIP TO
Île-de-France Terroir, p. 20; Antonin Carême, p. 156; Paris in the Soup, p. 266.

The Goldsmiths Who Set Our Tables

From the noblest tables to bourgeois tables, Parisian goldsmiths left their lasting mark on tableware.

—MARIE-LAURE FRÉCHET

An elite profession since the Middle Ages

Goldsmithing was a prosperous and renowned profession in Paris during the Middle Ages, as artisans fashioned precious metals into luxury items that became the treasures for churches and noble families. More than five hundred of these professionals were established on the Île de la Cité and in the Marais. The profession was regulated, including the quality of the gold and silver used. Louis XIV reformed their status in 1679 by restricting their number to three hundred, and he imposed the rule that only one master artist out of two could hand down the know-how from father to son. During the nineteenth century, grand goldsmithing houses began to appear with the advent of the bourgeoisie classes. Only a few survive today.

QUAI DES ORFÈVRES Located between Pont Saint-Michel and Pont-Neuf, this quay is so named because, as soon as it was completed in 1643, about fifty tableware and jewelry craftsmen and merchants set up shop here. Most of these businesses moved when the quay was overhauled in 1810. In 1871, the Paris police criminal investigation division moved into the iconic building of the Palais de Justice at the now-famous address 36, quai des Orfèvres (Paris 1st), which acts as the backdrop in many French movies and TV shows today.

Never without their hallmarks

THE GUARANTEE HALLMARK

The hallmark for each of these artisans is affixed by the governmental organization that guarantees the precious metal content of the object. Since 1838, the silver guarantee hallmark has been the head of Minerva facing right.

THE SILVERSMITH'S MARK

Example of a hallmark

The manufacturer applies its hallmark to the object. According to the law of 19 Brumaire year VI (November 9, 1797), the craftsman's initial and a symbol for each manufacturer is to be placed inside a diamond. The symbol may also include the location where the object was created, such as done with knives, and the signature of the craftsman.

Maison Christofle

📍 *9, rue Royale, Paris 8th*

- **1830**
Born into a family of industrialists specializing in precious metals, Charles Christofle takes over the family jewelry manufacturing business.

- **1832**
He creates his hallmark and moves to rue de Bondy (now rue René-Boulanger, Paris 10th) to make jewelry and, starting in 1844, becomes a goldsmith.

- **1851**
With his silver and goldsmithing patents in hand, he assures the company's reputation thanks to an order of four thousand pieces for Napoléon III; he also begins supplying objects to foreign sovereigns.

- **1877–1971**
Christofle opens a new factory in Saint-Denis before transferring the business to Normandy. The Saint-Denis factory is now listed as a historical monument. Christofle is part of the evolution of tableware through his creation of new pieces (tea service, wine carts, etc.) and through supplying tableware for major ocean liners and Paris's Ritz Hotel. He also supplies the Élysée, the presidential residence.

- **SINCE 2012**
The company belongs to the Chalhoub luxury group.

Other goldsmiths

MAISON PUIFORCAT

📍 *48, av. Gabriel, Paris 8th*

This business was founded at 14, rue Chapon (Paris 3rd), in 1820 by brothers Émile and Joseph-Marie Puiforcat and their cousin Jean-Baptiste Fuchs. The company's notoriety continued into the next century with their descendant Jean Puiforcat. Since 1993, the company has belonged to the Hermès group and continues production in its workshop in Pantin (Seine-Saint-Denis).

MAISON ODIOT

📍 *7, rue Royale, Paris 8th*

Founded in 1690 in Paris, it established its fame under the reign of Louis XV, thanks to Jean-Baptiste-Gaspard Odiot, one of the top goldsmiths of his time. Passed down for several generations until 1906, the company supplied many high-end customers, such as Said Pasha, the viceroy of Egypt.

MAISON LAPPARRA

📍 *157, rue du Temple, Paris 3rd*

Founded in 1893 by Antoine Lapparra at 3, rue de la Perle (Paris 3rd), this business was taken over in 2014 by Odile Casset de la Chesneraie and is still in operation.

SKIP TO
Sèvres: The Tableware of Grand Tables, p. 86; Le Train Bleu, p. 125; Tableware Dealers, p. 378.

Assorted Christofle silver service pieces

This emblematic Parisian goldsmith has created many pieces of silverware starting in the nineteenth century to today. Here are the most beautiful pieces in its collection.

Queens of the Stovetop

Culinary icons and publishing mavens, Parisiennes Ginette Mathiot and Françoise Bernard made cooking more accessible at home. Here are their side-by-side profiles. —MARIELLE GAUDRY

Ginette Mathiot
real name Geneviève Mathiot
(1907–1998, Paris)

Françoise Bernard
real name Andrée Jonquoy
(1921–2021, Paris)

AN ACCIDENTAL VOCATION

1925: Despite her protestant family's desires that she study medicine and plan to marry, she studies home economics.

1930: Albin Michel, one of France's leading publishers, wants to publish a book on healthy eating and approaches Hélène Delage, professor of culinary arts at the Collège Paul-Bert. She declines the offer and instead suggests Ginette Mathiot, whom she saw often at the École Normale de l'Enseignement Ménager (School of Home Economics).

1953: She is an executive assistant at Unilever and becomes a culinary consultant for the company's advertising group. She has the pleasant physique of the modern housewife, so she is asked to portray "Françoise Bernard," a name that combines the two most common names of the time.

1956: The SEB company asks her to write a practical guide to recipes for the pressure cooker (more than ten million copies are sold).

COOKBOOK CHAMPIONS

BESTSELLER—*Je sais cuisiner* (Albin Michel, 1932): More than 7.5 million copies sold.

NUMBER OF RECIPES: 1,900

PREFACE: In the preface is a quote from Brillat-Savarin—a nod to his longevity!
"Those who know how to eat are comparatively ten years younger than those to whom this science is unfamiliar."

APPROACH: Short, simplified recipes. Includes ingredients list, preparation and cooking times, and serving sizes always for six people. No photography.

BESTSELLER—*Les Recettes facile* (Hachette, 1965): More than 1.5 million copies sold.

NUMBER OF RECIPES: 750

PREFACE: Includes a dozen lines that get straight to the point of the book's objectives.
"Keep it [this book] in your kitchen, very close to your salt box. My only ambition is that you use one as often as the other."

APPROACH: Well-developed recipes. Includes ingredients list, difficulty, preparation and cooking times, tips, and serving sizes for a minimum of four people. No photography.

THE RECIPE FOR HACHIS PARMENTIER (SHEPHERD'S PIE)

These two famous French cooks each offered their own version of this dish. The type of meat used was the only difference.

Serves 6

PREPARE THE POTATOES
Place 2¼ pounds (1 kg) peeled starchy potatoes in a pot of cold, salted water. Bring to a boil and cook for 20 minutes. Drain, and press the potatoes through a fine-mesh strainer. Add 4 tablespoons (60 g) butter and 2 cups (500 ml) milk. Using a wooden spoon, stir to thoroughly combine.

PREPARE THE HACHIS
Ginette Mathiot
Meat: 10½ ounces (300 g) stewed beef and 3½ ounces (100 g) bacon. In a pan, cook 1 chopped onion in butter until translucent. Soak 3½ ounces (100 g) bread crumbs in a scant ½ cup (100 ml) warm milk. Chop the meats and incorporate them with the onion, bread crumbs, and chopped parsley. Incorporate 1 whole egg. Season with salt and pepper.

Françoise Bernard
Meat: about 14 ounces (400 g) leftover cooked meat. Chop 1 onion. Cook very gently in a pan for 10 minutes with a half tablespoon butter. Chop the meat with 1 garlic clove. Add them to the pan and cook for a few minutes. Season with salt and pepper.

ASSEMBLE THE DISH
Grease an oven-safe gratin dish with butter. Spread half the mashed potatoes into the bottom of the dish. Add the chopped meat, then spread the remaining potatoes on top. Sprinkle with grated Gruyère cheese or bread crumbs and dot the top with pieces of butter. Preheat the oven to 425°F (220°C) and bake for 15 minutes, or until the cheese is melted and golden.

Parisian Gnocchi

It's not what you think! There is no semolina or potatoes in this gnocchi, as is found in the version of France's neighbor Italy. The Parisian version uses choux pastry and was a common dish made by Parisians through the 1970s. —ILARIA BRUNETTI

THE RECIPE

Season: fall to winter **Difficulty** ● ● ○

SERVES 4

For the gnocchi
1 cup (250 ml) milk
5 tablespoons (75 g) unsalted butter
1 pinch of salt
1 pinch of white pepper
1 pinch of nutmeg
1 cup (125 g) all-purpose flour
3 large (150 g) eggs
¼ cup (25 g) grated Gruyère cheese

For the Mornay sauce
1¾ cups (450 ml) milk

3 tablespoons unsalted butter
¼ cup plus 1 tablespoon (45 g) all-purpose flour, well sifted
2 large (60 g) egg yolks
⅔ cup (70 g) grated Gruyère cheese
Salt

For finishing
½ cup (50 g) grated Gruyère cheese

Equipment
Pastry bag
Large plain piping tip
Slotted spoon or skimmer
Whisk
Gratin baking dish

Made with choux pastry poached in boiling water then gratinéed, these little gnocchi promise a comforting soft texture. Here is a classic version by Thomas Brachet, chef at bistro Les Arlots.*

Make the gnocchi: In a saucepan, bring the milk to a boil with the butter, salt, pepper, and nutmeg. Off the heat, add the flour all at once. Stir until the mixture detaches completely from the sides of the pan. Incorporate the eggs one at a time. Add the cheese and stir to incorporate.

Transfer the batter to a pastry bag fitted with a large plain piping tip. Pipe the gnocchi into a pot of salted, simmering water. Using a knife moistened with water, snip off the batter into small portions (⅓ to ⅔ inch/1 to 2 cm in length) as you pipe it into the water ❶. Cook the gnocchi for 5 minutes, remove using a slotted spoon, and set aside to drain ❷.

Make the mornay sauce: In a saucepan, bring the milk to a boil. In a separate saucepan, melt the butter over low heat. Add the flour to the butter. Cook for 2 minutes while whisking. Gradually whisk in the very hot milk. Off the heat, whisk in the egg yolks one at a time. Add the cheese and whisk to incorporate. Return to the heat for 3 to 5 minutes while stirring. Season with salt, mixing well until some of the moisture has cooked off.

Assemble and finish: Preheat the oven broiler. Spread a little of the Mornay sauce into the bottom of a baking dish. Add the gnocchi, then cover with the remaining sauce ❸. Sprinkle with cheese and bake for 10 minutes, or until golden brown.

THE CHEF'S TOUCH

Thomas Brachet offers panfried gnocchi with porcini mushrooms served with poultry juices. In the dough, he replaces the milk with the same amount of fromage blanc (a soft, fresh cheese) for an even softer texture.

* Les Arlots—136, rue du Faubourg-Poissonnière, Paris 10th.

WHERE DO THEY COME FROM?

From Italy? In *L'Apicius moderne* (1790) by Francesco Leonardi, a recipe is documented for gnocchi cooked in water, which consists of pieces of choux pastry cooked in water, a béchamel sauce, and baked au gratin using Parmesan.

From Austria-Hungary? Gnocchi in choux pastry can be found in recipes for soups with puffed fritters added, or in desserts, such as the Salzburger Nockerln.

WHAT IS PARISIAN ABOUT THEM?

The use of béchamel or Mornay sauce—with its variation enriched with egg yolks and cheese created by chef Joseph Voiron at Café Durand around 1860—is defined in culinary texts as a "Parisian sauce."

Maison Verot
📍 *3, rue Notre-Dame-des-Champs, Paris 6th +
2 locations*
As an individual version, made with a Mornay sauce.

La Causerie
📍 *31, rue Vital, Paris 16th.* €€
The chef arranges them with a colony of parsleyed escargots.

SKIP TO
Claude Lebey, p. 215; The Chouquette and Its Cousins, p. 278.

Chicken Recipes

Whether originating in the city or the countryside, these three recipes from the Paris region proudly represent the history and terroir of Île-de-France. Let's explore three little-known comfort dishes that celebrate chicken.

—ILARIA BRUNETTI, AIMIE BLANCHARD, THOMAS DARCOS

Le poulet du père Lathuille
(chicken with artichokes)

THE RECIPE

Season: fall   **Difficulty** ● ● ●

SERVES 6 TO 8

2¼ pounds (1 kg) potatoes

1 pound 2 ounces (500 g) Camus artichoke hearts (or the Gros Vert de Laon) or other variety

3⅓ pounds (1.5 kg) chicken breasts

10 tablespoons (150 g) unsalted butter

Salt and freshly ground black pepper

3 to 4 sprigs flat-leaf parsley

Equipment

12-inch (30 cm) pan with a handle and low sides

This recipe delighted fashionable Parisian society before evolving into a home-style dish.

Peel the potatoes and slice them into ¹⁄₁₀- to ⅛-inch-thick (2 to 3 mm) rounds. Cut the artichoke hearts into ⅓-inch (1 cm) cubes. Cut the chicken breasts into 6 to 8 pieces each.

In a skillet, melt 3 tablespoons of the butter over low heat and arrange the chicken pieces in the pan snug against each other side by side. Fill any empty gaps between the chicken pieces with the diced artichoke pieces ❶. Arrange the potato rounds on top in a thoughtful pattern, overlapping them ❷. Distribute 3 tablespoons of the remaining butter on top in small pieces. Season with salt and pepper. Cook, covered, for 30 minutes over medium heat.

Pour off the cooking juices into a bowl. Place a serving plate upside down on top of the pan and quickly invert the pan while securing the plate with your hand. Return the pan to low heat. Add the reserved cooking juices and slide the mixture back into the pan (the potatoes are now on the bottom). Distribute the remaining 4 tablespoons butter over the top, cover, and cook for 20 to 30 minutes.

Pour off the cooking juices into a bowl. Carefully invert the chicken mixture back onto the serving plate (the potatoes are now on top) ❸. Sprinkle with chopped parsley. Serve sliced into wedges.

Menu from Père Lathuille, nineteenth century.

A CABARET THAT WENT DOWN IN HISTORY

The Lathuille family were cattle and poultry breeders living in Batignolles (at the time outside the Paris city limits). To avoid paying the tax of 1780 on farm products entering Paris, they opened a cabaret (today 7, avenue de Clichy, Paris 17th) in 1790, inviting Parisians to cross the border. Over the years, the cabaret was transformed into a restaurant that became renowned for its cuisine—especially this chicken dish, made with artichokes and potatoes. The establishment became a café-concert in the nineteenth century until it closed in 1906.

THE HOME OF FIGHTERS . . .

The battle of Place de Clichy against the Russians and Prussians, marking the end of the Napoleonic Empire, took place in 1814 in front of the restaurant. Serving as General de Moncey's general headquarters, the guinguette provisioned the French soldiers: "Eat! Drink everything! At least the Russians won't have it!" said owner Jean-Marie Lathuille, a proud patriot who left the cannonball that struck his restaurant's cashier stand where it landed. The building appears in the painting *La Barrière de Clichy. Défense de Paris, le 30 mars 1814* (1820) by Horace Vernet.

. . . AND A HAUNT OF ARTISTS

In the second half of the nineteenth century, Père Lathuille's cabaret became one of the meeting places for impressionist artists. Manet painted a young couple sitting at one of its tables: *Chez le père Lathuille* (1879).

Chez le père Lathuille, Édouard Manet, 1879.

❶

❷

❸

Poulet Franchard

(chicken with herbs and mushrooms)

THE RECIPE

Season: spring
Difficulty ● ○ ○

SERVES 4

9 ounces (250 g) button mushrooms

1 lemon

2 sprigs tarragon

1 bunch flat-leaf parsley

1 bunch chervil

1 free-range chicken, cut into pieces

5½ tablespoons (80 g) unsalted butter

Salt and freshly ground black pepper

1 tablespoon flour

Just over ¾ cup (200 ml) chicken broth

4 slices pain de campagne (rustic loaf with rye)

2 cloves garlic

This is a simple casserole dish with all the comforting flavors of chicken and mushrooms.

Coarsely chop the mushrooms. Lightly spritz them with some lemon juice. Chop the tarragon, parsley, and chervil. Combine the mushrooms and herbs in a bowl **❶**.

In a Dutch oven set over high heat, brown the chicken pieces in the butter **❷**. Add the mushrooms and herbs. Season with salt and pepper and stir to combine. Sprinkle the flour over the meat and mushrooms and stir to coat **❸**. Add the broth and cook, covered, for 1 hour over low heat.

Toast the bread slices and rub them with the garlic cloves. Cut them into squares of about 1 inch (3 cm) to make croutons.

Serve the chicken with the sauce from the pan and the croutons.

Restaurant Franchard.

A RECIPE FOR A RUSTIC RENDEZVOUS

At the beginning of the twentieth century, in Fontainebleau forest near the ruins of the Franchard abbey, Sunday strollers would stop at inns to enjoy local dishes. With its mushrooms and fresh herbs, the poulet Franchard offered all the comforts of a rustic dish in which the very famous (now closed) restaurant Franchard specialized. The restaurant was featured in Jacques Deray's *Le Gang* with Alain Delon (1977) in a scene depicting a shootout between the police and the Tractions Avant gang.

Poularde à la briarde

(chicken in cider and mustard)

THE RECIPE

Season: winter
Difficulty ● ○ ○

SERVES 6

1¾ pounds (800 g) carrots

2 onions

8½ tablespoons (120 g) unsalted butter

2 cups (500 ml) chicken broth

1 (4-pound/1.8 kg) chicken, cut into 8 pieces

2 tablespoons peanut oil

3 cups (750 ml) Briard cider or other hard cider

2 cups (500 ml) heavy cream

4 tablespoons moutarde de Meaux or similar strong mustard

Salt and freshly ground black pepper

This is a dish that celebrates the rich flavors of chicken, cider, and the famous moutarde de Meaux. The result is a simple yet satisfying supper.

Peel and slice the carrots and onions. In a skillet, melt 5½ tablespoons (80 g) of the butter in a scant ½ cup (100 ml) of the broth. Cook the carrots in the liquid over low heat while stirring until the liquid has evaporated and the carrots are glazed.

In a Dutch oven set over high heat, brown the chicken pieces in the oil. Once browned, remove them and set aside. In the same Dutch oven, add the sliced onions and a scant ¼ cup (50 ml) of the broth and cook over low heat until the onions are softened and lightly browned. Add the chicken to the pan and then add the cider and the remaining broth. Simmer for 40 minutes, or until the chicken is cooked through and tender. Transfer the chicken pieces to a serving dish.

Reduce the cooking juices by half. Add the cream, mustard, and the remaining butter to the pan. Season with salt and pepper. Stir until the sauce is thick and creamy. Add the glazed carrots to the sauce, stir to coat, and pour over the chicken pieces.

THE FABULOUS HEN FROM MULTIEN

This recipe comes from one of the richest plains of France in the Île-de-France region, located between Haute-Brie and Valois. It combines three local products: chicken, Briard cider, and mustard (moutarde de Meaux). Traditionally, it is prepared with a chicken that has been force-fed (*gavage*) a month before it is slaughtered, giving it a very flavorful and fatty flesh.

SKIP TO
Île-de-France
Terroir, p. 20.

Gabin, the Boss from Pantruche*

*Pantruche: a popular surname in Paris in the eighteenth and nineteenth centuries, derived from the slang for Pantin.

Jean Gabin, one of France's greatest actors, was a true gourmand. Let's take a short tour of where he could be found at the tables of Paris. —MARCELLE RATAFIA

Voici le temps des assassins by Julien Duvivier

La Belle Équipe by Julien Duvivier

❶ LES HALLES
Gabin, the chef

📍 *Corner of rue Mondétour, Grande-Truanderie, Paris 1st*

In *Voici le temps des assassins* (*Deadlier Than the Male*), Gabin was a renowned chef at the head of a restaurant in Les Halles. The film's screenwriter managed to persuade the actor to take the role by offering him a tempting morsel: the role of chef, in tribute to his passion for delectable food willingly shared with his acting companions Bernard Blier and Lino Ventura.

"So get rid of the Château Yquem and give them a Monbazillac for 400 francs, it will save them money, we are not in Massachusetts!"
—*Voici le temps des assassins*, 1956

Archimède le clochard by Gilles Grangier

❷ CHAMPS-ÉLYSÉES
Gabin, craving home cooking

📍 *La Calavados—40, av. Pierre-Ier-de-Serbie, Paris 8th*

As a cop in early retirement in *Le Pacha*, Gabin the boss is feeling lost in the Parisian night: The hippies have thrown out the dancers in the dance halls, and Gabin gets stuck in the company of escort girls and their customers at the legendary Calavados, a chic restaurant in Paris's 8th arrondissement. On the menu: Iranian caviar and lobster swimming in a very Nouvelle Cuisine dish. "I'm not hungry," he gruffs; it's not the same as a simple blanquette.

"And who is looking after Albert?"
—*Le Pacha* (*Pasha*), 1968

❸ MOUFFETARD
Gabin, the educated drunk

📍 *Rue Mouffetard, Paris 5th*

In a film based on an idea by Gabin, Archimède the bum traipses around in hole-filled espadrilles and enters the bistros of Mouffetard with his cocky chattering. A bum who is not always inspiring with his words, he makes attempts at insightful thoughts, but more especially to get bottles of white wine, not chilled, and preferably on the house. Tired of his usual cheap wine and meals of sausage, he is offered a feast of champions with his friend Arsène (Darry Cowl) at a nice table in Les Halles.

"This second bottle, will you take it out the ice? It's not a Nautilus! Any body immersed in a liquid is pushed up from the bottom to top equal to the weight of the volume of liquid displaced. No ice!"
—*Archimède le clochard* (*The Magnificent Tramp*), 1959

❹ EAST PARIS
Gabin, a guinguette boss

📍 *Porte des Lilas, Paris 19th*

In his early days, Gabin played a bad boy who lies about. He knocks back glasses of beer in the north of Paris while waiting for the Popular Front to make him meet his *Belle Équipe*. In this film, he opens a guinguette with his buddies on the banks of the Marne.

Touchez pas au grisbi by Jacques Becker

❺ PIGALLE
Gabin, the gangster gourmet

📍 *Rue de Douai, Paris 9th*

In the 1950s, Gabin was no longer the hero of the working classes. He had white hair and a paunch. He returned to the screen by playing a gangster in *Touchez pas au grisbi*. As a kind kingpin, he chose the restaurant where he meets up with his gang around a feast at Bouche, in Pigalle.

"I have no bread, you'll make do with a cracker."
—*Touchez pas au grisbi*, 1954

SKIP TO
Les Guinguettes, p. 72.

Odd Food Jobs

At the end of the nineteenth century during times of crisis and hardship, some Parisians managed to put bread on the table by inventing unusual jobs related to food. Here are some of the most scandalous among them. —MARCELLE RATAFIA

Cockscomb maker

In the nineteenth century, cockscombs were highly sought after. They were a popular ingredient in vol-au-vent and stews. To compensate for the recurrent shortage of these gallinaceous tops, someone had the bright idea to make them. To accomplish this, a putty was made of beef, mutton, or blanched veal then stamped out using a cookie cutter. Once finished, the forged combs looked like the real thing.

Food scraps vendor

This job from the nineteenth century consisted of collecting leftover scraps from bourgeois homes and upscale restaurants and selling them on the street, either in the form of a buffet of leftovers or by mixing everything together in a large pot. A little boeuf bourguignon here, some leftover stew there, a bit of tête de veau, a sardine bone or two, a drizzle of vinaigrette, and voilà—a taste of home, right?

Meat rental company

The word *barbaque* appeared in 1873. According to the *Gazette des tribunaux*, this term meant "nickname for a fake butcher from La Chapelle." At that time, some unscrupulous restaurateurs enlisted the services of "meat renters." In order to bait frequent customers into their establishments, butchers and bistro owners would display gleaming red cheap cuts of meat in their windows. At the end of the day, they would return the meat to the "renters" and make room on their plates and in their cases for pale and poorly smelling cuts to sell instead.

Soup spitter

In French, the "eyes" of a soup are those delicious droplets of fat that collect on the surface of stews from the meat used. However, some cooks would simulate this with a most awful deception: spitting a bit of fish oil from between the teeth directly into the pot. Why such terrible treachery? To save having to use real pork or marrow in the recipe, of course! The restaurant boss in Pierre Perret's song "Tord-Boyaux" did the same: "He spits in the pot / to make eyes in the broth."

Turkey-leg painter

Imagine: you show up at the butcher shop to buy a nice roasted turkey, but the turkey is looking a little pallid. Not very appetizing, right? Don't fret! A gifted artist will apply makeup to its legs for you, and you'll be all set to go. Observed amusingly by writer and journalist Privat d'Anglemont, this unusual way of making a living, along with other such jobs, was chronicled in his famous *Paris anecdote* (1854).

SKIP TO
Les Halles: The Belly of Paris, p. 113; A Parisian Way of Speaking, p. 250.

And more . . .

› **The "guardian angel"** was paid to escort inebriated customers to their homes to keep them out of the gutter.
› **The *cabaretier,*** street vendors who operated small stands called pieds humides, would buy used grounds from high-end cafés to make an ersatz coffee to earn a bit of change.

Nicolas Appert (1749–1841)

Appert, a Generous Inventor

This master Parisian confectioner popularized his revolutionary idea for preserving foods. —MARIELLE GAUDRY

"Confiseur," a way to "confit"

At his father Claude's Auberge du Cheval Blanc in Châlons-sur-Marne, Nicolas frequently faced waste and shortages, two problems that threatened the family business. As a teenager, he knew he wanted to become a confiseur.

Confiserie (which today refers to sweets or candies), in the language of the eighteenth century related to the term *confit*, to "conserve." To *confire* was to add a "foreign substance suitable for preventing fermentation and putrefaction" (*Le Livre de tous les ménages*, 1810), which could be sugar, salt, alcohol, vinegar, or fat. But this method changed the flavor of the food, plus it was not suitable for all foods. Finding a way to preserve all types of food became an obsession for Nicolas Appert.

"[The] result is to have, in each bottle and at little cost, a good selection of foods that reminds us of the month of May in the midst of winter. . . ."

—Grimod de la Reynière, *Almanach des gourmands*, 1806

Appert, a predestined name?

Apperie means "to open" in Latin. In 1795, in his workshop in Ivry-sur-Seine, Nicolas submerged his glass bottles (champagne bottles with wide necks) filled with vegetables, fruits, meat, and even milk, into a bain-marie and sealed them with a cork secured by a wire. Eureka! An airtight container + boiling water = appertization (the canning process). In 1802, Nicolas Appert moved to Massy to surround himself in vegetable gardens to grow and preserve his own produce.

The champagne bottle.

The "Tour de France" of preserved foods

AT THE END OF 1805, he undertook a tour of France to collect orders and distribute samples of his preserved foods. The French navy tested this effectiveness at sea. Whether rolling, pitching, or sailing through storms, nothing would alter these preserved foods. The conclusion was unanimous.

ON MARCH 15, 1809, a report of the Société d'Encouragement pour l'Industrie Nationale formalized his discovery.

THE FOLLOWING YEAR, the Minister of the Interior, Montalivet, made him a deal: an incentive of twelve thousand francs in return for the publication of his invention. The details would appear in *Le Livre de tous les ménages, ou l'Art de conserve, pour plusieurs ans, tous les substances animales et végétals* (1810) because he cared as much about teaching as many people as possible about how to preserve foods as he did selling his own jars.

A Poor Benefactor

Although he had an award-winning invention, he did not patent it. The British soon began using a tin container because it was less expensive than bottles. Canning's popularity skyrocketed, and not to the benefit of its inventor. The poor "benefactor of humanity," as he was symbolically titled, died destitute on June 1, 1841. His body was placed in a mass grave.

SKIP TO
Charcutier-Caterers, p. 318.

Homard à l'Américaine
American-Style Lobster

This lobster and tomato dish was the darling of Parisian restaurants in the nineteenth and early twentieth centuries. Today, it's enjoying a resurgence in upscale eateries. —MARIE-AMAL BIZALION

THE RECIPE

Season: spring to summer
Difficulty ● ● ○

SERVES 4

2 live lobsters, about 1 pound 12 ounces (800 g) each

9½ tablespoons (140 g) unsalted butter

Salt

Scant ¼ cup (50 ml) olive oil

Scant ½ cup (100 ml) cognac

6 tomatoes

2 shallots, chopped

1 clove garlic, chopped

1⅔ cups (400 ml) white wine

Chili powder

⅔ cup (150 ml) veal broth

¼ bunch parsley, chopped

Auguste Escoffier codified this recipe in his *Guide culinaire* in 1903. This is a simplified and lighter version.

Freeze the lobsters for 30 minutes before cutting them up.

Split the lobsters lengthwise in half using a large knife ❶. Remove and break up the pincers. Discard the grain sac (behind the head). Remove the intestines and combine them with 6½ tablespoons (90 g) of the butter ❷.

Season the lobster pieces with salt and sear them over high heat in the oil and the remaining butter. Cook, while stirring, until the pieces turn bright red ❸. Skim off any impurities and flambé with the cognac (pour the cognac on top and light with a long match), then add the tomatoes, shallots, garlic, wine, chili powder to taste, and broth.

Cook, covered, for 10 to 12 minutes over low heat. Remove the lobster and some of the cooking juices and set aside to keep warm. Reduce the remaining sauce in the pan by one-third. Add the butter and intestines mixture and whisk to combine.

Arrange the lobster pieces on a serving dish and coat with the sauce. Sprinkle with parsley.

J. Grange, 1940s.

A PARISIAN HODGEPODGE

According to gastronomic writer Curnonsky, it was Pierre Fraysse, chef of Peter's restaurant (Passage des Princes, Paris 2nd), who created this recipe in 1860 after returning from the United States. Surprised by the late-night arrival of some customers to his restaurant, he quickly cut up a lobster and cooked it in a spicy sauce and called it "à l'américaine" (American-style). At Le Bonnefoy, chef Constant Guillot had been coating lobster with such a sauce since 1853, so its origins remain unclear. One thing is certain, however: the first written record of it occurs in 1856 in *La Cuisine classique* by Urbain Dubois and Émile Bernard. In 1873, Alexandre Dumas offered a recipe credited to his friend Vuillemot in *Le Grand Dictionnaire de la cuisine*. Both describe a poached lobster, not seared, as codified by Escoffier.

BUT ISN'T IT "À L'ARMORICAINE"?

No! In the nineteenth century, tomato and olive oil were popular for Provençal cooking but almost unknown to the Bretons in Armorica (Brittany). Lobster was caught in Armorican nets, hence the use of the word when referring to the dish.

"An American woman was unsure of how to cook a lobster. 'Let's put it off until later,' referring to it as lobster *à l'américaine*."

—Alexandre Vialatte, in his columns for *La Montagne*, *Vialatte à La Montagne*, 2011

TOP
LETS
EAT
PARIS!
ADDRESSES

Les Enfants Rouges
📍 *9, rue de Beauce, Paris 3rd.* €€€

In spring, Japanese chef Dai Shinozuka surrounds it with green asparagus and peas.

Chez Michel
📍 *10, rue de Belzunce, Paris 10th.* €€€

Chef Masahiro Kawai, "Masa," offers it whole, 1⅓ to 1½ pounds (600 to 700 g), depending on Breton fishermen's daily catch.

La Grande Cascade
📍 *Allée de Longchamp, Paris 16th.* €€€€

To homogenize the texture, Frédéric Robert stops the cooking of the tails (after six minutes) and the pincers (after twelve minutes) by placing them in an ice bath.

SKIP TO
Urbain Dubois, p. 148; Curnonsky, p. 276.

The Macaron

Originally, it was a small cookie made of almond paste, sugar, and egg white. The Parisian version became an international star, but its story remains obscure.

—LOÏC BIENASSIS

THE RECIPE

Season: year-round
Difficulty ● ● ●

MAKES 15 MACARONS

For the macaron shells
⅔ cup (75 g) almond flour
¾ cup (75 g) confectioners' sugar
1 teaspoon cocoa powder
1 large (30 g) egg white

For the Italian meringue
1 large (30 g) egg white
1 tablespoon plus 1 teaspoon (20 ml) water
¼ cup plus 2 tablespoons (75 g) granulated sugar

For the chocolate ganache
⅓ cup plus 1 tablespoon (90 g) whipping cream (preferably 30% fat)
2½ teaspoons (10 g) granulated sugar
3 ounces (90 g) 70% cacao dark chocolate, chopped
¾ ounce (20 g) milk chocolate, chopped
1 tablespoon (20 g) unsalted butter, cut into cubes
1 pinch fleur de sel sea salt

Equipment
Stand mixer
Thermometer
Pastry bag
Plain piping tip
Fine-mesh strainer

Le Pastry chef extraordinaire Ludo Pastry offers an unmatched chocolate macaron recipe.

Make the macaron shells: In a bowl, combine the almond flour, confectioners' sugar, and cocoa powder. Add the egg white and stir to thoroughly combine.

Make the Italian meringue: In a stand mixer fitted with the whisk attachment, add the egg white. In a saucepan, heat the water and granulated sugar together to 237°F (114°C). Start beating the egg white on maximum speed. When the syrup reaches 244°F (118°C), pour it slowly into the mixing bowl with the mixer running (avoiding the whisk) and beat until the meringue has cooled; when the whisk is pulled up and turned on its side, the meringue should curve downward slightly at the tip.

Add one-third of the meringue to the almond-flour mixture and incorporate it using a silicone spatula. Add the remaining meringue and combine ❶.

Preheat the oven to 325°F (170°C). Scrape the batter into a pastry bag fitted with a plain piping tip and pipe 30 rounds 1-inch (2.5 cm) in diameter on a baking sheet lined with a silicone baking mat ❷. Let stand for 20 minutes. Bake for 12 minutes. The shells must form a beautiful "foot" (ruffled bottom) when baked. Let the shells cool on the baking sheet.

Make the chocolate ganache: In a saucepan over medium-high heat, bring the cream and granulated sugar to a boil. Combine the chocolates in a bowl. Pour the hot cream in thirds over the chocolates, stirring with a silicone spatula until combined. The ganache should be smooth and creamy. When the ganache reaches room temperature, stir in the butter and fleur de sel sea salt. Set aside to crystallize for 30 minutes at room temperature.

Assemble: Turn half the shells bottom side up. Using a pastry bag, pipe ganache onto the inverted shells. Close them with a second shell and set aside for at least 2 hours to mature before enjoying.

FROM MACARONI TO MACARON

The word *macaron* appeared in the French language at the beginning of the fifteenth century as a translation of the Italian word *maccheroni*, which designated pasta of various shapes.

FIRST RECIPES

The first recipe that is dated comes from an English work from 1617, *A Daily Exercise for Ladies and Gentlewomen* by John Murrell. But the recipe concerned *French Macaroones*. The first recipe in French dates to 1652 in the second edition of François Pierre de La Varenne's *Cuisinier françois*. The long shape of these cakes evoked *maccheroni*, no doubt where the confection earned its name.

THE LONG EVOLUTION OF THE PARISIAN VERSION
A LIGHTENED MERINGUE

Émile Darenne and Émile Duval mentioned it in 1909: "The macarons to which Italian meringue or royal icing have been added are smooth and shiny" (*Traité de pâtisserie moderne*).

Over the course of the twentieth century, recipes emerged where the use of meringue (Italian) grew, such as the macarons royaux that Pierre Lacam and Paul Seurre presented in the *Nouveau mémorial de la pâtisserie* in 1934.

In a word, the recipe for today's shells emerged during the interwar period.

TWO SHELLS COME TOGETHER

The idea of joining together two macaron shells dates to at least the late nineteenth century. A recipe for "soft macarons" from 1913 notes that "filled macarons" are made "quite commonly": just out of the oven, they are stuck directly to each other, but sometimes a filling is used. In *Le Nouveau Mémorial de la pâtisserie*, two small disks made of Succès batter (meringue with a nut flour) are sandwiched together with a pistachio buttercream.

THE GERBET MACARON

The famous Parisian "sandwich" macaron is also known as the Gerbet macaron. The Parisian pastry chef by this name had a shop on rue du Bac (Paris 7th) at the end of the nineteenth century, but his recipe had nothing in common with the one we know today.

SKIP TO
Ladurée, p. 225;
Pastry Shops, p. 312.

AND PARIS IN ALL THIS?

In 1900, Pierre Lacam's *Le Mémorial historique et géographique de la pâtisserie* described the "macarons de Paris," a soft macaron that "is generally made in Paris." However, this was far from the product produced today.

FIRST DESFONTAINES

In 1960, Pierre Desfontaines, at the head of Ladurée, fashioned macarons using two light, beige shells, stuck together. Along with his pastry chef Marcel Thébert, he decided to incorporate cocoa powder into these shells and join them with a thin layer of ganache and make them larger, nearly the size of a hand. Over the years, variations in flavor were added: coffee, raspberry, pistachio, praline, lemon, orange, and more. And Ladurée also made them in a small size, sold by weight. Thus began the saga of the modern Parisian macaron.

THEN CAME HERMÉ

Both national and global success for the macaron occurred in the mid-1990s with Pierre Hermé. The pastry chef at Fauchon (1985–1996) and Ladurée (1997), he enriched the macaron fillings and invented many new flavors and combinations: chestnut, coconut, lime and basil, rose, lychee and raspberry, etc.

THE BEST MACARONS IN PARIS

Raspberry, vanilla, chocolate, pistachio . . . In a blind taste test of sixty-eight macarons in these four flavors across Paris and Île-de-France, these were the winners.

Raspberry

Angelina
📍 *226, rue de Rivoli, Paris 1st + 6 locations*
Shell: soft, dark pink.
Filling: supple, very fruity.

Pierre Hermé
📍 *72, rue Bonaparte, Paris 6th + 22 locations*
Shell: crackly, rounded.
Filling: creamy, delicate raspberry jam.

La Grande Épicerie de Paris
📍 *38, rue de Sèvres, Paris 7th*
📍 *80, rue de Passy, Paris 16th*
Shell: soft, not very sweet.
Filling: assertive fruit flavor.

Chocolate

Pierre Hermé
📍 *72, rue Bonaparte, Paris 6th + 22 locations*
Shell: crackly, dusted with cocoa.
Filling: slight sweetness, slight cocoa bitterness.

La Grande Épicerie de Paris
📍 *38, rue de Sèvres, Paris 7th*
📍 *80, rue de Passy, Paris 16th*
Shell: soft.
Filling: creamy, flavor of chocolate cake.

Le Jardin Sucré
📍 *156, rue de Courcelles, Paris 17th*
📍 *10, pl. Paul-Grimault, Cernay-la-Ville (Yvelines)*
Shell: smooth, delicate.
Filling: touch of vanilla.

Vanilla

Pierre Hermé
📍 *72, rue Bonaparte, Paris 6th + 22 locations*
Shell: crackly.
Filling: intense vanilla.

Carette
📍 *4, pl. du Trocadéro-et- du-11-Novembre, Paris 16th*
📍 *7, pl. du Tertre, Paris 18th*
Shell: rounded, delicate.
Filling: balanced, flavorful in vanilla.

Le Jardin Sucré
📍 *156, rue de Courcelles, Paris 17th*
📍 *10, pl. Paul-Grimault, Cernay-la-Ville (Yvelines)*
Shell: smooth, delicate.
Filling: intense vanilla.

Pistachio

La Grande Épicerie de Paris
📍 *38, rue de Sèvres, Paris 7th*
📍 *80, rue de Passy, Paris 16th*
Shell: soft, not very sweet.
Filling: subtle and balanced.

Carette
📍 *4, pl. du Trocadéro-et-du-11-Novembre, Paris 16th*
📍 *7, pl. du Tertre, Paris 18th*
Shell: rounded, delicate.
Filling: intense pistachio.

Le Jardin Sucré
📍 *156, rue de Courcelles, Paris 17th*
📍 *10, pl. Paul-Grimault, Cernay-la-Ville (Yvelines)*
Shell: smooth, delicate.
Filling: intense pistachio.

Paris: A Moveable Feast

During the 1920s, Paris was the El Dorado of the American intelligentsia who fled Prohibition. Ernest Hemingway not only refined his taste for alcohol during this time but also developed his palate for fine foods.

—STÉPHANE SOLIER

An American in Paris

1899
Born in Oak Park, Illinois.

MAY 1918
While on the Italian front during the Great War, he discovers Paris.

DECEMBER 1921 TO AUGUST 1923
First stay in Paris as a correspondent along with his wife, Hadley.

JANUARY 1924 TO MARCH 1928
Second stay in Paris as a novelist, with his wife, Hadley, and their son John, then with his second wife, Pauline.

APRIL–JULY 1929
Third time in Paris, with Pauline.

1930s
Short stays in Paris.

AUGUST 25, 1944
Liberation Day, followed up with a long stay in Paris.

1954
Wins the Nobel Prize in literature.

1956
Makes a trip to France, coming through Paris.

1961
Commits suicide in Ketchum, Idaho.

1964
Posthumous publication of *A Moveable Feast.*

Declaration of love for Paris

"If you are lucky enough to have lived in Paris as a young man, then wherever you go for the rest of your life, it stays with you, for Paris is a moveable feast."

—*A Moveable Feast (MF)*, 1964

Lover of Île-de-France

FRYING GUDGEONS FROM THE SEINE

"These are eaten fried, whole, and I could devour plates full. . . . we ate them bones and all."

—*MF*, chapter 7

BISTRO PÂTÉ

"We had lunch at the square Louvois at a very good, plain bistro. . . . We spread paté on the good bistro bread and drank white wine."

—*MF*, chapter 10

WILD BOAR PÂTÉS EN CROÛTE

"Dear Papa, . . . the countryside outside Paris and beyond to Picardy is very beautiful. . . . I ate wild boar twice. It's excellent. It is cooked here in paté en croûte with carrots, onions, mushrooms in a thin brown crust. . . ."

—Letter to Clarence Hemingway, Paris, May 1922

TOP 5 HEMINGWAY RESTAURANTS AND THEIR MENUS

1. Restaurant Prunier
9, rue Duphot, Paris 1st
OYSTERS
CRAB À LA MEXICAINE
SANCERRE

2. Restaurant Michaud
29, rue des Saints-Pères, Paris 6th
TOURNEDOS & POMMES FRITES
CHERRY TART
CARAFE OF WINE

3. Brasserie Lipp
151, blvd. Saint-Germain, Paris 6th
POTATO SALAD WITH OLIVE OIL & CERVELAS
SAUSAGE WITH MUSTARD SAUCE
BEER

4. Le Nègre de Toulouse
159, blvd. du Montparnasse, Paris 6th
CASSOULET
WINE FROM CAHORS

5. "The best and most expensive restaurant in the Latin Quarter"
Hemingway did not remember the name of the restaurant, Paris 5th
FLAT OYSTERS FROM MARENNES
TOURNEDOS BÉARNAISE & POMMES FRITES
CHÂTEAUNEUF-DU-PAPE

The art and happiness of eating oysters

"As I ate the oysters with their strong taste of the sea and their faint metallic taste that the cold white wine washed away, leaving only the sea taste and the succulent texture. . . . I lost the empty feeling and began to be happy and to make plans."

—*MF*, chapter 2

SKIP TO
Les Guinguettes, p. 72; Outdoor Cafés, p. 368; Brasserie Lipp, p. 259.

HEMINGWAY'S GOURMAND PARIS AND ITS SURROUNDINGS

HIS CAFÉS AND BARS

LEFT BANK

→ LATIN QUARTER / SAINT-GERMAIN-DES-PRÉS

① "A Good Café on the Place St-Michel"
A café au lait, a café crème, or a rum Saint-James by himself.

② Les Deux Magots
6, place Saint-Germain-des-Prés, 6th
A dry sherry with James Joyce.

→ MONTPARNASSE

③ La Closerie des Lilas
171, blvd. du Montparnasse, 6th
"One of the best coffees in Paris." A beer or a café crème alone, a whisky with the poet Evan Shipman, a whisky-soda with F. Scott Fitzgerald, a Chambéry-Cassis with his wife, Hadley.

④ Le Dôme
108, blvd. du Montparnasse, 14th
A *demi-blonde* (lager) with the painter Pascin.

⑤ Le Dingo Bar
10, rue Delambre, 14th
Champagne with F. Scott Fitzgerald, a Long Island Iced Tea.

⑥ La Coupole
102, blvd. du Montparnasse, 14th
A drink on the terrace to celebrate the liberation of Paris.

⑦ La Rotonde
105, blvd. du Montparnasse, 6th
A drink on the terrace with Henry Miller, F. Scott Fitzgerald, or George Gershwin.

⑧ Le Select
99, blvd. du Montparnasse, 6th
A breakfast alone; coffee with writers Morley Callaghan, Robert McAlmon, Robert Desnos, or artist Isamu Noguchi; whiskeys shared in the evening.

⑨ Le Falstaff
42, rue du Montparnasse, 14th
Beers (and a boxing match) with Morley Callaghan and F. Scott Fitzgerald (1929).

RIGHT BANK

⑩ Ritz Hotel Bar
15, place Vendôme, 1st
The future Hemingway Bar
"When I dream of afterlife in heaven the action always takes place in the Paris Ritz!" A drink with F. Scott Fitzgerald, fifty dry martinis to celebrate the liberation of the Ritz and of Paris.

⑪ Bar at the Hôtel de Crillon
10, place de la Concorde, 8th
A Jack Rose cocktail while waiting for Lady Brett Ashley, a character from *The Sun Also Rises* (1926).

⑫ Café Neapolitan
1, blvd. des Capucines, 9th (now closed)
A drink with the boxer Larry Gains, a coffee with Robert Cohn, or a Pernod with Georgette Hobin, a character from *The Sun Also Rises* (1926).

⑬ Harry's New York Bar
5, rue Daunou, 2nd
A Bloody Mary, perhaps created at Hemingway's request to avoid having alcohol breath . . . and marital discord.

⑭ Café de la Paix
5, Place de l'Opéra, 9th
A whisky on the terrace with the character from *My Old Man* (1923).

ON THE OUTSKIRTS

⑮ Bar at the Hippodrome d'Enghien—*Val-d'Oise*
Champagne with his wife, Hadley, after the races.

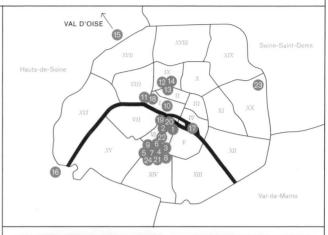

Le Select—99, blvd. du Montparnasse, 6th

RESTAURANTS AND BOULANGERIES

ON THE OUTSKIRTS

⑯ Restaurant La Pêche Miraculeuse
49, route de Vaugirard, Meudon, Hauts-de-Seine

CENTRAL PARIS

⑰ Restaurants on Île Saint-Louis

⑱ Prunier
9, rue Duphot, 1st
Today called Goumard.

⑲ Michaud
29, rue des Saints-Pères, 6th
Today called Le Comptoir des Saints-Pères.

⑳ Brasserie Lipp
151, blvd. Saint-Germain, 6th

㉑ Le Nègre de Toulouse
159, blvd. du Montparnasse, 6th
Today called L'Apèro.

㉒ Le Pré aux Clercs
30, rue Bonaparte, 6th

㉓ Restaurant-dancing at Stade Anastasie
136, rue Pelleport, 20th
Now closed.

㉔ Boulangerie Les Blés d'Ange
151, blvd. du Montparnasse, 6th
Now closed.

Le Dôme—108, blvd. du Montparnasse, 14th

Celery Remoulade

This lovely marriage between celery root and remoulade sauce has become a classic appetizer among Parisian bistros. —**CHARLES PATIN O'COOHOON**

THE RECIPE

Season: fall to winter **Difficulty** ● ○ ○

SERVES 4

For the mayonnaise	½ celery root
1 large (20 g) egg yolk	½ lemon
1 teaspoon Dijon mustard	1½ tablespoons moutarde de Meaux Pommery or similar strong mustard
Just over ¾ cup (200 ml) grapeseed oil	
1 tablespoon sherry vinegar	Salt and freshly ground black pepper
Salt and freshly ground black pepper	¼ bunch flat-leaf parsley

This irrefutably good celery remoulade recipe by Bouillon Pigalle* is as good as their oeuf mayonnaise.

Make the mayonnaise: In a bowl, whisk the egg yolk with the Dijon mustard while very slowly streaming in the oil to make a creamy emulsion. Gently warm the sherry vinegar in a saucepan over low heat and season with salt and pepper. Pour the vinegar into the mayonnaise while whisking vigorously so that the mixture remains thick.

Peel the celery root and squeeze a bit of lemon juice over it. Cut the celery root into large pieces and grate them.

Coat the grated celery root in the mayonnaise and Pommery mustard combined. Season with salt and pepper.

Arrange a mound of the celery remoulade in the center of a plate. Top with parsley leaves. Serve.

*Bouillon Pigalle—22, blvd. de Clichy, Paris 18th.

TOP LET'S EAT PARIS! ADDRESSES

La Poule au Pot
📍 *9, rue Vauvilliers, Paris 1st.* €€€
Chef Jean-François Piège offers an admirable classic version.

Grande Brasserie
📍 *6, rue de la Bastille, Paris 4th.* €€
Adrien Spanu serves a creamy celery remoulade with oeuf mayonnaise amid her seasonal dishes in a bucolic space.

Le Bistrot de Paris
📍 *33, rue de Lille, Paris 7th.* €
This authentic bistro lends a tangy touch to its impeccable remoulade by adding Granny Smith apples.

FROM SALAD DRESSING TO EMULSION

Chronology of the remoulade, the ancestor of mayonnaise:

- **1705**
François Massialot in *Le Cuisinier royal et bourgeois* describes a vinaigrette called rémoula made of anchovies, capers, and herbs.

- **1735**
In *Le Cuisinier moderne*, Vincent La Chapelle provides the recipe for sausse en Rémoulade, which he emulsifies with a cold velouté and mustard.

- **1806**
André Viard in *Le Cuisinier impérial* replaces the velouté with "two egg yolks" "that you will stir with your remoulade."

WHAT ABOUT THE CELERY?

It's difficult to date when celery root (celeriac) and remoulade sauce were first married. Celery root has been cultivated in France since the nineteenth century and has found a privileged place among vegetable growers in the Paris Basin.

WHERE DOES ITS NAME COME FROM?

› According to the nineteenth-century lexicographer Achille Delboulle, the word *rémoulade* was derived from the Picard *ramorache*, meaning *raifort* (horseradish) in 1528, borrowed from the Italian *ramolaccio*, a term probably transmitted by Italian cooks.

› According to Joseph Favre in his *Dictionnaire universel de cuisine pratique* (1905), the term comes from the verb *remoudre* (to regrind), the ingredients being ground twice in a mortar.

A SMALL LITERARY INVENTORY

"I have an hors d'oeuvre of my choice: five slices of sausage or radishes or shrimp or a dish of celery remoulade."
—Sartre, *La Nausée*, 1938

"The celery remoulade was disgusting, and my wife was really a very bad cook. I couldn't take it anymore. I shot."
—Chantal Pelletier, *Tirez sur le caviste*, 2006

"That evening again Jasselin, after putting Michou to bed, went to the table and sat in his usual place, waiting for his wife to bring the celery remoulade; he had always loved celery remoulade."
—Michel Houellebecq, *La Carte et le Territoire*, 2010

SKIP TO
Egg with Mayo, p. 262; Bistros, p. 352.

Talleyrand vs. Cambacérès: Diplomacy and Good Food

Their mission was to embody the glory and power of France from the opulence of Parisian palaces. —AIMIE BLANCHARD

Charles-Maurice de Talleyrand-Périgord

Jean-Jacques-Régis de Cambacérès

Talleyrand		Cambacérès
Former Bishop of Autun, Minister of External Relations (1799–1807), Vice-Grand Elector (1807–1814), Minister of Foreign Affairs (1814–1815), Prince of Bénévent.	**STATUS**	Archchancellor, second consul of Napoléon (1804–1815), Duke of Parma.
The beef filet à la Talleyrand, with truffles, foie gras, and macaroni. **Burgundian snails,** served to Tsar Alexander I in May 1814.	**FAVORITE DISHES**	**Potage à la Cambacérès:** chicken velouté with crayfish butter, crème fraîche, squab quenelles, and crayfish tails. **Partridge half-grilled, half-roasted.** **Thinly sliced warm foie gras** in apple croustade and Madeira sauce.
Brie: "The only master that Talleyrand has never betrayed is Brie cheese" (an opponent).	**KING OF CHEESES**	**Parmesan:** "The Duke of Parma [Cambacérès] leaves / No more hotel, no more courtier / Monseigneur *mange du fromage** / But it is no longer Parmesan" (epigram of 1814 in opposition to Cambacérès). **"Manger du fromage" [eats cheese], figuratively meaning "to be unhappy."*
Sweet wines: sherry, dry Madeira that he would cut with water to drink for breakfast and that he would drink after his soup.	**WINES**	**Bordeaux and Burgundy wines:** he had one of the best cellars in the Empire.
The caricature by James Gillray in *Tiddy-Doll, the Great French-Gingerbread-Baker; Drawing Out a New Batch of Kings, His Man Hopping Talley, Mixing Up the Dough* (1806) depicts Napoléon and Talleyrand kneading and shaping their policy for conquering continental Europe.	**AS SEEN IN ART**	In *Les Châtiments* (1853), Victor Hugo wrote: "Les goinfres courtisans, les altesses ventrues / Toute gloutonnerie et toute abjection / Depuis Cambacérès jusqu'à Trimalcion." [the sycophant pigs, their paunchy royal highnesses / All gluttony and all abjection / From Cambacérès to Trimalcion].

Ambassadors for France

Napoléon maintained his military habits and rarely spent more than half an hour at the table. With the Empire, it was necessary to invent a new protocol. To do this, the Empire would rely on two gracious hosts that could make gastronomy a political weapon and Paris a prestigious springboard for the art of French cuisine on the international stage.

Rivalry of the palates

Talleyrand and Cambacérès stole each other's cooks, argued over dishes, and disparaged each other's tables. Each had their disciples, and gastronomic Paris was divided into two camps:

› **TALLEYRAND** at the Hôtel de Galliffet (Paris 7th) and at Hôtel Saint-Florentin (Paris 1st). He surrounded himself with big names: Antonin Carême, Jean Avice, and Anacréon, whom he poached from Cambacérès to prepare dinners for thirty-six guests four times a week with sixteen to eighteen dishes.

› **CAMBACÉRÈS** at the Hotel Molé (formerly de Roquelaure, Paris 7th). He knew how to mix politics at the table, with a dinner of fifty guests, twice a week, with sixteen to eighteen courses.

SKIP TO
Bries, p. 39; Antonin Carême, p. 156; Paris in the Soup, p. 266.

The Taste of the Prix Goncourt

It's been more than a century since this famous literary prize was first awarded at restaurant Drouant in Paris, and this annual event centers around not just words but also dishes.
—EMMANUEL RUBIN

Waiting for the Prix Goncourt, 1975.

A little history

Edmond Goncourt and Jules Goncourt, brothers who became writing collaborators and produced several books, conceived the idea of the Académie Goncourt (Goncourt Literary Society) in 1867. Edmond bequeathed his estate after Jules's death to provide for the academy's creation with the mission of promoting and celebrating French authors, but also as an alternative award for writers not recognized at the time by the Académie Française (the body whose primary mission is to promote the French language through literary rewards and the publishing of dictionaries). The Académie Goncourt comprises only ten members (none of whom may be a member of the Académie Française) who meet to select the winners. The Prix Goncourt is considered France's most prestigious literary prize and was first awarded in 1903.

The Goncourt brothers, 1854–1855.

Lunch with the Goncourts with Philippe Jaccottet, Prix Goncourt for poetry in 2003.

A table for the Goncourt

From its beginnings, the young academy set out to find the season's best writers while also seeking an appropriate eating establishment conducive to feeding the jury's necessary discussions. The jurors first met at the Grand Hôtel in Champeaux, then at the Café de Paris, but these locations did not quite meet their needs. On October 31, 1914, eleven years after the introduction of the Prix Goncourt, the jury settled in at the restaurant Drouant, located on rue Gaillon (Paris 2nd), a modest bistro-bar founded in 1880 by the Alsatian Charles Drouant. The restaurant enjoyed an excellent reputation for its generous oyster platters, especially among the "aristocracy" of the time, including the Daudets, Renoir, Rodin, Pissaro, Rosny, the Clemenceaus, Octave Mirbeau, and Claude Monet.

From the belly of the Goncourt brothers . . .

A careful reading of the *Journal*, a diary published by the brothers (1851–1896), attests to their frequenting restaurants. Jules and Edmond loved Les Frères Provençaux and Le Véry at the Palais-Royal, and they were regulars at Maison Dorée, snubbing the tables d'hôtes or the Duval bouillons that were fashionable during the time. They praised Café Riche and participated, starting in 1862, in the twice-monthly dinners held at the restaurant Magny and later at Le Brébant.

. . . to the belly of the Prix Goncourt

In 1903, when asked to give an opinion on the new Goncourt Literary Society, academician Émile Faguet offered a blunt remark: "An Acadé-miette!" (*miette* means "crumb" in French). The importance placed by the academy's jurors on the meal during deliberations is undeniable and sometimes controversial: "Is this what we call the cuisine of literary prizes?" a statement from Robert Sabatier, fourth "couvert" (member) until 2012, after a review of the menu. His comment reflects the remark by André Stil, first couvert until 2004: "The Goncourt, influenced? Yes, by the quality of the cuisine, a necessary supplement to literature. You can't award anything or anyone when your mouth is watering while anticipating lobster in a sauce or a Pauillac rack of lamb."

THE SELECTION PROCESS

Action
Every Tuesday there is a meeting of the ten jurors to add to the list of literary selections.

Time
A winner of the Prix Goncourt is announced the first week of November. The winner receives only ten euros but can count on financial successes through media exposure and book sales as a result of being awarded the prize.

Place
The Drouant restaurant, the silent eleventh juror, without whom the Goncourt formula would lack any taste.

Menu of the third Goncourt dinner, 1903.

Cutlery vs. armchairs

Just as the Académie Française is embodied in its fauteuils (armchairs) representing the seats of its forty elected members, the Goncourt members are represented by couverts (cutlery). Starting in 1961, each new member's name is engraved in Italics on a set of cutlery passed down from former members to the next as a symbolic gesture of continuity among the members. Régis Debray, the seventh couvert, followed Hériat and Tournier. Patrick Rambaud, the fifth couvert, followed Aragon and Boulanger. Assouline was the tenth couvert; before him was Mac Orlan and Mallet-Joris.

The 100th anniversary menu

NOVEMBER 5, 2014—ONE O'CLOCK

To celebrate its hundredth year at Drouant, the menu of the 2014 Goncourt served, according to the requirements: oysters, foie gras, high-quality products and "furry game in even-numbered years, feathered in odd-numbered years," as chef Antoine Westermann states. On the menu, hare, and on the honors list, Lydie Salvayre for her novel *Pas pleurer* (Seuil).

· Amuse-bouche
· Scallops and gelée de poule with black pepper from Madagascar
· Roasted Breton lobster with Reinette apples
· Seaweed steamed sea bass and oyster tartare, confit of red beets and panfried duck liver in sherry vinegar
· Boudin and rabbit saddle, civet sauce, and celery mousseline
· Goat cheese from Dominique Fabre
· Norwegian omelet

And the chefs for the affair?

These were true professionals, discreet and charged with orchestrating the tradition. The ritual is that the cook comes to greet the Goncourt at the end of the monthly lunch and proposes to the secretary the next menu. Here debates and clashes ensue. Louis Grondard, long at the head of the Drouant kitchen brigade, recalls: "Two or three months after my arrival, faced with the uproar and indecision caused by my proposals, couvert François Nourissier finally told me, '*Do what you want, chef!*'" Grondard's successor for twelve years, Antoine Westermann, added: "I perk up my ears when the Goncourts talk about literature. We also talk about cooking. They are all gourmets." According to Westermann, in a beautiful humility that contrasts with this small universe of egos: "Without the Goncourt, Drouant would merely be a good restaurant. Thanks to the prestige of the award, our restaurant is known all over the world."

The last word

The former and hedonistic president, Bernard Pivot, stated: "Drouant brings together literature and the stomach." In 1949, Julien Gracq, author of the famous pamphlet *La Littérature à l'estomac*, attacked the literary mores of the time and the race for fame through literary prizes. He refused the Goncourt in 1951 for his novel *Rivage des Syrtes*.

A feast of prizes

In Paris, where there's a prix, there's a restaurant.

– PRIX RENAUDOT
The same day as the Goncourt, also at Drouant, Paris 2nd.

– PRIX MÉDICIS
The first Friday of November, for a long time at the Crillon and now at La Méditerranée ❶, Paris 6th.

– PRIX FEMINA
The first Wednesday of November, at the Crillon ❷, Paris 8th.

– PRIX INTERALLIÉ
The second week of November, at Lasserre ❸, Paris 8th.

– PRIX DE FLORE
In mid-November, at Café de Flore, Paris 6th.

– PRIX DÉCEMBRE
At the end of October or beginning of November, formerly at Le Meurice, Paris 1st, then for a long time at Lutetia, Paris 6th.

– PRIX CAZES
In November, at Brasserie Lipp ❹, Paris 6th.

– PRIX WEPLER
In mid-November, at Le Wepler, Paris 18th.

– PRIX DES DEUX MAGOTS
The last Tuesday of January, at Les Deux Magots, Paris 6th.

– GRANDS PRIX DE L'HUMOUR NOIR
Every Shrove Tuesday, Le Procope ❺, Paris 6th.

– PRIX DE LA CLOSERIE DES LILAS
In April, at La Closerie des Lilas ❻, Paris 6th.

– PRIX ROGER NIMIER
The second week of May, at Fouquet's, Paris 8th.

– PRIX FRANÇOISE SAGAN
End of May or beginning of June, at La Société, Paris 6th.

SKIP TO

La Closerie des Lilas, p. 112; Café de Flore or Les Deux Magots?, p. 256; Liberated Gourmands, p. 289.

A Parisian Way of Speaking

When it comes to good food and good wine, the *Parigots* (Parisians) have invented their own way of speaking. —AURORE VINCENTI

Jargon and greasy spoons

What became traditional Parisian slang originated in the language of roughnecks and hooligans in Parisian suburbs at the end of the nineteenth century. The areas of Ménilmuche, Belleville, and La Butte (Montmartre), at the time, represented a melting pot of slang and jargon. But other great Parisian ways of speaking were born in the world of bectance (food) and biture (drinking) amid the great Parisian food halls, such as Bercy's wine halls and in central Paris around the meat markets at La Villette (Villetouze) and Les Halles.

The tradition of the "cris de Paris"

Since the Middle Ages, various street vendors in Paris announced their presence and hocked their merchandise by shouting in the streets. In the sixteenth century, these cries were immortalized by Clément Janequin in the song "Voulez ouÿr les cris de Paris?" ["Do You Want to Hear the Cries of Paris?"]:

"Do you want to hear the cries of Paris? Where are these poor wretches? Very hot pâtés, who will take a look? White wine, claret wine, ruby wine for six sous. Slices of headcheese. I sell them, I offer them for just a little white wine. Dainty pastries . . . !"

Louchébem, the largonji of butchers

Louchébem, loucherbem, or louch'bem was the butchers' jargon that evolved in the slaughterhouses and markets of La Villette and Les Halles de Paris in the mid-nineteenth century. To speak this language, you had to learn to carve up your words. Although butchers may have been comfortable handling knives for carving up their meats, they were not the ones who invented this method of chopped-up words. They adopted their largonji (argot, or slang) language from that of crooks and shady characters. *Loufoque* and *loucedé* (crazy and sneaky, respectively) are two words in *largonji* that are used in French today!

THE RULES FOR SPEAKING

● Take the initial consonant of the word and place it at the end of the word. Add in its place an *l* and, at the end of the word, a slang suffix: -*èm*, -*ès*, -*oque*, -*uche*, -*ique*, etc.

● Thus, the word *jargon* becomes
→ *argonj*
→ *largonj*
→ *largonji*;

and *boucher* (butcher) becomes
→ *oucherb*
→ *loucherb*
→ *loucherbem*.

Louchébem is alive!

Between 2016 and 2020, 226 butchers from Paris and the inner suburbs were interviewed about their use of louchébem. More than half admitted they still occasionally speak louchébem, and some even regularly. *Vive le louchébem!*

—Valérie Saugera, "Louchébem: la pérennité d'un argot à clé," *La Linguistique*, vol. 57, no. 2, 2021

SKIP TO
Les Halles: The Belly of Paris, p. 113; The Adventures of Bercy, p. 302; Butcher Shops, p. 316.

FOOD SLANG

MARCELLE RATAFIA

ON THE MENU

Mouise: its first meaning is "misery" or "excrement," but this is also a bad, lumpy soup. The name derives from *mouesse* (coarse jam) in the dialect of Doubs and *moues* (porridge) in the dialect of southern German.

Le craint-l'air: a fish.

Verdouze: vegetables.

Le cric-à-bite: reputed aphrodisiac thanks to its effectiveness as a vasodilator (causes sexual arousal).

Le sifflard: also called the "sauce," sauciflard, or saucisson (cured sausages eaten sliced with aperitifs).

Le brignolet: synonymous with northern origins of bricheton (bread).

Le claquosse: also called calendos or claque-merde, this is the king of cheeses: Camembert, whose aroma "claque" (stinks) for the uninitiated.

La criolle or crignole: perhaps a contraction of "carrion," designating bidoche or barbaque—meat!

Les musicians: beans.

La piquante: the fork.

Le puant: also called fromji or fromtogom, it is the diminutive of frometon (cheeses).

IN THE KITCHEN

Le fouille-au-pot: the commis in a professional kitchen.

La cuistance: the kitchen.

Le bourre-cochons: a restaurateur whose clientele is not exactly top choice.

La bibine: first meaning an unpretentious establishment where the food is very cheap, but today referring to a mediocre drink.

BOF: the beef-egg-cheese merchants, the aristocrats of Les Halles

TIME TO EAT

C'est la polka des mandibules: it's a feast.

Bléchard: disgusting (pejorative derivative of blèche: soft, overripe, bad).

Becter à la table qui recule: to be starving.

Chenu: excellent (literally "white from old age," regarding the hair, because a wine's maturity often gives it value).

C'est pas le frère à dégueulasse: it's delicious!

Fleurir le cimetière à poulets: fill your belly.

Morfiler: literally "sharpen" (the appetite, of course!), synonymous with briffer, gousser, or tortorer, to change up what you eat.

CHEERS!

Un asticot de cercueil: half liter of beer.

Un petit déj' de déménageur, un malage de boueux: big glass of red wine.

Un kilbus: a liter of wine.

Une roteuse, une limonade de linspré ("prince" in louchébem): a bottle of Champagne.

Un bébé rose: strawberry milk.

Un Château Lapompe: sirop de parapluie ("umbrella juice"), i.e., water.

Listrobouic: a bistro (in louchébem).

A cahoua au lard: a coffee washed down with absinthe.

Un lait de panthère: a glass of strong alcohol.

NOT WHAT IT SOUNDS LIKE ("FAUX AMIS")

Un quart de brie: a long nose.

Une bavette: a snitch; in prison slang, a hanged snitching inmate.

Une râpe à fromage: a thick mustache.

La blanquette: silverware.

Une mouillette: a criminal enterprise risking disappointment.

A mironton: a slightly wacky person, not to be confused with a miroton, the beef dish in sauce.

Un pied de cochon: a bad trick that you play on someone.

Mettre au beurre dans les épinards: supplement your income, as an "honest woman," engaging in occasional prostitution.

Une boîte de six: a police van.

Les Assiettes: the Court of Assizes (criminal trial court).

Être bon comme la romaine: to be very vulnerable, ready to be arrested (aussi tendre que la laitue—"as delicate as lettuce").

Se trouver dans une scarée béchamel: to suffer setbacks.

Avoir des lunettes en peau de saucisson: to no longer see clearly (because of drinking).

GENDARMES AND THIEVES

La maison poulaga: in 1871, the barracks of the city were built on the former site of the poultry market. Legend has it that the nickname *"poulet"* was partly due to the uniform: at one time, the capes of the security agents gave them a birdlike appearance, especially on their bicycles (their capes flying in the air).

Les boeuf-carottes: there are three theories for the origins of this nickname for the investigative police. They are known for letting suspects "simmer" for a long time; because the dish is cheap, it's the only dish a policeman can afford once they've been laid off; unlike these inspectors, the officers of the Palais de Justice have time to partake in their favorite dish at Le Soleil d'Or, the brasserie across the street from the judicial building.

Croquer de la Tour Pointue: "work for." The expression applies to informants or snitches.

Le demi-sel: an inadequate roughneck.

Le julot casse-croûte: a pimp working from day to day.

La vache: traitor for sale to the highest bidder, ready to give up "manger son bifteck" (eat his steak, meaning keep silent) for a remission of sentence or a hot meal, having an unfortunate tendency to "attaquer le rôti" (attack the roast) or to "se mettre à table" (sit at the table), in other words to confess.

The Manqué

This is a very simple yet great classic dessert among Parisian households. Parisians even use the traditional round cake pan for baking it. —MARIE-LAURE FRÉCHET

1 **2** **3**

THE RECIPE

Season: year-round
Difficulty ●○○

SERVES 8

9 tablespoons (125 g) unsalted butter, plus more for greasing

8 large (160 g) egg yolks

1¼ cups (250 g) granulated sugar

1 pinch of salt

2 cups (250 g) all-purpose flour

8 large (240 g) egg whites

Confectioners' sugar

Equipment

1 round cake pan measuring 9½ inches (24 cm) in diameter

Here is a version of this cake that is a little less sweet than the original recipe to suit modern tastes.

Grease the cake pan with butter. Preheat the oven to 350°F (180°C). In a bowl, whisk together the egg yolks, granulated sugar, and salt until the mixture turns pale yellow **1**. Melt the butter over low heat. Skim off any foam from the top and drizzle the butter into the bowl **2** while whisking. Gradually incorporate the flour.

Beat the egg whites to stiff peaks and gently incorporate them into the batter using a spatula **3**. Scrape the batter into the prepared pan (the batter should fill the pan about two-thirds full). Bake for 40 minutes, or until the tip of a knife inserted into the center comes out clean.

Unmold the cake and let cool on a rack. Dust with confectioners' sugar before serving.

ITS VARIATIONS

This cake can be embellished with praline (nuts boiled in sugar then dried and ground): After 20 minutes of baking time, sprinkle about 2 ounces (50 g) of praline on top, then continue baking for 20 minutes. You can also flavor the batter with lemon zest or rum.

LE MANQUÉ, PROUST'S OTHER MADELEINE

"[The] ladies of the nearby châteaux . . . came to Mass 'in their carriages,' not without buying on the way back, at the pastry shop on the square . . . some of these cakes round like towers, protected from the sun by a window shade—'Manqués,' 'Saint-Honorés' and 'Génoises,'—whose lingering and sweet aromas remained, for me, intertwined with the bells of High Mass and the gaiety of Sundays."

—Marcel Proust, preface by the translator, in John Ruskin, *Sésame et les lys* (*Sesame and Lilies*), Mercure de France, 1906

A LITTLE HISTORY

In 1842, an assistant of the famous pastry shop Félix, located on rue Vivienne in Paris, wanted to make a gâteau de Savoie (Savoy cake, a light sponge cake), but his egg whites became grainy. It is unknown if the apprentice or the boss added the melted butter to save the mixture. When it came time to name the cake, the pastry chef exclaimed: "C'est un gâteau manqué!" ("It's a failed cake!")

BEHIND THE LEGEND

The term *manqué*, as relates to pastry, dates to at least the seventeenth century. At the time, it described cookies, which were certainly very different from the cake known by the name today. In 1803, Grimod de la Reynière mentioned petits manqués with orange flower water in *L'Alambic littéraire* (1803).

Starting in the eighteenth century, a recipe appears very close to that of today's manqués in *Le Cannaméliste français* (1751) by Joseph Gilliers, and in *Le Cuisinier royal, ou l'Art de faire la cuisine* (1820), a bestseller by André Viard.

THE TRADITIONAL PAN

SIDES
Straight sides, 1½ inches (4 cm) high

DIAMETER
Between 9½ and 11 inches (24 and 28 cm)

This pan is a staple piece of equipment for any kitchen. If not making a manqué, the pan is perfect for baking a cheesecake, a tarte Tatin, or other sponge cake.

SKIP TO
Grimod de la Reynière, p. 222.

Gaston Lenôtre (1920–2009)

The Pastry Chef of the Century

Gaston Lenôtre revolutionized the world of pastry and made Paris the capital of all things sweet. His credo? "Good flavor and a beautiful appearance!" —**MARIE-LAURE FRÉCHET**

Off on the right foot

Gaston was born on May 28, 1920, in Saint-Nicolas-du-Bosc (Eure). From the start, his future looked bright for a culinary career, as his mother was a pastry chef for Baron de Rothschild and his father was a saucier chef in a grand Parisian hotel.

A tireless researcher

A hard worker with a fantastic palate, Gaston would seek out innovations, such as the first refrigerated display cases he spotted in Italy, and the ingenious idea of connecting the oven to the shop by a ventilation hose to attract customers with delicious aromas.

A precursor

› He was attentive to the quality of his products, which he shopped for himself at Les Halles and Rungis.
› He was adept at lighter recipes, such as his buttercream in which he incorporated a pâte à bombe and a meringue.
› He popularized Bavarians and fruit mousses.

A supportive wife

"Colette was 51 percent of my success," said Gaston Lenôtre of his first wife. She would watch over the windows and attend to packaging and the outfits of the salesclerks, which were designed for a time by the couturier André Courrèges.

His iconic cakes

❶ LE CONCORDE: three layers of chocolate meringue, chocolate mousse, decorated with "fairy fingers" (meringue sticks). A tribute to the legendary French aircraft and more broadly to Air France, which he supplied in the 1970s.

❷ L'OPÉRA: consisting of a Joconde sponge cake soaked in coffee with layers of chocolate ganache and coffee buttercream.

❸ LA FEUILLE D'AUTOMNE: a cake made with meringue and chocolate mousse, topped with thin ruffles of dark chocolate.

❹ LE SUCCÈS: a cake consisting of two meringue disks with almond flour, topped with praline buttercream, and decorated with crushed nougatine.

LE COLOMBIER: a cake made from almond paste and candied fruits, covered with sliced almonds. Its name is a tribute to the doves of peace.

LE CASINO: a sponge cake rolled around a kirsch-flavored Bavarian, served with raspberry coulis.

The king of entrepreneurship

1947
Opens his pastry shop in Pont-Audemer (Eure).

1957
Opens his first Parisian boutique at 44, rue d'Auteuil (Paris 16th). The industrialist Marcel Dassault is a customer and helps spread the word.

1964
Creation of the catering and reception department.

1971
Creation of the Lenôtre school in Plaisir (Yvelines).

1976
Took over Pré Catelan. Chef Frédéric Anton was awarded three Michelin stars in 2007.

2022
Now eleven Lenôtre boutiques worldwide with more than two hundred chefs (including four MOFs), the largest team in France. His establishment received distinction with the label Entreprise du Patrimoine Vivant for its artisan quality and excellent production processes.

Lenôtre boutique in Berlin in the 1980s.

SKIP TO
The Financier, p. 155; The Macaron, p. 242; The Bûche de Noël, p. 277.

Steak Tartare

This recipe has become the dish par excellence in brasseries and a Parisian classic known throughout world. —**CHARLES PATIN O'COOHOON**

Parisian genealogy

- **1880**
  Jules Verne adapted his novel *Michel Strogoff* for the stage, and it was a triumph at the Théâtre du Châtelet (Paris 1st). It's a tale about a barbarian captain, appointed by Tsar Alexander II to carry a letter from Moscow to Irkutsk to warn the tsar's brother of the arrival of a band of Tartars. Although he did not invent steak tartare, Jules Verne certainly helped popularize it. During Act 2, this dialogue unfolds:
  Postmaster: *I can offer you sir the kulbat.*
  Blount: *What is that . . . kulbat?*
  The postmaster: *A pâté made with pounded meat and eggs.*

- **1910**
  Dr. O'Followell, a member of the Paris Faculty of Medicine, publishes in his book *Zomothérapie et viande crue* a recipe for chopped raw meat, strained, and seasoned with egg yolk, herbs, and spices.

- **1938**
  In *Larousse gastronomique*, Prosper Montagné describes steak *à la tartare* as a steak taken from the filet or the sirloin and chopped, seasoned with salt and pepper, and served raw with a raw egg yolk.

Poster by *Michel Strogoff* at the Théâtre du Châtelet, 1880.

Let's ride!

Tartar horsemen are credited with pounding raw horse meat by placing it under their saddles to tenderize it. In 1238, the army, led by Batu Khan, grandson of Genghis Khan, besieged Russia and introduced chopped meat, referred to as "steak tartare."

The avatars of tartare

If you come across these versions in a Parisian brasserie, run!

STEAK TARTARE WITH EGG YOLK IN A SHELL ON TOP
This risks food poisoning due to the possible presence of bacteria on the shell.

ITALIAN TARTARE
Embellished with shavings of Parmesan. Just like spaghetti Bolognese, there's nothing Italian about it.

TARTARE "ALLER-RETOUR"
This is tartare seared on both sides. Steak tartare is raw, a normal steak is cooked. You must choose!

Ingredients for steak tartare

- RAW BEEF
- EGG YOLK
- DIJON MUSTARD
- CHOPPED SHALLOTS
- CHOPPED CAPERS
- CORNICHONS
- PARSLEY
- TABASCO SAUCE
- WORCESTERSHIRE SAUCE

Let's mix it up

Here is a short list of the debates that can change the prep.

BEEF OR HORSE?
Purists enjoy it made from horse meat, which is less fatty than beef and was abundant after World War I. But since the 1960s, beef is most often used. Aux Deux Amis (Paris 11th) offers a horse-meat tartare once a week.

WITH A KNIFE OR A MEAT GRINDER?
Chef Bernard Loiseau claimed that a meat grinder causes the meat to lose its blood and warms it. Chopping it finely with a knife offers a beautiful texture that releases the flavors and aromas of the meat. The meat grinder creates a melting texture provided the grid used is not too small (holes between ⅓ and ¼ inch/6 and 8 mm). It's up to you!

SERVED PREPARED OR UNPREPARED?
It's difficult to enjoy a dish in a restaurant if it hasn't been cooked or prepared for you. Ask the server to prepare it for you!

"In Paris, my favorite steak tartare is from La Closerie des Lilas. It is perfectly prepared, seasoned, and served."
—Marc Lambron, "Steak tartare," *La Règle du jeu*, No. 75, 2011

SKIP TO
Bistros, p. 352;
Brasseries, p. 356;
Restaurants for
Meat Lovers,
p. 362.

Les Fines Gueules

♀ *43, rue Croix-des-Petits-Champs, Paris 1st*

Cut: 7 ounces (200 g) center rump; Charolais.
Chopping: knife.
Seasonings: house-made green pesto.

Ma Bourgogne

♀ *19, pl. des Vosges, Paris 4th*

Cut: 9–10 ounces (250–280 g) flank steak; Normande, Limousin, or Aubrac.
Chopping: medium-grid grinder.
Seasonings: egg yolk, Worcestershire sauce, ketchup, mustard, Tabasco, salt, pepper.

Aux Vins des Pyrénées

♀ *25, rue Beautreillis, Paris 4th*

Cut: 4¼–5¼ ounces (120–150 g) rump steak; Angus, Normande, or Simmental.
Chopping: knife.
Seasonings: egg yolk, capers, onion, parsley, cherry blossom shoots, traditional and old-fashioned mustards, Espelette pepper, Tabasco, salt, pepper.

Le Bon Georges

♀ *45, rue Saint-Georges, Paris 9th*

Cut: 9 ounces (250 g) eye of round; Blonde d'Aquitaine.
Chopping: knife.
Seasonings: neutral oil, salt, pepper.

Bien Élevé

♀ *47, rue Richer, Paris 9th*

Cut: 5¼–6⅓ ounces (150–180 g) strip sirloin; Angus.
Chopping: knife.
Seasonings: egg yolk, oil, capers, cornichons, shallots, creamed corn, cashews, sweet onions, basil pesto.

Bidoche

♀ *7, rue Jean-Pierre-Timbaud, Paris 11th*

Cut: 5¼–6 ounces (150–170 g) eye of round or bottom sirloin; Limousin or Bazadaise.
Chopping: knife.
Seasonings: egg yolk, parsley, white onion, house-made ketchup.

Les Provinces

♀ *20, rue d'Aligre, Paris 12th*

Cut: 7 ounces (200 g) shoulder; Limousin or Charolais.
Chopping: large-grid grinder.
Seasonings: capers, cornichons, Tabasco, ketchup, mayonnaise, fleur de sel sea salt.

Le Severo

♀ *8, rue des Plantes, Paris 14th*

Cut: 9 ounces (250 g) flank steak; Limousin or Charolais.
Chopping: medium-grid grinder.
Seasonings: egg yolk, shallots, ketchup, Worcestershire sauce, Tabasco, olive oil, salt, pepper.

La Table d'Hugo Desnoyer

♀ *28, rue du Docteur-Blanche, Paris 16th*

Cut: 9 ounces (250 g) rump filet; Limousin.
Chopping: knife.
Seasonings: shallots, chives, scallions, olive oil, lime juice, salt, pepper.

Café de Flore or Les Deux Magots?

CAFÉ DE FLORE— 📍 172, blvd. Saint-Germain, Paris 6th

NUMBER OF SEATS
213 indoors and 82 on the terrace.

OPENED
1885. It owes its name to a sculpture of Flora, the goddess of flowers and spring from Greco-Roman mythology, which, at the time, was located across the boulevard.

ITS FAME
Guillaume Apollinaire was the first, just before World War I, to make it his favorite place. He shared company with André Breton and Louis Aragon. This is where the surrealist movement began. The café would eventually be frequented by Pablo Picasso, Alberto Giacometti, Marcel Carné, and Jean-Louis Barrault. Simone de Beauvoir, who at one time was a regular at Le Dôme in Montparnasse, made the second floor her haunt.

THE DECOR
The are two levels. Art deco touches mingle with the classic red moleskin banquettes and the elegant floor mosaic. Outside there is a large wall of greenery.

THE AMBIENCE
Less touristy than its neighbor. Café de Flore is still a café for Parisians. The menu has not changed for years, but Parisians commune here to reinvent the world, to meet, and to observe the mixture of people and styles rather than just to eat.

THE LITERARY PRIZE
The Prix de Flore, cofounded in 1994 by Frédéric Beigbeder and Carole Chrétiennot, is intended as an "anti-literary prize." A winner receives a check for 6,150 euros and is invited to drink a glass of Pouilly-Fumé every day at the café for a year.

ON THE PLATE
› **Welsh rarebit:** melted cheddar cheese tops a slice of bread and is baked.
› **The club sandwich.**
› **Salade carciofi:** salad, artichokes, San Daniele ham, and Parmesan.

IN THE GLASS
› **Pouilly-Fumé Ladoucette.**
› **Le Flore signature cocktail:** red fruits coulis, Grand Marnier, cognac, Champagne.

IN THE CUP
› **Cafés Richard coffee:** raised to €4.90 in 2022.
› **The chocolat chaud** (**hot chocolate**) **"spécial Flore"** (€7.80): consistent quality and wonderfully served in a small silver pot.

THE SERVICE
Exquisite, elegant, and cheeky at the same time. Male servers are dressed in a black spencer jacket (short jacket with pockets and rounded sides) and a white apron and carry trays.

THE FILM
In 2011 on location at the café, Jean-Marc Vallée filmed a melodrama with Vanessa Paradis that takes place between Paris and Quebec City, titled *Café de Flore.*

If you are a true Parisian, your preference is either Café de Flore or Les Deux Magots—it's one or the other, rarely both. Although this seems a bit snobbish, that's the way it is, and it's nothing new. Just 144 feet (44 m) separate these two legendary cafés situated on Boulevard Saint-Germain. —ELVIRA MASSON

LES DEUX MAGOTS— 📍 6, pl. Saint-Germain-des-Prés, Paris 6th

NUMBER OF SEATS
130 indoors and 144 on the terrace.

OPENED
1885. Its name comes from the two Chinese figurines perched on the indoor central column that have been there since 1873, when a silk shop was located here prior to the opening of the café.

ITS FAME
When the former dry goods store became a café-bar in 1885, friends Paul Verlaine, Arthur Rimbaud, and Stéphane Mallarmé would meet here. After the creation of the café's literary prize in the 1930s, the café became the hub for intellectuals, including Louis Aragon, Elsa Triolet, Pablo Picasso, Fernand Léger, and Jacques Prévert. Simone de Beauvoir was also a regular. One of the rooms bears the name of one of her novels: *Les Mandarins*.

THE DECOR
An art deco interior with moleskin banquettes and green velvet curtains and large terraces, one of which, with the garden, has views of the oldest church in Paris.

THE AMBIENCE
The café is now a little more frequented by tourists and a little less by Parisians. The café has adapted to current tastes and has evolved its menu to include pastries by Pierre Hermé.

THE LITERARY PRIZE
Created in 1933, on the day André Malraux was awarded the Prix Goncourt, the Prix des Deux Magots was intended to be less academic than the Prix Goncourt. The first winner was Raymond Queneau for *Le Chiendent*, awarded by a jury that counted Georges Bataille, Robert Desnos, and André Derain among its members. The current prize is €7,750.

ON THE PLATE
› **Beef tartare:** an emulsion of fresh herbs and tomato confit.
› **Farmstead chicken breast:** flavored with truffle, served with pommes Darphin (a potato cake).

IN THE GLASS
› **Le Jazzy:** the signature cocktail made with Chambord, Veuve Clicquot Champagne, and fresh raspberries.

IN THE CUP
› **Cafés Richard coffee:** raised to €4.90 in 2022.
› **The chocolat des Deux Magots à l'ancienne:** is splendid and nicely served (€9).

THE SERVICE
Perfect: whether you are a Parisian or a tourist, everyone is treated the same. The male servers are dressed in a black spencer jacket and a white apron and carry trays.

THE FILM
In *The Intouchables* (2011) by Éric Toledano and Olivier Nakache, Bakari (Omar Sy) and Philippe (François Cluzet) discover each other on the terrace of the café.

SKIP TO
Gainsbourg at the Table, p. 264; Liberated Gourmands, p. 289.

Blanquette de Veau
Veal in White Sauce

Despite its complex geographical origin, it was in Paris that this stewed dish became part of bourgeois cuisine before becoming an iconic and popular dish.
— **CHARLES PATIN O'COOHOON**

THE RECIPE

Season: fall
Difficulty ● ● ○

SERVES 4

2¼ pounds (1 kg) veal (mixture of shank, chuck, flank, chuck tender)

2 carrots

20 small grelot onions, or spring onions with the green portion removed

9 ounces (250 g) button mushrooms, quartered if large

1 large white onion

3 cloves

1 bouquet garni

1 teaspoon black peppercorns

Salt

Scant ⅔ cup (150 ml) crème fraîche

2 large (40 g) egg yolks

1 tablespoon lemon juice

For the white roux

1½ tablespoons unsalted butter

3 tablespoons all-purpose flour

White rice, for serving (optional)

Here is the recipe for a perfect classic blanquette de veau, with its thick, ivory-colored sauce, inspired by Jean Sévègnes.*

Cut the veal into 2-inch (5 cm) cubes. Peel the carrots and grelot onions. Slice the carrots on the diagonal. Clean the mushrooms and cut off the bottom part of the stems.

Arrange the meat in a cooking pot and add just enough water to cover it. Bring to a boil and reduce the heat. Skim any impurities from the surface to obtain a clear broth. Stud the white onion with the cloves (stick the pointed ends into the flesh of the onion). Add the onion and the bouquet garni to the pot. Cover and cook over low heat for 1 hour.

Add the carrots and grelot onions (if they are spring onions, add them at the same time as the mushrooms) and the peppercorns. Season with salt and cook, covered, for 1 hour.

Add the mushrooms and cook for another 30 minutes.

Make the white roux: In a saucepan, melt the butter without letting it brown. Off the heat, add the flour all at once and whisk to combine. Return to the heat and cook for 2 minutes; the roux will thicken and be white in color.

Using a large slotted spoon or skimmer, remove the meat, onion with the cloves, and bouquet garni. Using a whisk, incorporate the white roux in the broth. Add half the crème fraîche and whisk to combine. Place the meat, onion with the cloves, and bouquet garni back in the pot and increase the heat.

In a bowl, combine the egg yolks with the remaining crème fraîche and the lemon juice. Just before serving, pour the yolk mixture into the pot and stir to combine. Serve immediately with white rice.

* Le Café des Ministères
83, rue de l'Université, Paris 7th

TOP
LET'S EAT PARIS!
ADDRESSES

Le Bistrot Paul Bert
📍 *18, rue Paul-Bert, Paris 11th.* €€
Tender pieces of veal (foreribs, shank, breast), cream sauce, and asparagus (in season).

Le Villaret
📍 *13, rue Ternaux, Paris 11th.* €€
Chuck tender of veal from Lozère, well-thickened sauce.

MAM
📍 *22, rue Fourcroy, Paris 17th.* €€€
A blanquette symphony (shoulder, breast, neck) infused with coffee by chef Stephanie Le Quellec.

A BLANQUETTE INSPECTION

› This recipe may have been inspired by the brouets de volaille (a broth with chicken) of the Middle Ages, in which pieces of meat were poached and then served with an emulsion of egg yolks, almonds, and bread crumbs.

› According to another theory, this was a method of preparing leftover veal served with a white sauce, and whose origin is claimed by several regional traditions (Normandy, Lyon, Poitou). The first written recipe appears in *Le Cuisinier moderne* by Vincent La Chapelle (1735).

› The modern recipe appears at the end of the nineteenth century, made using raw veal cooked in a broth, attributed to the Parisian Jules Gouffé (*Le Livre de cuisine*, 1867). The dish soon conquered the capital's bourgeois kitchens.

> **"M'man, who knew telepathically I was coming, simmered blanquette de veau made for great occasions."**
> —Frédéric Dard/San-Antonio, *Le Trouillomètre à zéro*, 1987

SKIP TO
Beef Bourguignon, p. 133; When Hollywood Dines in Paris, p. 286.

BRASSERIE LIPP

For some, it's one of the great Parisian establishments; for others it's provocative. Brasserie Lipp has been a mirror of Parisian life for almost 150 years.

—NICOLAS D'ESTIENNE D'ORVES

BRASSERIE LIPP
151, Bd Saint-Germain. 151   MÊME · MAISON   BRASSERIE BALZAR
49. Rue des Ecoles. 49

From Alsace to Auvergne, by way of Aveyron

In 1880, the Alsatian Léonard Lipp opened Brasserie des Bords du Rhin. Starting in 1900, the establishment changed names and hands. In 1920, Marcelin Cazes from Aveyron acquired the now-named Brasserie Lipp, which went from ten to eighty tables. Brasserie Lipp was purchased in 2001 by the restaurant group of Olivier Bertrand, a native of Auvergne, so the brasserie now remains in Auvergnat hands.

In the owner's words

"I can say that, starting from that point forward, Lipp had three types of clientele: at noon came the businessmen and merchants from the district who wanted to have lunch in a quiet and serious place; from five o'clock to eight o'clock, writers, booksellers, publishers, magistrates, civil servants, doctors, and artists would come from their work to converse and relax in front of half pints or aperitifs . . . and in the evening was the fashionable set."

—Marcelin Cazes,
50 ans de Lipp, 1966

GUEST BOOK

LITERATURE
Verlaine, Léon-Paul Fargue, Apollinaire, Gide, Saint-Exupéry, Hemingway, Cendrars, Genet, Vian, Sagan, Camus. Genet stole a manuscript from Bataille, and Pivot dined here after hosting the TV show *Apostrophe.*

POLITICS
Maginot, Herriot, Laval, Blum, Pompidou, Giscard. In 1965, Moroccan opponent of French imperialism Mehdi Ben Barka was abducted here.

ARTS
Jouvet, Chazot, Hitchcock, Grace Kelly, Belmondo father and son, Chagall father and daughter (Marc Chagall's daughter Ida's water broke here in 1955!).

A literary prize

In 1935, Dr. Étienne Fatou founded the Prix Cazes with a jury made up of Paul Salmon, Georges Blond, Thierry Maulnier, and Robert Brasillach. The prize was intended to honor an author who had not yet been recognized. Winners today are awarded a check for four thousand euros and a credit account at the brasserie in the amount of eight hundred euros. Jean Marchat and Marcel Herrand were the first awardees. Kléber Haedens, Albert Paraz, Jean Chalon, François Cavanna, Jean-Paul Enthoven, Gérard de Cortanze, Richard Millet, and Louis-Henri de La Rochefoucauld followed.

Hell or heaven?

Brasserie Lipp is a place to see and be seen. In their slightly tilted position, the mirrors allow you to spy across the room from table to table. But the ascent (or "banishment") to your table depends on the host, who offers you a table in "paradise" (the ground floor) or in "hell" (the top floor), depending on the distribution of the "good" tables. The Cazes specialized in this discreet way of distributing their clientele. The emblematic director Claude Guittard stepped down from the post in 2021 after twenty-nine years.

TO SEE

The floral glazed tiles: works of Maison Fargue, the parents of the poet Léon-Paul.

Its two clocks: set ahead seven minutes so that customers are never late for their appointments.

Its all-male staff: except for the coat check attendant.

TO TRY

The dishes on its unchanging menu: Stuffed pig's foot, andouillette, tête de veau (calf's head) on Fridays, sauerkraut with pork shank, herring Bismarck, cervelas (sausage) remoulade, millefeuille, fresh pineapple.

SKIP TO
Paris: A Moveable Feast, p. 244; Brasseries, p. 356.

259

Traditions in Vegetable Farming

Two complementary cultivation systems at one time supplied the capital with vegetables: plots located on the former inner-city marsh areas, which grew small, spring vegetables; and the surrounding plains, which specialized in the cultivation of large vegetables. —XAVIER MATHIAS

Inner-city vs. outer-city cultivation

The purpose of vegetable plots in and around Paris from past eras was to meet the demand of the growing Parisian population. Geographical proximity was a considerable advantage for perishable and fragile vegetables, which would eventually face urbanization as one of its first challenges.

› **Inner-city plots** grew delicate and expensive vegetables to sell at Les Halles, which served as an appointed space.

› **Outer-city plains (those beyond the town walls)** sold "large vegetables," which were taken to the Carreau des Halles twice weekly, but without an appointed space. In 1895, 95 percent of the fruits and vegetables consumed in Île-de-France came from this region.

Caillebotte family at Les Halles de Créteil, 1957.

Cabbage cart, Aubervilliers, early twentieth century.

A city garden plot.

Monsieur Bordier in the plain of Vertus, 1906.

SKIP TO
Île-de-France
Terroir, p. 20.

THE GENIUS OF DAVERNE AND MOREAU
Many of today's organic produce farmers were inspired by the methods of the Paris-region vegetable growers of the nineteenth century thanks to the book *Manuel pratique de la culture maraîchère* by Daverne and Moreau, published in 1845 and updated by Jean-Martin Fortier, a Quebecois and champion of bio-intensive gardening within small plots. As early as 1869, thanks to gardener and journalist William Robinson, the English were strongly inspired by these methods.

Paris: 1,400 acres (600 ha) of cultivation excellence

The marsh areas of Paris, described by English vegetable gardeners as the "French market garden system," represented, in the mid-nineteenth century, 6 percent of the area within the city limits. The average plot size was about 43,000 square feet (4,000 sq m), with one worker taking care of only about 11,000 square feet (1,000 sq m). Although traditional vegetable farmers could take care of two or three crops per bed grown per year, vegetable farmers in the Paris region could manage up to eight crops, an unmatched level of productivity.

A BONUS FOR SPRING VEGETABLE PRODUCERS

Paris's vegetable farmers fed the capital under the assumption that all their production would be offloaded at Les Halles de Paris. Measured in terms of kilos, crates, or units, the volumes sold were extraordinary. These were the spring vegetables, which were fresh, colorful, and fragrant products, and which contributed to Parisian gastronomy achieving its favorable status. White onions, lettuce, mini round carrots, tender haricots verts, and sweet garden peas were no longer the prerogative of the aristocracy or the bourgeoisie.

Family of vegetable farmers at 5, rue de l'Union, La Courneuve, 1907.

THE CHALLENGES OF SPRING VEGETABLE PRODUCERS

Farmers who grew spring vegetables had been demonstrating for more than 150 years that with warm layers, raised domed flower beds, cloches, cold frames, and eventually greenhouses, they could control temperatures practically mechanically and "force" crops to grow. An even more remarkable feat is that through patient phenotypic selection (utilizing genetic diversity that appears naturally within a population), they could rely on photoperiodism (the recurring cycle of light and dark periods of constant length). Thus, to grow onions that needed long days, they could create varieties capable of growing in short days, which were, therefore, more suitable for growing during the early (spring) days. The famous Blanc de Vaugirard onion is a perfect example.

Outer-city producers

Despite inner-city production, reinforcement from produce cultivated in the surrounding outer plains was still essential, including those in Aubervilliers, Courbevoie, the plain of Vertus (currently Saint-Denis), Croissy, Montesson, and Chatou. Spring peas were grown in the west, beans in the southwest, cabbages mainly in the north, etc. The plains areas played a fundamental role in supplying Paris until the second half of the twentieth century.

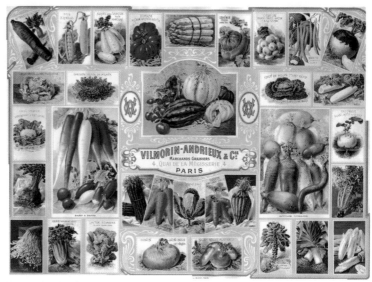

Catalog of seeds Vilmorin-Andrieux, early twentieth century.

URBAN VEGETABLES

One hundred fifty varieties of vegetables bear the name of more than seventy communes in Île-de-France.

List:

Paris artichoke	Paris blonde Batavia lettuce
Asparagus from Argenteuil	Lettuce from Val d'Orge
Red Long Lisse de Meaux carrot	Peppermint from Milly-la-Forêt
Meaux curly endive	Turnip from Croissy
Vaugirard cabbage	Yellow turnip from Montmagny
Brussels sprouts from Rosny	White onion from Vaugirard
White cucumber from Bonneuil	Large sorrel from Belleville
Fin de Meaux cucumber	Dandelion from Montmagny
Cornichon vert petit de Paris (pickling cucumber)	Leek of Gennevilliers
Giant spinach from Viroflay	Peas from Clamart
Crochu de Montmagny (small red bean)	Peas from Marly
	Michaux de Nanterre peas
Flageolet bean from Étampes	Belle de Fontenay potato
Romaine ballon from Bougival (romaine lettuce)	Improved tomato from Montlhéry
	Grosse Lisse aka Trophy tomato

THE BEGINNINGS OF "SOILLESS" PRODUCE FARMS; WAS THIS A BLESSING?

Humans and goods were, at one time, transported by animals, so the quantity of available manure in the city was abundant. Fortunately, inner-city produce farmers, using their layering techniques, could recycle this plentiful organic matter on-site. The small handcarts full of vegetables on the way in left behind, on their way out, a valuable deposit of manure available for collecting. Rather than acting as a "parasite" that devours organic matter from the countryside only to send it back outside the city limits in plastic garbage bags, the city was a virtuous organism capable of appreciating what was once waste by turning it into a valuable resource. Inner-city vegetable gardeners, therefore, cultivated "soilless" crops or, in other words, crops far from natural soils and in what was often made up of backfill, and they did so naturally. Perhaps this is a source of inspiration for today's cultivation methods.

Oeuf Mayo
Egg with Mayo

It's difficult to imagine a more iconic Parisian bistro dish than the famous oeuf mayonnaise. —SÉBASTIEN MAYOL

THE RECIPE

Season: year-round
Difficulty ●○○

SERVES 2

For the eggs
3 large eggs of good quality, in their shells, at room temperature
Salt
Vinegar

For the mayonnaise
1 tablespoon whole-grain mustard
1 splash sherry vinegar
1 large (20 g) egg yolk
Salt and freshly ground black pepper
Scant ⅔ cup (150 ml) neutral-flavored oil (peanut, sunflower, or rapeseed)

For the garnish
1 shallot
1 scallion

The simplest recipes are sometimes the most difficult to make, so for this recipe be sure to follow Sébastien Mayol's directions.*

Prepare the eggs: Fill a saucepan with a large amount of water. Add a generous amount of salt and some vinegar. Bring to a boil, and carefully lower the eggs into the boiling water. Cook for 8 minutes and 40 seconds. Immediately transfer the eggs to a bowl of ice water to stop the cooking.

Make the mayonnaise: Stir together the mustard, vinegar, and egg yolk. Add a pinch of salt and pepper. Using a handheld whisk or stand mixer with a whisk attachment, beat the mayonnaise while slowly drizzling in the oil to achieve a smooth and creamy consistency by the time all the oil is added.

Peel and halve the eggs. Place three egg halves on a serving plate, one with the yolk facing up. Generously spoon the mayonnaise on top of the two halves with the yolks facing down. Peel and finely chop the shallot and scallion and sprinkle them over the eggs.

*Head of the bistro Oh Vin Dieu (HQ of ASOM)—19, rue Treilhard, Paris 8th, and copresident of ASOM.

1 PREPARATION, 3 PRESENTATIONS

As an entremet
In the original version called oeufs en salade (eggs on lettuce), hard-boiled or soft-boiled eggs were placed on lettuce leaves and topped with a vinaigrette. These were green entremets (historically small dishes served between courses,) that followed the roast. Joseph Menon provided a recipe in his *Soupers de la Cour* (1755), including a version in the spirit of today's dish using soft-boiled eggs topped with an emulsion of honey, vinegar, garum spiced with pepper, lovage, and pine nuts, from the Roman cookbook *Apicius* (*L'Art culinaire*, VII, 17, 3).

As a side dish
Starting in the late nineteenth century, this combination was served accompanying poultry or cold fish dishes with the mayonnaise presented separately, as advocated by Auguste Escoffier in *Le Guide culinarie* (1903).

As a cold starter
Oeufs mayonnaise placed on toasted bread slices or lettuce and embellished with a choice of cornichons, tarragon, anchovies, capers, and olives became a starter thanks to A. Bautte, chef of the Hans Crescent Hotel in London.

ASOM
In 1987, food critic Claude Lebey created the Association pour la Sauvegarde de l'Oeuf Mayonnaise (ASOM) to glorify and preserve the history and integrity of the dish. The association was revived after its founder's retirement in 2013 and once again produced a champion for the best oeuf mayonnaise, awarded in 2018.

"Over the years, I have developed an official doctrine for this bistro starter. After many readings and conversations, I know, for example, that an oeuf mayonnaise, when presented on a Parisian table, normally has three hard-boiled egg halves, no more and no less. I also argue that the true oeuf mayonnaise rejects these additions that today's bistro owners love to include: lettuce leaves and a potato salad. . . ."

—Benoît Duteurtre, *Le Retour du Général* (2010)

SKIP TO
Brasseries, p. 356.

THE BEST OEUFS MAYO IN PARIS

D'chez eux
📍 *2, av. de Lowendal, Paris 7th*
Cook time: 7 minutes.
Mayonnaise: creamy with a coating consistency.
Garnish: mixed diced vegetables.

Le Voltaire
📍 *27, quai Voltaire, Paris 7th*
Cook time: 10 to 12 minutes.
Mayonnaise: creamy with a coating consistency.
Garnish: raw vegetables.

Oui Mon Général!
📍 *14, rue du Général-Bertrand, Paris 7th*
Cook time: 8 minutes 45 seconds.
Mayonnaise: thick, with a good amount of mustard.
Garnish: varies seasonally, pumpkin seeds, toasted bread slices.

Le Griffonnier
📍 *8, rue des Saussaies, Paris 8th*
Cook time: 8 minutes.
Mayonnaise: smooth, with a good amount of mustard.
Garnish: potato salad and tomato segments.

Oh Vin Dieu
📍 *19, rue Treilhard, Paris 8th*
Cook time: 8 minutes 40 seconds.
Mayonnaise: a coating consistency, with a good amount of mustard.
Garnish: pickled vegetables, arugula.

Le Bon Georges
📍 *45, rue Saint-Georges, Paris 9th*
Cook time: 8 minutes 20 seconds.
Mayonnaise: Fallot mustard base, oil infused with lemon zest.
Garnish: green salad.

Les Arlots
📍 *136, rue du Faubourg-Poissonnière, Paris 10th*
Cook time: between 8 minutes 40 seconds and 9 minutes 40 seconds.
Mayonnaise: creamy.
Garnish: potatoes, cornichons, chives, watercress.

Caves Pétrissans
📍 *30 bis, av. Niel, Paris 17th*
Cook time: between 8 minutes 30 seconds and 10 minutes, depending on size.
Mayonnaise: creamy, following Monsieur Lebey's suggestion.
Garnish: a few green lettuce leaves.

Bouillon Pigalle
📍 *22, blvd. de Clichy, Paris 18th*
Cook time: 10 minutes.
Mayonnaise: thick and well seasoned, to counter the fat of the egg.
Garnish: spinach.

Gainsbourg at the Table

Although we remember him for his scandalous notoriety, French pop artist Serge Gainsbourg was also an aesthete who had very keen ideas about what he liked to eat. —ELVIRA MASSON

In the kitchen on rue de Verneuil

For more than twenty years, the famous singer lived at 5 bis, rue de Verneuil (Paris 7th). The apartment, with its black walls, is kept precisely as it was before the singer suddenly passed away in 1991. Jane Birkin, his longtime romantic partner, loved to cook for his family, making both French and English dishes, but Gainsbourg also liked to dabble in the kitchen. His favorite recipe? Irish stew, which he shared in 1969 on the program *Quatre Temps** after confessing: "I have a lot of specialties."

*Source: INA video archive, 1969.

The program (INA) on which Gainsbourg shared his Irish stew recipe, 1969.

His shops

In his corner of Paris with its villagelike feel, Gainsbourg would frequent:

› **food shops** on rue du Bac, including the Félix Potin food shop and Nicolas wine shop.

› **restaurants and cafés** (Brasserie Lipp, Café de Flore) and **clubs** (Castel, Le Bilboquet).

He chose this area in the city not "by chance or for snobbery . . . [but because] as a former student of the Beaux-Arts, he appreciated [his] aesthetics. . . ."

—Jacky Jakubowicz and Emmanuelle Guilcher, *Le Paris de Gainsbourg*, Éditions Alexandrines, 2020.

His favorite restaurant: Le Bistrot de Paris

› Located at 33, rue de Lille (Paris 7th), this was a superb Parisian brasserie during his time and is still impeccable today. Frequented by André Gide and Paul Valéry, this is where Paris's smart set would gather when it was taken over by Michel Oliver, star TV chef in the 1960s. Gainsbourg sat at table 46, facing the bar under the glass roof. He would pass a metal spindle where he would stick a five-hundred franc note before sitting down.

› Gainsbourg came here to celebrate the publication in 1980 of his only novel, *Evguénie Sokolov* (Gallimard).

› He dined here with daughter Charlotte Gainsbourg and his companion Bambou the day before he died of a heart attack.

› He frequented another local restaurant, now gone, Le Galant Vert, which was very fashionable in the 1980s.

Jane Birkin and Serge Gainsbourg at Brasserie Lipp in Paris.

Gainsbourg at Maxim's

1930s

Gainsbourg's father, Joseph Ginsburg, is an excellent pianist and performs regularly at Maxim's.

1950s

Serge frequents Maxim's wearing an Yves Saint Laurent suit and a denim shirt.

1963

He is a regular customer, and writes the song "Maxim's": as a dedication to the restaurant.

1968

During their short but passionate romance, the singer treats Brigitte Bardot with Champagne dinners before slipping off to finish the evening at trendy places such as Rasputin, a Russian cabaret near the Champs-Élysées, or at New Jimmy's, the cabaret of his friend Régine.

1971

Crazy in love with Jane Birkin, who had just given birth to their daughter, Charlotte, Serge proposes a large wedding of about nine hundred guests at Maxim's, but Jane turns down the offer and the couple remains unmarried.

Jane Birkin and Serge Gainsbourg at Regine's, Paris, March 22, 1971.

"Le Paris de Serge Gainsbourg" (INA), 1965.

A SLAVIC SOUL

Gainsbourg's mother, Brucha Goda Besman-Ginsburg, nicknamed Olia or Olga, cooked borscht and piroshkis (filled buns). Serge would take her out for Russian-themed evenings, drinking and eating at Rasputin, the Russian cabaret-restaurant on rue de Bassano (Paris 8th) where they would run into a host of characters from famous stars to taxi drivers.

Hotel life

L'HÔTEL

◉ *13, rue des Beaux-Arts, Paris 6th*

A year, an album, a little girl—during the work on his house on rue de Verneuil, Gainsbourg lived at L'Hôtel with Jane for a year where he composed, in 1971, his legendary album *Histoire de Melody Nelson*. His daughter Charlotte took her first steps here, which was also Oscar Wilde's last home in 1900.

RITZ

◉ *15, pl. Vendôme, Paris 1st*

After his separation from Jane Birkin in 1980, he became a resident here for a short while, often accompanied by daughter Charlotte until he asked permission from the hotel to use the bar's famous matches in their navy blue matchbooks in his film *Charlotte Forever* (1986). The Ritz refused, and the prestigious guest's immediate response was: "We're packing our bags and we're outta here!"

LE RAPHAËL

◉ *17, av. Kléber, Paris 16th*

In 1986, Gainsbourg moved to Le Raphaël located on avenue Kléber (Paris 16th), which would become his new favorite hotel and his second home, especially at the bar where he would enjoy his favorite cocktail, the Gibson (one part vermouth, two parts gin, two small onions on a toothpick).

SKIP TO
Maxim's, p. 82;
Félix Potin, p. 99;
The Parisian Taste for Wine, p. 224;
Brasserie Lipp, p. 259.

Paris in the Soup

The capital has the finest collection of vegetable soups (potage) in France, and many of them bear the name of the vegetable-growing communes in Île-de-France. —**FRANÇOIS-RÉGIS GAUDRY**

GENERAL INSTRUCTIONS

All the following recipes serve 6.

Chicken broth can be replaced with water for a vegetarian version.

If the soups become too thick, thin them by adding a little water.

As a nice extra, add a few pieces homemade croutons made by toasting cubes of crusty bread in a little butter.

Argenteuil

VEGETABLE: Asparagus.

ORIGIN: Argenteuil (Val-d'Oise) was the cradle for the cultivation of a wide variety of white asparagus in the seventeenth century. When the vegetable was abundant, the best part of the asparagus was sold, and the leftover stems were used to make this soup.

RECIPE

Peel 12 medium white asparagus (about 1⅓ pounds/600 g) using a vegetable peeler. Cut off the tips (about 2⅓ inches/6 cm) and set them aside in cold water. Cut the stems into pieces and sauté them for a few minutes in a saucepan with 3 tablespoons (50 g) butter, without letting them brown. Add 3 cups (750 ml) water, season with salt, and cook for 15 to 20 minutes over low heat. Meanwhile, cook the asparagus tips for 7 to 10 minutes in a pot of boiling salted water. Drain and set aside. Blend the soup using an immersion blender and strain. In a bowl, thoroughly combine 4 large (80 g) egg yolks with 1¼ cups (300 ml) crème fraîche. Pour this mixture into the soup, stirring with a whisk until smooth. Add the asparagus tips to warm them, stirring carefully to distribute them.

Cressonière

VEGETABLE: Watercress.

ORIGIN: Cultivated since the early nineteenth century in the Paris region, watercress became an emblematic vegetable of the markets at Les Halles. Restaurateurs and cooks of the bourgeoisie prepared it in salads or soups.

RECIPE

In a saucepan, cook 1 minced onion over low heat with 1 tablespoon (2 g) butter for 10 minutes, covered. Wash 1 bunch watercress and trim the stems, maintaining 2 inches (5 cm) of the stem.

Peel 14 ounces (400 g) potatoes and cut them into ⅓-inch (1 cm) cubes. Add 4 cups (1 L) water or chicken broth and add the watercress and potatoes. Season with salt and cook for 20 minutes, covered. Blend using an immersion blender with about a half tablespoon unsalted butter and a scant ½ cup (100 ml) crème fraîche. Serve.

Crécy

VEGETABLE: Carrot.

ORIGIN: Crécy-la-Chapelle (Seine-et-Marne) is famous for its cultivation of carrots called "de Meaux" (a variety with a long root and an orange color tending toward red).

RECIPE

Peel 1 pound 2 ounces (500 g) carrots, slice them, and sauté them for several minutes in a saucepan with 3 tablespoons (50 g) butter. Add 1 medium chopped onion, 1 pinch of salt, and 1 pinch of sugar. Cover and cook, stirring frequently, for 15 to 20 minutes over low heat. Add 4 cups (1 L) chicken broth and ⅔ cup (100 g) cooked rice (or about 2 cups/100 g stale bread) and cook uncovered, simmering for 20 to 25 minutes. Blend using an immersion blender with about a half tablespoon unsalted butter. Serve.

Choisy

VEGETABLE: Lettuce.

ORIGIN: Choisy (now Choisy-le-Roi, Val-de-Marne) has been known since the seventeenth century for the quality of its lettuce. In the eighteenth century, Louis XV often stayed at the chateau de Choisy and encouraged their cultivation.

RECIPE

Sauté 1 sliced onion in a saucepan with 2 tablespoons (30 g) butter. Add 3 cups (750 ml) chicken broth, 2 cups (500 ml) milk, and 2 large starchy potatoes peeled and cut into pieces. Season with salt. Cook, simmering, until the potatoes are tender. Add fresh, washed lettuce leaves (9 to 10½ ounces/250 to 300 g) and bring to a boil again and cook for 5 minutes. Blend using an immersion blender and serve.

Saint-Germain

VEGETABLE: Pea (not split peas, although dry has commonly replaced fresh peas in recipes).

ORIGIN: This soup did not originate from Saint-Germain-en-Laye, although this commune, located in Yvelines, was one of the first areas specializing in the cultivation of peas. Instead, it originates from Count Claude-Louis de Saint-Germain, who devoted himself to agriculture.

RECIPE

Shell 2¼ to 3⅓ pounds (1 to 1.5 kg) fresh peas to obtain 1½ to 1¾ pounds (700 to 800 g) shelled peas. Cut 1¾ ounces (50 g) good-quality thick bacon into lardons (thick cubes). Sauté the lardons in a saucepan for 5 minutes over medium heat, only lightly browning them. Drain off most of the fat from the pan. Add the peas and sauté for 3 minutes. Add 4 cups (1 L) water, 1 bouquet garni, and season with salt. Once it begins to simmer, cook gently, simmering, for 15 minutes. While the peas are cooking, remove a small ladle of peas and set them aside. Blend the soup using an immersion blender with about a half tablespoon unsalted butter; strain. Spoon the reserved whole peas into the bottom of serving dishes and ladle the soup on top. Serve with a few chervil leaves on top.

Germiny

VEGETABLE: Sorrel.

ORIGIN: Adolphe Dugléré, the chef at Café Anglais, invented this soup in 1869 as a tribute to one of his customers, the Comte de Germiny, governor of the Bank of France. Sorrel (oseille) was a widespread plant in the Paris region and was colloquial for "silver."

RECIPE

Finely chop 14 ounces (400 g) sorrel into thin strips. Cook in a saucepan over low heat with 3 tablespoons (50 g) butter. Add 4 cups (1 L) chicken broth. Blend using an immersion blender. In a bowl, beat 4 large (80 g) egg yolks with 1¼ cups (300 ml) crème fraîche. Pour this mixture into the soup, stirring with a whisk, until smooth. Heat slightly without boiling. Serve.

Parisien

VEGETABLES: Leek and potato.

ORIGIN: This is a rustic peasant soup from the Paris region but has been ennobled under the name potage bonne femme in cookbooks of the nineteenth century and the first half of the twentieth century, when butter and cream were eventually added.

RECIPE

Peel 3 leeks, keeping only 2 inches (5 cm) of the bottom portion of the greens. Chop the green and white portions and cook for 15 minutes, covered, in 1 tablespoon (20 g) butter without letting them brown. Add 6 cups (1.5 L) water, season with salt, and bring to a boil. Peel 1 pound 2 ounces (500 g) starchy potatoes, cut them into medium pieces, and add them to the boiling water. Gently simmer for 20 minutes. Serve sprinkled with chervil leaves.

Freneuse

VEGETABLE: Turnip.

ORIGIN: Freneuse (Yvelines) has specialized in the cultivation of turnips since the eighteenth century.

RECIPE

Peel 1⅓ pounds (600 g) turnips and 2 potatoes. Cut them into small pieces and sauté them in a saucepan with 3 tablespoons (50 g) butter. Add 3 cups (750 ml) chicken broth, season with salt, cover, and cook for 30 minutes over low heat. Blend using an immersion blender with about a half tablespoon unsalted butter. Serve.

SKIP TO
Île-de-France Terroir, p. 20;
Adolphe Dugléré, p. 305.

267

The Tarte Bourdaloue

A crumbly sweet pastry dough, an almond cream, and sliced pears . . . It's a match made in heaven in Paris's most famous tart. —VALENTINE OUDARD

THE RECIPE

Season: fall to winter
Difficulty ● ● ○

SERVES 6

For the poached pears

2 red Bartlett pears
Juice of 1 lemon
1⅔ cups (400 ml) water
1¼ cups (125 g) superfine sugar
1 Tahitian vanilla bean

For the tart dough (for 2 tarts)

13 tablespoons (180 g) unsalted butter, plus more for greasing and finishing
1 teaspoon fine salt
1 teaspoon honey
1 large (20 g) egg yolk
Scant ¼ cup (50 ml) water
1¼ cups (160 g) all-purpose flour
⅔ cup (90 g) cornstarch

For the almond cream

7 tablespoons (100 g) unsalted butter, at room temperature
1 cup (100 g) confectioners' sugar, plus more for finishing
1 cup (125 g) almond flour
1 tablespoon cornstarch
2 tablespoons agricultural dark rum
2 large (100 g) eggs
⅓ cup (80 g) whipping cream, very cold

Equipment

One 7-inch (18 cm) round tart pan
Pie weights

"Tartelettes à la Bourdaloue," *Cuisine artistique: étude de l'école moderne*, Urbain Dubois, 1882.

Sébastien Gaudard's pastry shop* is just a stone's throw from rue Bourdaloue. He makes a traditional version of this tart.

Make the poached pears: The day before, peel the pears and sprinkle them with lemon juice. Cut the pears in half. Bring the water and superfine sugar to a boil in a saucepan. Split and scrape the vanilla bean lengthwise in half and scrape out the seeds using the tip of a knife. Add the seeds to the hot syrup. Place the pear halves in the syrup and let simmer for 5 minutes. Check that the pears are tender all the way through. Set aside for 12 hours at room temperature.

Make the tart dough: In the bowl of a stand mixer fitted with the paddle attachment, beat the butter until creamy. Add the salt, honey, egg yolk, and water and beat to combine. Incorporate the flour and cornstarch until the dough is homogeneous. Separate the dough into two even portions (freeze one portion for another use). Wrap the remaining dough portion in plastic wrap and refrigerate for 2 hours. Preheat the oven to 325°F (170°C). Roll out the dough to about 1/10 inch (1.5 mm) thick. Grease the pan with butter and line it with the dough. Prick the dough all over, using a fork, and place a piece of parchment paper on top of the dough. Add the pie weights on top of the parchment paper. Bake for 25 minutes. Let cool.

Make the almond cream: In a bowl, combine the butter, sugar, flour, cornstarch, rum, and eggs. In the bowl of a stand mixer fitted with the whisk attachment, beat the cream to medium-firm peaks then carefully incorporate it into the mixture.

Assemble: Preheat the oven to 350°F (180°C). Remove the pears from the syrup and set them aside to drain. Cut the pears into 8 slices, making sure to hold them together. Scrape the almond cream into the baked tart crust and evenly spread it out. Slide the sliced pear halves on top, evenly spaced. Brush the pears with a little melted butter. Bake for 40 minutes. Let cool and dust with confectioners' sugar.

*Pâtisserie des Martyrs—22, rue des Martyrs, Paris 9th.

A LITTLE HISTORY

The church of Notre-Dame-de-Lorette (Paris 9th) is bordered to the left by rue Fléchier and to the right by rue Bourdaloue, the names of two famous preachers under Louis XIV. Located at 7, rue Bourdaloue was the popular Lesserteur pastry shop.
> The shop's pastry chef, Nicolas Bourgoin, delighted customers with a memorable almond-based tart. Pierre Lacam attributes the creation of the tarte Bourdaloue to him, even though this tart had no sliced almonds.
> Joseph Favre, founder of the Académie Culinaire de France in 1883, attributed the creation to pastry chef Fasquelle, Bourgoin's successor. First made with apricots, it was eventually made using pears, which are now the standard.

TARTE AMANDINE OR BOURDALOUE?

Tarte Amandine, made famous by pastry chef Ragueneau and his tirade in Edmond Rostand's *Cyrano de Bergerac* (1897), is an almond tart made of almond cream and sliced almonds. There is a version, tarte amandine aux poires (pears amandine), which is often confused with tarte Bourdaloue.

HOW DO YOU TELL THEM APART?

In tarte amandine, the pears are diced and sprinkled over the almond cream.

TOP
LET'S EAT PARIS!
ADDRESSES

Stohrer
📍 *51, rue Montorgueil, Paris 2nd*
A classic: a sweet shortcrust, almond cream, sliced pears, sliced almonds.

Sain
📍 *13, rue Marie-et-Louise, Paris 10th*
Sweet shortcrust, whole pears poached in syrup, almond cream, and caramel laitier (caramel with milk added).

Nicolas Bernardé
📍 *2, pl. de la Liberté, La Garenne-Colombes (Hauts-de-Seine)*
Sweet shortcrust, light almond cream, pears poached in syrup and vanilla.

SKIP TO
Île-de-France Terroir, p. 20;
Pastry Shops, p. 312.

BERTHILLON

For more than half a century, this Paris institution on Île Saint-Louis, one of the city's islands, has handed down the art of sorbet and ice cream making from generation to generation. —MARIE-LAURE FRÉCHET

MAISON PARISIENNE
29–31, RUE SAINT-LOUIS-
EN L'ÎLE, 4TH ARR.

Raymond Berthillon.

Flavors and colors

Among more than seventy flavors, the most emblematic are:

RAYMOND BERTHILLON'S FAVORITE

 Vanilla ice cream

THE MOST ICONIC

 Wild strawberry sorbet

THE ESSENTIALS

 Chocolate ice cream

 Cocoa sorbet

A FAVORITE

 Pink grapefruit sorbet

HAPPY MARRIAGES

 Ginger-caramel ice cream

 Peachy–mint leaf sorbet

 Yuzu yogurt ice cream

 Lemon verbena sorbet

INDULGENT

 Gingerbread ice cream

 Speculoos ice cream

EXOTIC

 Sesame ice cream

 Roasted pineapple sorbet with basil

Berthillon's sorbet, with a little theater

In his hospital room where everyone has gathered to socialize, Cyrille, the hero of *Une visite inopportune* by Copi, is aware he's going to die, so he decides to celebrate with friends as a last hurrah. In a what is a rather ludicrous spectacle, he welcomes into his room his crazy friends and family, who bring gifts of food.

NURSE
Another gift from your sister-in-law!

HUBERT
—A sorbet from Berthillon!

NURSE
I've never seen a sorbet of this size! Your sister-in-law is a true aristocrat! […]

CYRILLE
—Hubert, ice cream spoons.

PROFESSOR
One tablespoon will be enough for me, thank you! Mmmm! A fraise des bois sorbet! It reminds me of my nanny's perfume in Deauville . . . Mmmm . . . What a great artist Berthillon is!

—Copi, *Une visite inopportune* (1987), scenes 17–18

The sign

Inside the *B* of the company's Gothic-font logo is a hidden *D* for "Dangles," the name of Raymond Berthillon's mother-in-law. The logo also contains a *C* for "Chauvin."

A family affair

In 1954, Raymond Berthillon, at the time a baker, arrived to help his mother-in-law run the café-hotel Le Bourgogne located on Île Saint-Louis (Paris 4th). He brought his ice cream machine and created recipes that delighted the neighborhood schoolchildren. In 1961, Henri Gault and Christian Millau praised this "astonishing ice cream maker hidden in a bistro on Île Saint-Louis." Berthillon passed on his expertise to his son-in-law Bernard Chauvin and his granddaughter Muriel Delpuech, who still run the business today.

The Golden Rule

Berthillon is probably the only glacier (ice cream maker) that closes in summer. It was Aimée-Jeanne Berthillon, Raymond's wife, who implemented this tradition so that she could enjoy her children and grandchildren and allow the staff to rest. The shop is closed for five weeks only, from the second half of July through August.

Every day, 260 gallons (1,000 L) of ice cream and sorbets are made on-site, divided equally to supply the shops and retailers.

SKIP TO
Le Procope, p. 281; Ice Cream Shops, p. 332.

Sir, a Glass of Water, Please!

The water in Paris is safe to drink, whether it comes from springs or is drawn from the river. This feat took eight centuries to accomplish.

— JACQUES BRUNEL

Drinking the Seine: an ancient story

- **AROUND 360**
  The emperor Julien, while staying in Lutetia, wrote that he liked the water from the Seine.

- **IN THE FOURTEENTH CENTURY**
  The river and well water in what is now Europe's largest city is contaminated by waste. It is better to drink wine (or vinegar) with the water.

- **EARLY SEVENTEENTH CENTURY**
  To stave off alcoholism and quench the thirst of the Louvre district, Henri IV builds a vacuum pump on the Pont Neuf named La Samaritaine in memory of the Samaritan woman who offered Jesus a drink (1).

- **IN 1676**
  A second pump (2) is installed on Pont Notre-Dame and serves twenty-nine nearby fountains. The water is delivered by water carriers using yokes.

- **IN 1802**
  Paris is constantly thirsty. Bonaparte supplies the city with the purer waters of the Ourcq by digging a new canal.

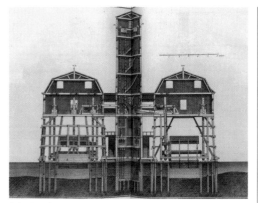
2. Profile of the Notre-Dame pump, in *l'Encyclopédie* by Diderot and d'Alembert.

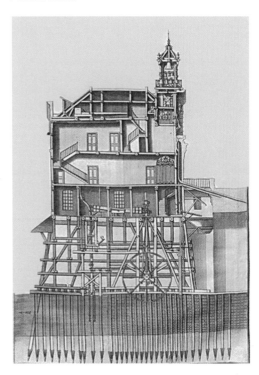
← 1. Profile of La Samaritaine pump (1739).

A concealed heritage

To supply the water, 1,200 miles (2,000 km) of pipes form an underground city where there are lakes, such as the one made famous in *The Phantom of the Opera* under the Opéra Garnier, and the Montsouris reservoir with eighteen hundred pillars, which is a must-see for its "truitomètres" (essentially "trout-o-meters") that allowed the quality of the water to be determined based on the health of the fish.

The Médicis aqueduct, the largest historical monument in France, includes twenty-one "regards," aboveground stone entries through which a person could descend to check the water.

PARIS BOTTLED UP
Today, Lutécia is the only Île-de-France natural mineral water. It comes from the springs in Saint-Lambert-des-Bois (Yvelines) in the Chevreuse Valley.

In search of pure water

LEFT BANK

From the time of the Roman Empire, the Left Bank drew pure water from the Plateau de Saclay to the Cluny thermal baths via the Médius aqueduct 9 miles (15 km) long. On the same route, in 1623, a new aqueduct supplied water to the Luxembourg Palace of Marie de Médicis.

RIGHT BANK

There were deposits of pure water on the hills of the city: Belleville, Le Pré-Saint-Gervais, Montreuil, etc. Starting in the twelfth century, the nuns of Saint-Lazare channeled the water and created Paris's first fountain. The Belleville aqueduct was built soon after. Due to lack of maintenance, the water flowing through the aqueduct to the fountains tasted very briny. The name of the Maubuée fountain (Paris 4th) means "dirty laundry." Later, water from the Seine was recycled by others for free (almost). The pioneers of the water faucets would have a hard time convincing Parisians about the healthiness of paid water.

Artesian wells

In the nineteenth century, advances in technology allowed deep drilling and tapped into ancient and pure water with a temperature of 82°F (28°C) from 1,900 feet (600 m) below the surface. These artesian wells created new fountains, the most famous of which is in Grenelle, Place Georges-Mulot (Paris 15th). There are only three still in operation, which provide water without chlorine, nitrates, or limestone (but a tad murky and loaded with iron). Parisians arrive with armloads of bottles to fill at:
- the fountain at Butte-aux-Cailles, Place Paul-Verlaine (Paris 13th).
- the fountain at Passy, Square Lamartine (Paris 16th).
- the fountain at Square de la Madone (Paris 18th).

A bottle of "grand cru"

When you enjoy a bottle of Parisian water, you are enjoying a "Château Lapompe"! This name, made in jest, and its other variations (Château Chirac, Château Delanoë, and Château Hidalgo) are a funny way to refer to a carafe d'eau (carafe of tap water) that is ordered at restaurants by customers wishing to save a few euros.

Where does Paris's water come from?

Tap water in Paris is treated with activated charcoal and originates from the springs of several rivers:
› **Loing** for the central districts, › **Avre** for the northwest, › **Vanne** for the southwest, › the **waterways of the Seine and Marne** after many treatments. This is the case for the more working-class sections of east Paris

(18th, 19th, and 20th arrondissements, and parts of the 10th, 11th, and 12th).

Paris ranks sixth in urban water quality after Toulouse, Bordeaux, Lyon, Strasbourg, and Nantes, which, when considering the capital's three million inhabitants, is quite an achievement.

AVERAGE COMPOSITION (MG/L)	
CALCIUM	90
MAGNESIUM	6
SODIUM	10
POTASSIUM	2
BICARBONATES	220
CHLORIDES	20
FLUORINE	0.17
SULFATES	30
NITRATES	29
AND TINY TRACES OF AGRICULTURAL POLLUTANTS	

WALLACE'S NYMPHS

Paris was adept at creating works of art around its water sources within the city. In addition to the historic basins and fountains, uniformly designed water fountains during the nineteenth century are thanks to one man: Richard Wallace. This wealthy Scottish Francophile and philanthropist financed mass-produced public fountains.

Modest in size but easy to spot (8 feet 11 inches/ 2.71 m high), solid, and inexpensive, they were first designed by Wallace then made in cast iron and painted green, the color of vegetation. There are several designs.

LARGE STYLE
In this large fountain, four caryatids (draped statues of women, representing Goodness, Charity, Simplicity, and Sobriety) surround a trickle of water. Loved by Parisians, ninety-seven of these fountains survive today, located throughout all districts.

Since 2011, several Wallace fountains have been painted in bright colors (pink, red, yellow, and blue), especially in the 13th and 20th arrondissements, adding a pop of color and making them easy to spot.

SKIP TO
The River Saga, p. 300.

SMALL COLUMNAR
Smaller and more economical, the four caryatids of the large style are replaced by columns. Only two of these fountains remain, found on rue de Rémusat (Paris 16th) and avenue des Ternes (Paris 17th).

Water signs

Many city streets and arteries of all sizes recall Paris's aquatic and fluvial past.

SMALL PUSH TAP
This fountain releases water using a tap that must be pushed. They can be seen adorning the squares and gardens throughout the city.

The Pot-au-Feu

The term *pot-au-feu* (pot on the fire) designates both the cooking vessel and the contents of this meat-and-vegetable recipe that was once a special-occasion dish for the working classes and a common dish of bourgeois cuisine. —PIERRICK JÉGU

THE RECIPE

Season: fall to winter
Difficulty ● ○ ○

SERVES 8

For the aromatics

2 onions

2 carrots

2 leeks

2 stalks celery

2 turnips

2 cloves

1 bouquet garni

2 cloves garlic

For the meats

1¾ pounds (800 g) chuck tender

1¾ pounds (800 g) beef shank

1¾ pounds (800 g) upper shoulder (blade)

1¾ pounds (800 g) top rib

1¾ pounds (800 g) bone marrow

Coarse salt

Fine salt

For the vegetables

8 small potatoes

8 small carrots

8 turnips

2 stalks celery

4 leeks (white portion only)

Salt

Michelin-starred chef Jean-François Piège delivers an exemplary version of this bourgeois classic.*

Prepare the aromatics: Peel and wash the onions, carrots, leeks, celery, and turnips. Cut the onions in half and sauté them in a saucepan until browned. Stud one of the browned onion halves with the cloves (stick the pointed ends into the flesh of the onion).

Prepare the meats: Trim the pieces of meat from their bones and trim away any excess fat. Truss the meat as necessary. Place the bones in ice water.

In a large pot, bring 5 quarts (5 L) of cold, salted water to a boil with the bones, bouquet garni, and garlic. As soon as the water begins to boil, add the meat. Remove the bones and the marrow 5 minutes after the water starts to boil. Cook over very low heat for 4½ hours. Regularly skim off any foam and impurities that collect on the surface; the broth should be clear and a light golden color.

Prepare the vegetables: Wash and peel the potatoes, carrots, and turnips. Strip away any fibrous threads from the celery stalks and cut the celery and leek whites into large pieces. Remove some of the cooking broth and begin cooking the carrots, turnips, celery, and leeks in the broth 30 minutes before the end of the meat cooking time. Add the potatoes to a pot of cold, salted water and bring to a boil and cook until they are tender.

Add the pieces of meat to a large shallow serving platter. Arrange the vegetables around the meat and drizzle the meat and vegetables with the cooking juices.

*À l'Épi d'Or – 25, rue Jean-Jacques-Rousseau, Paris 1st.

Adèle sert le pot-au-feu Dodin-Bouffant, illustration by Joseph Hemard in *La Vie et la Passion de Dodin-Bouffant,* Marcel Rouff, 1924.

VOCABULARY

In a letter to her daughter dated 1763, Madame de Sévigné wrote from Paris after a restless night: "I had the pot au feu, it was an oille* and a consommé, which was cooked separately." Could this be the origin of the expression "pot-au-feu," whose conventional definition was entered in the *Dictionnaire de l'Académie* in 1798?

*Borrowed from Spanish, *olla* (in the expression "olla podrida"): a highly spiced meat-and-vegetable stew.

IN PRINT

From Cadine, in *Le Ventre de Paris,* to Gervaise, in Zola's *L'Assommoir* (1877), the pot-au-feu was a special-occasion dish for Parisian commoners: "At half past three, the pot-au-feu was boiling in a large pot, prepared by the restaurant next door . . . and it trembled for a long time, discreetly. . . . The pot-au-feu kept singing and humming, with its belly in the sun."

—*L'Assommoir,* chapter 7, 1876

TOP ADDRESSES

Chez René

📍 *14, blvd. Saint-Germain, Paris 5th.* €

Served every Thursday, and claimed to be the best in Paris; a generous plate in a setting surrounded with drawings by Yves Saint Laurent.

Le Roi du Pot au Feu

📍 *34, rue Vignon, Paris 9th.* €

Served year-round made with vegetables simmered nearly eight hours. A bowl of consommé is also on the menu.

Le Quincy

📍 *28, av. Ledru-Rollin, Paris 12th.* €€

On the winter menu, served in a casserole dish. Broth clarified by the traditional method using mirepoix (diced vegetables) and egg whites, cooked separately from the vegetables.

L'Os à Moelle

📍 *3, rue Vasco-de-Gama, Paris 15th.* €€

Prepared with chuck (top blade or flat iron), oxtail, and ox cheek. Broth colored with two blackened onions, vegetables cooked separately, bone marrow served on the side.

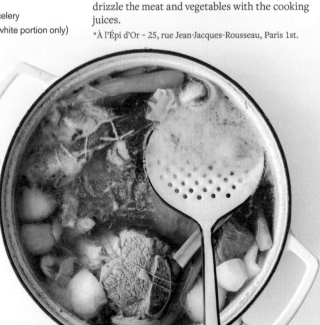

SKIP TO
The Invention of the Restaurant, p. 61.

Places of Worship and Culinary Destinations

Paris has several hundred places of worship whose religious communities welcome us into their spaces and invite us to enjoy foods connected to their rituals. —SEBASTIEN PIÈVE

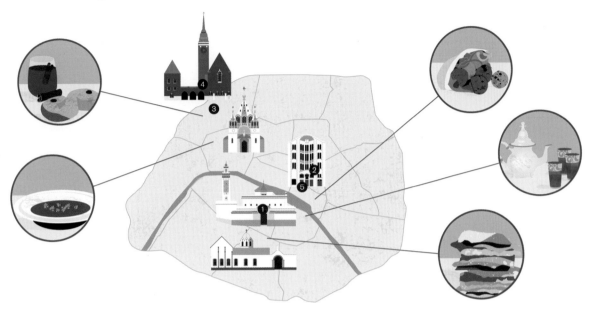

Guilty pleasures in a monastery

❶ Monastère de la Visitation and the monastic artisans' shop

📍 *68–68 bis, av. Denfert-Rochereau, Paris 14th*

There are still monasteries in Paris of cloistered Catholic men and women who dedicate their lives to prayer and work . . . and sometimes to making delicacies. The Monastère de la Visitation is the largest in terms of area, with a community of active Visitandine nuns. A monastic artisans' shop is located within the monastery and offers products made in monasteries from all over France, including foods and beverages, both savory and sweet.

TO TRY

Savory or sweet cookies prepared by the Annonciades of Thiais (Val-de-Marne).

A falafel in a synagogue

❷ Synagogue on rue Pavée

📍 *10, rue Pavée, Paris 4th*

The synagogue on rue Pavée was built in the early twentieth century by the famous architect Hector Guimard, a Frenchman and champion of Art Nouveau. The synagogue is in the historic Marais sector where a Jewish district is located around rue des Rosiers.

TO TRY

L'As du Fallafel

📍 *34, rue des Rosiers, Paris 4th*

Falafels, the popular deep-fried fritters of chickpeas and herbs and spices typically enjoyed in a pita-style bread, can be found in abundance in food stands located in the immediate surroundings of the synagogue.

Orthodox foods

❸ Saint-Alexandre-Nevsky Orthodox Cathedral

📍 *12, rue Daru, Paris 8th*

This building was the first permanent Russian Orthodox place of worship in Paris. After attending the Divine Liturgy in the cathedral and listening to beautiful a cappella songs in Slavonic, a visitor can explore À la Ville de Pétrograd, opposite the church. This century-old institution serves many traditional dishes, including vegetarian during Orthodox Lent.

TO TRY

À la Ville de Pétrograd

📍 *13, rue Daru, Paris 8th*

Enjoy borscht, a beet soup, and okroshka (a cold soup with diced vegetables and aromatic herbs).

Christmas in a Swedish church

❹ Swedish Church of Paris

📍 *9, rue Médéric, Paris 17th*

This Lutheran Protestant temple, built in the early twentieth century, is characterized by its redbrick facade, and it plays an important religious role for the Franco-Swedish community in the city. Every year a Christmas market is held in the building during Advent, culminating in the ceremonies and processions of Saint Lucia (celebrated on December 13).

TO TRY

Glögg (spicy mulled wine), enhanced with lussekatter (buns that are yellow from saffron and symbolize light).

Tea in a mosque

❺ Great Mosque of Paris

📍 *2 bis, pl. du Puits-de-l'Ermite, Paris 5th*

Hispano-Moresque in style, the Great Mosque of Paris is the oldest Muslim place of worship in metropolitan France. A restaurant and a tearoom are attached to it.

TO TRY

Traditional mint tea served with Middle East–inspired pastries. These are particularly honored during festive meals that mark the breaking of the fast during the month of Ramadan.

SKIP TO
Paris, a Cosmopolitan City, p. 164.

The Royal Vegetable Garden

To satisfy the excesses of Louis XIV, the gardener La Quintinie turned a swampy plot into the largest vegetable garden in Europe. Today, it is still home to hundreds of varieties of vegetables and fruit trees. —CHARLOTTE LANGRAND

Royal ambitions

The Sun King was clear: just like his châteaus, the vegetable garden of Versailles must reflect the greatness of the monarch and dazzle the world. Louis XIV therefore commissioned Jean-Baptiste de La Quintinie, a lawyer from Charente with a passion for gardening, to grow a lavish garden, the "King's vegetable garden," to replace a swamp. In 1678, thousands of workers drained the land and filled it with nourishing soil.

A pioneer in gardening

La Quintinie proved to be a pioneer in the evolution of vegetable-farming techniques. He helped cultivate spring crops by improving pruning techniques. He once said, "This garden must cover

the table," and it produced tons of fruits and vegetables each day to feed the royal family (150 people).

The culture of "out of season"

To satisfy royal appetites and whims, La Quintinie managed to grow vegetables through force by using detachable greenhouses, glass garden frames and cloches, and espaliering and trellising. Lettuces were harvested in January, figs and strawberries in spring, and asparagus in winter.

A little java?

Using seeds from a coffee tree gifted by the mayor of Amsterdam to Louis XIV, Louis XV's gardener, François II le Normand, planted twelve coffee trees standing 13 feet (4 m) high in the greenhouse to be able to serve the king coffee from his garden.

A pearl of urban agriculture

The court would gather on the large terrace to admire the "spectacle of nature."

> The vegetable garden was built as a stage on an area of 22 acres (9 ha): a quadrilateral of 7 acres (3 ha) constituted the Grand Carré, divided into sixteen small square plots of vegetables arranged around the central basin and surrounded by twenty-nine gardens growing fruit trees, vegetables, and berries.

> This island of greenery in the heart of the city was totally artificial: shaped for optimal planting, it was crossed with about 2 miles (3 km) of walls to protect the plants from the wind and create microclimates inside the vegetable garden, increasing the temperature in some places by two to three degrees.

> The garden had 450 fruit varieties and 300 vegetable varieties: Bon-Chrétien, Angelys, Cuisse-Madame pears; Calville blanc d'hiver, Api, Reinette apples; plums from Monsieur and Sainte-Catherine. Some varieties dated from the sixteenth and seventeenth centuries, although new species were regularly introduced.

Still going

The vegetable garden has been maintained for three hundred years by generations of gardeners who today preserve this heritage by adapting it to the ecological challenges of the time. The École Nationale Supérieure du Paysage manages the site and has launched an enormous renovation project to preserve the original walls, replant trees, and reduce the use of phytosanitary products. Classified as a historical monument in 1926, this shining example of vegetable gardening has been open to the public since 1991 for classes and visits.

SKIP TO
Traditions in Vegetable Farming, p. 260; Urban Farms, p. 338.

The Moka

The Moka is a classic cake that deserves a prominent place in the windows of Paris pastry shops. —AIMIE BLANCHARD

RECIPE · PARIS CUISINE · RECIPE

THE RECIPE

Season: year-round
Difficulty ● ● ●

SERVES 8

For the génoise sponge

1 tablespoon butter

2½ tablespoons all-purpose flour

4 large (200 g) eggs

½ cup plus 2 teaspoons (110 g) sugar

¾ cup plus 2 tablespoons (110 g) all-purpose flour

For the soaking syrup

1 brewed espresso measuring a scant ¼ cup (50 ml)

3 tablespoons sugar

Scant ¼ cup (50 ml) rum

For the buttercream

1 vanilla bean

2 large (100 g) eggs

2 large (40 g) egg yolks

1 brewed espresso measuring a scant ¼ cup (50 ml)

1 cup (200 g) sugar

16 tablespoons (225 g) unsalted butter, room temperature

For finishing

1 cup (100 g) sliced almonds

Equipment

9¾-inch (25 cm) cake pan

Stand mixer

Thermometer

Ribbon piping tip

Sifter

Carrefour de l'Odéon, Paris, 1850.

For coffee lovers who want a cross between a tiramisu and an opéra cake—meet the Moka.

Make the génoise sponge: Grease the cake pan using the butter and flour. Preheat the oven to 375°F (190°C). In the bowl of a stand mixer fitted with the whisk attachment, beat the eggs and sugar until thickened and pale yellow. Place the bowl in a bain-marie over low heat. Whisk vigorously until the temperature reaches 104°F (40°C); remove the bowl from the water bath and place the bowl back on the stand mixer. Beat for several minutes until tripled in volume and completely cooled. Sift in the flour and carefully fold it in using a silicone spatula. Once the flour is fully incorporated, scrape the batter into the prepared pan. The batter should fill the pan two-thirds full. Bake for 20 minutes, or until risen and pale golden across the top. Set the cake on a rack to cool for 5 minutes. Unmold it onto a cooling rack to cool completely.

Make the soaking syrup: In a saucepan, bring the espresso and sugar to a boil. Let cool and add the rum.

Make the buttercream: Split the vanilla bean lengthwise in half and scrape out the seeds using the tip of a knife. In the bowl of a stand mixer fitted with the whisk attachment, beat the eggs, egg yolks, and vanilla bean seeds on low speed (speed 1). Heat the espresso and sugar together to 244°F (118°C) and add the mixture into the eggs with the mixer running. Increase the mixer speed to medium-high and beat until completely cooled. Add the butter and beat until fully incorporated.

Assemble and finish: Toast the sliced almonds. Cut the génoise cake horizontally into three even layers. Soak the first layer with some of the soaking syrup and spread some of the buttercream on top. Place a second génoise layer on top, and repeat, followed by the third layer of génoise.

Cover the top and sides of the cake with a generous amount of buttercream and apply the sliced almonds to the sides. Using any remaining buttercream, decorate the cake using a ribbon piping tip. Refrigerate the cake for 1 hour and serve.

A LEFT BANK PASTRY SHOP

At the end of the nineteenth century, there were doubts about the origins of this cake, whose first mentions are found in the eighteenth century. With the popularity of coffee during the late seventeenth and eighteenth centuries, Parisian pastry shops quickly incorporated coffee flavors into various desserts. The recipe for the modern Moka cake may have originated at the Quillet pastry shop on rue de Buci (Paris 6th), sold under the name gâteau Quillet, available in pistachio or coffee cream versions. A few steps away at Odéon, the Guignard pastry shop claimed the cake's origins in 1857.

> **"The best known, simplest, and one of the most loved among [desserts] is, without a doubt, le gâteau moka. . . . And today there is no pastry shop that doesn't make one."**
>
> —G. Dumont, *La Pâtisserie,* 1911

THE COFFEE-COLORED PASTRY TRINITY

Three steps and three layers: that's what it takes to make this cake. With its light sponge and buttercream coating sweetened with coffee aromas, its color is as appealing as its flavor.

| BUTTERCREAM |
| GÉNOISE |
| BUTTERCREAM |
| GÉNOISE |
| BUTTERCREAM |
| GÉNOISE |

> **"The maître d' suggests desserts:**
>
> **'Tonight, we have from the pastry case: éclairs, mokas, cream puffs, just as before the war . . .'**
>
> **'That's it,' said Caracalla, 'bring the pastries.'**
>
> **'How many cakes?'"**
>
> —Roger Vailland, *Drôle de jeu,* 1945

SKIP TO
A P'tit Noir, Please, p. 130; Pastry Shops, p. 312.

Curnonsky (1872–1956)

The Prince of Gastronomes

For him, gastronomy became a principality. —**BRUNO FULIGNI**

His life and career

› Maurice Edmond Sailland was born in Angevin. At the age of eighteen, he moved to Paris to study literature. Thanks to his grandmother Marie Chevalier, who cooked "as good as the birds sing," he developed an educated palate.

› Starting in 1895, he earned his stripes through collaborations with the French writer Henry Gauthier Villars (aka Willy), penning novels, plays, reports, and gastronomic articles.

› Starting in 1903, he lived in a simple apartment at 14, square Henri-Bergson (Paris 8th). The apartment had no kitchen, no dining room, and no wine cellar. He loved this simple way of life without fuss.

› In 1927, the magazine *La Bonne Table & Le Bon Gîte* organized a ballot by which, out of 3,388 official gourmands, 1,823 elected him "the prince of gastronomes."

› In 1956, he died after falling from the window of his third-floor apartment.

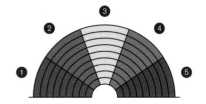

The gastronomic spectrum

Curnonsky wrote: "In gastronomy, . . . there is a far right, a right, a center, a left, and a far left."
—*Souvenirs littéraires et gastronomiques*, 1958.

❶ FAR LEFT
The neo-cuisine of visionaries who are curious about exotic cuisines.

❷ LEFT
Cuisine without fuss.

❸ CENTER
Bourgeois cuisine and regional cuisine, which can be enjoyed in restaurants.

❹ RIGHT
Traditional cuisine you enjoy at home.

❺ FAR RIGHT
Grand cuisine, the food of diplomacy.

A night owl of gastronomy

Curnonsky almost never ate breakfast. He dined late and spent his nights writing and his mornings sleeping. Well known throughout Paris, he could be spotted with friends:
- at Le Chat Noir with Alphonse Allais in Montmartre (Paris 8th).
- at Brasserie Weber (Paris 1st), closed in 1961.
- at the bar at Café de la Paix (Paris 9th) until 3 a.m.
- at Café Vachette (Paris 5th) with Pierre Louÿs.
- at Café d'Harcourt (Paris 5th) with Colette.

Veal medallions Curnonsky

Cut truffles into thin strips and sauté them in butter. Add crème fraîche and cook until reduced and thickened. This is the sauce. From a rack of veal, cut medallions (5¼ ounces/150 g per person) and sauté them in clarified butter. Arrange on a serving plate, and cover with cooked asparagus tips topped with the truffle sauce.

A potato cake served on the side on the plate will ensure none of the sauce is lost.

Members of the Académie des Gastronomes, 1929.

The critic

1900
Leaves for the Far East with a press delegation where he discovers "admirable" Chinese cuisine. On his return, *Le Journal* and *Le Matin* ask him to write food columns.

1921–1930
The "gastronomad" travels around France by car with his friend Marcel Rouff. Together they write *La France gastronomique: guide des merveilles culinaires et des bonnes auberges françaises* in twenty-eight volumes.

1928
Creates the Académie des Gastronomes with his friends, a cenacle for gourmets comparable to the Institut de France.

1933
Condenses, along with Austin de Croze, *La France gastronomique* into a single work, *Le Trésor gastronomique de France*.

1947
Together with Madeleine Decure, launches the magazine *Cuisine de France*, which eventually becomes *Cuisine et Vins de France*.

Aphorisms

"Cooking is when you allow things to taste as they are."
"The secret to good health: the reasonable practice of all excesses and the polite abstention from all sports."
"The cuisine of Périgord is without butter and without reproach."

SKIP TO
Claude Lebey, p. 215; Club of One Hundred, p. 230.

The Bûche de Noël

It's a dramatic end to any Christmas meal. The bûche de Noël (also known as the yule log) regained popularity in the 2000s and has been transformed into a variety of modern designs. —JACQUES BRUNEL

A Parisian cake

The origins of this cake trace to a pastry chef who was inspired by countryside traditions of burning a log in the hearth from Christmas until the Epiphany on January 6 to ensure a prosperous year. This cake dedicated to this Christmas tradition has two possible creators:
› an apprentice pastry chef from Saint-Germain-des-Prés around 1834.
› pastry chef Pierre Lacam from Périgord, chef at Ladurée, who worked for the Prince of Monaco. Along with his son-in-law, he founded the pastry shop Seurre on rue des Martyrs (Paris 9th) and published, in 1900, *Le Mémorial historique et géographique de la pâtisserie*, containing the first recipe for a bûche de Noël.

The concept

A flat sponge cake is topped with cream, rolled, covered with more cream, then scored to look like wood bark on a log. In the late 1830s, chef Auguste Julien of the Chiboust pastry shop (rue Saint-Honoré, Paris 1st), during a trip to visit his colleague Lorsa in Bordeaux, is said to have discovered, from an Italian worker from Genoa, the technique for the sponge cake, which consists of beating the batter while placed over low heat. He popularized it under the name "génoise" (Genoese).

COLLABORATIONS

Since the early 2000s, pastry chefs and designers have been collaborating on bûches de Noël, competing each year for the most creative.

① 2006: Bûche de Noël (block of wood) by Philippe Starck (French designer) for Lenôtre. €94

② 2009: Bûche de Noël (handbag) by Alexis Mabille (French stylist) for Angelina. The bow is the Lyon designer's favorite accessory. €60

③ 2011: "Un Noël à Paris . . . par Sempé" (French cartoonist) for Lenôtre, inspired by the Pont des Arts. €125

④ 2012: "Street art" by Jérôme Mesnager (painter, artist of *Homme en blanc*) for Benoît Castel. €40

⑤ 2014: "Salon gourmand" by Maison Pierre Frey (manufacturer of upholstery fabrics) for Lenôtre. €130

⑥ 2015: "La Bûche à Trésors" by Pascale Mussard (artistic director of Petit H, Hermès) for Lenôtre. €130

⑦ 2018: "Panda Chocolaté" by Richard Orlinski (French artist, sculptor, and musician) for Pierre Gagnaire at Fouquet's. €95

⑧ 2019: Bûche de Noël (children's toys) by Gilles & Boissier (architects) for the Mandarin Oriental. €98

⑨ 2020: "Cyclope" by Tal Lacman (designer) and Maurizio Galante (Italian couturier and designer) for Benoit Castel, inspired by the *Ultraman* series. €50

⑩ 2021: "Totem" by Matali Crasset (French designer) for Benoît Castel. €50

⑪ 2022: "Tout-Paris" by Octave Marsal (French artist) for Pierre Hermé. €250

SKIP TO
Capital Chairs, p. 122; Pastry Shops, p. 312.

The Chouquette...
and Its Cousins

Its success has never waned and has inspired many classics
of Parisian pastry. —MARIE-LAURE FRÉCHET

THE RECIPE

Season: year-round
Difficulty ● ● ○

**MAKES ABOUT
20 CHOUQUETTES**

Ingredients

Scant ⅔ cup (150 ml) water

1 pinch of salt

1 tablespoon (15 g)
granulated sugar

3 tablespoons (45 g)
unsalted butter

¾ cup minus 1 teaspoon
(90 g) high-protein all-
purpose flour or bread flour
or T65 flour

3 large (150 g) eggs

⅛ cup (150 g) pearl sugar

Equipment

Pastry bag

½-inch (11 mm) plain
piping tip

**Here is an amazing recipe for chouquettes that
requires a bit of skill when it comes to handling
the pastry bag.**

Preheat the oven to 350°F (180°C) convection heat.

In a saucepan, bring the water, salt, granulated
sugar, and butter to a boil. When the mixture
begins to boil, add all the flour at once. Cook for
2 minutes, stirring vigorously, until the dough
begins to dry out some.

Off the heat, stir in the eggs one by one. The dough
should be smooth, shiny, and detach from the sides
of the pan ❶.

On a baking sheet lined with parchment paper and
using a pastry bag, pipe balls the size of a large
walnut in staggered rows ❷. Sprinkle generously
with the pearl sugar ❸.

Bake for 30 minutes. Let cool for 5 to 10 minutes in
the oven with the oven turned off, then transfer to
a rack to cool.

DEFINITION

The first mention of a
cabbage-shaped pastry
sprinkled with pearl
sugar appears under
the name "*chou*" in
Antoine Furetière's
Dictionnaire universel
in 1690: "a kind of
very swollen pastry,
made with eggs,
butter, and rose
water. It is sprinkled
on top with what is
similar to dragée."
In its commercial
version, it is the holy
grail of the hero in
Muriel Barbery's *Un
gourmandise* (2000),
who searches to find a
flavor from childhood
before dying.

THE ORIGIN OF
CHOUX PASTRY

› In *Livre des mestiers*
of the provost of
Paris, Étienne Boileau
(1268) makes popelin
(or poupelin), a kind
of very popular small
cake made from eggs
and flour. The dough,
cooked on the fire, was
called pâte à chaud,
which evolved into pâte
à choux (choux pastry).

› **In 1607,** *Le Thrésor
de santé* mentioned a
savory version, "les
petits choux de Paris,"
with a dough made
from fatty cheese, eggs,
and flour and heavily
beaten.

› **In 1739,** Joseph
Menon's *Nouveau Traité
de la cuisine* presented a
recipe for choux pastry
as we know it today and
which inspired pastry
chefs of the nineteenth
century, including the
great Antonin Carême.

Mamiche

📍 45, rue Condorcet,
Paris 9th

📍 32, rue du Château-
d'Eau, Paris 10th

A squat pastry, well
baked, slightly sweet.

Granine

📍 54, rue Oberkampf,
Paris 11th

Well domed, the choux
pastry is squat and
sprinkled with large
sugar crystals.

**Boulangerie
Chambelland**

📍 14, rue Ternaux,
Paris 11th

📍 Corner Bien épicerie
bio [organic]—61, rue
de la Pompe, Paris 16th

Organic and gluten-
free, the choux pastry
is soft, with a balanced
sweetness.

Léonie

📍 96, rue de Lévis,
Paris 17th

Golden, with a good
taste of butter, the
choux is generous and
light.

Pain Pain

📍 88, rue des Martyrs,
Paris 18th

A small dark golden
shape, a light texture.

❶ THE CROQUEMBOUCHE

A tower composed of choux puffs, draped in threads of cooked sugar. The base seems to have evolved during the nineteenth century; Antonin Carême is credited with originating its shape, although the first mention of croquembouche made with choux puffs appears in 1818 in *La Pâtissière de la campagne et de la ville*, by Pierre Quentin.

Sébastien Gaudard

📍 *1, rue des Pyramides, Paris 1st*
📍 *22, rue des Martyrs, Paris 9th*

On a thin nougatine base, four choux puffs (per person) are filled with light vanilla cream and covered with a hard caramel.

❷ THE ÉCLAIR

An elongated choux pastry filled with flavored pastry cream (chocolate, coffee, etc.) and decorated with a fondant glaze. The description from the eighteenth century is found in *Les Dons de Comus* by François Marin (1739) under the entry "cartouches." In the nineteenth century, it was called pain à la duchesse, bâton royal, or pain au chocolat. It owes its name to the fact that it is eaten quickly (*éclair* meaning "lightning" or "flash").

L'Éclair de Génie

📍 *122, rue Montmartre, Paris 2nd*
📍 *14, rue Pavée, Paris 4th*
📍 *35, blvd. Haussmann, Paris 9th*

This very talented pastry shop cleverly revisits the classics. New selections are offered each week.

❸ THE RELIGIEUSE

A pastry consisting of two stacked choux puffs of a different size, each filled with a flavored pastry cream. The "neck" is decorated with piped buttercream and is reminiscent of a nun's habit (hence its name "religieuse," meaning "nun"). Legend says it was invented in the Parisian Café Frascati in 1856.

Maison Pradier

📍 *6, rue de Bourgogne, Paris 7th + 9 locations*

The 80 percent cacao chocolate religieuse is balanced with firm choux pastry, sweet icing, and aerial pastry cream with intense cocoa flavors.

❹ THE SALAMBO

Oblong-shaped choux pastry created in reference to the success of an opera by Ernest Reyer (1890) based on Gustave Flaubert's novel *Salammbô* (1862). It is filled with vanilla or kirsch pastry cream and topped with a caramel glaze. When it is glazed with green fondant and topped with chocolate sprinkles, it is called the "gland" due to its acornlike appearance. A letter from Maxime Du Camp to his friend Flaubert dated March 30, 1863, quotes Maison Boissier as the creator of "a new petit-four with cream called 'Salammbô.'"

La Vieille France

📍 *5, av. de Laumière, Paris 19th*

A flavorful pastry cream with kirsch and a choux pastry covered with crackly caramel.

❺ PROFITEROLES

This timeless dessert, consisting of choux puffs filled with vanilla ice cream and served topped with melted chocolate, appeared as early as the nineteenth century in the writings of Grimod de La Reynière. According to some, Antonin Carême filled puffs with pastry cream instead.

Grande Brasserie

📍 *6, rue de la Bastille, Paris 4th*

The house serves three choux puffs covered with a craquelin top and filled with Bourbon vanilla ice cream and topped with a slightly sweet dark chocolate sauce made from 70 percent cacao Sao Tomé chocolate.

SKIP TO
The Paris-Brest, p. 120; The Saint-Honoré, p. 206; Parisian Gnocchi, p. 235.

Beef Miroton

The art of using leftover beef gave birth to this carefully prepared recipe. —SACHA LOMNITZ

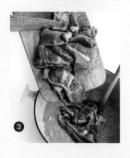

THE RECIPE

Season : spring and summer   **Difficulty** ●○○

SERVES 4

18 ounces (500 g) cooked beef stew meat or roast beef	2 tablespoons apple cider vinegar
10½ ounces (300 g) yellow onions	1¼ cups (300 ml) beef broth
2 tablespoons unsalted butter	Salt and freshly ground black pepper
2 tablespoons all-purpose flour	Steamed potatoes, for serving (optional)

Looking for a way to use leftover cooked meat from beef stew or a roast? Here is a simple and family-style approach to achieve it.

Cut the meat into very thin slices. Peel and slice the onions.

In a pot over medium-low heat, melt the butter. Add the onions and sauté until softened and translucent; do not brown them.

Add the flour and stir ❶. Add the vinegar and continue stirring while adding the broth. Bring to a boil ❷.

When the onions are well cooked down, lower the heat, and simmer for 15 to 30 minutes, covered.

Add the meat ❸, and cook over low heat for about 30 minutes (up to 1 hour if using roast beef). Adjust the seasoning and serve. Serve with steamed potatoes on the side, if desired.

HIS MAJESTY, THE OX
Made from leftover cooked stew meat or roast beef, boeuf miroton figured prominently in the procession of the Boeuf Gras (Fatted Calf) that was led, until the early twentieth century, through the streets of Paris during celebrations on the Thursday of mid-Lent. Followed by a troupe of onions and carrots and amid shouts from parade goers, during what was also known as the *fête du Boeuf villé*, the animal was walked through the city to the La Villette slaughterhouses where its meat was sold, usually for double the price.

IS IT SPELLED *MIROTON* OR *MIRONTON*?
The term *miroton* is of unknown origin but appeared in François Massialot's *Le Cuisinier royal et bourgeois* (1691) well before the famous refrain "*Mironton, mironton, mirontaine*" from the eighteenth-century popular folk song "*Malbrough s'en va-t-en guerre*" ("Marlborough Is Going to War"). The words *miroton* and *mironton* have nothing in common, except that the former is sometimes spelled as the latter, making it an amusing point of confusion.

ACROSS PAGES ACROSS PARIS . . .
Zazie d'Queneau, the cheeky ten-year-old character in the film *Zazie dans le métro* (1959), is on an exploration through Paris when she meets a "cop raised by his mother on a solid tradition of boeuf miroton." This is also the dish that Madame Maigret lovingly concocts in her apartment at 132, boulevard Richard-Lenoir, in a novel by Georges Simenon, and that Madame Cibot cooks up in the Marais on rue de Normandie in the building where cousin Pons lived in Balzac's novel a century earlier (1847).

"This was leftover boiled beef scraps bought from a roaster who dealt in secondhand scraps, fricasseed in butter with thinly sliced onions until the butter was absorbed by the meat and onions so that this dish . . . had the appearance of being fried."

—Honoré de Balzac, *Le Cousin Pons*, 1847

SKIP TO
The Balzac Eating Guide, p. 84; Les Halles: The Belly of Paris, p. 113; A Parisian Way of Speaking, p. 250.

LE PROCOPE

The history of the first literary café in Paris is linked to the arrival of coffee from the Middle East—but the café's origins are Italian. —ILARIA BRUNETTI

MAISON PARISIENNE
13, RUE DE L'ANCIENNE-
COMÉDIE, 6TH ARR.

RESTAURANT
Le Procope
Fondé en 1686

◉ TO SEE

The magnificent facade with its wrought-iron balconies, which became a historical monument in 1962.

The bicorne hat that belonged to Napoléon Bonaparte (on the stairs).

The Salon Rousseau, to sit under the portrait of the philosopher.

🍴 TO TRY

The tête de veau en cocotte comme en 1686 (calf's head in a casserole as done in 1686)

The coq au vin "ivre de juliénas" (chicken in red wine) served in a copper casserole dish.

SKIP TO

A P'tit Noir, Please, p. 130; Ice Cream Shops, p. 332; Coffee Roasters, p. 372.

A strong coffee history

Francesco Procopio Cutò arrived in Paris from Sicily in 1670 and secured his first job as clerk for an Armenian coffee shop. A few years later, he opened his own stall selling coffee at the Saint-Germain fair. In 1686, Cutò, now going by the name Procope, purchased a renowned bathhouse from a man named Gregory and transformed it into a luxurious space that would become his legendary café Le Procope.

The end of a legend

In 1716, Procopio's son inherited the business, but it closed definitively in 1890. After serving as a space for various activities (headquarters of a literary circle, a bouillon, and more), café Le Procope was renovated in 1957 to become the eighteenth century–style restaurant it is today.

The inventor of ice cream?

Procope had an interesting lineage. His grandfather, a fisherman, created a machine to make granitas (ice confections he prepared using snow from Mount Etna, with honey and fresh fruit juices), which had become very fashionable at the time. Cutò improved the recipe by replacing the honey with sugar and adding salt to keep the mixture frozen longer. The multiflavored ice creams he served at Le Procope quickly became famous throughout Paris.

Quench the thirst . . .

At Le Procope, guests could order myriad beverages, including coffee, the new trendy drink recently imported from Turkey; wine; and (since Francesco Procopio Cutò was a master limonadier and spirit distiller) alcoholic beverages such as "rosée du soleil," a mixture of spices macerated in brandy, "liqueur du parfait amour," and "populo," made with spices and wine.

. . . and nourish the mind

Although another establishment Café Grégoire was attracting artists and aristocrats of the time, Le Procope became the first true literary café in Paris, frequented by many artists, philosophers, and politicians. Stories somewhere between truth and legend state that d'Alembert and Diderot had the idea of composing their *Encyclopédie* here and that Benjamin Franklin wrote the Treaty of Alliance with France and articles of the American Constitution here. Le Procope became the meeting place of the club des Cordeliers and revolutionaries, the Phrygian cap was displayed here for the first time, and it was the favorite café of the Romantics Musset, Sand, and Balzac.

A sumptuous decor

Procope was attentive to the decor of his café, with its marble tables, crystal chandeliers, precious tapestries, windows, and mirrors. Even the servers dressed in a style of the East with their fur hats.

To See and to Drink

A walk along the streets of Paris is a feast for the eyes, and there are seemingly endless places to stop along the way for a little refreshment. Here are ten stops that are just a thousand steps or fewer from some of the most emblematic places in the capital. —ALEXIS GOUJARD

Garden of the Palais-Royal

👣 143 STEPS
→ **ENYAA**

📍 37, rue de Montpensier, Paris 1st. €€€

Sake and Champagne, two best friends of Japanese cuisine, have been served here since 2017.

TO DRINK

A compendium of well-known labels (Kakureï and Daïna sake, Champagnes from De Sousa, Selosse, Savart, Coulon, and more).

TO EAT

Sashimi, tempura, eel cooked with binchō-tan.

👣 314 STEPS
→ **JUVENILES**

📍 47, rue de Richelieu, Paris 1st. €€

Open since 1987, this establishment has been one of the pioneers of wine bistros.

TO DRINK

The Scottish owner's first love for the Rhône (Jamet, Clape, Vieux Télégraphe).

TO EAT

Scotch egg, calamari à la plancha, roasted guinea fowl.

The Eiffel Tower

👣 OVERHEAD
→ **LE JULES VERNE**

📍 5, av. Gustave-Eiffel, Paris 7th. €€€€

Since 1983, on the second floor of the Eiffel Tower, this establishment has offered a high-level wine list and cuisine.

TO DRINK

Choose options from the list curated by Benjamin Roffet, MOF (Best Craftsman of France) 2011 and best sommelier of France 2010. Classic and well-suited vintages.

TO EAT

Chef Frédéric Anton's starred cuisine, in five to seven courses.

👣 714 STEPS
→ **CAVE VINO SAPIENS**

📍 145, rue Saint-Dominique, Paris 7th. €€

Since 2014, an eat-in wine bar well stocked with old vintages and natural wines.

TO DRINK

Burgundies of Romanée-Conti, Lignier, Mugneret-Gibourg, natural Alsatian wines by Pierre Frick.

TO EAT

Duck legs from Beleslou farm, smoked dry sausage.

Notre Dame de Paris

👣 714 STEPS
→ **L'ÉTIQUETTE**

📍 10, rue Jean-du-Bellay, Paris 4th. €€

Perched on Île Saint-Louis, this evolving wine cellar has been delighting since 2012.

TO DRINK

100 percent organic, biodynamic, and natural wines from nearly 170 winemakers.

TO EAT

Whelks-mayo, pollack, and wood-fired chicken.

👣 1,000 STEPS
→ **LA TOUR D'ARGENT**

📍 15–17, quai de la Tournelle, Paris 5th. €€€€

The legendary cellar of La Tour d'Argent was founded in the sixteenth century and brings together the greatest wines that an oenophile could ever taste, as noted in 1867 by Alfred Delvau in his guide *Les Plaisirs de Paris*.

TO DRINK

320,000 bottles in the wine cellar. Everything in the cellar has been there since the end of the nineteenth century.

TO EAT

The pressed duck or the sole cardinal.

Sacré Coeur Basilica

👣 386 STEPS
→ **LA BONNE FRANQUETTE**

📍 18, rue Saint-Rustique, Paris 18th.

An institution in Montmartre since 1925. It has a guinguette atmosphere and great wines.

TO DRINK

Champagne Drappier, Cornas de Balthazar, Château-Chalon de Macle, Chinon de Philippe Alliet.

TO EAT

Bistro-style food including pistachio sausage, escargot, beef estouffade, etc.

👣 929 STEPS
→ **COMESTIBLES & MARCHAND DE VINS**

📍 65, rue du Mont-Cenis, Paris 18th. €

Open since 2013 and offering a large selection of bottles and magnums of vins vivants (living wines) at low prices.

TO DRINK

Côte-Roannaise de Sérol, Terrasses-du-Larzac du Mas Jullien, PGI Alpilles du Domaine Hauvette.

TO EAT

Tapas de cecina, lomo Iberico (dry-cured pork), guindillas (a pepper), and boudin Béarnais (blood sausage).

Pantheon

👣 714 STEPS
→ **LES PAPILLES**

📍 30, rue Gay-Lussac, Paris 5th. €€

Tasty cuisine and great classic and natural wines have been titillating the taste buds here since 2003.

TO DRINK

Bollinger, Châteauneuf-du-Pape de Beaucastel, Sancerre de Riffault, Cornas de Thierry Allemand.

TO EAT

Gorgeous bistro cuisine, Domaine Le Voisin duck stew.

👣 857 STEPS
→ **LE LOUIS VINS**

📍 9, rue de la Montagne-Sainte-Geneviève, Paris 5th. €€

Offering cozy chesterfield banquettes, comforting dishes, and a tidy wine list since 2013.

TO DRINK

Chablis de Dauvissat, Pauillac de Pichon Comtesse, Côte-Rôtie de Gangloff, Cahors de Cosse-Maisonneuve.

TO EAT

Veal crusted pâté and foie gras, porcini mushrooms in persillade, shellfish cannelloni.

SKIP TO
Tour d'Argent, p. 132; Restaurants of the Eiffel Tower, p. 138; Spotlight on Sole, p. 290.

Brioche

Whether from Paris or Nanterre, the ethereal brioche, a bread enriched with butter and egg, is a satisfying addition to any Parisian breakfast table. —MARIE-LAURE FRÉCHET

THE RECIPE

Season: year-round
Difficulty : ●○○

MAKES 1 LARGE BRIOCHE

There is no milk in this traditional brioche, as is typically included in boulangerie versions.

1½ teaspoons (10 g) fresh yeast

2 cups (250 g) all-purpose or T55 flour, or pastry flour or T45 flour, plus more for dusting

2 tablespoons plus 1¼ teaspoons (30 g) sugar

¾ teaspoon (5 g) salt

4 large (200 g) eggs

1 tablespoon plus 1 teaspoon (20 g) water

9 tablespoons (130 g) unsalted butter, room temperature, plus more for greasing

Equipment

Stand mixer

One 8½-inch (22 cm) fluted brioche mold or 1 loaf pan

La Brioche by Édouard Manet, 1870.

Crumble the yeast and add it to the bowl of a stand mixer fitted with the dough hook. Add the flour, sugar, salt, and 3 (150 g) of the eggs. Knead for 4 minutes on low speed (speed 1) and for 5 minutes on speed 2. Add the water if the dough becomes too dense. Knead in the butter . Turn the dough out onto a floured work surface and shape it into a ball. Cover it with a clean towel and let rise for 30 minutes. Turn the dough (fold it over onto itself) and set aside again to rise for 30 minutes. When the dough has doubled in volume, turn it again to release any gases, and transfer it to a wide container. Cover and refrigerate for 8 hours. The next day, place the dough onto a floured work surface and cut it in half using a bench scraper.

FOR A LARGE PARISIAN-STYLE BRIOCHE WITH A HEAD

Cut away one-fifth of the dough. Shape the two dough pieces into a large and small ball, then cover them with a cloth and set aside for 30 minutes. Grease a fluted brioche

mold by brushing the inside with softened butter using a pastry brush. Pierce the large ball through the center to make a ring. Roll out the small ball into a pear shape. Place the large ball ring in the bottom of the mold. Push the small ball into the center with the narrower end down into the ring. Using your fingers, pinch the two dough pieces together at the seam to adhere them.

FOR A NANTERRE BRIOCHE

Divide the dough into 8 portions of the same weight. Shape each portion into a ball and place them staggered in a greased loaf pan .

In a bowl, beat the remaining egg. Using a pastry brush, glaze the dough with the egg wash. Set aside for 1½ hours, covered, to rise. Preheat the oven to 350°F (180°C), conventional heat (no fan). Glaze the dough balls again with the egg. Bake for 15 minutes for the Parisian brioche or 20 to 25 minutes for the Nanterre brioche. Let stand for at least 5 minutes before unmolding.

THE PARISIAN

Composed of a ball topped by a smaller one called the "head," this brioche also comes in a large format for sharing. The painters Chardin (in 1763) and Manet (in 1870) paid tribute to it in their works.

THE NANTERRE

Consists of eight balls placed snuggly into two rows in a rectangular mold. Its origin dates to Saint Geneviève, patron saint of Nanterre, around 450 CE, and the blessed breads that celebrated her worship. Famous all over, including in Paris, they were sold by street vendors, as depicted by Jean-Jacques Rousseau's *Rêveries du promeneur solitaire* (1782).

A MAJOR DIFFERENCE

Historically, brioche breads were found throughout France, but in Paris, brewer's yeast was used as early as the eighteenth century to help the bread rise, ensuring an airy texture.

SKIP TO
Holy Croissant!, p. 226; Bakeries, p. 308.

Nanterre brioche.

The Croque-Monsieur

Made with bread, cheese, and ham, this hot and comforting sandwich is a sure bet to enjoy in Parisian restaurants and at home. — FRANÇOIS-RÉGIS GAUDRY

THE RECIPE

Season: year-round   **Difficulty** ●○○

MAKES 2 CROQUE-MONSIEURS

2 tablespoons crème fraîche

1 teaspoon mustard

1 pinch of Espelette pepper

1 pinch of freshly grated nutmeg

Salt and freshly ground black pepper

6 slices bread (3 slices per croque-monsieur)

8 slices very thin ham, or 4 slices very thick ham

3 ounces (90 g) 12-month Comté, grated

2 tablespoons (30 g) unsalted butter

Equipment

Microplane grater

Plastic wrap

This recipe by the creative cook Suzy Palatine is a delicious variation of the classic, made using crème fraîche instead of béchamel, Comté cheese, and not two slices of bread but three.

In a bowl, combine the crème fraîche, mustard, Espelette pepper, nutmeg, and a small pinch of salt and black pepper ❶.

Spread the cream mixture generously on one side of 2 slices of bread, then on both sides of a third slice ❷.

Construct the croque-monsieur in this order from the bottom: a slice of bread with a single-side of spread, half the ham and Comté, the slice of bread with a double-side of spread, the remaining ham and Comté, the final slice of bread with a single-side of spread, to close the sandwich ❸. Repeat to make a second croque-monsieur. Wrap the croque-monsieurs in plastic wrap and set aside in a cool place for 30 minutes while making an accompaniment, such as a salad.

Preheat the oven to 350°F (180°C). Unwrap the croque and melt the butter and brush it on top. Bake for 10 minutes, or until the bread is golden. Serve immediately.

A POPULAR SPECIALTY

Variations abound for this popular comfort food: using slices of French or Japanese pain de mie (Pullman loaf sandwich bread), covered, or not, with a thick layer of cheese and béchamel, accompanied by fries or a salad, topped with a fried egg (which then makes it a croque-madame), and sometimes embellished with chicken and tomato. Despite all the schools of thought, the sandwich's popularity in Parisian cafés, sporting venues, train station eateries, and even quality bistros is undeniable.

A LITTLE HISTORY

Its story is not verified, but according to René Girard, in *Histoire des mots de la cuisine française* (1947), the croque-monsieur was created in 1910 at the Bel Âge, a café on boulevard des Capucines. One day, running out of baguette, boss Michel Lunarca was preparing a sandwich with pain de mie. A customer reportedly asked him about the meat. It's "de la viande de monsieur!" (the meat of Sir!), the bistro owner replied, as if to thumb his nose at the local reputation he had of being a cannibal. The expression "croque-monsieur" appeared on his menu. It's difficult to believe this story, however, because there were repeated mentions of the "croque-monsieur" as early as 1891 to designate the newest popular sandwich in the news.

A PROUSTIAN DISH

Marcel Proust mentions the croque-monsieur in *À l'ombre des jeunes filles en fleurs* (*In the Shadow of Young Girls in Flower*), published in 1919: "And when we came out of the concert, as if on the way back to the hotel, we stopped, my grandmothers and I, to exchange a few words with Madame de Villeparisis, who told us that she had ordered for us at the hotel 'des croque-monsieur' and eggs cooked in cream."

SKIP TO
Île-de-France
Terroir, p. 20;
Bistros, p. 352.

THE BEST CROQUE-MONSIEURS IN PARIS

Sébastien Gaudard
📍 *1, rue des Pyramides, Paris 1st*
Bread: Pullman loaf.
The cheesy filling: Comté from Marcel Petite (Doubs), a savory pastry cream.
Ham: jambon blanc, from the Linard charcuterie (Aveyron).

Vins des Pyrénées
📍 *25, rue Beautreillis, Paris 4th*
Bread: brioche-style Pullman loaf from bakery Les Délices de Parmentier (Paris 11th).
The cheesy filling: Gouda, béchamel.
Ham: Prince de Paris.

Carré Pain de Mie
📍 *5, rue Rambuteau, Paris 4th*
Bread: house-made Pullman loaf.
The cheesy filling: 15-month Comté, béchamel.
Ham: Prince de Paris.

Maison Mulot
📍 *76, rue de Seine, Paris 6th*
Bread: house-made Pullman loaf.
The cheesy filling: farmstead Emmental, crème d'Isigny (fresh cream).
Ham: jambon blanc de Paris.

Pierre Hermé
📍 *Café-Restaurant Beaupassage, 53–57, rue de Grenelle, Paris 7th*
Bread: Pullman loaf from Shiba's (Vitry-sur-Seine, Val-de-Marne).
The cheesy filling: Comté, crème fraîche, inspired by Gaston Lenôtre.
Ham: Prince de Paris.

Fric-Frac
📍 *79, quai de Valmy, Paris 10th*
📍 *4, rue des Trois-Frères, Paris 18th*
Bread: multigrain loaf by MOF (Best Craftsman of France) chef Frédéric Lalos.
The cheesy filling: Emmental, Mornay sauce.
Ham: jambon de Paris cooked au torchon (wrapped in a cloth and poached).

When Hollywood Dines in Paris

Whether on the big or small screen, Paris is a rich backdrop to movies and television shows, and it serves as a source of inspiration for American fiction. — CHARLES PATIN O'COOHOON

The Ratatouille recipe

In one of the greatest restaurants in Paris, Rémy, a little rat who is passionate about cooking, dreams of becoming a chef. Brad Bird's 2007 film, the eighth production for Pixar Studios, was inspired by French places and personalities.

THE CHARACTERS

Colette Tatou, sous-chef
Inspiration: Hélène Darroze

Auguste Gusteau, five-star chef
Inspiration: Bernard Loiseau, Paul Bocuse, and Auguste Escoffier

Anton Ego, food critic
Inspiration: French-style food criticism, culminating under the guise of Louis Jouvet

THE VOICES

Cyril Lignac and Guy Savoy were the voices of Lalo and Horst, respectively, two of the kitchen chefs.

THE RESTAURANTS

To prepare for the film, the camera team, led by Sharon Calahan, took nearly forty-five hundred shots of Paris, many of them at Le Procope (Paris 6th), La Tour d'Argent (Paris 5th), Taillevent (Paris 8th), Chez Michel (Paris 10th), and Hélène Darroze (Paris 6th).

THE CRITIC'S CRITIQUE

On the release of the film, François Simon wrote in the August 1, 2007, edition of *Le Figaro*:
"In this movie is a miserable rosette of eggplant, zucchini, and tomatoes (reminiscent of the pinkie-in-the-air nouvelle American cuisine during the years 1997–98), far from the slowly stewed and melt-in-the-mouth ratatouille that we know. It makes you wonder, and not without delight, if any rat could become a film director."

THE RATATOUILLE?

The star dish of the film is not a ratatouille but instead confit byaldi, made of peppers, onions, tomatoes, garlic, and olive oil, traced to American chef Thomas Keller, itself inspired by the confit byaldi of French chef Michel Guérard.

Hollywood at the table

Hollywood has repeatedly seated itself at Parisian tables. Here is a short inventory of films and their directors:

MIDNIGHT IN PARIS, BY WOODY ALLEN (2011)
The place: Aux Lyonnais—2, rue Saint-Marc, Paris 2nd
The scene: Gil (Owen Wilson) sips a bottle of Haut-Brion with Dalí (Adrien Brody), Luis Buñuel (Adrien de Van), and Man Ray (Tom Cordier) in this gem set in the nineteenth century.

SOMETHING'S GOTTA GIVE, BY NANCY MEYERS (2004)
The place: Le Grand Colbert—2, rue Vivienne, Paris 2nd
The scene: Harry Sanborn (Jack Nicholson) joins Erica Barry (Diane Keaton) for a birthday dinner.

THE ARISTOCATS, BY WOLFGANG REITHERMAN (1971)
The place: Le Café de la Paix—5, pl. de l'Opéra, Paris 9th
The scene: the gang of cats and the mouse Roquefort run past this iconic café, where a man sipping a bottle of red thinks he is hallucinating.

LOVE IN THE AFTERNOON, BY BILLY WILDER (1957)
The place: The Ritz Paris—5, pl. Vendôme, Paris 8th
The scene: billionaire Frank Flanagan (Gary Cooper) seduces Ariane Chavasse (Audrey Hepburn) in this famous Parisian grand hotel.

AN AMERICAN IN PARIS, BY VINCENTE MINNELLI (1952)
The place: Café Huguette
The scene: Jerry Mulligan (Gene Kelly) lives above this colorful Parisian café re-created from scratch in the studios of Hollywood.

MARATHON MAN, BY JOHN SCHLESINGER (1976)
The place: Le Dôme—108, blvd. du Montparnasse, Paris 14th
The scene: feeling threatened, Doc (Roy Scheider) has a rendezvous with his superior Janeway (William Devane).

The Planet Hollywood Adventure

On August 25, 1995, Sylvester Stallone and Arnold Schwarzenegger opened their concept Planet Hollywood at 78, avenue des Champs-Élysées, a 43,100-square-foot (4,000 sq m) restaurant dedicated to American cinema. Between the shark from *Jaws* and Sean Connery's costume in *Highlander,* guests would chow down on burgers and tacos. In February 2008, faced with soaring rent prices, the restaurant closed.

TV series in restaurants

Here is a small inventory of episodes of American TV series shot in Paris.

BEVERLY HILLS 90210
Created by Darren Star—Season 3, Episode 3, 1992

The set: Le Chardonnay, a replica of Brasserie Vagenende (Paris 6th) on Melrose Avenue in West Hollywood
The meal: Donna (Tori Spelling) and Brenda (Shannen Doherty) order a veal dish, the only one whose title they understand, but it ends up being veal brain.

MODERN FAMILY
Created by Christopher Lloyd II and Steven Levitan—Season 11, Episode 13, 2021

The set: L'Oiseau Blanc, The Peninsula Paris—19, av. Kléber, Paris 16th
The meal: the Pritchett-Dunphy-Tucker clan meets under the glass roof of this Parisian luxury hotel and enjoys a gastronomic meal.

SEX AND THE CITY
Created by Darren Star—Season 6, Episode 20, 2004

The set: Kong—1, rue du Pont-Neuf, Paris 1st
Lunch: Carrie (Sarah Jessica Parker) and Juliette (Carole Bouquet) have a glass of red wine. Carrie delights in the fact that Juliette finds the chairs by Philippe Starck "hideous."

DYNASTY
Created by Josh Schwartz and Stephanie Savage—Season 2, Episode 14, 2019

The set: Café Marly—93, rue de Rivoli, Paris 1st
The meal: facing the Louvre, Fallon Carrington (Elizabeth Gillies), Sammy Jo (Rafael de La Fuente), and Steven Carrington (James Mackay) share a glass of wine.

Following Emily

Shown on Netflix since 2020, *Emily in Paris* follows the Parisian wanderings of Emily Cooper (Lily Collins), who has landed straight from Chicago to work in Paris. She falls in love with Gabriel (Lucas Bravo), a cook. Here is a guided tour of her favorite places.

1 BISTROT VALOIS
📍 *1, pl. de Valois, Paris 1st*

2 LE CAFÉ MARLY
📍 *93, rue de Rivoli, Paris 1st*

3 LE TOUT-PARIS
📍 *8, quai du Louvre, Paris 1st*

4 LE FLORE EN L'ILE
📍 *42, quai d'Orléans, Paris 4th*

5 BOULANGERIE MODERNE
📍 *16, rue des Fossés-Saint-Jacques, Paris 5th*

6 CAFÉ DE LA NOUVELLE MAIRIE
📍 *19, rue des Fossés-Saint-Jacques, Paris 5th*

7 RISTORANTE TERRA NERA
📍 *18, rue des Fossés-Saint-Jacques, Paris 5th*
Gabriel's restaurant Les Deux Compères—the focus of many of the show's storylines—is, in reality, the restaurant Terra Nera. On the menu? The "Tagliata di manzo Emily," in homage to the series.

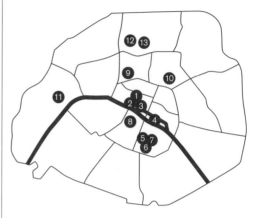

8 CAFÉ DE FLORE
📍 *172, blvd. Saint-Germain, Paris 6th*

9 TORTUGA
📍 *25, rue de la Chaussée-d'Antin, Paris 9th*

10 LULU LA NANTAISE
📍 *67, rue de Lancry, Paris, 10th*

11 CAFÉ DE L'HOMME
📍 *17, pl. du Trocadéro-et-du-11-Novembre, Paris 16th*

12 HÔTEL PARTICULIER MONTMARTRE
📍 *23, av. Junot, Pavillon D, Paris 18th*

13 LA MAISON ROSE
📍 *2, rue de l'Abreuvoir, Paris 18th*

The Fontainebleau

This creamy and simple specialty composed of whipped cream and fromage blanc (a soft, fresh cheese) has a few secrets to reveal. —PIERRE COULON

THE RECIPE

Season: year-round
Difficulty ● ○ ○

MAKES 4 DESSERTS

1 cup plus 2 tablespoons (260 g) whipping cream

3 tablespoons (40 g) crème fraîche

¾ cup (200 g) fromage blanc

Equipment

Handheld electric mixer

This is a creamy combo of cream and fromage blanc, by Pierre Coulon.*

In a bowl, combine the cream and crème fraîche. Beat the mixture into the consistency of whipped cream. Add the fromage blanc all at once and continue beating until soft peaks with tips that just barely bend ("bec d'oiseau," or bird's beak) form on the surface.

The mixture is traditionally presented pressed into cheesecloth and served with a coulis or red fruits, or, more simply, served in ramekins.

ITS VARIATIONS

With chestnut cream, salted butter caramel, and even lemon curd or halva added, the Fontainebleau is an ideal base for adding flavors. To flavor it, simply take half of the mixture and combine it with 3½ ounces (100 g) chestnut cream or 1¾ ounces (50 g) salted butter caramel or 3½ ounces (100 g) crumbled halva. Place the mixture at the bottom of the ramekins and spoon the remainder on top to create two layers.

Voiture de laitier, 1910.

"BUMPY" BEGINNINGS

According to legend, in the eighteenth century, a dairyman on rue Grande in Fontainebleau (Seine-et-Marne) had the idea of beating the foam that formed on the surface of the containers of cream during the bumpy cart ride when he transported the cream over cobblestoned streets. These cream-based preparations became more popular, especially during the time of François Vatel, who invented Chantilly cream, and were served over desserts with beaten egg whites, such as crémet d'Anjou.

IN THE TWENTIETH CENTURY

As a dairy-based dessert, the Fontainebleau's increased popularity was a natural consequence of the invention of a mechanism by the Barthélémy family to separate cream onto the surface of milk, which also naturally gently whipped it. This technique remained a secret, and so did the machine, as it was never commercialized.

One strict characteristic: The cream mixture has no added milk or cheese and must have a mousselike texture.

AN EMBLEM

In the 1990s, dairies successfully revived the Fontainebleau. They beat cream and added fromage blanc to lend it acidity and to differentiate it from whipped cream. Each manufacturer selects their own proportions of the two ingredients.

Since 2016, the Fromagers de France (an organization of dairy farmers) has been organizing a Fontainebleau competition.

TOP · LET'S EAT PARIS! · ADDRESSES

Quatrehomme
📍 *62, rue de Sèvres, Paris 7th + 4 locations*
A very light mousse, not too sweet.

Taka et Vermo
📍 *61 bis, rue du Faubourg-Saint-Denis, Paris 10th*
Airy, with slight acidity.

* Laiterie de Paris
The business of the author of this page.
📍 *74, rue des Poissonniers, Paris 18th*
Sweet and light, plain or flavored according to the seasons.

SKIP TO
Île-de-France Terroir, p. 20; From Cattle Farms to Dairies, p. 77.

Liberated Gourmands

Beauvoir, Duras, Sagan: these three illustrious twentieth-century women of letters shared a common love for Paris's Left Bank restaurants. — ELVIRA MASSON

Simone de Beauvoir, the spiritual customer (1908–1986)

HER WORKTABLE

La Coupole (102, blvd. du Montparnasse, Paris 14th). Here she wrote her novel *L'Invitée* (*She Came to Stay*) from 1943, in which she immortalized the restaurant. "'You can get hamburger steak at La Coupole,' says Gerbert resolutely. . . . Gerbert looked tenderly at the facade of La Coupole; the play of light captivated his heart almost as melancholy as a jazz tune."

HER FAVORITE TABLE

Les Deux Magots (6, pl. Saint-Germain-des-Prés, Paris 6th). She spent her time here observing customers, as evidenced by a letter to Nelson Algren: "On my way back, I came across Jean Genet, the vagabond-thief, who was very kind and very funny but prevented me from working."

HER RENDEZVOUS TABLE

Le Café de Flore (172, blvd. Saint-Germain, Paris 6th). Because it was better heated than her room, she worked here during the day and spent her evenings here with Jean-Paul Sartre, Olga Kosakiewicz, Maurice Merleau-Ponty, Albert Camus, and Jean Genet.

HER TABLE FOR TWO

Le Dôme (108, blvd. du Montparnasse, Paris 14th). She would meet with Sartre here twice a week, where they would spend the evening on the terrace.

Marguerite Duras, the magician in the kitchen (1914–1996)

HER WORKTABLE

Le Café de Flore (172, blvd. Saint-Germain, Paris 6th) just downstairs from her apartment. She would meet here with communist militants.

HER FAVORITE TABLE

Le Petit Saint-Benoît (4, rue Saint-Benoît, Paris 6th) and **Le Pré aux Clercs** (30, rue Bonaparte, Paris 6th). She lived all her life in the heart of Saint-Germain-des-Prés and loved to dine on the terraces in her neighborhood.

HER RENDEZVOUS TABLE

Hers! She cooked a lot, and all the time. She knew how to cook everything. The "Rue Saint-Benoît Groupe," postwar intellectuals, would meet at her home to debate, act, and have a little lunch. Some of her recipes were captured in a book, *La Cuisine de Marguerite*, published after her death by her son Jean Mascolo and eventually banned by her last companion and literary executor, Yann Andréa. "I don't tell them [people] I love them, I don't kiss them, I'm not a tender person, so I make food for others."

HER TABLE FOR TWO

Le Duc (243, blvd. Raspail, Paris 14th). This was where she had her last meeting with François Mitterrand. They maintained a political and literary relationship throughout their lives.

Françoise Sagan, the nibbling socialite (1935–2004)

HER WORKTABLE

Le Café Cujas (now closed, Paris 5th). At the age of eighteen, she skipped her classes at the Sorbonne next door and wrote her first novel, *Bonjour tristesse* (1954).

HER FAVORITE TABLE

Le Moniage Guillaume (now closed, Paris 14th). She often had lunch here with Sartre near the end of her life. He was blind at the time, and guests remember Sagan cutting his meat.

HER RENDEZVOUS TABLE

Chez Régine (49, rue de Ponthieu, Paris 8th), and later at New Jimmy's (now closed, Paris 14th) and Castel (15, rue Princesse, Paris 6th). Much more a partier than a gourmand, she would leave restaurants and cafés for jazz clubs, where her brother took her dancing.

HER TABLE FOR TWO

Brasserie Lipp (151, blvd. Saint-Germain, Paris 6th). She was a regular and would meet here with the writer and critic Philippe Sollers, head of the magazine *Tel Quel*, who asked her to lunch after reading one of her novels.

SKIP TO
Colette, p. 76; Café de Flore or Les Deux Magots?, p. 256.

Spotlight on Sole

More accustomed to sandy bottoms than to Parisian cobblestones, this flat fish has given birth to many great dishes served up in the capital. — CHARLES PATIN O'COOHOON

Sole on scene

The love story between Paris and sole is an ancient one. Remains of *Solea solea* (common sole) were found during the sixteenth century in the basements of upscale neighborhoods of ancient Lutetia. Remains of sole and flounder were recovered during the 1992 excavations in the Jardin du Carrousel (Paris 1st). In the sixteenth century, wealthy Parisians ate fish instead of meat more than 150 days out of the year, and evidence reveals that sole occupied a significant place in their diet. Louis XIV enjoyed them with crayfish or truffles in his seventeenth-century royal court. In *L'Art de la cuisine française* (1833), Antonin Carême offered 41 recipes. Auguste Escoffier offered 189 recipes for sole in his *Guide culinaire*. Since these times and today, *Solea solea* has been a major player on the menus of some of the most prestigious Parisian establishments. Being experienced with preparing sole is often a must for any great chef.

Sole Albert

ORIGIN

Named after Albert Blaser, nicknamed "the prince of maître d's and the maître d' of princes," served in the dining room at Maxim's from 1934 to 1959.

COMPOSITION

Sole is breaded and braised on a bed of shallots, drizzled with a vermouth sauce.

Sole à la Bercy

ORIGIN

Bercy, the district dedicated to the wine trade, is the birthplace of sauce Bercy.

COMPOSITION

Sole is drizzled with a reduction of shallots simmered in white wine and fish stock.

Sole Cardinal

ORIGIN

The recipe was created in the 1950s at La Tour d'Argent by chef Pierre Descreux.

COMPOSITION

Sole fillets are served with a crayfish stuffing the color of cardinals' robes.

Sole Dugléré

ORIGIN

This classic is named after its creator, Adolphe Dugléré, one of the greatest chefs of the twentieth century. He developed the recipe when he was at the head of Café Anglais.

COMPOSITION

Pieces of sole are served with a tomato-based sauce with white wine.

Sole à la Joinville

ORIGIN

Auguste Hélie, cook of the Prince of Joinville (the son of King Louis-Philippe) and author of the *Traité général de la cuisine maigre* (1896), is said to have created this recipe as homage to the prince.

COMPOSITION

Sole fillets are served with a mushroom-and-crayfish sauce thickened with heavy cream.

Sole Jules Janin

ORIGIN

In 1855, chef Urbain Dubois developed this recipe as a tribute to the famous drama critic and author of the foreword to Antonin Carême's *Cuisinier parisien* (1828).

COMPOSITION

Sole is poached in white wine; accompanied by poached mussels, truffle slices, and crayfish tails; and drizzled with a sauce tortue (Madeira, thyme, bay leaf, rosemary, mushrooms).

Sole Marguery

ORIGIN

Jean-Nicolas Marguery—who lent his name to the restaurant he acquired in 1867—is the creator of this dish. Its reputation became widespread thanks to the American James Buchanan Brady, who sent a friend's son to be hired under a fake name so he could get the recipe.

COMPOSITION

Sole fillets are served with a creamy sauce with white wine, accompanied by mussels and crayfish.

Sole Murat

ORIGIN

After a hunting trip, Napoléon I and his brother-in-law Joachim Murat dined at Maxim's. Taken aback by their unannounced arrival, the chef improvised a sole dish using leftovers from the dinner service.

COMPOSITION

Sole fillets are sautéed in butter and served with potatoes, artichoke hearts, and tomato slices.

Sole à la Pompadour

ORIGIN

With the help of her cooks, the Marquise de Pompadour created several recipes, including this sole dish that she served to King Louis XV at Château de Choisy on November 4, 1747.

COMPOSITION

Sole fillets are wrapped around chopped truffles and drizzled with a crayfish sauce.

Sole à la Normande

ORIGIN

Although its name doesn't provide a clue, this recipe, from 1837, is a Parisian creation of chef Langlais at Au Rocher de Cancale.

COMPOSITION

Sole is poached, covered with a sauce enriched with Isigny butter, and surrounded by mussels, shrimp, oysters, and mushrooms.

Trim, clean, and remove the black skin from a 14-ounce (400 g) sole. Wash the sole. Poach 4 oysters and their water without their shell in a scant ½ cup (100 ml) white wine for 1 minute. Reserve the cooking liquid. Cook 14 ounces (400 g) bouchot (pole-cultivated) mussels and keep the cooking liquid. Clean 4 button mushroom caps and sauté them. Reserve the cooking liquid. Shell 3½ ounces (100 g) shrimp and sauté them in ½ tablespoon butter. In a skillet, bring a scant ½ cup (100 ml) white wine and the reserved cooking liquids to a boil. Add 1 chopped shallot and the sole, white skin side up. Sauté for 5 minutes. Remove the sole and set aside in a serving dish and keep warm. Reduce the liquid by a third and add just over ¾ cup (200 ml) fresh cream. Reduce further. Strain the sauce and stir in 2½ tablespoons (40 g) butter. Add the shelled mussels, oysters, shrimp, and mushrooms. Ladle this mixture over the sole and serve.

Sole Urbain Dubois

ORIGIN

Chef at the court of the King of Prussia, Urbain Dubois dubbed this recipe, created in the mid-nineteenth century, in his own name.

COMPOSITION

Stuffed with crayfish tails with sauce Nantua and covered with a pike forcemeat, the soles are accompanied by breaded scallops and served with a sauce Normande.

TOP
· LET'S EAT PARIS! ·
ADDRESSES

LES BONNES MANIÈRES DE LA SOLE MEUNIÈRE

This is certainly the most typical sole recipe in Paris: floured, panfried in a little butter, and drizzled with a squeeze of lemon.

La Luna

📍 *69, rue du Rocher, Paris 8th.* €€

In this seafood temple, chef Michel Choisnel prepares a large line-caught sole served whole.

L'Écailler du Bistrot

📍 *22, rue Paul-Bert, Paris 11th.* €€

This is the seafood outpost of Bertrand Auboyneau's bistros, where a whole, grilled sole is served.

Le Duc

📍 *243, blvd. Raspail, Paris 14th.* €€€

The sole at this seafood house is generously accompanied and presented in fillets.

Le Dôme

📍 *108, blvd. du Montparnasse, Paris 14th.* €€€

This famous brasserie in Montparnasse serves a beautiful grilled whole sole.

SKIP TO
Urbain Dubois, p. 148; The Adventures of Bercy, p. 302; Adolphe Dugléré, p. 305.

Galette des Rois
King Cake

Popular in a large portion of the northern half of France, the so-called "Parisian" galette des Rois is a disk filled with frangipane encased in puff pastry. Is it a time-honored tradition? Not really. — LOÏC BIENASSIS

THE RECIPE

Season: year-round
Difficulty ● ● ○

SERVES 6

For the pastry cream

1 vanilla bean

½ cup plus 1 teaspoon (130 ml) whole milk

1 tablespoon plus 1 teaspoon (20 g) sugar

1 large (20 g) egg yolk

1 tablespoon plus 1 teaspoon (12 g) cornstarch

2½ teaspoons (12 g) unsalted butter

For the frangipane cream

3 tablespoons (50 g) unsalted butter, room temperature

¼ cup (50 g) sugar

2 tablespoons (15 g) all-purpose flour

½ cup (50 g) almond flour

1 large (50 g) egg

2 tablespoons rum (optional)

1⅓ pounds (600 g) Puff Pastry (p. 58), or 2 store-bought puff pastry disks

For finishing

2 large (40 g) egg yolks

Equipment

Pastry bag

Plain piping tip measuring ⅔ inch (16 mm)

2 cake rings measuring 9½ and 10¼ inches (24 and 26 cm) in diameter

1 edible bean

Should the galette be filled with frangipane or almond cream? French pastry chef Jean-Philippe Marsan has chosen sides in this exquisite recipe.

Make the pastry cream: Split the vanilla bean lengthwise in half and scrape out the seeds using the tip of a knife. In a saucepan, heat the milk, vanilla bean seeds and empty pod, and half (2 teaspoons/10 g) of the sugar. Bring to a simmer.

In a bowl, combine the egg yolk and remaining sugar. Add the cornstarch and stir to incorporate. Add the hot milk while whisking. Pour the mixture into a saucepan set over medium heat, whisking continuously. After 20 seconds of boiling, remove from the heat and add the butter. Stir thoroughly to combine. Transfer to a heatproof bowl, gently press plastic wrap onto the surface, and refrigerate until completely cooled.

Make the frangipane cream: In a bowl, combine the butter and sugar. Add the all-purpose and almond flours. Stir in the egg and rum, if using.

Whisk the pastry cream to smooth the texture and incorporate it into the frangipane mixture. The final frangipane cream must be homogeneous.

Fill a pastry bag with the frangipane cream and place the bag in the refrigerator to keep cool.

Assemble and finish: Roll out the puff pastry into rectangles measuring 12 by 24 inches (30 by 60 cm) and ⅛ inch (3 mm) thick. Using a sharp knife and the cake rings, cut out a disk measuring 9½ inches (24 cm) and a disk measuring 10¼ inches (26 cm) in diameter 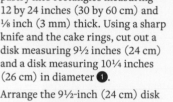.

Arrange the 9½-inch (24 cm) disk on a piece of parchment paper and, starting from the center, pipe a spiral of frangipane cream 6 inches (16 cm) in diameter . Place the bean in a random spot on the cream. Lightly moisten the edges of the disk with water. Arrange the 10¼-inch (26 cm) disk on top and press the edges of the two dough disks together to seal them and enclose the cream. Set aside in the freezer for 10 minutes. In a bowl, whisk the egg yolks.

Brush the top of the dough with the egg yolks and set aside for 30 minutes in a cool place.

Meanwhile, preheat the oven to 350°F (180°C).

Brush the top of the cake again with the egg yolk. Using the tip of a toothpick, score a pattern of your choice into the top  .

Bake for about 45 minutes, or until dark golden and puffed into layers.

SKIP TO
The Mille-Feuille, p. 58; Antonin Carême, p. 156; Pastry Shops, p. 312.

ANCIEN RÉGIME

In eighteenth-century Paris—and certainly well before—breads enriched with butter and eggs, similar to today's brioche, were baked golden and round into which a fève (bean) was inserted. At the time, these were called gâteaux des Rois, not galettes.

PUFF PASTRY

The "gasteaux fueilletez" has been made in Paris since most likely the sixteenth century, although it is difficult to determine what they consisted of exactly. The making of modern puff pastry was described for the first time in 1651 in *Le Cuisinier françois* by François Pierre de La Varenne. In 1653, the anonymously penned *Pastissier françois* gave the recipe for the gâteau feuilleté, puff pastry cake: "Spread the pâte feuilleté on paper that is not greased. Give this dough the thickness of the width of a finger or a thumb & cut the dough all around with a knife to round it into the shape of a cake. Glaze it on top & put it in the oven." It is not out of the question that pastries like this were enjoyed during Epiphany.

WHEN FRANGIPANE BECAME THE NORM

Cake recipes combining puff pastry and almonds are ancient, such as the tourte de franchipanne in *Cuisinier françois* for which La Varenne recommended a cream mixing pistachios and almonds.

There is mention of galette or gâteau des Rois with frangipane at the end of the nineteenth century. In 1938, *Larousse gastronomique* snubbed it again: "In Paris and in all the neighboring provinces of Île-de-France, it is a galette feuilletée [puff pastry galette] that is the galette des Rois." However, this dry puff pastry galette (without a filling) was the exception and not the rule at the end of the twentieth century. The "Parisian" galette des Rois is now made with frangipane, and now the lover of galette feuilleté must ask for a "galette sèche" (dry galette).

NINETEENTH CENTURY

In 1815, Antonin Carême explained how to make a gâteau de plomb au chocolat, a pastry sometimes served for the Feast of Kings. Still, in the mid-nineteenth century, there are recipes found using pâte brisée (a flaky tart dough), while the galette feuilleté tends to appear in cookbooks. The former version has "ordinary" layers, light in butter, with four turns, while the latter is more luxurious, fattier, with more turns, and therefore more puffed.

THE GALETTE IN THE MOVIES

In Christophe Honoré's *Les Chansons d'amour* (2007), Jeanne Pommeraye (Chiara Mastroianni) is crowned victor over a Parisian galette des Rois during a Sunday meal on a cloudy Paris day.

THE BEST GALETTES DES ROIS IN PARIS

Boulangerie de la Tour

📍 *2, rue du Cardinal-Lemoine, Paris 5th*
Light flaking and a fragrant and unctuous frangipane.

Des Gâteau and du Pain

📍 *89, rue du Bac, Paris 7th*
📍 *63, blvd. Pasteur, Paris 15th*
Crisp inverted puff pastry, generous cream made with almonds from Provence.

Pâtisserie Cyril Lignac

📍 *24, rue Paul-Bert, Paris 11th + 5 locations*
Caramelized puff pastry and a creamy almond-milk cream.

Pierre Hermé

📍 *53-57, rue de Grenelle, Paris 7th + 22 locations*
Lightly caramelized puff pastry and almond cream with toasted sliced almonds.

Mamiche

📍 *45, rue Condorcet, Paris 9th*
📍 *32, rue du Château d'Eau, Paris 10th*
Crisp puff pastry and generous frangipane.

Atelier P1

📍 *157, rue Marcadet, Paris 18th*
Inverted puff pastry, intense cream with whole almonds.

B.O.U.L.O.M

📍 *181, rue Ordener, Paris 18th*
Inverted puff pastry and frangipane with crème brûlée and almonds.

293

LUTETIA AT THE TABLE

Thanks to archaeological excavations within Paris in recent years, we can take a deeper look into the cooking pots of Gallo-Roman Lutetia. —STÉPHANE SOLIER

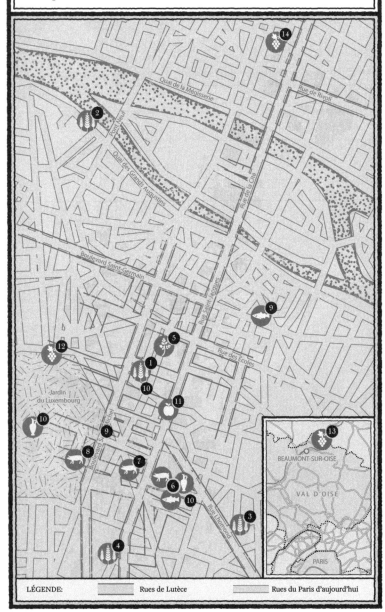

LÉGENDE: Rues de Lutèce   Rues du Paris d'aujourd'hui

GRAINS
(*soft wheat, hard wheat, spelt, rye*)
Makes up the basis of the diet in the form of porridges, breads, flatbreads, fermented drinks (cervoise).

❶ Neighborhood bakery (granary and ovens)

❷ Grain fields (river deposits) with granary

❸ Domestic flour millstones

❹ Domestic ovens in individual habitats

LEGUMINOUS PLANTS, VEGETABLES, AND AROMATIC PLANTS
Frequent complement to the grain base.
› field beans, legumes, lentils
› carrots, kohlrabi, chard, lettuces
› Fennel, celery, coriander, oregano, savory, dill

❺ Granary (remains of fruits and seeds)

MEATS
This is the third important food group. Pork, ox, and goat are the primary sources of meat, but traces of Gallic customs using dog and horsemeat are found. Depending on the social status of its inhabitants, the quality and type of the meat and change across sites. The consumption of cheese, especially using goat's milk, is attested to by the presence of ceramic faisselles (straining molds) and by the evidence of a goat farm in the city (archaeozoological studies).

❻ Common habitats (leftover pigs, lamb, farm birds)

❼ Modest and peripheral neighborhood (remains of mature sheep)

❽ Neighborhood with special cultural status (pig remains, hunting game: roe deer, hare, stag; no horse or dog remains)

FISH AND MOLLUSKS
Lesser consumption and linked to the social status of the consumers.

❻ Common habitats (remains of Channel flatfish, eels, freshwater fish, oysters, and mussels)

❾ Common habitats (many remains of oysters from Calvados)

OLIVE OIL AND GARUM (FISH SAUCE)
Imported from the Mediterranean as evidenced by the amphorae discovered in large quantities.

❻ ❿ Rubbish pits

FRUITS
Several varieties are introduced under Roman influence (grapevines, figs, peaches), wild nuts and fruits (hazelnuts, blackberries, etc.), and fruits cultivated since the Gallic era (pears, apples, walnuts, chestnuts). **"People in the region have a sunnier winter. They grow a quality vine in their region and some have already managed to have fig trees."** —Emperor Julian, *Misopogon*, VII, 7, fourth century

⓫ Peach pits

WINE
Valued by the Gauls and imported from the Mediterranean. The discovery of second-century vines in the Val-d'Oise and amphorae production on the right bank of Lutetia attests to early local viticulture.

⓬ Burial of the sculpture l'homme du Sénat, a Gallic auxiliary horseman (with wine amphorae)

⓭ Vine plots

⓮ Potter's workshop (regional wine amphorae)

A short chronology of ancient Paris

› **Before the Roman conquest**
Dependent upon a more important stronghold suspected to have existed under what is today the city of Nanterre, a Gallic settlement was present on Paris's Île de la Cité.

› **52 BCE**
Conquest of Lutetia, as referred to by the Romans, by Caesar's troops.

› **Early First Century CE**
Founding of Roman Lutetia and its extension onto the Left Bank.

› **Thirteenth Century CE**
Apogee of the Gallo-Roman city.

› **Late Third–Early Fourth Century CE**
Construction of the city's rampart and the palace on Île de la Cité. Emperors Julian and Valentinian stay here.

SKIP TO
The Thousand-Year Saga of Île-de-France Wines, p. 78.

The Niflette of Provins

This tartlet, which commemorates All Saints' Day, has a well-established tradition and pride of place among the inhabitants of Provins, a town situated not too far from Paris. Let's take a look at this crisp and creamy confection. —MARIELLE GAUDRY

La Grande Rue du Val, Provins (Seine-et-Marne), 1907.

THE RECIPE

Season: fall
Difficulty ●○○

SERVES 6

10½ ounces (300 g) Puff Pastry (p. 58)

For the pastry cream

2 cups (500 ml) milk

3 large (150 g) eggs

½ cup (100 g) sugar

3 tablespoons (25 g) all-purpose flour

2 tablespoons plus 2 teaspoons (25 g) cornstarch

1 large (20 g) egg yolk, for glazing

2 tablespoons (30 ml) orange flower water

Equipment

Pastry bag

1 round cookie cutter 2¾ inches (7 cm) in diameter

Dominique Gaufillier,* a baker and pastry chef in Provins, offers his traditional recipe for the niflette.

In a saucepan, bring the milk to a boil. In a bowl, thoroughly combine the eggs and sugar. Stir in the flour and cornstarch until thoroughly combined. Pour the hot milk over the egg mixture while whisking. Pour the mixture into the saucepan and bring to a boil while whisking continuously until thickened. Scrape the mixture into a heatproof bowl and set aside in the refrigerator with a piece of plastic wrap pressed against the surface. Once the pastry cream is cold, stir in the orange flower water.

Preheat the oven to 400°F (200°C). Roll out the puff pastry to a thickness of ¾ inch (2 cm). Cut out disks 2¾ inches (7 cm) in diameter using the cookie cutter.

Place the disks on a baking sheet. Scrape the pastry cream into the pastry bag. Brush the edges (about ⅓ inch/1 cm) of the dough disks with the egg yolk and pipe the pastry cream in the center.

Bake for about 30 minutes, or until puffed and golden. Serve warm.

* Boulangerie-Pâtisserie Gaufillier—2, rue Victor-Garnier, Provins (Seine-et-Marne).

WHAT IS IT?

A tart 2⅓ to 4 inches (6 to 10 cm) in diameter made of puff pastry and filled with pastry cream. Traditionally flavored with orange flower water, the cream can also be flavored with vanilla or just plain with no flavoring. It is best enjoyed warm, when it's crisp and moist.

AN INDULGENCE TO CONSOLE

The confection is thought to date to the Middle Ages. During All Saints' Day (November 1), a small pastry was distributed to orphans as they left the cemetery after visiting their parents' gravesites. Their keepers would tell them *"Ne flete"* ("Do not cry" in Low Latin), the origin of its name. These beginnings are debated, however, because of the niflette's use of pastry cream and puff pastry, for which written recipes do not appear in France until the seventeenth century.

Since 2018, Provins has replaced its Saint-Martin's fair with the niflette festival since the pastry has become a town specialty.

THIRTEEN TO A DOZEN

Over a period of a month and a half around All Saints' Day, the niflettes are sold individually or by the half dozen, but most often by the dozen. If a dozen is ordered, tradition dictates that a thirteenth is added to the box as an offering in the spirit of its origins.

Le Ruban Rouge
📍 21, rue Hugues-le-Grand, Provins (Seine-et-Marne)

A generous cream and a crisp puff pastry. There is a version with vanilla from Papua New Guinea with a bright taste.

Le Comte de Champagne
📍 10, pl. du Maréchal-Leclerc, Provins (Seine-et-Marne)

A voluptuous cream, sprinkled with confectioners' sugar, and an ethereal puff pastry.

SKIP TO
Portugal, p. 169; Pastry Shops, p. 312.

A DISTANT COUSIN?

The niflette is often compared to the pastel de nata.

	NIFLETTE	PASTEL DE NATA
ORIGIN	Provins (Seine-et-Marne)	Portugal
TIME OF YEAR	Around All Saints' Day	Year-round
FILLING	Pastry Cream	Flan sprinkled with confectioners' sugar and cinnamon

LA COUPOLE

As a temple of art deco and a classic rendezvous of the Roaring Twenties, this extravagant brasserie made Montparnasse a legend. —ESTELLE LENARTOWICZ

Indian Lamb Curry

Season: spring
Difficulty ● ● ○

SERVES 6

4½ pounds (2 kg) boneless lamb shoulder

5 tablespoons sunflower oil

1 onion

1 banana

2 cloves garlic

2 tablespoons curry

1 teaspoon paprika

¼ cup (20 g) shredded coconut

Salt

1 tablespoon all-purpose flour

1¼ cups (300 ml) lamb jus

1 bouquet garni

2 golden apples

1 large tomato, chopped

Fresh herbs (optional)

1½ cups (300 g) long-grain rice

9 ounces (250 g) mango chutney

For the achars
(pickled vegetables)

7 ounces (200 g) cauliflower

⅓ ounce (10 g) carrots

¼ orange

¼ lemon

2 tablespoons sunflower oil

2 tablespoons vinegar

⅓ ounce (10 g) haricots verts (string beans)

1 teaspoon curry

1 red chile

1 pinch ground paprika

1 pinch ground ginger

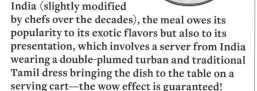

This has been a star dish on the restaurant's menu since 1927 and embodies the cosmopolitan soul of La Coupole. Prepared according to an authentic recipe from the Madras region of India (slightly modified by chefs over the decades), the meal owes its popularity to its exotic flavors but also to its presentation, which involves a server from India wearing a double-plumed turban and traditional Tamil dress bringing the dish to the table on a serving cart—the wow effect is guaranteed!

Cut the lamb into cubes. In a flameproof casserole dish, sauté the lamb pieces in the oil without browning them. Peel and chop the onion, banana, and garlic and add them to the casserole dish with the curry, paprika, and coconut. Season with salt and let simmer for 10 minutes over low heat. Sprinkle the flour over the ingredients to help bind the sauce. Add the jus and 4 cups (1 L) of water. Add the bouquet garni. Cover and simmer for 1½ hours. Remove the lamb pieces and the bouquet garni. Stir the sauce. Peel and cube the apples and sauté them. Add them to the sauce with the chopped tomato. Continue cooking over very low heat until ready to serve. Sprinkle with fresh herbs, as desired. Cook the rice.

Make the achars: Chop the cauliflower and carrots. Wash the orange and lemon and cut them into small wedges. In a saucepan, add the oil, vinegar, and orange and lemon wedges, and bring to a boil. Add the vegetables and spices and gently cook until softened. Let cool. Serve the meat and sauce while hot, accompanied by the rice. Serve the achars and the mango chutney on the side.

LA COUPOLE

Stretching down the boulevard

In 1927, Ernest Fraux and René Lafon, brothers-in-law from Auvergne, built a beautiful restaurant designed by the architects Barillet and Le Bouc. Situated in a former coal warehouse at 102, boulevard du Montparnasse, this long, luxurious space is nearly 8,600 square feet (800 sq m) and serves up to a thousand people a day. The 16-foot high (5 m) ceiling (built at this height to help corral cigarette smoke away from diners) is an Art Deco wonder.

Where does its name come from?

The name was chosen simply to be in keeping with the theme of the other restaurants in the district: Le Dôme and La Rotonde.

Celebrity dishes

› In 1968, student-uprising leader Daniel Cohn-Bendit climbed onto a table to order lobster.

› In 1995, former president François Mitterrand was served the famous Indian curry, his last meal in the city.

› Pop singing legend Serge Gainsbourg would sip a "102" here (a double Pastis 51).

› Writer-director Jean-Paul Belmondo enjoyed the tartare here until his final days.

Table 149

The proximity to the coat check and the passing young women made this Jean-Paul Sartre's favorite table. When he would dine here with Simone de Beauvoir, they would leave astronomical tips.

🔍 TO SEE

FIVE DETAILS OF
LA COUPOLE

The floor: composed of magnificent ceramic mosaics with colorful Cubist motifs.

The chandeliers: of imposing geometric lines made by master glassmaker Jean Perzel.

The statue: *La Terre* stands in the middle of the room. The two figures sculpted in bronze by Louis Derbré replaced the old central fountain.

The pillars: there are thirty-three, symmetrical and uniform and decorated with frescoes painted by artists of the time, such as Jeanne Rij-Rousseau and Marie Vassilieff.

The ballroom: on the lower level, where Josephine Baker and the greatest orchestras performed.

SKIP TO
Art Nouveau or
Art Deco?, p. 160.

Gibelotte de Lapin
Rabbit Stew

The gibelotte is a traditional stew whose origins trace to the commune of Suresnes and the nineteenth-century walls that surrounded Paris. —SACHA LOMNITZ

THE RECIPE

Season: fall to winter
Difficulty ● ○ ○

SERVES 6 TO 8

1 pound 2 ounces (500 g) fresh pork belly

9 ounces (250 g) button mushrooms

9 ounces (250 g) small grelot onions

5½ tablespoons (80 g) unsalted butter

1 large rabbit weighing 3⅓ to 4 pounds (1.5 to 1.8 kg), cut into sections

1 tablespoon flour

1¼ cups (300 ml) vegetable or chicken broth

1¼ cups (300 ml) white wine

1 bouquet garni

Salt and freshly ground black pepper

This is a fricassee that starts by sautéing the meat to prevent it from falling apart and to give it a nice color. The dish then finishes with braising to keep the flesh tender and moist.

Cut the pork belly into large cubes. Clean and trim the mushrooms. Peel the onions.

In a Dutch oven, lightly brown the butter. Add the cubed pork belly and rabbit pieces and cook until browned. Remove the meat from the pan and set aside.

Add the flour to the pan and stir, on the heat, using a wooden spoon, until the butter and flour are a nice dark brown color (add more flour if needed). Add the broth, white wine, bouquet garni, and rabbit and pork pieces. Season with salt and pepper. Cook for 1½ hours, covered. After 1 hour of cooking, add the mushrooms and onions. Remove the bouquet garni. Serve with fresh pasta or steamed potatoes.

JUST ACROSS THE RIVER

Gibelotte de lapin originated in the 1860s at the Auberge du Père Lapin, located in the hills of Suresnes (Hauts-de-Seine) with a view of the Eiffel Tower. People came here on Sundays from across the Seine to enjoy the pleasant white wines from the local vineyards, plus they could enjoy them without paying the wine tax since the area was not part of Paris at the time.

RABBITS EVERYWHERE

When Paris was surrounded by tax-collection barriers and the Thiers wall, which were replaced by the periphery several decades ago, rabbits abounded around the capital. A popular method of preparation was to sauté them with shallots, white wine, and parsley. And if no rabbit could be found, a cat might do the trick . . . making it a gibelotte de gouttière ("alley cat" stew)!

LAPINS WEREN'T JUST RABBITS

Although the Auberge du Père Lapin made the gibelotte a specialty, the dish was also created as a tribute to the excavators who dug Mount Valérien to erect the fort. These workers were nicknamed the lapins.

Au Père Lapin
depuis 1861

Au Père Lapin

📍 10, rue du Calvaire, Suresnes (Hauts-de-Seine). €€

In the kitchen at Au Père Lapin, chef Guillaume Delage continues the house tradition with a lapin de gibolette using farmstead rabbit from Vendée, accompanied by mashed potatoes.

SKIP TO
Île-de-France Terroir, p. 20.

Couscous

The capital has long enjoyed this North African dish—at the risk of betraying its origins. —FRANÇOIS-RÉGIS GAUDRY

Royal couscous

> It's called "royal," because it includes several meats—chicken, lamb, meatballs, merguez sausage—arranged in a crown on the serving dish, which would be heresy for inhabitants of North Africa, who never mix the couscous with the meats that are grilled separately. It is impossible to date when the expression "royal couscous" came into use, but it seems it was a Parisian invention by the Algerian-born French community, which has a large presence in Île-de-France.

> Chez Bébert popularized the dish in the 1960s. Founded in 1956 on rue du Faubourg-Montmartre (Paris 9th) by Albert Nizard from Tunisia, this couscous restaurant gave rise to others, located on boulevard du Montparnasse (Paris 14th) and boulevard Pereire (Paris 17th), opened by Nizard's sons, Jean-Luc and Mike.

Moroccan Pavilion, Colonial Exposition, Paris, 1931.

Since when has Paris been dabbling in couscous?

> Although couscous was at first an exotic dish from distant lands, it came into fashion when cultures of the Middle East became popular. In *La Cuisine de tous les pays* (1872), chef Urbain Dubois proposed the recipe for couscous des Arabes, made with leg of mutton, broth, vegetables, couscous, and grated Parmesan cheese.

> Parisians were introduced to this specialty during the Universal Exposition of 1889. Couscous vendors set up on the Esplanade des Invalides (Paris 7th). In 1931, the Moroccan pavilion offered multiple couscous dishes à la carte from its restaurant.

> During the Belle Époque, the gourmet food shop Hédiard offered couscous, as mentioned in the book *L'Art du bien manger* (published around 1900): "Couscouss [sic] . . . and the Middle East at home. But we do not eat authentic couscous in Paris, whether purchased at Hédiard at Place de la Madeleine or sent by an Arab chef."

> Couscous became popular in Paris in the second half of the twentieth century thanks to successive waves of migration due to the influx of labor from the Maghreb and the return of the French from Algeria after Algeria gained its independence in 1962.

The components of royal couscous

Assortment of grilled meats

Couscous

Golden raisins

Chickpeas

Vegetables in broth

Harissa

"We prepared supper. Good couscous and a lot of potages . . . were prepared properly by Fripesauce, Hochepot, and Pilleverjus, cooks of Grangousier."

—Rabelais, *Gargantua* (translated by Marie-Madeleine Fragonard), XXXVII, 1534

SKIP TO
Paris, a Cosmopolitan City, p. 164.

THE BEST COUSCOUS IN PARIS

Mama Nissa (Algeria)

📍 *14, rue Mandar, Paris 2nd*

MAKFOUL (KABYLE COUSCOUS)

Couscous: barley.
Accompaniments: five steamed seasonal vegetables, beef meatballs, and a poached egg.
Broth: no broth.

Chez Omar (Algeria)

📍 *47, rue de Bretagne, Paris 3rd*

ROYAL COUSCOUS

Couscous: barley.
Accompaniments: merguez sausage, lamb skewers, and beef and lamb méchoui.
Broth: turnips, carrots, zucchini, onions, and celery.

Le Tagine (Morocco)

📍 *13, rue de Crussol, Paris 11th*

COUSCOUS MÉCHOUI

Couscous: wheat, fine.
Accompaniments: méchoui suckling lamb leg from the Pyrénées.
Broth: turnips, carrots, and small zucchini from Morocco.

Le Taïs (Algeria)

📍 *129, blvd. de Ménilmontant, Paris 11th*

LAMB COUSCOUS

Couscous: wheat, fine and medium.
Accompaniments: lamb confit and kebabs.
Broth: tomatoes, turnips, zucchini, chickpeas, celery, and carrots.

Chez Mamane (Algeria)

📍 *27, rue des Cinq-Diamants, Paris 13th*

ROYAL COUSCOUS

Couscous: wheat, fine.
Accompaniments: shoulder and leg of lamb, merguez sausage (veal and beef), and chicken from the butcher shop Villette Sud.
Broth: tomatoes, carrots, turnips, celery, onions, garlic, coriander, cumin, ras el-hanout spice blend, paprika, and white pepper.

À Mi-Chemin (Tunisia)

📍 *31, rue Boulard, Paris 14th*

ROYAL COUSCOUS

Couscous: wheat, fine.
Accompaniments: merguez sausage (by Hugo Desnoyer), veal meatballs, and lamb knuckle confit.
Broth: seasonal vegetables, carrots, and butternut squash or eggplant, and ras el-hanout spice blend.

Le Caroubier (Morocco)

📍 *82, blvd. Lefebvre, Paris 15th*

FASSI COUSCOUS

Couscous: wheat, fine and medium.
Accompaniments: onion compote, raisins, almonds, cinnamon, orange blossoms, confectioners' sugar, and, in season, dates.
Broth: no broth.

Le Kouriet (Algeria)

📍 *23, rue Viala, Paris 15th*

TRADITIONAL COUSCOUS

Couscous: wheat, medium.
Accompaniments: lamb skewers, lamb méchoui.
Broth: carrots, zucchini, fennel, turnips, chickpeas, leeks, beef bones and fat, and ras el-hanout spice blend.

Chez Nini (Tunisia)

📍 *24, rue Saussier-Leroy, Paris 17th*

HOUSE-MADE COUSCOUS

Couscous: wheat, medium.
Accompaniments: beef meatballs, flat iron steak or beef shank, and merguez sausage.
Broth: carrots, zucchini, and turnips.

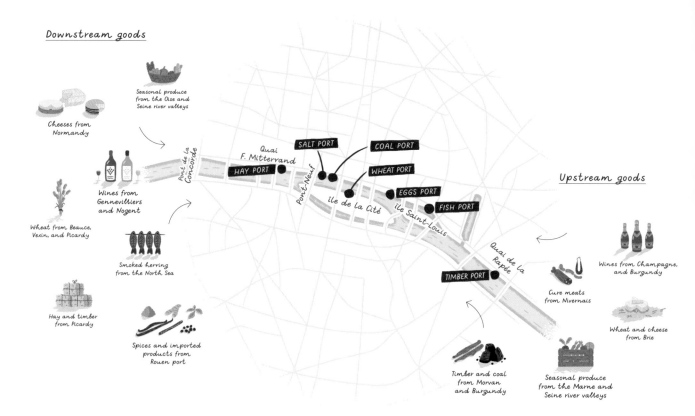

Downstream goods

Cheeses from Normandy

Seasonal produce from the Oise and Seine river valleys

SALT PORT

COAL PORT

Quai F. Mitterrand

WHEAT PORT

HAY PORT

Wines from Gennevilliers and Nogent

Pont de la Concorde

Pont-Neuf

Île de la Cité

EGGS PORT

Île Saint-Louis

FISH PORT

Upstream goods

Wheat from Beauce, Vexin, and Picardy

Smoked herring from the North Sea

Quai de la Rapée

TIMBER PORT

Wines from Champagne and Burgundy

Cure meats from Nivernais

Hay and timber from Picardy

Spices and imported products from Rouen port

Wheat and cheese from Brie

Timber and coal from Morvan and Burgundy

Seasonal produce from the Marne and Seine river valleys

The River Saga

FROM TRANSPORT …

Although many cities are built on rivers, Paris is the only one to qualify its region as an island (Île-de-France), and the water that crosses it has long defined the capital. —JACQUES BRUNEL

The *Fluctuat nec mergitur* Motto

The boat adorning the coat of arms of the city of Paris and the motto *fluctuat nec mergitur* (beaten by the waves, but does not sink) comes from the commercial group of the Nautes, shipowners and sailors who, until the Middle Ages, were a river guild that assured and regulated river traffic. Activity on Paris's river has endured nearly six thousand years, according to the discovery of ten canoes exhumed in Bercy. Carved with flint axes from tree trunks up to 20 feet (6 m) long, the canoes were used to carry people and goods or for fishing. In Roman times, the boatmen of Lutetia imported olive oil from southern areas via the Seine and the Saône.

Muddy Paris

CONTINUAL CIRCULATION, fueled by the instability of the Seine and its frequent floods, justified the name "Lutetia," which in Gaulish meant "muddy." Except for its hills and islands, Paris was built on marshes.

IN THE MIDDLE AGES, there were many ponds in the city, often filled with waste, which people crossed on planks.

TO CLEAN UP, Paris worked to contain the Seine (the first quays appeared during the Renaissance) in order to convert the swampy marshes into fruit and vegetable plots and to bury the small rivers that acted as sewers for human waste.

The nourishing Seine

Trade along the river resumed around the year 1200 as the orchards and vegetable gardens of northern Paris and the vineyards of the Left Bank were no longer sufficient to provide everything needed for inhabitants. The land routes, a rough and infamous terrain, were used to transport fresh fish and livestock herds (poultry, pigs, goats) which, before being slaughtered, would fatten themselves on the meadows (the "pré d'embouche") of Île aux Vaches (now Île Saint-Louis). The rest were entrusted to the river: "a moving path," according to Blaise Pascal, although in only one direction. Once the cargo was sold, the boats from Burgundy were chopped into firewood. The flat-bottom barges arriving with goods from Normandy or the Picardy region were hauled—by the strength of men, oxen, or horses—upstream, with chains blocking the passage over bridges and tollways. Before the arrival of the railway, the river provided Paris with two-thirds of its supplies.

... TO FISHING

The Seine also was a source of food. The quantity of fish taken from the Seine over its history was often miraculous.

Eels, salmon, sturgeons

Parisians ate fish for nearly a third of the year because of fasting required for religious practices, including during Lent on Fridays. Before the Romans introduced carp, originating from the Danube, the Seine and its tributaries were full of bleak, eel, barbel, bream, trout, pike, roach fish, chub, salmon, sturgeon, and other fish. In the twelfth century, monks acclimatized fish from eastern Europe (tench, perch, freshwater burbot, etc.) and, as around the abbeys at Royaumont, Maubuisson, and Chaalis, the ponds needed merely to be drained to access all they had to offer.

Fishing on the banks of the Seine

The rivers' best fishing spots were near mills, whose breaks would trap fish, but the mill owners (often lords) prevented access. In Paris, large funnel nets surrounded one of the arches of the Pont-Marie to capture an abundance of eels, so highly prized they were sometimes used as currency.

Near the end of the twelfth century, overfishing and excess driftwood led to the virtual disappearance of salmon and sturgeon in the Seine. However, the opening of the canals to other river basins (the Rhine, Loire, Rhône, etc.) brought new water species (ruffe, common nase, freshwater pike perch) that are now endemic.

The return of the fish

Although suffering from pollution since the Middle Ages due to tanners, washing, sewers, boats, and industrial waste, the Seine would naturally clean itself as it flowed. Thanks to the advent of wastewater treatment techniques, treatment plants, and monitoring, crowds of fishermen around forty years ago would come to the squares Barye (Paris 4th) and Vert-Galant (Paris 1st) to the shops that sold corks and boxes of larvae for fishing. However, only eel and carp were fished. Today thirty-two species of fish are in the Seine. In Choisy-le-Roi in 2020, fishermen caught a 12-foot (2.40 m) catfish.

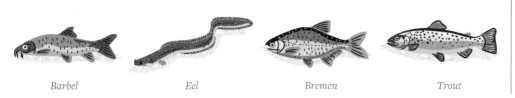

Barbel *Eel* *Bremen* *Trout*

FISHING SPOTS IN PARIS

MODUS OPERANDI FOR FISHING THE SEINE
Bring a fishing card and respect the fishing seasons. Fish caught from the Seine must be released, as they are rich in heavy metals, parasites, and polychlorinated biphenyls (PCBs), a toxic material.

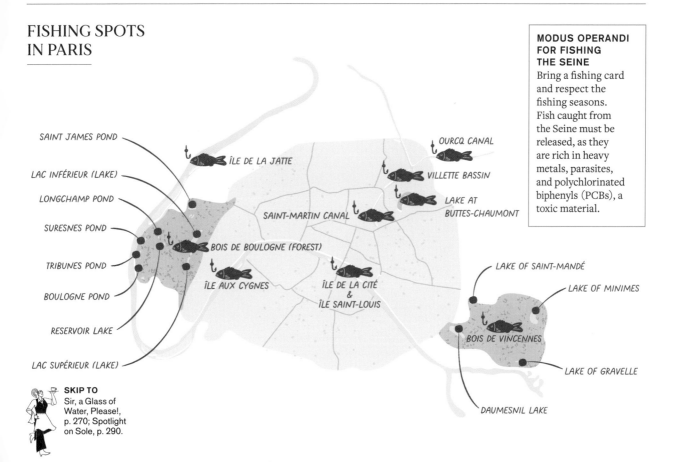

SAINT JAMES POND

LAC INFÉRIEUR (LAKE)

LONGCHAMP POND

SURESNES POND

TRIBUNES POND

BOULOGNE POND

RESERVOIR LAKE

LAC SUPÉRIEUR (LAKE)

ÎLE DE LA JATTE

OURCQ CANAL

VILLETTE BASSIN

SAINT-MARTIN CANAL

LAKE AT BUTTES-CHAUMONT

BOIS DE BOULOGNE (FOREST)

ÎLE AUX CYGNES

ÎLE DE LA CITÉ & ÎLE SAINT-LOUIS

LAKE OF SAINT-MANDÉ

LAKE OF MINIMES

BOIS DE VINCENNES

LAKE OF GRAVELLE

DAUMESNIL LAKE

SKIP TO
Sir, a Glass of Water, Please!, p. 270; Spotlight on Sole, p. 290.

The Adventures of Bercy

The warehouses of Bercy were for a long time the hub of wine trade in Paris. This district's name also became the name of a famous sauce.

—SACHA LOMNITZ AND AURORE VINCENTI

Halle aux Vins, quai Saint-Bernard (Paris 5th), 1928.

A little history

The name Bercy evokes many ideas. For some, it reminds them of wine; for others, the Accor sports arena. Bercy is the name of a former longtime-independent commune that was located outside the wall of the farmers-general. The commune was integrated into Paris in 1860. Thanks to its ideal geographical location at the time, the wines that arrived in Bercy were exempt from taxes, which explains the significant development of its cellars during the nineteenth century.

Addresses of the past

Bercy was at first a working-class commune, but at the end of the nineteenth century, both the working classes and Paris high society found the area to be an ideal rural setting for walking or enjoying a drink. From Pont de Bercy to the current avenue des Terroirs-de-France, guinguettes and auberges, places of leisure, multiplied in number. Les Terrasses, which attracted rowers, Les Marronniers, and Le Soleil d'Or were some of the places that exemplified "joyful Bercy."

Bercy, the wine capital

Bercy was once the largest wine and spirits market in the world. In 1878, the current Cour Saint-Émilion served as an enormous warehouse and point of sale for beverages transported by the Seine or by rail in cask wagons and bottled nearby.

Bercy and rue Alphonse-Murge

The Bercy district has fed the imagination and French language in regard to alcohol. The expressions in French "to be born on the slopes of Bercy," "to have the disease of Bercy," or "to be bersillée" all suggest a state of drunkenness. What is less known is that the verb *se murger* (to get drunk) also originates in this area. Rue Alphonse-Murge, now demolished, ran along the Bercy warehouses. The street's name gave birth to the expression "walk along the walls of rue Murge" after overimbibing in neighborhood cabarets. Who is Alphonse? The poor guy probably had nothing to do with it.

Bercy sauce

This is one of the emblematic sauces, made using white wine, in the repertoire of French cuisine. Escoffier treated fish and meat à la mode Bercy differently in his *Guide culinaire*: fish (whiting, shad, carp, tench, sole, etc.) were accompanied by a "Bercy sauce" (a reduction of shallots, white wine, and fish stock), while meats (steak, veal liver, testicles, veal kidneys, etc.) were essentially served with a "Bercy butter" (beurre en pommade [a cold softened butter] mixed with a reduction of white wine, shallots, chopped parsley, and diced marrow).

THE RECIPE   Season: year-round   Difficulty ● ○ ○

Bercy sauce can accompany fish or meat. It is prepared with fish stock or meat stock, depending on the chosen protein.

SERVES 4

2 shallots

2 to 3 sprigs flat-leaf parsley

Just over ¾ cup (200 ml) white wine

1 cup (250 ml) fish or beef stock

7 tablespoons (100 g) unsalted butter, cold

Salt and freshly ground black pepper

Chop the shallots and parsley.

In a saucepan set over low heat, cook the shallots in the white wine until all of the liquid has evaporated. Add the stock. Stir in the butter while whisking vigorously to create an emulsion and thicken the sauce. Season with salt and pepper and stir in the chopped parsley. Serve.

A place for working ...

At the end of the nineteenth century, Bercy was buzzing with nearly seven thousand workers. Merchants, coopers, and carriers worked side by side with all necessary trades, making up a veritable city within a city. There was even a trade referred to as the "jaune d'oeuf" (egg yolk), the nickname given to the person who resold the yolks of eggs whose whites had been used to clarify the wine.

... and for eating

The Bercy food stalls offered their famous fried foods and matelotes, stews made with freshwater fish caught in the Seine and cooked in wine. This is also the origin of entrecôte Bercy with a marchand de vin sauce (a shallot, butter, and wine sauce) and whiting with Bercy sauce (shallots cooked in wine).

The end of the warehouses

Built in 1800, the cellars were rebuilt in 1820 using the materials of the old hôtel particuliers (private urban homes) along rue de Bercy after a fire. In 1964, after a century of prosperity, the leases were not renewed. The warehouses were gradually abandoned and partly destroyed during the construction of the Palais Omnisport arena in Bercy. The last cellars, the L'heureux cellars (currently Pavillons de Bercy), were listed in the Supplementary Inventory of Historic Monuments in 1985.

A warehouse of wine barrels at the Halle aux Vins.

Rue du Petit-Bercy.

Rue du Port-de-Bercy.

The large cellars (currently the Museum of Fairground Arts).

The main alley of Bercy Village today.

🔍 TO SEE

The original forty-six cellars, which today are an outdoor and pedestrian shopping center.

The six large cellars in buhrstone, brick vaults, and metal structures, located on the edge of rue des Pirogues where the Museum of Fairground Arts is located.

On the ground of the Cour Saint-Émilion, the rails installed in 1849 were used by the train carrying wine to Bercy station.

In the Yitzhak Rabin garden of Bercy Park, the 350 vines planted in 1996, which produce 66 gallons (250 L) of wine per year.

SKIP TO
The Thousand-Year Saga of Île-de-France Wines, p. 78; A Parisian Way of Speaking, p. 250; The River Saga, p. 300.

Béarnaise Sauce

This warm sauce flavored with tarragon is one of the French classics, but its beginnings were far from Béarn. —FRANÇOIS-RÉGIS GAUDRY

RECIPE · PARIS CUISINE · RECIPE

THE RECIPE

Season: year-round **Difficulty** ● ● ●

SERVES 6

9 ounces (250 g) unsalted butter	8 large (160 g) egg yolks
½ bunch tarragon	Scant ½ cup (100 ml) water
½ bunch chervil	Salt
4 shallots	**Equipment**
Scant ¼ cup (50 ml) white wine vinegar	1 saucepan 9¾ inches (25 cm) in diameter (prepared as a bain-marie)
Scant ¼ cup (50 ml) white vinegar	1 pan 8 inches (20 cm) in diameter
Freshly ground black pepper	Fine-mesh strainer

This sauce requires a bit of skill and patience. Here is a classic version, ideal to accompany a steak or firm-flesh fish.

Clarify the butter: Melt the butter over low heat and strain it once it looks clear (do not brown it).

Strip the tarragon leaves from their stems and set the stems aside. Chop the tarragon leaves with the chervil. Peel and chop the shallots.

In a very small saucepan, simmer the shallots with the vinegars, a large pinch of pepper, and the tarragon stems over low heat ❶. Reduce, covered, until the vinegar evaporates completely; the shallots must be translucent but not browned. Remove the tarragon stems.

Add the egg yolks and water ❷. Season with salt. Place the pan in the heated bain-marie and whisk vigorously to obtain a sabayon (the mixture will be thick and billowy). The sauce is done when the bottom of the pan becomes visible while whisking. Drizzle in the clarified butter and whisk to obtain the texture of a mayonnaise.

Adjust the seasoning, if needed, and add the chopped herbs ❸. Serve warm.

Le Pavillon Henri IV, Saint-Germain-en-Laye (Yvelines).

WHAT IS IT?

A warm, emulsified sauce based on hollandaise sauce. The recipe appeared in 1856 in *La Cuisine classique* by Urbain Dubois and Émile Bernard. In *Le Petit Cuisinier moderne* (1890), Gustave Garlin presented a recipe for "Parisian Béarnaise sauce"! This differs from classic Béarnaise by the addition of anchovy butter.

WAS IT AN ACCIDENT?

In the mid-nineteenth century, Jean-Louis-François Collinet, chef at Pavillon Henri IV, messed up a shallot reduction that he fixed by adding egg yolks and various condiments. The Béarnaise was born, named as such because of the bust of Henri IV, a native of Béarn, that was on display in the dining room.

ITS COUSINS

Occitane Sauce (created by André Daguin at the Hôtel de France in Auch, Gers). The butter is replaced by foie gras fat.

Choron Sauce (created by Alexandre Choron at the restaurant Voisin in the nineteenth century). With added tomato.

Paloise Sauce Tarragon is replaced with mint.

Foyot Sauce (created by Nicolas Foyot, chef of Foyot in Paris in the nineteenth century). Finished with a glace de viande.

TOP · LET'S EAT PARIS! · ADDRESSES

Le Voltaire
27, quai Voltaire, Paris 7th. €€€
A creamy Béarnaise with wild turbot à la plancha.

Bistrot Paul Bert
18, rue Paul-Bert, Paris 11th. €€
The Béarnaise classic served with Irish prime rib.

Pavillon Henri IV
19–21, rue Thiers, Saint-Germain-en-Laye (Yvelines). €€€
Prepared with a mixture of vinegar from Reims and balsamic vinegar, to accompany the Salers beef filet.

SKIP TO
The "Fifth Quarter" of Paris, p. 221; Brasseries, p. 356.

Adolphe Dugléré (1805–1884)

The Mozart of the Kitchen

Between his time at Café Anglais and his culinary creations, this little-known chef was one of the major toques of the nineteenth century.
—CHARLES PATIN O'COOHOON

Conquering Paris

He was a great French chef whom Rossini nicknamed the Mozart of cooking. And yet there is no known portrait of him. At the age of twenty, Adolphe Dugléré, encouraged by his father, chef Jean Dugléré, left Bordeaux to cook in Paris. He succeeded his master Antonin Carême in the kitchens of the Rothschilds until 1848, when he was appointed chef of Les Trois Frères Provençaux, a mecca of Parisian gastronomy in the Palais-Royal district. In 1866, he became head of the Café Anglais, one of the most popular restaurants in the capital.

> **"Three suppers a week at the Café Anglais and I know everything being said in Paris."**
> —According to Henri Martineau, in *Stendhal : Oeuvres complètes et annexes*, Éditions Arvensa

He was close to Balzac and advised Alexandre Dumas in the writing of his *Grand Dictionnaire de cuisine*. An art lover, he had a rich collection of paintings by the masters Rubens, Corot, and Delacroix.

Le Café Anglais, 1858.

Le Café Anglais

Opened in 1802 at the corner of boulevard des Italiens and rue Marivaux, this restaurant became, starting in 1855, the most famous restaurant of the Second Empire. Its twenty-two salons and private cabinets attracted the most fashionable members of nineteenth-century society, from Alfred de Musset to Barbey d'Aurevilly to Alexandre Dumas. At that time, there were many references to the Café Anglais in several masterpieces of literature:

> **"While he was talking to her, standing against the door on the right, Hussonnet appeared on the left side, and, noting this of Café Anglais: 'It's a pretty establishment! Let's have a bite, yes?'"**
> —Gustave Flaubert, *L'Éducation sentimentale*, 1869

> **"Going up the spiral staircase of the cellars of the Café Anglais, we met, at the busiest hour, the excellent Dugléré, the distinguished practitioner whom I have consulted more than once as a gastronomic oracle and to whom I owe the menus placed under his name at the end of this Dictionnaire."**
> —Alexandre Dumas, *Le Grand Dictionnaire de cuisine*, article "Vins," subsection "Cave-Décantage," 1873

Le Café Anglais, praised by the cook Françoise in Marcel Proust's *À l'ombre des jeunes filles en fleurs* (*In the Shadow of Young Girls in Flower*; 1918)—"a restaurant where it seemed to have a very good bourgeois cuisine"—is undoubtedly that of Adolphe Dugléré, since Françoise refers to the glory days of the establishment.

---

1 sauce, 3 dishes

Adolphe Dugléré was a formidable instructor, a great organizer in the kitchens, and curious about exotic ingredients. He placed sauces at the forefront in his cooking repertoire and named iconic recipes in honor of his customers.

LA SAUCE DUGLÉRÉ
Traditionally, this sauce is served over sole, brill, or turbot. To make it, melt 2½ tablespoons butter in a saucepan. Add ⅓ cup flour (45 g) to make a brown roux. Add a scant ½ cup (100 ml) white wine, then 1¼ cups (300 ml) fish stock, 4 crushed tomatoes, 1 chopped shallot, 1 chopped garlic clove, and 1 bouquet garni. Reduce the heat to medium. Season with salt and pepper. Serve ladled on top of the fish.

POULARDE À L'ALBUFERA
The inspiration: marshal Louis-Gabriel Suchet, Duke of Albufera.
The composition: a stuffed chicken, poached, filled with truffle sauce, chicken meatballs, kidneys, and rooster's comb.

LA POMME DE TERRE ANNA
The inspiration: Anna Deslions, a famous courtesan.
The composition: a round "cake" of sliced potatoes, buttered and baked.

LE POTAGE GERMINY
The inspiration: the governor of the Bank of France.
The composition: a creamed vegetable soup, with sorrel.

SKIP TO
The Invention of the Restaurant, p. 61; Fries Forever!, p. 142; Paris in the Soup, p. 266.

Le Cordon Bleu

The school has taught the highest level of culinary arts for almost 130 years, starting in Paris, then spreading to all corners of the globe. —SACHA LOMNITZ

📍 *13–15, quai André-Citroën, Paris 15th*

The Cordon Bleu kitchens, Paris, 1905.

Once upon a time …

Le Cordon Bleu was founded in 1895, the year in which journalist Marthe Distel launched *La Cuisinière Cordon Bleu* magazine to promote "healthy and good family cooking" for housewives. It was an immediate success, and the institute offered free cooking classes for subscribers in a space at Galerie d'Orléans at the Palais-Royal. From that moment, the school was born … and kept growing … and kept moving (from rue du Champ-de-Mars in the 7th, to rue Léon-Delhomme in the 15th, to quai André-Citroën where it is now).

In the movies

- *Sabrina* (1954), by Billy Wilder: Audrey Hepburn plays a student at Le Cordon Bleu in the title role.
- *Julie and Julia* (2009), by Nora Ephron: Julie (Amy Adams) challenges herself to make all the recipes from the famous cookbook by Julia Child (played by Meryl Streep).

The whims of language

› Originally, "le cordon bleu" was the name given to the ribbon of the knights of the Order of the Holy Spirit during the Wars of Religion who met regularly as a "club of gourmands."
› Over the centuries, the term developed a metaphorical meaning to refer to a group or institution considered superior and honorable. The Académie Française used an example as "cordon bleu of fine spirits," a metaphor it incorporated into its dictionary in 1832.
› The meaning in the sense of a "bonne cuisinière" (good cook) appears in *L'Hermite de la Chaussée-d'Antin, ou Observations sur les moeurs et les usages parisiens au début du XIXᵉ siècle* by Étienne de Jouy (1814) before being used more commonly by Balzac (*La Rabouilleuse*, 1842), Baudelaire (*La Fanfarlo*, 1847), and George Sand (*Histoire de ma vie*, 1855).

Opening to the world

The institute has always been at the forefront of innovation, from both a technical and educational perspective. In 1897, the school welcomed foreign students who then, in their home countries, would spread the interests and knowledge of French gastronomy. Julia Child taught French cuisine on American television in 1962 as part of her show *The French Chef*. From 1933, the school spread throughout the world, to London, New York, and Shanghai.

Diplomatic successes

• **1948**
Accreditation by the Pentagon in Washington, DC, for professional training of young American soldiers after their service in Europe.

• **1953**
The "Coronation chicken," created by two instructors from the London school, is served to foreign dignitaries at the coronation dinner of Queen Elizabeth II.

• **2000**
Trains Australian chefs in preparation for the Sydney Olympics.

First in the number of culinary institutes around the world

---

35 schools in more than 20 countries

20,000 students of more than 100 nationalities trained each year

---

1 objective: the promotion of French gastronomic heritage

Big names

From the beginning, Marthe Distel brought together chef-instructors and accomplished professionals, including Charles Driessens, to lead the first courses at the Palais-Royal. Even today, the one thousand students trained each year in Paris rub shoulders with great chefs such as Éric Briffard, Philippe Groult, Fabrice Danniel, and Franck Ramage, the former assistant head sommelier at the Crillon Hotel.

Le 13–15, quai André-Citroën

› **A highly innovative** eco-friendly building, with beehives and an 8,600-square-foot (800 sq m) vegetable garden with fresh ingredients used in the cooking classes.
› **A shop** where you can find kitchen equipment and products recommended by Le Cordon Bleu chefs.
› **Le Cordon Bleu café**.

Current kitchens at Le Cordon Bleu in Paris, with MOF chef Éric Briffard.

SKIP TO When Hollywood Dines in Paris, p. 286.

Check, Please!

In French, the bill received at the end of a meal is called the "carte à payer," "note," or "addition." Here is a little history regarding this dreaded piece of paper. —MARCELLE RATAFIA

Pain in the wallet

The nineteenth century was the beginning of the heyday for restaurants, but also of the tally presented at the table at the end of a meal, unlike with fixed price menus at inns of the time. Before the advent of the cash register and the introduction of the term *addition*, slang had an ad hoc word for the carte à payer: "Slang has been enriched with a charming word. The addition, also known as 'carte à payer,' has been called, for some time, the 'douloureuse' [literally "damage"]," mused an article in *Le Figaro* in 1862.

The grand disillusion

In *Illusions perdues* (*Lost Illusions*; 1837–1843), Balzac describes Lucien de Rubempré, a young man from the country who had gone to the capital and dined at Le Véry at the Palais-Royal, enjoying a very Parisian supper consisting of Bordeaux wine, fish, partridge, macaroni, and, most especially, Ostend oysters. "His illusions were shattered when the bill arrived and he owed fifty francs, a sum he assumed would take him far in Paris. Instead, his dinner cost him what was the equivalent of a month's pay at home." This scene became a Romantic motif: In *Bel-Ami*, by Maupassant (1885), we find the young hero penniless in the same precarious position but saved by the lovely Madame de Marelle who "threw . . . her purse into his hands" to pay "l'addition" of 130 francs for their meal at Café Riche.

A pricey bet

Nicknamed the "high-society busybody" by his friends and "Fiel-Castel" (*fiel* meaning "venom") by others, the Count of Viel-Castel was renowned for his Anglophobia. In 1837, he bet a British lord that he could consume a five-hundred-franc meal at the very chic Café de Paris. At stake? His honor, except the bill amounted to three thousand francs! He chose the most expensive dishes: potage of wild game, carp milt, quail in puff pastry, trout from Geneva, essence of crayfish, pheasant covered in ortolans, pyramid of truffles, compote from the West Indies, and more, all washed down with Tokaji wine and Clos Vougeot from Burgundy. Victorious, Fiel-Castel dashed off, leaving the lord to settle the "douloureuse."

L'addition, Not a Chic Word?

The expression "l'addition" offends the Parisian ear because it's too "mathematical." The animator Jean Nohain, around 1920, dined with his father, the poet Franc-Nohain, who asked him to ask for "la note," pointing out that the term *addition* was not very chic. His son complied and, misinterpreting his father's request to exaggerate instead, bellowed out through the dining room: "And l'ADDITION for monsieur!"

SKIP TO
The Invention of the Restaurant, p. 61; The Balzac Eating Guide, p. 84.

BAKERIES Les Boulangeries

Paris is known as the City of Light, but some could argue it's also the city of bread. The capital's twenty arrondissements, as well as its immediate outer areas, have a plethora of bakeries that are worth a visit. —FARAH KERAM

The bread of Paris

Paris has always been home to many options for bread. There were the communal ovens of the Middle Ages, the itinerant fairground bakers of the eighteenth century, the upscale bakeries of the nineteenth century, and shops with bakeries in the basement below their storefronts. And when the bread runs out, Parisians have proven through history that they can revolt. "We will not run out of bread anymore! We will bring back the bakers and the baker's apprentice." This was the victory song of French women of the people bringing the king, queen, and dauphin from Versailles to Paris on October 6, 1789.

THE HISTORIC PLACES

① Poilâne

◆ 38, rue Debelleyme, Paris 3rd

◆ 8, rue du Cherche-Midi, Paris 6th

◆ 49, blvd. de Grenelle, Paris 15th

◆ 39, rue de Lévis, Paris 17th

◆ 83, rue de Crimée, Paris 19th

In the Poilâne family, the founder's granddaughter Apollonia leads the way as the worthy and dedicated heir of this bakeshop, which opened in 1932. In all their locations, natural sourdoughs are uniquely shaped, and each one, without exception, is branded with the now famous *P*. Since the shop's beginnings, the wood-fired oven has been the shop's preferred method for baking, fueled by recycled and offcut pieces of wood: a resolutely modern taste of olden times.

SPECIALTY

The Poilâne round loaf, quite simply.

BAGUETTE?

Not since 1932.

② Gana

◆ 65, rue de Clichy, Paris 9th

◆ 121, rue de la Roquette, Paris 11th

◆ 92, rue de Charonne, Paris 11th

◆ 106, blvd. Voltaire, Paris 11th

◆ 212, rue de la Convention, Paris 15th

◆ 22, rue Brochant, Paris 17th

◆ 60, rue Duhesme, Paris 18th

◆ 159, rue Ordener, Paris 18th

◆ 226, rue des Pyrénées, Paris 20th

◆ 31, rue Raymond-du-Temple, Vincennes (Val-de-Marne)

Within the Parisian family of bakers, Ganachaud is one of the biggest names. The parent company Gana was founded in 1960 on the hills of the Ménilmontant district and has since continued to expand throughout Paris. On its shelves are dozens of breads, including many specialty breads made from organic flour and consistently good all-butter viennoiseries (flaky pastries).

SPECIALTY

The millstone bread, made with Gana flour ground on their stone mill, manufactured by Astrié, in their shop on rue Brochant (Paris 17th).

BAGUETTE?

Yes, the Gana flûte (a long loaf), the emblem of the shop and the first bread created by its founder, Bernard Ganachaud.

③ La Gambette à Pain

◆ 86, av. Gambetta, Paris 20th

Behind a magnificent period-style storefront, Jean-Paul Mathon oversees the operations. Thanks to slow kneading and high-quality flours, the breads here reveal all their aromas and offer fragrant flavors. The shop also offers sweet delicacies that have the unique feature of being made with T80 flour (a whole wheat flour) and not white flour. It is also rumored that Mathon trained Christophe Vasseur, the owner of the renowned Parisian bakery Du Pain et des Idées.

SPECIALTIES

The "mon pain préféré," available by the slice, and the "mouna," an orange flower water brioche: two must-haves of the bakery.

BAGUETTE?

Yes, called the gambette, naturally.

THE TOP BAKERIES

④ Des Gâteaux et du Pain

◆ 89, rue du Bac, Paris 7th

◆ 63, blvd. Pasteur, Paris 15th

Lovers of undercooked breads, pass on by! At Claire Damon's bakery, chef-baker David Granger makes organic breads with natural sourdough with extended baking times. The result? A caramelized effect that delivers a crunch and unique flavor. There is always something delicious to taste,—including a wide range of breads made with fruits and seeds.

SPECIALTY

The Polka, a traditional bread with a forty-eight-hour fermentation.

BAGUETTE?

Yes, slightly caramelized.

⑤ Mamiche

◆ 45, rue Condorcet, Paris 9th

◆ 32, rue du Château-d'Eau, Paris 10th

Cécile Khayat and Victoria Effantin excel in the art of bread-making experimentation. Since 2017, the two owners, heading up the bakeries with the longest lines in the capital, have been turning out all kinds of loaves, generous sandwiches at low prices, butter-based pastries, and creations that combine sweet and savory that have become iconic, such as their pain au chocolat flûte with demi-sel butter, and the pain perdu.

SPECIALTIES

The large bread sold by the slice in its whole-grain or plain version and all their pastries (especially the pain au chocolat, the cookie, and the brownie).

BAGUETTE?

Yes, and incredibly crisp!

⑥ Benoît Castel

◆ 72, rue Jean-Pierre-Timbaud, Paris 11th

◆ 11, rue Sorbier, Paris 20th

◆ 150, rue de Ménilmontant, Paris 20th

A leader among France's bakers for decades, he owes his long success to well-sourced ingredients, his product range, and his creativity in the business, which is constantly on the forefront. The bakery deserves a special mention for recycling their unsold breads and transforming them into a bread that bears the sweet name "pain d'hier et de demain" ("bread of yesterday and tomorrow").

SPECIALTY

Le Pain du Coin, his signature bread.

BAGUETTE?

Yes, ultracrisp!

NATURAL BREADS

⑦ Boulangerie Archibald

◆ 28, rue des Fossés-Saint-Bernard, Paris 5th

This is the temple of natural breads on the Left Bank. On the shelves of this bakery, managed by Ève Roizen and Louis-Marie Dupuis, are breads of consistent quality with delicious flavors, including the campagne au levain (a rustic natural sourdough made with whole rye) and the gluten-free loaf made with rice flour and buckwheat flour.

SPECIALTY

The Balthazar (from ancient grains), kneaded by hand.

BAGUETTE?

No, but for addicts, go for the Parisian sourdough made of einkorn wheat, which lends the effect of an (excellent) baguette "tradition."

⑧ Sain Boulangerie

◆ 15, rue Marie-et-Louise, Paris 10th

As a tribute to the nearby Saint-Martin canal, Anthony Courteille named his signature bread the Saint-Martin. A mixture of rustic wheat flour, einkorn flour, and chestnut flour, this loaf is available in two formats representative of the bakery's die-hard natural style. The products are flawless, with flours made from local ancient grains. The pastries are ethereal: the house-made puff pastry used in the flaky pastries is irresistible. And the choice of sponge cakes is unmatched.

SPECIALTIES

All the creations that combine breads and spices, such as harissa, preserved lemon, and Kalamata olives.

BAGUETTE?

Yes. Crisp, with a smoky taste.

Benoît Castel, Paris 20th.

⑨ Fermentation Générale

📍 *37, rue de la Folie-Méricourt, Paris 11th*

In this small shop decorated in light hues, everything is about fermentation, from breads to focaccia to jars of vegetables to bottles of natural wine. Every day, Valentin Orgeas churns out, from within his microbakery, a range of wheat-flour breads made from rustic varieties, and he even offers more unknown blends, such as Tunisian boulou, made from flour, egg, brown sugar, almonds, grapes, orange flower water, bitter almonds, orange, and sourdough.

SPECIALTIES

The Barbu de Roussillon and its slight smoky taste; focaccia and fougasses.

BAGUETTE?

No.

⑩ Boulangerie Persephone

📍 *102, blvd. Diderot, Paris 12th*

In her tiny bakery, Christel Régis makes about fifteen breads, as well as brioches and delicacies, using organic flours, filtered and dynamized water, and natural sourdough. The Hadès, the buckwheat, the rye, and the walnut stone-ground wheat loaf all nourish the body, mind, and soul.

SPECIALTIES

The Persephone, with its smoky taste, spelt sourdough, spelt and semi-whole grains, and the Hadès.

BAGUETTE?

Yes, sourdough.

⑪ Atelier P1

📍 *157, rue Marcadet, Paris 18th*

Julien Cantenot's mantra is "Time, long fermentations, and quality ingredients." In his bakery, this enthusiast has deconstructed the boundary between the bakeshop and the sales counter. Everyone can observe the heap of "P1s" being made: the P1 pain de mie and the P1 de riz et graines, a clever mixture of rice flour, rice sourdough, psyllium, flaxseed, sesame seed, and oatmeal. In a die-hard commitment to the profession, Atelier P1 offers sourdough bread-making workshops for all ages.

SPECIALTY

The pain de métail (a mix of rye, wheat, barley, and sometimes oats).

BAGUETTE?

No.

Shinya Pain

📍 *41, rue des Trois-Frères, Paris 18th*

An alchemist of ancient flours and a renowned baker, Shinya Inagaki, a native of Japan, chose Montmartre as his new home to make his varied offerings. The pain de métail, the buckwheat bread, and the scones made from natural sourdough are divine, as is the focaccia. A tip for newcomers: Bring patience, as the line is often as long as the list of items.

SPECIALTY

The Barbu du Roussillon bread.

BAGUETTE?

No.

⑫ Boulangerie Pajol

📍 *83 bis, rue Philippe-de-Girard, Paris 18th*

At the head of this bakery are Maxime Bussy (Bricheton) and Vincent Bedel, two passionate bakers who work with rustic flours and natural sourdoughs. The breads have very thick crusts and beautiful hydration rates, and are flavorful with a long shelf life. Everything is thought of.

SPECIALTIES

The seed bread is addictive; the pain de mie and the brioche are the too-good-to-miss specialties of the house.

BAGUETTE?

No.

⑬ Pain Paris

📍 *95, rue de Meaux, Paris 19th*

Vanessa Dezallé, who made a career change to become a baker, opened her bakery in spring 2022 close to Buttes-Chaumont park where she kneads, shapes, and bakes her breads with generous crumbs and organic flours from the Moulin de Colagne in Lozère. In addition to daily breads (einkorn, pain de campagne, seed breads, whole wheat flour and ancient grain breads), each day marks the appearance of an ephemeral loaf, such as the crisp chestnut bread. Sweet tooths will be happy here, too, with babka, cinnamon rolls, and cookies occupying a prominent place in her cases.

SPECIALTIES

Khorasan wheat bread, also called Kamut, with a delicate taste of walnuts and hazelnuts, and the brioche.

BAGUETTE?

No.

⑭ Le Bricheton

📍 *50, rue de la Réunion, Paris 20th*

As the spearhead of this lively and very Parisian bakery, Maxime Bussy has chosen to work only with so-called ancient flours; add to this the quality of the water obtained from the capital's artesian wells, the salt (also sourced), and the kneading by hand to shape unique breads. Natural wines and raw-milk cheeses to fill your basket can be found in the refrigerator case.

SPECIALTIES

The Bricheton, the signature bread, and the bardu that can be enjoyed like brioche.

BAGUETTE?

We dare you to ask them!

⑮ Éléments

📍 *3, rue Victor-Letalle, Paris 20th*

In the lower Ménilmontant, Claire Escalon, a former interior designer, designed and built her bakery, where she offers a range of breads made from organic rustic flours and natural starters using rye, rice, and einkorn, all at unbeatable prices. Here lovers of breads made from grains and multigrains will be delighted. The sourdough Schwarzbrot and other rice-buckwheat flour breads are amazing.

SPECIALTY
The round pain de campagne in its plain version or with seeds, soft and crisp at the same time.

BAGUETTE?
Yes, but in the form of "branches" with fruits or stalks filled with olives, tomato, or squid ink, depending on the season.

⑯ La Rue Palloy
📍 *50 ter, rue Palloy, Clichy (Hauts-de-Seine)*
Since 2017, Amaury Fieutelot and his partner, Sibille Gempp, have been delighting the inhabitants of Clichy with whole-grain tourte (with a forty-eight-hour fermentation!) and raw-milk flan pâtissier. The house grinds its own flour on a stone mill, which is visible from inside the shop.

SPECIALTY
The surprising and addictive sourdough oatmeal bread.

BAGUETTE?

The classic (made from T80 flour from their mill) or buckwheat (30 percent buckwheat from its miller).

⑰ Le Fournil Éphémère L'Atelier
📍 *11, rue de l'Église, Montreuil (Seine-Saint-Denis)*
What was supposed to be a short romance turned into an institution in lower Montreuil. In 2014, François Massonnet and Gaultier Vexlard set up shop in an old abandoned marble factory to sell organic sourdough bread three nights a week—a "temporary" project. Today, six days a week, the bakery and its natural breads delight locals and others from all around.

SPECIALTIES
German breads, mastered to perfection; focaccia.

BAGUETTE?
The Carabistoule, a baguette "tradition" with natural starter from Kamut.

NEIGHBORHOOD BOULANGERIES

⑱ Boulangerie Terroirs d'Avenir
📍 *3, rue du Nil, Paris 2nd*
📍 *17, blvd. Morland, Paris 4th*
📍 *8, rue Paul-Bert, Paris 11th*
📍 *90, rue Jean-Pierre-Timbaud, Paris 11th*
Within the large Terroirs d'Avenir group, a French success story that now has several shops, the bakery rises to the occasion. There is an abundant choice of pastries and breads made from organic French flours from rustic grains.

SPECIALTIES
The bread with einkorn and the bardu with a texture similar to that of brioche.

BAGUETTE?
Yes, sourdough.

⑲ Ten Belles
📍 *53, rue du Cherche-Midi, Paris 6th*
📍 *10, rue de la Grange-aux-Belles, Paris 10th*
📍 *17–19, rue Breguet, Paris 11th*
Now internationally renowned, this bakery

cofounded by the Franco-British trio Anna Trattles, Alice Quillet, and Anselme Blayney offers breads whose shelf life—four to five days—beats the competition. On the list of choices: the classic ancient grains from the Ferme de Montaquoy whose flours are stone-ground, and whole wheat bread and focaccia. Coffees are offered to enjoy on-site.

SPECIALTY
The classic bread, which can also be found served in many Parisian restaurants.

BAGUETTE?
No, but the classic can be used perfectly for dipping.

⑳ Léonie Bakery
📍 *15, av. Trudaine, Paris 9th*
📍 *96, rue de Lévis, Paris 17th*
Heading this bakery is Kamel Saci, a passionate baker who traveled to various capitals to train in bakeries and share knowledge. He makes excellent breads and pastries that employ all he's learned.

SPECIALTY
Vollkornbrot (a German multigrain bread).

BAGUETTE?
Yes, several kinds and all sourdough.

㉑ Le Temps et Le Pain
📍 *7, rue Mouton-Duvernet, Paris 14th*
Baker Alexis Borychowski acts as an alchemist and offers a range of loaves using organic flours from the Siluire flour mill, controlled hydrations, and plenty of passion. Between the millstone bread, the signature, and the nut and fruit versions, the choice is often difficult.

SPECIALTY
Kamut, with a beautiful golden color.

BAGUETTE?
Yes, and as crisp as can be.

SKIP TO
Poilâne, a Family History, p. 136.

La Flûte Gana, Paris 20th.

PASTRY SHOPS Les Pâtisseries

With all these pastry shops, we've placed our bets that there is no capital sweeter than Paris! — **VALENTINE OUDARD**

A sweet story

During the seventeenth century, confectioners and pastry chefs opened their first specialized shops.

At the end of the eighteenth century, on rue Vivienne (Paris 2nd), pastry chef Sylvain Bailly hired a young apprentice: Antonin Carême, the father of modern pastry.

In the nineteenth century, Parisian pastries experienced a boom under the influence of two phenomena:
› The legacy left by Antonin Carême, who captivated the minds of France and Europe with his architectural pieces.
› The establishment of a beet sugar factory in Passy (Hauts-de-Seine) by botanist Benjamin Delessert in the early nineteenth century. In 1812, Napoléon welcomed the creation of this new agro-industrial sector, which was very promising for France, by awarding Delessert the Legion of Honor. This discovery of making sugar from beets contributed to a drop in the price of sugar and popularized pastry, which prior to this time was reserved for wealthy classes.

THE HISTORIC PLACES

Angelina
📍 26, rue de Rivoli, Paris 1st + 6 locations

Since its opening in 1903, Angelina has remained the temple for lovers of Mont Blanc and hot chocolate.

THE MUST-TRY

The Mont Blanc, created by Anton Rumpelmayer, the founder of the business, which has become the pinnacle of French pastry.

A FAVORITE

The old-style hot chocolate that honors three cacaos with origins in the African countries of Niger, Ghana, and Ivory Coast.

Ladurée
📍 16, rue Royale, Paris 1st + 29 locations

Founded in 1862, the establishment continues to forge the capital's sweet reputation. Today, the 2011 world pastry champion Julien Alvarez heads the business and continues to move its success forward for the long term.

THE MUST-TRY

Macarons, the go-to for tourists.

A FAVORITE

The Bayadère (an ode to the almond), created for the pastry shop's 160th anniversary.

Stohrer
📍 51, rue Montorgueil, Paris 2nd

This is one of the oldest pastry shops in Paris still open. Surrounded by paintings from Paul Baudry, choose t from all the emblematic and historic pastries in the capital.

THE MUST-TRY

Le Russe (praline buttercream and dacquoise).

A FAVORITE

The kugelhopf, for its softness and the delicious flavor of the butter.

CHEF SIGNATURES

Cédric Grolet
📍 6, rue de Castiglione, Paris 1st
📍 35, av. de l'Opéra, Paris 2nd

Since arriving at Le Meurice in 2012, Grolet has been named winner of Best Pastry Chef in 2015 on the show *Le Chef* and selected best pastry chef in the world in 2018 (*50 Best*). He is one of the sweet universe's most talented and fashionable pastry chefs.

THE MUST-TRY

His incredible trompe-l'oeil creations.

A FAVORITE

The Saint-Honoré (phyllo dough, caramel choux puffs, and vanilla pastry cream) made to order.

Philippe Conticini
📍 31, rue Notre-Dame-de-Nazareth, Paris 3rd
📍 37, rue de Varenne, Paris 7th
📍 42, rue de l'Annonciation, Paris 16th

Conticini enjoys a global reputation and has elevated French pastry and introduced major innovations.

THE MUST-TRY

The Saint-Honoré tart.

A FAVORITE

The lemon tart with creamy buckwheat praline.

Jacques Genin
📍 133, rue de Turenne, Paris 3rd
📍 27, rue de Varenne, Paris 7th

A tart by Jacques Genin should never be missed.

THE MUST-TRIES

The lemon-basil tart, and the chocolate caper praline tart.

A FAVORITE

The mango–passion fruit soft caramel.

Christophe Michalak
📍 16, rue de la Verrerie, Paris 4th
📍 8, rue du Vieux-Colombier, Paris 6th
📍 60, rue du Faubourg-Poissonnière, Paris 10th

He worked at several grand pastry houses, and he modernized pastry with his rock 'n' roll creations and the opening, in 2013, of his Michalak Masterclass and Takeaway.

THE MUST-TRY

Vanilla apricot choux.

A FAVORITE

Kosmik (66 percent cacao chocolate mousse and pecan praline).

Yann Couvreur
📍 23 bis, rue des Rosiers, Paris 4th
📍 137, av. Parmentier, Paris 10th
📍 145, rue Saint-Charles, Paris 15th
📍 25, rue Legendre, Paris 17th
📍 87, rue de Fontenay, Vincennes (Val-de-Marne)

A young prodigy of the dessert scene, Couvreur conquered Paris with his elegant low-sugar and generous pastries.

THE MUST-TRY

Isatis tart (vanilla ganache, almond cream, and pecan praline).

A FAVORITE

The Madagascar vanilla mille-feuille, with an unforgettable finesse.

Pierre Hermé
📍 72, rue Bonaparte, Paris 6th + 22 locations

The king of the macaron continues to work tirelessly to explore new, sweet nuances.

THE MUST-TRY

The Ispahan, as a pastry or as a frozen version: rose, lychee, and raspberry make up a deliciously successful trio.

A FAVORITE

The Estela (buckwheat shortbread, praline with pine nuts, ganache, and Chantilly cream infused with Scots pine buds, sage-lovage-mint-coriander gelée).

Jean-Paul Hévin
📍 23 bis, av. de la Motte-Picquet, Paris 7th + 7 locations

Hévin is one of the most ardent defenders of chocolate flavors, and he explores them from A to Z.

THE MUST-TRY

The chocolate tart.

A FAVORITE

The pomme de terre (resembling a potato, an amazing trompe-l'oeil made from candied fruit and dark chocolate).

Des Gâteaux et du Pain—Claire Damon
📍 89, rue du Bac, Paris 7th
📍 63, blvd. Pasteur, Paris 15th

The ambitious and talented Claire Damon pays tribute to plants by highlighting seasonal fruits and working with ingredients representing all French terroirs.

THE MUST-TRY

The J'adore la Fraise (strawberry in a sponge, voluptuous cream, tangy compote, and airy mousse).

A FAVORITE

Angel Wings, flavored with orange flower water.

Hugo & Victor
📍 40, blvd. Raspail, Paris 7th

Hugues Pouget is a committed craftsman. He uses natural fruit powders and spices to color his macarons, setting aside natural and synthetic extracts, and works wonderfully with seasonal fruits and citrus fruits.

THE MUST-TRY

The Arlequin tart, made up of ten different slices with seasonal flavors.

A FAVORITE

The grapefruit Tarte Pétales, a tribute to this wonderful citrus fruit.

The Mont Blanc at Angelina.

Ladurée macarons.

Le Russe at Stohrer.

The Raspberry, by C. Grelot.

The tarte au chocolat, by J. P. Hévin.

The Saint-Honoré, by P. Conticini.

The lemon-basil tart, by J. Genin.

The apricot-vanilla choux, by C. Michelak.

The Isatis tart, by Y. Couvreur.

The Ispahan, by P. Hermé.

The J'Adore la Fraise, by C. Damon.

The Arlequin tart, by Hugo & Victor.

The Mussipontain, by S. Gaudard.

The Équinoxe, by C. Lignac.

The chocolate éclair, by KL Pâtisserie.

Sébastien Gaudard

📍 22, rue des Martyrs, Paris 9th

📍 Salon de thé des Tuileries, 1, rue des Pyramides, Paris 1st

The art of combining the delicious with the beautiful. This is a tidy shop with the charm of olden times and a short menu that pays tribute to Gaudard's native Lorraine.

THE MUST-TRY

The Mussipontain.

A FAVORITE

The Black Forest cake (Gaudard is one of the few Parisian locations to offer it).

Cyril Lignac – Gourmand Croquant

📍 24, rue Paul-Bert, Paris 11th + 5 locations

The pastry chef focuses on pastry with a geometric look and a play of textures—crunchiness, creaminess, airiness, meltness. The results are addictive, simple, indulgent, and compelling.

THE MUST-TRY

The Équinox.

A FAVORITE

The simple marshmallow bears.

KL Pâtisserie

📍 78, av. de Villiers, Paris 17th

In the metallic-gray backdrop of his pastry shop–tearoom, Kevin Lacote masterfully produces the classics.

THE MUST-TRIES

Chocolate éclair, lemon tart, mille-feuille, and gâteaux de voyage (cakes to carry).

A FAVORITE

The flan pâtissier and its incredibly light pastry.

MAM

📍 22, rue Fourcroy, Paris 17th

Stéphanie Le Quellec's kitchens produce excellent pastries. As the head of the kitchens that open to the shop, Pierre Chirac brilliantly executes a classical repertoire.

THE MUST-TRIES

The lemon tart and citrus confit, the baba with muscovado sugar, the flan pâtissier.

A FAVORITE

The incredible texture of the madeleines with chestnut honey.

Gilles Marchal

📍 9, rue Ravignan, Paris 18th

Born in Lorraine, he spent time in the kitchens of the grand Parisian luxury hotels and is today the emblematic pastry chef of Montmartre.

THE MUST-TRY

The éclair.

A FAVORITE

Filled madeleines (Sicilian pistachio, lemon, salted-butter caramel).

HOTEL PASTRY SHOPS

Ritz Paris Le Comptoir

📍 38, rue Cambon, Paris 1st

The talented pastry chef at the Ritz, François Perret, shines with his intelligent and daring way of associating the codes of luxury hotel pastries with takeout.

THE MUST-TRY

The Mille-Feuille To Go! Never easy to cut, this one can be enjoyed anywhere.

A FAVORITE

The marbled cake beverage among his series of pastry-inspired drinks (a drinking version of all the classics).

Pâtisserie Brach de Yann Brys

📍 1-7, rue Jean-Richepin, Paris 16th

Come here if for no other reason than to feast with the eyes. The MOF (Best Craftsman of France) pastry chef stands out for his creativity and the beauty of his cakes. Beyond his mastery of the tourbillon technique (a spiral technique achieved on a turntable), his pastries are of rare finesse and elegance.

THE MUST-TRY

The yuzu tart.

A FAVORITE

The calisson for the almondy sweetness and vanilla cream.

THE NEW GUARD

Julien Dechenaud

📍 11, rue Paul-Bert, Paris 11th

📍 16, rue du Rendez-Vous, Paris 12th

📍 32, rue Robert-Giraudineau, Vincennes (Val-de-Marne)

Julien Dechenaud is the son of a chocolatier. He spent time under chocolate masters Jean-Paul Hévin, Patrick Roger, and Alain Ducasse, so he has chocolate in his veins. His refined chocolate tablets reveal an elegant intensity, and his pastries leave not only long-lasting impressions of flavor but also the desire to quickly return.

THE MUST-TRY

The praline chocolate tart.

A FAVORITE

The nonconched Brazilian chocolate bar (raw chocolate with brown sugar that lends softness and crispiness).

Cinq Sens— Nicolas Paciello

📍 114, rue Saint-Charles, Paris 15th

This pastry chef whose past includes stints at luxury hotels offers a sensory journey that awakens the appetite.

THE MUST-TRY

The chocolate éclair.

A FAVORITE

The moist, marbled cake with intense chocolate flavor.

Le Jardin Sucré

📍 156, rue de Courcelles, Paris 17th

📍 10, pl. Paul-Grimault Cernay-la-Ville (Yvelines)

Mélanie L'Héritier and Arnaud Mathez have managed to elevate their macarons to the top of the Parisian pastry game.

THE MUST-TRY

The pistachio and orange flower water tart.

A FAVORITE

The black sesame macaron with the perfect hint of salt.

Jeffrey Cagnes

📍 24, rue des Moines, Paris 17th

Cagnes is the pastry chef who modernized the Stohrer pastry shop and opened his first boutique in 2021. His talents span from pastry to breads to chocolate.

THE MUST-TRY

The Saint-Honoré.

A FAVORITE

The praline-peanut bar is addictive.

Stéphane Glacier

📍 39, rue du Général-Leclerc, Bois-Colombes (Hauts-de-Seine)

MOF (Best Craftsman of France) Stéphane Glacier shares his passion for sweets both in his ice creams and cakes, and in his pastry school.

THE MUST-TRY

Le petit Antoine (crispy praline, hazelnut dacquoise, chocolate crémeux, milk chocolate Chantilly cream, thin wafers of milk chocolate).

A FAVORITE

The choux chouquette.

FOREIGN INSPIRATIONS

Bontemps

📍 57, rue de Bretagne, Paris 3rd

The entire Bontemps pastry shop is a must-try!

THE MUST-TRIES

The Romy lemon-hazelnut tart, the red fruits and orange flower water tart, the gianduja tart.

A FAVORITE

The very intense lemon cake.

Maison Aleph

📍 20, rue de la Verrerie, Paris 4th

📍 63, rue des Abbesses, Paris 18th

In her Levantine shop, Myriam Sabet seeks out the best ingredients for her exotic pastries, ice creams, and sorbets.

THE MUST-TRIES

The pastry nests, vanilla flan pâtissier, and galette des rois.

A FAVORITE

The knafeh.

Pages Blanches

📍 11, blvd. de Courcelles, Paris 8th

Pastries with Franco-Japanese notes, a sharp selection of seasonal products, and creative products that center on tea.

THE MUST-TRY

The flan pâtissier, caramelized as you wait.

A FAVORITE

The very light Japanese fraisier.

ONLINE PASTRY SHOPS

Claire Heitzler & Producteurs

📍 9, rue du Parc, Levallois-Perret (Hauts-de-Seine)

www.patisserie-claire.com

Voted best pastry chef of the year several times, the talented Claire Heitzler stands out for her low-sugar recipes and her deep respect for ingredients. This is evidenced by her new click-and-collect address, through which she pays tribute to the producers with whom she works.

THE MUST-TRY

The gâteau de l'amitié yuzu (yuzu cake).

A FAVORITE

Mont Blanc with candied clementine and calisson.

Nina Métayer Delicacy

www.delicatisserie.com

After working at Le Meurice, Jean-François Piège's Grand Restaurant, and Café Pouchkine, pastry chef and baker Nina Métayer opened her first boutique in 2020. Her pastries are poetic and bold.

THE MUST-TRY

Cheesecake or mille-feuille.

A FAVORITE

The Olivier at Easter time, a chocolate and olive oil cake.

The lemon tart from MAM.

Éclairs, by G. Marchal.

The mille-feuille from Le Comptoir at the Ritz.

The yuzu-filled tart from Brach.

The chocolate éclair from Cinq Sens.

The pistachio tart from Le Jardin Sucré.

The Saint-Honoré, by Jeffrey Cagnes.

The chocolate praline tart, by J. Dechenaud.

The Petit Antoine, by S. Glacier.

The red fruit tart from Bontemps.

The pastry nests from Maison Aleph.

The flan pâtissier from Pages Blanches.

BUTCHER SHOPS Les Boucheries

From the forecourt of Notre Dame to the slaughterhouses of La Villette to the Grande Boucherie des Halles, butcher shops can be found all over the city as an integral part of Parisian culture. Here are several locations to get to know.

—CHARLES PATIN O'COOHOON AND MARILOU PETRICOLA

From Île de la Cité to La Villette

In the Middle Ages, near the square in front of Notre Dame de Paris, the first butcher shop in Paris opened close to the Seine to allow the animals to drink and butchers to wash the blood.

In the fourteenth century, the Grande Boucherie was located around the historic district of Grand Châtelet. The boucherie was demolished in 1416 and replaced by four butcher shops by order of King Charles VI. The animals were mostly slaughtered in the street: "*The blood drips in the streets, it thickens under your feet and your shoes become red with it,*" reported Louis-Sébastien Mercier in 1783.

In 1808, Napoléon I signed a decree ending these "personal killings" in the capital and creating five public slaughterhouses to put an end to the disorder.

In 1867, the general slaughterhouses of La Villette officially opened.

Horse butchery

Émile Decroix, a soldier and veterinarian, fought two battles: one against the use of tobacco and the other in favor of hippophagy, the consumption of horsemeat. In 1866, he opened the first horse butcher shop in Paris. Four years later, there were about fifty such shops. On the site of the old hippophagy market, in the Georges-Brassens Park (Paris 15th), a sculpture of the bust of Decroix still stands. Eating horsemeat has gone out of fashion in Paris, and fewer than ten horse butchers remain in Île-de-France. Their old storefronts, recognizable by their red mosaics, are still visible. Among them is the Jacques Leban butcher shop, an institution since 1971, where you can purchase horse steak, minced meat, sausage, and horse from Meaux.

⚲ 89, rue Cambronne, Paris 15th

The Butcher of Paris

⚲ 39, rue de Bretagne, Paris 3rd

Located at the covered market of Les Enfants Rouges, this butcher shop owned by Louis-Marie Martin and Robin Bassin exclusively serves French-sourced meats, sourced from several farms.

CHOICE CUTS

Corsican veal from the Abbatucci family; beef "Salangus," a cross between Salers and Angus; organic Gascon pork.

Viande Viande

⚲ 206, rue Saint-Martin, Paris 3rd

The French-sourced meats raised in the open air arrive here whole, ready to be broken down by Édouard Haguet and Adrien Quennepoix on the large central chopping block. The meat is left in the window to age.

CHOICE CUT

The aged ground steak, a marvel of flavor and melting tenderness.

La Boucherie Gardil

⚲ 44, rue Saint-Louis-en-l'Île, Paris 4th

Jean-Paul Gardil and his son Wilfried have been wielding their knives behind their magnificent storefront since 1981, which has remained mostly in its original state. Here you'll get good advice and French-sourced meats from the Marais Poitevin, Limousin, and Gers.

CHOICE CUTS

Black chicken from Astarac-Bigorre, Rex du Poitou rabbit.

Au Bell Viandier

⚲ 4, rue Lobineau, Paris 6th

At the covered market of Saint-Germain, Serge Caillaud attracts regulars with his jovial manner and his beautiful cuts of pork, veal, beef, and lamb, made into pâtés-croûtes and terrines.

CHOICE CUT

In hunting season, the partridge terrine.

Maison Le Bourdonnec

⚲ 43, rue du Cherche-Midi, Paris 6th

⚲ 51, rue de Lévis, Paris 7th

⚲ 208 bis, rue de Grenelle, Paris 17th

Since running his first butcher shop in 1987 at only nineteen years old, Yves-Marie Le Bourdonnec has delighted his customers with French-sourced meats bought directly from the farm and with impeccable cuts and careful aging.

CHOICE CUT

The forty-day prime rib.

Les Viandes du Champ-de-Mars

⚲ 122, rue Saint-Dominique, Paris 7th

Behind the chopping block, Jean-Marie Boedec offers lamb from Sisteron, salt-meadow veal from Corrèze, and Wagyu beef.

CHOICE CUT

Simmental prime rib from Bavaria.

Boucheries Nivernaises

⚲ 99, rue du Faubourg-Saint-Honoré, Paris 8th

Charles de Gaulle was one of the first customers of the Bissonnet family and paid for his meat using his own checkbook. Located at the foot of the Élysée, this seventh-generation butcher still provides venues and luxury hotels with exceptional cuts from French livestock.

CHOICE CUT

The rump heart of Norman cows.

Boucherie D. Chainay

⚲ 43, rue du Château-d'Eau, Paris 10th

Beef from Aquitaine, milk-fed veal from Corrèze, lamb from Limousin . . . For more than twenty years, Denis Chainay has been working the old-fashioned way in this shop dating from 1912, decorated from top to bottom with marble, a material historically used to help keep the meat cold.

CHOICE CUTS

Upper shoulder, eye of round, neck—all classic cuts, but excellent.

Boucherie Larrazet

⚲ 85 bis, blvd. de Magenta, Paris 10th

At the covered market of Saint-Quentin, Jean-Louis Larrazet presents Aubrac beef, Lozère lamb, farm-raised Label Rouge (Red Label) pork from Limousin, Landes chicken, and veal from Corrèze.

CHOICE CUT

The shoulder of lamb for confit.

Viande & Chef

⚲ 38, rue de Lancry, Paris 10th

Simon Bricard's teams work in front of the customer, in complete transparency, breaking down French, farmstead, and rustic breeds to offer top-quality meat and ready-made meals. Every week, there are barbecue workshops!

CHOICE CUT

Kintoa pork from Pays Basque.

Boucherie Moderne

⚲ 249, blvd. Voltaire, Paris 11th

Using mostly meat from Normandy but also some stock from Spain and Scotland, John Gillot proudly uses all parts of the animal and visits his breeders.

CHOICE CUT

The aged Norman prime rib, with deliciously marbled fat.

L'Atelier de la Viande

⚲ 55, rue Claude-Decaen, Paris 12th

Organic, French, and farmstead products are on sale here by Ouadi Jriri, who offers a selection of specialized meats and, behind the window, aged cuts, such as Angus or Aubrac beef and lamb's knuckle. There are also several house-made preparations: sausage, merguez sausage, roast beef, and stuffed meats.

CHOICE CUTS

Homemade marinated chicken, lamb, or beef skewers.

Hugo Desnoyer

⚲ 45, rue Boulard, Paris 14th

⚲ 28, rue du Dr Blanche, Paris 16th

The butcher here personally chooses the breeders he buys from and has perfect mastery of his trade while doling out good advice to customers. All these traits have made Hugo Desnoyer an essential butcher for consumers and Michelin-starred restaurants.

CHOICE CUT

The Limousin sirloin.

Boucherie Caman Père et Fils

📍 155, av. de Suffren, Paris 15th

You'll find Limousin beef, pork from Brittany, lamb from Sisteron and Corrèze, poultry and rabbit, a few selections of Spanish charcuterie, and some prepared dishes in this elegant family butcher shop with carefully arranged windows. Everything is managed by Fabrice Caman.

CHOICE CUT

Veal Orloff, a well-executed classic.

Romain Leboeuf

📍 37, av. Félix-Faure, Paris 15th

Romain Leboeuf, MOF (Best Craftsman of France) butcher, continues the family story in his neighborhood butcher shop. The meat comes from Augy-sur-Arbois (Cher) from Thierry Lamouroux, his favorite breeder.

CHOICE CUTS

Beef aged on-site and oyster steak.

Boucherie Mozart

📍 48, av. Mozart, Paris 16th

Pascal Bouttier offers a large selection of French-sourced meats directly from the producer, black pork from Bigorre, and suckling veal. There are also charcuterie and prepared foods as well as many poultry selections.

CHOICE CUTS

Culoiseau chickens.

Billot Club

📍 105, av. de Saint-Ouen, Paris 17th

Before opening this shop, Augustin Savouré toured France to meet the best breeders. His shop is recognizable by its green awning.

CHOICE CUTS

The Laotian pâté and the black-pork sausage.

Boucherie Meissonier

📍 8, rue Meissonier, Paris 17th

The president of the Paris butchers' union,

Véronique Langlais also runs her own butcher shop. There is a host of roasts, stuffed meats, aged beef ribs, and many other delectable surprises.

CHOICE CUT

The Rubia Gallega beef rib from Spain is marbled to perfection.

Boucherie Timothée Sautereau

📍 25, rue Ramey, Paris 18th

Trained at the renowned butcher Le Bourdonnec, Timothée Sautereau offers a wide choice of French and Spanish meats delivered whole and broken down on-site. Aged beef is available but also ground steaks using less noble pieces.

CHOICE CUT

The aged pork spare ribs.

Boucherie Le Lann

📍 242 bis, rue des Pyrénées, Paris 20th

In 2013, former employee Laurent Courtiol took over from Christian Le Lann and continues the journey of this excellent hundred-year-old butcher shop in Ménilmontant.

CHOICE CUTS

Salt-meadow lamb from Mont-Saint-Michel, Gascon chickens from Arnaud Tauzin, and black pork from Bigorre.

Les Apaches

📍 21, rue des Gâtines, Paris 20th

From the ceiling hang large sausages and bouquets of dried herbs. On the shelves are marbled Landes pork round, homemade sausages, and house-made pulled pork tourte. Vincent Deniau and François Guillemin offer French-sourced meats bought directly from the producers.

CHOICE CUT

Plate short ribs from Limousin cattle dry-aged on the bone for thirty days.

Les Apaches, above and below left.

Viande Viande.

Hugo Desnoyer.

Romain Leboeuf.

Boucheries Nivernaises.

Billot Club.

CHARCUTIER-CATERERS
Les Charcuteries-Traiteurs

From large shops to small neighborhood artisans, these locations delight for everyday meals and special occasions.
—**MARIE-LAURE FRÉCHET AND CHARLES PATIN O'COOHOON**

The charcutiers

The first statutes representing the profession of butcher date to the letters patent of January 17, 1475, recorded in the Register of Châtelet. The butchers at that time held a monopoly on the sale of cooked pork. In return, they had to pay a fee. Eventually, they could no longer supply enough meat for Paris's growing population. The butchers appealed to the fairground community of butchers in Nanterre (the cheap restaurants, or gargots), which brought together about twenty families of butchers who provided Paris with pork for more than three centuries.

The traiteurs (caterers)

In the Middle Ages, the traiteur was a "merchant who trades," or in other words negotiates. In the seventeenth century, the term meant the person "who prepares, who provides food for money." Under the Ancien Régime, traiteurs specialized in weddings and banquets before eventually preparing meals for loyal customers. During the Revolution, deprived of their clientele within the nobility, Parisian traiteurs were ousted by "restaurateurs" who opened establishments where people could go out to eat.

The charcutiers-traiteurs

Until 1790, the profession of butcher was regulated by a corporation. After the corporation's suppression in 1791, the charcuterie trade bureau was created in Paris in 1805. In 1891, the Syndicat Général de la Charcuterie Française was created, chaired by Eugène Jumin (there is a street named after him in the 19th arrondissement). In the twentieth century, the profession evolved and expanded to the preparation of ready-made meals. In 1992, the union became the Confédération Nationale des Charcutiers-traiteurs et Traiteurs (CNCT).

The tourte vigneronne (winegrower's savory pie) from Maison Thielen.

The boudin noir from Durand.

The oreiller de la Belle Aurore from Maison Verot.

Fauchon vs Hédiard, Head-to-Head at La Madeleine

Now gone, the two legendary Parisian houses enlivened the Place de la Madeleine for more than a century. Hédiard, the bourgeois shop, against Fauchon, the more upper-class establishment.

"Y en a marre du Fauchon, du Hédiard, du saumon, du caviar" ("I'm tired of Fauchon, Hédiard, salmon, and caviar")

—Les Inconnus, "Auteuil Neuilly Passy," 1991

FAUCHON

⬥ *24–30, pl. de la Madeleine, Paris 8th*

OPENING OF THE BUSINESS
1886, by Auguste Félix Fauchon.

OPENING ON PLACE DE LA MADELEINE 1886

SIZE 5,380 square feet (500 sq m).

COMPOSITION
Shop and restaurant.

SPECIALTIES
Inventive products such as LU cookies and Maggi bouillon cubes, but also French grocery products, a catering service, and a pastry case considered a hallmark in the industry.

CLOSURE 2020.

HÉDIARD

⬥ *21, pl. de la Madeleine, Paris 8th*

OPENING OF THE BUSINESS
1854, by Ferdinand Hédiard.

OPENING ON PLACE DE LA MADELEINE 1880

SIZE 16,100 square feet (1,500 sq m).

COMPOSITION
Shop and restaurant.

SPECIALTIES
This "shop of the colonies and Algeria" historically offered peppers, teas, coffees, exotic fruits, and a catering service (foie gras, terrines, small bites, savory pies, salads, etc.).

CLOSURE 2015.

HISTORIC CATERERS

Dalloyau

⬥ *101, rue du Faubourg-Saint-Honoré, Paris 8th + 6 locations*

Charles Dalloyau, while in the service of the Prince of Condé, was poached by Louis XIV because of the quality of his bread. After the Revolution, Jean-Baptiste Dalloyau established his shop. He offered cooked dishes to be delivered to homes, in an aristocratic manner. The establishment now enjoys an international reputation.

SPECIALTIES
The Opéra cake; the praline Dalloyau.

Lenôtre

⬥ *44, rue d'Auteuil, Paris 16th + 9 locations*

Pastry chef Gaston Lenôtre started a traiteur in 1964. The Lenôtre establishment now has four hundred chefs including seven MOFs (Best Craftsmen of France). It caters more than six thousand events each year. It also manages the Parisian restaurant Le Pré Catelan, run by chef Frédéric Anton.

SPECIALTY

Le Succès (a cake of layered nut meringue).

Maison Pou

◇ 16, av. des Ternes, Paris 17th

The address has been the same since 1830. Particularly famous for its charcuterie, the establishment is now run by Guy Feryn and his son Aurélien. In 2009, the headcheese, a family specialty, won as champion of France in its category.

SPECIALTIES

The salmon koulibiac, the lobster terrine.

Potel et Chabot

www.poteletchabot.com

In 1820 in Paris, Jean-François Potel, master pastry chef, and Étienne Chabot, renowned cook of the court of France, joined forces to create a catering house for at-home meals. Building on their success, they bought shops, including the oldest Parisian traiteur, Chevet, where Escoffier had his beginnings. Glorified particularly in thanks to its organizing the banquet of mayors in 1900 (twenty-three thousand place settings, set up in the Tuileries Garden), it has become a gold standard for important Parisian receptions.

SPECIALTIES

Pike soufflé, lobster choux, and tournedos Rossini.

CHARCUTIERS-CATERERS

Maison Verot

◇ 38, rue de Bretagne, Paris 3rd

◇ 3, rue Notre-Dame-des-Champs, Paris 6th

◇ 7, rue Lecourbe, Paris 15th

Since 1930 and Jean Verot's first charcuterie shop in Saint-Étienne, four generations of the Verot family have succeeded one another. Today, Gilles and his son Nicolas continue to

make the establishment a hallmark for pâtés en croûte, rillettes, and prepared creations.

A SPECIALTY

The oreiller de la Belle Aurore (a square pâté en croûte), when in season.

Lastre Sans Apostrophe

188, rue de Grenelle, Paris 7th

Formerly of La Tour d'Argent and world champion of pâté en croûte in 2012, Yohan Lastre and his partner, cabinetmaker Marion Sonier, fashion an incredible collection of pâtés en croûte and several specialties, such as fougasse from Saint-Mamert-du-Gard and a superb leeks vinaigrette.

SPECIALTY

The pâté en croûte of duck, foie gras, and pistachio.

Arnaud Nicolas

◇ 47, av. de la Bourdonnais, Paris 7th

◇ 125, rue Caulaincourt, Paris 18th

Offering tourte de couchon (pork pie), Lyon sausage, and terrine grand-mère, as well as charcuterie cooked and made without preservatives or nitrites, this MOF (Best Craftsman of France) charcutier also sets up the restaurant adjoining his 7th-arrondissement shop.

SPECIALTY

The essential dish: chicken and duck fois gras pâté en croûte.

Au Chochon Rose

◇ 137, rue Saint-Charles, Paris 15th

Marbled ham, pork headcheese, savory pies in puff pastry, ready-made meals, roasted chickens, and an armada of salads: here Dominique Bignon presents all the greats of a charcutier-caterer.

SPECIALTIES

Champion headcheese of France, roasted suckling pig.

Joly Traiteur

◇ 89, rue Cambronne, Paris 15th

In his Cambronne laboratory-shop, the MOF (Best Craftsman of France) charcutier Pascal Joly and his son Florian make natural charcuterie (nitrite-free, allergen-free, preservative-free, etc.) and impeccably prepared dishes: Bavarian salmon and local farm-raised vegetables from Saint-Jacques.

SPECIALTY

The headcheese Oreille d'Or, champion of France 2014.

Durand Traiteur

2, rue d'Avron, Paris 20th

Christian Durand, the 2019 headcheese champion of France, perfectly executes the classic repertoire of the charcutier-caterer in his shop at Nation.

SPECIALTIES

House-made kettle chips, boudin Parisien (one-third blood, one-third onions, one-third pork).

Maison Thielen

◇ 21, rue des Martyrs, Paris 9th

◇ 24, rue de la République, Vanves (Haut-de-Seine)

The young Alsatian Stéphane Thielen made a reputation for himself in Vanves before opening a second location in the 9th. On the shelves are rabbit terrine, Strasbourg sausages, braised ham, and savory meat pies along with excellent sauerkraut.

SPECIALTY

The tourte vigneronne (winegrower's savory pie) made with pork and Riesling.

The chicken and fois gras pâté en croûte, by A. Nicholas.

The praline Dalloyau from Dalloyau.

The lobster terrine from Maison Pou.

Le Succès from Lenôtre.

The headcheese from Joly Traiteur.

The oreiller de la Belle Aurore from Lastre Sans Apostrophe.

CHEESE SHOPS Les Fromageries

Paris is in love with all things dairy. Here are some of the best cheesy locations. — PIERRE COULON

Crémerie Terroirs d'Avenir

📍 8, rue du Nil, Paris 2nd

📍 17, blvd. Morlan, Paris 4th

Before opening their first boutiques, Alexandre Drouard and Samuel Nahon embarked on a tour of France for products supplied to restaurants. Since then, their creamery Terroirs d'Avenir has been importing rare cheeses that complete an already well-sourced range. They prioritize products from ancient breeds.

AFFINAGE CAVE

Their aging cellar occupies an old underground passage that connected different shops along the street. It has humidity and temperature control.

THE CRÈME DE LA CRÈME

- The chèvre ficu (goat cheese), fresh, racy, wrapped in a fig leaf.
- The creamy Tomme de Bois Joubert with Bretonne Pie Noire cow's milk.
- The Pustier from Montjay farm, aged in summer savory.

Fromagerie Laurent Dubois

📍 97–99, rue Saint-Antoine, Paris 4th

📍 47 ter, blvd. Saint-Germain, Paris 5th

📍 2, rue de Lourmel, Paris 15th

📍 58, rue d'Auteuil, Paris 16th

Coming from a large family of dairymen and cheesemakers, Laurent Dubois opened his shop in 1996 after touring around France to choose his producers. He maintains a precise range of cheeses that he ages on-site in his cellars. Passionate about cooking and pastry, he has developed many cheese creations inspired by his travels and the seasons. He was rewarded with the title of MOF (Best Craftsman of France) in 2000.

AFFINAGE CAVE

Each shop has a refrigerated aging cellar of about 20 square feet (5 sq m).

THE CRÈME DE LA CRÈME

- The southwest sheep's-milk tommes, aged in-house.
- Roquefort quince paste.
- Tomme d'Oudry, a mild goat cheese.

Fromagerie Quatrehomme

📍 62, rue de Sèvres, Paris 7th

📍 26, rue des Martyrs, Paris 9th

📍 4, rue du Rendez-vous, Paris 12th

📍 32, rue de l'Espérance, Paris 13th

📍 9, rue du Général–Leclerc, Issy-les-Moulineaux (Hauts-de-Seine)

With Nathalie and Maxime Quatrehomme, the third generation of cheesemakers continues the tradition of one of the oldest locations in Paris. Since 1953, the Quatrehommes have been running a shop, and they offer more than four hundred labels. In 2000, the first year cheesemongers were eligible, Marie Quatrehomme became the first female MOF (Best Craftsman of France).

AFFINAGE CAVE

Located in the 7th arrondissement 270 square feet (25 sq m), and entirely natural.

THE CRÈME DE LA CRÈME

- The smoked goat cheese made with Nikka whisky.
- The melting sheep's tomme from Laruns.
- Bleu de Bellevue, a Breton cheese with fenugreek seeds and toasted aromatics.

Fromagerie Taka & Vermo

📍 61, rue du Faubourg-Saint-Denis, Paris 10th

At Taka & Vermo, Laure Takahashi and Mathieu Vermorel are at the head of what is one of the city's most enjoyable fromageries. In their aging cellars, they make cow's-milk, goat's-milk (what a selection!), and sheep's-milk cheeses along with aging tommes they discover during their travels. Many cheese preparations elevate the choices. It's an elegant location, full of flavors, with attentive service and undoubtedly one of the best values for the money in the capital.

AFFINAGE CAVE

The 64-square-foot (6 sq m) aging cellar located in the basement of the fromagerie was built when the shop opened. It has all the tools necessary for controlling the affinage of cheeses they sell in the shop.

THE CRÈME DE LA CRÈME

- The Saint-Clément, a goat's-milk cheese made entirely from cream.
- Sheep's tomme by Stéphane Chetrit.
- Fresh goat's-milk cheese with yuzu.

Fromagerie Goncourt

📍 1, rue Abel-Rabaud, Paris 11th

📍 14, rue de la Jonquière, Paris 17th

After taking a bike tour of France to meet producers, Clément Brossault opened his fromagerie with specialized products. Here the seasons and animal welfare are emphasized. There are no goat's-milk cheeses in winter. There are just a few labels for sale, but they are well sourced. Raclette is offered year-round. This is a Corsican range of products to die for.

AFFINAGE CAVE

Just 55 square feet (5 sq m) make up this aging cellar with a hygrometric control system that diffuses water vapor among the cheeses.

THE CRÈME DE LA CRÈME

- The Pavé des Pyrénées, a characteristic goat's-milk cheese (in spring).
- Raclette de Savoie (in summer).
- The Estive du Jura, a cooked-paste cheese made with spring milk (in autumn).
- The Brebis (sheep's) Crémeux from Pays Basque (in winter).

Fromagerie Chez Virginie

📍 54, rue Damrémont, Paris 18th

📍 125, rue Caulaincourt, Paris 18th

A dairyman's daughter, Virginie Boularouah started working with cheese at the age of twenty-seven after a career as a translator. In her century-old shop, she has developed true expertise as an affineur. The cheeses age between two natural straw mats that produce beautiful colors and flavors in the cheeses' interior.

AFFINAGE CAVE

A refrigerated cellar of 269 square feet (25 sq m), founded a hundred years ago, with a ventilation and hygrometric control system.

THE CRÈME DE LA CRÈME

- The dense and elegant Pouligny blue cheese.
- The decadent spoon-scoopable Saint-Félician.
- The Clos de Montmartre, aged in vine shoot ash from vines on Butte Montmartre.

AND . . .

Androuet

📍 134, rue Mouffetard, Paris 5th + 9 locations

Founded in 1909 by Henri Androuët, on rue d'Amsterdam (9th), this business was one of the first to offer regional cheeses to Parisians. It was taken over by Stéphane Blohorn in 2005.

Barthélémy

📍 51, rue de Grenelle, Paris 7th

Supplier of the Élysée and Matignon, the emblematic Nicole Barthélémy passed the business in 2021 to Claire Griffon. The shop offers aged cheeses and cheese creations.

Alleosse

📍 13, rue Poncelet, Paris 17th

Since 1976, three generations have succeeded each other in managing this fromagerie. Below the shop is an underground space spanning 2,600 square feet (250 sq m) and divided into four aging cellars.

Fromagerie La Fontaine

This is one of the oldest fromageries in Paris. It has been located at 75, rue Jean-de-La-Fontaine (16th) since 1890. Prior to current owners Clara Solvit and Lucien Dumond, six generations of cheesemakers succeeded each other. It is a safe bet that Marcel Proust, born just twenty paces from this institution now classified as a historical monument, was a regular.

Roquefort quince paste, by Laurent Dubois.

The Pavé des Pyrénées and the Estive du Jura from Fromagerie Goncourt.

The Clos Montmartre from Chez Virginie.

The chèvre ficu from Crémerie Terroirs d'Avenir.

Fresh yuzu goat's-milk cheese from Taka & Vermo.

The smoked Nikka whisky goat's-milk cheese from Fromagerie Quatrehomme.

FISH MERCHANTS
Les Poissonneries

Here is a selection of fish merchants making waves in the capital. — **CLARISSE TEYSSANDIER**

A fishy story

Before the fourteenth century in Paris, the majority of fish consumed by the population was freshwater fish from the Seine or Marne or salted or dried fish. With the evolution of transportation, Picardy and Normandy became primary suppliers to the capital. Starting in the mid-nineteenth century, the fish pavilion at Les Halles became the epicenter for Parisian fishmongers. With the expanse of neighborhood markets, as decreed under Haussmann, and the relocation of the city's wholesale food markets to Rungis, local fishmongers took over as the suppliers of fresh fish to Paris.

Poissonnerie Terroirs d'Avenir

◦ *8, rue du Nil, Paris 2nd*
◦ *17, blvd. Morland, Paris 4th*

Historically located on rue du Nil, the Terroirs d'Avenir team has been campaigning since 2008 to supply Parisian plates with products from sustainable fishing sources and to promote small-scale French coastal fishing. Here pride of place is given to lesser-known species, such as rough scad and bonito tuna.

BEST FROM THE NET
• Diver Saint-Jacques scallops, caught by Laurent Jehanno and Tomy Journals.
• The Île-de-France freshwater pike perch net-caught by Yoann Bertolo in the Yvelines and Val-d'Oise.

Poissons

◦ *46, rue des Gravilliers, Paris 3rd*

After working at Maison Vanhamme, Arnaud Agostini opened his own shop in 2019. His passion is raising awareness of sustainable fishing techniques. Providing total transparency about his suppliers is at the heart of his approach.

BEST FROM THE NET
• Shrimp from Noirmoutier.
• The seafood paella on Saturday.

Poissonnerie Moby Dick

◦ *50, rue du Cherche-Midi, Paris 6th*

Founded by actor Gérard Depardieu, the most famous sea wolf in French cinema, Poissonnerie Moby Dick highlights seasonal fishing from small boats off the Atlantic coast.

BEST FROM THE NET
• Seafood couscous, Thursday, Friday, and Saturday.
• Line-caught bluefin tuna.

Poissonnerie Viot

◦ *6, rue Lobineau, Paris 6th*

After spending time in the Yves Camdeborde's kitchens, Marie-Victoire and Arthur Viot swam against the tide by opening a dried-fish market in 2021. Their products are preserved without ice. As a result, the fish has an extended shelf life, and the texture is better. They also mature fish in the cold room of their shop.

BEST FROM THE NET
• The aged ikejime-killed catfish.
• Grilled dried sardines enjoyed on-site.

Ebisu

◦ *81, rue du Faubourg-Saint-Denis, Paris 10th*
◦ *30, rue du Chemin-Vert, Paris 11th*

Patrick Fernandez is one of the pioneers of ikejime in Paris. This fish-slaughtering technique from Japan, which consists of neutralizing the nervous system of the fish and emptying its blood as soon as it comes out of the water, makes it possible to preserve its freshness longer. The catering area is run by the fishmonger's Japanese wife and offers Japanese specialties. Yebisu, the shop's outpost, opened in 2021 in the 10th.

BEST FROM THE NET
• The chirashi, using the catch of the day.
• Ikejime-killed gray sea bream.

Poissonnerie du Dôme

◦ *4, rue Delambre, Paris 14th*
◦ *61, rue Damrémont, Paris 18th*

At the helm of this historic fish market in Montparnasse is Julien Chartrain, who took over the business in 2012 following his father-in-law. Obsessed with the freshness and quality of products, he favors small French-sourced seasonal fishing.

BEST FROM THE NET
• Gray shrimp from the Vendée.
• House-made Taramasalata with cod roe.

Lecourbe-Marée

◦ *93, rue Lecourbe, Paris 15th*

This fish market is a family story begun by Damien Lejeune, MOF (Best Craftsman of France) fishmonger-scaler 2007. There is a refined selection of fish and shellfish from small-boat fishermen.

BEST FROM THE NET
• Bouchot (pole-cultivated) Morisseau mussels from Mont-Saint-Michel.

• Slow-cooked fish soup, using the catch of the day.

Maison Vanhamme

◦ *103, rue de la Tour, Paris 16th*
◦ *15, rue Pierre-Guérin, Paris 16th*

Born into a family of fishmongers and scalers for four generations, Arnaud Vanhamme has seawater in his blood. An MOF (Best Craftsman of France) since 2011, he offers a rigorous selection of catches from small fishing boats from the Atlantic and Mediterranean coasts.

BEST FROM THE NET
• Line-caught sea bass.
• Sand sole.

La Poissonnerie de Passy

◦ *1, rue Bois-le-Vent, Paris 16th*

Ikejime-slaughtering processes and large pieces of rare fish are offered here. Located in the Passy market, Christophe Hierax has been working with exceptional products since 2002. Among his regular clients are Alain Ducasse, Christian Le Squer, and Pascal Barbot. There is raw fish to take away or to enjoy on the spot.

BEST FROM THE NET
• The ikejime-killed Vendée pollack.
• Utah Beach oysters from Normandy.

Poissonnerie Daguerre Marée

◦ *4, rue Bayen, Paris 17th*

Anne-Sophie Gautret took over this family business with her husband, Sylvain Carré. On the shelves are daily arrivals from French coastal fishing. The specialty of the house is fish smoked and salted on-site several times a week.

BEST FROM THE NET
• The sar from the island of Oléron.
• The bouchot (pole-cultivated) mussels from Mont-Saint-Michel.

Poissonnerie Goube

◦ *Marché des Bergères, 151–153, av. du Président-Wilson, Puteaux (Hauts-de-Seine), Wednesday and Saturday*
◦ *Marché Chantecoq, 59, rue Eugène-Eichenberger, Puteaux (Hauts-de-Seine), Thursday and Sunday*
◦ *Windsor Market, 5, rue Windsor, Neuilly-sur-Seine (Hauts-de-Seine), Wednesday, Friday, and Sunday*

Best Craftsman of France and fishmonger-scaler Jordan Goube has made excellent service his signature. He pays particular attention to sourcing, with fish supplied mainly from small French fishing boats.

BEST FROM THE NET
• Roasted Brittany monkfish.
• Brittany turbot en portefeuille (served filled and folded)

Montreuil sur Mer

◦ *15, rue de l'Église, Montreuil (Seine-Saint-Denis)*

Guillaume Gréaud, Simon Turmel, and Yannick Costa landed in Montreuil in 2020. Here you won't find shrimp or cod. Instead, the establishment chooses to highlight wild and abundant fish from small French fishing sources.

BEST FROM THE NET
• Ribs of line-caught tuna.
• The brandade using line-caught hake.

Poissonnerie de Passy, above and at right.

Poissonnerie Terroirs d'Avenir.

Poissonnerie Lecourbe-Marée.

Poissonnerie Terroirs d'Avenir.

Poissonnerie du Dôme.

Poissonnerie Vanhamme.

Poissonnerie du Dôme.

PRODUCE MARKETS
Les Primeurs

Paris is plentiful with fresh fruit-and-vegetable markets where quality is paramount. Here is a small selection of some of the best. —MORGANE MIZZON

The history of the term
› Seventeenth century: *primeurs* means "early (spring) fruits and vegetables."
› Late-eighteenth and nineteenth centuries: *primeur* refers to the "first season of certain fruits."
› Twentieth century: by association, primeur—or primeuriste—becomes the name for the fruit-and-vegetable merchant, then for the shop itself.

Retail sales of fresh fruits and vegetables
Until World War II, fruits and vegetables could be purchased in two places in Paris:
› at the "fruitier" or more often the "fruitière," which also sold dairy products.
› at the "marchand des quatre-saisons" (four-seasons merchant), a street vendor who transported fruits and vegetables on handcarts from Les Halles.

Berrie.

M.I.A.M.

Miyam.

Les Primeurs d'Excellence
♀ 48, rue Saint-Honoré, Paris 1st
♀ 23 and 97, rue Saint-Antoine, Paris 4th
♀ 50, av. Mozart, Paris 16th
♀ 216, rue des Pyrénées, Paris 20th
♀ 18, rue Henri-Barbusse, Levallois-Perret (Hauts-de-Seine)
♀ 37, rue de Chézy, Neuilly-sur-Seine (Hauts-de-Seine)

From raspberries from Corrèze to Indian mangos, fruits and veggies are always abundant here. This market has a solid reputation among professionals and the general public.

THE TOP OF THE BASKET
Potatoes from the island of Ré, organic carrots from Île-de-France.

Primeur Terroirs d'Avenir
♀ 7, rue du Nil, Paris 2nd
♀ 17, blvd. Morland, Paris 4th
♀ 5, rue Paul-Bert, Paris 11th
♀ 84, rue Jean-Pierre-Timbaud, Paris 11th
♀ 123, rue des Dames, Paris 17th
♀ 9, rue du Capitaine-Dreyfus, Montreuil (Seine-Saint-Denis)

Founded by Alexandre Drouard and Samuel Nahon, this shop became a haunt for chefs and the general public. Fruits and vegetables are procured using ultra-advanced sourcing.

THE TOP OF THE BASKET
Citrus fruits from Mathieu Vessières (Pyrénées-Orientales).

Miyam
♀ 82, rue Beaubourg, Paris 3rd
♀ 161, rue du Faubourg-Saint-Antoine, Paris 11th
♀ 69, rue de la Convention, Paris 15th
♀ 11, rue du Poteau, Paris 18th

At the head of this store, which promotes no waste, are the Sebbag siblings, who take the shop's withering vegetables and cook them to consume. The result is less than 1 percent food waste.

THE TOP OF THE BASKET
Fruits, vegetables, and cheeses from 150 French producers.

Harry Cover
♀ 208, rue de Grenelle, Paris 7th

This fourth-generation primeur is now run by

Gérard Loli and his son Julien, who select the best vegetables from Rungis and offer them by weight or made into soups.

THE TOP OF THE BASKET
A wide selection of French-grown organic fruits and vegetables.

Berrie
♀ 39, rue Saint-Lazare, Paris 9th
♀ 21, rue des Martyrs, Paris 9th
♀ 45, rue des Moines, Paris 17th

You can find everything in this "small neighborhood supermarket" set up by Jérémy Geneau, Olivier Tatin, and Guillaume Aubailly—three childhood friends from Berry.

THE TOP OF THE BASKET
Fruits and vegetables from Valdemar Barreira (Yvelines).

Zingam
♀ 75, rue du Chemin-Vert, Paris 11th
♀ 51, rue de la Fontaine-au-Roi, Paris 11th
♀ 74, rue des Martyrs, Paris 18th

Lelio Stettin and Tania Grawitz offer local fruits and vegetables, beautiful charcuterie, and cheeses.

THE TOP OF THE BASKET
Rhubarb from the Grand Laval farm (Drôme).

Humphris
♀ 2, rue Milton, Paris 9th

In the Humphris family, Nicolas, the father, grows organic fruits and vegetables and makes breads from ancient-grain flours on his farm in Heurteloup (Yvelines). Dan, the son, sells them among a range of authentic products.

THE TOP OF THE BASKET
Ginger (from Indre) from Herba Humana.

Chez Victor
♀ 73, rue Pernety, Paris 14th

Since 2017, Victor Brun has been offering fruits, vegetables, cheeses, and jams sourced within a radius of less than 60 miles (100 km).

THE TOP OF THE BASKET
The mini zucchini from Sophie Fils (Yvelines).

Le Comptoir des Producteurs
♀ 25, rue Mouton-Duvernet, Paris 14th

Founded by the Charraire family and based in Rungis, this primeur is the go-to for Parisian chefs. It offers delivery in Paris.

THE TOP OF THE BASKET
Aromatic herbs from Bastelica (South Corsica).

M.I.A.M.
♀ 168, rue de Crimée, Paris 19th
♀ 52, rue Curial, Paris 19th

Opened in 2018, the Marché Indépendant d'Alice Audebrand and Marie Van Hemelryck has no majority owner, allowing them to compensate the fruit and vegetable growers more fairly. On the shelves are organic and local products and citrus fruits from Sicily, plus Italian cheeses.

THE TOP OF THE BASKET
Smoked Gouda from the Lyon affineur Janier, and Picardy chard from Bio-Mesnil farm.

SPICE SHOPS
Les Comptoirs à épices

For several centuries, the capital has offered a plethora of spices.
Here's a short guide. — SAMIR OURIAGHLI

Heratchian Frères.

Épices Roellinger.

Izraël.

Épices Roellinger.

A Little History

In the Middle Ages, *épicier* literally referred to the spice merchant, and sugar and honey were part of what was offered. Since the eighteenth century, specialists have become generalists and the word has changed somewhat from its original meaning.

Le Comptoir des Poivres

📍 *6, rue Villedo, Paris 1st*

This is a shop with two sides. Japanese products are offered as well as a plethora of peppers and chiles. The establishment also sells a selection of almost seventy specialty items, including black peppercorns from Putumayo and white peppercorns from Kampot.

AN EXTRA PINCH

The land of the Rising Sun rubs shoulders here with a range of piquant products, such as yuzu kosho and Japanese red curry.

Épices Roellinger

📍 *51 bis, rue Sainte-Anne, Paris 2nd*

Former Michelin three-starred chef Olivier Roellinger embarked, in 1982, on his spice adventures, then passed his passion for them down to his daughter Mathilde, who took over the management of this Parisian shop dating to 2009.

AN EXTRA PINCH

More than twelve varieties of vanilla and sixty spice blends are masterfully created to brighten up everyday dishes.

Izraël

📍 *30, rue François-Miron, Paris 4th*

This is a modern-day Ali Baba's cave of products! Located in the Marais since 1947, Izraël offers a wide choice of exotic products, including a hundred spices from the Maghreb, the Middle East, and Asia. The charming shop can seem a bit overwhelming at first

with its myriad products stashed here and there, but with a little exploring, customers realize it's a meticulously organized Eastern bazaar.

AN EXTRA PINCH

Old-fashioned spice offerings sit next to jars with a deliciously retro look.

La Compagnie Française des Poivres et des Épices

📍 *7, rue de Furstemberg, Paris 6th*

Nestled in the heart of Saint-Germain-des-Prés, this boutique opened in 2018 is a peaceful haven. Seeming part herbalist and part perfumery, it offers more than sixty peppers, including Malabar pepper, and a hundred spices and spice blends, such as Madras curry.

AN EXTRA PINCH

Lift the delicate glass cloches to smell the irresistible aroma of spices.

Heratchian Frères

📍 *6, rue Lamartine, Paris 9th*

This institution invites us to go back in time. The Mediterranean borders have been well represented here for nearly a century (sumac from Turkey, za'atar from the Middle East). Generations of Turks, Lebanese, Greeks, and Parisians in search of products not found elsewhere have crossed its threshold.

AN EXTRA PINCH

In this jumble of products, customers can purchase spices by weight.

DELICATESSENS
Les Épiceries Fines

Nowadays, delicatessens take varied and sometimes surprising forms. Here is a nonexhaustive inventory of shops where not only are the foods of the finest quality, but the spaces themselves are, too. —LOÏC BALLET*

Origins

The birth of the Parisian épicerie fine (delicatessen) as we know it today has its roots in the post-Revolutionary period. The bourgeoisie gradually adopted the attributes of the nobility, and social codes changed. With the abolition of privileges, apothecaries no longer had a monopoly on the sale of spices that were thought to have medicinal benefits. This is true also for sweet treats, such as chocolate, candied fruits, and jams. These expensive items could then be found on the shelves of retailers who thus offered rare, high-quality products to a wealthy clientele in search of something more exotic.

Industrialization, a godsend for groceries

Throughout the nineteenth century, tremendous technical and scientific progress transformed the grocery. Transport by train and boat made it possible to import rarer and more unusual foodstuffs to Europe. In the large cities, the grocery became a veritable showcase for a wide selection of products from all over the French empire. But the invention that truly opened the possibilities for a variety of products on shop shelves was the food-preserving process invented by Nicolas Appert. This invention filled the shelves with all sorts of terrines, jars, and canned items.

Le Comptoir de la Gastronomie

📍 *34, rue Montmartre, Paris 1st*

Founded in 1894 and a standout from others thanks to its sumptuous facade, this fine-foods temple, originally intended for professionals in the catering trades, has gradually opened to the public with great success.

THE MUST-SEE

Delicious artisanal foodstuffs sold in jars, such as the sublime veal Axoa in the colors of the Pays Basque.

G. Detou

📍 *58, rue Tiquetonne, Paris 2nd*

On the storefront is the message "Everything for pastry and cooking." Gérard Detou's grocery is

a go-to for professionals and civilians alike, with a lot of equipment as well as a large selection of food items.

THE MUST-SEE

Couverture chocolates; dried nuts, such as unsalted pistachios; natural flavorings; pistachio and rose pastes; and so much more.

Maison Plisson

📍 *93, blvd. Beaumarchais, Paris 3rd*

Founded in 2015 by Delphine Plisson with a background in fashion, this grocery is now a true brand in the form of shops, kiosks, and even snacks.

THE MUST-SEE

The artichoke cream with Périgord black truffle by Maison Plisson and L'Épicurien.

La Petite Épicerie de la Tour

📍 *13, quai de la Tournelle, Paris 5th*

La Tour d'Argent, a legendary restaurant, opened a specialty grocery store on the ground floor in 2016.

THE MUST-SEE

The verrines of Crêpes Mademoiselle (in a blend of Grand Marnier, Cointreau, imperial mandarin, butter, and Fine Champagne cognac), an iconic dessert at La Tour d'Argent.

La Grande Épicerie de Paris

📍 *38, rue de Sèvres, Paris 7th*

📍 *80, rue de Passy, Paris 16th*

In the spirit of department stores, this shop opened in 1923 under the name Comptoir de l'Alimentation within Le Bon Marché, founded in 1852. Named La Grande Épicerie de Paris in 1978, it covers 30,000 square feet (2,800 sq m), with nearly thirty thousand items. It is the largest grocery store in the world.

THE MUST-SEE

The Force Basque condiment produced by Maison Arostéguy, 100 percent produced in Biarritz, made with fleur de sel sea salt, Espelette pepper, pink peppercorns, and parsley. *Caliente!*

L'Épicerie Fine Rive Gauche

📍 *8, rue du Champ-de-Mars, Paris 7th*

A stone's throw from the Eiffel Tower, Nathalie and Pascal Mièvre have been passionately running one of the most beautiful groceries in the capital

G. Detou.

Causses, above and at right.

La Grande Épicerie de Paris.

for nearly twenty years. Their offerings include Berthillon ice cream and Thai curry pastes.

THE MUST-SEE
The cooking stocks (fish fumet, veal stock, etc.) from Ariaké, all 100 percent natural, made in France and Holland.

Causses
⦿ *99, rue Rambuteau, Paris 1st*
⦿ *222, rue Saint-Martin, Paris 3rd*
⦿ *55, rue Notre-Dame-de-Lorette, Paris 9th*

Founded in 2011 by Alexis Roux de Bézieux from Lyon, this is a delicatessen in the style of a mini-mart, or perhaps it's a mini-mart in the style of a delicatessen. It offers a wide range of products, including vegetables, cheeses, meats, and savory items—everything is here.

THE MUST-SEE
The deliciously crisp and ultrathin shiitake chips are a real find.

Le Printemps du Goût
⦿ *59, rue de Caumartin, Paris 9th*

Printemps du Goût opened in 2018 as the gastronomic counterpart to one of the pillars of fashion in Paris, Le Printemps department store. On the seventh and eighth floors of Printemps de l'Homme (the men's department) can be found a grocery laid out as an eatery from the nineteenth century, and a marketplace offering fresh products. As a bonus, there is a terrace for enjoying a breathtaking view.

THE MUST-SEE
The truffles of Maison Balme, absolutely incomparable, and cultivated for more than 110 years in the heart of Provence.

Julhès
⦿ *54–56, rue du Faubourg-Saint-Denis, Paris 10th*
⦿ *59, rue du Faubourg-Saint-Martin, Paris 10th*
⦿ *28, rue du Faubourg-Poissonnière, Paris 10th*

⦿ *129, blvd. Voltaire, Paris 11th*
⦿ *31, rue Saint-Maur, Paris 11th*
⦿ *120, rue de Charonne, Paris 11th*

Nicolas and Sébastien Julhès took over their parents' small Parisian shop opened in 1996 on rue du Faubourg-Saint-Denis. Today, the brothers are not only grocers but also bakers, pastry chefs, traiteurs, cheesemakers, wine merchants, and even distillers.

THE MUST-SEE
Batch #1 gin, inspired by François Coty's Cyprus perfume, launched in 1917, in the style of a classic London dry gin with juniper, bergamot, and coriander.

La Fédération Française de l'Apéritif
⦿ *2, rue de Paradis, Paris 10th*
⦿ *50, rue des Dames, Paris 17th*

It all started in 2006 with a joke between friends when Paul-Antoine Solier, Arnaud de Broves, and Quentin Chapuis created the (very young) Fédération Française de l'Apéritif. The idea was to gather in one place everything needed to make an aperitif worthy of the name: wines, beers, cheeses, cookies, etc., all from 350 handpicked producers—and it worked!

THE MUST-SEE
The elderflower liqueur by Giffard, an incomparable delight (but to be enjoyed in moderation).

Les Résistants Épicerie-Cave
⦿ *29, rue du Château-d'Eau, Paris 10th*

After opening their two restaurants (Les Résistants and L'Avant-Post), this group of friends tripled their offerings by opening this shop in the 10th, offering farmstead products.

THE MUST-SEE
The vegetables from La Ferme ô VR in the Manche, the Corsican black pig (porcu nustrale) charcuterie by Stéphanie Frombolacci and Pierre-Antoine Battini, not to mention the rich selection of natural wines.

Native Delicatessen
⦿ *55, rue de la Fontaine-au-Roi, Paris 11th*

Native Delicatessen's mission since 2013 has been to discover the untreated, distinct flavors native to the world's oldest peoples: plants, spices, preparations, and plants known to the Inuit, American Indians, ancient tribes of Tasmania and Lapland, etc. The idea came from Richard Lebon and Alexandre Wolf Grauer, who held the position of Europe's cultural delegate of the Six Nations of the Iroquois Confederacy.

THE MUST-SEE
A jam from the Arctic Circle made from peat-bog brambleberries.

Julhès, Paris 11th.

THE SHOPPING LIST

Here is a short list of prepared products made in Paris
→ *Prince de Paris ham*
→ *La Confiture parisienne*
→ *Plaq chocolate*
→ *Beers from Brasserie Goutte-d'Or*
→ *Honey from Un Apiculteur Près de Chez Vous*
→ *Spirits from La Distillerie de Paris*

* *Founder of L'Épicerie de Loïc B, which offers regional, handpicked, quality products originating from and produced in France at good prices.*
⦿ *7, rue Sedaine, Paris 11th*

CONFECTIONERIES
Les Confiseries

The ancestors of what we know today as candies were consumed for their medicinal benefits and served in the court of kings. Here are a few locations to satisfy any sweet tooth. —MARILOU PETRICOLA

Sweet Paris

› **End of the fourteenth century:** Europe organizes its sugar trade. As a result, recipes for candied fruit, dragées, and nougats are perfected. Confectionery is becoming more popular in Europe.

› **Starting in the seventeenth century:** confectionery shops open in Paris for a very rich clientele who love pastilles and other sweets.

› **Early nineteenth century:** the development of producing sugar from beets makes sugar more common and confectionery products accessible to the masses. Rue des Lombards (Paris 1st and 4th) specializes in the art of the confiseur (confectioner), a term derived from *confire*, which means to preserve items not only in sugar but also in salt, vinegar, wine, brandy, or fat.

Invented in Paris

Each region of France boasts its own local artisanal sweets, and Île-de-France is no exception: the Boule de Boissier, the Badines de Paris from Fouquet, the Coquelicot (poppy) of Nemours, the fondant of the rue des Lombards, the Cacahuète Feuilletée (with the flavor and shape of a peanut), nuts and . . . the lollipop. In 1923, Georges Evrard, founder of the Pierrot Gourmand brand, placed a ball of cooked sugar on a stick to avoid getting his fingers sticky.

Confectioner-chocolatier Fouquet.

Käramell.

Fifi La Praline.

Rue des Lombards, the Historic Center for All Things Sweet

In *Les Français peints par eux-même: Encyclopédie morale du XIXe siècle* (1840–1842), a man named Andréas wrote a long description about rue des Lombards, which smelled like a sugar factory: *"At the other end of the world, there is a street where all the products of the globe meet, extend, and overlap. . . .*

In summer, they candy the fruits, crystallizing them, turning them, on rue des Lombards, into transparent jellies. A provincial housewife would recoil in terror when she saw her cherries, strawberries, currants, which she peels one by one, treated as the damned will be one day, that is to say all together poured into an immense cauldron. These [sweets] are intended to supply all of Paris at sixteen cents a pound. Around a long square table are settled about fifty workers whose work varies according to the products of the confectioner's trade: today using folding machines with reams of glossy paper; tomorrow they will strip roses for the entire season and build chocolate pyramids for the twelve arrondissements, the provinces, and abroad. There are no more ambidextrous workers who have more taste for their profession than confectioners. . . .

In addition to its annual and daily occasions, which includes baptisms, engagements, patron-saint festivals, and all other ceremonies where candies play a role, and besides its clandestine supplies of the most brilliant and busiest stores in Paris, rue des Lombards has, as far as its pralines and gifts are concerned, a day, or a week even, when it is unaffordable, where it sells, perhaps solely, to nearly all the twelve arrondissements. New Year's Day seems invented just for her."

Le Bonbon au Palais

◊ *19, rue Monge, Paris 5th*

Anise from Vosges, Nantes rigolettes (a fruit bonbon), menhirs from Brittany (bites of chocolate in the shape of menhirs), sottises from Valenciennes (sugar candies of various flavors): all of sweet France can be found in this candy shop that offers more than three hundred varieties. Be sure to quiz the owner, who knows the fascinating history of each one.

SPECIAL TREAT

The fresh marshmallow from Toulouse and its twenty different flavors.

Les Bonbons

◊ *6, rue Bréa, Paris 6th*

This very small shop, remaining nearly intact since 1980, offers a choice of four hundred varieties of regional confections (bergamot from Nancy, calissons from Aix, etc.) and foreign confections (Spanish turron, Belgian Napoléon candies, Italian Leone pastilles, and more).

SPECIAL TREATS

The classic licorice and the sugar fondant.

Maison Boissier

◊ *77, rue du Bac, Paris 7th*

◊ *48, rue de Passy, Paris 16th*

Opened in Paris in 1827, this confectioner has long made its iconic sweets and candied chestnuts in-house. Modified in 2008, it now only assembles on-site, with production being handled by craftsmen selected in France.

SPECIAL TREAT

The unbeatable Boule de Boissier, a large red ball with a hard shell and flowing center with Montmorency cherry, originally designed for women who wanted to suck on a treat while attending the opera.

À la Mère de Famille

◊ *35, rue du Faubourg-Montmartre, Paris 9th*
+ 14 locations

Although it is now more recognized as a

À la Mère de Famille, Paris 9th.

chocolate factory, it was a confectioner in the eighteenth century. The shop still offers about thirty varieties of sweets.

SPECIAL TREAT

The Négus de Nevers, a light caramel candy of chocolate or coffee encased in a hard caramel, still handmade in the historic shop in Burgundy.

Fouquet Confiseur Chocolatier

♦ 36, rue Laffitte, Paris 9th
♦ 23, rue François-Ier, Paris 8th

In the small workshop of the shop on rue Laffitte, cocoa beans are still worked using the strength of the chef's hands. The Chambeau family, who have operated the business since 1852, created the Badines de Paris, which are sticks of pure dark chocolate, but production stopped in the 1990s. In addition to a hundred varieties of

sweets, the shop offers a wide range of chocolates.

SPECIAL TREAT

Soft caramels, classic or candied ginger, chocolate, vanilla, or pistachio.

Käramell

♦ 15, rue des Martyrs, Paris 9th

Sweden's Lena Rosen offers 180 kinds of Scandinavian sweets in her shop, with an emphasis on licorice, the käramell ("candy" in Swedish) emblematic of her native country.

SPECIAL TREAT

Licorice is available here in an unprecedented number of choices: in sticks, syrups, with chocolate, and even in savory items.

Fifi La Praline

♦ 11, rue Taylor, Paris 10th

Jean-Philippe Casteuble, aka Fifi, a former chocolatier, rides his

blue scooter to deliver the sweets from his childhood, including the praline (or prasline) of Montargis, not to be confused with the chouchou à la cacahuète, an almond confection from the seventeenth century.

SPECIAL TREAT

The unmatched l'amande and its variations of pistachio, hazelnut, and pecan.

Chocolatier Servant

♦ 30, rue d'Auteuil, Paris 16th
♦ 22 bis, rue de Chartres, Neuilly (Hauts-de-Seine)

Created in 1913, this shop offers eighty varieties of old-fashioned sweets from France's regions: Diane de Poytiers nougats, pralines from Montargis, violettes from Toulouse, coquelicots from Nemours. Remaining faithful to the artisans from the past, the

shop works to perpetuate this French heritage.

SPECIAL TREATS

Raspberry, apricot, and orange pâte de fruits; glacéed chestnuts; and Barnier Froufrous, small squares filled with jam.

Kubli

♦ 17, rue Gustave-Eiffel, Morangis (Essonne)

When in 1900 the Swiss Jacques Kubli moved to Paris's 13th arrondissement, he took his recipes for iconic sweets with him. Since 1973, the company has been based in Morangis (Essonne) and has gained international renown. The production is always artisanal.

SPECIAL TREAT

The Délice Cacahuète (peanut), invented by Jacques Kubli. The lamination is always done by hand.

BOMBES AND CANDIES

In his collection *Choses vues*, published posthumously (1887–1900), Victor Hugo celebrated on January 6, 1871, during the siege of Paris, the Boissier shop: "At dessert yesterday, I offered candy to women and said, 'With thanks to Boissier, my dear colombes, Happy at your feet, we fall, for the strong are seduced by the bombes and the weak by the sweets.'"

CHOCOLATE SHOPS
Les Chocolateries

Paris and its chocolate shops have a history that stretches back more than two hundred years. Here are some sinfully chocolaty locations. —EZEKIEL ZÉRAH

A chocolate tradition

François Marquis, a very famous chocolatier of his time, opened his chocolate shop in 1818 at Passage des Panoramas and became the "patented supplier of all the courts of Europe." His magnificent wooden storefront is still at number 57. In his novel *Nana* (1880), Émile Zola described "perfumes of vanilla rising from the basement of a chocolatier"; this was no doubt François Marquis's shop. The Goncourt brothers and actress Sarah Bernhardt snapped up the elegant boxes made of wood, leather, fine gold, and hand-painted silk. The chocolate tablet was also a Parisian invention. Jean-Antoine-Brutus Menier, founder of Maison Menier, based in the Marais and now also Noisiel in Seine-et-Marne, made the first chocolate tablet in 1836.

THE HISTORIC PLACES

① Debauve & Gallais

📍 *33, rue Vivienne, Paris 2nd*

📍 *30, rue des Saints-Pères, Paris 7th*

Today, it is still possible to taste Marie-Antoinette's favorite chocolate. In 1779, Sulpice Debauve, then a pharmacist, mixed headache medicines with cocoa butter. The queen loved them, calling them "pistoles," and its inventor was made the king's official chocolatier. Along with his nephew Jean-Baptiste Auguste Gallais in 1800, he opened the shop that would, over the centuries, seduce the likes of Napoléon I (who was fond of his chocolate almonds), Marcel Proust, and Sonia Rykiel.

SPECIAL CREATION
Chocolate in the shape of a fleur-de-lys, the symbol of the shop, created in 1825 for the coronation of Charles X. Made with 60 percent cacao dark chocolate and caramel ganache.

② À la Mère de Famille

📍 *35, rue du Faubourg-Montmartre, Paris 9th + 14 locations*

This former confectioner is now more focused on chocolate (with more than a thousand items!). The shop opened in 1760, and its storefront is classified as a historical monument. The expertise has been handed down through the changes of owners since the time of Marie-Adélaïde Bridault, to whom the store's name pays tribute.

SPECIAL CREATION
Le Palet Mère de famille, a dark chocolate ganache made from 75 percent cacao dark chocolate from Haiti, coated in dark chocolate.

THE ESSENTIALS

③ Jacques Genin

📍 *133, rue de Turenne, Paris 3rd*

📍 *27, rue de Varenne, Paris 7th*

With his caramels, marshmallows, nougats, and chocolates, Genin could have remained in the shadows as supplier to the best restaurants in the capital, but he preferred to make a name for himself and opened his first shop to the public in 2008.

SPECIAL CREATIONS
Chocolate candy with capers with its hint of sea salt from Guérande and chocolate candy infused with fresh mint.

④ La Maison du Chocolat

📍 *225, rue du Faubourg-Saint-Honoré, Paris 8th + 6 locations*

The French chocolate industry owes much to Robert Linxe, the founder of this company in 1977, who was one of the very first to use cacaos of certain grands crus and reduced quantities of sugar and cream in his chocolates. Since 2012, the artistic direction has been entrusted to MOF (Best Craftsman of France) chocolatier Nicolas Cloiseau. The shop is the height of chic, and they sell a micro-box of just two chocolates to whet your appetite.

SPECIAL CREATIONS
Rigoletto (chocolate with a caramelized milk chocolate mousse) and fruit ganaches (black currant from Burgundy).

⑤ Jean-Paul Hévin

📍 *23 bis, av. de la Motte-Picquet, Paris 7th + 7 locations*

This former pastry chef of Joël Robuchon at Nikko (Paris 2nd) has been a gold standard of chocolate in both in France and Japan since the late 1980s.

SPECIAL CREATIONS
The Pomelo with fresh grapefruit, the Carapuna with two honeys, and the Woman with green tea and bergamot; plus chocolate candies mixing herbs and cheeses.

⑥ Le Chocolat Alain Ducasse

📍 *40, rue de La Roquette, Paris 11th (the production facility) + 19 locations*

The chocolate shop of the famous chef Alain Ducasse has become a true standard in the industry, with the help of chocolate maker Nicolas Berger. The house roasts its own cocoa beans.

SPECIAL CREATIONS
The old-fashioned pralines (they quickly become addictive) and the tablet filled with 45 percent cacao milk chocolate and creamy caramel.

⑦ Au Bonbon Royal

📍 *56, rue Jouffroy-d'Abbans, Paris 17th*

The chocolate candies of this brand, launched in 1992 by Philippe Ploquin, can be seen in the film *Chocolat* (Lasse Hallström, 2011) with Johnny Depp and Juliette Binoche. The shop along the long street (rue Jouffroy-d'Abbans) is deliciously old-fashioned.

SPECIAL CREATIONS
Marshmallow bears coated in dark or milk chocolate, the Glaçon (a thin Swiss meringue shell that surrounds a melting praline), kirsch-soaked cherries coated in chocolate.

⑧ Patrick Roger

📍 *47, rue Houdan, Sceaux (Hauts-de-Seine) + 8 locations*

The "Rodin of chocolate" has been showcasing his talent since 2004 in his shops decorated with life-size animals carved in cacao. He spends hundreds of hours polishing these pieces in his workshop in Sceaux (Hauts-de-Seine).

SPECIAL CREATIONS
The colored half-spheres, the Instinct (almond praline, hazelnut, almond pieces, and nougatine, coated with dark chocolate), the Pavé de Mai (a 20-oz/ 600 g trompe-l'oeil "cobblestone" filled with almond praline).

THE NEW GUARD

⑨ Edwart Chocolatier

📍 *244, rue de Rivoli, Paris 1st*

📍 *17, rue Vieille-du-Temple, Paris 4th*

📍 *67, rue des Dames, Paris 17th*

📍 *10, rue Bayen, Paris 17th*

The hat-wearing Edwin Yansané designs creations with rare flavors (praline with Madras curry, ganache with makrut lime zest, and praline with monkey bread). You must taste the popcorn-praline chocolate tablet.

SPECIAL CREATIONS
The Cilantro, a hazelnut praline with coriander seed.

⑩ L'Instant Cacao

📍 *3, rue des Petits-Champs, Paris 1st*

A cozy bean-to-bar shop open since 2018 where you can see Marc Chinchole at work fashioning bars from fair-trade cacao, plus enjoy hot chocolate on-site.

SPECIAL CREATION
The Emmoni, a 75 to 78 percent Bolivian cacao dark chocolate bar.

⑪ Plaq

📍 *4, rue du Nil, Paris 2nd + 5 locations*

This new Parisian bean-to-bar phenomenon opened in 2019 on one of the most popular food lovers' streets in the capital. Here the simplicity of the packaging downplays the indulgences, which include the milk chocolate bar from Kerala (India), the maple sugar bar, and the pistachio chocolate bar.

SPECIAL CREATION
The 76 percent cacao Chuao tablet from Venezuela.

⑫ Les Copains de Bastien

📍 *90, rue de Maubeuge, Paris 10th*

Since 2021, this bean-to-bar brand trains those unemployed to become chocolatiers thanks to the know-how of its traveling craftsman who scours the globe for flavors. Tablets are particularly popular with connoisseurs.

SPECIAL CREATION
The 70 percent cacao single-origin tablet from Mexico.

⑬ Alléno & Rivoire

📍 *9, rue du Champ-de-Mars, Paris 7th*

Chef Yannick Alléno and pastry chef Aurélien Rivoire opened this innovative chocolate shop in 2021. By using birch tree sap instead of sugar, they significantly reduced the glycemic index of their chocolates. The confit fruits are also worth the visit.

SPECIAL CREATION
The Clover, two chocolate shells in the shape of a clover filled with a chocolaty sauce and a crispy praline. Available in six flavors.

ICE CREAM SHOPS Les Glaciers

This tour of Paris's ice cream shops is sure to warm your heart. —MARILOU PETRICOLA

THE HISTORIC PLACES

Berthillon

📍 31, rue Saint-Louis-en-l'Île, Paris 4th

Founded in 1954 by Raymond Berthillon, the shop is now run by his son-in-law and granddaughter.

THE SCOOP

You'll find seventy classic flavors and ice creams made with little air for dense textures. It's the only ice cream shop closed in August.

PRODUCTION

1,320 gallons (5,000 L) per week.

ICONIC CONES

Vanilla ice cream, wild strawberry sorbet, and chocolate sorbet.

Dans Les Bacs

📍 109, rue du Bac, Paris 7th

Founded in 1955 by Sam Yoël. His grandson, Julien Yoël, now runs the shop.

THE SCOOP

Choose among sixty flavors, twenty of which are made with seasonal fruits. There are classic flavors and some savory flavors (Camembert, Beaujolais Nouveau, and others). The ice creams are processed with little air so are very dense and indulgent, and the sorbets have an intense taste of fruit.

PRODUCTION

260 gallons (1,000 L) per week.

ICONIC CONES

The vanilla ice cream and the extra dark chocolate sorbet.

Raimo

📍 59–63, blvd. de Reuilly, Paris 12th

Founded in 1947 by Antoine Raimondo, this is the oldest artisanal ice cream shop in Paris. The first recipes were inspired by those of the great prewar luxury hotels where the founder's father worked.

THE SCOOP

Look for 55 flavors available in the shop and 176 on the website. There are classic flavors, but also unexpected flavors (goat's milk and basil, Selim pepper, Ruinart Champagne).

PRODUCTION

1,320 gallons (5,000 L) per week.

ICONIC CONES

Vanilla ice cream and strawberry-basil sorbet.

CHEF SIGNATURES

La Glacerie Paris

📍 13, rue du Temple, Paris 4th

Founded in 2018 by David Wesmaël, an ice cream MOF (Best Craftsman of France) and world team pastry champion.

THE SCOOP

There are thirty-five flavors in the store, including various grand cru vanillas and chocolates. Ingredients are as local as possible, and the ice creams are processed with little air.

PRODUCTION

260 gallons (1,000 L) per week.

ICONIC CONES

Mango-vanilla ice cream (created during the World Pastry Championship in 2006), pistachio ice cream from Sicily, and blackberry sorbet (blackberry and raspberry).

Une Glace à Paris

📍 15, rue Sainte-Croix-de-la-Bretonnerie, Paris 4th
📍 16, pl. des Abbesses, Paris 18th

Founded in 2015 by Olivier Ménard and Emmanuel Ryon, MOF (Best Craftsman of France) in ice cream and world pastry champion.

THE SCOOP

About twenty flavors in winter and forty-five in summer. Original flavors (pumpkin, wild pollen from Colombia) and sorbets (orange-carrot-ginger, black currant–mint–cinnamon). The texture is airy, the taste sharp.

PRODUCTION

530 gallons (2,000 L) per week.

ICONIC CONES

Vanilla ice cream, Alphonso mango sorbet, buckwheat-nougatine ice cream.

THE CREATIVES

Bachir

📍 58, rue Rambuteau, Paris 3rd
📍 7, rue Tardieu, Paris 18th

Founded in 1936 in Bikfaya in Lebanon and in 2017 in Paris by two brothers, Maurice and Édouard Bachir.

THE SCOOP

Twelve flavors of organic and Lebanese ice creams, milk based and mastic (a natural resin from certain trees), which gives them an elastic and very melting texture.

PRODUCTION

210 gallons (800 L) per week.

ICONIC CONE

Ashta fior di latte ice cream with orange flower water, covered with crushed pistachios.

Glazed

📍 19, rue Geoffroy-Saint-Hilaire, Paris 5th
📍 54, rue des Martyrs, Paris 9th

After founding his ice cream truck in 2012, Henri Guittet opened his first boutique in 2014.

THE SCOOP

Each shop offers twenty-five flavors of soft and creamy ice creams and sorbets. The team's originality (Glazed and Confused, Porn Cop, and I Shot the Sherry are some of their original flavors) has sealed their reputation.

PRODUCTION

210 gallons (800 L) per week.

ICONIC CONES

Mister Green (pistachio and black sesame cream) and Dirty Berry (raspberry, lime, sumac sorbet).

Folderol

📍 10, rue du Grand-Prieuré, Paris 11th

This shop was founded in 2020 by Jessica Yang and Robert Compagnon. In English, *folderol* means "useless but beautiful."

THE SCOOP

Offers natural wines and ice creams. Twelve flavors for scooping, fifteen to thirty in to-go containers, which change every day. The flavors are assertive and the texture firm, served in house-made cones with a crumbly texture.

PRODUCTION

40 gallons (150 L) per week.

ICONIC CONES

Olive oil ice cream, banana raw-cream ice cream, vanilla ice cream, and chocolate ice cream.

La Glace Alain Ducasse

📍 38, rue de la Roquette, Paris 11th + 17 locations

Founded in 2021 under the leadership of chef Alain Ducasse, with ice cream maker Matteo Casone at the helm.

THE SCOOP

Ice cream is prepared in front of the customer and in small quantities. Candied fruits, infusions, baked: the chef applies the same techniques as a cook or pastry chef for ice creams, which have strong flavors and a distinct chew.

PRODUCTION

79 gallons (300 L) per week.

ICONIC CONES

The vanilla trio ice cream (using Madagascar, Mexican, and Tahitian vanillas), the fresh-herb sorbet.

ITALIAN

Pozzetto

📍 39, rue du Roi-de-Sicile, Paris 4th
📍 16, rue Vieille-du-Temple, Paris 4th

Founded in 2005 by Maura Burlando, a native of Turin, who could not find ice cream in Paris to satisfy her demanding palate.

THE SCOOP

Twelve flavors made from ingredients from Italy, including three that change regularly. Typical Italian flavors: fior di latte, nocciola, and stracciatella, but also strawberry and fig sorbets.

PRODUCTION

396 gallons (1,500 L) per week.

ICONIC CONES

Gianduja ice cream and pistachio ice cream.

Il Gelato del Marchese

📍 2, rue de Condé, Paris 6th + 8 locations

Founded in 2014 by Veronika and Renato Squillante Montoro, originally from Rome.

THE SCOOP

Sixteen flavors that change according to the season. The ice creams are minimally aerated and not very sweet, and the sorbets are especially fruity.

PRODUCTION

130 to 790 gallons (500 to 3,000 L) per week.

ICONIC CONES

Iranian pistachio ice cream and passion fruit sorbet.

Fresh herb sorbet from La Glace Alain Ducasse.

Strawberry-basil sorbet from Raimo.

Vanilla ice cream from Berthillon.

Olive oil ice cream from Folderol.

Mister Green from Glazed.

Gianduja ice cream from Pozzetto.

Chocolate sorbet from Bac à Glaces.

Pistachio ice cream from
Il Gelato del Marchese.

Buckwheat-nougatine ice cream
from Une Glace à Paris.

Ashta orange flower water ice cream from Bashir.

WINE SHOPS Les Cavistes

Whether historic or contemporary, these wine shops stock the best bottles in the capital. —GWILHERM DE CERVAL

Caves Legrand.

THE
HISTORIC PLACES

Caves Legrand

📍 *1, rue de la Banque,
Paris 2nd*

Originally a spice store, this wood-paneled cellar founded in 1880 witnessed the birth of the wine merchant's profession during the Liberation. A true visionary, Lucien Legrand believes in terroirs and travels the vineyards of France to meet the producers he highlights during his tasting events.

LABELS

4,500.

EMBLEMATIC CUVÉE

Château Latour, 1893, premier grand cru classé de Pauillac.

Les Caves du Panthéon

📍 *174, rue Saint-Jacques,
Paris 5th*

Since 2009, Olivier Roblin has been at the helm of this small cellar founded in the 1940s that looks like an apothecary shop. He serves a careful selection of independent winemakers.

LABELS

1,000.

EMBLEMATIC CUVÉE

La Romanée, grand cru 2012, from Domaine du Comte Liger-Belair.

La Grande Épicerie de Paris

📍 *38, rue de Sèvres,
Paris 7th*

This establishment opened in 1978 as La Grande Épicerie de Paris but was at first a small food purveyor annex to Le Bon Marché starting in 1923. The 5,900-square-foot (550 sq m) wine cellar, also founded in 1923 and restored in 2012, offers a wide selection, ranging from prestigious Champagne labels to signature wines.

LABELS

8,000.

EMBLEMATIC CUVÉE

Chablis grand cru Les Preuses 2008 from Domaine Vincent Dauvissat.

Les Caves de Taillevent

📍 *228, rue du Faubourg-Saint-Honoré, Paris 8th*

Valérie Vrinat, granddaughter of the founder of the restaurant Le Taillevent, diversified her family's activities by opening this wine shop on rue du Faubourg-Saint-Honoré in 1987. The shop relocated in 2014 to a more spacious location and is full of old vintages.

LABELS

2,000.

EMBLEMATIC CUVÉE

Vosne-Romanée premier cru Aux Brûlées 2000 from Domaine Leroy.

Les Crus du Soleil

📍 *146, rue du Château, Paris 14th*

Since 1998, Serge Lacombe has been warming the Montparnasse district with his sunny vintages. Its exclusively southern selection from Languedoc and Roussillon can also be enjoyed at Les Rouquins, the connected restaurant.

LABELS

300.

EMBLEMATIC CUVÉE

Cartagena, the fortified wine from Mas Jullien.

NATURAL
WINE SELLERS

Caves Augé

📍 *116, blvd. Haussmann, Paris 8th*

Located in the heart of Haussmannian Paris, this magnificent odds-and-ends shop, founded in 1850, is one of the first wine cellars to claim a selection mixing "classic" Bordeaux châteaus with natural wines.

LABELS

More than 4,000.

Liquiderie Cave.

Rock Bottles.

EMBLEMATIC CUVÉE

Cornas Reynard 2015 from Domaine Thierry Allemand.

La Cave du Château

📍 *31, av. Franklin-Delano-Roosevelt, Paris 8th*

Behind its aristocratic airs, the cellar (adjacent to the restaurant Le Clarence, owned by Domaine Clarence Dillon and managed by Prince Robert of Luxembourg) was founded in 2015. The shop offers a specialized selection, rich in signature natural wines.

LABELS

3,000.

EMBLEMATIC CUVÉE

Les Béguines, extra brut Champagne from La Closerie.

Le Verre Volé

📍 *67, rue de Lancry, Paris 10th*

Cyril Bordarier is a pioneer. On the banks of the Canal Saint-Martin, he founded, in 2000, the first "cave à manger" (eat-in wine shop) in the capital. Here the plate is as elevated as the beautiful selection of vins vivants (living wines).

LABELS

2,000.

EMBLEMATIC CUVÉE

Fleurie 2014 from Domaine Yvon Métras.

La Cave des Papilles

📍 *35, rue Daguerre, Paris 14th*

Now operated by Ewen Le Moigne, this emblematic winery was founded in 1996 by Gérard Katz and brings together one of the most dedicated natural wine selections of the last twenty years.

LABELS

1,500.

EMBLEMATIC CUVÉE

Arbois-Pupillin Poulsard 1989 by Maison Pierre Overnoy.

La Cave de Belleville

📍 *51, rue de Belleville, Paris 19th*

Founded in 2015, this wine cellar in Belleville, founded by a group of natural wine converts, compiles a beautiful collection of biodynamic labels presented on substantial shelves.

LABELS

1,500.

Caves Augé.

EMBLEMATIC CUVÉE

Le Rouge 2020 from Domaine Nicolas Suteau.

THE NEXT
GENERATION

Liquiderie Cave

📍 *9, rue des Trois-Bornes, Paris 11th*

Behind a dazzling blue facade, Julien Maillet has been offering since 2017 a selection of vins vivants (living wines) that go against the norm. He showcases even more with a second business not far from this location, Liquiderie Bar.

LABELS

550.

EMBLEMATIC CUVÉE

Fier Hérétique 2020 from Domaine La Sorga.

Delicatessen Cave

📍 *136, rue Amelot, Paris 11th.*

For this brand founded in 2016, Mireille Langlois and her son Gabriel seek out their bottles with great care and have an obvious penchant for their native Beaujolais.

LABELS

1,000.

EMBLEMATIC CUVÉE

Pouilly-Fuissé 2008 from Maison Valette, Clos de Monsieur Noly.

Rock Bottles

📍 *22, rue du Ruisseau, Paris 18th*

Used to making deliveries himself, Oliver Gage swapped his scooter in 2021 for a location near Sacré Coeur. This specialized cellar is an incubator for young natural gems.

LABELS

450.

EMBLEMATIC CUVÉE

Bonne Étoile 2020 from Domaine Petite Nature.

Koikonboi?

📍 *58, rue Custine, Paris 18th*

Hidden in the heart of Butte Montmartre, this shop founded in 2019 by Charlie Ragot has already become a must-visit.

LABELS

300.

EMBLEMATIC CUVÉE

Chante Pinot, a natural sparkling wine from France Domaine Josmeyer.

MICROBREWERIES
Les Microbrasseries

Beer brewing in the Paris region is in full swing, driven by newbies to the trade as well as the established pioneers. —DOMINIQUE HUTIN

THE PIONEERS

Brasserie Goutte d'Or

📍 *28, rue de la Goutte-d'Or, Paris 18th*

Founded in 2012, this is the oldest artisanal brasserie in Paris.

Brasserie La Baleine

📍 *17, rue Henri-Duvernois, Paris 20th*

This microbrewery, founded in 2013, creates a dozen beers on lees, fermented in the bottle.

Brasserie Gallia

📍 *35, rue Méhul, Pantin (Seine-Saint-Denis)*

Brasserie Nouvelle Gallia was founded in 1890 on rue Sarrette (Paris 14th) and became the most prominent of the Parisian brasseries. It was demolished in 1968 but reopened in 2009 in Pantin.

THE BREWERS

① Fauve

📍 *64, rue de Charonne, Paris 11th*

With the opening of Fauve, it's as if a colorful whirlwind of ephemeral beers appeared in the heart of Paris to drench the 11th arrondissement in suds. It's a "brewed on-site, drunk on-site" concept. They offer vibrant labels designed by artists and beer recipes for connoisseur brewers who want to try homebrewing. It's an artsy, funky, uplifting brewpub.

TOP FOAM

The ephemeral nature of the local beers here beckons you to return. Or, with a bit more patience, wait to taste their beers brewed in barrels. In the meantime, there is the perfect "Love Story," a NEIPA (New England India Pale Ale) brewed partly with oats and punched up with Sabro, Mosaic, and

Simcoe hops (6.5% ABV, IBU UNKNOWN).

② Brasserie de l'Être

📍 *7 ter, rue Duvergier, Paris 19th*

Certified organic, the beers at l'Être catch both the eye (thanks to their fantastic creature-themed black-and-white labels) and the palate (with their attention to yeasts), letting time do the rest.

TOP FOAM

Salamandra, a seasonal cloudy blonde-orange beer with yeast, pepper, pear, and woody aromas on the nose. Punchy and easygoing despite its spirited profile (organic, 6.5% ABV, IBU UNKNOWN).

③ Les Bières de Belleville

📍 *9, rue Jean-Baptiste-Dumay, Paris 20th*

Local brewers Vincent Montagut and Mathieu Parnaud have chosen to use 500 ml bottles "for the idea of sharing, which equals two glasses or a pint" and for ecological purposes: the cost of a glass is more economical, which is a win-win for customers, who are now offered beers in refundable bottles.

TOP FOAM

The Piaf (a nod to Édith!), a supple, amiable, and hoppy sipping blonde. Nice balance (3.9% ABV, IBU UNKNOWN).

④ Brasserie La Voisine

📍 *Rue du Pont-des-Landes, Coignières (Yvelines)*

The small size of its production site puts the "micro" in microbrewery; it is managed by the thirty-something Harmony Voisin, who launched her career using a homebrewing kit for amateurs. With her business now matured,

her product revolves around the use of local hops in a permanent range of six organic beers crafted with careful attention.

TOP FOAM

Yolande is a "triple" with a caressing texture that expands with almond notes and is delicate on the palate without being abrasive (8.5% ABV, IBU UNKNOWN).

⑤ Outland

📍 *54, rue André-Tessier, Fontenay-sous-Bois (Val-de-Marne)*

A pioneer, Outland follows a formula of no residual sugar, US inspirations, and above all, a buzzing activity around the brewery. The bar (which offers small bites on weekends), continual collaborations, collective initiatives, and the annual ritual of the Bloc Party, a half-wild, half-playful festival, make this place a blast.

TOP FOAM

Tasty with light alcohol and exuberant citrus aromas, its sessions IPA with a strong color is both dense and light, with a bitterness that doesn't overwhelm (3.9% ABV, IBU 35).

⑥ Volcelest

📍 *28, rue du Roseau, Le Perray-en-Yvelines (Yvelines)*

Represented with a stag's head, these beers have been brewed in the Chevreuse Valley since 2008, and this brewery, located in the regional natural park, has experienced good growth. Using experiences from his past as a winemaker working in several countries, Emmanuel Rey respects the science of fermentation in beer making, which has earned him more freedom and creativity. The offerings are punctuated with

mainstay beers as well as seasonal ones in a wide, accessible range whose production is well controlled.

TOP FOAMS

A blonde brewed with oats with a citrus note enhanced with exotic fruits (5% ABV, IBU 10). A pale ale with an earthy, accessible character (organic, 6% ABV, IBU 18).

⑦ La Parisienne

📍 *29, rue Cartier-Bresson, Pantin (Seine-Saint-Denis)*

Managing a crop of hundreds of hops growing in the city, La Parisienne proudly claims to be the "first hop grower" in Paris. The business is dedicated to several concepts (organic beers, waste recycling, bottle deposits, etc.), making this Parisienne the queen of bubbles.

TOP FOAM

Empress Joséphine, an imperial pilsner that imposes its tactile flavors with a delicate vegetal bitterness. Beautifully balanced, incredibly fresh (7% ABV, IBU 50).

⑧ L'Instant

📍 *24 bis, rue du Pré-des-Aulnes, Pontault-Combault (Seine-et-Marne)*

Its three founders are of Franco-Belgian-Bulgarian origins, ex-roommates, and ex–Sciences Po classmates. Other European-inspired combinations inspire the offerings in this forward-thinking brasserie.

TOP FOAM

With malts de la Brie and Alsatian hops (Mistral), the Française is a "typically French" pale ale that is ample, with hints of yellow fruit (5.6% ABV, IBU 35).

⑨ 77Craft

📍 *12, rue de l'Église, Villiers-sous-Grez (Seine-et-Marne)*

In this tiny village is a buzzing beehive of brewing activity directed by Marie and Miguel Garcia, which coexists with the town's hops farm. Visit for their organic, unfiltered, unpasteurized, and refermented beers served in bottles.

TOP FOAM

The Hoppy Mini, which should be blind tasted against other beers! This oddity offers a merely symbolic amount of alcohol, without any thinness, and with a super combination of bitterness and freshness (organic, 1.9% ABV, IBU UNKNOWN).

PLACES DEDICATED TO BEER

IBU

📍 *20, cour des Petites-Écuries, Paris 10th*
📍 *144, rue Oberkampf, Paris 11th*

This temple of beer compiles ten craft beers on tap whose selection rotates, and about fifty options in bottles or cans.

La Fine Mousse

📍 *4 bis–6, av. Jean-Aicard, Paris 11th*

Between a beer bar and its restaurant focused on pairings, this dual-purpose location is a top offering for beer in Paris.

La Liquiderie

📍 *7, rue de la Présentation, Paris 11th*

Passionate about craft beers and natural wines, Julien Maillet has set up a loft that serves about twenty beers on tap.

SKIP TO
Subterranean Breweries, p. 47.

 ①
 ②
 ③
 ④
 ⑤
 ⑥
 ⑦
 ⑧
 ⑨

URBAN FARMS
Les Fermes Urbaines

Paris's urban farms help establish links between city life and agriculture with myriad projects, ranging from supplying food to restaurants and consumers to offering educational experiences. Here is a sampling of Paris's well-established urban farms. —ZAZIE TAVITIAN

Ferme Urbaine Flora Tristan.

La Sauge.

La Caverne.

Fermes d'Espoir.

La Caverne.

La Sauge.

La Caverne

⚲ 24–26, rue Raymond-Queneau, Paris 18th

THE PROJECT

In 2017, Jean-Noël Gertz planted a mushroom farm in a former 99,000-square-foot (9,200 sq m) parking lot. Oyster mushrooms, shiitakes, button mushrooms, and endives are grown organically and aboveground, in the dark. The concept was also created in Lyon and Bordeaux.

Les Fermes d'Espoir

⚲ Ferme pédagogique de la butte Pinson—16, rue Suzanne-Valadon, Montmagny (Val-d'Oise)
⚲ Petite ferme de la Goutte-d'Or—16, rue de Jessaint, Paris 18th
⚲ Ferme du jardin d'Éole—19, rue d'Aubervilliers, Paris 18th
⚲ Ferme universitaire P13—130, av. Jean-Baptiste-Clément, Villetaneuse (Seine-Saint-Denis)

THE PROJECT

Providing new perspectives to young people who have been incarcerated was the impetus behind the Parc de la butte Pinson farm created in 2015 by Julien Boucher. It's located on 1,080 square feet (100 sq m) of abandoned forest and is also home to previously abused animals. A permaculture garden and educational farm complete this unique network that also promotes social integration.

Plantation Paris

⚲ 37, rue des Cheminots, Paris 18th

THE PROJECT

On the 75,000 square feet (7,000 sq m) of this rooftop farm, managed by Sarah Msika and Sidney Delourme since 2019, there is a greenhouse heated from the energy released from the building's data center, and a 16,000-square-foot (1,500 sq m) vegetable garden growing seventy varieties without the use of chemicals.

Ferme Urbaine Flora Tristan

⚲ Collège public Flora Tristan—4, rue Galleron, Paris 20th

THE PROJECT

This project was created by Nadine Lahoud with the goal to educate students about agriculture and gardening. The Veni Verdi association decided to turn the roof of a middle school into an urban agriculture laboratory where students and volunteers can put their hands in the soil.

Les Bergers Urbains

⚲ 3–7, rue Albert-Marquet, Paris 20th

THE PROJECT

With their herd of about thirty sheep, Julie-Lou Dubreuilh and Guillaume Leterrier brought animals back to the city. In addition to reducing weeds around the area, the herd creates a bond with the inhabitants while also serving as a source of nourishment. Every year on St. Michael's Day, some of these Bleus du Maine sheep, which are exclusively grass-fed and raised for up to eighteen months, are slaughtered and sold directly to chefs and gourmets.

La Sauge: La Prairie du Canal + Terre Terre

⚲ La Prairie du canal—55, rue de Paris, Bobigny (Seine-Saint-Denis)
⚲ Terre Terre—223, blvd. Félix-Faure, Aubervilliers (Seine-Saint-Denis)

THE PROJECT

In this meadow managed since 2015 by Swen Déral and Antoine Devins, the area's neighbors, students, and volunteers have been learning to plant and grow organic herbs, fruits, and vegetables, which are then sold to individuals. People also visit to enjoy a drink and relax.

Zone Sensible

⚲ 112, av. de Stalingrad, Saint-Denis, (Seine-Saint-Denis)

THE PROJECT

Located just a few steps from the metro, this green farm is situated on the former plain of Virtus where more than 350 families grew vegetables during the nineteenth century. Franck Ponthier, a passionate gardener, grows nearly 250 plant species and produces honey here. The space offers an agricultural and artistic program, designed by Olivier Darné, its creator.

SKIP TO
Île-de-France Terroir, p. 20; Traditions in Vegetable Farming, p. 260.

COVERED MARKETS
Les Marchés Couverts

From Tuesday to Saturday all day and until noon on Sunday, the covered markets of Paris are a beehive of activity with delicious choices among their food stalls and food counters. — ANTONY COINTRE AND XAVIER VAN KERREBROUCK

Under cover

The first covered market was founded in the twelfth century in the current Les Halles district in Paris. To alleviate the growing congestion caused by the market, Napoléon I built four other covered markets in 1811, an undertaking that Napoléon III continued. Often demolished and rebuilt, some of these original food temples are still thriving.

Marché des Enfants Rouges

♀ 39, rue de Bretagne, Paris 3rd

CREATION DATE

1615, making it the oldest food market in Paris

HISTORY

The name "enfants rouges" (red children) comes from the hospice-orphanage created here in 1524 by Marguerite de Navarre and the red capes the little residents wore. The hall, classified as a historical monument, rests on sixteen oak pillars constructed by Perceval Noblet, the king's master carpenter.

STANDOUT STALLS

The fruit-and-vegetable stall of Jardin des Délices, the chopping block of the Butcher of Paris, and Alain Miam Miam's sandwiches.

Marché Saint-Germain

♀ 4–6, rue Lobineau, Paris 6th

CREATION DATE

1817

HISTORY

From its origins in 1511 to its modifications into a covered market under Napoléon I, the market settled into its current look in 2017.

STANDOUT STALLS

The butcher of Bell Viandier, the Viot fish stall, and the organic fruit-and-vegetable stall of Le Marché de la Terre.

Marché Saint-Quentin

♀ 85 bis, blvd. Magenta, Paris 10th

CREATION DATE

1835, as the largest covered market in Paris

HISTORY

Rebuilt in 1866 by the architect Pierre-François-Nicolas Philippon, the halls are made of pink brick with green cast-iron arcades and skylights.

STANDOUT STALLS

The Petit Bateau fish stall, the Larrazet butcher shop, the Vitis Vinifera winery specializing in rare grape varieties, and the Oh Africa restaurant with mafé (an African meat and fish dish).

Marché Saint-Martin

♀ 31–33, rue du Château-d'Eau, Paris 10th

CREATION DATE

1854

HISTORY

In December 1879, the snowpacked roof collapsed and destroyed the building, which was rebuilt several times until its current form in 1989.

STANDOUT STALLS

The German grocery Der Tante Emma-Laden; the fish stall Le Canot' Vendéen; and Le Refectory, serving up burgers.

Marché Beauvau

♀ Place d'Aligre, Paris 12th

CREATION DATE

1643

HISTORY

It took its current form in 1843 with its magnificent "boat hull" frame designed by Marc-Gabriel Jolivet, an architect employed for the city. It is classified as a historical monument.

STANDOUT STALLS

The artisanal roaster Early Bird, the butcher Guignard, and the épicerie-traiteur Miss Lunch.

Marché Couvert de Passy

♀ Place de Passy, Paris 16th

CREATION DATE

1857

HISTORY

The hall was erected in the heart of the old village of Passy in 1857 and rebuilt in 1955.

STANDOUT STALLS

The Passy fish stall, the Passy butcher, the cheesemaker Androuet, and the fruit-and-vegetable stall of Gautier.

Marché Couvert des Batignolles

♀ 96 bis, rue Lemercier, Paris 17th

CREATION DATE

1867

HISTORY

The covered hall was demolished. The market is now on the ground floor of a contemporary building.

STANDOUT STALLS

The Bacillus bakery, the butcher Pilote, Les Fromages des Batignolles for cheeses, and the shared plates at Chez Serge et Mimi.

Marché des Ternes

♀ 8 bis, rue Lebon, Paris 17th

CREATION DATE

1868

HISTORY

Built on the site of an old farm, these Baltard-style halls are located on the building's ground floor.

The Saint-Quentin covered market.

STANDOUT STALLS

The cheesemaker Beillevaire, the poultry of Fermette des Ternes, the fish stall Marées 115, and the prepared foods of Diwan Beirut (Lebanese) and Chez Kim (Asian).

Marché Couvert La Chapelle

♀ 10, rue de l'Olive, Paris 18th

CREATION DATE

1883

HISTORY

The Baltard-style hall, built by Auguste-Joseph Magne on the site of the "Marché aux Vaches Grasse," was transformed into a food market after 1920.

STANDOUT STALLS

The organic fruit-and-vegetable stall Sebbah Primeurs, the fish stall Maison Bleue, and the Senegalese dishes from Les Délices d'Assia.

FOOD COURTS

Ground Control

♀ 81, rue du Charolais, Paris 12th

Located in a recycling center covering 64,600 square feet (6,000 sq m), this food hall and boutique center brings together Caribbean, Malian, and Italian eateries and a shop dedicated to rural products.

HOBA

♀ 43, rue Bernard-Buffet, Paris 17th

This large glass hall with a terrace houses five resident chefs who offer a tour of international street foods.

PALACE HOTELS
Les Tables de Palace

Palace hotels are part of Parisian heritage, and their restaurants are often their most beautiful showcase. —HADRIAN GONZALES

Le Cinq.

Now that's a palace!

Not every hotel in France can claim the prestigious title of "palace." Since 2010, France has been the only country in the world to regulate the definition of a "palace" (*palace* refers to a luxury hotel, unlike the word *palais*, which denotes a royal palace or court). This designation is granted for five years by the minister of tourism. It honors, upon application, five-star hotels "with exceptional characteristics relating in particular to their geographical location, their particular historical and aesthetic interest and heritage, as well as the services offered." Among their most basic services is dining. As of January 1, 2022, only thirty-one establishments in France are part of this exclusive group, including twelve in Paris.

Le Meurice

📍 *Le Meurice Alain Ducasse—228, rue de Rivoli, Paris 1st. €€€€*

THE LOCATION

Founded in 1835, this was the first Parisian palace. The four large windows of the restaurant overlook the rue de Rivoli and the Tuileries Gardens.

THE BEST TABLE

On the ground floor, at the end of a secret dining room, a curtain opens onto a large bay window overlooking the kitchens. This "chef's table" accommodates up to ten guests.

THE CHEF

In 2020, the "Ducasse boy" Amaury Bouhours succeeded Jocelyn Herland, who left to join Jean Imbert at Plaza Athénée. Prior to these chefs, the palace was the stronghold of the great Yannick Alléno (2003–2012).

THE PASTRY CHEF

Cédric Grolet, the pastry chef with four million social media followers, delights the eyes and taste buds with his trompe-l'oeil fruits.

THE ICONIC DISH

Lightly seared Noirmoutier duarade (sea bream) and grilled carrots, julienned and pickled, served on a "pillow" of ice.

ECCENTRICITY

A regular guest of the hotel requested, without making a reservation, a gastronomic marathon lasting from breakfast to dinner. Because the dining rooms were full, the nonstop meal was set up in a suite. The amount of the bill remains a secret.

Ritz Paris

📍 *L'Espadon—15, pl. Vendôme, Paris 1st. €€€*

THE LOCATION

Although it does not carry the official "palace" label, this is truly the palace of all palaces, opened in 1898 by César Ritz in the magnificent Place Vendôme square. The flagship restaurant, L'Espadon, has been nestled at the back of the hotel on the rue Cambon side since 1956. It underwent a grand restoration in 2023.

THE BEST TABLE

To date, table 12 is the most coveted.

THE CHEF

Eugénie Béziat, trained in the southwest of France at chef signature restaurants Michel Sarran and Michel Guérard, executes her dishes in the footsteps of Auguste Escoffier, preceded by Michel Roth and Nicolas Sale.

THE PASTRY CHEF

Since 2015, François Perret has been reconstructing iconic French delicacies: a barquette, a marble cake, and so much more.

THE ICONIC PASTRY

The madeleine with a meltingly soft center.

ECCENTRICITY

For Christmas Eve 1955, Coco Chanel asked for "a soup and a large piece of bread." Her guest that evening, writer Michel Déon, stated that the maître d' "seemed abominably shocked" but agreed to serve them. Could the definition of true luxury be simplicity?

Lutetia

📍 *Brasserie Lutetia— 45, blvd. Raspail, Paris 6th. €€€*

THE LOCATION

This masterpiece of Art Nouveau is the only palace on the Left Bank. Today, it no longer has a gourmet restaurant but a beautiful brasserie spanning 4,300 square feet (400 sq m), with a balcony and a patio.

THE BEST TABLE

The discreet no. 38, which has four seats with a panoramic view of the room.

THE CHEF

Formerly with Le Grand Véfour, Patrick Charvet beautifully executes a contemporary seafood-centric menu.

ICONIC DISHES

There is more than one, including the wild sea bass tartare with calamansi lemon and olive oil, blue lobster roasted in its juices, and sole meunière with capers and herbs.

ECCENTRICITY

One afternoon in the 1990s, Gérard Depardieu went to the kitchen and, in front of a stunned kitchen crew, prepared himself pasta with basil. Back in the restaurant with his plate, the actor got down on one knee and handed it to his companion, Carole Bouquet, and said: "I made you pasta, my love."

Four Seasons Hôtel George V

◊ Le Cinq—31, av. George-V, Paris 8th. €€€€

THE LOCATION

At the end of a gallery, two majestic wrought-iron doors open onto forty-five Louis XVI medallion chairs gilded in gold leaf: this is Le Cinq, "the" exceptional three-Michelin-star dining experience within this luxury hotel in Paris's Golden Triangle.

THE BEST TABLE

In the back, on the right, overlooking the room and the hotel's marbled courtyard.

THE CHEF

Christian Le Squer has maintained his three Michelin stars here since 2016.

THE ICONIC DISH

The chef pays tribute to his native Brittany with a fabulous line-caught sea bass, caviar, and lait ribot (fermented buttermilk) from his childhood.

ECCENTRICITY

On February 4, 2013, Joe Biden, then vice president of the United States, declined an invitation to eat at the Élysée Palace, preferring to sit down with his family at the George V to enjoy the shoulder of lamb confit by chef Éric Briffard (2008–2014).

The reason for what was something of a diplomatic blunder? His son's birthday.

Le Bristol Paris

◊ Épicure—112, rue du Faubourg-Saint-Honoré, Paris 8th. €€€€

THE LOCATION

On the ground floor of an Art Deco building, 790 feet (240 m) from the Élysée, the Michelin three-starred restaurant Épicure enchants at each service.

THE BEST TABLE

On sunny days, on the terrace.

THE CHEF

Wearing the top toque since 1999, the tremendous Éric Frechon has the distinction of having the longest stint leading the kitchen of a Parisian palace.

THE ICONIC DISH

Pasta stuffed with black truffle, artichoke, and duck foie gras served au gratin with an aged Parmesan cheese.

ECCENTRICITY

A regular customer loves this recipe so much that with each visit, his menu is the same: the stuffed pasta as a starter, a main course, and dessert. The portions are adapted.

Le Crillon

◊ L'Écrin—10, pl. de la Concorde, Paris 8th. €€€

THE LOCATION

Place de la Concorde. The majestic classical hotel, erected in 1758, houses the twenty-seat restaurant Écrin on the ground floor.

THE BEST TABLE

No. 4, with a banquette and armchairs, perfectly placed to admire the ballet of the service.

THE CHEF

The Savoyard Boris Campanella inherited the toque worn before him by two giants of French gastronomy, Christian Constant (1988–1996) and Jean-François Piège (2004–2009).

ICONIC DISHES

Far from what might be considered luxury: the chickpea purée soup with walnut praline, blue lobster with forest fruits.

ECCENTRICITY

For his marriage proposal, a customer asked the head sommelier, Xavier Thuizat, to get, within forty-eight hours, three bottles of wine (a Pétrus, a Romanée-Conti, and a Château Latour from 1989), which was his future wife's birth year. The sommelier managed to find two of the three bottles. The Château Latour was delivered by the owner by car from Belgium. He arrived one hour before the deadline.

Plaza Athénée

◊ Jean Imbert at the Plaza Athénée—25, av. Montaigne, Paris 8th. €€€€

THE LOCATION

Opened in 1913, the hotel, with its front facade garlanded with red geraniums, claims that twenty thousand gold leaves were required to decorate its gourmet dining room.

THE BEST TABLE

The exceptional 40-foot-long (12 m) marble table d'hôte, or chef's table, an exclusive location in front of the kitchen service window.

THE CHEF

Jean Imbert delights with his antimodern cuisine inspired by the grimoires of Carême, Escoffier, and Gouffé.

THE ICONIC DISH

The vol-au-vent with sweetbreads, kidneys, rooster's comb, crayfish, mushrooms, and poultry quenelles, all under a puff pastry lid.

ECCENTRICITY

In 1997, obsessed with orange, Michael Jackson had his suite redecorated in the color, and on one night when he called room service he ordered pumpkin soup.

Le Meurice, above.

Le Bristol Paris, above.

BISTRONOMY ESTABLISHMENTS
Les Bistrots de Chef(fe)s

These establishments offer the friendly atmosphere of a bistro combined with signature, chef-inspired dishes. Here is an overview of bistronomy's flagship locations. —HUGO DE SAINT PHALLE AND CHARLES PATIN O'COOHOON

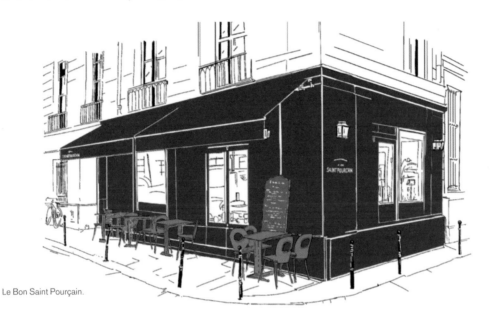

Le Bon Saint Pourçain.

La Régalade Saint-Honoré

📍 106, rue Saint-Honoré, Paris 1st. €€

THE CHEF

Bruno Doucet took over Yves Camdeborde's La Régalade before moving to the center of Paris.

THE BISTRO

The crackly and melting pork, parsleyed veal liver, and a memorable rice pudding can all be enjoyed amid the decor of exposed stone and historic wood beams.

Marcore

📍 1, rue des Panoramas, Paris 2nd. €€

THE CHEF

Marc Favier trained with Jean-François Piège and Frédéric Anton, then went solo at his restaurant Bouillon before landing at this spot now devoted to bistronomy.

THE BISTRO

Within a setting of black marble and alabaster lighting, the ground floor (the floor above is a starred restaurant) serves well-crafted dishes whose flavors reveal an immense amount of skill in sauces and cooking.

Elmer

📍 30, rue de Notre-Dame-de-Nazareth, Paris 3rd. €€

THE CHEF

Simon Horwitz, alumnus of L'Oustau de Baumanière (Bouches-du-Rhône), has cooked around the globe, including in Australia, Peru, and Japan.

THE BISTRO

The menu gives pride of place to wood-fired cooking and the art of rotisserie. In the dining room, sommelier Sébastien Perrot makes excellent recommendations.

Les Enfants Rouges

📍 9, rue de Beauce, Paris 3rd. €€

THE CHEF

Daï Shinozuka, originally from Japan, cooked alongside Yves Camdeborde and Stéphane Jégo.

THE BISTRO

Behind the emblematic red storefront can be found tasty cuisine, such as tender langoustine ravioli and wild mushrooms, made using local market products.

Le MaZenay

📍 46, rue de Montmorency, Paris 3rd. €€

THE CHEF

With his wife, Lan, Denis Groison opened this amazing bistro in the Marais in 2015.

THE BISTRO

Wild snails with herbs and seasonal game are among the choices here, where exemplary ingredients, a true mastery of cooking, and Asian touches are the norm.

Capitaine

📍 4, imp. Guéménée, Paris 4th. €€

THE CHEF

Baptiste Day, great-grandson of a sea captain, set sail on a course paved with Michelin stars (at Ambroisie, Astrance, and Arpège) and now skillfully navigates his own kitchens.

THE BISTRO

Offering seafood dishes as well as garam masala brill and poulette (young chicken) with lemon and olives.

Baca'v

📍 6, rue des Fossés-Saint-Marcel, Paris 5th. €€

Following in the footsteps of her Limousin-native cooks Taillevent and Drouant, Émile Cotte has opened this friendly location of her dreams.

THE BISTRO

With a wine-bar ambience, friendly casual dishes, and expert know-how, the chef sends out such plates as duck-pistachio pâté and a playful surf-and-turf vol-au-vent.

KGB (Kitchen Galerie Bis)

📍 25, rue des Grands-Augustins, Paris 6th. €€

THE CHEF

First trained by William Ledeuil before becoming his business partner, Martin Maumet leads the kitchens of this annex to Ze Kitchen Galerie.

THE BISTRO

The chef cooks dishes personal to him, with Asian influences. The setting is artsy loft-style decor.

Le Bon Saint Pourçain

📍 10 bis, rue Servandoni, Paris 6th. €€€

THE CHEF

Since 2015, Mathieu Techer has been making the classics resonate perfectly at this location opened by the prolific restaurateur David Lanher.

THE BISTRO

Tablecloths, Baumann chairs, and a short menu: line-caught bluefin tuna carpaccio, duck breast with Apicius spices, and poultry from Cour d'Armoise poultry farm.

THE CHEF

Le Comptoir du Relais

📍 *9, carr. de l'Odéon, Paris 6th.* €€€

THE CHEF

Bruno Doucet continues the culinary theme established here by Yves Camdeborde.

THE BISTRO

The terrace and dining room create a cozy space where you can enjoy a brilliant bistro lineup.

Bistrot Belhara

📍 *23, rue Duvivier, Paris 7th.* €€

THE CHEF

Thierry Dufroux rubbed shoulders with the greatest chefs (Guérard, Ducasse, and others) before moving home in 2013.

THE BISTRO

A mosaic floor, velvet banquettes, and comforting dishes reflect the delicious flavors from France's southwest terroir.

L'Ami Jean

📍 *27, rue Malar, Paris 7th.* €€€

THE CHEF

Stéphane Jégo, Yves Camdeborde's former second-in-command at La Régalade, is as boisterous as he is creative.

THE BISTRO

Here the pig is cooked from head to toe, as is wild game (of fur or feathers). This is high-flying rock 'n' roll bistronomy in a provincial inn–style setting.

Le Café des Ministères

📍 *83, rue de l'Université, Paris 7th.* €€€

THE CHEF

His background would make most chefs swoon, but Jean Sévègnes has turned away from Michelin-starred restaurants to open this model bistro with his wife, Roxane.

THE BISTRO

A solid classical repertoire, carried by the emblematic vol-au-vent (sweetbreads, free-range poultry, spinach) in a modest and modern ambience.

Pottoka

📍 *4, rue de l'Exposition, Paris 7th.* €€

THE CHEFS

Sébastien Gravé, from Bayonne, and Louise Jacob from Landes, make France's southwest dishes shine.

THE BISTRO

The bistronomy-style dishes often take on a Basque accent in a playful menu.

Le Mermoz

📍 *16, rue Jean-Mermoz, Paris 8th.* €€

THE CHEF

The American Thomas Graham's challenge was to replace the excellent Manon Fleury, the previous chef, and his mission has been accomplished with flying colors.

THE BISTRO

Monkfish Wellington and mussel soup with yuzu make up a tour de force menu in the comfort of a beautiful 1930s bistro.

Neva Cuisine

📍 *2, rue de Berne, Paris 8th.* €€

THE CHEF

Parisian by adoption, Beatriz Gonzalez, a native of Mexico, opened this location in 2011 before doubling her offerings with Coretta (Paris 17th).

THE BISTRO

Colorful plates and spot-on flavors make this a consistently tip-top location for the best tables in the neighborhood.

Le Pantruche

📍 *3, rue Victor-Massé, Paris 9th.* €€

THE CHEF

Franck Baranger has built a small bistro empire (Caillebotte, Belle Maison, Le Coucou). This is where it all began.

THE BISTRO

An incredible Grand Marnier soufflé and a board with a consistent quality-to-price ratio in an authentic Parisian decor.

Captaine.

KGB.

Marcore.

Pottoka.

Baca'v.

Le Café des Ministères.

Papillon.

Nosso, above and at right.

Les Petits Parisiens.

Caius.

Sardanac.

Rooster.

Candide

📍 35, rue Sambre-et-Meuse, Paris 10th. €€

THE CHEFS

Alessandro Candido and Camille Guillaud provide the cooking and the service.

THE BISTRO

With well-executed small plates for lunch, the menu reveals all its creativity for dinner. On Wednesdays, there is spit-roasted chicken. There is an open kitchen, plus bare wooden tables and pretty tiles for decor.

Chez Michel

📍 10, rue de Belzunce, Paris 10th. €€

THE CHEF

Following in the footsteps of the iconic Thierry Breton, the Japanese chef Masahiro Kawai has been leading this "punk bistro" since 2015.

THE BISTRO

An ancient-inn atmosphere where you can enjoy dishes with Breton, Japanese, and Hispanic influences. Translation: fish-chorizo soup, wild abalone from Trégor with garlic and parsley.

Pouliche

📍 11, rue d'Enghien, Paris 10th. €€

THE CHEF

From a pharmacist to the chef at a luxury hotel, Amandine Chaignot had quite a journey before opening Pouliche in 2019.

THE BISTRO

An elegant three-room kitchen with dishes that emphasize vegetables. On Wednesdays, the chef even offers a 100 percent vegetarian menu.

Le Servan

📍 32, rue Saint-Maur, Paris 11th. €€

THE CHEF

Opened in 2014, this stellar spot is run by the Levha sisters, Tatiana in the kitchen and Katia in the dining room.

THE BISTRO

Ceiling moldings and large bay windows for the decor and, on the plate, creative cuisine with influences from Asia and Russia (such as zakouski, meaning "appetizer" in Russian).

Le Petit Keller

📍 13, rue Keller, Paris 11th. €

THE CHEF

Formerly of Nanashi, Kaori Endo cooks bistro cuisine with occasional Japanese touches.

THE BISTRO

In a 1950s interior with Formica tables, this place serves up hazuki bean hummus, pork rillettes with five flavors, and menchi-katsu (breaded beef meatball), among other offerings.

Amarante

📍 4, rue Biscornet, Paris 12th. €€

THE CHEF

The shy Christophe Philippe is deeply dedicated to classic French cuisine.

THE BISTRO

Sitting among red leatherette and retro tiles, go for the offal, treated as a choice product, such as the well-made veal, used from head to toe (brains, tongue, caul, sweetbreads, etc.).

Nosso

📍 22, prom. Claude-Lévi-Strauss, Paris 13th. €€

THE CHEF

Brazilian Alessandra Montagne's talents command respect.

THE BISTRO

The cooking here is sincere and executed in a responsible and bright manner in a feel-good location with contemporary design.

L'Assiette

📍 181, rue du Château, Paris 14th. €€

THE CHEF

David Rathgeber, a self-proclaimed goof, is an outstanding technician and was part of Alain Ducasse's largest teams.

THE BISTRO

The distinguished decor pleases the eye, as do the

perfect plates in a style somewhere between rustic and chic.

Les Petits Parisiens

49, av. Jean-Moulin, Paris 14th. €€

THE CHEF
After opening Les Petits Princes in Suresnes (Hauts-de-Seine), restaurateur Arnaud Duhem and chef Rémy Danthez doubled the bet in the location of the historic La Régalade.

THE BISTRO
Wooden furniture and floor mosaics create a cozy atmosphere for enjoying terrines and impeccable plates.

Le Beurre Noisette

68, rue Vasco-de-Gama, Paris 15th. €€

THE CHEF
Chef Thierry Blanqui is tactful and humble, two personality traits that have helped make his bistro a standout since 2001.

THE BISTRO
A bar, parquet floor, and cloth napkins set the ambience here. This bistro satisfies appetites with its classic menu punctuated with clever twists.

Disciples

136, blvd. Murat, Paris 16th. €€

THE CHEFS
After his historic Apicius (Paris 16th), chef Jean-Pierre Vigato brilliantly continues his classical orchestrations, accompanied by his disciple Romain Dubuisson.

THE BISTRO
Within the bright dining room and on the large terrace parade delicately roasted squab and admirable tête de veau (calf's head).

Caius

6, rue d'Armaillé, Paris 17th. €€

THE CHEF
Jean-Marc Notelet spices up his plates with Indian and Nepalese touches. He spent time in the kitchens of Gérard Boyer and Marc Meneau.

THE BISTRO
Well-seasoned plates emphasizing fresh market vegetables, all enjoyed in an intimate and chic dining room.

Papillon

8, rue Meissonier, Paris 17th. €€

THE CHEF
Christophe Saintagne, a Norman, is the former Michelin three-starred executive chef of Le Meurice (Paris 1st). He also spent time in the kitchens of Alain Ducasse.

THE BISTRO
Traditional, simple, and healthy, with international influences, the menu expresses itself skillfully in all repertoires using choice ingredients. A modern decor.

Rooster

137, rue Cardinet, Paris 17th. €€

THE CHEF
Frédéric Duc, from Marseille, left Racines in New York (where he was nicknamed "rooster") to settle in Paris.

THE BISTRO
An old betting café where the chef serves a generous, lively, and comforting bistronomy-style menu.

Chantoiseau

63, rue Lepic, Paris 18th. €€€

THE CHEFS
In their bistro situated on Butte Montmartre, brothers Nicolas and Julien Durand pay tribute to the inventor of the modern restaurant.

THE BISTRO
Solid on the classics with some creative touches.

Le Maquis

53, rue des Cloÿs, Paris 18th. €

THE CHEFS
Paul Boudier and Albert Touton spent time in impressive kitchens, such as Chateaubriand.

THE BISTRO
The decor is in its original state. The place buzzes with conviviality around plates that have a sense of celebration.

Mensae

23, rue Melingue, Paris 19th. €€

THE CHEF
Thibault Sombardier, a finalist on *Top Chef*, received a Michelin star at Antoine in 2012 and heads three restaurants.

THE BISTRO
The frogs' legs, taramasalata, and praline chocolate mousse are already iconic dishes.

Le Baratin

3, rue Jouye-Rouve, Paris 20th. €€

THE CHEF
Every day for thirty years, with her apron tied behind her, Raquel Carena has worked faithfully here in her small kitchen.

THE BISTRO
The best sweetbreads in Paris in a spot recognizable by its pretty sea-green facade. There is a love for natural wines here, on an exceptional menu created by Philippe Pinoteau, aka Pinuche.

Sadarnac

17, rue Saint-Blaise, Paris 20th. €€

THE CHEF
Lise Deveix, originally from Saint-Germain-en-Laye (Yvelines), spent time in grand establishments such as Le Taillevent (Paris 8th) before opening her restaurant.

THE BISTRO
Red, blue, and green velvet; black marble; and dreamy wallpaper create a welcoming decor for enjoying plates focused on local products.

The Grandes Dames of Parisian Cooking

These women have left their mark on Paris's gastronomic scene.

OLYMPE VERSINI
Born in Paris, she was the self-taught chef of the Michelin-starred Restaurant d'Olympe (now closed) from 1979 to 1988. She was also a great success in media.

GHISLAINE ARABIAN
Ambassador of Flemish cuisine and starred chef from 1992 to 1998 at Le Pavillon Ledoyen (Paris 8th), she took over Les Petites Sorcières (Paris 14th) in 2007.

MARTHE AND FERNANDE ALLARD
Founder of the bistro Allard (Paris 6th) in 1932, Marthe, who maintained two stars for thirty years, passed the baton to her daughter-in-law Fernande (*pictured above*) in the 1940s.

FLORA MIKULA
Originally from Avignon, she's the chef and owner of several restaurants in Paris, including her own inn, Auberge Flora, from 2012 to 2020 (Paris 11th, today Hôtel La Finca).

First Female TV Chef

Adrienne Biasin was the head chef of the emblematic bistro in Les Halles, Chez la Vieille, with "la vieille" ("the old woman") being a nickname she inherited from the age of twenty-two for her traditional cuisine. Author of several cookbooks, she was the first woman to host a cooking show on TF1 called *La Table d'Adrienne* (1982–1983). With her household classics, she delighted Michou, François Mitterrand, Jacques Chirac, Lino Ventura, and so many other regulars.

GRAND RESTAURANTS
Les Grands Restaurants

Offering decor, service, dishes, and wine lists on a grand scale, these exceptional locations make lunch or dinner a truly remarkable experience. —FRANÇOIS-RÉGIS GAUDRY AND CHARLES PATIN O'COOHOON

CHEF SIGNATURES

These restaurants are run by some of the finest chefs in Parisian gastronomy.

Kei

◊ 5, rue du Coq-Héron, Paris 1st. €€€€

In a sparkling decor of marble and crystal, Kei Kobayashi, a child of Nagano, dreams in French gastronomy and revisits it through dishes that are now icons, such as "le jardin de légumes croquant" (a festive plate of fresh vegetables), and lobster grilled over hot Japanese oak and hardwood.

Plénitude

◊ Hotel Cheval Blanc—8, quai du Louvre, Paris 1st. €€€€

With three Michelin stars for La Vague d'Or in Saint-Tropez, Arnaud Donckele repeated the experience in Paris in 2022 just six months after opening. This is a grandiose experience around the "absolutes": the jus, vinaigrettes, and other "quintessential" sauces. Stellar desserts are executed by Maxime Frédéric, and there are breathtaking views of the Pont-Neuf.

L'Ambrosie

◊ 9, pl. des Vosges, Paris 4th. €€€

Feuillantine of langoustine in curry sauce, sea bass "petals" with artichoke and caviar—the signature dishes abound on the menu of Bernard Pacaud, a modest virtuoso (who has earned three stars since 1986) tucked away in the former Hôtel de Luynes.

Guy Savoy

◊ Monnaie de Paris—11, quai de Conti, Paris 6th. €€€€

Six rooms decorated with contemporary artwork overlooking the Seine, a chef elevated to ambassador of French gastronomy, and a grand neoclassical cuisine featuring sumptuous sauces.

L'Arpège

◊ 84, rue de Varenne, Paris 7th. €€€€

Within a tapestry of hand-embroidered and garden armchairs, the new bucolic decor is up to par with the irresistible cuisine of Alain Passard. His dishes, executed with fresh ingredients from his three vegetable gardens, are dazzling, but he is also an unparalleled roaster and pastry chef.

Alléno Paris

◊ 8, av. Dutuit, Paris 8th. €€€€

Since 2014, Yannick Alléno has been the owner of the emblematic Pavillon Ledoyen. Among his extractions, fermentations, and excellent sauces, this three-starred chef paints a canvas of modernity. The premises are also home to L'Abysse, a sushi counter (two stars), and Pavyllon, a gourmet dining counter (one star), making this the most starred establishment in the world.

La Scène

◊ 32, av. Matignon, Paris 8th. €€€

At the helm of a table of thirty seats in a chic vintage yacht–style ambience, Stéphanie Le Quellec skillfully executes her repertoire in her open kitchen.

Le Gabriel

◊ La Réserve Paris—42, av. Gabriel, Paris 8th. €€€

In a luxuriously refurbished former hôtel particulier (private urban home), Jérôme Banctel prepares lively and precise dishes inspired by his native Brittany and his many travels, especially through Japan.

Le Grand Restaurant

◊ 7, rue d'Aguesseau, Paris 8th. €€€

As you walk in, you pass through the metal lace door representing the map of Paris to spot the open kitchen with blocks of Carrara marble, the contemporary dining room, the impressive geometric glass roof, and the twenty tasting seats of the "territories of France" and "slow-cooked dishes" of Jean-François Piège. Suckling calf is slow cooked over walnut shells with chanterelle mushrooms.

Le Clarence

◊ 31, av. Franklin-D.-Roosevelt, Paris 8th. €€€

Facing the Grand Palais, in a majestic nineteenth-century hôtel particulier (private urban home) completely restored by Domaine Clarence Dillon in Bordeaux (owner of Château Haut-Brion), Christophe Pelé orchestrates a harmony of brilliance and creativity within a classic repertoire.

Pierre Gagnaire

◊ 6, rue Balzac, Paris 8th. €€€€

Possessing three stars since 1996, this chef, a native of Saint-Étienne, is one of the greatest artists on the Parisian gastronomic scene. Always on point, constantly reinvented, and flanked by small "satellite" creations, his dishes provide a thrill.

Le Pré Catelan

◊ Rte. de Suresnes, Bois de Boulogne, Paris 16th. €€€€

In a Napoléon III decor created by Pierre-Yves Rochon, Frédéric Anton—he earned three Michelin stars in 2007—creates signature pieces for a refined cuisine.

THE GRAND CLASSICS

Through their decor, their cuisine, and their service, these establishments are all classics.

La Tour d'Argent

◊ 15, quai de la Tournelle, Paris 5th. €€€

This Parisian gastronomic temple has stood on the banks of the Seine since 1582. The restaurant's reputation is not just for its pressed duck but also for chef Yannick Franques's tireless creations that continue the tradition, such as sole cardinal, "Trois empereurs" foie gras, and the stunning wine list.

Le Relais Louis XIII

◊ 8, rue des Grands-Augustins, Paris 6th. €€€

An MOF (Best Craftsman of France), Manuel Martinez executes Bresse poultry with Albufera sauce, lobster ravioli, foie gras, and lobster quenelle, all with fervor and accuracy in a space steeped in history, built on the cellars of the former Grands-Augustins convent.

Marsan

◊ 4, rue d'Assas, Paris 6th. €€€

In an elegant setting of light woodwork and drapery, the cuisine of chef Hélène Darroze is focused on ingredients and always prepared with extreme accuracy.

Lasserre

◊ 17, av. Franklin-D.-Roosevelt, Paris 8th. €€€

From his squab André Malraux to the stuffed pasta, chef Jean-Louis Nomicos continues the tradition of this legendary location, opened in 1942 by René Lasserre.

Le Taillevent

◊ 15, rue Lamennais, Paris 8th. €€€

In the Duke of Morny's former private residence with opulent decor and a rich wine cellar, Italian Giuliano Sperandio creates a beautifully traditional gastronomic experiences.

La Grande Cascade

◊ All. de Longchamp, Paris 16th. €€€

Since 2006, Frédéric Robert has been showcasing great classic cuisine in this 1900 pavilion: black truffle and foie gras pasta, beef from Salers with Choron sauce, sweetbreads, and turtle soup.

Maison Rostang

◊ 20, rue Rennequin, Paris 17th. €€€

Opened in 1978 by the Rostang family, this iconic restaurant was taken over by Stéphane Manigold in 2019. Chef Nicolas Beaumann perpetuates a classic cuisine full of finesse.

Plénitude.

Le Gabriel.

Kei.

L'Arpège.

La Grande Cascade.

Le Grand Restaurant.

Maison Rostang.

Guy Savoy.

La Scène.

Parisian Personalities of Nouvelle Cuisine

After writing the *Guide Julliard de Paris* in 1963, Henri Gault and Christian Millau founded Nouvelle Cuisine in 1973.

ANDRÉ GUILLOT
Set up in 1952 at the Auberge du Vieux Marly in Marly-le-Roi (Yvelines). Gault and Millau considered this chef's style the precursor to Nouvelle Cuisine.

JEAN DELAVEYNE
"The wizard of Bougival" opened the restaurant Le Camélia in Bougival (Yvelines) in 1957.

ALAIN SENDERENS
First chef, in 1985, then owner of Lucas-Carton (Paris 8th), he was one of the first to offer food and wine pairings. His great signature dish: Apicius duck.

PAUL MINCHELLI
The founder of the restaurant Le Duc (Paris 14th) was one of the first to serve raw fish in Paris.

CLAUDE PEYROT
Chef of the Vivarois (Paris 16th, now closed) from 1966, he held three Michelin stars from 1973 to 1982.

MICHEL GUÉRARD
The three-star chef of Les Prés d'Eugénie in Eugénie-les-Bains (Landes) began his career at Le Pot-au-Feu (now closed) in Asnières-sur-Seine (Hauts-de-Seine), where his "salade gourmande" was invented.

CHEF-DRIVEN RESTAURANTS
Les Tables d'Auteurs

Behind these restaurant walls hides the unique repertoire of a chef with a commanding personality.

— FRANÇOIS-RÉGIS GAUDRY AND CHARLES PATIN O'COOHOON

THE SIGNATURES

The chef's name is enough to attract gourmets to these stellar establishments.

Granite

⚲ 6, rue Bailleul,
Paris 1st. €€

In this establishment opened by restaurateur Stéphane Manigold, Tom Meyer (La Chèvre d'Or, Maison Pic, and others) gives free rein to his inspirations around carefully sourced local products. You'll find a chic and contemporary decor with natural materials and a richly endowed cellar.

Fleur de Pavé

⚲ 5, rue Paul-Lelong,
Paris 2nd. €€

In his kitchen, chef Sylvain Sendra designs masterful plates inspired by his extensive travels to everywhere from Thailand to Lebanon. Among the superb ingredients are rare vegetables from the farm of Asafumi Yamashita (Yvelines).

Frenchie

⚲ 5, rue du Nil,
Paris 2nd. €€

In 2008, Grégory Marchand was the first to settle at rue du Nil, which has become one of the best streets for gourmets in Paris. Since that time, the chef has been exuding creativity in a relaxed, gastronomic atmosphere.

Solstice

⚲ 45, rue Claude-Bernard,
Paris 5th. €€

A former instructor at the Ferrandi school and cofounder of Semilla and Freddy's (Paris 6th), Eric Trochon has headed his own establishment since 2019. With his Korean partner Mijin Ryu, this MOF (Best Craftsman of France) chef creates a contemporary cuisine using carefully sourced ingredients that follow the seasons.

Quinsou

⚲ 33, rue de l'Abbé-
Grégoire, Paris 6th. €€

Humble and shy, Antonin Bonnet follows his destiny in this space of rustic elegance. The cuisine presents the best ingredients from freshwater fishing and traditional cultivation methods without ever distorting them. There is one prix fixe menu.

Auguste

⚲ 54, rue de Bourgogne,
Paris 7th. €€

Chef Gaël Orieux stands at the helm of this excellent seafood-centric establishment located near Les Invalides. In an elegant setting that evokes the sea, he serves refined and dedicated cuisine, using only nonendangered species.

David Toutain

⚲ 29, rue Surcouf,
Paris 7th. €€€

Mentored by Marc Veyrat and Alain Passard, this Norman chef showcases plants with striking mastery in a contemporary setting dominated by raw wood. His smoked eel with black sesame cream is now an iconic dish.

Garance

⚲ 34, rue Saint-Dominique,
Paris 7th. €

A stone's throw from Les Invalides, Guillaume Muller leads this gustatory journey with a fine selection of bottles and dishes composed of products from his farm in Haute-Vienne.

L'Atelier Joël Robuchon

⚲ Hotel du Pont-Royal—5
rue de Montalembert,
Paris 7th. €€€

Axel Manes's plates are first eaten with the eyes while sitting at one of the forty seats at the counter of this open kitchen. The classics come in small portions.

Tomy & Co

⚲ 22, rue Surcouf,
Paris 7th. €€

Receiving Michelin stars in 2019, Cambodian-born chef Tomy Gousset has turned his restaurant into a gourmet and locavore bistro. On the menu are signature dishes that rotate with the seasons: gnocchi with black truffle in winter and with chanterelles, roasted apricots, and lemon verbena in summer.

Akrame

⚲ 7, rue Tronchet,
Paris 8th. €€

Near La Madeleine, chef Akrame Benallal established his restaurant in a contemporary setting with dark tones. The dishes, inspired by global cuisines, make an impact. Wine list recommendations are by sommelier Sarah Bodianu.

NESO

⚲ 6, rue Papillon,
Paris 9th. €€

Moving, frenzied, and ambitious are just some words that come to mind when describing the heavily tattooed Guillaume Sanchez, who shines with his inspirations and extraordinary techniques here. This is a stunning experience in a beautiful and modern space. The menu will surprise.

Pétrelle

⚲ 34, rue Pétrelle,
Paris 9th. €€

Inside Jean-Luc André's high-society den, chef Lucie Boursier-Mougenot and sommelier Luca Danti ensure a high-flying bistronomy-style experience in a romantic boudoir atmosphere. Cleverly constructed plates are tinged with Mediterranean flavors and complemented by a natural wine list.

Eels

⚲ 27, rue d'Hauteville,
Paris 10th. €€

A former chef under William Ledeuil, Adrien Ferrand expresses all his talents in his neo-bistro that is full of inventiveness. Smoked eel, licorice, apple, and hazelnut always have a place on the menu. The chef draws his inspirations from around the globe.

Le Chateaubriand

⚲ 129, av. Parmentier,
Paris 11th. €€

Do not be fooled by the simplicity of this antique bistro: Iñaki Aizpitarte is a dynamite chef with flashes of brilliance, a hero of the Parisian bistronomy scene. Gourmands come to experience the unique menu and the rich selection of natural wines.

FIEF

⚲ 44, rue de la Folie-
Méricourt, Paris 11th. €€

Victor Mercier made his FIEF ("Fait Ici En France") a bastion of French terroirs. Here no food is imported, which does not limit this chef in showing all his creativity and precision in menus with such titles as "Amour Végétal" and "Omnivore Conscient."

Rigmarole

⚲ 10, rue du Grand-Prieuré,
Paris 11th. €€

Behind a long walnut-wood counter, French American chef Robert Compagnon and his Taiwanese American partner Jessica Yang orchestrate a cuisine at the crossroads of cultures (French, Italian, and Japanese). There are items grilled over Japanese oak, and pastas to die for.

Septime

⚲ 80, rue de Charonne,
Paris 11th. €€

An atelier with industrial charm offering a rich wine list composed by partner Théo Pourriat and cuisine by Bertrand Grébaut with vibrant inspirations, strong ecological convictions, and impeccable technique. A must for any gourmet visiting Paris.

Table

⚲ 3, rue de Prague,
Paris 12th. €€€€

Blogger, author, and self-taught chef Bruno Verjus translates his immense gastronomic experiences onto his table without separation between the kitchen and the dining room. All techniques are employed here, from the classic to the modern. The beautiful ingredients include fish from the island of Yeu and lamb from the Pyrénées. There is a huge list of natural wines.

Auguste.

Solstice.

Septime.

Neso.

Eels.

FIEF.

Pétrelle.

Tomy & Co.

Quinsou, above and at right.

Substance.

Gramme.

Yam'Tcha.

Bellefeuille

📍 *5, pl. du Chancellor-Adenauer, Paris 16th.* €€€

On the ground floor in a natural setting in the Hôtel Saint James Paris, chef Julien Dumas (formerly of Lucas-Carton) delivers a menu that oscillates between plants and sea with irreproachable ingredients.

Comice

📍 *31, av. de Versailles, Paris 16th.* €€

Within a neo-bourgeois decor (antique furniture and Art Deco silverware), Noam Gedalof (in the kitchen) and Etheliya Hananova (in the dining room), a Canadian couple, offer a unique menu where ingredients are cooked with accuracy and sensitivity.

Substance

📍 *18, rue Chaillot, Paris 16th.* €€

Semifinalist of *Top Chef* 2021 Matthias Marc started his adventure under the leadership of restaurateur Stéphane Manigold. He composes a sincere, effervescent, and balanced cuisine in which French tradition meets his Jura roots. There is an exceptional wine list of more than a thousand labels.

Nomicos

📍 *16, av. Bugeaud, Paris 16th.* €€

Jean-Louis Nomicos creates a Mediterranean-inspired menu that is generous and comprehensive. His signature pasta with truffle and foie gras is served alongside center-cut pollack fillets in bouillabaisse.

Anona

📍 *80, blvd. des Batignolles, Paris 17th.* €€

The name is in homage to the cherimoya (aka "anone"), an exotic fruit known as much for its good flavor as for its health benefits, which sets the tone of the restaurant. In a refined decor, Thibaut Spiwack has been executing creative and responsible dishes since 2019.

Jacques Faussat

📍 *54, rue Cardinet, Paris 17th.* €€

Here chef Jacques Faussat, from Ger, orchestrates a masterful menu of ingredients with several signature dishes: potato mille-feuille and foie gras, and hot almond soufflé.

Frédéric Simonin

📍 *25, rue Bayen, Paris 17th.* €€

In his establishments with the allure of a Parisian apartment, MOF (Best Craftsman of France) chef Frédéric Simonin offers simplicity and sophistication. His cuisine, while mastering the classics, gives way to creativity with Japanese touches.

La Table du 11

📍 *8, rue de la Chancellerie, Versailles (Yvelines).* €€

Just a stone's throw from the Palace of Versailles, Jean-Baptiste Lavergne-Morazzani practices royal cuisine in a cozy space with neo-fifties influences that is lively, timeless, and executed with clarity. The Cave du 11 (at the same address) and the Bistrot du 11 (10, rue de Satory) complete the picture.

Ochre

📍 *56, rue du Gué, Rueil-Malmaison (Hauts-de-Seine).* €€

It was a meteoric rise for Baptiste Renouard, former *Top Chef* candidate with an imposing résumé (Lasserre, Robuchon, Alléno), who became a starred chef. He is capable of small miracles and bold risks in his refined tasting room.

L'Escarbille

📍 *8, rue de Vélizy, Meudon, (Hauts-de-Seine).* €€€

Roasted turbot, pressed squab, and watercress purée are just some of the dishes in Régis Douysset's gastronomic repertoire at his restaurant located in an old train station café.

Villa9Trois

📍 *71, rue Hoche, Montreuil (Seine-Saint-Denis).* €€€

Lacquered veal sweetbreads and venison bagna càuda (a hot dish made from garlic and anchovies) are among the plates of chef Camille Saint-M'Leux that can be enjoyed by the fire or on the tree-lined terrace of this unpretentious establishment.

L'Ours

📍 *10–12, rue de l'Église, Vincennes (Val-de-Marne).* €€€

In a decor of wood, metal, and stone, Jacky Ribault

The Crillon Generation

Chef of the restaurant Les Ambassadeurs at the Hôtel de Crillon (Paris 8th) between 1988 and 1996, Christian Constant built a brigade of sous-chefs and young cooks who set out on their own as ambassadors of French gastronomy.

📍 *10 pl. de la Concorde, Paris 8th*

CHEF	AT THE CRILLON	TODAY
Yves Camdeborde	Executive sous-chef	Bistronomy pioneer, TV host, and restaurateur
Éric Frechon	Executive sous-chef	Executive chef of Épicure—Le Bristol (three stars, Paris 8th)
Thierry Breton	Chef de partie tournant	Chef owner of La Pointe du Grouin (Paris 10th)
Jean-François Rouquette	Chef de partie saucier	Executive chef of Pur' at the Park Hyatt Paris-Vendôme (Paris 1st)
Thierry Fauchet	Demi-chef de partie	Chef owner of L'Os à Moelle (Paris 15th) and Le Barbezingue (Châtillon, Hauts-de-Seine)
Emmanuel Renaut	Demi-chef de partie	Executive chef of Flocons de Sel (three stars, Megève, Haute-Savoie)
Jean-François Piège	Commis garde-manger	Chef of Le Grand Restaurant (Paris 8th), La Poule au Pot (Paris 1st), Épi d'Or (Paris 1st), and Clover Grill (Paris 1st)
Christophe Felder	Pastry chef	Pastry book author
Gilles Marchal	Pastry sous-chef	Founder of the pastry shop Gilles Marchal (Paris 18th)
Laurent Jeannin	Pastry sous-chef	Former pastry chef of Épicure—Le Bristol (three stars, Paris 8th); he died in 2017

has set up an elegant space where he serves a cuisine highlighting rustic inspirations, delicate execution, and foreign influences.

L'Or Q'Idée

📍 14, rue Marcel-Rousier, Pontoise (Val-d'Oise). €€€

At the foot of the church in the city center, the former *Top Chef* winner Naoëlle d'Hainaut, who spent time in the kitchens of Le Bristol, Paris 8th, directs a gastronomic and modern score in a refined setting with Scandinavian inspirations.

INTERNATIONAL INSPIRATIONS

These restaurants serve up dishes with global influences.

Palais Royal Restaurant

📍 110, galerie de Valois, Paris 1st. €€€

Under the colonnades of the Palais-Royal, Philip Chronopoulos, former chef of L'Atelier Robuchon (Paris 8th), delivers a creative cuisine that sometimes resonates with his native Greece.

Yam'Tcha

📍 121, rue Saint-Honoré, Paris 1st. €€

Yin and yang are in balance here between the cuisine of chef Adeline Grattard and the tea pairings of Chi Wah Chan. In a decor of wood, Carrara marble, and gold leaf, the dishes are the perfect symbiosis of the art of cooking and preparation of local French products with Chinese techniques.

Ze Kitchen Gallery

📍 4, rue des Grands-Augustins, Paris 6th. €€

Since 2002, in this colorful loft with the feel of an art gallery, William Ledeuil has been putting forth a unique gastronomic repertoire, a culinary Esperanto inspired by Asia enhanced

with lemongrass, root vegetables, citrus fruits, fresh herbs, and spices. This is one of the most stimulating dining experiences in Paris.

Double Dragon

📍 52, rue Saint-Maur, Paris 11th. €

The second address of the Levha sisters (the other is Le Servan) promises a double dose of fun! In the open kitchen behind the counter of their Asian canteen are plates with Korean-Filipino influences—all flavorful and lively.

Pierre Sang in Oberkampf

📍 55, rue Oberkampf, Paris 11th. €€

Born in Seoul, this adopted Auvergnat composes, behind the long counter, a unique menu of French inspirations with Korean techniques and influences. He doubled and then tripled the setting at rue Gambey (Paris 11th) with a chic eatery and a gourmet restaurant.

MoSuke

📍 11, rue Raymond-Losserand, Paris 14th. €€

Former *Top Chef* winner Mory Sacko (formerly of Mandarin Oriental) delivers a cuisine that meets at the crossroads of his Malian origins, his passion for Japan, and French gastronomy.

Alan Geeam

📍 19, rue Lauriston, Paris 16th. €€

In a refined setting, self-taught chef Alan Geeam pays a moving tribute to French cuisine without neglecting the Lebanese influences of his origins; offering fixed menus of five or seven courses.

Le Faham

📍 108, rue Cardinet, Paris 17th. €€

In a cozy, muted dining room in turquoise tones, Reunionese Kelly Rangama (a former Top

Chef) and her pastry chef husband, Jérôme Devreese, present a refined and colorful cuisine with overseas influences.

JAPANESE-STYLE

This generation of Japanese chefs pays tribute to the French repertoire.

Yoshinori

📍 18, rue Grégoire-de-Tours, Paris 6th. €€

Chef Yoshinori Morié brilliantly rubs shoulders with French gastronomy with his classic cuisine featuring Japanese touches in a traditional Parisian setting with a wood-beamed ground floor and vaulted cellar.

Cuisine

📍 50, rue Condorcet, Paris 9th. €€

In this twenty-seat bistro decorated by the Italian architect Federico Masotto, Japanese chef Takao Inazawa practices a cheerful and generous bistronomy-style cuisine accented with Japanese flavors. His partner Benoît Simon pours a cheerful selection of vins vivants (living wines).

Abri

📍 92, rue du Faubourg-Poissonnière, Paris 10th. €€

With skills honed at L'Atelier Robuchon and Le Taillevent, Katsuaki Okiyama skillfully handles his knife in his twenty-seat bistro, serving up an instinctive cuisine that keeps up with the times—French inspired and often improvised— in an *omakase*-style (depending on his mood).

Pages

📍 4, rue Auguste-Vacquerie, Paris 16th. €€

In his Franco-Japanese space near the Arc de Triomphe, Japanese chef Ryuji Teshima pays delicious tribute to French gastronomy with incredible techniques and ingredients.

L'Axel

📍 43, rue de France, Fontainebleau (Seine-et Marne). €€€

In a simple and elegant decor, chef Kunihisa Goto's Japanese-style French classics are perfectly executed, as evidenced by his Wagyu beef and Bintje croquettes.

CHEF-DRIVEN COFFEE SHOPS

From breakfast to lunch, these locations are as convincing in the cup as on the plate.

Gramme

📍 86, rue des Archives, Paris 3rd. €

It has "Parisian cuisine" in its subtitle, offering a coffee shop where delicious Lomi coffees, kombuchas, and house-made lemonades accompany generous plates with English and Levantine influences, all by chef Marine Gora. There are excellent cookies and pastries.

Mokonuts

📍 5, rue Saint-Bernard, Paris 11th. €

Moko Hirayama manages the sweet dishes and Omar Koreitem manages the savory dishes, elevating this coffee shop to the top. Between Japanese and Levantine influences, the shop offers high-quality cookies and creative dishes. Dinner is possible as a private booking.

BISTROS Les Bistrots

Classic decor and saucy dishes are the winning combo at these popular Parisian eateries where comfort food is on the menu. —PIERRE-YVES CHUPIN

À l'Épi d'or.

La Poule au Pot

◊ 9, rue Vauvilliers, Paris 1st. €€€

Jean-François Piège took possession of this bistro in 2018, offering "typically French" bourgeois cuisine with excellently sourced ingredients and old-fashioned charm.

SERVED UP

Slow-cooked chicken, parsleyed frogs' legs, escargot, and île flottante (poached meringues floating on a vanilla custard sauce). What could be more comforting?

À l'Épi d'Or

◊ 25, rue Jean-Jacques-Rousseau, Paris 1st. €€

This institution in the Les Halles district has changed its chef without changing its decor one iota. A weekly fixed menu is offered. Perhaps the best chocolate mousse in Paris.

SERVED UP

Liver mousse, house-made fries, skate with capers.

Au Vieux Comptoir

◊ 17, rue des Lavandières-Sainte-Opportune, Paris 1st. €€

Classic decor and food that keeps regulars coming back thanks to a traditional menu, exceptional charcuterie, and a large selection of wines.

SERVED UP

Tatin of boudin noir (blood sausage), boeuf bourguignon, andouillette, onion soup gratinée.

Le Rubis

◊ 10, rue du Marché Saint-Honoré, Paris 1st. €

With barrels lined up against the entrance, this bistro is a popular stop in the neighborhood.

SERVED UP

Hareng pommes à l'huile (herring mixed with cooked potatoes), kidneys cooked in port, and wine by the carafe.

Le Saint-Amour

◊ 19, rue Étienne-Marcel, Paris 1st. €€

A former butcher, Erick Lenoir lovingly runs this bistro with its crazy layout. He is alone at the controls, and everything he serves is good.

SERVED UP

House-made terrine, stew, offal.

La Bourse et la Vie

◊ 12, rue Vivienne, Paris 2nd. €€

It took an American chef, Daniel Rose, to elevate this former bar. At lunch, the daily appetizers and the house-made fries are a great success. At dinner, traditional recipes and saucy dishes attract regulars.

SERVED UP

Leeks vinaigrette with Piedmont hazelnuts, tête de veau (calf's head) with sauce ravigote.

Aux Crus de Bourgogne

◊ 3, rue Bachaumont, Paris 2nd. €€€

The location opened in 1902, and André Malraux lovingly modified it, returning its luster and excellent service. Servers in the dining room wear white jackets with a stitched name tag and, in the kitchen, only the classics are prepared, with up-to-date touches.

SERVED UP

Pâté en croûte, oeufs en meurette (poached eggs in red wine sauce), vol-au-vent, profiteroles.

Chez Georges

◊ 1, rue du Mail, Paris 2nd. €€€

Oeuf mayonnaise has been served here since 1964, along with beef headcheese and grilled kidneys Henri IV–style. The service is charming, and the wines were chosen by the owner with the same passion as for his collection of nineteenth-century paintings.

SERVED UP
Kidneys, sweetbreads with morels, rum baba.

Le Rubis

📍 14, rue Léopold-Bellan, Paris 2nd. €

Bistro chairs, black Formica tables, photos on the wall: there is nothing flashy here, including the lunch and dinner menu, with plates served up by Tommaso Brandini.

SERVED UP
Fresh cod with beurre blanc sauce, veal tripe, panna cotta.

Parcelles

📍 13, rue Chapon, Paris 3rd. €€

In a former neighborhood haunt (Taxi Jaune), Sarah Michielsen and Bastien Fidelin express their passion for the bistro setting with its exposed wood beams and stones, solid-wood counter, and white tablecloths.

SERVED UP
Pâté en croûte, tête de veau (calf's head) carpaccio, veal-anchovy tartare, and an amazing wine list.

Le Petit Célestin

📍 12, quai des Célestins, Paris 4th. €€

Scores of old drinking songs still adorn the walls of this historic bistro. Yanice Mimoun sends out classics of the genre: aged cheeses and a good choice of wines.

SERVED UP
Hangar steak, house-made fries, and jus.

Benoît

📍 20, rue Saint-Martin, Paris 4th. €€

The decor is so typically bistro-style, and on two levels. The classic dishes are well done, and the attentive service make this spot a must-visit.

SERVED UP
Sautéed sweetbreads, profiteroles Benoît.

Chez René

📍 14, blvd. Saint-Germain, Paris 5th. €€

Walls covered with gallery posters, tablecloths, and old-fashioned service make this a comfy choice. The menu stands out and is unchanging as the chef rolls out brasserie classics.

SERVED UP
Grilled marrowbone with thyme flowers, boeuf bourguignon, île flottante (poached meringues floating on a vanilla custard sauce) with pink pralines.

La Rôtisserie d'Argent

📍 19, quai de la Tournelle, Paris 5th. €€€

The rotisserie occupies a major place here and allows the chef to display an undeniable expertise in cooking meats. Worth mentioning is the purée, one of the best in Paris. The end of the meal does not disappoint, with pastries from La Tour d'Argent's pastry shop.

SERVED UP
Oeuf mayonnaise, pike quenelles André Terrail, roasted squab with thyme.

Allard

📍 41, rue Saint-André-des-Arts, Paris 6th. €€€

The weekly menu is faithful to the classics during the time of Fernande and André Allard, who ran the bistro for nearly forty years. Alain Ducasse took over in 2013 and saved this Saint-Germain-des-Prés institution.

SERVED UP
Cassoulet, chicken in vin jaune, frogs' legs.

Chez Dumonet— Restaurant Joséphine

📍 117, rue du Cherche-Midi, Paris 6th. €€€

Lucile and Jean-Christian Dumonet treat their customers with generous plates that respect tradition and reflect the Dumonets' expertise for choosing the best ingredients and cooked to perfection.

SERVED UP
House-made fresh duck foie gras, veal sweetbreads and new potatoes, millefeuille Jean-Louis.

Au Vieux Comptoir.

La Poule au Pot, above and at right.

À l'Épi d'Or

Aux Crus de Bourgogne.

Aux Bons Crus.

Wadja

📍 *10, rue de la Grande-Chaumière, Paris 6th. €€*

Launched in 1942 by a native of Poland, this historic location in Montparnasse with its unchanged decor is always full. Manning the kitchen is a young chef with solid skills sending out appetizing and generous plates.

SERVED UP

Soup Agnès Sorel, eel carpaccio.

Chez Marcel

📍 *7, rue Stanislas, Paris 6th. €*

Among the delightful conglomeration of objects and elbow-to-elbow tables, there is an unchanging menu directed by Pierre Cheucle offering Lyon specialties, which are pork-based, and home-style dishes.

SERVED UP

Cervelat sausages with pistachio, pike quenelle with sauce Nantua (crayfish sauce), cervelle de canut (seasoned fromage blanc, a Lyonnaise specialty), pink praline tart.

Au Petit Tonneau

📍 *20, rue Surcouf, Paris 7th. €€*

Simple decor, unchanged for years, welcomes the many Americans who arrive to (re)discover the standard-bearers of French gastronomy. The dishes are authentic and the portions generous. Desserts are traditional.

SERVED UP

Duckling, kidneys, blanquette, and other classics.

Café Lignac

📍 *139, rue Saint-Dominique, Paris 7th. €€*

The handover of this bistro from Christian Constant (from Tarn-et-Garonne) and Cyril Lignac (from Aveyron) was a smooth one. The menu of the new chef still includes Christian's cassoulet, and the atmosphere has not changed. It's the best.

SERVED UP

Sweetbreads vol-au-vent, tarte Tatin with crème crue (crème fraîche).

L'Affable

📍 *10, rue de Saint-Simon, Paris 7th. €€*

Olivier Hélion, the stylish owner and bon vivant, welcomes customers who have often become friends in this stylish bistro. The kitchen lovingly prepares beautiful ingredients with flawless presentation.

SERVED UP

Veal sweetbreads with anchovies, chocolate soufflé.

Oui Mon Général!

📍 *14, rue du Général-Bertrand, Paris, 7th. €€*

The right ingredients perfectly prepared for the love of good food are the two principles from which Stéphane Reynaud never deviates. The wine list is successfully ambitious.

SERVED UP

Tête de veau (calf's head) carpaccio, suckling pig in caul fat, and a rich mash of potatoes.

Le Bistrot de Paris

📍 *33, rue de Lille, Paris 7th. €€*

This historic location has regained its panache thanks to a convincing culinary purpose, 100 percent authentically French waiters, and a very Parisian ambience.

SERVED UP

Marinated smoked herring in potatoes, panfried calf's liver with shallots confit in vinegar, profiteroles.

Chez Monsieur

📍 *11, rue du Chevalier-de-Saint-George, Paris 8th. €€€*

A chic bistro with good bottles, and waiters in white shirts, ties, and striped aprons. The wine list is assembled by Carole Colin and Denis Jamet, at the head of the prestigious restaurant Les Climats.

SERVED UP

Six Burgundy snails cooked in beurre blanc, traditional veal blanquette served in a casserole, fresh profiteroles with real hot chocolate sauce.

Le Griffonnier

📍 *8, rue des Saussaies, Paris 8th. €€*

Camped behind his counter, Cédric Duthilleul, the charismatic boss, offers a generous cuisine with his daily specials that follow the seasons. The wine list impresses with its exceptional old vintages.

SERVED UP

Oeuf mayonnaise, panfried andouillette in a Sancerre sauce.

Le Bon Georges

📍 *45, rue Saint-Georges, Paris 9th. €€*

Benoît Duval-Arnould, the owner, has set his sights on wines with a cellar bringing together the best from the vineyard. In the kitchen, the chef has unparalleled skill in the choice of ingredients and preparation.

SERVED UP

Oreiller de la Belle Aurore (an extravagant pâté en croûte), lièvre à la royale (hare), chocolate mousse.

Le Beaucé

📍 *43, rue Richer, Paris 9th. €€*

Behind a flamboyant facade hides a lovely bistro with a bar, exposed stones, and a tiled floor. In the kitchen, Marius Bénard is a real fan of offal.

SERVED UP

Terrine de campagne (country-style terrine), brains meunière, oeuf mayonnaise, whole sweetbreads.

Les Canailles

📍 *25, rue La Bruyère, Paris 9th. €€*

Chef Tetsu Yoshida's cuisine is inspired by the seasons. The welcome is friendly, the service impeccable, the plates prepared with care, the wine list fun with choices by the glass.

Le Bon Georges.

SERVED UP

Beef tongue carpaccio with gribiche sauce.

Les Arlots

📍 *136, rue du Faubourg-Poissonnière, Paris 10th. €€*

A mosaic floor, a long counter, a shelf full of wines, and wooden furniture welcome you in Thomas Brachet's classic gold-standard Parisian bistro. More than one hundred wines are available, but there is no wine list.

SERVED UP

Saucisse-aligot from Arlots (sausage with aligot, a purée of cheese and potato).

Auberge Pyrénées Cévennes

📍 *106, rue de la Folie-Méricourt, Paris 11th. €€*

Although this auberge has changed chef and owner on occasion, nothing else changes: wood beams, a collection of copper pans, hunting trophies, and towels folded into a fan set in drinking glasses. The menu can be described as between *L'Art de la cuisine* by Antonin Carême and *Le Grand dictionnaire de cuisine* by Alexandre Dumas.

SERVED UP

Kidney and sweetbreads, pâté en croûte, pig's foot, Paris-Brest, tarte Tatin (stunning).

Bistrot Paul Bert

📍 *18, rue Paul-Bert, Paris 11th. €€*

Bertrand Auboyneau's bistro is an institution. Beautiful traditional cuisine, enlivened with original touches, generous portions, careful preparation, and a stunning wine list.

SERVED UP

Cromesquis de cochon (pork fritters), blanquette de veau, Paris-Brest.

Le Repaire de Cartouche

📍 *8, blvd. des Filles-du-Calvaire, Paris 11th. €€*

Rodolphe Paquin dominates by his size (he is almost 6 feet 7 inches/2 m tall!). He has a sincere cooking style and taste for sharing. His terrines, such as his pâté en croûte, are made to be shared among friends. The wine list has great options, and the kitsch decor is worth seeing.

Lamb terrine with figs, panfried pigs' feet crépinette (a sausage patty encased in a membrane).

Le Quincy

📍 28, av. Ledru-Rollin,
Paris 12th. €€

Even though the world changes, this establishment stays the same. The kitchen continues serving up classics such as chicken in vin jaune and morels, just like it always has. The cooking and sauces are spot on.

SERVED UP

Caillette from Ardèche (a cross between a pâté and a meatball wrapped in caul fat), roasting chicken, and pigs' feet and stuffed tripe.

Aux Enfants Gâtés

📍 4, rue Danville,
Paris 14th. €€

In this space for just twenty settings, chef Frédéric Bidault, formerly of Lasserre, presents braised dishes surrounded with reduced jus and savory jellies. Each dish is a playful selection of cooking skills worthy of some of the finest restaurants.

SERVED UP

Vitello tonnato and a large winter cabbage cooked in a casserole.

Le Radis Beurre

📍 51, blvd. Garibaldi,
Paris 15th. €€

Good bread, good butter, and seasonal products all handled with delicacy and a touch of whimsy. This is a safe bet in the neighborhood.

SERVED UP

Seared pigs' feet with duck foie gras, rice pudding with caramel sauce and flaky sea salt.

Bélisaire

📍 2, rue Marmontel,
Paris 15th. €€

It's a bistro with a simple appearance but with dishes full of flavors and finesse. Matthieu Garrel explores the delights of his native Brittany here. Seafood is omnipresent on his menu, but products from the land are not overlooked.

SERVED UP

Lièvre à la royale (hare), roasted John Dory with sautéed spinach, mashed potatoes, and champagne sauce.

L'Accolade

📍 208, rue de la Croix-Nivert, Paris 15th. €€

In this charming bistro, you'll be welcomed like a friend. A deliberately short menu for a French bistro–style cuisine with some exotic touches. The wine list is particularly well chosen.

SERVED UP

63°C oeuf en meurette (delicately poached eggs in a red wine sauce), Madagascar vanilla and salted butter caramel mille-feuille.

Le Grand Pan

📍 20, rue Rosenwald,
Paris 15th. €€

From the lièvre à la royale (hare) served in fall to the lobster served in summer, chef Benoît Gauthier masters cooking and flavors. His bistro is a blast from the past. The two rooms are separated by a central bar, a good spot to settle in.

SERVED UP

Mauléon veal chop, lièvre à la royale.

Le Cassenoix

📍 56, rue de la Fédération, Paris 15th. €€

A collection of antique objects for the decor and a cuisine well in tune with its time, enlivened thanks to a chef who knows how to play up the home-style dishes. Listed on the board is a nice selection of wines at affordable prices.

SERVED UP

A melting pork cheek, cabbage Belle-Hélène, and house-made ice cream.

Victor

📍 101 bis, rue Lauriston, Paris 16th. €€

An irresistible charm, a warm welcome, and a cellar bringing together both grands crus—some served by the glass—and more accessible labels.

SERVED UP

House-made pâté en croûte, caramelized roasted apple, sablé Breton tart with Granny Smith coulis.

Brigitte

📍 16, av. de Villiers,
Paris 17th. €€€

An elegant bistro whose ambience is defined by the dining room with cozy nooks inviting discreet discussions and the service by apron-clad waiters. A cuisine respectful of the seasons, with plates focused on flavor and an eye-pleasing presentation. A beautiful wine list with a relevant choice of wines by the glass, constantly updated.

SERVED UP

Hangar steak with Béarnaise sauce, Monsieur Paul's gaufre (waffle) with house-made whipped cream and chocolate sauce.

Caves Pétrissans

📍 30 bis, av. Niel,
Paris 17th. €€€

This institution, created at the end of the nineteenth century, maintains its certain elegance representative of the Fourth Republic. Why change a formula that works? Daily (or weekly) specials and traditional dishes (excellent house-made charcuterie) are offered as part of the hearty menu. Exceptional wine cellar.

SERVED UP

Tête de veau (calf's head—maybe the best in Paris), veal kidney flambéed with Armagnac.

Goupil Le Bistro

📍 4, rue Claude-Debussy, Paris 17th. €€€

Bourgeois bistro traditions are represented here and served to a serious clientele of aficionados who applaud the place enthusiastically. Plates are served up on a wide terrace or in one of the three dining rooms. The dishes are nearly timeless and as well presented as they are generous.

SERVED UP

Chateaubriand with peppercorn sauce and sautéed potatoes, vanilla vacherin and cherries.

Le Cadoret

📍 1, rue Pradier,
Paris 19th. €

A figure in the Belleville gastronomic scene, Léa Fleuriot runs this welcoming bistro with her brother Louis-Marie. She offers absolute comfort with her straightforward food, for which her talents are well suited.

SERVED UP

Leeks vinaigrette, Scotch egg, house-made rillettes, and fish fritters with tartar sauce.

Café Lignac.

Le Bistrot de Paris.

Auberge Pyrénées Cévennes, above and at right.

BRASSERIES Les Brasseries

Whether historic or newly established, these large-scale restaurants embody the Parisian art of living. —FRANÇOIS-RÉGIS GAUDRY

THE HISTORIC PLACES

Le Grand Colbert

⚲ 2, rue Vivienne, Paris 2nd. €€

This hot spot is worth a visit to see its classified facade, carved pilasters, Pompeian frescoes, and floor mosaics. It's also worth a visit for its sole meunière, veal blanquette (veal in white sauce), and house-roasted chicken and house-made fries. There is also an oyster bar.

Vaudeville

⚲ 29, rue Vivienne, Paris 2nd. €€

A former café of the eponymous theater where *La Dame au camélia* by Albert Dumas fils triumphed, this Art Deco temple combines marble, opaline chandeliers, and a mosaic floor. On the menu is a wide choice of seafood and all the safe bets: Norman steak tartare and andouillette AAAAA, not to mention tête de veau (calf's head).

Bofinger

⚲ 5–7, rue de la Bastille, Paris 4th. €€

Founded in 1864 by Frédéric Bofinger, a pioneer of draft beer, this institution with historical decor (a stained-glass dome, copper railings, marquetry panels) has maintained its original Alsatian accent with onion soup with Muenster cheese, flammekueche (pizzalike flatbread), mussels in Riesling, glazed kugelhopf, and a large selection of sauerkraut.

Mollard

⚲ 115, rue Saint-Lazare, Paris 8th. €€

Independently owned since its opening in 1895 opposite the Saint-Lazare train station, this Art Nouveau jewel dazzles with its decoration classified as a historical monument and impresses with its oyster bar and traditional specialties: Chateaubriand Béarnaise, veal kidneys flambéed with cognac, baked Alaska.

Floderer

⚲ 7, cours des Petites-Écuries, Paris 10th. €€

"The cathedral of Alsatian cuisine since 1818," says the slogan. In fact, apart from the opulent Strasbourg sauerkraut, this German tavern decorated with molded woodwork, stained-glass windows, and coffered ceilings serves the Parisian classics: seafood, Charolais steak tartare, fresh frites (fries), dark-rum baba.

THE INSTITUTIONS

Le Balzar

⚲ 49, rue des Écoles, Paris 5th. €

Founded in 1886, as the institution claims. Or was it in 1931? One thing is certain: with its globe-domed lights from the 1930s and modernist tiles, this is the Sorbonne students' favorite brasserie, frequented by Barthes, Lacan, Sartre, and Beauvoir. The bistro-style menu cheerfully includes celery rémoulade, harengs pommes à l'huile (herring mixed with cooked potatoes), beef bourguignon, and profiteroles.

Chez Savy

⚲ 23, rue Bayard, Paris 8th. €€

"A reliable business since 1923": this is the motto of this small brasserie just near the Champs-Élysées serving up knife-chopped steak tartare, duck confit with sautéed potatoes, sole meunière, and rice pudding.

Le Stella

⚲ 133, av. Victor-Hugo, Paris 16th. €€

A sunny terrace, an oyster bar, and top-notch service. This traditional brasserie delights with top sirloin steak with shallots, oeuf mayonnaise, onion soup, and île flottante (poached meringues floating on a vanilla custard sauce).

CHIC BRASSERIES

Chez Les Anges

⚲ 54, blvd. de la Tour-Maubourg, Paris 7th. €€

Founded in 1952 by Armand Monassier, and owned in the 1980s by Paul Minchelli, this brasserie is now led by Jacques Lapicière. Its decor, designed by François Champsaur, is chic and comfortable, and it offers traditional cuisine: sole de Saint-Gilles-Croix-de-Vie meunière, parsleyed pâté de tête (country-style headcheese pâté), and bistronomy-style dishes (coquille Saint-Jacques from Brittany and truffled parsnip purée).

Les 110 de Taillevent

⚲ 195, rue du Faubourg-Saint-Honoré, Paris 8th. €€€

Between the solid oak and the golden frescoes of a chic Pierre-Yves Rochon setting, this posh table offers 110 wines, sold by the glass and kept in a refrigerated cabinet 23 feet (7 m) long. Here is found neotraditional cuisine: vol-au-vent with sauce financière (Madeira and truffle sauce), panfried sweetbreads, Chartreuse soufflé.

Mimosa

⚲ 2, rue Royale, Paris 8th. €€€

Jean-François Piège is at the helm of this large space with neo–Art Deco and Côte d'Azur styles. The menu is inspired by foods in the spirit of the Riviera: deviled eggs, pistou pasta, lobster grilled over embers, petits farcis (small stuffed vegetables), and aged meats cooked over a wood fire. There is a beautiful terrace in the courtyard of the Hôtel de la Marine.

Girafe

⚲ 1, pl. du Trocadéro-et-du-11-Novembre, Paris 16th. €€€

After Monsieur Bleu at the Palais de Tokyo, Laurent de Gourcuff launched this seafood-focused brasserie in the heart of the Cité de l'Architecture. It's a space with a cozy decor (created by Joseph Dirand in a 1930s style), a large choice of shellfish, local wines, and dishes with Japanese-Peruvian inspirations. The terrace faces the Eiffel Tower.

NEO-BRASSERIES

Le Gallopin

⚲ 40, rue Notre-Dame-des-Victoires, Paris 2nd. €€

An authentic brasserie, opened in 1976, and relaunched by Mathieu Bucher. The Victorian woodwork, the 1900s glass roof, and the Delft earthenware-tile fireplace have regained their brilliance. The menu pays homage to the bourgeois tradition: beef filet au poivre, baked Alaska, and contemporary inspirations including salmon miso and creamy spicy cod.

Grand Brasserie

⚲ 6, rue de la Bastille, Paris 4th. €€

Previously known as Petit Bofinger, it retains the Art Deco charm. The rest is the creativity of new boss Adrien Spanu, offering nostalgic cuisine (cromesquis escargot, batter-dipped and fried croquettes), house-made terrine, Liège coffee, southern touches (tomate à l'antiboise, stuffed tomatoes), grand aïoli, and a commanding selection of natural wines.

Terminus Nord

⚲ 23, rue de Dunkerque, Paris 10th. €€

Founded in 1925 opposite the Gare du Nord, this brasserie has regained all the brilliance of its interior and Art Deco mirrors under the direction of English decorator John Whelan. The brasserie sends out the classics: onion soup gratinée, parsleyed calf's liver, sole meunière, and île flottante (poached meringues floating on a vanilla custard sauce).

Brasserie Bellanger

⚲ 140, rue du Faubourg-Poissonnière, Paris 10th. €

This is the folkloric and typical allegory of the Parisian brasserie: traditional kitsch decor, waiters dashing between the tables, and seasonal cuisine based on products arriving directly from French producers. Leeks vinaigrette, oeuf mayonnaise, skate wing from Grenoble, sausage with mashed potatoes—all the classics are on call.

And . . .

Brasserie Dubillot

⚲ 222, rue Saint-Denis, Paris 2nd. €

Brasserie Martin

⚲ 24, rue Saint-Ambroise, Paris 11th. €

Grand Brasserie.

Brasserie Bellanger.

Terminus Nord.

Le Balzar.

Girafe.

Le Grand Colbert.

Mollard.

Les 110 de Taillevent.

Bofinger.

Le Dôme *vs* La Rotonde

These two historic restaurants face each other on the boulevard du Montparnasse. And they compete on the culinary and intellectual scenes.

LE DÔME	LA ROTONDE
108, blvd. du Montparnasse, Paris 14th	105, blvd. du Montparnasse, Paris 6th

FOUNDED

In 1897 or 1898 by Paul Chambon, from Auvergne.	In 1903, taken over in 1911 by Victor Libion, from Auvergne.

THE OWNERS

Maxime and Édouard Bras, brothers from Auvergne.	Serge and Gérard Tafanel, brothers from Cantal.

THE DECOR

Created by Slavik and implemented by designer Axel Huynh. White tablecloths, bouquets of fresh flowers, and 100 seats in the dining room. A terrace of greenery with 30 seats.	Chic and comfortable, with red velvet banquettes, white tablecloths, soft lighting, and 158 seats in the dining room. Corner terrace with 36 seats.

THE CUISINE

Japanese chef Yoshihiko Miura orchestrates great traditional plates focused on the sea: roasted turbot with Béarnaise sauce, blue lobster flambéed with cognac, Marseille bouillabaisse. €€€	Chef Franck Gonnet sends out great classics: organic oeuf mayonnaise, Burgundy escargots, haddock with Nantes butter, leg of lamb from Lozère with sage. Oyster bar. €€

THE REGULARS

Amélie Nothomb and Jean-Christophe Grangé (Albin Michel is 262 feet/80 m away), Franz-Olivier Giesbert, Pierce Brosnan, and Bono during each of their stays in the capital.	Publishers, writers, journalists, and politicians. On April 23, 2017, Emmanuel Macron celebrated his victory here during the first round of the presidential election.

SKIP TO

La Closerie des Lilas, p. 112; Le Train Bleu, p. 125; Au Pied de Cochon, p. 361; Brasserie Lipp, p. 259; La Coupole, p. 296; Seafood Spots, p. 364.

CAFÉS Les Cafés

Parisian par excellence, cafés sometimes do much more than serve coffee, they set the table in their own style. —YVES NESPOULOUS

Le Bougainville.

Sunset.

Café du Coin.

Chez Jeannette.

The "caffé" houses

Since their appearance in Paris in 1671, the "maisons de caffé" have gradually become a scene for all social classes, growing in Paris from about three hundred cafés in 1716 to more than three thousand at the end of the eighteenth century.

Alongside the "aristocratic" cafés that created the legend of a social and sociable Paris,* natives of Auvergne operated the first artisan shops during the Second Empire, but they closed because of the industrial revolution. The cafés were thus transformed into wood and coal depots, with hot coffee served as a bonus. These spots were referred to as cafés-charbons, or bougnats. The cafés of the working-class neighborhoods were popular because of their sociable character. Blue-collar workers would gather here to warm up, eat, and socialize among their native culinary and musical traditions. As such, the café became an emblem of Parisian life that was adopted by all social classes and artists, contributing to the Parisian legend.
* *Tout Paris au café* written by Maxime Rude in 1877.

"Cafés became part of the Parisian legend."
—Léon-Paul Fargue, *Refuges*, 1942

Le Bougainville

9 5, rue de la Banque, Paris 2nd. €

THE PLACE
On the edge of the chic Galerie Vivienne is this very popular café whose neon lights, faceted columns, and Formica counter have stood the test of time but remained in fashion.

SERVED UP
Impeccable classics: house-made terrine, Aubrac steak tartare, petits farcis (small stuffed vegetables), tart of the day, and the finest charcuterie and cheeses from Auvergne.

Le Petit Vendôme

9 8, rue des Capucines, Paris 2nd. €€

THE PLACE
In the heart of this luxury district, this bar has been in its original state since the 1960s, with a mixed clientele and a decor with a piggy motif.

SERVED UP
This bistrolike café serves up simple fare: onion soup gratinée, Burgundy escargots, fried andouillette, grilled pigs' feet, and legendary sandwiches with ham sliced from the bone.

Café Compagnon

9 22–26, rue Léopold-Bellan, Paris 2nd. €€

THE PLACE
After Le Richer and Le 52, coffee roaster–restaurateur Charles Compagnon created an elegant spot buzzing with life amid the decor of red marble from Alicante and the solid oak trim. The drinking chocolate is made on-site, the coffee roasted in-house, and authentic wine selections curated by the owner.

SERVED UP
Bistronomy-style dishes at lunch and dinner (sashimi of peanut and Banka trout, a farm-raised trout from Pays Basque; white tuna and raspberry), and simple fare all day (terrine, Bayonne ham).

Le Progrès

9 1, rue de Bretagne, Paris 3rd. €

THE PLACE
An emblematic Parisian bar-tabac (a neighborhood pub) from the Haut-Marais, this corner café, under red neon lights, enlivens the district with its large terrace and all-day service.

SERVED UP
Only the classics: croque pain Poilâne (croque-monsieur made with Poilâne bread), organic oeuf mayonnaise, and an armada of salads (Caesar, peasant, lentils, and many more).

Café de la Nouvelle Mairie

19, rue des Fossés-Saint-Jacques, Paris 5th. €€

THE PLACE
Located around the Pantheon, where good finds are rare, this café of Aveyron ancestry is a delight among the neighboring record stores.

SERVED UP
Nicely bistrolike, to accompany the string of natural wines: baby leeks with honey vinaigrette, pork sauté with paprika, rhubarb clafoutis, and more.

Tram Café

9 47, rue de la Montagne-Sainte-Geneviève, Paris 5th. €€

THE PLACE
Located on the slopes of Sainte-Geneviève, this is an inspired café-

bookstore with large tables overlooking a tree-lined courtyard.

SERVED UP

Tasty contemporary flavors including mullet ceviche, attractive house-made pastries (for takeout), vegetable aïoli, and a mega croque-monsieur.

Le Select

⚲ *99, blvd. du Montparnasse, Paris 6th. €€*

THE PLACE

Is it an American bar, a café, or a brasserie? There is a bit of all three in this Montparnasse-style establishment where people have come to see and be seen since 1923, from 7 a.m. to 2 a.m.

SERVED UP

Preparing the classics with no surprises but with respect: charcuterie from Maison Conquet, asparagus omelet, Thai tuna tartare, veal chops with chanterelles, tarte Tatin, and more.

Café de la Paix

⚲ *5, pl. de l'Opéra, Paris 9th. €€€*

THE PLACE

Opened in 1862 by Empress Eugénie, this is the former mecca of artsy Paris (Oscar Wilde, Maupassant, and Hugo were regulars). The café is in the purest Napoléon III style and continues to delight, wrapping the corner at the foot of the Opéra Garnier.

SERVED UP

A collection of seafood, foie gras "Café de la Paix," onion soup, grilled sole, club sandwich, and steak tartare—served all day.

Chez Jeannette

⚲ *47, rue du Faubourg-Saint-Denis, Paris 10th. €*

THE PLACE

A long Formica countertop, crown molding, and a chandelier—this is the big brother of Mansart, Sans Souci, and Brasserie Barbès that has become,

from early morning to late at night, a buzzing neighborhood scene.

SERVED UP

Steak tartare, terrines, salads, egg mayonnaise, fried sausage—all the classics.

Delaville Café

⚲ *34–36, blvd. de Bonne-Nouvelle, Paris 10th. €€*

THE PLACE

In the former spot of the sumptuous Marguery restaurant from the 1870s, the Delaville has planted a green terrace among cozy bars, private rooms, and a microbrewery on the Grands Boulevards.

SERVED UP

A taste of the East: labneh, grilled pepper, tahini, prawn tempura, Italian beef carpaccio, Lebanese yogurt, orange flower water flavors.

Au Petit Panisse

⚲ *35, rue de Montreuil, Paris 11th. €*

THE PLACE

In the Aligre market district, this is an ideal Parisian café with its beautiful tiles, vintage walls, spiral staircase, and elbow-to-elbow atmosphere.

SERVED UP

Bistro dishes by Jeff Schilde offer tasty creativity: soft-boiled egg and cream of monkfish liver, roasted sea bream and tahini sauce, and crème caramel.

Café du Coin

⚲ *9, rue Camille-Desmoulins, Paris 11th. €*

THE PLACE

A café from the past revived by the gang known for its popular bars (Grégory Back, Raman Suzat, and Florent Ciccoli), with a large Formica countertop where you can have a drink.

SERVED UP

Little jewels of inventiveness: mini pizzas, churros, and ajo blanco (a Spanish cold white soup) made with haddock milk, grilled buckwheat cream, and nectarine crumble.

Tram Café.

Au Petit Panisse.

Café Compagnon.

Café de Luce

⚲ *2, rue des Trois-Frères, Paris 18th. €€*

THE PLACE

A well-established café in lower Montmartre, with a dream terrace under the trees of Place Charles-Dullin.

SERVED UP

Attended to all day by chef Amandine Chaignot: good croissants, sea bream crudo with lime, frogs' legs with almonds, knife-chopped steak tartare and great frites (fries), house-made tarts.

Sunset

⚲ *100, rue Ordener, Paris 18th. €*

THE PLACE

Located just three steps from the town hall offices of the 18th arrondissement, this nice hole-in-the-wall café has pointillism-style walls and a Generation X clientele.

SERVED UP

Flavorful and shareable plates: red lentil fritters and chimichurri, tuna tartare, horseradish Chantilly cream, pineapple cheesecake, all to be enjoyed after (or before) strong cocktails. Sunday brunch is a must.

Les Pères Populaires

⚲ *46, rue de Buzenval, Paris 20th. €*

THE PLACE

A furnished neighborhood canteen serving up breakfast, snacks, aperitifs, and music for the evening.

SERVED UP

From high-level to simple dishes to lunch at very low prices: labneh and roasted tomatoes, pork spare rib with honey and fennel, apricot crumble, and tapas in the evening.

HOTEL RESTAURANTS
Les Restaurants d'Hôtel

Whether quaint or luxurious, in the city center or in the suburbs, these Parisian hotels elevate the dining experience. —YVES NESPOULOUS

Hôtel Grand Amour.

Mob Hotel.

Hôtel des Grands Boulevards.

Hôtel Molitor.

Les Costes

◊ 239, rue Saint-Honoré, Paris 1st. €€€€

THE PLACE

Velvety rooms by Jacques Garcia with a patio, a house playlist, and an attentive staff. This has been a hot spot for fashionistas and jet-setters since its creation in 1995 by Les Costes.

SERVED UP

Without reproach and for all (luxury) tastes: asparagus with sauce mousseline, caviar, veal chops with morels, Cyril Lignac's éclair.

Hotel des Grands Boulevards

◊ 17, blvd. Poissonnière, Paris 2nd. €€€

THE PLACE

In 2018, the Experimental Group entrusted the decoration of its hotel to Dorothée Meilichzon, offering a terrace with a vegetable garden, a rooftop patio, and a restaurant under a glass roof.

SERVED UP

Italian flavors (by Giovanni Passerini) that hit all the right notes: goat with zucchini, roasted octopus, avocado-lemon-ginger condiment, pineapple pavlova, and more delights.

Hôtel Amour/Hôtel Grand Amour

◊ 8, rue de Navarin, Paris 9th. €€

◊ 18, rue de la Fidélité, Paris 10th. €€

THE PLACE

Opened in 2006 with vintage furniture, the hotel became the gold standard for trendy, playful Paris. Nine years later, its sister Grand Amour rises to the same occasion.

SERVED UP

An eclectic neo-brasserie style with all-day service. Zucchini fritters, grilled calamari with saffron, chocolate mousse at Grand Amour.

Hôtel Rochechouart

◊ 55, blvd. de Rochechouart, Paris 9th. €€€

THE PLACE

A grand Art Deco hotel from 1929 restyled in 2020 by the duo from Festen design group, with a superb dining room and rooftop overlooking Sacré Coeur.

SERVED UP

A very convincing selection within the chic brasserie category. Oeuf mayonnaise with caviar, Colbert whiting fish, île flottante (poached meringues floating on a vanilla custard sauce). In summer, Italian plates are served on the rooftop.

Café Les Deux Gares

◊ 1, rue des Deux-Gares, Paris 10th. €

THE PLACE

A bistro in all its splendor, opposite the hotel that opened in 2020, overlooking the tracks of Gare de l'Est.

SERVED UP

Dishes constructed by Jonathan Schweizer, who joyfully prepares vegetables and striking side dishes: haricots verts, apricots, dill flowers, and burnt garlic.

Hôtel Molitor

◊ 13, rue Nungesser-et-Coli, Paris 16th. €€

THE PLACE

With a terrace overlooking the legendary outdoor swimming pool, this establishment opened in 1929, closed in 1989, then was resurrected as a luxury hotel in 2014.

SERVED UP

A world tour on the plate: tapas, ceviche of line-caught fish, vitello tonnato (sliced veal in a creamy sauce served chilled) streaked with squid ink, aged prime rib, banana-caramel banoffee.

Terrass'

◊ 12–14, rue Joseph-de-Maistre, Paris 18th. €€€

THE PLACE

The Edmond, the restaurant located high up in Montmartre, opened in 1911 and offers a rooftop patio with deck chairs and one of the most "wow" views of the city.

SERVED UP

Friendly foods, like the puff pastry tart with vinegared chanterelles, creamy trofie alle vongole (a short twisted pasta), praline éclair.

Hôtel Particulier

◊ 23, av. Junot, pavillon D, Paris 18th. €€€

THE PLACE

Well hidden in an old bourgeois residence at the top of Butte Montmartre, five suites, a restaurant, a cocktail bar, and a small paradise-like garden.

SERVED UP

The dishes are refined: sea bream tartare with preserved lemon, veal chops with thyme, vanilla-raspberry mille-feuille.

Mama Shelter Paris La Défense

◊ 10, rue Jean-Jaurès, Puteaux (Hauts-de-Seine). €€

THE PLACE

On the fourteenth floor of the latest Parisian Mama Shelter hotel, the penthouse restaurant offers contrast with its hyped-up multicultural decor and the skyline of Paris.

SERVED UP

Creations by *Top Chef* finalist Pierre Chomet: sea bass carpaccio, coquillettes with mostello ham (pasta), crying tiger with Angus hangar, yuzu meringue pie.

Mob Hotel

◊ 6, rue Gambetta, Saint-Ouen (Seine-Saint-Denis). €

THE PLACE

The Karlito canteen is Cyril Aouizerate's latest creation, opened in 2017 behind the flea markets of Saint-Ouen, a connected "village" of brick and wood, with a rooftop vegetable garden, library, concerts, and an open-air cinema.

SERVED UP

Organic and 100 percent Italian. Antipasti, beef polpettes, pizzas, pastas, and limoncello cheesecake.

LATE-NIGHT SPOTS
Les Tables Nocturnes

Until the mid-nineteenth century, restaurants rarely remained open after 11 p.m. To find a place to hang out, night owls had to choose from scandalous locations more conducive to nightlife. — **MARCELLE RATAFIA**

Le Mabillon.

Clandestine suppers

In the 1860s, the cafés on the boulevards became luxury restaurants. Although they were supposed to close at 2 a.m., they would continue to serve customers who arrived to drink, play, and eat in the rooms. Hill's Tavern, for example, was so popular that the establishment wouldn't allow any unknown customers to enter. To gain access, the regulars whispered to the servers the name of one of the private rooms: Shakespeare, Calderon, Byron, as examples. The scandalous nature of discreet suppers became sensationalized after the serial publication of Zola's La Curée in 1871, which was suspended for a time. Readers could discover Renée Saccard having dinner in the "salon blanc" of Café Riche, alone, or with her stepson lover.

Midnight bread

During the Belle Époque, the Châteaudun bakery supplied sustenance for night owls around Pigalle while Racine bakery was a beacon for the late-night streets around Odéon. At 2 a.m., the bakery became La Tartine du Père Beauvy, full to bursting with students of the Beaux-Arts, medical students out for pleasure, and disheveled partygoers. The solo barkeep would make mountains of sandwiches to order. In Nuits à Paris (1889), the nightman Rodolphe Darzens describes the gesture of the sandwich maestro, deaf to the noise emitted by the clientele: "He holds his big knife without letting go . . . he uses it to split the buns, spreads on them a light smear of butter, then places on them a thin, pink strip of ham."

Au Pied de Cochon

⚲ 6, rue Coquillière, Paris 1st. €€

🕐 24 hours a day

Since 1947, this institution in Les Halles has continuously delighted workers, partygoers, presidents, showbiz stars, and even the France rugby team. On the menu is pigs' feet (of course) and charcuterie and onion soup gratinée.

Le Babylone bis

⚲ 34, rue Tiquetonne, Paris 2nd. €€

🕐 8 p.m. to 6 a.m.

On the walls are photos of celebrities who have arrived to enjoy Creole and Caribbean dishes until the early hours: Lenny Kravitz, Manu Payet, the Twins, Stevie Wonder, and Rihanna, among others.

Le Bienvenu

⚲ 42, rue d'Argout, Paris 2nd. €€

🕐 12:30 p.m. to 2 p.m. and 7 p.m. to 5 a.m.

This small Moroccan restaurant offers couscous and tagines to taxi drivers, postal workers, and journalists who start or end their day at dawn.

Le Mabillon

⚲ 164, blvd. Saint-Germain, Paris 6th. €€

🕐 8 a.m. to 5 a.m.

Very early for breakfast or brunch on Sunday, all the rest of the day and until 5 a.m. to enjoy brasserie dishes and cocktails in an elegant and cozy setting.

L'Alsace

⚲ 39, av. des Champs-Élysées, Paris 8th. €€

🕐 9 a.m. to 4 a.m. on weekends, 9 a.m. to 2 a.m. on weekdays

Sauerkraut and Alsatian wine and brasserie classics, including seafood platters.

Le Rey

⚲ 130, rue de la Roquette, Paris 11th. €€

🕐 7:30 a.m. to 4 a.m.

Brasserie dishes that satisfy nocturnal appetites. Continuous service at all hours.

Le Dalou

⚲ 30, pl. de la Nation, Paris 12th. €€

🕐 5 a.m. to 3 a.m.

Traditional brasserie dishes, mussels, and oysters served until 3 a.m. for night owls and artists; classic breakfast from 5 a.m.

RESTAURANTS FOR MEAT LOVERS
Les Restaurants de Viande

Between the very typical Parisian bistros with their meat dishes, eat-in butcher shops, and all the newcomer steak houses, meat lovers are spoiled for choice in the capital. — JACQUES BRUNEL

The legend of steak frites

Steak frites is one of the favorite dishes of the French, and it is an emblem of the Parisian bistro. The dish's popularity originates in England, where beef reigns. A pioneer in cattle breeding and transport, England introduced butchery vocabulary (steak, rosbif, etc.) into the French language. Easy, quick to cook, though expensive, the "biftèque" (beef steak) has long been the delicacy of butchers (the restaurant Au Boeuf Couronné opened in 1865 near the slaughterhouses of La Villette, and Le Louchébem opened five years later in Les Halles), the rich, and hearty eaters, registering in the imagination as the most vital and carnal aspects of eating. In a postwar period under American influence, grilled steak (with its very "French" fries) became a proletarian dish for routiers (truck drivers). From 1850 to 2022, per capita meat consumption in France increased from 50 to 190 pounds (23 to 85 kg) per year! Today, food trends encourage us to be less carnivorous, and perhaps this is for the better.

THE PIONEERS

The Louchébem

📍 31, rue Berger, Paris 1st. €€

This folkloric bistro's name is the term for butchers' slang (louchébem). The bistro is popular with tourists, and after enjoying excellent bone marrow, try a piece of (well) grilled 100 percent French beef. There is a wide selection of charcuterie.

CHOICE SELECTION
Skirt steak from the Blonde d'Aquitaine, which is extra tender and well marbled.

Au Boeuf Couronné

📍 188, av. Jean-Jaurès, Paris 19th. €€

A vestige of the butchery activities around La Villette, this brasserie, which is more than a hundred years old, elevates beautiful beef cuts aged twenty days, from cows raised in France: marbled rib eye (14 oz/400 g), pavé des mandataires steak (11oz/300 g, as a fillet).

CHOICE SELECTION
Served for two, the grilled prime rib (2½ lb/1,200 g and most often Norman beef) is accompanied by soufflé potatoes, a now-rare delicacy.

MEAT-CENTRIC BISTROS

Bien Élevé

📍 47, rue Richer, Paris 9th. €€

The Angus beef from Châteauneuf is most definitely well raised within the area's extensive farm in the Pas-de-Calais, where natural grazing and animal welfare are paramount. Aged for forty days, its exceptional meat is ideally cooked in a Josper grill (a hybrid grill and oven).

CHOICE SELECTION
The meltingly textured rib eye with its deep flavors accompanied by fries cooked in beef fat.

Le Flamboire

📍 54, rue Blanche, Paris 9th. €€€

This shabby-chic little spot serves exceptional well-aged Aubrac meats shipped by the Conquet brothers in Laguiole. It is a sight to see the meat cooking in the splendid wood-fired hearth, which gives it a divine, slightly smoky taste.

CHOICE SELECTION
The grilled prime rib, tender and juicy.

Le Severo

📍 8, rue des Plantes, Paris 14th. €€

This charming bistro is dedicated to French and Bavarian meats that William Bernet, the butcher-restaurateur, ages (thirty days for the fillet, eighty for the prime rib) and Chef Beguin prepares grilled or tataki. There is a nice selection of wines.

CHOICE SELECTION
Beef tenderloin, peppercorn sauce, served with fries.

STEAKHOUSES

Clover Grill

📍 6, rue Bailleul, Paris 1st. €€€

The top of its kind, by Jean-François Piège: chic and clever decor (marble tables), starters, stunning desserts, and a collection of high-quality meats selected by Olivier Metzger: Bavarian, Black Market beef from Australia, Blonde d'Aquitaine, all of which you can admire in the window before enjoying.

CHOICE SELECTION
Baltic Black rib eye aged with beechwood, served with buttered mashed potatoes.

Le Beef

📍 33, rue des Rosiers, Paris 4th. €€

In the heart of the Marais, this carnivorous location offers various purebred meats from ethical breeding, aged on shells in the cellar, and then cooked in grapeseed oil before being finished in herbed clarified butter.

CHOICE SELECTION
The Simmental rump steak pavé that lingers on the palate.

Beef Bar

📍 5, rue Marbeuf, Paris 8th. €€€

An Art Nouveau gem with mosaics and a glass ceiling, the decor is as posh as the grilled steaks served: Wagyu and Black Angus, but also French beef, such as the marinated hanger steak grilled on the barbecue accompanied by chimichurri rojo.

CHOICE SELECTION
The French-beef Chateaubriand, 21 ounces (600 g) for two, with house-made mashed potatoes.

EAT-IN BUTCHER SHOPS

Bidoche

📍 7, rue Jean-Pierre-Timbaud, Paris 11th. €€

Blue walls and wooden tables greet you in this space. Alexandre de Toulmon, the butcher-chef, loves the pasture-raised breeds from France's southwest regions: the Limousin and the Bazas, both tender and refined.

CHOICE SELECTION
A place of three chosen cuts (11 oz/300 g), grilled up and served with fries cooked in beef fat.

Boucherie Les Provinces

📍 20, rue d'Aligre, Paris 12th. €€

In this pocket-sized space, you can choose a cut of French beef, carefully aged, nicely grilled à la plancha by butcher Christophe Dru, and enjoy it at one of the few tables. There are also delightful pork dishes and organic wines.

CHOICE SELECTION
The Irish hanger steak, with new potatoes.

La Table d'Hugo Desnoyer

📍 28, rue du Docteur-Blanche, Paris 16th. €€

The star of butchers and butcher to the stars, Hugo Desnoyer has set up, near his stall, three tables in the shape of a chopping block where sixteen people can feast on his selected cuts that he has expertly aged and sliced and grilled in a way that shows love for his craft.

CHOICE SELECTION
The suckling veal chop from Corrèze (12 oz/350g) with seasonal vegetables.

SKIP TO
Le Relais de Venise, p. 109; Butcher Shops, p. 316.

The mixed-cuts plate from Bidoche.

The prime rib from Au Boeuf Couronné.

The skirt steak from Louchébem.

The strip sirloin from Bien Élevé.

The beef tenderloin from Le Severo.

The suckling veal chop from Hugo Desnoyer.

The Irish hanger steak from Boucherie Les Provinces.

The prime rib from Clover Grill.

The prime rib from Le Flamboire.

The Chateaubriand from Beef Bar.

SEAFOOD SPOTS
Les Tables Marines

Whether you prefer fresh water or salt water, you'll be sure to find a pearl among the capital's seafood establishments.

—CHARLES PATIN O'COOHOON AND MARILOU PETRICOLA

La Cagouille.

Divellec, above and below.

Le Rech.

Clamato.

A fragile commodity

The population of Paris has consumed fish since the Middle Ages, especially for religious reasons, but the city of Paris has imposed regulations around the sale of fish only since the thirteenth century. Fresh fish sold from March to October must be sold on the day of its arrival in the capital. During the rest of the year, fish must be sold within two days, a rule that favors the ports of Normandy and northern France due to their temperatures and proximity to the capital.

THE HISTORIC PLACES

La Méditerranée

⊙ 2, pl. de l'Odéon, Paris 6th. €€€

This brand, created by Jean Subrenat in 1942, quickly became a popular place for the Parisian smart set. It awards the annual Medici literary prize.

THE DECOR

Choose between the large, bright, and warm dining room and private lounges. The Mediterranean is represented here, served on plates designed by Jean Cocteau, and on the frescoes on the wall, painted by the artist Christian Bérard.

SERVED UP

Marinated sardines, rockfish soup, Breton sole meunière, red mullet with black tagliatelle.

Divellec

⊙ 18, rue Fabert, Paris 7th. €€€

Founded in 1983 by Jacques Le Divellec, this fish-loving institution, frequented by politicians, was taken over by chef Mathieu Pacaud.

THE DECOR

Green plants, blue mosaic flooring, comfortable blue-gray and teal banquettes.

SERVED UP

The royal seafood platter, blue lobster from Brittany, large fish to share (salt-crusted sea bass, young turbot with sauce Béarnaise, and John Dory cooked on a block of Himalayan salt).

Rech

⊙ 217, blvd. Saint-Germain, Paris 7th. €€€

Adrien Rech arrived in Paris from Alsace in 1925 and opened a grocery-café-restaurant at 62, avenue des Ternes where guests could enjoy oysters—it was an immediate success! Taken over by Alain Ducasse in 2007, the location was set up in the heart of the Maison de l'Amérique Latine in 2021.

THE DECOR

Tableware by Belgian designer and ceramist Pieter Stockmans, sea-centric decor in wood and brass, and bay windows.

SERVED UP

A thick cut of monkfish seared in butter, the legendary skate wing with capers, a giant coffee or chocolate éclair.

Helen

⊙ 3, rue Berryer, Paris 8th. €€

The great seafood classics rub shoulders here, depending on the catch: capon (a large scorpionfish 20 in./50 cm long), pulpito (small octopus with tender flesh), or denti (from the sea bream family).

THE DECOR

A refined location adorned with white tablecloths and blue velvet.

SERVED UP

Young turbot roasted with sage and pancetta, a small bouillabaisse of red mullet, suquet de poisson (a Catalan-style fish stew).

La Luna

⊙ 69, rue du Rocher, Paris 8th. €€

Since 1992, Catherine Delaunay has carefully selected the fish and shellfish that chef Michel Choisnel prepares in this temple of the sea.

THE DECOR

Carpet, benches, and armchairs, all in red, white tablecloths, and pop-art posters on the walls.

SERVED UP

Line-caught fish for two grilled over coals or, for a touch of exoticism, gilthead sea bream in banana leaf.

Marius et Janette

⊙ 4, av. George V, Paris 8th. €€€

Docked in the heart of the Golden Triangle, this institution salutes the sea under the leadership of chef Laurent Audiot.

THE DECOR

With its large room all in varnished wood, fishing rods and portholes on the walls, the restaurant has the appearance of a luxurious yacht.

SERVED UP

Beautiful panfried small-catch sole with demi-sel butter, linguine with clams, rockfish soup.

Le Chardenoux

📍 *1, rue Jules-Vallès, Paris 11th. €€*

A historic bistro founded in 1908 by the Chardenoux family. Today, Cyril Lignac creates the sea-loving menu.

THE DECOR

In this recently renovated historical monument, the superb pewter and wrought-iron moldings and borders rub shoulders with the floral ceiling created by Swedish architect-designer Martin Brudnizki.

SERVED UP

Lobster roll in a soft brioche bun, langoustine ravioli.

Le Cagouille

📍 *10, pl. Constantin-Brancusi, Paris 14th. €€*

Although its name means "snail" in Charente, it is fish that earns the reputation for this establishment created in 1981 by Gérard Allemandou, now run by André Robert.

THE DECOR

The covered terrace and the cozy interior (woodwork and fishing nets) make you forget the proximity to Montparnasse.

SERVED UP

Blunt jackknife clams in lemon butter, sea trout steak, grilled young turbot.

Le Duc

📍 *243, blvd. Raspail, Paris 14th. €€€*

Though the restaurant was opened by Jean Minchelli in the late 1960s, the nautical menu is part of the new culinary wave: less sauce, less cooking, and raw fish.

THE DECOR

The woodwork, carpets, and fish engravings on the wall immerse diners in a chic marine atmosphere.

SERVED UP

Steamed turbot, red mullet meunière, John Dory fillets with vodka butter.

Sur Mer.

Le Rech, above and at right.

Le Wepler.

Le Collier de la Reine.

Dessirier

📍 *9, pl. du Maréchal-Juin, Paris 17th. €€€*

This fish temple opened in 1883. Since 1996, it has been the flagship of the sea by the Rostang family.

THE DECOR

A chic brasserie with mirrors of different shapes and materials, banquettes, and white tablecloths.

SERVED UP

The bouillabaisse in two courses, the sea bass steak cooked rare.

Le Wepler

📍 *14, pl. de Clichy, Paris 18th. €€*

Specializing in seafood since 1892, this legendary brasserie founded by Conrad Wepler has welcomed writers and painters sitting around its huge oyster platters.

THE DECOR

Art Deco decor, moleskin banquettes, a *W* logo engraved on the windows and chandeliers. The poem *L'Étranger* by Charles Baudelaire is inscribed on an interior wall.

SERVED UP

A richly stocked seafood platter, sauerkraut.

THE NEW GUARD

Le Collier de la Reine

📍 *57, rue Charlot, Paris 3rd. €€*

The team Savoir Vivre (of Déviant and Vivant 2) rubs shoulders in this trendy seafood brasserie. There is an excellent natural wine cellar below.

THE DECOR

Orderly banquettes and filtered light.

SERVED UP

Huge seafood platters (Prince, King, or Queen) or more land-based options, such as eggs à la moscovite (boiled eggs with sardine, truffle, and caviar), artichoke-stuffed cabbage.

Sur Mer

📍 *53, rue de Lancry, Paris 10th. €€*

A pocket-sized restaurant where chef Olive Davoux cooks with great precision, adapting to arrivals and the product delivered, favoring small-boat catches.

THE DECOR

A one-room kitchen with a few tables set outside.

SERVED UP

Dishes to share, oysters with spicy sauce, raw scallops, whole fish.

Clamato

📍 *80, rue de Charonne, Paris 11th. €€*

Behind a green storefront hides this seafood-centric spot by Bertrand Grébaut and Théophile Pourriat (Septime).

THE DECOR

A seaside atmosphere with a large picture window, wooden ceiling, tiled floor, and large corner counter.

SERVED UP

Shellfish, ceviche, tataki, and whole fish from sustainable fishing sources, to share and to wash down with a vin vivant (living wine) from the wine list.

L'Écailler du Bistrot

📍 *22, rue Paul-Bert, Paris 11th. €€*

The little brother to Bistrot Paul Bert gives pride of place to oysters, all for the choosing from the slate board hanging on the wall, each classified by origin.

THE DECOR

Beautiful earthenware tiles on the wall and blue mosaic on the floor.

SERVED UP

Seafood platter, Kari Gosse–style blue lobster with house-made fries.

VEGETARIAN EATERIES
Les Tables Végétales

Slowly but surely, the trend of plant-based eating has swept through the capital. Here's a selection of eateries where you can graze on your favorite vegetables. —CHARLES PATIN O'COOHOON AND MARILOU PETRICOLA

Origins of vegetarianism in Paris

Anglo-Saxon and German-influenced vegetarianism gained a foothold in Paris in 1850. The "Pythagorean," or "vegetable-based," diet found its fervent defenders in high society and intellectual circles thanks to arguments for hygiene and religious justification. Vegetarianism spread to social salons, though not yet to restaurants at the time. In Zurich, Hiltl, the world's first vegetarian restaurant, opened in 1898. The 1970s and the hippie movement saw the first such establishments open in the capital with the restaurant Aquarius (Paris 14th) and Grand Appétit (Paris 4th), both now permanently closed.

THE PIONEER

Le Grenier de Notre-Dame

📍 *18, rue de la Bûcherie, Paris 5th.* €€

Opened in 1978 when the idea of a meat-free meal was in its infancy. Here you can enjoy couscous, cassoulet, or a burger fashioned from organic products and often gluten-free.

VEGETARIAN RESTAURANTS

La Guinguette d'Angèle

100% GLUTEN FREE

📍 *34, rue Coquillière, Paris 1st* €

📍 *7, rue Cadet, Paris 9th.* €

From her tiny shop and her takeout counter, former naturopath Angèle Ferreux-Maeght offers delicious gluten-free lunch boxes made with superfoods to enjoy while sipping detoxing juices.

Bob's

📍 *Parent company: Bob's Juice Bar—15, rue Lucien-Sampaix, Paris 10th.* €

www.bobsjuicebar.com

It's a juice bar, bagel bar, and cake bar—American Marc Grossman has managed to re-create the atmosphere of trendy healthy coffee shops in New York.

IMA Cantine

📍 *39, quai de Valmy, Paris 10th.* €

You could spend the day here tasting all there is to offer, from fluffy pancakes made with ricotta to tapas for aperitifs, salads, tarts, and crêpes with Mediterranean influences.

Le Daily Syrien Veggie

📍 *72, rue du Faubourg-Saint-Denis, Paris 10th.* €

The standard for falafel and poultry liver sandwiches has doubled down with this vegetarian location offering first-rate meze: hummus, lentil purée, za'atar cake, and cheese-filled turnovers.

Sapid

📍 *54, rue de Paradis, Paris 10th.* €

In this all-wood interior eatery by Romain Meder and Marvic Medina, well-sourced vegetables are offered alongside plant-based seafoods low in fat but rich in flavor, and the desserts are not too sugary. Served with unique blends of detox juices.

Sezono

📍 *13, rue Jacques Louvel-Tessier, Paris 10th.* €

Chef Ai Loan showcases vegetables on her plates, respecting the seasons and local farm-fresh products. The locamole is a must-try: in place of avocado, a mixture of broccoli and split peas is enlivened with herbs and preserved lemon.

Soya

📍 *106, quai de Jemmapes, Paris 10th.* €€

📍 *20, rue de la Pierre-Levée, Paris 11th.* €€

A shop and lunch counter where the offerings are healthy and flavorful and can be enjoyed in pleasant spaces. A firm favorite is the large plate of mezes, an assortment of vegetables, makis, soyafels (soy-based falafels), dips, and pickled vegetables.

Le Mezzé du Chef

📍 *80, rue de Ménilmontant, Paris 20th.* €

In this shop painted in red, the chef orchestrates a plethora of vegetable mezes: hummus, eggplant caviar, and the specialty, cig köfte (a meatball made from nuts, tomato, bell pepper, and spices).

VEGAN RESTAURANTS

Wild and the Moon

100% GLUTEN FREE

📍 *25, rue des Gravilliers, Paris 3rd.* €+ *8 locations*

The decor features cream-colored walls and plants on the ceiling. Cold-pressed juices and smoothies as rich in flavor as they are in nutrients are available, as are granola bowls, sandwiches, salads, and burgers, all gluten-free, organic, and free of refined sugars.

Le Potager Du Marais

📍 *26, rue Saint-Paul, Paris 4th.* €€

Since 2003, a creative 100 percent plant-based cuisine, with organic ingredients and many gluten-free dishes: mushroom tart, seaweed tartare, etc.

Abattoir Végétal

📍 *9, rue Guisarde, Paris 6th.* €

In this former butcher shop, meat is replaced by healthy and colorful dishes made from organic, seasonal, and local products and almost entirely gluten-free. For an aperitif, try the vegetable cheese board from Jay & Joy.

So Nat

📍 *5, rue Bourdaloue, Paris 9th.* €

Zohra Levacher cooks succulent bowls and vegetarian pitas with an approach that limits waste while working with local producers.

Le Potager de Charlotte

📍 *12, rue Louise-Émilie-de-La-Tour-d'Auvergne, Paris 9th.* €€

📍 *21, rue Rennequin, Paris 17th.* €€

The Valentin brothers, restaurateurs and naturopaths, deliver a creative cuisine punctuated by seasonal offerings. You can taste yummy rigatoni and avocado styled as deviled egg using hummus.

Plan D—Dwich & Glace

22, rue des Vinaigriers, Paris 10th. €

Try an insane blend of seasonal vegetables between two slices of soft bread toasted in olive oil. The oat-milk sundae deserves mention.

Sol Semilla

100% GLUTEN FREE

📍 *23, rue des Vinaigriers, Paris 10th.* €

At this plant-based, organic, and gluten-free eatery, the bowls are filled with superfoods: spirulina, a source of fiber, and acai, replenishing. Everything is carefully sourced with a sustainable approach.

Tien Hiang

📍 *14, rue Bichat, Paris 10th.* €

Pad Thai, phò, and bò bún are among the options of southeast Asian cuisine here—but made using soy protein. They may fool the eye, but delicious flavors are revealed. This was the first Asian vegetarian restaurant in Paris, opened in the 1990s.

Le Potager de Charlotte.

Plan D—Dwich & Glace.

Abattoir Végétal.

Elsa et Justin.

La Guinguette d'Angèle, above and at right.

Soya.

Plan D—Dwich & Glace.

OUTDOOR CAFÉS
Les Guinguettes

These open-air cafes and taverns ring nostalgic for seventeenth- and eighteenth-century Paris when they flourished as a gathering place for the laboring class. Today, when sunny days arrive along the banks of the Marne and Seine, some establishments still offer the opportunity to dance to an accordion tune after lunch. —**MARILOU PETRICOLA**

Do you speak guinguette slang?

RIPAILLER
To have a feast

GRENOUILLER
To drink a lot

GAMBILLER
To dance

La Bonne Franquette

📍 *18, rue Saint-Rustique, Paris 18th. €€*

Open since the sixteenth century (formerly Aux Billards en Bois).

DECOR
Two terraces, an interior with walls covered in the works of artists who were regulars (Renoir, Monet, Zola, Cézanne; Van Gogh painted *La Guinguette à Montmartre* in 1886), and a huge interior garden with a central linden tree.

RIPAILLER
Beef bourguignon, escargots, onion soup gratinée.

GRENOUILLER
More than two hundred labels of wines and spirits.

GAMBILLER
Every evening there is singing by the piano, and special events organized throughout the year include a day to celebrate wine. The slogan here: "Love, eat, drink, and sing."

Chez Gégène

📍 *162 bis, quai de Polangis, allée des Guinguettes, Joinville-le-Pont (Val-de-Marne). €€*

Founded by Eugène Favreux in 1918.

DECOR
Red-and-white checkered tablecloths, a glass ceiling, a dance hall, and a terrace on the banks of the Marne.

RIPAILLER
Fried foods, rack of lamb, foie gras toast.

GRENOUILLER
A glass of Sauvignon Blanc or red Burgundy.

GAMBILLER
On Saturday and Sunday afternoons from early April to mid-December, dance to the sound of the accordion.

La Guinguette Auvergnate

📍 *19, av. de Choisy, Villeneuve-Saint-Georges (Val-de-Marne). €*

Open since 1988 (formerly Café Buvette de la Station).

DECOR
A large pale pink building, located on the banks of the Seine, with a shaded terrace and multicolor flags.

RIPAILLER
Traditional plates of charcuterie, lamb chops, skirt steak with shallots—the food is oriented toward land rather than sea.

GRENOUILLER
A glass of Saint-Pourçain.

GAMBILLER
During lunch or dinner on weekends, dance to French, accordion, folk, or jazz music.

La Guinguette de l'île du Martin-Pêcheur

📍 *41, quai Victor-Hugo, Champigny-sur-Marne (Val-de-Marne). €€*

Open since 1991.

DECOR
String lights in the weeping willows, round tables covered with green checkered tablecloths set in the grass, an arbor and summer garden: it's a veritable real-life Renoir painting, with lawn darts and a pétanque court to boot.

RIPAILLER
Roasted free-range chicken, panna cotta.

GRENOUILLER
A red or white Sancerre Domaine Serge Laporte.

GAMBILLER
At any time of the year, outdoor games, concerts, and karaoke.

Chez Fifi

📍 *2, blvd. Maurice-Berteaux, Neuilly-sur-Marne (Seine-Saint-Denis). €€*

Open since 2000.

DECOR
Green plastic chairs and a large painted storefront, a bit rustic, along the nearby shore of the Marne.

RIPAILLER
Moules-frites (mussels and fries). "The king of mussels, that's Fifi!"

GRENOUILLER
A dry white wine, Domaine Pré Baron (Loire Valley).

GAMBILLER
Saturdays and Sundays and every day during good weather there are rock or flamenco concerts; tea dances and balls set to accordion music occur once a month.

La Guinguette de l'Écluse, le Martin-Pêcheur

📍 *Chemin de l'Écluse, Neuilly-sur-Marne (Seine-Saint-Denis). €*

Open since 2012.

DECOR
The restaurant, which turns into a dance floor, appears to be covered with a huge, upturned boat hull. In the grass on the banks of the Marne is a terrace set under the arbor.

RIPAILLER
Hake fillet, grilled skirt steak with shallot.

GRENOUILLER
White Sancerre, red Saumur, or rosé Gaillac.

GAMBILLER
On Monday afternoons, couples dance to accordion music or to a variety of concerts. On Saturday night, it's cabaret.

And . . .

Although it does not claim to be a guinguette, the Maison Fournaise remains a popular location on the banks of the Seine, once frequented by Monet, Manet, Degas, and Renoir, the latter of whom painted *Le Déjeuner des canotiers* (1880–1881) here. Maupassant was also a regular. One of his quotes is painted on the wall at the entrance. Today, the Maison Fournaise is a peaceful hotel-restaurant on the banks of the Seine and an impressionist museum.

Nouvelle Maison Fournaise—Île des Impressionnistes, Chatou (Yvelines). €€

Chez Gégène.

GREASY SPOONS Les Bouibouis

Very often still with their original decor, these off-the-radar locations delight regulars with prices that can't be beaten. Here is a small list of very-low-price Paris eateries. — JORDAN MOILIM

NEIGHBORHOOD BARS

Au Bon Coin
📍 49, rue des Cloÿs, Paris 18th

A bistro with offerings for less than €15! The Bras family has served oeuf mayonnaise, tartare, boudin purée, and headcheese vinaigrette for more than three generations. You can wash the food down with natural wine from a beautiful list put together by Jean-Louis, the youngest of the family.

Chez Pradel
📍 168, rue Ordener, Paris 18th

Coco, the chef-owner, serves an authentic home-style cooking for lunch and dinner to many regulars with whom he has become friends. And the food has remained affordable. The top sirloin au poivre and fries can be enjoyed for just €11.50.

Le Bar Fleuri
📍 1, rue du Plateau, Paris 19th

Martial and Joëlle Moro, a brother and sister, fell in love with this neighborhood bar more than twenty years ago. Since then, nothing has really changed. Customers sip pints on the terrace among a deliciously old-fashioned decor. The house-made roasted chicken and fries is a staple at an unchanging price of €6.86, or the exact conversion of 45 francs from the old days.

SOUP KITCHENS

La Cantine de Babelville
📍 77, rue de la Fontaine-au-Roi, Paris 11th

In this restaurant operated by the association La Coop

La Table du RECHO.

Mijotée, political refugees and migrants looking for work cook an unbeatable menu with one of the best "mafés" (an African meat and fish dish) in the capital at less than €7, served with a portion of rice and a few pieces of alloco (fried plantains).

La Table du RECHO
📍 51, blvd. Exelmans, Paris 16th

This former barracks transformed into a homeless shelter welcomes refugee residents for a meal for less than €15. Meals are inspired by the countries of origin of its guests.

SOMETHING UNIQUE

My Noodles
📍 129, blvd. du Montparnasse, Paris 6th

It's hard to resist the spectacle of noodles being made by Anaïs and Jacques in the window of this restaurant. Specialists in ramen, the duo serves house-made soup with these famous noodles cooked to order, a good beef broth, a little chile, bok choy, and slices of fried chicken, all for less than €10.

Le Taïs Ménilmontant
📍 129, blvd. de Ménilmontant, Paris 11th

Seating in this historic Algerian canteen in the Paris neighborhood of Ménilmontant is elbow to elbow. It is a haven of regulars where you can taste hearty couscous and tagines (€7 to €12). The grill stand serving meat skewers in the window (lamb, chicken, mutton) is a must.

Feel Ling
📍 24, rue Lauriston, Paris 16th

Near the Étoile, Sophie Ya, a brilliant self-taught chef, offers, at every lunch, the best fixed-price menu in the neighborhood (€11 and €13), with influences drawn from all over Asia: pad Thai, caramel pork with tofu skin, and the divine house-made gyozas.

A Nosa Casa Galicia
📍 91, rue du Ruisseau, Paris 18th

This discreet Spanish-origin (Galicia) haunt is open Friday to Sunday only, when you can taste, for less than €10, Galician octopus, a delicious Spanish tortilla, or the classic patatas bravas served with their garlic mayo.

Lagoa
📍 13, rue Montcalm, Paris 18th

Chef Clara Goncalves cooks dishes that combine her Brazilian origins with her husband's Portuguese roots. On the menu is feijoada, a pork-ear salad, and the famous bacalhau de cebolada, a generous fried cod steak on a bed of onions and cooked bell peppers. There is a fixed-price lunch menu for €12.50.

Alexi 20
📍 21, rue de Bagnolet, Paris 20th

Since 1986, May Chabene has been at the helm of this Lebanese gourmet-to-go shop. Regulars recommend tasting the "patate," a potato baked before being briefly deep-fried and then topped with ground beef and hummus, all wrapped in a pita. The Graubünden meat sandwich (€6) is also a good option.

TABLES BY THE FIRE
Les Tables au Coin du Feu

Delicious food by a cozy fire is an idyllic setting for a meal in Paris. —SAMIR OURIAGHLI

During the chill of winter, who doesn't dream of a cozy fireplace?

We don't notice them on warm days, but we realize how much we miss the ambience and warmth of a fireplace once the weather cools through changing seasons. These locations within the capital have earned a place on the UNESCO World Heritage list for their comforting fires, which were almost banned in 2015. Here are some spots for pleasurable moments by the fire.

RESTAURANTS

Atelier Maître Albert

📍 1, rue Maître-Albert, Paris 5th. €€€

"Here the aromas of wood, fireplaces, and rotisseries are a magnificent prelude to delicious food," says Michelin-starred chef Guy Savoy, who in 2003 took over this restaurant, located a stone's throw from Notre Dame. Inside, a monumental fireplace features two sublime rotisseries and decor by the architect Jean-Michel Wilmotte.

STYLE AND USE
A fireplace for ambience in a medieval style.

ON THE MENU
Farm-raised spit-roasted chicken, beef ribs with Béarnaise sauce.

Le Flamboire

📍 54, rue Blanche, Paris 9th. €€€

This restaurant is one of the few in Paris to offer wood-fired grills (oak and beech). Since 2012, all meats are carefully prepared by the skilled hands of Jean-Yves Chesneau (from Aveyron), a master roaster and the

Le Flamboire.

Hôtel Providence Paris.

Atelier Maître Albert.

owner. He is the only one who officiates at the fire for the thirty seats.

STYLE AND USE
A large fireplace for cooking.

ON THE MENU
A selection of French-beef ribs: Norman, Limousin, Charolais, and Aubrac.

Robert et Louise

📍 64, rue Vieille-du-Temple, Paris 3rd. €€

A true haven of peace in the heart of the trendy Marais district. The decor has remained the same since 1958. The fire crackles in the middle of a cozy and warm room.

STYLE AND USE
The brick cooking fireplace offers a rustic and authentic feel.

ON THE MENU
The steak house version of traditional French cuisine.

Le Coupe-Chou

📍 11, rue de Lanneau, Paris 5th. €€

In the heart of the Latin Quarter, this restaurant, comprising four houses dating from the sixteenth to the seventeenth centuries, offers four rooms with a fireplace. Opened in 1962, the setting takes you back to the time of the kings.

STYLE AND USE
Medieval-style pleasure fireplaces. Most are made of stone except one from solid wood.

ON THE MENU
Traditional cuisine.

HOTELS

Café Laurent de l'Hôtel d'Aubusson

📍 33, rue Dauphine, Paris 6th

A mecca of the literary and artistic life of Paris since 1960, it became a

jazz club frequented by Boris Vian, Juliette Gréco, and Jacques Prévert.

STYLE AND USE
An elegant fireplace in Burgundian stones lit from October to April.

ON THE MENU
During the day, you can drink coffee or tea in majestic calm. In the evening, from Monday to Saturday, make way for jazz concerts.

Salon Proust at the Ritz Hotel

📍 15, pl. Vendôme, Paris 1st

Located in Place Vendôme, the Ritz offers a fireplace nestled in the Proust salon with its incredible library. It's an ideal spot for quiet conversation by the fireplace.

STYLE AND USE
Marble fireplace.

ON THE MENU
A refined snack or tea, recommended by a tea sommelier, that might even make the British royal family jealous.

Hôtel Providence Paris

📍 90, rue René-Boulanger, Paris 10th

Close to the hustle and bustle of the Grands Boulevards, this adorable hotel is a peaceful oasis with its Empire-style furniture, velvet armchairs, and a few touches of rococo. Places by the fire are highly prized but limited.

STYLE AND USE
For pleasure, offering dark woodwork.

ON THE MENU
From coffee to cocktails.

TEAROOMS
Les Maisons de Thé

Paris is experiencing the emergence of independent tearooms and tea shops, offering customers teas from direct sources as well as a gastronomic experience. —LYDIA GAUTIER

French tea

In the middle of the seventeenth century, tea appeared in France. Appreciated at the time for its medicinal virtues and its exoticism, tea was a very expensive commodity and was consumed mainly by the aristocracy. Under the Second Empire, salons de thé (tearooms) began to open. At the end of the nineteenth century, the popularity of Japanese culture made tea drinking fashionable, and the Parisian elites became passionate about the Far East and the culture surrounding tea drinking.

THE HISTORIC PLACES

Musée du Thé de Mariage Frères

⦿ 30, rue du Bourg-Tibourg, Paris 4th

A great place for lovers of antiques from the East and West, with teapots and sample cases.

THE CUP OF TEA
Champasak smoked green tea from the Bolaven plateau (Laos).

École du Thé du Palais des Thés

7, rue de Nice, Paris 11th

Whether a tea neophyte or connoisseur, everyone can learn the secrets of tea in a fun and sensory way here.

THE CUP OF TEA
One of the spring crus of the Darjeeling appellation from northern India.

TEAHOUSES

Terre de Chine

⦿ 49, rue Quincampoix, Paris 4th

Run by Lyne Wang since 1997, this tea shop offers teas from a network of small producers.

THE CUP OF TEA
Yan Luo Po Hirondelle green tea from Anhui province, China.

Le Parti du Thé

⦿ 34, rue Faidherbe, Paris 11th

Since 2007, Pierre Lebrun's recurring theme has been to make tea accessible and uninhibited. There are more than three hundred types to purchase here.

THE CUP OF TEA
The soft and vegetal Kabusecha from the island of Kyushu in Japan.

Maison de Thé et Céramiques Neo. T.

⦿ 89, rue des Martyrs, Paris 18th

Valérie Stalport is passionate about Japanese teas, pu-erh (fermented tea), and others. In the spirit of an art gallery, she displays the work of young ceramists and offers their work for sale among her teas.

THE CUP OF TEA
The tannic dark pu-erh tea Sheng Wawee from Thailand, vintage 2020.

TEAROOMS (SALONS DE THÉ)

Ogata

⦿ 16, rue Debelleyme, Paris 3rd

In this temple of all things Japanese, you can enjoy hot and cold teas by Sabō, accompanied by savory and sweet dishes.

THE CUP OF TEA
Gyokuro, a rare green tea, shaded from the sun, with an unmatched mild flavor, in three courses.

Thé-ritoires

⦿ 5, rue de Condé, Paris 6th

To accompany your tea, don't miss Arnaud Bachelin's scones, served with clotted cream and homemade marmalade.

THE CUP OF TEA
A woody and minerally rock blue tea, Da Hong Pao from Fujian province.

Wistaria Tea House

⦿ 6, rue du Pont-de-Lodi, Paris 6th

It's a visit through Southeast Asia when entering this tea shop (cha yi guan), which opened its doors in September 2021 under the leadership of Sophie Lin, director of the historic Wistaria Tea House in the heart of Taipei, founded in 1981.

THE CUP OF TEA
The Dong Ding Oolong 1999, with sweet and vanilla vegetal notes.

Plaza Athénée

⦿ 25, av. Montaigne, Paris 8th

Take a seat in La Galerie at the Plaza Athénée for a "Tea & Snack" orchestrated by pastry chef Angelo Musa and a passionate tea team led by Benoît Marin.

THE CUP OF TEA
The Comte Grey, an Earl Grey made with black tea from Nepal and bergamot essential oil.

Les Pipelettes

⦿ 31, rue Brézin, Paris 14th

Aline Fellmann offers homemade cuisine, with tea prepared according to the rules of the art.

THE CUP OF TEA
The velvety dark pu-erh Tonka.

RESTAURANTS

La Halle aux Grains de la Maison Bras

⦿ 2, rue de Viarmes, Paris 1st. €€€

In a setting with a view across Paris's rooftops, Michel and Sébastien Bras delight guests with grains and teas infused in bottles.

THE CUP OF TEA
The woody Qimen Kao black tea made from Qimen tea and cacao husks.

Yam'Tcha

⦿ 121, rue Saint-Honoré, Paris 1st. €€€

Michelin-starred chef Adeline Grattard and her partner, Chi Wah Chan, have been orchestrating tea and food pairings throughout their gastronomic menu since 2009.

THE CUP OF TEA
The flowery Jasmine Pearls white tea from China.

SHOP

Paris Rendez-Vous

⦿ 29, rue de Rivoli, Paris 4th

Organic herbal teas and teas selected by the author of this page. The concept: ten neighborhoods, ten moments, ten ambiences.

La Halle aux Grains.

Thé-ritoires.

Les Pipelettes.

COFFEE ROASTERS
Les Torréfacteurs

From the opening of Le Procope to the rise of coffee shops, coffee has always been of particular importance in Parisian culture, society, and life. —ALICE BOSIO

TRADITIONAL ROASTERS

Far from Anglo-Saxon fashions and influences, these locations have been haunts with retro charm for Parisians for decades.

Verlet

♀ *256, rue Saint-Honoré, Paris 1st*

Opened in 1880, this is the oldest coffeehouse in Paris. It was acquired in 1921 by Auguste Woerhlé, known as Verlet, who turned it into an elegant salon whose decor has not changed. Its century-old roaster is located behind the gardens of the Palais-Royal.

THE BEAN TO GRIND

Sainte-Hélène coffee, with caramelized notes, a rarity for which Verlet has exclusive rights in France.

Caron

♀ *32, rue Notre-Dame-de-Nazareth, Paris 3rd*

Created in 1974, this roaster is operated by Anne Caron, voted best roaster of France in 2017. The location boasts traditional know-how with slow roasting to develop the aromas of its ethically sourced specialty coffees.

THE BEAN TO GRIND

Caron coffee, a blend of four Arabica grands crus, with tangy notes and aromas of brioche, caramel, and chocolate.

La Caféothèque de Paris

♀ *52, rue de l'Hôtel-de-Ville, Paris 4th*

This coffee room, roasting space, and school located on the banks of the Seine was opened by Gloria Montenegro, a pioneer of Parisian-origin coffees.

THE BEAN TO GRIND

Finca El Injerto coffee (Guatemala), with lemony, spicy, woody, and caramelized notes.

La Brûlerie des Gobelins

♀ *2, av. des Gobelins, Paris 5th*

A former wine bar, it has been filling the outskirts of Mouffetard with its amazing aromas since 1957. Purveyor of organic and fair-trade specialty coffee, it has a gleaming coffee shop in the very chic La Samaritaine department store.

THE BEAN TO GRIND

Guji coffee (from Ethiopia), with notes of black currant, blueberry, and rhubarb.

Café Lanni

♀ *54, rue du Faubourg-Saint-Denis, Paris 10th*

♀ *61, av. Mozart, Paris 16th*

♀ *125, av. de Clichy, Paris 17th*

♀ *1, rue du Poteau, Paris 18th*

Founded in 1947, this family roaster was taken over by Olivier Cahen, the creator's son, and supplies consumers and professionals with freshly roasted coffees.

THE BEAN TO GRIND

Ethiopian high-altitude washed coffees, with tangy notes.

NEW ROASTERS

Part of the new wave of coffee, these establishments roast sustainable Arabica grands crus, served in the best coffee shops, bistros, and even Michelin-starred restaurants in Paris and beyond.

Terres de Café

♀ *150, rue Saint-Honoré, Paris 1st*

♀ *14, rue Rambuteau, Paris 3rd*

♀ *36, rue des Blancs-Manteaux, Paris 4th*

♀ *67, av. de la Bourdonnais, Paris 7th*

♀ *33, rue des Batignolles, Paris 17th*

Christophe Servell, the son and grandson of roasters, opened his first roasting house in 2009 in the Marais. Today, at the head of five locations, he offers a wide range of thirty specialty pure-origin or blend French coffees. The roasting is now done in Bezons (Val-d'Oise).

THE BEAN TO GRIND

Los Pirineos-Pacamara coffee (El Salvador), with notes of passion fruit, mango, and flowers.

L'Arbre à Café

♀ *10, rue du Nil, Paris 2nd*

♀ *61, rue Oberkampf, Paris 11th*

♀ *49–51, rue du Commandant-Mouchotte, Saint-Mandé (Val-de-Marne)*

Hippolyte Courty, who just sixteen years ago was not a coffee drinker, promotes a French and sustainable vision of coffee. His comprehensive, single-varietal selections make him the supplier of chefs such as Pierre Hermé and Anne-Sophie Pic. He is also a producer thanks to his plantations in Peru.

THE BEAN TO GRIND

The Iapar Red coffee from Brazil, grown biodynamically, with great mildness, freshness, and sensuality, with chocolate and almond aromas.

Coutume

♀ *47, rue de Babylone, Paris 7th*

♀ *54, rue du Faubourg-Saint-Honoré, Paris 8th*

♀ *Galeries Lafayette—40, blvd. Haussmann, Paris 9th*

♀ *56, rue du Faubourg-Saint-Denis, Paris 10th*

♀ *80, rue de Passy, Paris 16th*

♀ *2, esp. du Général-de-Gaulle, Courbevoie (Hauts-de-Seine)*

♀ *43, rue de la Commune-de-Paris, Romainville (Seine-Saint-Denis)*

Founded by Australian Tom Clark, the first Café Coutume was on rue de Babylone offering pure-origin grands crus. It was eventually joined by six other meticulously skillful coffee shops. The roasting space has recently moved to Romainville (Seine-Saint-Denis).

THE BEANS TO GRIND

Ethiopian coffees and pink bourbon from Colombia, with great aromatic richness of dominating floral and fruity notes.

Lomi

♀ *3 ter, rue Marcadet, Paris 18th*

This roasting space was launched in 2010 north of Paris by Aleaume Paturle and Paul Arnephy, an MOF (Best Craftsman of France) roaster. The establishment was quickly followed up with a coffee shop and an accessories shop, then a school, particularly popular with professionals. A second roasting location was set up in the Drôme department.

THE BEAN TO GRIND

The signature blend for espresso "J'ai Deux Amours," rounded, with flavors of chocolate and roasted hazelnut.

Belleville Brûlerie

♀ *14 bis, rue Lally-Tollendal, Paris 19th*

Launched in 2013 by Thomas Lehoux and David Flynn in a micro-workshop near Buttes-Chaumont, Belleville Brûlerie has grown and had to relocate in 2017. Under the careful roasting of Mihaela Iordache, the business continues to specialize in blends, tinged with a bit of humor.

THE BEAN TO GRIND

Château Belleville coffee, a blend inspired by the world of red wine, with mature fruit notes and a developed body.

COFFEE-SHOP ROASTERS

With their Scandinavian decor and tattooed baristas who serve up everything from Chemex to lattes, these specialists developed reputations in coffee shops before launching their own roasters.

Ten Belles

♀ *53, rue du Cherche-Midi, Paris 6th*

♀ *10, rue de la Grange-aux-Belles, Paris 10th*

♀ *17–19, rue Bréguet, Paris 11th*

After shaking up the coffee-shop world for nearly ten years, trio Anna Trattles, Alice Quillet, and Anselme Blayney have been roasting their own coffee since the end of 2019 at the premises of their friends' brasserie Deck & Donohue in Bonneuil-sur-Marne (Val-de-Marne).

THE BEAN TO GRIND

SHG coffee for Igualdad Mujeres Hombres (Colombia), with both complex and acidic cocoa notes with a great deal of body and roundness.

KB Coffee Roasters

📍 53, av. Trudaine, Paris 9th

📍 25, rue Amelot, Paris 11th

Located in Pigalle, this is one of the first coffee-shop roasters to open in France. In 2015, Nicolas Piégay and Rémi Bompart started roasting before opening a second coffee shop, Back in Black, close to the Bastille in 2019. Only pure origins are roasted.

THE BEAN TO GRIND

La Senda coffee (Guatemala), with subtle notes of freshly cut flowers and black tea, nectarine, and orange sweets.

La Compagnie du Café

📍 19, rue Notre-Dame-de-Lorette, Paris 9th

Former business attorney Romain Fabry converted to a coffee afficionado with this half-coffee-shop-half-workshop location in 2015. An organic product and sustainability and responsibility are at the heart of his business.

THE BEAN TO GRIND

Greengo (Rwanda), a washed red bourbon with notes of cocoa butter, with a persistent touch of tropical fruits.

Café Compagnon

📍 22–26, rue Léopold-Bellan, Paris 2nd

Not content with shaking up Parisian bistronomy, Charles Compagnon has been roasting his own beans in his establishment in Courances (Essonne) since 2017. Served and sold at Richer (2, rue Richer, Paris 9th), 52 (52, rue du Faubourg-Saint-Denis, Paris 10th), and Café Compagnon (22–26, rue Léopold-Bellan, Paris 2nd), the coffee is pure origin and organically grown.

THE BEAN TO GRIND

Fedecoreva coffee (Guatemala), with acidic notes of red fruits combined with the sweet aroma of cocoa.

Verlet, above and at right.

L'Arbre à Café.

Ten Belles.

La Compagnie du Café.

Brûlerie des Gobelins.

Hexagone

📍 121, rue du Château, Paris 14th

Launched in 2015 by four friends, including Stéphane Cataldi (who manages the roasting in Brittany) and Chung-Leng Tran (a barista), this stop, where you can also enjoy a kakigōri (a Japanese dessert), has become a staple in the neighborhood.

THE BEAN TO GRIND

Aricha Yirgacheffe coffee (Ethiopia), with notes of white flowers, apricot, and citric acidity.

WHERE TO DRINK SPECIALTY COFFEE

Although they do not roast their own beans, these places source their beans from the best roasters.

Télescope

📍 5, rue Villedo, Paris 1st

In his café, Nicolas Clerc was one of the first to serve specialty coffees in Paris, since 2013.

Loustic

📍 40, rue Chapon, Paris 3rd

This coffee shop owned by the British espresso specialist Channa Galhenagé was opened in 2013. The coffees of the Belgian roaster Caffènation are accompanied by scones, sandwiches, and other fare.

Chanceux

📍 57, rue Saint-Maur, Paris 11th

Farah Laacher and Thomas Lehoux (cofounder of Belleville Brûlerie and Ten Belles) have set up a café-épicerie where what's in the cup (specialty coffees) is at the same level of quality as what's on the plate (great sandwiches and light bites).

Kabane

📍 23, rue Faidherbe, Paris 11th

Make way for a comprehensive menu from European roasters in this charming setting.

La Main Noire

📍 12, rue Cavallotti, Paris 18th

This industrial loft serves delicious organic lattes, Australian-style brunches, and specialty coffees from European roasters.

COCKTAIL BARS
Les Bars à Cocktails

As the birthplace of legendary cocktails and with its enormous diversity of bars, Paris has been at the forefront of the spirits scene for a century. —CÉCILE FORTIS

THE PIONEERS

Hemingway Bar, Ritz Hotel

⚲ *15, pl. Vendôme, Paris 1st*

Legendary. Filled with leather armchairs and Ernest Hemingway's trophies, the bar owes its status to its unique atmosphere and top-notch service. This institution also owes its appeal to Colin Field, the unbeatable master of the house.

THE SIGNATURE COCKTAIL

The Serendipity (Calvados, Champagne, apple juice, fresh mint, simple syrup).

Harry's New York Bar

⚲ *5, rue Daunou, Paris 2nd*

Bought in 1923 by bartender Harry MacElhone, Harry's New York Bar is the oldest cocktail bar in Paris.

THE SIGNATURE COCKTAIL

The Bloody Mary, invented here, according to the legend.

PALACE HOTEL BARS

La Langosteria, Hôtel Cheval Blanc

⚲ *8, quai du Louvre, Paris 1st*

Of the three bars at Hôtel Cheval Blanc, the Langosteria, the Italian restaurant dedicated to seafood, is the most spectacular with its large circular bar, a view of all of Paris, and cocktails very dolce vita.

THE SIGNATURE COCKTAIL

The Portofino (gin, Taggiasca olive oil, dry vermouth, pesto).

Les Ambassadeurs, Hôtel de Crillon

⚲ *10, pl. de la Concorde, Paris 8th*

Thanks to its very eighteenth-century style of marble, gilt, and crystal chandeliers and its resolutely luxe service with innovative cocktails and DJ-hosted evenings, the bar at the Hôtel de Crillon dominates the Parisian cocktail scene.

THE SIGNATURE COCKTAIL

The Nonoka (Talisker single-malt Scotch, Bols Elderflower, sake, caraway, bergamot).

Le Bulgari Bar

⚲ *30, av. George-V, Paris 8th*

The Bulgari Hotel impresses with its backlit bar and extended menu, but it's the aperitivo that reaches truly great heights.

THE SIGNATURE COCKTAIL

The Negroni (gin, vermouth, bitters), a true classic.

THE "NEW WAVE"

Danico

⚲ *6, rue Vivienne, Paris 2nd*

Nestled at the back of Daroco, the chic pizzeria in the Galerie Vivienne, Danico is one of the most prominent Parisian cocktail bars. Nico de Soto, also owner of Mace in New York, is renowned for his creativity and high-octane milk punches.

THE SIGNATURE COCKTAIL

The For Christ Sake! (sake, jackfruit and black rice syrup, coconut milk, egg).

Golden Promise

⚲ *11, rue Tiquetonne, Paris 2nd*

Located in the basement of the Maison du Saké, the Golden Promise is an insider's spot. Within its vaulted cellars, you can enjoy always-well-crafted cocktails along with legendary whiskeys, including many considered collectors' items.

THE SIGNATURE COCKTAIL

The Old-Fashioned made with Blanton's and served with a chocolate spoon.

Little Red Door

⚲ *60, rue Charlot, Paris 3rd*

Thanks to its conceptual menus, the LRD has established itself as a staple on the international cocktail scene. It further distinguishes itself with its "from farm to glass" approach.

THE SIGNATURE COCKTAIL

The Walnut (Glasshouse whisky, Baldoria rosso dry vermouth, walnut shrub, sparkling wine).

Prescription Cocktail Club

⚲ *23, rue Mazarine, Paris 6th*

One of the flagship locations of the Experimental Cocktail Group, the pioneer of the new French mixology wave. With its new cosmic theater look and its creative cocktails, the Prescription lights up the Left Bank more than ever.

THE SIGNATURE COCKTAIL

The Flores Sagradas (vodka, vermouth with bergamot, amaretto, flower syrup, lemon).

CopperBay

⚲ *5, rue Bouchardon, Paris 10th*

Since it dropped anchor in the 10th arrondissement, CopperBay has made a name for itself thanks to its cocktails inspired by the food and talents of Aurélie Panhelleux, one of the three partners, as much of a technician in her craft as she is welcoming in her demeanor.

THE SIGNATURE COCKTAIL

The Roquetini (vodka, cherry tomatoes, arugula, lemon, white balsamic, black pepper).

Le Syndicat

⚲ *51, rue du Faubourg-Saint-Denis, Paris 10th*

Behind a storefront covered with posters, this cocktail bar promotes the richness and diversity of French spirits. The cocktails are exclusively made from French products. Le Syndicat also owes its success to its crazy look and its supercharged atmosphere.

THE SIGNATURE COCKTAIL

The Dame de Fer (gin, Champagne syrup, cider foam, and iron oxide).

Fréquence

⚲ *20, rue Keller, Paris 11th*

Here turntables sit on the counter and a host of vinyls line the shelves in the back in place of bottles. The creative cocktails of Guillaume Quenza and Matthieu Biron are no less perfectly crafted. The welcome is hi-fi.

THE SIGNATURE COCKTAIL

The Seiji (umeshu, sake, pickled mango).

Cravan

⚲ *17, rue Jean-de-La Fontaine, Paris 16th*

Franck Audoux, former associate of chef Inaki Aizpitarte, has made this little Art Nouveau gem one of the strongholds of mixology. His classically inspired cocktails are of a rare precision and balance.

THE SIGNATURE COCKTAIL

The Yellow Cocktail (dry gin, Grandmont bitter gentian, yellow Chartreuse, lemon).

Combat

⚲ *63, rue de Belleville, Paris 19th*

Founded in Belleville in 2017 by Margot Lecarpentier, Combat quickly became a flagship spot on the Parisian cocktail scene. The atmosphere and cocktails are just like this iconic bartender: stylish and dedicated.

THE SIGNATURE COCKTAIL

The Impecâpre (tequila infused with capers, vermouth, walnut liqueur, gentian liqueur, lemon).

SPEAKEASIES

Candelaria

⚲ *52, rue de Saintonge, Paris 3rd*

This bar, hidden below a mini-taqueria, is the temple of cocktails and festive times. As for the notoriety of Carina Soto Velasquez, its emblematic cofounder, it knows no boundaries.

THE SIGNATURE COCKTAIL

The Guêpe Verte (tequila infused with chile, cucumber, coriander, agave syrup, lemon).

Moonshiner

⚲ *5, rue Sedaine, Paris 11th*

Take note, you have to cross through the refrigerated cold room of the Da Vito pizzeria to access the Moonshiner, one of the first Parisian speakeasies and sporting an Art Deco setting and a Prohibition-style atmosphere. This is the least well-kept secret of the capital because the cocktails are impeccable.

THE SIGNATURE COCKTAIL

The Vieux Carré (bourbon, cognac, vermouth, bitters), which spends some time here in the barrel.

The Serendipity, at the Ritz.

The Bloody Mary, at Harry's Bar.

The Nonoka, at the Crillon.

The Negroni, at Bulgari Hotel.

The Portofino, at Langosteria.

The Impecâpre, at Combat.

The Roquetini, at CopperBay.

The Yellow Cocktail, at Cravan.

The For Christ Sake!, at Danico.

The Seiji, at Fréquence.

The Old-Fashioned, at Golden Promise.

The Dame de Fer, at Le Syndicat.

The Walnut, at Little Red Door.

The Flores Sagradas, at Prescription Cocktail Club.

The Guêpe Verte, at Candelaria.

The Vieux Carré, at Moonshiner.

RENOWNED WINE CELLARS
Les Caves de Renom

Some grand restaurants and bistros have underground wine cellars that house incredible collections. —JÉRÔME GAGNEZ

PALACE HOTELS

George V

📍 *31, av. George-V, Paris 8th*

DATE OF CONSTRUCTION
1928

CELLAR DEPTH
49 feet (15 m)

CELLAR AREA
4,300 square feet
(400 sq m)

NUMBER OF BOTTLES
45,000

THE OLDEST BOTTLE
A Madeira Solera from
1792.

HISTORY
The hotel was built by
André Terrail (head
of La Tour d'Argent)
and George Wybo (the
architect of Printemps
Haussmann). The cellar
was dug out in the quarry
of the Chaillot hill, whose
stones were used for the
construction of the Arc de
Triomphe.

ANECDOTES
› A customer drank
298 bottles of Pétrus in
three years. The customer
is today in a prison in
Caracas.
› A record bill: One
evening a customer left
a check for €150,000.
He spent part of the night
drinking the greatest
wines (eighteen bottles)
with the hotel staff.

Le Bristol Paris

📍 *112, rue du Faubourg-
Saint-Honoré, Paris 8th*

DATE OF CONSTRUCTION
1978

CELLAR DEPTH
30 feet (9 m)

CELLAR AREA
1,044 square feet
(97 sq m)

NUMBER OF BOTTLES
58,500 bottles on-site
at Le Bristol; 110,000
bottles counting external
storage.

THE OLDEST BOTTLES
A Rivesaltes from 1875,
along with a few bottles
of Château Cheval Blanc
from 1937. A Petrus from
1961.

HISTORY
Built in the eighteenth
century by the Duke of
Noailles, builder of King
Louis XV, the private
mansion was made more
splendid when the Count
of Castellane bought it in
1829. In 1925, Hippolyte
Jammet turned it into a
hotel.

ANECDOTES
› In 2018, a loyal customer
offered the hotel a
magnificent Imperial (a
bottle holding 6 liters, the
equivalent of forty-two
glasses or eight bottles
of 750 ml) of Château La
Mission Haut-Brion 1923.
› The most important
bottles are housed in a
wrought-iron cabinet made
with the old railings of the
hotel's historic elevator.

STARRED RESTAURANTS

La Tour d'Argent

📍 *15, quai de la Tournelle,
Paris 5th*

DATE OF CONSTRUCTION
1830 for the first cellar,
1985 for the second

CELLAR DEPTH
17 feet (5 m) for the first
cellar, 30 feet (9 m) for
the second

CELLAR AREA
12,900 square feet
(1,200 sq m) divided into
two levels; the first level is
a rotunda of 8,600 square
feet (800 sq m), the
second is 4,300 square
feet (400 sq m)

NUMBER OF BOTTLES
300,000. In forty years of
"reign," sommelier David
Ridgway increased the
number of labels from
1,000 to 15,000.

THE OLDEST BOTTLE
A Clos de Griffier cognac
from 1788.

HISTORY
In 1940, when the
Germans were about to
take over the premises,
the owner's son, Claude
Terrail, closed in part of
the cellar to hide 500,000
bottles from the German's
reach.

ANECDOTE
In the 1920s, American
tycoon banker J. P. Morgan
stole an exceptional
bottle of fine Napoléon
cognac from 1805 that the
restaurant refused to sell
him. He left a blank check
to pay for it. He wrote a
letter of apology, however,
and the check was never
cashed.

Le Taillevent

📍 *15, rue Lamennais,
Paris 8th*

DATE OF CONSTRUCTION
1852

CELLAR DEPTH
13 feet (4 m)

CELLAR AREA
Almost 2,100 square feet
(200 sq m)

NUMBER OF BOTTLES
30,000 bottles among
nearly 3,000 labels.

THE OLDEST BOTTLE
A Château d'Yquem from
1893.

HISTORY
Located in the former
private mansion of the
Duke of Morny, half
brother of Napoléon III,
Le Taillevent is a tribute
to Guillaume Tirel dit
Taillevent, master of the
kings of France Philip VI,
Charles V, and Charles VI
in the fourteenth century.

ANECDOTE
The owner, Mr. Vrinat,
was the first to favor
Burgundy wines over
Bordeaux, which
encouraged the house to
forge strong links with the
great Burgundian estates.

BISTROS

Les Fines Gueules

📍 *43, rue Croix-des-Petits-
Champs, Paris 1st*

DATE OF CONSTRUCTION
1733

CELLAR DEPTH
17 feet (5 m) for the first
cellar and 33 feet (10 m)
for the second

CELLAR AREA
1,200 square feet
(120 sq m), spread over
two levels

NUMBER OF BOTTLES
20,000 bottles among
1,200 labels, collected
by the manager Arnaud
Bradol, mainly from
artisanal, organic, and
biodynamic vineyards.

THE OLDEST BOTTLE
A Coteaux-du-Layon
Domaine Cousin from
1959.

HISTORY
On the orders of the
Countess of Jaucourt, née
Marie-Josèphe de Graves,
the master mason
Sébastien Charpentier
built the cellar in Paris
stone, according to
plans by architect Pierre
Desmaisons.

ANECDOTE
While actor Jean
Rochefort was having
lunch standing at the
counter, the maître d'
asked him, "Would you
like a small glass of wine
with your salmon steak
and steamed vegetables?"
To which Rochefort
replied, "As a young man,
my doctor told me that I
drank my quota."

Vantre

📍 *19, rue de La Fontaine-
au-Roi, Paris 11th*

DATE OF CONSTRUCTION
Late nineteenth century

CELLAR DEPTH
13 feet (4 m)

CELLAR AREA
640 square feet (60 sq m)
in the restaurant and
970 square feet (90 sq m)
in four other cellars in Paris

NUMBER OF BOTTLES
10,000 bottles on-site with
2,500 labels on the menu.
35,000 bottles in total with
the other four cellars.

THE OLDEST BOTTLE
A Château Montrose from
1890.

HISTORY
Although old, the cellar
had never been used to
store wine before. The
current sommelier, Marco
Pelletier, is the one who
developed the cellar.

ANECDOTE
The great classic wines
stand next to the best
natural, foreign, and
small-production wines.

AND . . .

La Robe et le Palais

📍 *13, rue des Lavandières-
Sainte-Opportune,
Paris 1st*

This bistro with vins
vivants (living wines) lists
more than five hundred
labels on the menu. The
cellar contains a few
thousand labels.

Le Petit Sommelier

📍 *49, av. du Maine, Paris 14th*

Opposite Montparnasse
train station, sommelier
Pierre Vila Palleja's bistro
offers one of the most
extensive wine lists in
Paris.

Les Caves Pétrissans

📍 *30 bis, av. Niel, Paris 17th*

The fifth generation of
the family, owners since
1895, watches over one
of the most beautiful
cellars in the capital.

Cellar of Le Bristol.

Cellar of Vantre.

Cellar of Les Fines Gueules.

Cellar of La Tour d'Argent, above.

Cellar of Le Taillevent.

TABLEWARE DEALERS
Les Puces à Table

Though once considered old-fashioned, monogrammed silver cutlery and serving dishes are making a comeback. Let's zoom in on six antique dealers at the Serpette antiques market who offer fine collections of tableware from the nineteenth and twentieth centuries. —SYLVIE WOLFF

Les Tables d'Eva

⚲ *Serpette Market, aisle 4, stands 2 and 5; phone: 06 23 90 54 39*

Daughter, granddaughter, and great-granddaughter of antiques dealers, Eva Cwajg has always been fond of antique tableware and ceramics, which according to her are important objects for creating a convivial ambience at the table.

SPECIALTY ITEMS

Porcelain and glazed earthenware serving dishes from the late 1700s to the 1940s from the largest French and German manufacturers.

AND

Silver-plated and gilded silver cutlery, and glassware.

BESTSELLERS

The Tournai glazed earthenware serving dishes from the late eighteenth century, and the monogrammed Porcelaine de Paris serving dishes from the eighteenth century.

FAMOUS REGULAR CUSTOMERS

Chefs Alain Ducasse and Assaf Granit.

Les Tables d'Eva Côté Campagne

⚲ *Serpette Market, aisle 4, stands 2 and 5; phone: 06 23 90 54 39*

SPECIALTY ITEMS

The fourteenth-century glazed earthenware serving dishes and ceramics from Lunéville, Sarreguemines, and Gien French brands and Mintons and Wedgwood English brands.

AND

Lobster dishes, shellfish and fish plates, cabbage bowls.

BESTSELLER

Asparagus dishes.

FAMOUS REGULAR CUSTOMERS

Chefs Hélène Darroze and Jean-François Piège.

Jérôme Chedmail

⚲ *Serpette Market, aisle 3, stand 13; phone: 06 63 74 83 30*

According to Jérôme Chedmail, who has been selling from this market for more than twenty years, silver-plated and solid-silver flatware are no longer just for important family ceremonies but also for everyday use.

SPECIALTY ITEMS

The mismatched silver-plated cutlery and the nineteenth- and twentieth-century cutlery from the great French manufacturers Christofle, Ercuis, Boulenger, Puiforcat, Odiot, and others. Also, candlesticks and serving trays.

AND

Silver-plated dishes, soup tureens, ice buckets, asparagus tongs, teakettles.

BESTSELLER

The silver-plated champagne bucket.

FAMOUS REGULAR CUSTOMERS

Chefs Hélène Darroze and Thierry Marx.

Nicolas Giovannoni

⚲ *Serpette Market, aisle 6, stands 8 and 10; phone: 06 07 42 13 76*

Selling at Serpette since 1993, this collector of crystal champagne glasses and flutes offers almost museum-quality pieces.

SPECIALTY ITEMS

Water glasses, wineglasses, and coupe glasses in transparent or colored crystal, or faceted, cut, engraved, and monogrammed, by Baccarat, Saint-Louis, Lalique, Daum, Clichy, and Val Saint Lambert, a Belgian manufacturer.

AND

Limoges Bleu de Four porcelain serving dishes.

BESTSELLER

Baccarat stemmed glassware from the 1970s.

FAMOUS REGULAR CUSTOMERS

Set designer Vincent Darré and designer Christian Louboutin.

Alexis Allegro

⚲ *Serpette Market, aisle 2, stand 8; phone: 06 75 44 26 43*

He is one of the youngest sellers at Serpette, partial to objects of curiosity in solid silver.

SPECIALTY ITEMS

Decorative pieces in solid silver from the nineteenth and twentieth centuries from Puiforcat, Odiot, Buccellati, and Paul Storr, such as fish sauce servers, cowhide butter dishes, coupes made of shell, and pet name tags.

AND

Crystal or fine silver decanters and coupes from the nineteenth century.

BESTSELLERS

Scallop-shell menu holders and salt and pepper shakers with fish motifs.

FAMOUS REGULAR CUSTOMERS

Hubert de Vinols, architect of the Tables d'Exception website.

Objets de Hasard

⚲ *Serpette Market, aisle 2, stand 42; phone: 06 11 78 28 71*

Florence Pfenniger's family have been merchants here for four generations. Unlike relatives before her, she is particularly passionate about tableware from southern France.

SPECIALTY ITEMS

Provençal tableware by the most famous potters, including Robert Picault, Marius Giuge, Aegitna, from the 1950s to the 1980s.

AND

Biot vases and glassware.

BESTSELLER

Cérenne de Vallauris figure plates with fish and cherub motifs from the 1950s and 1960s.

FAMOUS REGULAR CUSTOMERS

Designers Philippe Starck and India Mahdavi, chef Hélène Darroze.

Les Merveilles de Babellou Antiquités

⚲ *Paul-Bert Market, aisle 1, stand 17*

François Casal has carved out a solid reputation as a supplier to many restaurants,and to collectors.

SPECIALTY ITEMS

From copper pans to jam-making kettles, duck presses and terrines, this stall has a large selection of professional equipment from the nineteenth and twentieth centuries.

AND

Glazed earthenware plates in trompe-l'oeil as snails, chestnuts, or shellfish.

BESTSELLERS

Old bars from Parisian bistros and copper flat-fish cookers and stewpots.

FAMOUS REGULAR CUSTOMERS

Chefs Anne-Sophie Pic, Jacky Ribault, and Pierre Gagnaire.

WHERE TO EAT ON-SITE?

Feuille de Chou

⚲ *70, rue des Rosiers, Saint-Ouen (Seine-Saint-Denis). €€*

Located in the heart of the MOB House, this brasserie focuses on organic and local products.

Bonne Aventure

⚲ *59, rue des Rosiers, Saint-Ouen (Seine-Saint-Denis). €€*

This two-room-kitchen set up opposite the Paul-Bert market is a vibrant natural-focused bistro operated by Alcidia Vulbeau.

Chez Arnaud

⚲ *85–87, rue des Rosiers, Saint-Ouen (Seine-Saint-Denis). €€*

At the entrance of the Biron market, Arnaud Schwizguebel serves nicely presented seasonal bistronomy-style dishes.

Kanopë

⚲ *39, rue Paul Bert, Saint-Ouen (Seine-Saint-Denis). €*

Set up in market's center, this organic pizzeria uses local products including dough made by the pizza world champion Thierry Graffagnino, organic flours from Moulins Familiales in the Paris region, artisanal mozzarella from Yvelines, and seasonal vegetables.

Porcelain serving dishes at Les Tables d'Eva.

Champagne buckets at Jérôme Chedmail.

Tournai serving dishes at Les Tables d'Eva.

Vallauris serving dishes at Objects de Chance.

A turbotière (flat-fish cooker) at Les Merveilles de Babellou Antiquités.

Asparagus serving dishes at Les Tables d'Eva.

Solid silver cutlery at Jérôme Chedmail.

The Serpette market.

KITCHEN SUPPLY STORES
Les Boutiques d'Ustensiles

These shops offering traditional kitchen equipment excite both amateur and professional cooks.
—MARIELLE GAUDRY

Similarities among the shops

› Most of these shops are in the Les Halles district, the historic location of Paris's food markets.
› They sell to the public, but they largely supply restaurant and hotel professionals in Paris, throughout France, and abroad.
› Their product turnover has been steadily increasing in recent years with a return to popularity of old-fashioned and manual cooking methods rather than the use of electric appliances.
› They strive to sell products made in France or Europe.

Mora

📍 13, rue Montmartre, Paris 1st
Since 1814.

OWNER
The Mora family.

THE SHOP
A spacious modernized shop where you can stroll through generously stocked shelves.

SPECIALTY
A cutting-edge pastry department.

BESTSELLERS
Silicone baking mats and molds, nitrous oxide canisters, pastry bags.

ANECDOTE
A customer who decided to equip his entire kitchen all at once spent more than five thousand euros in a single transaction.

E. Dehillerin

📍 18–20, rue Coquillière, Paris 1st
Since 1820.

OWNER
The Dehillerin family.

THE SHOP
A treasure trove spread over two floors that has remained unchanged and crammed from floor to ceiling. It would be easy to imagine Escoffier shopping here.

SPECIALTY
The most complete range of copperware on the market.

BESTSELLERS
Metal mini molds, dough sheeters, mandolines, Microplanes.

ANECDOTE
In 1912, the British shipping company White Star Line ordered a collection of utensils for the kitchens of the legendary ocean liner *Titanic*.

A. Simon

📍 48, rue Montmartre, Paris 2nd
Since 1884.

OWNER
Jean-Claude Thomas.

THE SHOP
A vast single-story store that seems like a warehouse, overflowing with brand-name equipment.

SPECIALTY
A design service for personalized tableware and knife sharpening.

BESTSELLERS
1¾-inch (4.5 cm) diameter copper fluted molds, stainless steel skillets, serrated paring knives, Japanese mandolines.

ANECDOTES
A plates juggler wanted to find a plate that weighed exactly 232 grams (about 8 ounces) for a future performance. A restaurateur inquired about the price for plates decorated with a photo of his backside!

Maison Lefranc

📍 26, blvd. des Batignolles, Paris 17th
Since 2015.

OWNER
Alexandre Valenza-Troubat.

THE SHOP
This small, well-organized, and recently opened shop has an old-style feel inside and out to match the feel of its traditional French cutlery.

SPECIALTIES
Offering an adjoining old-fashioned drugstore, cooking classes, and a fine-foods section.

BESTSELLERS
Salad spinners, Microplanes.

ANECDOTE
At the end of the 2020 COVID-19 lockdown, the shop recorded a record sale of forty-eight rolling pins, twenty-five dough sheeters, and a dozen cast-iron cooking pots in just two days.

Bellynck et Fils

📍 194, av. Jean-Jaurès, Paris 19th
Since 1936.

OWNER
The Bellynck family.

THE SHOP
Its canary yellow facade is unmissable. Inside, you maneuver your way between the vintage sideboards and the more modern shelves overflowing with flatware under a ceiling of pots and pans and butcher's hooks.

SPECIALTIES
Knives, butcher's hooks. The first dealer of Lacanche cooking ranges.

BESTSELLER
Knife sharpeners.

ANECDOTE
The shop supplied utensils to the slaughterhouses and cattle markets of La Villette just opposite (opened in 1867, definitively closed in 1974; today on the site is the Grande Halle). It continues to supply butcher shops as well as restaurants in the neighborhood.

AND

Verrerie des Halles

📍 15, rue du Louvre, Paris 1st
Since 1946, this wholesaler, tucked away in a courtyard, has been supplying kitchen equipment to catering and hotel professionals. No retail sales, but individual professionals can purchase.

J. Ducerf

📍 23, rue Pierre-Fontaine, Paris 9th
Since 1948, this specialist in traditional tableware has been primarily supplying hotels and restaurants. They offer porcelain, glassware, accessories, cookware, and electric appliances of several brands.

Francis Batt

📍 180, av. Victor-Hugo, Paris 16th
📍 22, rue des Huissiers, Neuilly-sur-Seine (Hauts-de-Seine)
Arriving from his native Vosges, Francis Batt took over a drugstore in 1976 that he transformed in 1982 into a kitchen utensil store. There is a wide choice of knives, cooking accessories, tableware, and small appliances behind its unmissable bright red facade.

La Bovida

📍 19, av. Corentin-Cariou, Paris 19th
Before moving its Parisian address to La Villette, the brand had its headquarters starting in 1936 on rue Montmartre, near Les Halles. Its name refers to the activity of transforming the innards of animals for use in charcuterie (casings). It has grown significantly (twenty-two stores in France now), mainly geared toward food professionals.

Mora.

A. Simon, above and below.

E. Dehillerin, above and below.

Maison Lefranc.

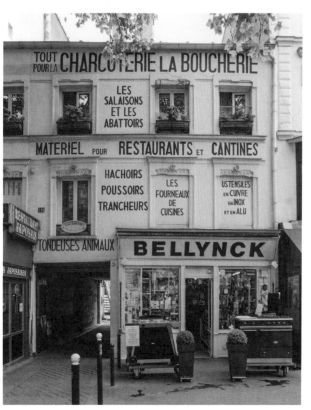

Bellynck et Fils.

INDEX BY ARRONDISSEMENTS

RECIPE INDEX

BIBLIOGRAPHY

Almeida-Topor. Hélène d'. *Le Goût de l'étranger: Les saveurs venues d'ailleurs depuis la fin du xviiie siècle*. Paris: Armand Colin, 2006.

Arago, Jacques. *Comme on dîne à Paris*. Paris: Berquet et Pétion, 1842.

Aries, Philippe, and Georges Duby, eds. *Histoire de la vie privée*. Paris: Seuil, 1999.

Aron, Jean-Paul. *Le Mangeur du xixe siècle*. Paris: Denoël, 1976.

Arranger, Benjamin. *Paris vu par les écrivains*. Paris: Arcadia, 2003.

Baecque, Antoine de. *La France gastronome: comment le restaurant est entré dans notre histoire*. Paris: Payot, 2019.

Barbary de Langlade, Jacques. *Maxim's*. Paris: Robert Laffont, 1990.

Béarn, Pierre. *Grimod de La Reynière*. Paris: Gallimard, 1930.

Beck, Robert, Ulrike Krampl, and Emmanuelle Retaillaud-Bajac, eds. *Les Cinq Sens de la ville du Moyen Âge à nos jours*. Tours: PUFR, 2013.

Becker, Karin. *Gastronomie et littérature en France au xixe siècle*. Orléans: Éditions Paradigmes, 2017.

Berard, Laurence, et al. *Ile-de-France: produits du terroir et recettes traditionnelles*. L'Inventaire du patrimoine culinaire de la France. Paris: CNAC/Albin Michel, 1993.

Binh, N. T. *Paris au cinéma: la vie rêvée de la capitale de Méliès à Amélie Poulain*. Paris: Parigramme, 2003.

Blanc, François. *Le Paris des pâtisseries*. Paris: Ducasse Éditions, 2020.

Blanc, Honoré. *Le Guide des dîneurs de Paris*. Paris: Chez les Marchands de Nouveautés, 1815.

Boudan, Christian. *La Vraie Cuisine parisienne*. Paris: Éditions de L'Epure, 2016.

Boussel, Patrice. *Les Restaurants dans "La Comédie humaine"*. Paris: Éditions de la Tournelle, 1950.

Briffault, Eugène. *Paris à table*. Paris: Hetzel, 1846.

Bure, Gilles de, and Eric Neuhoff. *Quand les brasseries se racontent*. Paris: Albin Michel, 2006.

Castelot, André. *L'Histoire à table, Si la cuisine m'était contée*. Paris: Plon/Perrin, 1972.

Christophe, Delphine, and Georgina Letourmy. *Paris et ses cafés*. Paris: Action artistique de la Ville de Paris, 2004.

Courtine, Robert. *La Vie parisienne. Cafés et restaurants des Boulevards 1814–1914*. Paris: Perrin, 1984./*Un gourmand à Paris*. Paris: Grasset, 1959.

Csergo, Julia, and Jean-Pierre Lemasson, eds. *Voyages en gastronomie: l'invention des capitales et des régions gourmandes*. Paris: Autrement, 2008.

Delord, Taxile, and Edmond Texier. *Paris-Restaurant*. Paris: Librairie d'Alphonse Taride, 1854.

Delvaille, Bernard. *Paris, ses poètes, ses chansons*. Paris: Seghers, 1977.

Delvau, Alfred. *Histoire anecdotique des cafés et cabarets de Paris*. Paris, E. Dentu, 1862./*Les Plaisirs de Paris: Guide pratique des étrangers*. Paris, Achille Faure, 1867.

Diwo, Jean. *Chez Lipp*. Paris: Denoël, 1981.

Dupont, Jacques. *Le Paris de Colette*. Paris: Alexandrines, 2017.

Durand Boubal, Christophe. *Café de Flore, mémoire d'un siècle*. Paris: Indigo, 1993.

Flandrin, Jean-Louis, and Massimo Montanari, eds. *Histoire de l'alimentation*. Paris: Fayard, 1996.

Gardeton, César. *Nouveau guide des dîneurs*. Paris: J. Breauté, 1828.

Gaston-Breton, Tristan, and Patricia Kapferer. *Rungis, le plus grand marché du monde*. Paris: Cherche Midi, 2006.

Gaudry, François-Régis. *Mémoires du restaurant: histoire illustré d'une invention française*. Paris: Aubanel, 2006.

Gault, Henri, and Christian Millau. *Guide Julliard de Paris*. Paris: Julliard, 1962./*Gault et Millau se mettent à table*. Paris: Stock, 1976.

Girveau, Bruno, ed. *À table au xixe siècle*. Paris: Réunion des Musées Nationaux/Flammarion, 2001.

Goudeau, Émile. *Paris qui consomme: tableaux de Paris*. Paris: Henri Beraldi, 1893.

Gourdeau, Jean-Claude. *Le transfert des Halles à Rungis*. Paris: JC Lattes, 1977.

Hancock, Claire. *Paris et Londres au xixe siècle: représentations dans les guides et récits de voyages*. Paris: CNRS Éditions, 2003.

Hazan, Éric. *L'Invention de Paris*. Paris: Seuil, 2012.

Heisse, Ulla. *Histoire du café et des cafés les plus célèbres* (translated from the German by S. Alloyer). Paris: Belfond, 1988.

Helal, Nathalie. *Le Goût de Paris . . . et de la région Ile-de-France*. Paris: Hachette Pratique, 2021.

Héron de Villefosse, René. *Histoire et géographie gourmandes de Paris*. Paris: Les Éditions de Paris, 1956.

Huart, Louis. *Museum parisien: Histoire physiologique, pittoresque, philosophique et grotesque de toutes les bêtes curieuses de Paris et de la banlieue*. Paris: Beauger et Cie, 1841.

Kemblowska-Dupieu, Danuta, and Nathalie Lambeaux-Lion. *Une histoire des cafés de Paris*. Łódź: Lodart, 2001.

Langle, Henri-Melchior de. *Le Petit Monde des cafés et des débits parisiens au xixe siècle: Évolution de la sociabilité citadine*. Paris: PUF, 1990.

Laurioux, Bruno. "Entre savoir et pratiques: le livre de cuisine a la fin du Moyen Âge." *Médiévales* 14 (spring 1988): 59–71./*Le règne de Taillevent*. Paris: Éditions de la Sorbonne, 1997.

Lebey, Claude. *À table! La vie intrépide d'un gourmet redoutable*. Paris: Albin Michel, 2012.

Letailleur, Gérard. *Histoire insolite des cafés parisiens*. Paris: Perrin, 2011.

Mac Donogh, Giles. *Brillat-Savarin, juge des gourmandises*. Chatou: L'Arganier, 2006.

Maillard, Lucien. *Ledoyen ou la conquête du goût*. [Paris]: L'Avant Mémoire, 1992.

Malki-Thouvenel, Béatrice. *Cabarets, cafés et bistrots de Paris: Promenade dans les rues et dans le temps*. Roanne: Horvath, 1987.

Marès, Antoine, and Pierre Milza. *Le Paris des étrangers depuis 1945*. Paris: Éditions de la Sorbonne, 1995.

Menjot, Denis, ed. *Manger et boire au Moyen Âge*. Paris: Belles Lettres, 1984.

Messiant, Jacques. *Estaminets d'antan et distractions populaires*. Hazebrouck: J. Messiant, 1980.

Michelin. *La Saga du Guide Michelin*. Paris: Michelin, 2004.

Moret, Frédéric. "Images de Paris dans les guides touristiques en 1900," *Le Mouvement social*, 160, 1992.

Muhlstein, Anka. *Garçon, un cent d'huîtres! Balzac et la table*. Paris: Odile Jacob, 2010.

Ory, Pascal. *Le Discours gastronomique français, des origines à nos jours*. Paris: Gallimard, 1998.

Pitte, Jean-Robert. *Gastronomie française: Histoire et géographie d'une passion*. Paris: Fayard, 1991.

Planiol, Françoise. *La Coupole: 60 ans de Montparnasse*. Paris: Denoël, 1986.

Prudhomme, Louis-Marie. *Voyage descriptif et historique de l'ancien et du nouveau Paris*. Paris: Chez l'Auteur, 1814.

Pujol, Catherine. *De la taverne au bar à vins: les cafés à Paris, analyse géographique de la ville par ses débits de boissons* (doctoral thesis), 1988.

Quellier, Florent. *La table des Français: Une histoire culturelle (xve– début xixe siècle)*. Rennes: PUR, 2007.

Rambourg, Patrick. *De la cuisine à la gastronomie: histoire de la table française*. Paris: Louis Audibert, 2005.

Rearick, Charles. *Paris Dreams, Paris Memories: The City and Its Mystique*. Redwood City, CA : Stanford University Press, 2011.

Revel, Jean-François. *Un festin en paroles: Histoire littéraire de la sensibilité gastronomique de l'Antiquité à nos jours*. Paris: Compagnie Jean-Jacques Pauvert, 1985.

Rey, Marie-Pierre. *Le premier des chefs: l'exceptionnel destin d'Antonin Carême*. Paris: Flammarion, 2021.

Rochette, Hélène. *Le Paris de Claude Sautet*. Paris: Parigramme, 2020.

Rowley, Anthony, ed. *Les Français à table: atlas historique de la gastronomie française*. Paris: Hachette Pratique, 1997.

Scarpa, Marie. *Le Carnaval des Halles: une ethnocritique du* Ventre de Paris *de Zola*. Paris: CNRS Éditions, 2000.

Soulié Frédéric. "Restaurants et gargotes." In *La Grande Ville: nouveau tableau de Paris, comique, critique et philosophique*, Paul de Kock et al. Paris: Marescq, 1843.

Spang, Rebecca L. *The Invention of the Restaurant*. Cambridge, MA: Harvard University Press, 2000.

Steiner, Anne. *Belleville cafés*. Montreuil: L'Échappée, 2010.

Tardieu, Marc. *Les Auvergnats de Paris*. Monaco: Rocher, 2001.

Terrail, Claude. *Ma Tour d'Argent*. Verviers: Marabout, 1975.

Toussaint-Samat, Maguelonne. *La très belle et très exquise histoire des gâteaux et des friandises*. Paris: Flammarion, 2004.

Van Rompu, Ludovic. *L'Atelier pâtisserie de Ludo: 60 grands classiques*. Paris: Marabout, 2022.

Vermond, Paul. "Les Restaurants de Paris." *Review de Paris*, 2nd series, 15 (1835): 109–121.

THE *LET'S EAT PARIS!* CREW

EDITORIAL DIRECTOR
François-Régis Gaudry
with
Charles Patin O'Coohoon
Stéphane Solier

COORDINATION
Camille Mennesson
Marielle Gaudry
with
Aimie Blanchard
Thomas Darcos
Marilou Petricola

SCIENTIFIC ADVISOR
Loïc Bienassis

ÉDITIONS MARABOUT
Élisabeth Darets
Christine Martin
Audrey Génin
assisted by
Emmanuel Le Vallois

ÉDITIONS RADIO FRANCE
Anne-Julie Bémont

PROOFREADING
Élise Peylet
Irène Colas
Émilie Collet
Tiffany Nortier

IMAGE ARCHIVES
Tiffany Nortier

ARTISTIC DIRECTION, GRAPHIC DESIGN & LAYOUT
Pierre Boisson
(Drink Studio),
Sidonie Bernard,
Line Monthiers
(Hic et Nunc Studio)

FOOD STYLIST (ICONIC RECIPES)
Sabrina Fauda-Rôle

RECIPE PRODUCTION
Thomas Darcos
Jean-Philippe Marsan

PHOTOGRAPHERS
Émilie Franzo
Marielle Gaudry
Rebecca Genet
Isabelle Kanako
David Japy
Pierre Javelle
Sandra Mahut
Joann Pai
Mathieu Pellerin

ILLUSTRATORS
Lucie Barthe-Dejean
Pierre Busson
Lucas Burtin
Jack Chadwick
Alice Charbin
Chez Gertrud
Charlotte Colin
Mathieu Demuizon
Alice Des
Grégory Franco—Cartographer
Marie Guillard
Iris Hatzfeld
L'Atelier Cartøgraphik
Caroline Laguerre
Antoine Moreau-Dussault
Sophie Rivière
Paul Sirand
Studio Fago
Anthony Tambourini
Hubert Van Rie

ACKNOWLEDGMENTS
Bellynck company
Anne-Julie Bémont
Laurence Bloch
Bouillon Pigalle
Sabine Bucquet
Géraldine Cerf de Dudzeele
Isabelle Chalet-Bailhache
Nadia Chougui
Yann Chouquet
Florence Claval
Isaure Cointreau
Lilian Combourieu
Flavie Costamagna
Carole Chrétiennot
Eric Dehillerin
Bruno de Sa Moreira
Yves Desfontaines
Sandrine Dietriche
Marion Effray
Romain Fabry
Clarisse Ferreres-Frechon
Émilie Flechaire
Yves Françoise
Pascaline Fresnel
Mélanie Gallais
Denise and Pierre Gaudry
Louis Gautier
Stéphane Guenaud
Soazig Guilmin
Séverine Guyonnet
Ralph Grossmann
La Coupole
Bernard Laurance
Romain Leboeuf
Pascal Le Bihan
Pierre Lecoutre
Lorenza Lenzi
Frédérique Lurol
Olivier Maurey
Sébastien Mayol
Romane Milione
Giulia Molari
Mora company
Philippe Oriol
Mikaël Petitjean
Alice Pineau
Apollonia Poilâne
Gianpaolo Polverino
Caroline Poulain
Florence Quignard-Debuisson
Julien Richard
Cécile Rives
Thomas de Roaldes
Guillaume Roubaud-Quashie
Roxane and Jean Sévegne
Valérie Solvit
Lauranne Thomas
Laura Tudal
TV Only
Adèle Van Reeth
Sibyle Veil
Cécile Velley
Anne-Isabelle Vignaud
Hugo Zabraniecki

CONTRIBUTORS
Aïtor Alfonso
Loïc Ballet
Loïc Bienassis
Marie-Amal Bizalion
Aimie Blanchard
Alice Bosio
Vincent Brenot
Jacques Brunel
Ilaria Brunetti
Gwilherm de Cerval
Handa Cheng
Cathleen Clarity
Antony Cointre
Matthieu Conquet
Pierre Coulon
Pierre-Yves Chupin
Thomas Darcos
Laurent Delmas
Christine Doublet
Nicolas d'Estienne d'Orves
Anne Etorre
Manon Fleury
Cécile Fortis
Marie-Laure Fréchet
Bruno Fuligni
Jérôme Gagnez
François-Régis Gaudry
Marielle Gaudry
Lydia Gautier
Antoine Gerbelle
Hadrien Gonzales
Alexis Goujard
Frédérick Ernestine
Grasser Hermé
Nadia Hamam
Christophe de Hody
Dominique Hutin
Pierrick Jégu
Farah Keram
Bruno Laurioux
Charlotte Langrand
Estelle Lenartowicz
Sacha Lomnitz
Marylène Malbert
Jean-Philippe Marsan
Elvira Masson
Chihiro Masui
Xavier Mathias
Sébastien Mayol
Camille Mennesson
Morgane Mizzon
Jordan Moilim
Jean-Pierre Montanay
Éric Morain
Yves Nespoulous
Benoît Nicolas
Valentine Oudard
Samir Ouriaghli
Beena Paradin Migotto
Charles Patin O'Coohoon
Marilou Petricola
Déborah Pham
Alessandra Pierini
Sébastien Pieve
Caroline Poulain
Marcelle Ratafia
Marie-Pierre Rey
Sun Roux
Théophile Roux
Emmanuel Rubin
Hugo de Saint Phalle
Annabelle Schachmes
Benoist Simmat
Stéphane Solier
Mina Soundiram
Zazie Tavitian
Clarisse Teyssandier
Antoine Tézenas du Montcel
Xavier Van Kerrebrouck
Aurore Vincenti
Sylvie Wolff
Ezéchiel Zerah

CHEFS AND COOKS
Florence Abelin
Paul Boudier
Thomas Brachet
Benoît Castel
Yann Couvreur
Jeremy Del Val
Leandro De Seta
Hugo Desnoyer
Romain Dubuisson
Manon Fleury
Marie-Laure Fréchet
Sébastien Gaudard
Jacques Genin
Stéphane Glacier
Dominique Guiltier
Pierre Lecoutre
Cyril Lignac
Nina Métayer
Benoît Nicolas
Suzy Palatin
Rodolphe Paquin
Jean-François Piège
Poilâne company
Jean Sévègnes
Albert Touton
Ludovic Van Rompu
Jean-Pierre Vigato

PHOTO CREDITS

Originally published in French as *On Va Déguster Paris*
Copyright On Va Déguster Paris
© Hachette Livre (Marabout), Vanves, 2022

Translated from the French by Zachary R. Townsend

All rights reserved. No portion of this book may be reproduced—mechanically, electronically, or by any other means, including photocopying—without written permission of the publisher.

Library of Congress Cataloging-in-Publication Data is on file.

ISBN 978-1-64829-321-4

Design by Marabout
Cover illustration by Mathieu Demuizon

Artisan books are available at special discounts when purchased in bulk for premiums and sales promotions as well as for fundraising or educational use. Special editions or book excerpts can also be created to specification. For details, please contact special.markets@hbgusa.com.

The publisher is not responsible for websites (or their content) that are not owned by the publisher.

The Hachette Speakers Bureau provides a wide range of authors for speaking events. To find out more, go to hachettespeakersbureau.com or email HachetteSpeakers@hbgusa.com.

Published by Artisan, an imprint of Workman Publishing Co., Inc., a subsidiary of Hachette Book Group, Inc.
1290 Avenue of the Americas
New York, NY 10104
artisanbooks.com

Artisan is a registered trademark of Workman Publishing Co., Inc., a subsidiary of Hachette Book Group, Inc.

Printed in China on responsibly sourced paper
First printing, September 2023

10 9 8 7 6 5 4 3 2 1